Managing Supply Chains

A LOGISTICS APPROACH

9e

JOHN J. COYLE
The Pennsylvania State University

•

C. JOHN LANGLEY, JR.
The Pennsylvania State University

•

ROBERT A. NOVACK
The Pennsylvania State University

•

BRIAN J. GIBSON
Auburn University

SOUTH-WESTERN
CENGAGE Learning·

Australia • Brazil • Japan • Korea • Mexico • Singapore • Spain • United Kingdom • United States

SOUTH-WESTERN
CENGAGE Learning·

Managing Supply Chains: A Logistics Approach, Ninth International Edition
John J. Coyle, C. John Langley Jr., Robert A. Novack, Brian J. Gibson

Vice President of Editorial, Business: Jack W. Calhoun

Editor-in-Chief: Joe Sabatino

Senior Acquisitions Editor: Charles McCormick, Jr.

Developmental Editor: Daniel Noguera

Editorial Assistant: Courtney Bavaro

Marketing Manager: Adam Marsh

Senior Marketing Communications Manager: Libby Shipp

Design Direction, Production Management, and Composition: PreMediaGlobal

Media Editor: Chris Valentine

Rights Acquisitions Specialist, Text and Image: Deanna Ettinger

Manufacturing Planner: Ron Montgomery

Senior Art Director: Stacy Shirley

Cover Designer: Patti Hudepohl

Cover Photo Credits:
  B/W Image: Big Stock Photo
  Color Image: Shutterstock Images/ kentoh

ExamView® is a registered trademark of eInstruction Corp. Windows is a registered trademark of the Microsoft Corporation used herein under license. Macintosh and Power Macintosh are registered trademarks of Apple Computer, Inc. used herein under license. © 2008 Cengage Learning. All Rights Reserved.

Library of Congress Control Number: 2011943157

International Edition:

ISBN 13: 978-1-111-53392-2

ISBN 10: 1-111-53392-X

Cengage Learning International Offices

Asia
www.cengageasia.com
tel: (65) 6410 1200

Australia/New Zealand
www.cengage.com.au
tel: (61) 3 9685 4111

Brazil
www.cengage.com.br
tel: (55) 11 3665 9900

India
www.cengage.co.in
tel: (91) 11 4364 1111

Latin America
www.cengage.com.mx
tel: (52) 55 1500 6000

UK/Europe/Middle East/Africa
www.cengage.co.uk
tel: (44) 0 1264 332 424

Represented in Canada by Nelson Education, Ltd.
www.nelson.com
tel: (416) 752 9100 / (800) 668 0671

Cengage Learning is a leading provider of customized learning solutions with office locations around the globe, including Singapore, the United Kingdom, Australia, Mexico, Brazil, and Japan. Locate your local office at: **www.cengage.com/global**

For product information: **www.cengage.com/international**

Visit your local office: **www.cengage.com/global**

Visit our corporate website: **www.cengage.com**

Printed in Canada
1 2 3 4 5 6 7 16 15 14 13 12

A very special note of thanks and appreciation is due to our families. John Coyle would like to thank his wife Barbara, their children John and Susan, and their grandchildren Lauren, Matthew, Elizabeth Kate, Emily, Ben, Cathryn, and Zachary. John Langley would like to thank his wife Anne, their children Sarah and Mercer, and their grandchildren Bryson and Molly. Bob Novack would like to thank his wife Judith and their children Tom, Elizabeth, and Alex. Brian Gibson would like to thank his wife Marcia and son Andy.

Brief Contents

Contents

Part V

Preface

Supply chain management and the closely related concept of logistics are necessary cornerstones of competitive strategy, increased market share, and shareholder value for most organizations. Now more than ever, students who are currently planning to pursue a career in business will benefit from a clear understanding of this field. Practicing managers will also find this text a beneficial and helpful resource because of its timeliness and the depth and breadth of the topics covered.

With this edition we have tried to cover, as comprehensively as possible, the changes in the way business is being done. In fact, the title of this edition—*Managing Supply Chains: A Logistics Approach*—reflects the ever-changing nature of this rapidly evolving field. The author team strives to offer you the most current, comprehensive thinking on supply chain management, combined with an authenticated, real-world logistics perspective. In keeping with the dramatic changes that have taken place in the global business environment and in the field of supply chain management, the organization of this edition again provides a logical framework for achieving a meaningful understanding of the concepts and principles of supply chain management. Additionally, it is important to understand that a major feature of this text is that not only is the discipline of supply chain management viewed from a logistics perspective but also that logistics is positioned as a set of key processes and functions that are viewed as essential to strategic and operational success with the broader supply chain concept.

Part I provides a framework for your understanding of supply chain management and some of its important related components. Chapter 1 is devoted to a comprehensive introduction to supply chain management. Chapter 2 presents an overview of all of the important dimensions of logistics and explains the relationship of logistics to supply chain management. Finally, Chapter 3 explores global supply chains and their relevance to global trade strategy and success.

Strategic factors are the focus of Part II. Chapter 4 leads off with a discussion of supply chain relationships and the use of third-party logistics services. Chapter 5, a chapter devoted to performance measurement and financial analysis, will help you understand how to use both performance and financial metrics to gauge efficiency and effectiveness. And finally, Chapter 6 examines the role and importance of information systems in the effective management of supply chains.

Part III addresses the key process areas within supply chain fulfillment. Chapter 7 discusses demand management, while Chapter 8 addresses the very closely connected topics of order management and customer service. Chapter 9 focuses on one of the most crucial assets on many companies' balance sheets—inventory management—revealing the costs of inventory and the most effective means of managing inventory. Transportation and distribution can be viewed as the glue that holds supply chains together, and effective strategies and technologies in these areas are the subjects of Chapter 10 and Chapter 11.

With Part IV, you'll be drawn into the world of supply chain planning, sourcing, and operations. Chapter 12 will give you the tools needed to analyze, design, and refine a supply chain network, while Chapter 13 focuses attention on key topics and issues relating to sourcing, procurement, supplier and vendor relationships, and the latest electronic technologies to be used in these areas. Chapter 14 on operations and Chapter 15 on reverse flows present entirely new material created for this edition.

The final chapter, in Part V, explores the major macro trends that will impact the future of logistics and supply chain management, as well as strategies for staying competitive in the future. Among the major types of strategies discussed are differentiation, financing, technology, relationships, and globalization. Last, some thoughts are included on the need for organizations of all types to transform and change their supply chains as conditions would suggest.

Features

- Learning Objectives at the beginning of each chapter provide students with an overall perspective of chapter material and also serve to establish a baseline for a working knowledge of the topics that follow.

- *Supply Chain Profiles* are the opening vignettes at the beginning of each chapter that introduce students to the chapter's topics through familiar, real-world companies, people, and events.

- *On the Line* features are applied, concrete examples that provide students with hands-on managerial experience of the chapter topics.

- *Supply Chain Sustainability* boxes have been added to highlight the critical role of supply chain management in conserving resources, reducing waste, and mitigating the environmental impact of fulfillment operations.

- *Supply Chain Technology* boxes help students relate technological developments to supply chain management concepts and logistics practices.

- End-of-chapter summaries and study questions reinforce material presented in each chapter.

- Short cases at the end of each chapter build upon what students have learned. Questions that follow the cases sharpen critical thinking skills.

Ancillaries

Available on the companion Web site, www.cengagebrain.com, are three essential resources:

- The *Instructor's Manual* includes chapter outlines, answers to end-of-chapter study questions, commentary on end-of-chapter short cases and end-of-text comprehensive cases, and teaching tips.

- A convenient *Test Bank* offers a variety of true/false, multiple choice, and essay questions for each chapter.

- *PowerPoint* slides cover the main chapter topics and contain graphics from the main text.

Student Resources

A rich library of Student's Resources is available on the companion Web site, such as:

- Suggested reading for Part 1 through Part 5
- Directory of Trade and Professional Organizations in Supply Chain Management
- Additional Cases
- A Guide of Careers in Logistics
- Glossary
- Games and more

Acknowledgments

The authors are indebted to many individuals at our respective academic institutions as well as other individuals with whom we have had contact in a variety of venues. Our university students and our executive program students have provided an important sounding board for the many concepts, techniques, metrics, and strategies presented in the book. Our faculty and corporate colleagues have provided invaluable insights and appropriate criticism of our ideas. Some individuals deserve special consideration: Dr. David A. Lindsley (University of Toledo), Mark J. Basile (DuPont Corporation), Dr. Joe B. Hanna (Auburn University), Dr. Chris Norek (Chain Connectors), Ms. Jessica Volpe (Penn State University), Mr. Tim Gross (Penn State University), Mr. Sammie Markham (Penn State University), Ms. Devin Maguire (Penn State University), and especially Ms. Jean Beierlein and Ms. Tracie Shannon (Penn State University). Special thanks and appreciation to Dr. Kusumal Ruamsook, Visiting Research Associate for the Center for Supply Chain Research at The Pennsylvania State University, for her invaluable support.

The ninth edition of this text will be the first one that does not list Dr. Edward Bardi as one of the co-authors. Ed was one of the two, original co-authors of the text when it was published in 1976. It is unusual for an educational book to have a life cycle that exceeds 35 years and has gone through many editions. Ed Bardi played an important role in the success of the text by helping to keep it innovative, timely and vital. Not one to postpone or procrastinate, Ed would usually finish his chapters first, and thereby provide incentive and pressure for his fellow co-authors to be more timely in meeting deadlines. He would also volunteer to do some of the more tedious and less glamorous (but important) sections of the text, for example, subject index, author index, glossary, etc. We have missed Ed's participation and contributions this time and hope that we have lived up to his expectations and standards. We want to express our appreciation and thanks and extend a wish for good health and joy to Ed and his wife, Carol, and their family.

We extend our appreciation to the members of our Cengage Learning team, who have been very professional and helpful with this textbook: Charles McCormick, Jr., Senior Acquisitions Editor; Daniel Noguera, Developmental Editor; Jennifer Ziegler, Content Project Manager; Rathi Thirumalai, Senior Project Manager; Gunjan Chandola, Senior Project Manager; Stacey Shirley, Art Director; Adam Marsh, Marketing Manager; and Elaine Kosta, Rights and Acquisitions Specialist.

Special thanks should be given to the following Professors who served as reviewers and who provided meaningful input for our ninth edition:

Jeffrey L. Bennett	Northwood University
John A. Caltagirone	Loyola University Chicago
Adam Conrad	Pennsylvania State University
Eddie Davila	Arizona State University
Kathryn Dobie	North Carolina A&T State University
Matt Drake	Duquesne University
S. Altan Erdem	Edison Community College
Christopher C. Esgar	Penn State University, Mont Alto Campus
Paul L. Ewell	Virginia Wesleyan College
Ephrem Eyob	Virginia State University
Martin Farris	University of North Texas

Lou Firenze	*Northwood University*
Michael J. Gravier	*Bryant University*
Joh J. Gregor	*Washington & Jefferson College*
Joe Hanna	*Auburn University*
Ahmad Hassan	*Morehead State University*
Balaji Janamanchi	*Texas A&M International University*
Jonatan Jelen	*Baruch College*
Walter Kendall	*Tarleton State University*
Marco Lam	*York College of Pennsylvania*
Ian M. Langella Atkin	*Shippensburg University*
Tenpao Lee	*Niagara University*
Cheng Li	*California State University, Los Angeles*
Walter Martin	*Wake Tech Community College*
John R. Mawhinney	*Duquesne University*
Ron Mesia	*Florida International University*
Saeed Mohaghegh	*Assumption College*
Martin Nunlee	*Delaware State University*
Anthony M. Pagano	*University of Illinois at Chicago*
Ann Rensel	*Niagara University*
Paul Skilton	*Washington State University*
Michael J. Stevenson	*Hagerstown Community College*
Robert S. Trebatoski	*Penn State University*
David Vellenga	*Maine Maritime Academy*
Simon Veronneau	*Quinnipiac University*
Haibo Wang	*Texas A&M International University*
William Waxman	*UHCL*
Jon Whitford	*Rio Hondo College*
Linda Wright	*Longwood University*
Rick Yokeley	*Forsyth Technical Community College*

About the Authors

John J. Coyle is currently director of corporate relations for the Center for Supply Chain Research and professor emeritus of logistics and supply chain management in the Smeal College of Business at Penn State University. He holds a BS and MS from Penn State and earned his doctorate from Indiana University in Bloomington, Indiana, where he was a U.S. Steel Fellow. He joined the Penn State faculty in 1961 and attained the rank of full professor in 1967. In addition to his teaching responsibilities, he has served in a number of administrative positions, including department head, assistant dean, senior associate dean, special assistant for strategic planning to the university president, and executive director of the Center for Supply Chain Research. He also served as Penn State's faculty representative to the NCAA for 30 years and to the Big Ten for 10 years. Dr. Coyle was the editor of the *Journal of Business Logistics* from 1990 to 1996. He has authored or coauthored 20 books or monographs and numerous articles in professional journals. He has received 14 awards at Penn State for teaching excellence and advising. In addition, he received the Council of Logistics Management's Distinguished Service Award in 1991; the Philadelphia Traffic Club's Person of the Year Award in 2003; and the Eccles Medal from the International Society of Logistics for his contributions to the Department of Defense and the Lion's Paw Medal from Penn State for Distinguished Service, both in 2004. Dr. Coyle currently serves on the boards of three logistics and supply chain service companies and on the Advisory Board of the NLDC and continues to be active in teaching in the Executive Education Programs at Penn State.

C. John Langley Jr. is clinical professor of supply chain management in the Smeal College of Business at Penn State University and also serves as director of development in the Center for Supply Chain Research. Previously, he served as the John H. Dove distinguished professor of supply chain management at the University of Tennessee and the SCL professor of supply chain management at the Georgia Institute of Technology. Dr. Langley is a former president of the Council of Supply Chain Management Professionals and a recipient of the Council's Distinguished Service Award. He has been recognized by the American Society of Transportation and Logistics as an honorary distinguished logistics professional for his long-term contributions and continuing commitment to the transportation logistics community, and he is a recipient of the Outstanding Alumnus Award from Penn State's Business Logistics Program. Dr. Langley received his BS in mathematics, MBA in finance, and Ph.D. in business logistics degrees, all from Penn State University. Dr. Langley has coauthored several books, including *Managing Supply Chains: A Logistics Approach*. Also, he is lead author of the annual *Third Party Logistics Study* and recently completed the *2012 16th Annual 3PL Study*. His research publications have appeared in journals such as the *Journal of Business Logistics, International Journal of Physical Distribution and Logistics Management, International Journal of Logistics Management*, and *Supply Chain Management Review*. Dr. Langley serves on the Boards of Directors of UTi Worldwide, Inc., Forward Air Corporation, and Averitt Express, Inc., in addition to several involvements on academic advisory boards to logistics organizations. He also is a member of the Program Faculty for the Kühne Logistics University in Hamburg, Germany, and of the Industrial and Professional Advisory Council (IPAC) at Penn State University and currently serves as education advisor for NASSTRAC.

Robert Novack is an associate professor of supply chain management in the Department of Supply Chain and Information Systems at Penn State University. From 1981 to 1984 he worked in operations management and planning for the Yellow Freight Corporation in Overland Park, Kansas, and from 1984 to 1986 he worked in planning and transportation at Drackett Company in Cincinnati, Ohio. Dr. Novack's numerous articles have been published in such publications as the *Journal of Business Logistics, Transportation Journal,* and *International Journal of Physical Distribution and Logistics Management.* He also is a coauthor of *Creating Logistics Value: Themes for the Future.* Active in the Council of Supply Chain Management Professionals, he has served as overall program chair for the annual conference, as a track chair, and as a session speaker as well as a member of numerous committees. Dr. Novack holds the CTL designation from AST&L and is a member of WERC. He earned a BS degree and an MBA in logistics from Penn State University and a Ph.D. in logistics from the University of Tennessee.

Brian J. Gibson holds the Wilson Family Professorship in supply chain management and is a program coordinator for the Department of Supply Chain and Information Systems Management at Auburn University. Previously, he served on the faculty of Georgia Southern University and as a logistics manager for two major retailers. He has received multiple awards for outstanding teaching, research, and outreach, most notably the Council of Supply Chain Management Professionals' Innovative Teaching Award in 2009. Gibson's research has been published in the *Journal of Business Logistics, Supply Chain Management Review, International Journal of Logistics Management, International Journal of Physical Distribution and Logistics Management,* and other leading publications. He is coauthor of *Transportation: A Supply Chain Perspective,* author of the electronic textbook *Supply Chain Essentials,* and lead author of the annual *State of the Retail Supply Chain Report.* Dr. Gibson currently serves on key committees for the Council of Supply Chain Management Professionals and the Retail Industry Leaders Association. Dr. Gibson earned a BS/BA from Central Michigan University, an MBA from Wayne State University, and a Ph.D. in logistics and transportation from the University of Tennessee.

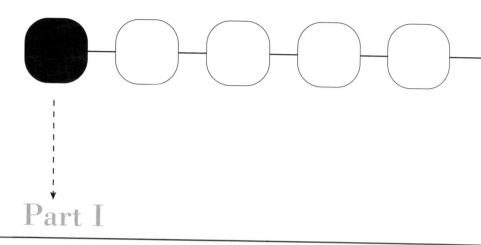

Part I

In his best selling book, *The World Is Flat,* Thomas Friedman, a staff writer for *The New York Times,* discusses 10 major forces that have helped to "flatten" the world from an economic perspective. One of the 10 forces is what he describes as supply chaining, a method of collaborating among businesses to manage the flow of goods, information, and cash to deliver "value" for the consumer. This type of collaboration has stretched vertically and horizontally on a global basis to become a cornerstone of competitive strategy for successful organizations in today's global marketplace.

Chapter 1 provides an introduction and overview of supply chain management. This chapter discusses the rationale for the attention that has been focused on supply chain management. It also depicts and explains the fundamentals of the concepts. The major issues or challenges for effective and efficient supply chains are explored in the chapter, and it provides the foundation for the chapters that follow.

Chapter 2 focuses on logistics processes that are very important for the effectiveness and efficiency of today's supply chains. Logistics processes and systems provide a cornerstone for the material flows, both forward and backward in the supply chain. **Chapter 2** explores both the macro and micro dimensions of logistics from the perspectives of "value add" and efficiency. The role and importance of logistics in private and public organizations are discussed, and special attention is devoted to the relationships and interfaces of logistics with other functional areas in a firm. In addition, this chapter examines approaches to analyzing logistics systems and presents techniques for short- and long-run analyses of logistics tradeoffs.

The global dimension of supply chains is presented in **Chapter 3**. The increased significance of global supply chains competing against global supply chains in world markets was indicated in **Chapter 1**. The role and complexity of the global supply chain are discussed in this chapter along with the changing importance of global trading partners. The unique characteristics of global trade services are also covered. The general issues as well as the specific requirements of global flows are discussed.

Overall, Part I provides the foundation and framework for the four remaining parts and their respective chapters.

Chapter 1

SUPPLY CHAIN MANAGEMENT: AN OVERVIEW

Learning Objectives

After reading this chapter, you should be able to do the following:

- Discuss the major change drivers in our economy and in the global marketplace.
- Understand the rationale for the development of supply chain management in leading organizations.
- Appreciate the importance and role of supply chain management among private and public organizations.
- Understand the contributions of a supply chain approach to organizational efficiency and effectiveness.
- Analyze the benefits that can accrue from implementing effective supply chain practices.
- Understand the major challenges and issues facing organizations developing and implementing supply chain strategies.

Supply Chain Profile   *SAB Distribution: A Sequel*

Sue Purdum, current president and CEO of SAB Distribution, was preparing to "pass the baton" to her successor, Susan Weber. Sue Purdum held her leadership role in SAB for over 10 years. She was credited with not only helping SAB to survive in a highly competitive economic environment but also with restoring its profitability with several strategic moves in the marketplace.

In a meeting with Susan, Ms. Purdum revisited the old adage in marketing strategy—"let's eliminate the middleman." SAB was definitely a classic, middle of the supply chain organization since it purchased consumer products from major manufacturers such as Kraft, Kimberly-Clark, Procter & Gamble (P&G), Unilever, etc., and sold them to smaller distributors, wholesalers, and retailers. Ms. Purdum indicated to Susan that SAB's survival depended upon the company reexamining its role in their supply chains and making appropriate strategic and tactical changes. This became the central mandate for Susan as she assumed her new role as CEO of SAB Distribution.

COMPANY BACKGROUND

SAB Distribution was established in 1949 in Harrisburg, Pennsylvania, by three World War II veterans who had served as supply officers in the U.S. Navy. They selected Harrisburg because of its central location in Pennsylvania and the mid-Atlantic region and because of its access by rail and highways. The founders of SAB—Skip, Al, and Bob—recognized the need for a food wholesaling company to serve medium and small-size retailers within a 100-mile radius of Harrisburg. Their vision proved to be correct, and the company grew and prospered in subsequent years. The company was incorporated in 1978, and a CEO, Pete Swan, was appointed in 1983 when the founders retired.

SAB's market area expanded into nearby states, and its product line was extended from nonperishable food items to also include perishables and nonfood consumer products. Ms. Purdum took over from Pete in 1995 when the company was at a major crossroad which could have led to the sale of the company. Ms. Purdum's career at SAB was marked by a series of competitive challenges that she navigated successfully. Now, as the end of the first decade of the twenty-first century approaches, SAB was again at a crisis point in terms of its survival.

EXECUTIVE COMMITTEE MEETING

As Susan looked across the table at her first SAB executive committee, she could see the concern in their eyes. They knew that she had a successful career at P&G in the supply chain area including global experience in Japan and other Pacific Rim countries, but could she make the transition to a smaller company with a different role in the supply chain?

SAB was faced with a number of challenges to its future existence. First and foremost, its customers had to compete against large retailers like Wal-Mart that could buy direct from the same consumer product manufacturers as SAB, i.e., "no middleman." Wal-Mart's buying advantage had to be offset in some way to keep SAB's customers competitive. In addition, globalization was impacting SAB's business because of an increase in imported products for the more diverse population of the United States and the ongoing search for lower-priced alternatives.

While the executives around the table were trying to assess the future viability of SAB, they also wondered whether they had a role to play under this new leader or if she would want to bring in her own executive team. Susan started the meeting, after her initial welcome, by stating "SAB needs this executive team, and I am hoping that all of you will stay the course.

I need your help and insights as we transition through these difficult times. We need to change, and I need you to help me with not only implementing the changes but also helping me to decide on appropriate changes. If you are afraid of change and would rather maintain the status quo, then your days at SAB are probably numbered. I need you to be 'agents of change' not 'keepers of the status quo.' Let me give you a brief overview of my vision of how we have to transform our company."

> When Sue Purdum assumed the role of CEO in 1995, she quickly analyzed our competitive environment and recognized the need to change our business practices. She focused initially upon efficiency in our warehouse operations to lower our cost of doing business. Then, she improved order fulfillment so that our customers received their orders quicker with less mistakes which lowered our customers' cost of doing business. At the same time, she developed partnerships with a core group of motor carriers to give them more volume which lead to lower rates and better service. Finally, she invested in information technology since she recognized that higher quality and more timely information would improve our forecasting with consequent reductions in inventory costs and improved order fulfillment.

> We will continue to try to improve in these same areas, but we need to go further, take a bigger step and transform our company. We need to analyze whether we can also provide viable services for larger retailers. Our niche has been the small to medium-size retailers, and we will continue to serve them efficiently and effectively. However, this group of retailers is losing market share to the larger retailers.

> Some of you may doubt our ability to serve larger retailers. Why do they need us since they buy in volumes as large or larger than ours? That view is myopic in that its focus is upon the traditional wholesaler/distributor business model. These large retailers all outsource part of their operations to what we commonly call third-party logistics companies who can provide services such as warehousing, order fulfillment, transportation, etc., at a lower cost or with better service than the large retailers.

> We have become pretty proficient in these areas thanks to you and your staff. If you couple that expertise with some strategic analysis of existing supply chains, I firmly believe that there are opportunities for SAB to help compress operations of existing or potential customers by eliminating duplicative echelons in some supply chains. You know that between the producer's plant and the retail store, there are often three to four distribution locations where products are stored and handled. That is our opportunity to serve this market niche. We just need to be more analytical and more proactive. Yes, it involves some risk, but less risk, in my opinion, than status quo. We also need to consider new customer opportunities such as restaurants.

The room was quiet at this point. Some individuals around the table felt uncomfortable because they felt that this vision was too daunting. Susan could sense the excitement of others who saw the logic of the opportunity and realized that SAB did not have an alternative if it wanted to survive.

Susan concluded with a quote: "If you do not change, you become extinct."[*] Looking at the group, she said, "We need to change our business model. Are you ready to help us go forward?"

---

*Spencer Johnson, *Who Moved My Cheese?* (G. P. Putnam's Sons, 1998).

Introduction

The last decade of the twentieth century was a period of rapid change for organizations, especially businesses. That rate of change has not slowed down and is actually increasing in the twenty-first century. The forces of change require organizations to be much more nimble and responsive; that is, organizations need to be able to transform themselves to survive in the intensely competitive global environment. The SAB case is a good example of this survivor mode, which forces companies to transform. It would have been driven out of business in the 1990s if it had not changed, and it now faces an even more daunting challenge, which will necessitate still bigger changes.

Several quotes cited in a previous edition of this book are still apropos at this point in time. They are as follows:

"Change is inevitable, but growth and improvement are optional."[1]

"You either change and get better or you slip and get worse, you cannot stay the same."[2]

"When the rate of change outside the organization is faster than inside, the end is near."[3]

Susan Weber, CEO of SAB, recognizes the wisdom of these comments. The case for change can be made by using the past and present giants of the retailing industry shown in Table 1.1.

Montgomery Ward lost its leadership position to Sears because it did not have the vision to understand that the exodus from the cities to the suburbs after World War II would cause it to lose sales volume at its large downtown stores. Sears developed a strategy to open multiple, smaller stores in the suburbs providing locational convenience and parking. In the 1970s when the U.S. economy was struggling with inflation and unemployment, Kmart replaced Sears as the retail leader with its emphasis upon price discounts. Then in the 1990s, Wal-Mart became the leading retailer with a multifaceted strategy based on discount pricing for brand name products, location in smaller communities, and more customer service. A key element in Wal-Mart's ability to discount brand name products was an understanding of the criticality of efficiency in its logistics and supply chain system from purchasing through delivery to its stores and a continual focus on improving its supply chain processes.

One could argue that most retailers are essentially supply chain companies since they buy products produced by others and sell these same products to their customers. While other factors such as merchandising, pricing, store location, and layout are very important, supply chain management and logistics are key ingredients for success in today's highly competitive global environment. Susan Weber (CEO, SAB) appears to

Table 1.1	Leading Retailers: 1930–2005
Montgomery Ward—1930s and 1940s	
Sears and Roebuck—1950s and 1960s	
Kmart—1970s and 1980s	
Wal-Mart—1990s to present	

comprehend the potential role that supply chains can play in making organizations successful. She also seems to understand that the dynamics of today's global environment require new thinking and perspectives.

At this juncture, an examination of the major external forces or change drivers shaping the economic and political environment is appropriate. We need to understand the impact of these forces of change on businesses and other organizations.

What Forces Are Driving the Rate of Change

We know that **supply chain management (SCM)** became a part of the vocabularies of CEOs, CFOs, COOs, and CIOs during the 1990s. The dynamics of the global environment changed dramatically during that decade, and organizations had to adapt to these changes or "die." Unfortunately, there were a number of casualties like some of the retailers previously mentioned.

Five major external forces seem to drive the rate of change and shape our economic and political landscape: globalization, technology, organizational consolidation, the empowered consumer, and government policy and regulation. The impact of these factors varies from sector to sector, but they are all important.

Globalization

Arguably, globalization is the most frequently cited change factor by business leaders, and it has replaced the post–World War II "cold war" as the dominant driving force for world economics. The concept of the "global marketplace" or global economy has taken on new meaning for all enterprises (profit and nonprofit; small, medium, and large) and for individual consumers during the last two decades.

Overall, globalization has led to a more competitively intense economic and geopolitical environment. This environment manifests itself in opportunities and threats, both economic and political. Some individuals have implied that there is no "geography" in the current global environment (figuratively speaking) or, perhaps more aptly, that time and distance have been compressed. So, for example, companies seeking to rationalize their global networks ask such questions as the following:

- Where in the world should we source our materials and/or services?
- Where in the world should we manufacture or produce our products and/or services?
- Where in the world should we market and sell our products and/or services?
- Where in the world should we store and/or distribute our products?
- What global transportation alternatives should we consider?

Some important issues or challenges for supply chains of the global economy are (1) more volatility of supply and demand, (2) shorter product life cycles, and (3) the blurring of traditional organizational boundaries. All three deserve some discussion.

Supply and demand have become more volatile for a number of reasons. Acts of terrorism, for example, can have serious implications for the flow of commerce. Companies have put in place security measures to protect their global supply chains and are prepared to act quickly to offset challenges to the flow of materials through their supply chains. Another example is the contamination of food products from countries such as

China. An interruption in the flow of products from China can cause serious shortages in the supply of food and other products. Natural catastrophes such as hurricanes, floods, earthquakes, etc., have become more problematic because of the scope and extent of global trade; therefore, they pose a significant potential problem. Other examples could be offered, but suffice it to say that challenges to supply and demand can be exacerbated in number and severity by the distances involved.

Longer-run issues of supply and demand also arise with the global competition of sources of supply and markets. The growth in steel production and automobile manufacturing in China and information technology in India has caused significant changes in U.S. markets in terms of economic impact. The global supply chains of the best companies must be adaptive and resilient to meet the challenges of the global marketplace.

Shorter product life cycles are a manifestation of the ability of products and services to be duplicated quickly. Technology companies are particularly vulnerable to the threat of their new products being reengineered. However, almost all products in our highly competitive global environment are faced with this issue. From a supply chain perspective, shorter product life cycles present a challenge for inventory management. Products that are duplicated will most likely face a faster reduction in demand and/or new pricing policies, both of which present challenges to effective inventory management. The risk of obsolescence in certain sectors of the economy as new products are developed is another challenge for inventory management.

The blurring of traditional organizational boundaries is the result of companies having to adjust or transform their business model or the way that they do business in a competitive global economy. To maintain their financial viability (read profitability), companies may have to outsource some parts of their operation to another domestic or global company that can provide what they need more efficiently and hopefully maintain the same quality. They may also add to their current operations to add value for customers. SAB is considering this strategy.

Outsourcing is not new. It has been going on for many decades. No organization is completely independent. The competitiveness of the global environment, however, has increased the scope of outsourcing both domestically and globally. As previously mentioned, companies need to analyze how they do business in order to stay competitive and financially viable. Nike, for example, outsources all of its manufacturing and has done so for many years. Airlines and hotels have outsourced their call centers. Many automobile and computer manufacturers outsource components or parts that they need for finished products. There are many examples of outsourcing for materials and services. From a supply chain and logistics perspective, the growth in outsourcing is very noteworthy because it increases the importance of effective and efficient global chains that are more complex and challenging.

Before discussing technology, mention should be made of the "BRIC factor" in our analysis of globalization and supply chains. BRIC is an acronym for the four countries of Brazil, Russia, India, and China. These four countries have a total population of about 2.8 billion, with China accounting for 1.3 billion of that total. These four countries, especially China and India, have been a leading force in the changing world marketplace in this era of globalization. They not only produce products and services for export, but they have also become major consumers of energy and other basic materials. The supply chains of most, if not all, companies have been affected by the emergence of the BRIC countries. Wal-Mart, for example, is by far the largest buyer of products produced in China, which is in sharp contrast to its 1970s slogan of "Made in America."

SAB Distribution has been impacted by globalization because a growing number of products that it buys and distributes are being produced in whole or in part in other countries even though a U.S. company is their source. SAB also needs to evaluate buying products directly from global producers. While this will add to the complexity of Wal-Mart's supply chains, it may enable the retail giant to provide more competitively priced products. Also, Wal-Mart may be able to satisfy the needs of its more diverse final customers. Similar to other U.S. companies, SAB is faced with both an opportunity and a threat in globalization.

A strong complement to the growth in the global economy has been the growth and development in the technology areas related to supply chains. Mention has been made of time and distance being compressed, and technology has certainly played a major role in making this happen. Technology will be discussed as the next external change factor.

Technology

Technology has had a major impact on supply chains as a facilitator of change as companies have transformed their processes. However, it is also a major force in changing the dynamics of the marketplace. Individuals and organizations are "connected" 24/7 and have access to information on the same basis via the Internet. Search engines such as Google have made it possible to gather timely information quickly. We have become what some individuals describe as the "click here" generation. We no longer have to wait for information to be "pushed out" to us via the media on their schedule; we can "pull" information as we need it. Vast stores of data and information are virtually at our fingertips.

It has been argued that technology has allowed individuals and smaller organizations to connect to the world's "knowledge pools" to create an unbelievable set of opportunities for collaboration in supply chains. A corollary of this phenomenon is that the world has become "flat." In other words, traditional underdeveloped countries such as China and India have become enabled and can participate in the global economy much more readily. The world is no longer tilted toward the developed countries such as the United States and European countries in terms of an economic advantage. Outsourcing to the less-developed countries has been enhanced by technology. Collaboration opportunities with individuals and companies throughout the globe have been enhanced. The flip side is that these economic advances have created market opportunities for U.S. companies. Consequently, the flow of commerce has become multidirectional. This factor also increases the need for efficient and effective supply chains.

Susan Weber, as SAB's new CEO, will have to fully exploit the opportunities presented by technology both on the procurement side of business and in serving customers. Her predecessor used technology to improve internal processes, e.g., warehouse operations and order fulfillment as well as transportation carrier collaboration. Susan will need to focus more externally to improve overall supply chain efficiency and effectiveness.

Organizational Consolidation

After World War II, product manufacturers became the driving force in supply chains. They developed, designed, produced, promoted, and distributed their products. They were usually the largest organizations in the supply chain in terms of sales volume, employees, buying power, locations, etc. They typically exerted their influence throughout the supply chain often to their specific economic advantage, especially in the distribution of their products.

During the 1980s and especially the 1990s, a significant change occurred in the relative economic power in a growing number of supply chains as mass retailers became increasingly larger. Retail giants such as Wal-Mart, Sears, Kmart, Home Depot, Target, Kroger, McDonald's, etc., became powerful market leaders. Wal-Mart, for example, was number one on the *Fortune* 500 list by the middle of the first decade of the twenty-first century. It had surpassed Ford, General Motors, and ExxonMobil with $350 billion plus of annual sales and was the number one employer in many states.

While other retailers are not as large as Wal-Mart, their size and economic buying power have increased significantly. An important aspect of the economic power shift toward the end of the supply chain is that many consumer product companies find that 15 to 20 percent of their customers account for 70 to 80 percent of their total sales. Wal-Mart, alone, may account for 10 to 20 percent of their total sales. Another interesting statistic is that if Wal-Mart was a country, it would be China's eighth largest trading partner.[4] This phenomenon is not just unique to the United States. For example, a list of the top 10 global retailers would include Carrefour, Metro, Ahold, and Tesco, all of which are headquartered in other countries.

The importance of the consolidation and power shift is that the large retailers are accorded special consideration from consumer product companies. For example, customized distribution services are provided such as scheduled deliveries, "rainbow" pallets [mixed array of products/stock-keeping units (SKUs)], advance shipment notices (ASNs), shrink-wrapped pallets, etc. These services allow retailers to operate more efficiently and often more effectively. The scale of the retailers can also provide economies (read cost savings) to the producers of the products.

In addition to customization, the retailer may be provided value-added services such as **vendor-managed inventory (VMI).** Essentially, this service usually means that the manufacturer will manage the inventory of its products and possibly related products at the retailer's warehouse(s) and reorder as appropriate for customer fulfillment. The manufacturer may also have a representative at the designated retail warehouse locations to assure accurate and timely delivery. The retailer should experience lower costs associated with inbound logistics, and the manufacturer should be able to offset its cost with increased sales (fewer stockouts, more complete orders, etc.).

Finally, more collaboration is being practiced between organizations in the supply chains to gain mutual cost savings and improved customer service. For example, sharing point-of-sale data is a powerful collaborative tool for mitigating the so-called bullwhip effect in the supply chain, which has multiple benefits to supply chain collaborators. Collaborative planning and forecasting for replenishment in the supply chain are other tools for reducing stockouts and overreaction to swings in demand levels. Companies sometimes can make simple changes at no extra cost to them, which will allow their vendors and/or their customers to reduce expenses. The power of information sharing cannot be overstated. This is a key area for SAB to exploit as it tries to adapt to its competitive environment.

The Empowered Consumer

Understanding consumer behavior has been a focus of marketing analysis and strategy development for many years. Typically, such analyses examine consumers in total and/or major groupings or segments to understand their needs and to respond to them with appropriate products and services. Such analyses have implications for logistics and supply chain management, but they have been viewed in the past by logisticians as having somewhat indirect impacts. Today, the impact of the consumer is much more direct for supply chains because the consumer has placed increased demands at the retail level for an expanded variety of products and services. For example, the availability of fresh fruits and vegetables year round which are frequently imported, a selection of many different variations of the same basic product, stores being open 24/7, etc., are all extras provided with very low margins on products. The supply chains have to be performing very efficiently to enable the retailer and other organizations in the supply chain to make a profit.

Today's consumers are more enlightened, educated, and empowered than ever before by the information that they have at their disposal from the Internet and other sources. Their access to supply sources has expanded dramatically beyond their immediate locale by virtue of catalogs, the Internet, and other media. They have the opportunity to compare prices, quality, and service. Consequently, they demand competitive prices, high quality, tailored/customized products, convenience, flexibility, and responsiveness. They tend to have a low tolerance level for poor quality in products and/or services. Consumers also have increased buying power due to higher income levels. They demand the best quality at the best price and with the best service. These demands place increased challenges and pressure on the various supply chains for consumer products.

The demographics of our society with the increase in two-career families and single-parent households have made time a critical factor for many households. Consumers want and demand quicker response times and more convenient offerings according to their schedules. The five-day services week from 9 AM to 6 PM for customers is no longer acceptable. The expectation for service is frequently 24/7 with a minimum of wait time. The age old axiom of "let the buyer beware" should probably be changed to "let the seller beware." Today's consumers do not have the loyalty of previous periods or much patience with inferior quality in any area. The Internet enables them to expand their buying alternatives and quickly make comparisons before they purchase. The associated transportation delivery service is usually expected to be provided quickly and conveniently.

Why is this consumer revolution so important in a supply chain/logistics context? The reason is that the supply chain/logistics requirements have dramatically increased. For example, if retail establishments have to be open for 24 hours seven days a week, their resulting tendency to order more frequently in smaller quantities places greater demands on the supply chains that serve them. Also, the pressure from consumers related to price puts pressure in turn on the supply chain to operate as efficiently as possible. The "power" of the consumer has caused much change in how supply chains function.

Government Policy and Regulation

The fifth external change factor is the various levels of government (federal, state, and local) that establish and administer policies, regulations, taxes, etc., which impact individual businesses and their supply chains. The deregulation of several important sectors of our economy that occurred in the 1980s and 1990s is a good example. These deregulated sectors include transportation, communications, and financial institutions—all of which are cornerstones of the infrastructure for most organizations.

Beginning in the late 1970s and into the 1980s, U.S. transportation was deregulated at the federal level in terms of economic controls such as rates and areas of service. The net effect was that it became possible for transportation services to be purchased and sold in a much more competitive environment. The results were frequently lower prices to users and better service. It became possible for carriers and shippers to negotiate and to make changes in their respective operations to allow carriers to operate more efficiently and lower their prices. New carriers entered the marketplace, particularly in the motor carrier industry. Certain sectors of transportation underwent consolidation through mergers and acquisition; most notable were the railroads and airlines. Transportation companies have also been allowed to offer more than just transportation services. Many motor carriers, for example, have declared themselves to be logistics services companies and offer an array of related services that can include order fulfillment, inventory management, warehousing, etc. They have moved aggressively ahead in the new business environment where companies view outsourcing and partnerships as potential strategic advantages.

The financial sector was also deregulated at the federal level. The distinction between commercial banks, savings and loan associations, and credit unions, for example, has blurred as these institutions have been allowed to broaden their array of services. Financial markets have become more competitive and, like the transportation sector, more responsive to customer needs. Brokerage and insurance companies have also been impacted by the deregulation of the broad financial industry, and some offer services similar to banks and vice versa.

The deregulation of financial institutions has fostered changes in how businesses can operate. For example, the opportunity to invest cash at the end of the day in the global overnight money market in periods of 6–10 hours made many companies more cognizant of the value of asset liquidity and asset reduction, especially inventory. Payment transactions for buyers and sellers have also changed dramatically with the alternatives in financial practices made possible by deregulation. The purchase cards used by many procurement departments for maintenance, repair, and operating (MRO) items are examples of the efficiencies that were made possible by deregulation. All of the above have contributed to the focus on cash flow previously discussed.

The communications industry was also made more competitive. This scenario was different since the major cause of change was a Supreme Court decision that split up the AT&T/Bell telephone system into regional companies, separated the "long-lines system" of AT&T, and made it accessible to other companies such as Sprint that wanted to sell telephone services. Like the other two industries discussed earlier, the communications industry has undergone much change and more is coming with the integration of related services such as cable, telephone, computers, and wireless access.

Businesses and the general consumer population are all being impacted by the many changes in this industry from cell phones and pagers to e-mail, text messaging, and the Internet. Communications efficiency and effectiveness have led to dramatic improvements and opportunities in logistics and supply chains. Examples include inventory visibility, quick response replenishment, improved transportation scheduling, rapid order entry, and so on. Supply chain practices have been improved leading to lower cost and better customer service. Some people argue that the best is yet to come with radio-frequency identification (RFID) and other technology.

SAB Distribution is being buffeted by all of these change drivers. The marketplace is much more competitive; consumers are much more demanding and knowledgeable. Globalization and deregulation have made SAB much more vulnerable in its regional

On the Line
Malt-O-Meal Company: Going National

Malt-O-Meal Company (MOM) is a small to medium-sized family-owned manufacturer (approximately $500 million per year) headquartered in Minneapolis, Minnesota. MOM has been an industry leader in providing quality, value-priced breakfast cereals to U.S. consumers since 1919. The company markets hot and ready-to-eat cereals under its own brand as well as private labels.

Over the last four years, Malt-O-Meal cereal sales have grown 40 percent in total pounds sold through traditional grocery store formats. This growth represents a market share change of approximately two points (on a total weight basis), from 3.2 percent to 5 percent of the $9 billion U.S. breakfast cereal market.

One driver of this growth has been the expanded distribution of the Malt-O-Meal brand. SKUs are increasing due to the addition of flavors, package types, and case configurations for new outlets like foodservice, mass merchants, and drug- and dollar-store formats. But this proliferation of SKUs and the unique requirements of nontraditional channels have added complexity to the existing business processes and the challenged supporting systems.

The company looked to its supply chain to deliver results for these growth initiatives while maintaining or reducing delivered cost and meeting service-level targets.

The supply chain organization at Malt-O-Meal is centralized and covers multiple production sites and distribution centers. It includes customer service, customer logistics, inventory planning, production planning, materials planning, procurement, distribution, and transportation. With this broad functional coverage, prioritization of supply chain initiatives is essential to success. MOM established its supply chain priorities based on three categories: customer focus (service), operational efficiency (cost/return on invested capital), and company culture (values).

SUPPLY CHAIN ORGANIZATION AND DEVELOPMENT

The supply chain organization has evolved to enable MOM to increase distribution of its brand. MOM has expanded the breadth of its supply chain by adding procurement to its responsibilities for end-to-end accountability. Packaging, commodities, and ingredients, for example, all have significant impact on the cost of goods sold and the delivered cost to the customer. For this reason, dollars conserved in these areas are available for investment in growth opportunities. In addition, MOM has created a customer logistics team to serve as points of contact to solve key customer supply chain issues. This has helped brand expansion by enabling effective customer collaboration and demonstrating service-level improvement.

MOM also restructured both its supply chain planning and execution (SCPE) group and the procurement group to focus efforts on creating executable operating plans that deliver desired results. SCPE was restructured to interface with internal customers: demand planning with sales, inventory planning with distribution, and production scheduling and materials management with manufacturing. Procurement was restructured to put an emphasis on strategic sourcing as well as transactional processes. Finally, to help ensure that it has future supply chain leaders, MOM recently began a leadership development initiative.

Source: Chris Norek, Wesley Gass, and Thomas Jorgenson, "You Can Transform Your Supply Chain, Too," *Supply Chain Management Review* (March 2007): 38. Copyright© 2007 Reed Business Information, a division of Reed Elsevier. Reproduced by permission.

marketplace and much less insulated against larger competitors. These change drivers represent both opportunities and threats for SAB, as well as for other businesses both large and small.

The rate of change has accelerated, as previously noted, with consequent negative impacts if organizations do not change accordingly. But such change can also have positive impacts if appropriate actions are taken. For example, the deregulation of transportation led to the demise of some very large, financially successful transportation companies that prospered in the era of regulation, but could not cope in the deregulated, competitive marketplace in the 1980s. On the other hand, new large and economically viable companies emerged in this more competitive environment such as Federal Express, Schneider National, and J.B. Hunt. They changed in response to the opportunities of the new environment.

The Supply Chain Concept

While references to supply chain management can be traced to the 1980s, it is safe to say that not until the 1990s did SCM capture the attention of senior-level management in numerous organizations. They recognized the power and potential impact of SCM to make organizations more globally competitive and to increase market share with consequent improvement in shareholder value.

Development of the Concept

It can be argued that supply chain management is not a brand new concept. Rather, supply chain management represents the third phase of an evolution that started in the 1960s with the development of the **physical distribution** concept that focused on the outbound side of a firm's logistics system. A number of studies[5] during the 1950s and 1960s indicated the potential of the systems concept. The focus of physical distribution was on total systems cost and analyzing tradeoff scenarios to arrive at the best or lowest system cost. As is explained in more detail in the next chapter, the system relationships among transportation, inventory requirements, warehousing, exterior packaging, materials handling, and some other activities or cost centers were recognized. For example, the selection and use of a mode of transportation, such as rail, impacts inventory, warehousing, packaging, customer service, and materials-handling costs; whereas motor carrier service would probably have a different impact on the same cost centers. The type of product, volume of movement, ship distances, etc., would influence which mode would have the lower total cost.

The initial focus on physical distribution or outbound logistics was logical since finished goods were usually higher in value, which meant that their inventory, warehousing, materials-handling, and packaging costs were relatively higher than their raw materials inputs. The impact of transportation selection was, therefore, usually more significant. Managers in certain industries such as consumer package/grocery products, high-tech companies, and other consumer product companies—as well as some academicians—became very interested in physical distribution management. A national organization, the **National Council of Physical Distribution Management (NCPDM),** was organized to foster leadership, education, research, and interest in this area.

The 1980s, as noted earlier, was a decade of change with the deregulation of transportation and financial institutions. The technology revolution was also well under way.

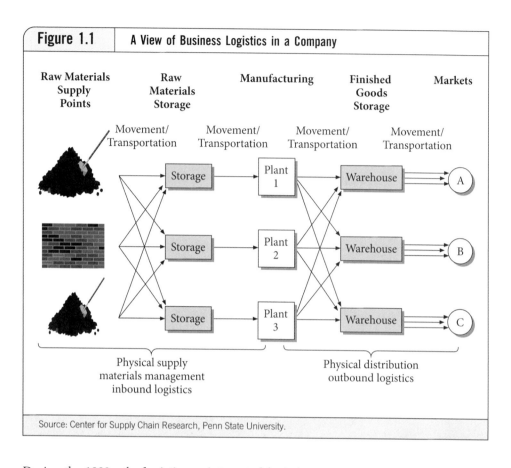

Figure 1.1 | **A View of Business Logistics in a Company**

Source: Center for Supply Chain Research, Penn State University.

During the 1980s, the **logistics** or **integrated logistics management concept** developed in a growing number of organizations. Logistics, in its simplest form, added inbound logistics to the outbound logistics of physical distribution (see Figures 1.1 and 1.2). This was a very logical addition since deregulation of transportation provided an opportunity to coordinate inbound and outbound transportation movements of large shippers, which could positively impact a carrier's operating cost by minimizing empty backhauls, leading to lower rates for the shipper. Also, international or global sourcing of materials and supplies for inbound systems was growing in importance. As previously noted, global transportation presents some special challenges for production scheduling. Therefore, it became increasingly apparent that coordination between the outbound and inbound logistics systems provided opportunities for increased efficiency and, perhaps, improved customer service.

The underlying logic of the **systems** or **total cost concept** was also the rationale for logistics management. However, the **value chain concept** had also been developed as a tool for competitive analysis and strategy. As can be seen in the value chain illustration in Figure 1.3, inbound and outbound logistics are important, primary components of the value chain; that is, they contribute value to the firm's customers and make the company financially viable. The more integrated nature of marketing, sales, and manufacturing with logistics is also an important dimension of the value chain. Logistics authors would usually include **procurement** as an element of logistics, as is indicated in Chapter 2, but the value chain depicts it as a support activity for all the primary activities. The rationale for the former is the opportunity for tradeoff analysis between procurement quantities, transportation volumes, inventory levels, and other related costs.

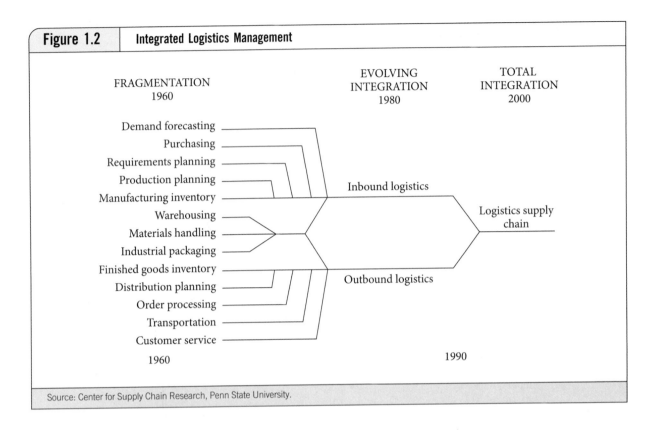

Figure 1.2 | **Integrated Logistics Management**

Source: Center for Supply Chain Research, Penn State University.

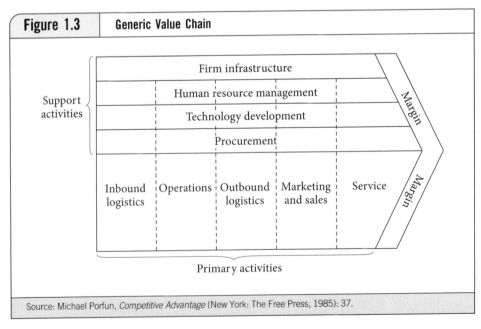

Figure 1.3 | **Generic Value Chain**

Source: Michael Porfun, *Competitive Advantage* (New York: The Free Press, 1985): 37.

As already stated, supply chain management came into vogue during the 1990s and continues to be a focal point for making organizations more competitive in the global marketplace. Supply chain management can be viewed as a pipeline or conduit for the efficient and effective flow of products/materials, services, information, and financials

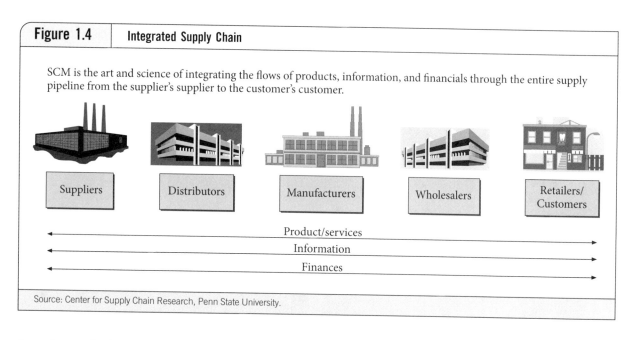

| Figure 1.4 | Integrated Supply Chain |

SCM is the art and science of integrating the flows of products, information, and financials through the entire supply pipeline from the supplier's supplier to the customer's customer.

Suppliers Distributors Manufacturers Wholesalers Retailers/Customers

Product/services
Information
Finances

Source: Center for Supply Chain Research, Penn State University.

from the supplier's suppliers through the various intermediate organizations/ companies out to the customer's customers (see Figure 1.4) or the system of connected networks between the original vendors and the ultimate final consumer. The extended enterprise perspective of supply chain management represents a logical extension of the logistics concept providing an opportunity to view the total system of interrelated companies for increased efficiency and effectiveness.

Before discussing and analyzing the supply chain concept in more detail, it is worth noting that a growing number of terms are being utilized by individuals and organizations that are presented as being more appropriate, comprehensive, and/or advanced than *supply chain management.* Such terms include *demand chain management, demand flow management, value chain management, value networks,* and *synchronization management,* etc. *Supply chain management* is viewed by some individuals to be narrowly focused and/or focused upon supplies and materials, not demand for finished products.

The definition of supply chain management proposed in this book is broad and comprehensive; therefore, demand and value are very relevant as well as synchronization of flows through the pipeline or supply chain. Thus, it could be argued that *supply chain, demand chain, value network, value chains,* etc., can be used as synonyms. Also, there appears to be a more widespread use and acceptance of the term *supply chain management* and the comprehensive viewpoint of supply chain management espoused in this chapter and throughout the book.

A logical question to be asked is why did supply chain management attract attention among CEOs, CFOs, COOs, CIOs, and other senior executives? A myriad of reasons can be given, but the business case for supply chain management was demonstrated by two well-known studies.

In the early 1990s, the Grocery Manufacturer's Association (GMA) commissioned a study by one of the large supply chain consulting organizations to research and analyze the supply chains of grocery manufacturers. Figure 1.5 illustrates one of the major findings of the study: on average, the industry had 104 days of inventory in its outbound supply chains.

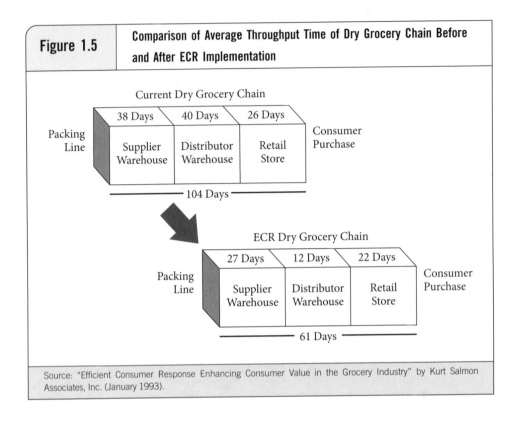

Figure 1.5 — Comparison of Average Throughput Time of Dry Grocery Chain Before and After ECR Implementation

Current Dry Grocery Chain

Packing Line | 38 Days | 40 Days | 26 Days | Consumer Purchase

Supplier Warehouse | Distributor Warehouse | Retail Store

104 Days

ECR Dry Grocery Chain

Packing Line | 27 Days | 12 Days | 22 Days | Consumer Purchase

Supplier Warehouse | Distributor Warehouse | Retail Store

61 Days

Source: "Efficient Consumer Response Enhancing Consumer Value in the Grocery Industry" by Kurt Salmon Associates, Inc. (January 1993).

The consulting company recommended a set of initiatives that would lead to reducing that to 61 days of inventory. There are two important points here. First, it was estimated that at least $30 billion per year would be saved by reducing pipeline inventory to 61 days. Such savings had the potential of having a significant impact upon consumer prices or what might be called "landed prices." Second, this study only considered part of the supply chain, which, therefore, understated the total potential. The potential savings of $30 billion demonstrated the power of optimizing the supply chain as opposed to just one individual company or one segment of the supply chain. The latter perspective often results in suboptimization of the whole supply chain with subsequent higher overall costs.

The other demonstration of the importance of focusing upon the supply chain came from the Supply Chain Council, which published a comparison for 1996 and 1997 of "best-in-class" companies (top 10 percent) and the median companies that were reporting their metrics to the council. As can be seen from Figure 1.6, in 1996, the supply chain–related costs of the best-in-class (BIC) companies were 7.0 percent of total sales, while the median company experienced 13.1 percent. In other words, the best-in-class companies spent 7.0 cents of every sales/revenue dollar for supply chain–related costs, while the median company spent 13.1 cents of every sales dollar on supply chain–related costs. In 1997, the respective numbers were 6.3 percent and 11.6 percent for best-in-class companies versus the median company. If we take a simple application of these numbers for a hypothetical company with $100 million in sales in 1997, being best in class would mean an additional $5.3 million of gross profit to an organization, which frequently would be the equivalent profit from an additional $80–$100 million of sales.

At this point, a more detailed analysis and discussion of the supply chain is appropriate. Figure 1.7 presents a simplified, linear example of a hypothetical supply chain.

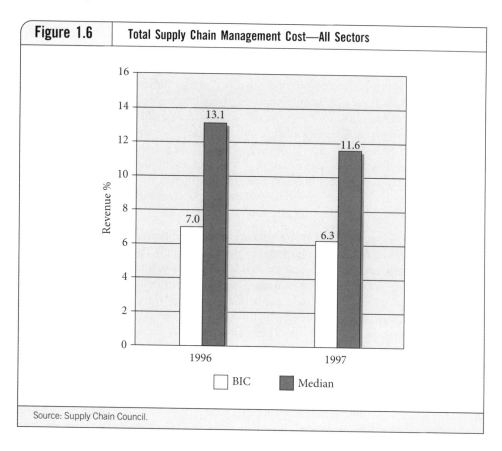

Figure 1.6 | **Total Supply Chain Management Cost—All Sectors**

Source: Supply Chain Council.

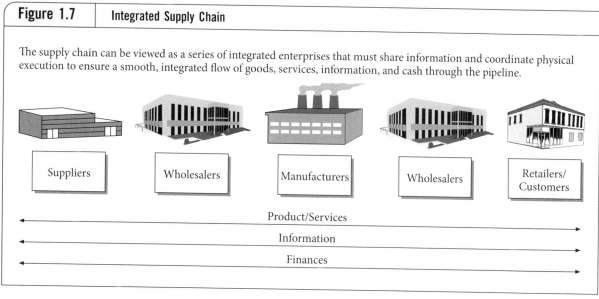

Figure 1.7 | **Integrated Supply Chain**

The supply chain can be viewed as a series of integrated enterprises that must share information and coordinate physical execution to ensure a smooth, integrated flow of goods, services, information, and cash through the pipeline.

Real-world supply chains are usually more complex than this example because they may be nonlinear and/or have more supply chain participants. Also, this supply chain does not adequately portray the importance of transportation in the supply chain. In addition, some companies may be part of several supply chains. For example, chemical companies provide the ingredients for many different products manufactured by different companies.

Figure 1.7, however, does provide sufficient perspective at this juncture to understand the basics of a supply chain. The definition that is a part of the illustration indicates several very important points. A **supply chain** is an extended enterprise that crosses the boundaries of individual firms to span the related activities of all the companies involved in the total supply chain. This extended enterprise should attempt to execute or implement a coordinated, two-way flow of goods/services, information, and financials (especially cash). The three flows enumerated at the bottom of the illustration are very important to the success of supply chain management. Integration across the boundaries of several organizations in essence means that the supply chain needs to function similar to one organization in satisfying the ultimate customer.

The top *flow—products and related services—has* traditionally been an important focus of logisticians and is still an important element in supply chain management. Customers expect their orders to be delivered in a timely, reliable, and damage-free manner; and transportation is critical to this outcome. Figure 1.7 also indicates that product flow is a two-way flow in today's environment because of the growing importance of reverse logistics systems for returning products that are unacceptable to the buyer, because they are damaged, obsolete, or worn out. There are numerous reasons for this growth in reverse systems, which are explored in Chapter 15, but there is no question that it is a growing phenomenon of supply chains. Note also that networks for reverse systems usually have to be designed differently than forward systems. The location, size, and layout of facilities are frequently different; and the transportation carriers need to be utilized differently. Consequently, third-party logistics companies that specialize in offering reverse flow systems have developed. They can provide a valuable service in appropriate situations.

The second flow indicated is the *information flow,* which has become an extremely important factor for success in supply chain management. Traditionally, we have viewed information as flowing in the opposite direction of products, that is, from the market/customer back to the wholesalers, manufacturers, and vendors. The information was primarily demand or sales data, which were the trigger for replenishment and the basis for forecasting. Note that, other than the retailer or final seller, the other members of the supply chain traditionally reacted to replenishment orders. If there were long time intervals between orders, the members of the supply chain were faced with much uncertainty about the level and pattern of the demand, which usually resulted in higher inventory or stockout costs, a phenomenon known as the **bullwhip effect.**

One of the realizable outcomes of supply chain management is the sharing of sales information on a more "real-time" basis, which leads to less uncertainty and, therefore, less safety stock. In a sense, the supply chain is being compressed or shortened through timely information flows back from the marketplace, which leads to a type of supply chain compression or inventory compression. In other words, inventory can be eliminated from the supply chain by timely, accurate information about demand. If point-of-sale (POS) data were available from the retail level on a real-time basis, it would help to mitigate the bullwhip effect associated with supply chain inventories and could significantly reduce cost.

Note that the illustration also indicates a two-way flow for information. In a supply chain environment, information flowing forward in the supply chain has taken on increased significance and importance. Forward information flow can take many forms such as advance shipment notices, order status information, inventory availability information, and so on. The overall impact has been to reduce uncertainty with respect to order replenishment, which also contributes to lowering inventory and improving replenishment time. A related aspect of forward information flow has been the increased utilization of barcodes and radio-frequency tags, which can increase inventory visibility and help reduce uncertainty and safety stock. The improved visibility of pipeline inventory also makes possible many opportunities for improved efficiency such as transportation consolidation and merge-in-transit strategies. The combined two-way flow of timely, accurate information lowers supply chain–related costs while also improving effectiveness/ customer service; but much more improvement can be made.

The third and final flow is *financials* or, more specifically, cash. Traditionally, financial flow has been viewed as one-directional—backward—in the supply chain or, in other words, payment for goods, services, and orders received. A major impact of supply chain compression and faster order cycle times has been faster cash flow. Customers receive orders faster, they are billed sooner, and companies can collect sooner. The faster cash-to-cash cycle or order-to-cash cycle has been a bonanza for companies because of the impact on working capital. In fact, some companies have negative working capital or what financial organizations refer to as "free" cash flow. They actually collect from their customers before they have to pay their vendors or suppliers. In companies such as Dell, where this period between collection and payment may be 30 to 45 days, the cash can be used for financial investment purposes or as another source of funding for product development or other improvements. Cash flow measures have become an important metric of the financial markets to gauge the viability or vulnerability of companies.

SAB Distribution is obviously part of a supply chain with an intermediate position between manufacturers and retailers. Wholesalers had a traditional role, which was buying products in volume quantities at volume prices and selling a mix of products in smaller quantities at higher prices to retailers. They frequently played a role in promoting and financing product sales in addition to distributing the item. Manufacturers and retailers depended upon them for efficiency in their operations. Large-scale retailers and manufacturers willing and able to provide more tailored, customized services have put wholesalers in jeopardy. SAB has felt this changing environment. It needs to reevaluate its role in relation to its retailers.

Supply chain management provides organizations with an opportunity to reduce cost (improve efficiency) and improve customer service (effectiveness). However, certain issues or challenges must be addressed before SCM will be successful.

Major Supply Chain Issues

The challenge to develop and sustain an efficient and effective supply chain(s) requires organizations to address a number of issues. We will discuss these issues briefly here, but they will be explored in much more depth in later chapters.

Supply Chain Networks

The network facilities (plants, distribution centers, terminals, etc.) and the supporting transportation services have long been considered important. However, the network system in a dynamic, global environment is critical. One of the challenges is the rapid changes that can take place. Companies and other organizations need a network system that is capable and flexible to respond and change with the dynamics of the marketplace whether in the short run or the long run.

Technology companies, for example, may have to move manufacturing operations to a different country in six to nine months because of changes that can occur which affect their cost and/or customer service. The need for flexibility frequently means leasing facilities, equipment, and maybe supporting services. At times, the flexibility may be required for a shorter duration—for example, a port strike, floods, hurricanes, etc. In either case, flexibility is a necessary requisite for success.

Wal-Mart and Home Depot received accolades for their ability to respond in 2005 to Hurricane Katrina and the flood disasters that occurred in New Orleans and the surrounding Gulf Coast area. Their respective supply chains distributed products when the Federal Emergency Management Agency (FEMA) was incapable. These same organizations analyze and change their networks in response to longer-run phenomena in the marketplace.

Complexity

Globalization and consolidation in supply chains that were previously discussed have caused an increased complexity for organizations in terms of SKUs, customer/supplier locations, transportation requirements, trade regulations, taxes, etc. Companies need to take steps to simplify, as much as possible, the various aspects of their supply chains. For example, the number of SKUs has expanded for many companies, which exacerbates problems for inventory management and order fulfillment. Consequently, companies have been rationalizing SKUs to eliminate the slow movers and/or items that do not contribute to profitability. Locations also need to be analyzed to eliminate high-cost operations. Customer service levels need to be rationalized as do vendors or suppliers. Layers of complexity develop and may seem necessary, but organizations need to continually evaluate those areas of complexity.

Inventory Deployment

Two interesting characteristics of supply chains are that inventory is often duplicated along the chain and the bullwhip effect arises. Consequently, SCM provides an opportunity to reduce inventory levels. The GMA study previously discussed in this chapter is a good example. Coordination or integration can help reduce inventory levels on horizontal (one firm) and/or vertical (multiple firms) levels in the supply chain. Strategies such as compression and postponement can also have a positive impact. Inventory deployment is a very important issue for supply chains because of the associated cost and related opportunities for increased efficiency.

Information

The technology and communication systems that are available to organizations today lead to the collection and storage of vast amounts of data, but interestingly enough, organizations may not be taking advantage of the abundant data to develop information systems to improve decision making. The accumulation and storage of data unless they are shared horizontally and vertically in the supply chain and used to make better decisions about inventory, customer service, transportation, etc., are almost useless. Information can be a powerful tool if it is timely, accurate, managed, and shared. It can be a substitute for inventory because it can reduce uncertainty. The latter is one of the major causes of higher inventory levels because it leads to the accumulation of safety stock. The challenge, frequently, is

On the Line — *How Supply Chain Variation Impacts Shareholder Value*

In today's global economy, companies are expected to provide competitive returns to shareholders. For publicly traded companies, the total return to shareholders is measured by the increase in stock price plus the dividends paid.

Clearly, a company's stock price is impacted by a variety of factors. However, in the long term, stock prices tend to be driven by company profits as measured by economic value added (EVA). EVA defines the true profit a company generates after deducting the total cost of doing business (i.e., operating costs, taxes, and cost of capital) from the revenues. Unlike the traditional financial measures, EVA enables managers to determine whether they are earning an adequate return. If the long-term trend in EVA is positive, a company earns a higher return than other investments of similar risk, and shareholder value is created.

The three basic drivers of EVA are revenue growth, cost reduction, and asset reduction. Supply chain management should be viewed as a powerful tool affecting all three drivers of financial performance/shareholder value. While holding the right mix of inventory could result in revenue growth, providing the same level of service with a lower amount of inventory (safety stocks) would result in shorter cash-to-cash cycle time and higher liquidity, allowing firms to grow faster and create shareholder value.

Variation in demand, supply, and lead times is a critical, but widely unrecognized, driver of inventory costs. Unfortunately, many managers are trained to think in terms of averages and do not fully appreciate the importance of the variation around those averages.

Such variation causes many of the costly supply chain disruptions and forces companies to keep excessive amounts of safety stocks. As supply chains become longer and more complex, it is even more important for companies to measure and control supply chain variation to improve their financial performance and maximize shareholder value.

Source: Farzad Mahmoodi, Clarkson University, and Heimo Losbichler, Steyr University (Austria), *World Trade Magazine* (September 5, 2006).

the sharing of information along the supply chain and the discipline to ensure the integrity of the data collected—a big challenge but one with much potential.

Cost/Value

Frequent reference has been made in this chapter to efficiency (cost) and effectiveness (value). A challenge for supply chains is the prevention of suboptimization. In today's environment, global supply chains compete against global supply chains, which means that the cost and value at the very end of the supply chain are what is important. If a competing supply chain is offering a comparable product at a lower cost and higher value, it does not matter if a company is effective and efficient but in the middle of another supply chain.

Consider SAB's situation. It has to be cognizant of the cost and value being offered by the large retailers who compete against its customers. It must think in terms of making its customers more competitive and/or attracting different customers where the synergies will lead to better outcomes. SAB's expertise in warehousing, distribution, and inventory management might be capitalized on for a new but related type of business. The supply chain perspective with vertical and horizontal views provides an opportunity to "think out of the box."

Organizational Relationships

Supply chain management emphasizes a horizontal process orientation that cuts across traditional functional silos within organizations and necessitates collaboration with external vendors, customers, transportation companies, 3 PLs, and others in the supply chain. In other words, internal collaboration or cooperation with marketing, sales, operations/manufacturing, and accounting/finance are very important as well as collaboration or cooperation with external organizations. Communication is critical to explain the opportunities for system tradeoffs that will make the supply chain more competitive. For example, the vice president of manufacturing may present a rationale for operating plants on a 24/7 basis to lower production costs, but what about the cost of warehousing and inventory of goods that have to be stored until sales are finalized? Looking at manufacturing cost in isolation could lead to higher overall system costs. In Chapter 2, we will explore the concept of systems analysis in more detail.

Performance Measurement

Most organizations have measures of performance or metrics in place to analyze and evaluate their efficiency and progress over different time periods. Sometimes, such measures are used for setting baseline performance objectives or expected outcomes, e.g., orders filled and shipped per day. Measurement is important, and more attention will be devoted to this topic in Chapter 5. At this juncture, it is important to recognize that lower-level metrics in an organization must connect directly to the high-level performance measures of the organization and the supply chain, which are usually net profit, return on investment, or assets and cash flow. In some instances, metrics are set that appear logical for the subunit of the organization but are suboptimal for the overall organization or supply chain. The previous example of the vice president running the plants 24/7 to achieve the lowest possible unit cost of products could have been saving 3 cents per unit on manufacturing, but the extra expense of holding excess inventory could have cost 4 to 5 cents per unit, thus lowering the company's net profit margin. The warehouse manager who is measured by the cost per cubic foot of units stored will be motivated to fill the warehouse to the ceiling (what is the tradeoff cost?).

Technology

Technology, as indicated previously, can be viewed as a change driver, but it is also important as a facilitator of change that will lead to improved efficiency and effectiveness. The challenge is to evaluate and successfully implement the technology to make the improvements desired. Sometimes technology is, figuratively speaking, thrown at a problem, which usually leads to frustration and then failure. The approach necessary is to analyze and adjust or change processes, educate the people involved, and then select and implement the technology to facilitate the changes in the processes. Skipping the first two steps is analogous to the frequently cited bad approach to strategic planning—ready, fire, aim. The technology available today is almost overwhelming, but analysis and planning are necessary to achieve the expected outcomes.

Transportation Management

Transportation can be viewed as the glue that makes the supply chain model function. The critical outcomes of the supply chain are to deliver the right product, at the right time, in the right quantity and quality, at the right cost, and to the right destination. Transportation plays an important role in making these "rights" happen. Another aspect

Supply Chain Technology

Transforming Supply Chain IT into "Business Technology"

When Nike, in a well-known fiasco, implemented its new supply chain software system in 2000, it lost $200 million. Its failure wasn't an anomaly, either. Gartner, Forrester, and other leading IT analysts regularly report systemic disconnects between IT and business processes that are responsible for poor returns on investment. The bottom line is that IT supply chain projects typically succeed only one in three times. No wonder execs view IT skeptically. On the flip side, Home Depot, Intel, Sun Microsystems, and others have achieved stellar results netting savings of millions when they used IT to revamp their supply chains. What is the different between success and failure? It lies not so much in what you do as in how you do it.

INTEL'S SOLVER INITIATIVE

Intel sought to improve its supply chain performance by introducing automated decisionmaking modules known as *solvers*. Solvers have been used for five years now in an environment with very dynamic markets and with many suppliers and manufacturing facilities.

The goals for the solvers initiative were to reduce the assembly test manufacturing schedule resets, reduce inventory, allocate product dies more efficiently, and deliver $2 million in optimization value. An after-implementation analysis showed that solvers were most effective for the less complex issues in product planning, resulting in a decision to put more emphasis on adapting the solvers for more complex issues with significant effects upon business processes of data quality requirements.

Using solvers saved Intel $39 million by reducing tactical planning. Improvements in cost management and supplier optimization saved another $26 million. By integrating business-to-business interactions with third-party boxing suppliers and standardizing shop-floor control solutions, Intel saved $3 million and enabled an integrated build plan process. Expanding that shop-floor control solution globally, along with developing better domestic shipping solutions and better performance metrics, saved an additional $21 million in transportation costs, according to Intel's analysis, published in the "2005 Information Technology Annual Performance Report."

At the same time, Intel was developing another supply chain program to establish closer ties with suppliers to thereby improve purchasing agility by creating a common approach to running the supply chain.

By replacing the myriad systems it used to source, requisition, procure, and account for materials and services with SAP's standard supplier relationship management framework and integrating it into Intel's existing ERP solutions, the hodgepodge was transformed into an agile enterprise solution platform.

The results of this teamwork began rolling out in late 2005. By year-end, Intel had completed three proofs of concept for the architecture and was 50 percent more agile in terms of aligning itself with industry expectations. Development time for enterprise solutions was cut from two years to five months for three projects undertaken on the new platform, and 19 other projects involved customers more closely in their development, which allowed faster completion with high levels of customer satisfaction. Deployment time for supply chain projects was cut by 75 percent, and software licensing and integration costs were also reduced.

Together, these two supply chain projects contributed $1 billion to Intel's "top-line growth or bottom-line improvements," according to its "2005 Information Technology Annual Performance Report."

Source: Gail Dutton, *World Trade Magazine* (September 5, 2006).

of the importance of transportation is related to some of the strategies that are being used by companies to remain competitive in today's economy—for example, just-in-time inventory, lean logistics and manufacturing, scheduled deliveries, etc. The challenge has been exacerbated by economic changes among transportation providers; shortages of drivers, higher fuel costs, and changes in driver hours regulations have led to what some individuals have called a transportation crisis or the "perfect storm." Transportation has gone from being a readily available "commodity" to potential users, especially in the 1990s, to today where transportation is scarce in some market areas.

Supply Chain Security

Safe, reliable delivery of products to customers is expected of the supply chain. In the past, this was often accepted as a given, but today it is a concern and potential challenge since 9/11. Globalization has obviously increased the risk of interruptions or shutdowns of supply chains. Consequently, organizations must be prepared in case of a terrorist attack. Such threats have changed some of the planning and preparation for supply chains that often include some type of scenario analysis that can consider possible threats, assess probabilities, and plan for alternatives.

SUMMARY

- Cash flow has become one of the most important measures of financial viability in today's global markets. Supply chains are an important determinant of improved cash flow since they impact order cycle time to customers.

- Supply chains are an important determinant of capital consumption since they impact working capital, inventory levels, and other assets such as warehouses.

- Efficient and effective supply chains can free up valuable resources and improve customer fulfillment systems so as to increase return on investment or assets and improve shareholder value.

- The rate of change in our economy has accelerated the necessity of continuing changes in organizations or even transformation to remain competitive.

- The rate of change has been driven by a set of external forces including but not limited to globalization, technology, organizational consolidation and shifts in power in supply chains, an empowered consumer, and government policy and regulations.

- The conceptual basis of the supply chain is not new. In fact, organizations have evolved from physical distribution management to logistics management to supply chain management.

- Supply chains are boundary spanning and require managing three flows—products, information, and financials (cash).

- Supply chain management is a journey, not a goal, and there are no "silver bullets" since all supply chains are unique.

- Information is power, and collaborative relationships internally and externally are a necessary ingredient for success.

- The performance of supply chains must be measured in terms of overall corporate goals for success.

- Supply chains need to focus on the customers at the end of the supply chain and be flexible and responsive.

- Technology is important to facilitate change, but it must follow a process and educate people to address problems and issues appropriately.

- Transportation management and security have become increasingly important in the twenty-first century because of changes that have occurred.

- Change with the changes, or you will be changed by the change!

STUDY QUESTIONS

1. Globalization and technology developments have led to what some individuals have described as a "flat world." What is the significance of the flat world concept? What is the impact of the flat world on supply chains?

2. The consolidation that has developed at the retail end of many supply chains has been described as the Wal-Mart effect. Why? What is the significance of retail consolidation for supply chains?

3. Consumers are considered to have much more influence in the marketplace today. What factors have lead to this "empowered consumer" situation? How has this factor changed supply chains in the last 10 to 15 years? Will this influence continue?

4. The influence and impact of federal, state, and local governments seem to be growing in importance for supply chains. Why? What are the most important dimensions of governmental control for supply chains?

5. Why should CEOs, COOs, CFOs, and CMOs be concerned about supply chain management in their organizations?

6. Supply chain managers should be concerned about three flows in their organizations. What are these three flows, and why are they important? How are they related to each other?

7. During the 1980s and 1990s, managing the transportation function in supply chains was recognized as being important but not critical. Has this perspective changed, and, if so, how and why?

8. Collaboration is a very critical ingredient for successful supply chains. Why? What types of collaboration are important? What are some of the challenges?

9. Why is information so important in supply chains? What are the challenges to the successful development and implementation of effective information?

10. What special role do networks play in supply chains? What are some of the challenges for efficient and effective networks?

NOTES

1. James Tompkins, speech presented at the Warehouse of the Future Conference (Atlanta, GA: May 2000).

2. Joe Paterno, football coach, speech presented at Penn State University (September 1998).

3. Anonymous, *Logistics* (July/August 2000): 43.

4. Charles Fishman, *The Wal-Mart Effect* (New York: Penguin Press, 2006): 5–7.

5. George Smerk, George Wilson, and John Spychalski, *Physical Distribution Management*, Vol. 1 (Bloomington, IN: Indiana University Press, 1964): 15–21.

CASE 1.1

Central Transport, Inc.

Jean Beierlein, president and CEO of Central Transport, had just met with Susan Weber, the new president and CEO of SAB Distribution. Jean had recently been promoted from COO at Central Transport. Her predecessor had worked closely with the former CEO of SAB Distribution when SAB had transferred its operations about seven years earlier to respond to changes in its competitive marketplace. Now, Susan was faced with new challenges and wanted the collaboration of Jean and Central Transport to transform again.

According to Susan, she had met extensively with the old and new members of her executive team (several old timers had left the organization when Susan had announced her planned changes) and had developed a tentative plan for modifying the strategic direction of SAB. Susan was convinced that SAB could attract some larger retailers in the mid-Atlantic states if it changed its business model to add services similar to third-party logistics companies, namely, warehousing, transportation delivery, and inventory management. However, Susan felt that she needed a major collaborator with experience in these areas. She also felt that it would be better if the collaborator was a company SAB had worked with previously on a successful basis and was willing to take on some new challenges.

Susan had decided to approach Wegmans Food Markets, Inc. as the final customer for these new services. Wegmans was a very successful company in the Northeast that was privately owned and had expanded carefully into new market areas over the last 10 years. It offered more value services to its customers, including an in-store bakery, deli, more take-out options, and in-store cooking demonstrations.

Susan was convinced that Wegmans had to be price competitive also to continue to grow in-store sales and expand its market opportunities. She felt that Dan Wegman would listen to her proposal to offer expanded services to help his company be more competitive. Now, she wanted control to join with SAB in making Wegmans a proposal.

Jean wants your help in developing a positive response to Susan.

CASE QUESTIONS

1. Why and how had the competitive market place for SAB changed in the last five to seven years?

2. What advantages might Central experience in the proposed new venture?

3. What issues would SAB and Central face in the proposed new approach?

Chapter 2

ROLE OF LOGISTICS IN SUPPLY CHAINS

Learning Objectives

After reading this chapter, you should be able to do the following:

- Understand the role and importance of logistics in private and public organizations.
- Discuss the impact of logistics on the economy and how effective logistics management contributes to the vitality of the economy.
- Understand the value-added roles of logistics on both a macro and micro level.
- Explain logistics systems from several perspectives.
- Understand the relationship between logistics and other important functional areas in an organization, including manufacturing, marketing, and finance.
- Discuss the importance of management activities in the logistics function.
- Analyze logistics systems from several different perspectives to meet different objectives.
- Determine the total costs and understand the cost tradeoffs in a logistics system.

Supply Chain Profile   *Jordano Foods*

Susan Weber, vice president for logistics at Jordano Foods (Jordano), had just sent the following e-mail to members of the executive committee of the company:

I just returned from a lengthy meeting with Chuck Chiarotti, CEO of SAB Distribution. Chuck is under great pressure from his board of directors to improve SAB's profitability. SAB has received a tender offer from another distributor to buy the company and several members of the SAB board have recommended that the offer be accepted. Chuck feels strongly that SAB can be "turned around," that is, profitability and growth can be improved. He is meeting with all of SAB's major suppliers and customers to request a more collaborative approach in their supply chain.

I am not certain that I understand all of the dimensions of supply chain management, but Chuck's ideas make sense to me. He feels that if he can work more closely with his major suppliers (we are SAB's second largest supplier) and major customers, a significant supply chain cost reduction can be achieved. He is also convinced that these cost reductions would not be at the expense of service. In fact, he gave examples of where organizations in a supply chain have reduced costs and improved service. I was concerned about how the cost savings would be shared. Chuck assured me that it would be a win-win approach. He feels strongly that most of the cost reductions should be applied to lowering product prices at the shelf to the consumer, making both us and SAB more competitive. This improved competitive position would result in increased revenue for all members of our supply chain, which would result in higher profits for all.

One way to look at Chuck's message is that the major supply chain members must not only improve their internal logistics operations but also coordinate their logistics activities with other supply chain members by collaborating and sharing information. I am going to ask Pete Mahoney, warehouse manager; Sue Kolbe, transportation manager; Alice Young, inventory manager; and Chris Glenn, customer service manager to serve as a facilitating group for our interactions with SAB. We will be holding weekly meetings and will update all directors and managers on our progress.

BACKGROUND ON JORDANO FOODS

Jordano Foods was founded in 1950 in Lewistown, Pennsylvania, by two brothers, Luigi and Mario Jordano. Their parents operated a restaurant in Burnham, Pennsylvania, featuring Italian cuisine. Marie Jordano was famous for her culinary skills. She developed her own recipes for pasta sauce, meatballs, fresh and dry pasta, and so on. Luigi and Mario worked in a restaurant prior to establishing Jordano Foods. The brothers felt that they could capitalize on the family recipes by selling pasta, sauces, and other related Italian food products to other restaurants in nearby communities in central Pennsylvania.

Their initial venture was so successful that they expanded their product line and began selling their products to small- to medium-sized wholesalers and distributors throughout Pennsylvania. They built a plant in Lewistown to produce their food products and subsequently built another plant in Elizabethtown, Pennsylvania, and a warehouse in Mechanicsburg, Pennsylvania.

CURRENT SITUATION

The 1990s and early 2000s were times of significant growth for Jordano. Mario and Luigi were still active in the company as president/CEO and chairman of the board, respectively. Revenue now exceeded $300 million per year, and a third plant had been built in the western part of Pennsylvania near Uniontown. A group of professional managers has been developed in the company to head up the major functional areas. Susan Weber was hired in 2005 to manage the logistics area, which had not received much attention prior to Susan's being hired. Her career at Procter & Gamble had provided her with experience in all aspects of logistics. Her experience with systems planning made her attractive to Mario Jordano when she was interviewed.

The transition to a relatively small company was initially a challenge for Susan. However, at this point in time, she was very comfortable in her role. Under her leadership, a number of initiatives in inbound transportation and inventory control had been implemented. She was very supportive of Chuck Chiarotti's collaborative approach. She had been involved in some of Procter & Gamble's initial collaborative efforts with suppliers. She wanted her working group to analyze how they could improve inbound and outbound logistics systems not only to operate more efficiently but also to provide better service to their plants (inbound) and customers (outbound), such as SAB.

Susan realized that the functional team she had appointed would need to operate with a systems perspective but also that the entire team would have to coordinate with manufacturing/processing and with marketing. She was concerned about the coordination with manufacturing and marketing because, traditionally, they had operated very independently and seemed reluctant to consider proposals she had made in the past for closer ties and discussions about tradeoffs among the areas.

Susan was trying to keep an open mind. She realized that the Jordano brothers had managed and developed the manufacturing and marketing functions during the formative years, and these two areas were regarded as cornerstones of the company's success. Logistics was a new functional area for Jordano. Skeptics within the company questioned logistics' value-add to the profitability and competitive position of Jordano.

Susan's "plate" was indeed "full" with both internal and external challenges and pressures to prove the importance of the logistics function. As you proceed through this chapter, identify areas where Jordano can improve its logistics processes and its supply chain relationships with SAB distributors.

Source: John J. Coyle, DBA. Used with permission.

Introduction

As previously mentioned, supply chain management has captured the attention and interest of many high-level executives. Logistics is misunderstood and often overlooked with the excitement surrounding supply chain management and all of the related technology that has been developed to support the supply chain. The glamour associated with the e-supply chain, e-tailing, e-business, and so on, seems to overshadow the importance of logistics in an organization and the need for efficient and effective logistics support in a supply chain. Logistics might be regarded by some individuals as mundane and staid when compared to supply chain initiatives such as collaboration and postponement.

Logistics professionals and other knowledgeable managers realize, however, that, in spite of all the hype about the Internet, successful organizations must manage order fulfillment to their customers effectively and efficiently to build and sustain competitive advantage and profitability. The much noted e-tailing problems of the 1999 Christmas season provide ample proof of the need for good, basic logistics systems and processes. Sophisticated front-end systems cannot stand alone in the competitive global marketplace of today—back office execution is critical for customer satisfaction. In fact, the speed of ordering via the Internet and other technologies exacerbates the need for an efficient and effective logistics system that can deploy appropriate levels of inventory, expedite completed orders to customers, and manage any returns. The often-quoted adage of "Good logistics is business power" is very appropriate because it helps build competitive advantage. If an organization cannot get its products to customers, it will not stay in business very long. This is not to say that quality products and effective marketing are not important. Both are obviously very important, but they must be combined with effective and efficient logistics systems for long-run success and financial viability.

The challenge is to manage the entire logistics system in such a way that order fulfillment meets and, perhaps, exceeds customer expectations. At the same time, the competitive marketplace demands efficiency—controlling transportation, inventory, and other logistics-related costs. As will be discussed, cost and service tradeoffs will have to be considered when evaluating customer service levels and the associated total cost of logistics, but both goals—efficiency and effectiveness—are important to an organization in today's competitive environment.

The concepts of supply chain management and logistics must be compared or, more appropriately, related to each other. In the preceding chapter, supply chain management was defined using a pipeline analogy with the start of the pipeline representing the initial supplier and the end of the pipeline representing the ultimate customer (see Figure 2.1). In other words, it was an extended set of enterprises from the supplier's supplier to the customer's customer.

Another perspective on supply chain management views it as a network of the logistics systems and related activities of all the individual organizations that are a part of a particular supply chain. The individual logistics systems obviously play a role in the success of the overall supply chain. The coordination or integration of the logistics systems in a supply chain is a challenge. The focus in this chapter is on the dimensions and roles of the individual logistics system, but always recognize that no logistics system operates in a vacuum. For example, the inbound part of a manufacturer's logistics system interfaces with the outbound side of the supplier's logistics system. The outbound portion of the manufacturer's logistics system interfaces with the inbound side of its customer's logistics system.

Having introduced the concept of logistics and its relationship to the supply chain, the next section will discuss the various definitions of logistics and the value-adding roles of logistics.

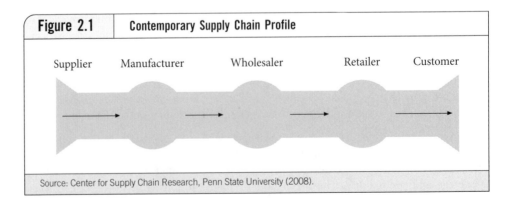

Figure 2.1	**Contemporary Supply Chain Profile**

Supplier   Manufacturer   Wholesaler   Retailer   Customer

Source: Center for Supply Chain Research, Penn State University (2008).

What Is Logistics?

The term **logistics** has become much more widely recognized by the general public in the last 20 years. Television, radio, and print advertising have lauded the importance of logistics. Transportation firms, such as UPS, DHL, and FedEx, frequently refer to their organizations as logistics companies and stress the importance of their service to overall logistics success. The Persian Gulf War of the 1990s probably contributed to increased recognition of logistics because of CNN news commentators' frequent mention of the logistics challenges associated with the 7,000-mile long "supply pipeline" to support the war effort in the Persian Gulf countries.

Another factor contributing to the recognition of logistics has been increased customer sensitivity to not only product quality but also to the associated service quality. For example, the previously mentioned problems during the Christmas season of 1999 associated with Internet retailers were widely publicized and often referred to as logistics system failures. But even prior to that time, when stores were out of stock of a particular item or a delivery of a package was not made on time, the logistics system would be blamed.

Even with increased recognition of the term *logistics,* however, there is still confusion about its definition. Some of the confusion can be traced to the fact that a number of terms are used by individuals when they refer to what has been described as logistics. For example, consider the following list of terms:

- Logistics management
- Business logistics management
- Integrated logistics management
- Materials management
- Physical distribution management
- Marketing logistics
- Industrial logistics
- Distribution

Logistics management is the most widely accepted term and encompasses logistics not only in the private business sector but also in the public/government and nonprofit sectors. In addition, service organizations such as banks, hospitals, restaurants, and hotels have logistics challenges and issues, and *logistics management* is an appropriate term in these industries.

Part of the definition problem is also traceable to the fact that logistics has been described by a variety of sources that have somewhat different perspectives. Table 2.1 illustrates a number of these definitions along with the corresponding perspective or connection.

For the purposes of this text, the definition offered by the Council of Supply Chain Management Professionals (formerly the Council of Logistics Management) is utilized. However, it is important to recognize that logistics owes its origins to the military, which has long recognized the importance of logistics activities for national defense.

The military definition of logistics encompasses supply items (food, fuel, spare parts) as well as personnel. The term *logistics* apparently became a part of the military lexicon in the eighteenth century in Europe. The logistics officer was responsible for encamping and quartering the troops as well as for stocking supply depots.[1]

The logistics concept began to appear in the business-related literature in the 1960s under the label of **physical distribution,** which had a focus on the outbound side of

Table 2.1	Logistics Definitions
PERSPECTIVE	**DEFINITION**
Inventory	Management of materials in motion and at rest
Customer	Getting the right product, to the right customer, in the right quantity, in the right condition, at the right place, at the right time, and at the right cost (called the "seven Rs of logistics")
Dictionary	The branch of military science having to do with procuring, maintaining, and transporting material, personnel, and facilities
International Society of Logistics	The art and science of management, engineering, and technical activities concerned with requirements, design, and supplying and maintaining resources to support objectives, plans, and operations
Utility/Value	Providing time and place utility/value of materials and products in support of organization objectives
Council of Supply Chain Management Professionals	That part of the supply chain process that plans, implements, and controls the efficient, effective flow and storage of goods, services, and related information from point of origin to point of consumption in order to meet customer requirements
Component support	Supply management for the plant (inbound logistics) and distribution management for the firm's customers (outbound logistics)
Functional management	Materials requirements determination, purchasing, transportation, inventory management, warehousing, materials handling, industrial packaging, facility location analysis, distribution, return goods handling, information management, customer service, and all other activities concerned with supporting the internal customer (manufacturing) with materials and the external customer (retail stores) with product
Common culture	Handling the details of an activity

Source: Adapted from Stephen H. Russell, "A General Theory of Logistics Practices," *Air Force Journal of Logistics* 24, no. 4 (2000): 15. Reproduced by permission.

the logistics system. During the 1960s, military logistics began to focus on engineering dimensions of logistics—reliability, maintainability, configuration management, life cycle management, and so on—with increased emphasis on modeling and quantitative analysis.[2] In contrast, the business or commercial applications were usually more focused on consumer nondurable goods related to marketing and physical distribution of finished products. The engineering-related logistics, as practiced by the military, attracted attention among businesses that produced industrial products that had to be maintained with repair parts over the life cycle of the product. For example, heavy machinery manufacturers, such as Komatsu, have developed world-renowned logistics systems for delivering spare parts to repair and maintain their vehicles. In fact, engineers developed a separate professional organization called the Society of Logistics Engineers (SOLE), which has had active participation from both military and commercial enterprises.

As indicated in the previous chapter, the business sector approach to logistics developed into inbound logistics (materials management to support manufacturing) and outbound logistics (physical distribution to support marketing) during the 1970s and 1980s. Then, in the 1990s, the business sector began to view logistics in the context of a supply or demand chain that linked all of the organizations from the supplier's supplier to the customer's customer. Supply chain management requires a collaborative, coordinated flow of materials and goods through the logistics systems of all the organizations in the network.

In the twenty-first century, logistics should be viewed as a part of management and has four subdivisions:[3]

- **Business logistics:** That part of the supply chain process that plans, implements, and controls the efficient, effective flow and storage of goods, service, and related information from point of use or consumption in order to meet customer requirements.

- **Military logistics:** The design and integration of all aspects of support for the operational capability of the military forces (deployed or in garrison) and their equipment to ensure readiness, reliability, and efficiency.

- **Event logistics:** The network of activities, facilities, and personnel required to organize, schedule, and deploy the resources for an event to take place and to efficiently withdraw after the event.

- **Service logistics:** The acquisition, scheduling, and management of the facilities/assets, personnel, and materials to support and sustain a service operation or business.

All four subdivisions have some common characteristics and requirements such as forecasting, scheduling, and transportation, but they also have some differences in their primary purpose. All four, however, can be viewed in a supply chain context; that is, upstream and downstream other organizations play a role in their overall success and long-run viability. The focus of this text is on logistics management in the business sector.

A general definition of logistics that could be used that appears to encompass all four subdivisions is as follows:

Logistics is the process of anticipating customer needs and wants; acquiring the capital, materials, people, technologies, and information necessary to meet those needs and wants; optimizing the goods- or service-producing network to fulfill customer requests; and utilizing the network to fulfill customer requests in a timely manner.

Having offered a definition of logistics, it is now appropriate to discuss how logistics adds value to an organization's products.

Value-Added Roles of Logistics

As Figure 2.2 illustrates, five principal types of economic utility add value to a product or service. Included are form, time, place, quantity, and possession. Generally, production activities are credited with providing form utility; logistics activities with time, place, and quantity utilities; and marketing activities with possession utility. Each will be discussed briefly.

Form Utility

Form utility refers to the value added to goods through a manufacturing or assembly process. For example, form utility results when raw materials or components are combined in some predetermined manner to make a finished product. This is the case, for example, when Dell combines components along with software to produce a computer to a customer's specifications. The simple process of combining these different components represents a change in the product *form* that adds value to a product.

In today's business environment, certain logistics activities can also provide form utility. For example, breaking bulk and mixing products, which typically take place at

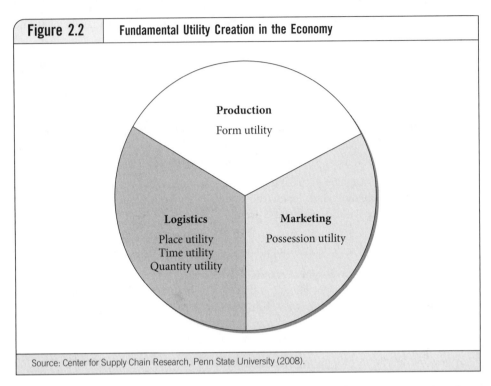

Figure 2.2 | **Fundamental Utility Creation in the Economy**

Source: Center for Supply Chain Research, Penn State University (2008).

distribution centers, change a product's form by changing its shipment size and packaging characteristics. Thus, unpacking a pallet of Kraft macaroni and cheese into individual consumer size boxes adds form utility to the product. However, the three principal ways in which logistics adds value are place, time, and quantity utilities.

Place Utility

Logistics provides place utility by moving goods from production surplus points to points where demand exists. Logistics extends the physical boundaries of the market area, thus adding economic value to the goods. Logistics creates place utility primarily through transportation. For example, moving Huggies diapers from a Kimberly-Clark manufacturing facility by motor carrier to markets where consumers need these diapers creates place utility. The same is true when steel is moved by rail to an automotive supplier to stamp automobile parts. The market boundary extension added by place utility increases competition, which usually leads to lower prices and increased product availability.

Time Utility

Not only must goods and services be available *where* customers need them but also at that point *when* customers demand them. This is called time utility, or the economic value added to a good or service by having it at a demand point at a specific time. Logistics creates time utility through proper inventory maintenance, the strategic location of goods and services, and transportation. For example, logistics creates time utility by having heavily advertised products and sale merchandise available in retail stores at precisely the time promised in the advertisement. This can be done by having the right products in inventory, having them stored close to the point of demand, or using a premium (faster) mode of transportation. Time utility is much more important today because of the emphasis on reducing lead time and minimizing inventory levels through logistics-related strategies such as just-in-time (JIT) inventory control.

On the Line — U.S. Providers Say Logistics in China Is on the Right Track

Recent media reports coming out of China indicate that the government plans to spend $440 billion over the next 30 years on upgrading highways and railroads. That bodes well for U.S. transportation and logistics companies like Schneider Logistics and YRC Worldwide, both of which are making significant progress in setting up their own China-based networks.

Executives for both companies said that China's planned investment should improve the limited transportation infrastructure and fragmented road networks that have made it difficult to gain supply chain visibility.

"From a ground-transportation standpoint, the environment in China continues to be highly fragmented, with limited visibility," said Jim Ritchie, president and CEO of YRC subsidiary Meridian IQ, which offers logistics and freight forwarding services in China. "What has happened in the last 12 months is that strategies are starting to form on how to develop cooperative agreements with [Chinese] transportation providers to create more synergy in the supply chain. By linking together the same service providers along different segments of the supply chain, we are starting to get better dependability and visibility."

Just 18 months ago, Ritchie said, it was very difficult to track freight in China from the time a shipment was turned over to a consolidator until it arrived at a port and was again consolidated into a container. But things have improved now that consolidators are working directly with suppliers, allowing service providers to monitor the whereabouts of customers' freight.

YRC has nearly 70 of its own trucks on the road in China and is mainly involved in freight forwarding- and logistics-related joint ventures. The company currently works with 39 Chinese transportation companies and provides inland transportation services for approximately 200 shippers. Schneider Logistics President Tom Escott agreed that supply chain visibility and reliability in China is improving. In the last 12 months, he noted, Chinese companies have been gaining a better sense of end-to-end supply chain management approaches.

"Supply chain functionality in North America includes national distribution, warehousing, and long-haul trucking," said Escott. "These things are still evolving in China, where customer needs tend to be more localized, with smaller shipping patterns. Suddenly, we are seeing a whole evolution of thinking in the [Chinese] market about distribution and managing supply chains."

Schneider Logistics, which opened a Shanghai office in 2005, is also involved in domestic logistics. Last month, the company received authority to set up shop as a domestic carrier and logistics service provider, making it the only North American operator to establish a domestic truckload business in China, according to company executives.

Source: Jeff Berman, *Logistics Management* (March 2007): 22.

Quantity Utility

Today's business environment demands that products not only be delivered on time to the correct destination but also be delivered in the proper quantities. So, the utilities of *when* and *where* must be accompanied by *how much*. Delivering the proper quantities of an item to where it is demanded is creating **quantity utility.** Logistics creates quantity utility through production forecasting, production scheduling, and inventory control. Take for example the importance of quantity utility in the automobile industry. Assume that General Motors will be assembling 1,000 automobiles in one day and it is using a JIT inventory strategy. This will require that 4,000 tires be delivered that morning to support the automobile production schedule. The tire supplier delivers 900 tires in time at the correct location. Even though the *when* and *where* utilities are created, the *how much* utility is not. Thus, GM will not be able to assemble the 1,000 cars as planned. So, logistics must deliver products at the right time, to the right place, and in the right quantities to add utility and economic value to a product.

Possession Utility

Possession utility is primarily created through the basic marketing activities related to the promotion of products and services. **Promotion** can be defined as the effort, through direct and indirect contact with the customer, to increase the desire to possess a good or to benefit from a service. The role of logistics in the economy depends on the existence of possession utility, for time, place, and quantity utilities make sense only if demand for the product or service exists. Marketing also depends on logistics, since possession utility cannot be acted upon unless time, place, and quantity utilities are provided.

Logistics Activities

The logistics definitions discussed previously indicate activities for which the logistics manager might be responsible. These activities might include the following:

- Transportation
- Warehousing and storage
- Industrial packaging
- Materials handling
- Inventory control
- Order fulfillment
- Demand forecasting
- Production planning/scheduling
- Procurement
- Customer service
- Facility location
- Return goods handling
- Parts and service support
- Salvage and scrap disposal

This list is quite comprehensive; some organizations with well-developed logistics departments might not place responsibility for all of these activities within the logistics area. However, decisions regarding these areas must utilize the systems view that is critical to logistics management.

Scope of Activities

The development of interest in logistics after World War II contributed to the growth in activities associated with logistics. Given the scope of this growth, it is worthwhile to discuss these activities and their relationship to logistics.

Transportation

Transportation is a very important activity in the logistics system and is often the largest variable logistics cost. A major focus in logistics is on the physical movement or flow of goods and on the network that moves the product. The network is composed of transportation organizations that provide service for the shipping firm. The logistics manager is responsible for selecting the mode or modes and carriers used in moving raw materials, components, and finished goods or for developing private transportation as an alternative.

Storage

A second area, which has a tradeoff relationship with transportation, is storage. Storage involves two separate, but closely related, activities: inventory management and warehousing. A direct relationship exists between transportation and the level of inventory and number of warehouses required. For example, if organizations use a relatively slow mode of transportation (for example, ocean), they usually have to hold higher inventory levels and thus have more warehousing space for inventory. An organization might consider using a faster mode of transportation (for example, air) to eliminate some of these warehouses and the inventory stored in them.

A number of important decisions are related to storage activities (inventory and warehousing), including how many warehouses, how much inventory, where to locate the warehouses, what size the warehouses should be, and so on. Because decisions related to transportation affect storage-related decisions, a decision framework to examine the tradeoffs related to the various alternatives is essential to optimize the overall logistics system.

Packaging

A third area of interest to logistics is industrial (exterior) packaging. Industrial packaging protects the product during transportation and storage and includes materials such as corrugated (cardboard boxes), stretch wrap, banding, bags, and so on. The type of transportation mode selected affects packaging requirements. For example, rail or ocean transportation typically requires additional packaging expenditures because of the greater possibility of damage in transit. For ocean transportation, additional packaging might be needed to prevent moisture from invading the product. In analyzing tradeoffs for proposed changes in transportation modes, logistics managers usually examine how the change will influence packaging costs. In many instances, changing to a premium transportation mode, such as air, will reduce packaging costs because there is less risk of damage.

Materials Handling

A fourth area to be considered is materials handling, which is also of interest to other areas in a typical manufacturing organization. Materials handling is important in warehouse design and efficient warehouse operations. Logistics managers are concerned with the movement of goods into a warehouse (from a transportation vehicle), the placement of goods in a warehouse, and the movement of goods from storage to order-picking areas and eventually to dock areas for transportation out of the warehouse.

Materials handling is concerned with mechanical equipment used for short-distance movement and includes equipment such as conveyors, forklift trucks, overhead cranes, and automated storage and retrieval systems (ASRS). Production managers might want a particular pallet or container type that is not compatible with logistics warehousing activities. Therefore, the materials handling designs must be coordinated in order to ensure congruity between the types of equipment used and the storage devices they are moving.

Inventory Control

A fifth area to examine is that of inventory control. Inventories can be found in both warehouses and manufacturing facilities. Inventory control has two dimensions: assuring adequate inventory levels and certifying inventory accuracy. Assuring adequate inventory levels requires logistics to monitor current inventory levels and either place replenishment orders or schedule production to bring inventory levels up to a predetermined level. For example, as a distribution center fills customer orders for shipment, current inventory levels are depleted. When these inventory levels reach a certain reorder point, replenishment orders are placed (either manually or electronically) to either another distribution center or to a manufacturing facility to bring current inventory levels to an acceptable level.

Another dimension of inventory control is certifying inventory accuracy. As inventory is physically depleted to fill customer orders, a facility's information system is electronically tracking the status of current inventory levels. To assure that the actual physical inventory levels match that shown in the information system, cycle counts are taken of selected items every period throughout the year. The result of the cycle count will either verify that the physical count and the information system count are in congruence (thus, no adjustments need to be made to the system) or they are different. In the later case, the discrepancy is investigated for its cause and the system is adjusted to reflect the actual physical count. Inventory accuracy is essential for assuring that customers' orders are filled complete and on time.

Order Fulfillment

Another activity area that logistics might control is order fulfillment, which generally consists of activities involved with filling and shipping customer orders. Order fulfillment is important to logistics because an important physical distribution factor is the time that elapses from when a customer places an order until the customer receives a satisfactory fulfillment of the order. This is also referred to as lead time.

For example, assume that the present order fulfillment process takes a total lead time of eight days for order transmittal, order processing, order preparation, and order shipment. Order processing might take four days, and order preparation might take an additional two days, which means that the goods need to be transported to the customer in two days. The short delivery time might require a premium mode of transportation (at a higher cost). An organization might consider adding technology to the order processing function to reduce it to a two-day time frame. This would allow the organization to use a less premium mode of transportation and still get the shipment to the customer in the agreed-upon eight-day lead time.

Forecasting

Another activity important to the logistics area is inventory forecasting. Accurate forecasting of inventory requirements and materials and components is essential to inventory control, manufacturing efficiency, and customer satisfaction. This is particularly true in organizations that use a JIT or material requirements planning (MRP) approach to controlling inventories. Logistics personnel should develop inventory forecasts in conjunction with marketing forecasts of demand to assure that proper inventory levels are maintained.

Production Planning

Another area of growing interest for logistics managers is production planning/scheduling, which is closely related to forecasting in terms of effective inventory control. Once a forecast is developed and the current inventory on hand and usage rate are determined, production managers can calculate the number of units to manufacture to ensure adequate market coverage. However, in organizations that have numerous products, manufacturing process timing and certain product line relationships require close coordination with logistics or actual control of production planning/scheduling by logistics.

Procurement

Procurement is another activity that can be included in logistics. The basic rationale for including procurement in logistics is that transportation costs relate directly to the geographic location (distance) of raw materials and component parts purchased for an organization's manufacturing needs. In terms of transportation and inventory costs, the quantities purchased would also affect total logistics costs. For example, buying component parts from China for a manufacturing facility located in the United States might have a lead time of several weeks. This would have a direct impact on the inventory levels that would need to be held at the manufacturing facility to prevent a plant shutdown. Using a premium mode of transportation to reduce this lead time would reduce inventory levels but would increase transportation costs. So, procurement decisions need to be made in consideration with total logistics costs.

Customer Service

Two dimensions of customer service are important to logistics: (1) the process of interacting directly with the customer to influence or take the order and (2) the levels of service an organization offers to its customers. From an order-taking perspective, logistics is concerned with having adequate inventory levels in the proper locations to meet the customer's order requirements. Also, logistics is concerned with being able to promise the customer, at the time the order is placed, when the order will be delivered. This requires coordination among inventory control, manufacturing, warehousing, and transportation to guarantee that any promises made when the order is taken as to delivery time and product availability will be kept.

The second dimension of customer service relates to the levels of service the organization promises its customers. These service levels might include order fill rates and on-time delivery rates. Decisions about inventories, transportation, and warehousing relate to customer service levels. While the logistics area does not usually completely control customer service decisions, logistics plays an extremely important role in ensuring that the customer gets the right product at the right time in the right quantity. Logistics decisions about product availability and lead time are critical to customer service.

Facility Location

Another area that is important to logistics is plant and warehouse site location. This topic will be discussed at some length in a later chapter. A site location change could alter time and place relationships between facilities and markets or between supply points and facilities. Such changes will affect transportation costs and service, customer service, and inventory requirements. Therefore, the logistics manager is concerned about facility location decisions.

Other Activities

Other areas might be considered a part of logistics. Areas such as parts and service support, return goods handling, and salvage and scrap disposal indicate the reality of logistics activities managed in organizations producing consumer durables or industrial products. In such cases, a very integrative approach is necessary. Logistics offers input to product design as well as to maintenance and supply services, since transportation and storage decisions affect these areas. These areas require the development of a reverse logistics system that will allow used, broken, or obsolete products to be returned to the supplier for disposition.

On the Line   *India's Logistics Challenges in a Nutshell*

As a percentage of GDP, logistics spending in India is estimated at 13 percent. This compares to around 10 percent in the United States and Europe. Such inefficiency reflects a transportation infrastructure that hasn't been able to keep pace with economic growth.

The Indian economy grew at a compound annual rate of 6.4 percent from 2000 through 2006, and by 8 percent over the past two years, according to the Centre for Monitoring Indian Economy Pvt. Ltd. (CMIE, http://www.cmie.com). The country's economy is expected to grow from 7 to 8 percent over the next three to five years.

From 2000 through 2006, Indian exports grew at an annual rate of 18.6 percent, driven by growth in the manufacturing, automotive, and textile sectors. Total imports grew at a similar rate over the same period, with nonpetroleum imports increasing by 17 percent.

The Indian logistics industry is highly fragmented. Carriers with fleets of less than five trucks account for over two-thirds of the total trucks owned and operated in India, according to market research firm Datamonitor (http://www.datamonitor.com) in a recent report, "India Logistics Outlook 2007."

Over 70 percent of the country's freight travels by road, and while the national highways account for only 2 percent of India's road network, they carry over 40 percent of its freight. As an indicator of road congestion, Datamonitor reports that commercial vehicles in India run at average speeds of 20 mph, compared to over 60 mph in Western Europe and the United States.

Rail transportation in the country is a monopoly managed by Indian Railways (http://www.indianrail.gov.in), with container movement managed by its subsidiary, Container Corporation of India Ltd. (Concor, http://www.concorindia.com). Rail cargo accounts for approximately 30 percent of cargo transported in terms of volume, and 11 percent of cargo in terms of value, reports SSKI, an investment bank headquartered in Mumbai (http://www.sski.co.in).

Despite a cost advantage, rail transportation has been slowly losing market share to roads, which SSKI analysts attribute to capacity constraints on key routes and better point-to-point service and better turnaround times offered by trucking companies. In an effort to improve the sector's competitiveness, the Ministry of Railways has begun to allow private companies to move containers by rail.

One major development that promises to change the face of logistics in India is the introduction of a value-added tax (VAT) structure, replacing a central state tax (CST). The present tax structure forces companies to set up warehouses in each state where they sell goods in order to reduce their tax burden. The change in the tax law would allow companies to set up more efficient hub-and-spoke distribution networks with larger regional warehouses. As a first step toward a complete phaseout targeted for April 2009, the CST was reduced to 2 percent in April 2007.

Source: Logistics Today (May 2007): 18. Reproduced by permission.

Logistics in the Economy: A Macro Perspective

The overall, absolute cost of logistics on a macro basis will increase with growth in the economy. In other words, if more goods and services are produced, logistics costs will increase. To determine the efficiency of the logistics system, total logistics costs need to be measured in relationship to gross domestic product (GDP), which is a widely accepted barometer used to gauge the rate of growth in the economy.

As indicated in Figure 2.3, logistics costs as a percent of GDP have declined since 1985 from 12.3 percent to 9.9 percent in 2006. In fact, logistics costs were closer to 20 percent of GDP in the early to mid-1970s. The low point occurred in 2003 with logistics costs being 8.6 percent of GDP. A modest increase in inventory costs starting in 2004 (as will be seen in Figure 2.5) coupled with a larger increase in transportation costs caused the percentage to increase for 2005 and 2006.

The reduction in logistics cost as a percent of GDP shown in Figure 2.3 has resulted from a significant improvement in the overall logistics systems of the organizations operating in the economy. This reduction in relative cost allows organizations to be more competitive since it directly impacts the cost of producing goods. It can be argued that the turnaround that occurred in the U.S. economy in the early 2000s was due in part to the reduction in relative logistics costs.

Some additional understanding of logistics costs can be gained by examining the three major cost categories included in this cost—warehousing and inventory costs, transportation costs, and other logistics costs. These can be seen in Figure 2.4. Warehousing costs are those associated with the assets used to hold inventory. Inventory costs are all the

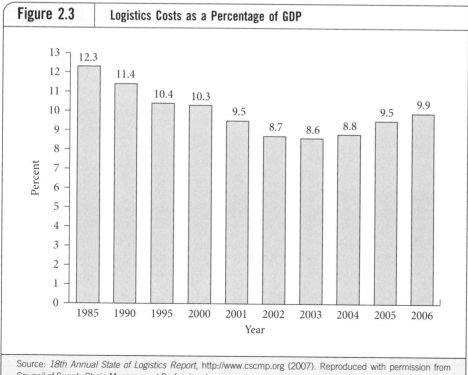

Figure 2.3 | **Logistics Costs as a Percentage of GDP**

Source: *18th Annual State of Logistics Report*, http://www.cscmp.org (2007). Reproduced with permission from Council of Supply Chain Management Professionals.

Figure 2.4	Total Logistics Costs—2006	
CARRYING COSTS—$1.857 TRILLION—ALL BUSINESS INVENTORY		**$ BILLION**
Interest		93
Taxes, obsolescence, depreciation, insurance		252
Warehousing		<u>101</u>
Subtotal		446
Transportation costs		
Motor carriers		
Truck—Intercity		432
Truck—Local		<u>203</u>
Subtotal		635
Other carriers		
Railroads		54
Water (international 32, domestic 8)		37
Oil pipelines		10
Air (international 15, domestic 23)		38
Forwarders		<u>27</u>
Subtotal		166
Shipper-related costs		8
Logistics administration		50
Total logistics cost		**1,305**

Source: *18th Annual State of Logistics Report*, http://www.cscmp.org (2007). Reproduced with permission from Council of Supply Chain Management Professionals.

expenses associated with holding goods in storage. Carrying costs include interest expense (or the opportunity cost associated with the investment in inventory), risk-related costs (obsolescence, depreciation), and service-related costs (insurance, taxes). Transportation costs are the total national expenditures for the movement of freight in the United States. The third category of logistics costs is the administrative and shipper-related costs associated with managing logistics activities and personnel.

Figure 2.4 probably underestimates the true costs of logistics in the economy because it does not appear to include some of the logistics activities that are discussed in this chapter. Nevertheless, the cost estimate provided in Figure 2.4 captures the major cost categories.

The declining trend for logistics cost relative to GDP shown in Figure 2.3 is very important to recognize. The decline started in the early 1980s and was closely

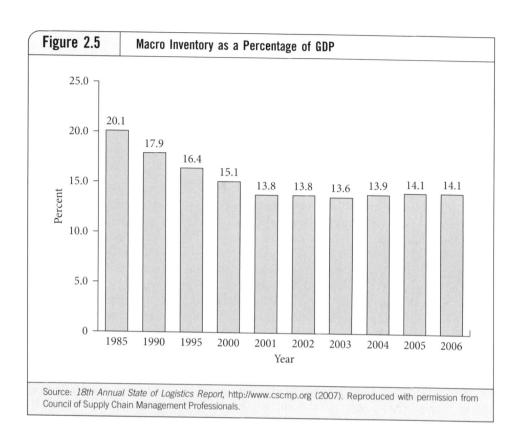

Figure 2.5 | **Macro Inventory as a Percentage of GDP**

Source: *18th Annual State of Logistics Report,* http://www.cscmp.org (2007). Reproduced with permission from Council of Supply Chain Management Professionals.

related to the deregulation of transportation, which permitted much more flexibility for carriers to adjust their freight rates and service in response to competition. A second factor contributing to the trend has been the improved management of inventory levels. This has been the result of more attention being focused on the investment in inventory and the better technology available to managers to make more effective inventory decisions.

On a macro basis, data are published on the ratio of inventory to GDP in the U.S. economy (see Figure 2.5). In other words, how much inventory do organizations carry to support GDP? Typically, it might be expected that inventory levels will increase with increased sales. Figure 2.5 indicates a very interesting trend of inventory levels declining relative to GDP. From 1985 through 2006, nominal GDP increased by 212.3 percent, while the value of all business inventories increased by 119.2 percent for the same period. This is a measure of efficiency and clearly indicates that organizations are improving in managing their inventory.

In addition to the managerial focus on managing inventory and transportation more efficiently, the total logistics system has received increased attention. It certainly appears that U.S. managers have realized the power of the message delivered by Peter Drucker in an article written in *Fortune* in 1962:[4]

> *Distribution is one of the most sadly neglected but most promising areas of American business.... We know little more about distribution today than Napolean's contemporaries knew about the interior of Africa. We know it's there, and we know it's big; and that's about all.... Most of our present concepts focus on production or on the stream of money and credit, rather than*

on the flow of physical goods and its economic characteristics.... To get control of distribution, therefore, requires seeing—and managing—it as a distinct dimension of business and as a property of product and process rather than as a collection of technical jobs. The industrial purchaser has to know his own business.... [H]e has to know what the product or supply he buys is supposed to contribute to his company's end results.... My purpose is to point to distribution as an area where intelligence and hard work can produce substantial results for American business. Above all, there is a need for a new orientation—one that gives distribution the importance in business design, business planning, and business policy its costs warrant.

The two largest cost categories in any organization's logistics system are transportation and inventory costs. As indicated, transportation is usually the single largest variable cost in any logistics system. Note the magnitude of the motor carrier share of the total freight expenditures shown in Figure 2.4—$635 billion versus $166 billion for all other modes of transportation. This level of expenditure is not based necessarily on the lowest transportation rates but reflects the value to shippers of the service provided by motor carriers. This point is discussed in Chapter 10 on transportation, but it is worth noting here because logistics management requires examining the total cost of logistics, not just one cost such as transportation.

Also worth noting is that one of the most frequent tradeoffs in logistics systems in an organization is between transportation and inventory costs. For example, an organization might be willing to pay much higher rates for air freight service because of the savings it will experience in inventory costs. In making this tradeoff evaluation, organizations are using a systems approach (which is discussed in more detail later in this chapter) to arrive at the lowest total cost solution.

Logistics in the Firm: The Micro Dimension

Another dimension of logistics is the micro perspective, which examines the relationships between logistics and other functional areas in an organization—marketing, manufacturing/operations, finance and accounting, and others. Logistics, by its nature, focuses on processes that cut across traditional functional boundaries, particularly in today's environment with its emphasis on the supply chain. Consequently, logistics interfaces in many important ways with other functional areas.

Logistics Interfaces with Manufacturing/Operations

A classic interface between logistics and manufacturing relates to the length of the production run. Manufacturing economies are typically associated with long production runs with infrequent manufacturing line setups or changeovers. These long runs, however, easily result in higher inventory levels of certain finished products and limited supplies of others. Thus, the ultimate manufacturing decision requires managers to carefully weight the advantages and disadvantages of long versus short production runs and their impacts on inventories. Many organizations today tend toward shorter production runs and doing whatever it takes to reduce the time and expense normally associated with changing production lines from one product to another. This is especially true for firms employing JIT or "lean" approaches to inventory and scheduling. The trend today is toward "pull" systems, manufacturing/logistics systems where the product is "pulled" in response to demand as opposed to being "pushed" in advance of demand. This practice lowers inventory levels, which can lower total logistics costs.

The production manager is interested in minimizing the effects of seasonal demand for products. Fully anticipating such demand is not always possible. Therefore, having the desired product quantities where and when needed is not always possible. For example, the chocolate candy industry is driven by a few "events" that are spread throughout the year, namely, Valentine's Day, Easter, Halloween, and Christmas. To keep costs low and avoid overtime and rush situations while meeting demand, production managers usually like to produce well ahead of the event and to produce a maximum amount of products. Such advance production might not be economically feasible because of inventory storage costs. However, production managers have to consider this problem in order to keep production costs low. Therefore, logistics, in conjunction with manufacturing, must be prepared to accept seasonal inventory that can begin to accumulate up to three months in advance of the event. The tradeoff here is between inventory costs and production costs.

Since the logistics manager is responsible for the inbound movement and storage of raw materials and components that will support production, logistics and manufacturing also interface on the supply side. A shortage or stockout could result in the shutdown of a manufacturing facility or an increase in production costs. The logistics manager should ensure that available quantities of raw materials and components are adequate to meet production schedules yet are conservative in terms of inventory carrying costs. Because of the need for this type of coordination, many organizations today have shifted the responsibility for production scheduling from manufacturing to logistics.

Another activity at the interface of logistics and manufacturing is industrial packaging, which many organizations treat as a logistics responsibility. In the context of manufacturing or logistics, the principal purpose that industrial packaging serves is to protect the product from damage. This is distinct from whatever value the consumer packaging might have for marketing or promotional reasons.

The interface between logistics and manufacturing is becoming more critical, given recent interest in the procurement of raw materials and components from offshore sources. Also, many organizations today are making arrangements with third-party manufacturers, "co-packers," or contract manufacturers to produce, assemble, or enhance some or all of the organization's finished products. These arrangements are especially prevalent in the food industry where some manufacturers produce only food items to be sold under someone else's label.

Logistics Interfaces with Marketing

Logistics is sometimes referred to as the other half of marketing. The rationale for this definition is that the physical distribution or outbound side of an organization's logistics system is responsible for the physical movement and storage of products for customers and thus plays an important role in selling a product. In some instances, physical distribution and order fulfillment might be the key variables in selling a product; that is, the ability to provide the product at the right time to the right place in the right quantities might be the critical element in making a sale.

This section briefly discusses the interfaces between logistics and marketing activities in each principal area of the marketing mix. The material is organized according to the four Ps of marketing—price, product, promotion, and place.[5] In addition, recent trends in the interface between logistics and marketing will be discussed.

Price

From a logistics perspective, adjusting quantity prices to conform to shipment sizes appropriate for transportation organizations might be quite important. Motor carriers, for example, publish minimum weight requirements for truckload lots—for instance, 20,000 pounds. The larger the shipment size, the lower the rate per pound charged by the transportation organization. In other words, a price discount schedule for shipping larger volumes at one time is important because the transportation organization experiences economies if the shipper tenders larger shipments.

Organizations selling products also typically provide a discount schedule for larger purchase quantities. If such discount schedules relate to transportation rate discount schedules in terms of weight, then both the shipper and customer might be able to reduce total transportation cost. For example, if an organization sells on a delivered-price basis (price includes transportation charges) and if its price schedule matches the transportation shipping requirements on a weight basis, the shipper should be able to get lower rates per pound with larger purchases and thus save money for the shipper and customer. So when an organization calculates the number of units that it wants to sell to a customer for a particular price, it should calculate how the weight of that number of units compares with the weight requirements for a transportation rate.

Although it is not always possible to adjust prices to meet transportation weight breaks and to have a quantity convenient to manage, organizations should investigate such alternatives. In some organizations, entire pricing schedules conform to various quantities that can be shipped by motor carriage and railroads or by other modes of transportation. Under the Robinson-Patman Act and related legislation, transportation cost savings are a valid reason for offering a price discount.

In addition, the logistics manager might be interested in the volume sold under different price schedules because this will affect inventory requirements, replenishment times, and other aspects of customer service. Although this is somewhat difficult to analyze, an organization might consider the logistics manager's ability to provide sufficient volumes within an attractive price schedule. Such a situation might be particularly true when price specials generate extra sales at particular times of the year. The logistics manager must be notified of such price specials so that he or she can adjust inventory levels to meet projected demand.

Product

Another decision frequently made in the marketing area concerns products, particularly their physical attributes. Much has been written about the number of new products that come on the market each year in the United States. Their size, shape, weight, packaging, and other physical dimensions affect the ability of the logistics system to move and store them. Therefore, the logistics manager should offer input when marketing is deciding on the physical dimensions of new products. The logistics manager can supply appropriate information about the movement and storage of new products. In addition to new products, organizations frequently refurbish old products in one way or another to improve or maintain sales. Very often, such changes might take the form of new package design and, perhaps, different package sizes. The physical dimensions of products affect the use of storage and movement systems. These dimensions affect the modes of transportation that an organization can use, equipment needed, damage rates, storage ability, use of materials-handling equipment such as conveyors and pallets, industrial packaging, and many other logistics aspects.

Frustration can mount for logistics managers when faced with a change in a product's dimensions that make the use of standard-size pallets uneconomical, or that use trailer or container space inefficiently or in a way that can damage products. For example, when Gillette first introduced the Daisy razor, the logistics group did not know that they would have to deal with light and bulky floor stand displays, with consequent low weight density. Not only would the floor stand displays not fit on the warehouse conveyors but they also had to be shipped at a price that was 150 percent higher than the existing transportation prices for the product itself. Gillette eventually corrected the situation, but it was an expensive lesson. These issues often seem mundane and somewhat trivial to executives making sales to customers, but they greatly affect an organization's overall success and profitability in the long run.

Prescribed rules do not exist to guide organizations in how to deal with these situations. However, keep in mind that collaboration can allow the logistics manager to provide input about the repercussions in these situations. The possibility exists that logistics can do nothing and that the sale is most important; but often the logistics manager can recommend small changes that make the product much more amenable to a logistics system's movement and storage capabilities while having no real effect on the sales of the product itself.

Another marketing area that affects logistics is consumer packaging. The marketing manager often regards consumer packaging as a "silent" salesperson. At the retail level, the package might be a determining factor in influencing sales. The marketing manager will be concerned about package appearance, information provided, and other related aspects; for a consumer comparing several products on a retailer's shelf, the consumer package might make the sale. The consumer package is important to the logistics manager for several reasons. First, the consumer package has to fit into the industrial package, or the external package. The size, shape, and other dimensions of the consumer package will affect the use of the industrial package. Second, the protection offered by the consumer package also concerns the logistics manager. The physical dimensions and the protection aspects of consumer packages affect the logistics system in the areas of transportation, materials handling, and warehousing.

Promotion

Promotion is a marketing area that receives much attention in an organization. Firms often spend millions of dollars on national advertising campaigns and other promotional practices to improve sales. An organization making a promotional effort to stimulate sales should inform its logistics manager so that sufficient quantities of inventory will be available for distribution to the customer. But even when logistics is informed, problems can occur. For example, when Gillette introduced the disposable twin-blade Good News razor, the company's original plan called for three consecutive promotions. The national launch promotion was to achieve sales of 20 million units. A later trade deal promotion was to net 10 million in sales, and Gillette expected a third promotional campaign to generate an additional 20 million—for a total of 50 million in sales. As it turned out, the first promotion sold 35 million, which was 75 percent over the original plan. Needless to say, this placed quite a burden on the logistics group to try to meet the additional demand.

A further analysis is necessary on the relationship between increasing sales and promotional strategies and their effect on the logistics area. Marketing managers often classify their promotion strategies into two basic categories: push or pull. Marketing can either "push" the product through the distribution channel to the customer or "pull" it through.[6] Distribution channels will be discussed in more detail later in this chapter. Distribution channels are composed of all the organizations that handle products after they are manufactured but before sale to the ultimate customer. They include organizations such as wholesalers and retailers.

Manufacturers frequently compete to get distribution channels to give their products the sales effort they feel their products deserve. For example, a breakfast cereal manufacturer might want to ensure sufficient space for its product on the retailer's shelf or that wholesalers will hold sufficient product quantities to satisfy retailers. Ultimately, the final consumer demand for a product will influence the retailer and the wholesaler. By selling popular products, both groups improve their profitability. The higher the product turnover, the more likely they are to make a profit; the more satisfied they are with a particular product, the more willing they are to give it space and a better position in the store.

Organizations can attempt to improve their sales by "pulling" their products through the distribution channel with national advertising. Promotional advertising attempts to create or stimulate sales to customers and to get customers into the retail store asking for a product they have seen advertised. The purchases will likely influence the retailer, and the retailer will influence the wholesaler from whom the retailer purchases. Some organizations feel that the best approach to promoting a product is to pull it through distribution channels by directly stimulating demand at the consumer level.

The other basic approach is the "push" method. Implied in the push approach is collaboration with the channels of distribution to stimulate customer sales. In other words, manufacturers might pay part of the local advertising costs or provide special store displays to stimulate sales. In collaborating with the wholesaler, a manufacturer might be able to offer retailers a special price at a particular time to stimulate product demand. The emphasis is on having the distribution channel work with the manufacturer. This contrasts with the pull approach, wherein the manufacturer stimulates demand somewhat independently of the retailer through national advertising.

Arguments can be made both for and against these two approaches. Most organizations combine the two approaches in their promotional efforts. From the perspective of the logistics manager, push and pull are often different as far as logistics system requirements are concerned. The pull approach is more likely to generate erratic demand that is difficult to predict and that might place emergency demands on the logistics system. National advertising has the potential to be extremely successful, but predicting consumer response to new products is often difficult. Such advertising might also strain the logistics system, requiring emergency shipments and higher transportation prices. Frequent stockouts might also result, requiring additional inventory. The Gillette situation is an example of such a case. On the other hand, a push approach might have a more orderly demand pattern. Collaboration with the retailer allows the manufacturer to fill the "pipeline" somewhat in advance of stimulated sales rather than quickly, on an almost emergency basis, as retailers and consumers clamor for some successfully promoted new product.

Place

The place decision refers to the distribution channels decision and thus involves both transactional and physical distribution channel decisions. Marketers typically become more involved in making decisions about marketing transactions and in deciding such things as whether to sell a product to wholesalers or to deal directly with retailers. For the logistics manager's perspective, such decisions might significantly affect logistics system requirements. For example, organizations dealing only with wholesalers will probably have fewer logistics problems than they will when dealing directly with retailers. Wholesalers, on the average, tend to purchase in larger quantities than do retailers and place their orders and manage their inventories more predictably and consistently, thereby making the logistics manager's decision less challenging. Retailers, and in particular small retailers, often order in small quantities and do not always allow sufficient lead time for replenishment before stockouts. Consequently, manufacturers might need to purchase premium transportation service to meet delivery needs.

Recent Trends

Perhaps the most significant trend is that marketers have begun to recognize the strategic value of place in the marketing mix and the increased revenues and customer satisfaction that might result from excellent logistics service. As a result, many organizations have recognized **customer service** as the interface activity between marketing and logistics and have aggressively and effectively promoted customer service as a key element of the marketing mix. Organizations in such industries as food, chemicals, pharmaceuticals, and technology have reported considerable success with this strategy.

Logistics Interfaces with Other Areas

While manufacturing and marketing are probably the two most important internal, functional interfaces for logistics in a product-oriented organization, there are other important interfaces. The finance area has become increasingly important during the last decade. The impact that logistics can have upon return on assets (ROA) or return on investment (ROI) is very significant (this will be discussed in greater detail in Chapter 5). ROA is defined as follows:

$$ROA = Revenue - Expenses/Assets$$

Or

$$ROA = Gross\ Profit/Assets$$

Logistics can positively impact ROA in several ways. First, inventory is both an asset on the balance sheet and an expense on the income statement. Reducing inventory levels reduces the asset base as well as the corresponding variable expenses, thus having a positive impact on ROA. Second, transportation and warehousing costs can also influence ROA. If an organization owns its warehouses and transportation fleet, assets will be increased. If these assets are reduced or eliminated, ROA will increase. Similarly, if an organization utilizes third parties for warehousing and transportation, variable expenses will be incurred. Reducing these expenses will also have a positive impact on ROA. Finally, the focus on customer service (which will be discussed further in Chapter 8) can increase revenue. As long as the incremental increase in revenue is larger than the incremental increase in the cost of customer service, ROA will increase.

Increasingly, CFOs in organizations have become very knowledgeable about logistics because of the impact that it can have on key financial metrics such as ROA or ROI. These metrics are important barometers for the external financial community to gauge the financial viability of an organization.

On the other hand, logistics managers have to justify increased investment in logistics-related assets using acceptable financial parameters related to "payback" periods.

Consequently, logistics managers must be knowledgeable about financial metrics and standards of performance.

Accounting is also an important interface for logistics. Accounting systems are critical for providing appropriate cost information for analysis of alternative logistics systems. Far too often in the past, logistics-related costs were not measured specifically and were often accumulated into an overhead account, which made it extremely difficult to systematically monitor logistics costs. The recent interest in customer profitability and the related cost accounting systems such as activity-based costing (ABC) has been beneficial to improving the quality of logistics data and analyses. Accounting systems are also critical for measuring supply chain tradeoffs and performance.

Logistics in the Firm: Factors Affecting the Cost and Importance of Logistics

This section deals with specific factors relating to the cost and importance of logistics. Emphasizing some of the competitive, product, and spatial relationships of logistics can help explain the strategic role of an organization's logistics activities.

Competitive Relationships

Frequently, competition is narrowly interpreted only in terms of price competition. While price is certainly important, in many markets customer service can be a very important form of competition. For example, if an organization can reliably provide customers with its products in a relatively short time period, then its customers can often minimize inventory costs. An organization should consider minimizing customer inventory costs to be just as important as keeping product prices low, since minimizing such costs will contribute to more profit or in turn enable the seller to be more competitive. Therefore, customer service is of great importance to the logistics area.

Order Cycle

A well-accepted principle of logistics management is that order cycle length directly affects inventory levels. Stated another way, the shorter the order cycle, the less inventory required to be held by the customer. Figure 2.6 shows this relationship. **Order cycle** can be defined as the time that elapses from when a customer places an order until the order is received. The order cycle includes activities such as order transmission, order receipt, order processing, order preparation (picking and packing), and order shipment. Figure 2.6 shows that longer order cycle times usually require higher customer inventories. For example, assume that a customer is using 10 units of a product per day and that the supplier's order cycle time is eight days. The customer's average inventory during order cycle time is 40 units (80/2). If the supplier can reduce the order cycle time to four days, the customer's average inventory is reduced to 20 units (40/2). Therefore, if an organization can improve customer service by shortening its order cycle time, its customers should be able to operate with less inventory. It follows, then, that such a cost reduction could be as important as a price reduction.

Substitutability

Substitutability very often affects the importance of customer service. In other words, if a product is similar to other products, consumers might be willing to substitute a

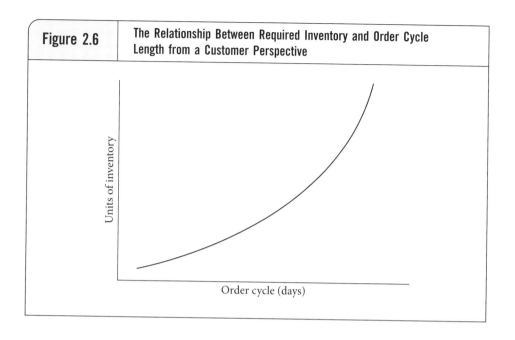

Figure 2.6	The Relationship Between Required Inventory and Order Cycle Length from a Customer Perspective

competitive product if a stockout occurs. Therefore, customer service is more important for highly substitutable products than for products that customers might be willing to wait for or back-order. This is one reason organizations spend so much advertising money making consumers aware of their brands. They want consumers to ask for their brands, and, if their brands are temporarily not available, they would like consumers to wait until they are.

Product substitutability varies greatly among industries. Usually, the more substitutable a product, the higher the customer service level required. As far as the logistics manager is concerned, an organization wishing to reduce its lost sales cost, which is a measure of customer service and substitutability, can either spend more on inventory or spend more on transportation.

Inventory Effect

Figure 2.7 shows that by increasing inventory costs (either by increasing the inventory level or by increasing reorder points), organizations can usually reduce the cost of lost sales. In other words, an inverse relationship exists between the cost of lost sales and inventory cost. However, organizations are usually willing to increase the inventory cost only until total costs start to increase. These organizations are typically willing to spend increasing amounts on inventory to decrease lost sales cost by larger amounts—that is, up to the point at which the marginal savings from reducing lost sales cost equal the marginal cost of carrying additional inventory.

Transportation Effect

A similar relationship exists with transportation as can be seen in Figure 2.8. Organizations can usually trade off increased transportation costs against decreased lost sales costs. For transportation, this additional expenditure involves buying a better service—for example, switching from water to rail, or rail to motor, or motor to air. The higher transportation cost could also result from shipping more frequently in smaller quantities

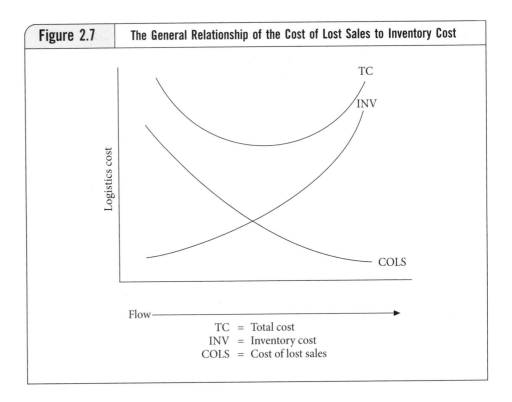

Figure 2.7　The General Relationship of the Cost of Lost Sales to Inventory Cost

TC = Total cost
INV = Inventory cost
COLS = Cost of lost sales

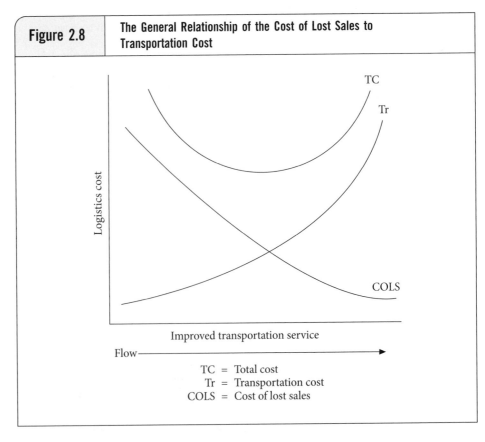

Figure 2.8　The General Relationship of the Cost of Lost Sales to Transportation Cost

TC = Total cost
Tr = Transportation cost
COLS = Cost of lost sales

at higher transportation prices. So, as indicated in Figure 2.8, organizations can reduce the cost of lost sales by spending more on transportation service to improve customer service. Once again, most organizations willingly do this only up to the point where the marginal savings in lost sales cost equals the marginal increment associated with the increased transportation cost.

Although showing inventory cost and transportation cost separately is convenient here, organizations often spend more money for inventory and for transportation almost simultaneously to reduce the cost of lost sales. In fact, improved transportation will usually result in lower inventory cost. In other words, the situation is much more inter-active and coordinated than is indicated here.

Product Relationships

A number of product-related factors affect the cost and importance of logistics. Among the more significant of these are dollar value, density, susceptibility to damage, and the need for special handling.

Dollar Value

Several product aspects have a direct bearing on logistics costs. First, the product's dollar value typically affects warehousing costs, inventory costs, transportation costs, packaging costs, and even materials-handling costs. As Figure 2.9 indicates, as the

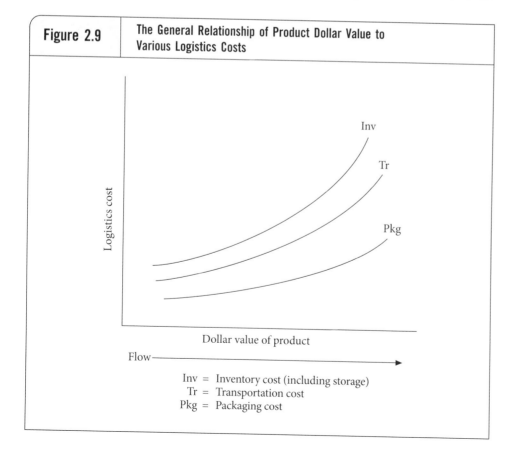

| Figure 2.9 | The General Relationship of Product Dollar Value to Various Logistics Costs |

Inv = Inventory cost (including storage)
Tr = Transportation cost
Pkg = Packaging cost

product's dollar value increases, the cost in each individual area also increases. The actual slope and level of the cost functions vary from product to product.

Transportation prices reflect the risk associated with the movement of goods. There is often more chance for damage with higher-value goods; damage to such goods will cost the transportation provider more money in the form of reimbursement to the owner. Transportation providers also tend to charge higher prices for higher-value products because their customers can typically afford to pay higher prices for transportation service. A relationship exists between the product value and the transportation price in transportation rate structures.

Warehousing and inventory costs also increase as the dollar value of products increases. Higher value means more capital invested in inventory, resulting in higher total capital costs. In addition, the risk factor for storing higher-value products increases the costs of obsolescence and depreciation. Also, since the physical facilities required to store higher-value products are more sophisticated, warehousing costs increase with higher dollar value products.

Packaging costs also usually increase because the organization uses protective packaging to minimize damage to the product. An organization spends more effort in packaging a product to protect it from damage or loss if it has higher value. Finally, materials-handling equipment used to meet the needs of higher-value products is very often more sophisticated. Organizations are usually willing to use more capital-intensive and expensive equipment to speed higher-value goods through the warehouse and to minimize the chance of damage.

Density

Another factor that affects logistics cost is density, which refers to the weight/space ratio of the product. An item that is lightweight compared to the space it occupies—for example, household furniture—has low density. Density affects transportation and warehousing costs, as shown in Figure 2.10. As density increases for a product, its transportation and warehousing costs tend to decrease.

When establishing their prices, transportation providers consider how much weight they can fit into their vehicles, since they quote their prices in dollars and cents per hundred pounds. Therefore, on high-density items, these providers can afford to charge a lower price per hundred pounds because they can fit more weight into their vehicle. For example, assume a motor carrier needs $5,000 in revenue from the freight that fills a 53-foot trailer. A low-density product might be able to fit 20,000 pounds into this trailer to fill it completely. The motor carrier would need to charge $25 per hundred pounds for this product. On the other hand, a high-density product might be able to fill the trailer at 40,000 pounds. The resulting price per hundred pounds would be $12.50.

Density also affects warehousing costs. The higher the density, the more weight can fit into an area of warehouse space—hence, the more efficient use of warehousing space. So, both warehousing cost and transportation cost tend to be influenced in the same way by a product's density.

Susceptibility to Damage

The third product factor affecting logistics cost is susceptibility to damage (see Figure 2.11). The greater the risk of damage to a product, the higher the transportation and warehousing cost. Because of a higher degree of risk and liability associated with

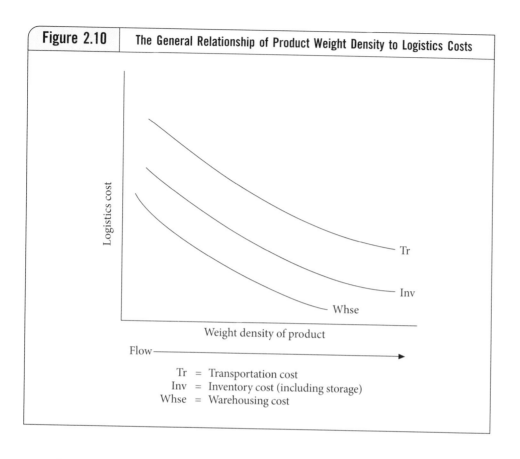

Figure 2.10 | The General Relationship of Product Weight Density to Logistics Costs

Logistics cost

Weight density of product

Flow

Tr = Transportation cost
Inv = Inventory cost (including storage)
Whse = Warehousing cost

more fragile goods, the higher are the prices charged by both transportation and warehousing providers. These providers might also charge higher prices because of measures they must take to prevent product damage.

Special Handling Requirements

A fourth factor, related to damage susceptibility but somewhat distinct, is special handling requirements for products. Some products might require specifically designed equipment, refrigeration, heating, or strapping. These special requirements will usually increase warehousing, transportation, and packaging costs.

Spatial Relationships

A final topic that is extremely significant to logistics is spatial relationships, the location of fixed points in the logistics system with respect to demand and supply points. Spatial relationships are very important to transportation costs, since these costs tend to increase with distance. Consider the following example, which Figure 2.12 illustrates.

Example

The firm located at point B has a $1.50 production cost advantage over Firm A, since Firm B produces at $7.00 per unit as opposed to $8.50 per unit for Firm A. However, Firm B pays $1.35 for inbound raw materials ($0.60 + $0.75) and $3.50 for outbound movement to the market (M), for a total of $4.85 in per-unit transportation charges. Firm A pays $0.90 for inbound raw materials and $1.15 for outbound movement, for a

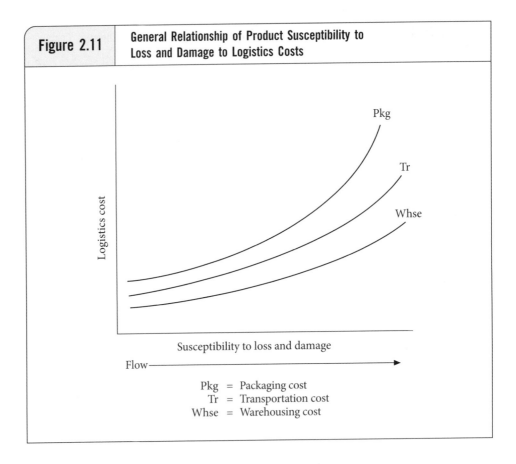

Figure 2.11 | General Relationship of Product Susceptibility to Loss and Damage to Logistics Costs

Pkg = Packaging cost
Tr = Transportation cost
Whse = Warehousing cost

total of $2.05 in per-unit transportation charges. Firm A's $2.80 transportation cost advantage offsets the $1.50 production cost disadvantage. Firm B might want to investigate alternative strategies for its logistics system in order to compete more effectively at M. For example, Firm B might base its $3.50/unit transportation cost for shipping to M on less-than-truckload prices (low-volume movements). Firm B might consider using a warehouse at M and shipping in full truckload quantities at lower transportation charges.

The distance factor or spatial relationships might affect logistics costs in ways other than transportation costs. For example, a firm located far from one or more of its markets might need to use a market-oriented warehouse to make customer deliveries in a satisfactory time period. Therefore, distance can add to warehousing and inventory carrying costs.

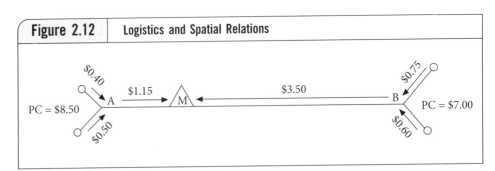

Figure 2.12 | Logistics and Spatial Relations

Distance or spatial relationships are of such importance to logistics that logistics responsibilities might include site location. For many organizations, warehouse location decisions are made based on distance to market, distance from suppliers, and access to transportation. Location, or site analysis, is considered in some detail later in this text.

Techniques of Logistics System Analysis

In this section, total cost analysis techniques for logistics are discussed. Only the more basic models are examined; more sophisticated techniques of total cost analysis are discussed later in this text. The basic approaches examined here unite some of the basic concepts discussed thus far and provide a background for much of the material in the remainder of this text.

Short-Run/Static Analysis

One general approach to total cost analysis for logistics is known as **short-run analysis.** In a short-run analysis, a specific point in time, or level of production, is chosen and costs are developed for the various logistics cost centers described previously. Multiple short-run analyses would be considered and then the system with the lowest overall cost would be selected, as long as it was consistent with constraints the organization imposed on the logistics area. Some authors refer to this short-run analysis as **static analysis.**[7] Essentially, they are saying that this method analyzes costs associated with a logistics system's various components at one point in time or one output level.

Example

Table 2.2 shows an example of static, or short-run, analysis. In this example, an organization is currently using an all-rail route from its plant and the associated plant warehouse to its customers. At the plant warehouse, the chemicals are bagged and palletized and shipped by rail to the customer. A proposed second system would use a market-oriented warehouse. The chemicals would be shipped from the plant to the market warehouse and then packaged and sent to the customer. Instead of shipping all goods by rail, the organization would ship them by barge to the market warehouse, taking advantage of low, bulk transportation prices. Then, after bagging, the chemicals would move by rail from the warehouse to the customer.

In this example, the tradeoff is lower transportation costs versus some increases in storage and warehousing. If the analysis is strictly static (at a specific level of output), the proposed system is more expensive than the current one. So, unless further analysis provided additional information more favorable to the proposed system, the organization would continue with its current system.

However, there are two reasons to favor the proposed system. First, there is no information about customer service requirements. The new market-oriented warehouse might provide better customer service, therefore increasing sales and profits and offsetting some of the higher costs of System 2.

Second, the organization might switch to System 2, even though it is experiencing lower costs with the current system (System 1), because the organization expects System 2 to result in lower costs in the future. This will require the use of **dynamic analysis,** which is the topic of discussion in the next section.

Table 2.2	Static Analysis of C&B Chemical Company (50,000 Pounds of Output)
PLANT LOGISTICS COSTS*	SYSTEM 1	SYSTEM 2
Packaging	$ 500	$ 0
Storage and handling	150	50
Inventory carrying	50	25
Administrative	75	25
Fixed cost	4,200	2,400
Transportation Costs		
To market warehouse	0	150
To customer	800	100
Warehouse Costs		
Packaging	0	500
Storage and handling	0	150
Inventory carrying	0	75
Administrative	0	75
Fixed cost	0	2,400
Total cost	$5,775	$5,950

*All amounts are in thousands of dollars.

Long-Run/Dynamic Analysis

While short-run analysis concentrates on specific time or level of output, dynamic analysis examines a logistics system over a long time period or range of output. Using the data from Table 2.2, a dynamic analysis can be undertaken. The results can be seen in Figure 2.13. For a mathematical solution, the equation for a straight line is used ($y = a + bx$). In this particular case, a would be the fixed costs of each system, and b would be the variable cost per unit. The x would be the output level. To solve for the output level at which the two systems are equal, an equation for each system is developed and they are set equal to each other in order to solve for x. As is shown below, the two systems are equal at 70,588 pounds of output and this becomes the point of indifference. This can also be seen in the graph in Figure 2.13.

System 1

Total Cost = Fixed Cost + Variable Cost/Unit × Number of Units

$y = \$4,200 + \$0.0315x$

System 2

$y = \$4,800 + \$0.0230x$

Tradeoff point

$$\$4,800 + \$0.0230x = \$4,200 + \$0.0315x$$
$$600 = 0.0085x$$
$$x = 70,588 \text{ pounds}$$

In this case, the organization is better off using System 1 at output levels up to 70,587 pounds. System 2 is less expensive at output levels greater than 70,588. At an output level of 70,588 pounds, both systems produce the same total costs.

A particular organization might consider more than two logistics systems at one time. Many examples show an organization considering three or sometimes four systems. The same basic methodology can be used for graphing and mathematically solving for the points of indifference regardless of how many systems are analyzed. In a particular situation involving two systems, the cost functions might not necessarily intersect. Hence, one function will be lower than the other over the entire range of output. When an organization considers three or more systems, two of them might intersect while the other occurs at a higher level in the quadrant. If there are three intersecting systems, two relevant intersection points or two relevant points of indifference usually occur. A third intersection would occur at a point above some other cost function and would not be relevant.

| Figure 2.13 | Dynamic Analysis |

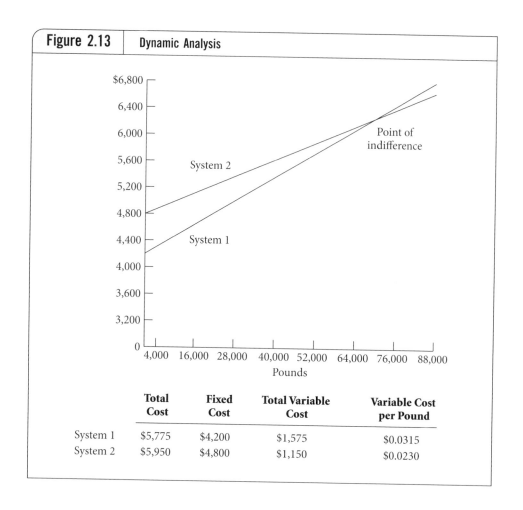

	Total Cost	Fixed Cost	Total Variable Cost	Variable Cost per Pound
System 1	$5,775	$4,200	$1,575	$0.0315
System 2	$5,950	$4,800	$1,150	$0.0230

Approaches to Analyzing Logistics Systems

The analysis of logistics systems frequently requires different views or perspectives of logistics activities. The best perspective to take depends on the type of analysis that is needed. For example, if an organization wants to analyze the long-run design of its logistics system, a view of logistics that focuses on the organization's network of node and link relationships would probably be most beneficial. On the other hand, if an organization is evaluating a change in a carrier or mode of transportation, it should probably analyze the logistics system in terms of cost centers. In this section, four approaches to analyzing logistics systems are discussed: (1) materials management versus physical distribution, (2) cost centers, (3) nodes versus links, and (4) logistics channels.

Materials Management versus Physical Distribution

The classification of logistics into materials management and physical distribution (inbound and outbound logistics) is very useful to logistics management or control in an organization. Frequently, the movement and storage of raw materials in an organization is different from the movement and storage of finished goods. For example, a drywall manufacturer transports gypsum and other bulk commodities to its plants in rail cars. Storage is very basic and consists of enclosed domes (located outside the plant) with an opening at the top through which the gypsum rock is transferred from the rail cars. Finished goods movement and storage for drywall is different. Transportation is usually provided by specially designed rail cars or flatbed motor carrier vehicles. Storage of the finished drywall product is totally inside the facility where pallets of drywall sheets are stacked and readied for loading. This internal storage is necessary to prevent the drywall from getting wet.

The different logistics requirements that might exist between materials management and physical distribution might have important implications for the design of an organization's logistics system. The design for each of these two activities might be quite different. In spite of these differences, close coordination between materials management and physical distribution is still critical.

Additional perspectives related to viewing logistics in terms of materials management/ inbound logistics and physical distribution/outbound logistics deserve consideration. In fact, from the inbound and outbound requirements perspective, organizations can be classified into four different types of logistics systems.

Balanced System

Some organizations have a reasonably balanced flow on the inbound and outbound sides of their logistics systems. In other words, they receive raw materials and components from suppliers in different locations and ship finished product to customers in various locations. Numerous raw materials are used to produce a variety of finished products. Similar modes of transportation (rail and motor) are used for both inbound and outbound movements. Consumer product companies such as Kraft and Unilever typically fit this description. While these organizations might emphasize the outbound side because of the importance of customer service, both inbound and outbound logistics are important.

Heavy Inbound

Some organizations have a very heavy inbound flow and a very simple outbound flow. An aircraft manufacturer such as Boeing is a good example. Boeing uses thousands of parts and components manufactured by hundreds of suppliers to assemble an aircraft. Multiple modes of transportation (rail, motor, air, and ocean) are used to move these parts to the assembly plant. Once the aircraft is assembled and tested, Boeing simply flies it to the customer (for example, United). The outbound process requires no warehousing, special transportation, or packaging. In contrast, the inbound side requires detailed scheduling, coordination, and planning to make sure that parts arrive when they are needed. Varying lead times from suppliers present a complex logistics challenge. Automobile manufacturers, using thousands of parts per car, also fit this model. Their outbound systems, while more complex than an aircraft assembler, are not nearly as complex as their inbound systems.

Heavy Outbound

A chemical company like ExxonMobil offers a good example of a logistics system with a heavy outbound flow. Inbound crude oil by-products, salt water, and other raw materials flow from a limited number of sources and frequently move in volume over relatively short distances. Inbound transportation modes might include motor, rail, ocean, and pipeline. On the outbound side, a wide variety of industrial products are manufactured that need storage, packaging, and transportation (motor, rail, ocean, and pipeline) to the final customer. Therefore, in an organization with a heavy outbound flow, the physical distribution side of the logistics system is more complex.

Reverse Systems

Some organizations have reverse flows on the outbound side of their logistics systems. This is true of organizations producing durable goods that the customer might return for trade-in, for repairs, or for salvage and disposal. Nokia, an assembler of cellular phones, is a good example of an organization with significant reverse systems. Organizations that deal with returnable containers also fit this model. The ink cartridges used in Hewlett-Packard printers would be a good example. Increased concern with the environment will require more organizations to develop reverse logistics systems to dispose of packaging materials from used products.

Cost Centers

A previous discussion mentioned the management activities that many organizations include in the logistics area, namely, transportation, warehousing, inventory, materials handling, and industrial packaging. By examining these activities as cost centers, trade-offs between them can be analyzed to determine the overall lowest cost or highest service logistics system.

The breakdown of logistics into various cost centers represents a second approach to logistics system analysis. Organizations frequently analyze logistics systems by dividing them into cost centers, since reducing total logistics costs and/or improving service most frequently occurs by trading off one cost center against another. For example,

Table 2.3	Analysis of Total Logistics Cost with a Change to a Higher Cost Mode of Transport	
COST CENTERS	**RAIL**	**MOTOR**
Transportation	$ 3.00	$ 4.30
Inventory	5.00	3.75
Packaging	3.50	3.20
Warehousing	1.50	0.75
Cost of lost sales	2.00	1.00
Total cost	$15.00*	$13.00*

*Costs per unit.

shifting the mode of transportation from rail to motor might result, because of faster and more reliable transit times, in lower inventory costs that offset the higher motor carrier price. Table 2.3 shows that the motor carrier price is higher than rail, but resulting reductions in other costs more than offset this higher transportation price. Another example might be increasing the number of warehouses in a logistics system, thereby increasing warehousing and inventory costs but possibly decreasing transportation and lost sales costs. As Table 2.4 shows, however, this might not produce the lowest cost solution.

Nodes versus Links

A third approach to analyzing logistics systems in an organization is in terms of nodes and links (see Figure 2.14). The **nodes** are fixed spatial points where goods stop for storage or processing. In other words, nodes are manufacturing/assembling facilities and warehouses where the organization stores materials for conversion into finished products or stores finished products for delivery to the customer (balancing supply and demand).

Table 2.4	Analysis of Total Logistics Cost with a Change to More Warehouses	
COST CENTERS	**SYSTEM 1 THREE WAREHOUSES**	**SYSTEM 2 FIVE WAREHOUSES**
Transportation	$ 850,000	$ 500,000
Inventory	1,500,000	2,000,000
Warehousing	600,000	1,000,000
Cost of lost sales*	350,000	100,000
Total cost	$3,300,000	$3,600,000

*Expected cost based upon probabilities of not having stock/inventory available when customers want it.

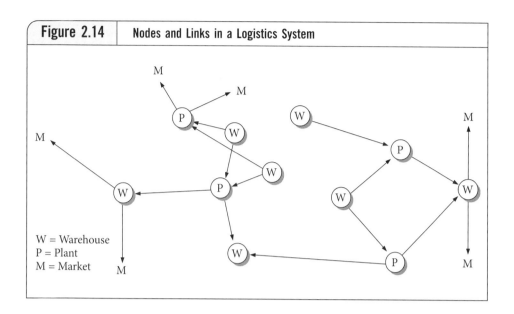

Figure 2.14 | **Nodes and Links in a Logistics System**

W = Warehouse
P = Plant
M = Market

Links represent the transportation network and connect the nodes in the logistics system. The network can be composed of individual modes of transportation (rail, motor, air, ocean, or pipeline) and of combinations and variations that will be discussed in Chapter 10.

From a node-link perspective, the complexity of logistics systems can vary enormously. One node system might use a simple link from suppliers to a combined plant and warehouse and then to customers in a relatively small market area. At the other end of the spectrum are large, multiple-product organizations with multiple plant and warehouse locations. The complex transportation networks of the latter might include three or four different modes and perhaps private as well as for-hire transportation.

The node-link perspective, in allowing analysis of a logistics system's two basic elements, represents a convenient basis for seeking possible system improvements. As has been noted, the complexity of a logistics system often relates directly to the various time and distance relationships between the nodes and the links and to the regularity, predictability, and volume of flow of goods entering, leaving, and moving within the system.

Logistics Channels

A final approach to logistics system analysis is the study of the **logistics channel,** or the network of intermediaries engaged in transfer, storage, handling, communication, and other functions that contribute to the efficient flow of goods. The logistics channel can be viewed as part of the total distribution channel, which includes both the logistics flow as well as the transaction flow which would be of specific interest to the marketing manager.[8]

The logistics channel can be simple or complex. Figure 2.15 shows a simple channel in which an individual producer deals directly with a final customer. The control in this

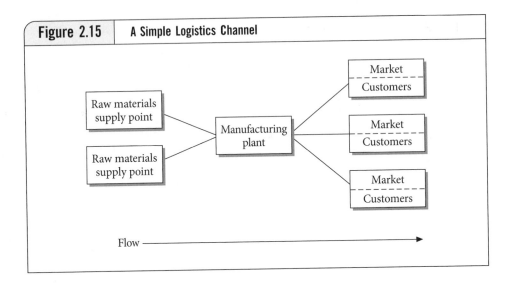

Figure 2.15   A Simple Logistics Channel

channel is relatively simple. The individual manufacturer controls the logistics flow since it deals directly with the customer.

Figure 2.16 presents a more complex, multi-echelon channel, with a market warehouse and retailers. The market warehouse could be a public warehouse. In this instance, the control is more difficult because of the additional storage and transportation provided by third-party organizations.

Figure 2.17 illustrates a complex, comprehensive channel. In this instance, the task of achieving an effective logistics flow in the channel is far more challenging. This figure very realistically portrays the situation confronting many large organizations operating in the United States and overseas.

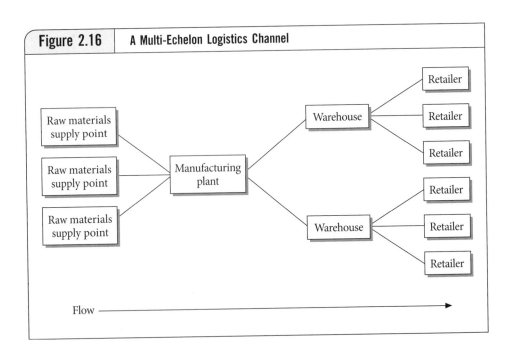

Figure 2.16   A Multi-Echelon Logistics Channel

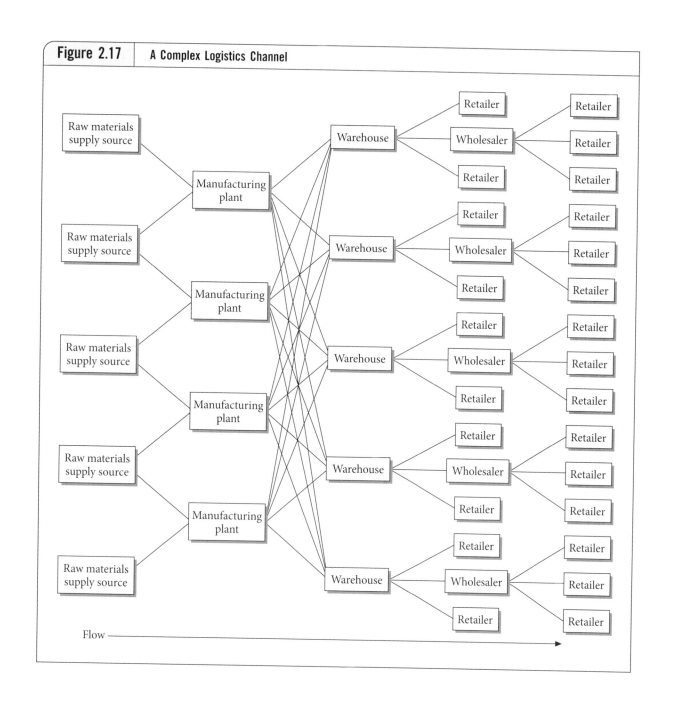

Figure 2.17 | **A Complex Logistics Channel**

Some instances involving production of a basic good like steel, aluminum, or chemicals might further complicate the situation because organizations might be a part of more than one channel. For example, the steel might be sold to auto manufacturers, container manufacturers, or file cabinet producers. Duplication of storage facilities, small-shipment transportation, conflict over mode choices, and other problems might contribute to inefficiencies in the channel. Communications problems might also exist.

Source: Jeff Berman, *Logistics Management* (May 2007): 20. Reproduced by permission.

Supply Chain Technology

Data Scrubbing: It's the Next Big Thing

While there have been many notable achievements in the logistics field—such as the evolution of the standard shipping container which helped spur global trade—the "next big thing" in logistics may be a bit harder to define, according to a recent report by Adrian Gonzalez, director of the Logistics Executive Council at ARC Advisory Group.

In his report, *The Next Big Thing in Logistics*, Gonzalez said that when he was recently asked what exciting developments were coming down the pike, his short answer was: "I don't know."

In the report, Gonzalez hypothesizes the world in the year 2035 and describes what he sees as "the emergence of standards-based logistics communication and process execution networks—a fancy way of describing the 'logistics utilities' that virtually every company uses to exchange electronic information and exchange business processes with their trading partners, customs, and regulatory agencies."

Gonzalez notes that over his eight years at ARC, the one constant theme he's heard is that collecting and cleaning data—a step critical in achieving his vision—is the most difficult and time-consuming step.

While data cleaning and collecting may not be viewed as sexy, Gonzalez said if it were addressed by shippers and logistics service providers in a standardized manner it could, in fact, be the "next big thing" in logistics technology.

Gonzalez told *Logistics Management* that data cleaning and collecting processes should receive far more attention than they're getting today. "Data quality—collecting and cleaning up data—is the number one issue [shippers and logistics service providers] are facing, and it's only getting worse," he says. "It's more of a roll up the sleeves, blue collar-type of thing, and companies just don't have it prioritized as well as they should," he adds.

Along with giving the issue more attention, another way to improve data cleaning and capturing processes is to work on a standards-based platform. Gonzalez likened a standards-based approach to the shipping container in the sense that the container brought value to all industry parties because it was a standard physical unit to build processes around.

"It doesn't have to be a single set of standards used across all industries," says Gonzalez. "It could be industry-specific, and if each company in a specific industry agrees to adhere to specific standards for things like messages and documents it will help to alleviate many of the data quality problems that are occurring."

He adds that making the internal investment—perhaps via the futuristic "logistics utilities"—may be the optimal way to go about this.

Logistics and Systems Analysis

An earlier section pointed out that improvements in analyses and methodologies have facilitated the development of logistics. One such improvement was systems analysis, or the systems concept. A convenient starting point for this section is a brief discussion of the basic nature of systems analysis.

Essentially, a system is a set of interacting elements, variables, parts, or objects that are functionally related to one another and that form a coherent group. The systems concept is something to which most individuals have been exposed at an early educational stage; for example, in science, students learn about the solar system and how relationships among the planets, the sun, and the moon result in day and night, weather, and so forth. In biology, students view the parts of the human body, such as the heart and blood, and their relationships as another system. In a power mechanics class, the internal combustion engine is explained as a system. Engine parts, such as pistons, might be made larger in size and more efficient but their very efficiency might overload other parts of the engine, causing it to break down. So the pistons had to be designed to work in harmony with other parts of the engine. In other words, the overall performance of the engine is more important than the performance of one part.

Cost Perspective

The preceding engine analogy provides insight into business system characteristics. If efficiency is measured in costs, an individual part of the system not operating at its lowest cost might contribute to the system's overall efficiency. For example, in a logistics context, water transportation might be the cheapest alternative available to an organization. If the organization optimizes transportation alone, then water movement would be the best approach. However, moving freight by water might require increased inventory holdings, with associated increases in warehousing space and other costs. These additional costs might be greater than the amount saved by using water transportation. In other words, the transportation decision has to be coordinated with related areas such as inventory, warehousing, and packaging to optimize the overall system, not just transportation. The general tenet of the systems concept is that the focus is not on individual variables but on how they interact as a whole. The objective is to operate the whole system effectively, not just the individual parts.

Levels of Optimality

Another aspect of the systems concept is that **levels of optimality** exist in an organization. At **optimality level I** (optimizing the organization), an organization should not optimize transportation at the expense of related logistics areas such as warehousing and packaging. At the same time, logistics is only one subsystem in an organization and, therefore, the organization should not optimize it at another area's expense. For example, the logistics manager might want to give five-day delivery to certain customers in order to eliminate some warehouses and inventory; but this might conflict with marketing, since the organization's competitors give three-day delivery service in the same delivery area. Clearly, an organization must work out some compromise after analyzing the situation. Logistics might have to accept the three-day service as a working constraint imposed because of competition and will have to design the best logistics system within this constraint. An individual or group at the organization's senior executive level has to examine the tradeoffs between marketing and logistics in terms of the total organization's efficiency or profit.

In addition to marketing, the organization must consider production, finance, and other areas (see Figure 2.18). In other words, the overall organization is a system that should be optimized. The organization might have to suboptimize internal subsystems to achieve the best overall position in the market. Generally, this means that logistics might work within constraints such as set delivery times, minimum production runs, and financial limits on warehouse improvements and construction. The goal is to

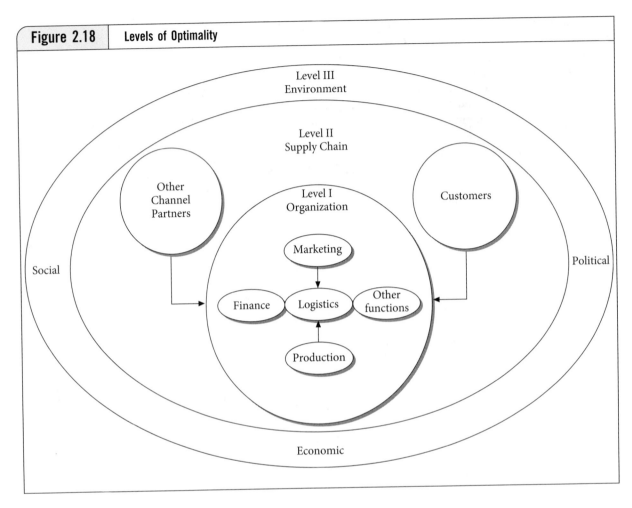

Figure 2.18   **Levels of Optimality**

identify the tradeoffs that exist within the organization and optimize the organization as a whole at optimality level I.

An organization is faced with constraints outside its own operations. **Optimality level II** consists of other organizations within the supply chain. Many times an organization is faced with constraints imposed by other supply chain members. These other supply chain members include suppliers (raw materials, components, and transportation providers) and customers (other manufacturers, wholesalers, and retailers). When an organization makes decisions to optimize at level I, it must also consider the impact of these decisions on the operation of the organizations in level II. For example, a manufacturer might decide to build pallets in its plant that are 60 inches high for delivery to its customer, since this pallet dimension is efficient for the manufacturer. However, a wholesale customer might not be able to store a pallet of this height and might require a 48-inch high pallet. A tradeoff decision must be made here taking into consideration the costs of the manufacturer versus the costs of the wholesaler. At optimality level II, tradeoff decisions need to be made that optimize the operation of the supply chain.

Finally, **optimality level III** involves the various constraints imposed by society and includes social, political, and economic influences. At this level of optimality, decisions must be made that optimize the organization and the supply chain subject to the requirements of society. For example, an organization with a private motor carrier fleet could minimize its transportation expenses if it allowed its drivers to operate its vehicles for 13 hours before they are required to rest. The political environment (regulations) only allows an 11-hour on-duty time for motor carrier drivers. As such, the organization would have to suboptimize its private fleet to optimize the requirements of society.

Obviously, logistics decisions are made considering multiple levels of optimality, and this results in some levels being suboptimized at the expense of other levels. Critical to logistics decisions, then, is the ability to understand all of the constituencies affected and then optimize at the level that is appropriate.

SUMMARY

- Logistics has developed as an important area or function of business since World War II. It has gone through several phases of development in achieving its present status.
- Logistics is a critical part of supply chain management. The coordination and, perhaps, integration of the logistics systems of all the organizations in a supply chain are necessary requirements for successful management of the supply chain.
- Logistics has a number of different definitions because of the broad-based interest in its activities and the recognition of its importance. The definition developed by the Council of Supply Chain Management Professionals is the primary definition used in this text.
- Logistics is an area of management that has four subdisciplines: business, military, service, and event.
- On a macro basis, logistics-related costs have been decreasing on a relative basis, which has helped the U.S. economy regain its competitive position on a global basis.
- Logistics adds place, time, and quantity utilities to products and enhances the form and possession utilities added by manufacturing and marketing.
- Logistics has an important relationship to manufacturing, marketing, finance, and other areas of the organization.
- Logistics managers are responsible for a number of important activities, including transportation, inventory, warehousing, materials handling, industrial packaging, customer service, forecasting, and others.
- Logistics systems can be viewed or approached in several different ways for analysis purposes, including materials management versus physical distribution, cost centers, nodes versus links, and channels. All four approaches are viable for different purposes.
- Logistics systems are frequently analyzed from a systems approach, which emphasizes total cost and tradeoffs when changes are proposed. Either a short- or a long-run perspective can be used.
- The cost of logistics systems can be affected by a number of major factors, including competition in the market, the spatial relationship of nodes, and product characteristics.

STUDY QUESTIONS

1. Compare and contrast the four subdivisions of logistics management.

2. Compare and contrast logistics management with supply chain management.

3. On a macro-economic basis, the ratio of inventory to sales has declined over the last 20 years. Is this good or bad? Why? What factors have contributed to this trend? Is this trend likely to continue in the future? Why or why not?

4. Logistics costs as a percentage of GDP have been decreasing in recent years. What factors have contributed to this relative decline? What does the future hold for logistics costs?

5. Discuss the ways in which logistics contributes to economic value in the economy and in an organization.

6. Manufacturing organizations have traditionally used long production runs as a means to gain a cost advantage in the marketplace. What is the impact of long production

runs on logistics? The current approach to manufacturing is to have shorter production runs and more setups. What impact does this approach have on logistics costs? Manufacturing costs? What are the tradeoffs?

7. Physical distribution has a special relationship to marketing. Why is this relationship so special? What is the nature of the overall relationship between logistics and marketing? Is the relationship becoming more or less important?

8. Logistics comprises a relatively large number of managerial activities. Discuss five of these activities and why they are important to logistics systems.

9. Compare and contrast the static analysis of logistics systems with dynamic analysis.

10. What product characteristics affect logistics costs? Discuss the effects of these characteristics on logistics costs.

NOTES

1. Stephen H. Russell, "Growing World of Logistics," *Air Force Journal of Logistics*, Vol. 24, No. 4(2000): 13–15.

2. Ibid.

3. Ibid.

4. Peter F. Drucker, "The Economy's Dark Continent," *Fortune* (April 1962): 103.

5. E. Jerome McCarthy and William E. Perrault, Jr., *Basic Marketing: A Managerial Approach*, 9th ed. (Homewood, IL: Richard D. Irwin, 1987): 46–52.

6. Philip Kotler, *Marketing Management: Analysis, Planning, and Control*, 5th ed. (Englewood Cliffs, NJ: Prentice-Hall, 1984): 463–464.

7. J. L. Heskett, Robert M. Ivie, and Nicholas A. Glaskowsky, Jr., *Business Logistics: Management of Physical Supply and Distribution* (New York, NY: Ronald Press, 1973): 454–469.

8. Roy Dale Voorhees and Merrill Kim Sharp, "Principles of Logistics Revisited," *Transportation Journal* (Fall 1978): 69–84.

CASE 2.1

Senco Electronics Company

Senco Electronics Company (Senco) is a U.S.-based contract manufacturer of laptop and personal computers. All of its current assembly operations are located in the United States and primarily serve the U.S. market. Transportation in the United States from Senco sites to its customers is primarily performed by motor carriers. Rising costs in its U.S. operations have caused Senco to begin construction of a new assembly plant in China. This plant will be used to satisfy the growing demand for laptop and personal computers in the United States. Traci Shannon, executive vice president of supply chain management for Senco, is concerned with how Senco will transport its products from China to the United States. "We've always had the luxury of a very well developed ground transportation infrastructure in the United States to move our products. Now we will be faced with moving enormous quantities of electronic products across several thousand miles of ocean. We really don't have that much experience with other modes of transportation." Skip Grenoble, director of logistics for Senco, was called on for his advice. "Obviously, we need to decide on whether to use ocean or air transportation to move our products from the new facility. Air transportation will cost more than ocean but will result in lower inventory costs because of the faster transit times. The opposite is true for ocean transportation. Moving products by air will also result in higher ordering costs since we will be ordering more often for replenishment for our U.S. distribution centers. Using either mode will require some fixed investment in loading/unloading facilities at both the new plant and our U.S. distribution centers. Projected annual demand from the new facility is 1.5 million pounds. However, we expect this demand to grow by 10 percent annually over the next five years. Although the air transportation system appears to be the more expensive option right now, we need to take into consideration our growth and how each mode will help us achieve our profit and service goals." The relevant cost information for each alternative is presented in the following table.

	OCEAN	AIR
Transportation costs	$ 50,000	$190,000
Inventory costs		
Carrying	40,000	15,000
Handling	15,000	19,000
Ordering	5,000	12,000
Fixed cost	410,000	350,000
Total costs	$520,000	$586,000

CASE QUESTIONS

1. If you were Skip Grenoble, which alternative would you advise Ms. Shannon to implement? What criteria would you use to arrive at your decision?

2. At what level of demand (in pounds) per year would these two alternatives be equal?

3. Graphically represent these two alternatives and their tradeoff point.

4. Which alternative would you recommend be in place to accommodate future demand growth?

CASE 2.2

Peanut Plantation

Peanut Plantation (Peanut) is a large processor of peanuts based in Atlanta, Georgia. Peanut's major products are roasted (plain and salted) peanuts distributed in 6-ounce bags and 18-ounce cans. Peanut's dominant market position was a result of its focus on product freshness and availability at stores. Peanut's product development department created a new peanut product that is cinnamon flavored. It was also able to reduce the amount of cholesterol in its peanuts, thus making the peanuts a more healthful snack. However, the new flavor shortened the shelf life of its products.

Peanut's marketing department decided to launch the new peanut product on the Friday before the Super Bowl. Advertisements were placed on television, on billboards, and in newspaper circulars one week before Super Bowl Sunday. A sweepstakes contest was also proposed that would award the contest winner a free trip for two to next year's Super Bowl. Each can of the cinnamon peanuts contained an insert with a serial number that could be matched with the winning number on Peanut's Web site.

To meet the estimated first week demand for the new product, manufacturing started making product one month before the introduction. Demand for the two days preceding the Super Bowl was estimated to be 2 million 18-ounce cans. Demand after the Super Bowl was estimated to be 1 million cans per week. Manufacturing capacity for the new product is 500,000 cans per week.

Peanut's price per can to its retail customers would be $1.50, which would allow for a gross margin of $0.75 per can. Peanut's cost to produce each can is $0.35. Inventory carrying costs per can are $0.05. Peanut's finance department was concerned that the heavy promotion and high build-up of inventories would eliminate almost all of the profit Peanut would make on each can. Their directive to the product manager was that the product had to maintain its profit, or it would be pulled from the market.

CASE QUESTIONS

1. What interactions needed to take place among the marketing, manufacturing, logistics, and finance departments? Explain the logistics department's role in the introduction of the new product.

2. Why is it necessary for the logistics department to be cognizant of all the details (quantity, timing) of the new product introduction? Discuss the issues that might arise (e.g., the drop in demand after the Super Bowl) and what responsibilities the logistics department would have as a result of these changes.

Chapter 3

GLOBAL DIMENSIONS OF SUPPLY CHAINS

Learning Objectives

After reading this chapter, you should be able to do the following:

- Describe the scope of a global company's supply chain network and understand what questions are appropriate for the network to function on a competitive basis.

- Understand the three major phases of globalization.

- Appreciate the complexity and magnitude of the operations of some successful global companies and why global expansion is important to their growth.

- Explain how technology and service specialists can help companies, especially small- to medium-size firms, penetrate the global marketplace.

- Appreciate the importance and magnitude of the trading partner countries of the United States.

- Understand the nature of global markets and competitive strategy.

- Explain the rationale for global security measures and the balance necessary to ensure that such security measures do not impede trade.

- Discuss global transportation options and strategic intermediaries.

Supply Chain Profile   *Red Fish, Blue Fish, LLP*

Fran Fisher was contemplating a significant career and business change. Basically, he was considering changing a hobby into a new business venture. For many years, he had been involved in the media communications business. While his specialty was in radio promotions and advertising, he had experience in television not only with promotions and advertising but also as a TV "personality" as a broadcaster of college sports events. He developed a small media consulting company which was located in Greensburg, Pennsylvania, about 30 miles from Pittsburgh.

Fran had always been interested in exotic fish and had several large display tanks in his office suite and at home in his study. He purchased fish mostly through a Pittsburgh wholesaler/distributor that also sold to selected individuals. He had also bought some fish through catalog offerings, and more recently, he had made some purchases from China via the Internet.

Several of Fran's friends had been asking his advice about buying exotic fish and the necessary equipment to have a setup like he has in his office. He had even been contacted by a local dentist who was having his office remodeled. The dentist, Andy Zimmerman, had read in the trade magazine for dentists that fish tanks were becoming popular as decorations and seemed to have a soothing impact on patients, especially children. Andy even offered to pay Fran a consulting fee for his initial advice on fish purchases and wanted him to consider doing the whole setup—buying fish and equipment and installing the tanks with appropriate compensation to follow.

Fran's media consulting business was declining, and he was concerned about the future. New Internet options such as YouTube, Facebook, and others were changing the media business, especially for small companies in small market areas. He needed to change his consulting business in some way or look for new opportunities. He decided to take advantage of Andy's offer and developed a three-phase proposal—selection of types and quantity of fish, purchase and setup of tanks and related equipment, and regular cleaning and maintenance of the tanks. Fran thought that his proposal might be too high priced, but Andy accepted the whole package and seemed pleased with the price that was proposed.

SIX MONTHS LATER

Andy's office was all set up, and he seemed very pleased overall. Fran received some inquiries from other local businesses and decided to pursue this new venture at least on a part-time basis initially. His wife, Charlotte, had expressed an interest in helping with the fish business with the exception of cleaning tanks. Fran had purchased Andy's fish and all the supporting equipment from China. He was actually surprised at how easy it was to search for suppliers via the Internet and the cost savings of buying from distributors in China. His nephew, Eric Lynch, was a logistics graduate of Penn State, and he had worked in the transportation business for many years. Eric advised Fran to use Federal Express, which turned out to be a very good recommendation.

Fran's Internet surfing also exposed him to some U.S. Web sites offering exotic fish for sale. He was surprised at the differential between the prices he had paid to purchase Andy's fish in China and what the domestic Web sites were charging for comparable fish. He thought the differential would provide him enough margin to make a profit on sales in the United States and even sales in Canada and Europe if he could develop a good Web site to display fish and related equipment.

Now it was time to address some basic issues about this new business venture. Eric was interested in joining the business to provide logistics and supply chain expertise. Charlotte had become proficient with handling purchases from China and other sources. Fran felt that his media experience would enable him to develop a good Web site for his new business, which he decided should be called Red Fish, Blue Fish. He was, however, concerned about working capital and cash flow.

Andy had offered to invest in the company when Fran told him about the new business. Eric believed that they could base their business model on Dell's approach. If they took orders via the Internet and immediately contacted their Chinese suppliers they could use overnight air freight delivery, which would minimize their inventory and the need for working capital. Fran felt that they could operate the business from his current offices. He also felt that business sales, like the one he did for Andy, could be quite lucrative, and the ongoing monthly maintenance fee would help his cash flow situation. He was even considering a collaborative arrangement with a local contractor, Jim Beierlein, who would do office and business installations since some remodeling was usually required. Also, Jim could help him with some of the special packaging if he had sales in Europe or Canada.

Introduction

Globalization was identified in Chapter 1 as being one of, if not *the* leading, external factors driving change of the economic landscape for not only for-profit companies but also for not-for-profit organizations. Global trading has been with us for centuries, but the scope and magnitude of the product, information, and financial flows today are almost mind boggling. For example, the value of trade between the United States and China has grown from $285 billion in 2005 to $343 billion in 2006, which represents a 20 percent increase in one year. This is indicative of the importance of global trade flows in the world economy and, in particular, to the U.S. economy.[1]

It has been argued that globalization was initially driven by countries (1400–1800) seeking materials and goods not available in their own land, but they also had imperialistic objectives of enhancing their economic and political power. The second era of globalization (1800–2000) was driven by companies seeking goods and materials, labor, economies of scale, and markets. This era produced multinational companies with global reach and enormous economic market power.[2]

The development and growth of large multinational companies really moved the world toward globalization. These companies were the ones that initially asked the following global questions first posed in Chapter 1:

- Where in the world should we procure or purchase raw materials, semifinished materials, components, services, etc.?
- Where in the world should we locate plants and/or supporting facilities to produce products and/or services to meet customer demand?
- Where in the world should we market and sell our products and/or services?
- Where in the world should we store and/or distribute our products or services?
- What global transportation and communication alternatives should we consider and use?
- What global partnerships or alliances should we establish for collaboration to improve our efficiency and effectiveness?

These questions should not be answered separately. They are too interrelated or synergistic and require the evaluation of alternative scenarios to answer all the questions for the optimal or best alternatives.

The scope of these questions provides an insight into the nature of being truly global. The established, successful multinational companies also created opportunities for smaller organizations to participate in the global marketplace as they "fine-tuned" their "business models" to improve efficiency and effectiveness. For example, the multinationals could purchase component parts needed for the finished products from a variety of sources in different countries. This became a common practice for auto and computer manufacturers. Companies, such as Nike, outsourced all of their manufacturing. The complexity of global trade sometimes required specialists not only in transportation but also in more specialized areas such as customs and tariffs. Such arrangements led to growing collaboration in the various supply chains.

In the second phase of globalization, companies headquartered in developed countries like the United States, Western Europe, Japan, etc., had an advantage in terms of infrastructure, educational systems, capital markets, etc. It has been suggested that the world was, figuratively speaking, tilted in favor of the developed countries. The economic advantage was such that the citizenry of the less-developed countries tended to migrate to the more developed countries, especially the United States. The well-educated and skillful immigrants added to the advantages enjoyed by the developed countries.[3]

The third era of globalization is said to have begun around the year 2000. The significant characteristic of this era is that it is being powered by individuals and smaller organizations in contrast to the countries of the first era and the large companies of the second era.[4] The critical ingredients for this new era have been the technological advances, especially in information technology and communications, which have connected the "four corners of the globe." Thus, with the enabling of more broad-based participation in the global economy without some of the massive infrastructure previously required, the world has indeed become flat. Again, the large, multinational companies have created "niche" opportunities for individuals and/or small organizations to collaborate in their supply chains.

One of the outcomes of this new global era is an "attack" on traditional, hierarchical organizational structures.[5] Businesses are being transformed into flatter, more horizontal, and more collaborative organizations that participate in more supply chains to add value and efficiency for consumers worldwide.

Chapter 1 argued that the rate of change has accelerated and is being fueled by a number of major external forces or change drivers. The synergism between globalization and technology, especially, has permanently changed the dynamics of the world's marketplace. The outcry in some quarters about outsourcing is 40 years too late and may be misguided. This new era has and will continue to spotlight supply chains as a critical part of the ability of organizations to compete economically, and it deserves special discussion.

Supply Chains in a Global Economy

In Chapter 1, a supply chain was depicted as being boundary spanning; that is, it encompasses a group of interrelated firms that should be focused on delivering the best "price/value" products and services to the ultimate customer at the end of the supply

On the Line

Adapting to Operating in Low-Cost Regions

Including low-cost regions in modern supply chains is now a given. But determining which regions to access for any particular purpose is still as much art as science. Ongoing discussions with key industry contacts suggest that different locations, countries, and regions have their own specific strengths (and weaknesses), and, even more importantly, regional positions shift over time.

Tracking and responding to the relative positions of low-cost regions will be an ongoing theme for global supply chain managers. Five years ago, China was *the* source for low-cost products; now, Vietnam is competing against inland China and parts of India for that same position. In terms of the importance of market proximity, whether to the United States, Europe, or emerging urban markets in India and China, it becomes even more necessary to understand how an area's character fits with a firm's global supply chain strategies.

How can buyers discover where to source materials, components, subassemblies, and finished goods? What makes a particular area attractive, and how long will it be before the next "hot" region appears on the horizon? How does a region structure itself to join the world economy in a mode that means sustainable growth and improvement for its citizens for years to come? These issues are on the agenda (or destined to be so) of supply and logistics managers all over the world.

Supply chain managers are now operating in a global business ecology. As the overseers of physical movements in the new economy, they face challenges within countries, between countries, and across regions. Researchers and managers need to cooperate so that everybody has the tools and insight needed to support continued economic success in a world where borders are still real, but transcending borders is the order of the day.

Source: Arnold Maltz, Arizona State University, *World Trade Magazine* (January 1, 2007).

chain. The supply chain also should manage three important flows, namely, materials/products, information, and financials. The best supply chains compete very successfully on a national and/or global basis.

Wal-Mart is frequently cited for its supply chain efficiency and effectiveness and rightly so. Consider, for example, that a computer manufacturer such as Hewlett-Packard will sell over 400,000 computers in one day through over 4,000 Wal-Mart stores to customers worldwide during the Christmas season. Each of the computers has component parts from a number of global providers, and the computers are usually assembled in several global locations. The synchronization of the three flows mentioned above that allows this to happen almost seamlessly is an amazing accomplishment.

Consider also that Americans spend over $35 million per hour, 24 hours per day, 365 days of the year in Wal-Mart stores, and the stores stock over 65,000 different items a year.[6] None of the above is meant to imply that the supply chains that Wal-Mart is a part of operate perfectly each and every time. In other words, Wal-Mart stores do experience shelf stockouts at times (hence the use of rain checks) or overstocks of some stock-keeping units (SKUs) occasionally.[7] However, considering the length and complexity of some of its supply chains, it minimizes such happenings using the tools, technology, and management skills discussed in this text.

The net effect of Wal-Mart's success with supply chain management has enabled it, as indicated in Chapter 1, to become the largest corporation in the world as measured by sales dollars of over $350 billion per year. Other companies have also been successful based to some extent on the efficiency and effectiveness of their supply chains, e.g., Apple, Dell, Procter & Gamble (P&G), IBM, Johnson & Johnson, General Electric, Kimberly-Clark, etc.

These companies and others have transformed themselves by changing their supply chains and their business models, which, in turn, has significantly changed the business landscape in the twenty-first century. Consider, for example, that some U.S. companies derive over 25 percent of their profit from global sales, which helps to mitigate declines or instability in domestic markets.

Adam Smith, who is credited with providing the economic rationale for capitalism in his famous book, *Wealth of Nations,* stated that division of labor or labor specialization is limited by the extent of the market or volume of demand.[8] In other words, economies and companies could improve their "wealth" by allowing specialization of tasks. The automobile assembly line is a good example of specialization wherein each individual performs a small task relative to the total product, but the output per individual is higher than if individuals each assembled a complete car. Smith's caveat, which is very relevant here, indicates that the advantage is true as long as you can sell the increased volume that is produced. We argued in 1976, in our first edition of this text, that an important role of logistics was to help extend the market area of countries or companies through improved efficiency to lower the "landed cost" in new market areas.

The logic of the rationale stated above is even more apropos for supply chains. It can be argued that supply chains help to establish the limits of what is competitively possible in the market. In other words, the cost and value at the end of the supply chain determine a firm's ability to compete in a marketplace. Good supply chains are "business power," and good supply chain managers are continually pushing the "limits" of their supply chains to be viable in both domestic and global markets.

Operating globally has become easier to accomplish for even individuals and small companies, as stated previously, because of the advances in information/communications technology and the continuing improvement of specialists such as UPS, FedEx, DHL, etc., that can provide global supply chain services at a very reasonable cost. A growing number of specialists and continuing improvements in information technology/communications are contributing to the flattening of the world. Obviously, large global companies are also contributing to this phenomenon.

It is safe to conclude that supply chains and supply chain management play an important role in the global economy and have helped to push the growth and success of companies that do "supply chaining" very well. The "train (globalization) is out of the station" and rolling down the tracks at increasing speed. Global supply chains impact all of us. We love the lower prices, the increased array of products, and the convenience (read 24/7, one-stop shopping, etc.), but we are critical of some of the outcomes when individuals lose their jobs, businesses are closed, etc. Many would argue that the advantages outweigh the disadvantages, e.g., the lower prices have saved consumers billions of dollars in purchase prices. There are tradeoffs (advantages and disadvantages), but there is no turning back. Successful organizations will continue to need effective and efficient supply chain management as they move ahead aggressively in the twenty-first century. The following chapters will address how such success can be accomplished.

In the next several sections of this chapter, we will discuss the magnitude of global operations and supply chains as well as some of the challenges and types of global supply chain services.

The Scope and Magnitude of Global Business

In Chapter 1, the concept of the world collapsing in terms of time and distance was presented. Obviously, the distance between New York City and Shanghai, China, is still the same, and these cities have not changed time zones. However, transportation, communications, and computer-related technology are making it much more convenient for business executives from different countries to meet face to face or via special information technology. The ability to connect to individuals and companies across the globe and to connect computer information systems on a 24/7 basis has provided unparalleled opportunity for collaboration horizontally and vertically in supply chains. This connectivity has allowed the type of interorganizational cooperation, visibility of flows, and real time adjustments necessary for efficient and effective supply chains.

The global data presented in this section reflect this new era. Table 3.1 presents trade data (total of imports and exports) for the top 10 U.S. trading partners. Some interesting and important relationships depicted in Table 3.1 should be noted. China is now our second largest trading partner, supplanting Mexico, which historically has been number 2. The trade volume with China was 18.2 percent of the total of the top 10 for 2006, and it increased its trade volume by 20 percent from 2005 to 2006. In 2000, China was number 4 on the top 10 list following Canada, Mexico, and Japan, and its trade volume with the United States has tripled since that time ($343 billion vs. $94 billion). This increase

Table 3.1	Top U.S. Trading Partners	
	VALUE OF TRADE ($ BILLIONS)	
COUNTRY	**2005**	**2006**
Canada	$ 499	$ 534
China	285	343
Mexico	290	332
Japan	194	208
Germany	119	130
United Kingdom	90	99
South Korea	72	78
Taiwan	56	61
France	57	61
Singapore	44	43
Total	$1,706	$1,889

Source: U.S. Bureau of the Census, Foreign Trade Statistics, 2007.

reflects the comments made previously about the growing importance of China. The total value of trade with these top 10 trading partners increased by 10.7 percent from 2005 to 2006, and since 2000 it has increased by about 53 percent in total value. Both of these percentage increases are reflective of the growing interdependence and the trade relationships with other countries. The data lend additional creditability to statements made previously about the importance of global supply chains.

India was mentioned in Chapter 1 in the context of globalization but does not appear in the top 10 countries listed in Table 3.1. India's strength has been in the area of information technology services, which tends to understate its importance for global supply chains. In 2005, 59 percent of U.S. corporate spending (off-shore) for information technology services was spent in India.[9] Interestingly, China, which is known for manufacturing various types of products, is attracting U.S. companies to establish research centers. Microsoft and Intel established research centers in Beijing in 1998, Google in 2005, and Rohm & Haas and Dupont in Shanghai in 2006.[10] The combined population of China and India, which is in excess of 2 billion people, makes them attractive as markets and as a source of imports. Consequently, it seems safe to conclude that global supply chain connections to both China and India will continue to grow. Large U.S. consumer product companies and retailers are already connected with sourcing and selling.

Even smaller companies, such as W. W. Grainger, a distributor of maintenance, repair, and operating (MRO) products, is "connecting" its supply chain to China as a source of products to buy and a market for distributing and selling its other products. Challenges and risks are associated with doing business with or in China and India, but the opportunities are enormous. Companies will change their business models because of these opportunities. Consider the partnership between IBM and Lenovo for IBM's personal computer business or Honda Motor in India which has used different partnering strategies for different product lines.

Once risks are identified, leading companies use a variety of strategies to manage them. These risk mitigation strategies are selectively applied depending on the impact and probability of each risk. Evidence is building that those firms that apply a rigorous risk management methodology are much more likely to see the promised benefits from a global outsourcing strategy, as well as realize the payback from their overarching globalization strategy.

Global Markets and Strategy

The global business environment has changed significantly and become much more conducive to business activity between and among different countries. Companies are not just importing and exporting products but are also locating plants and other facilities in other parts of the world. Honda and Toyota used to produce cars in Japan and ship them to the United States. Now their cars are, for the most part, produced in the United States for sale in North America. U.S. companies have also located plants in other countries.

As indicated in Chapter 1, tariffs and other trade barriers have been significantly reduced among many countries, allowing a much more competitive global economy.

This represents both a threat and an opportunity. Like deregulation of transportation, some companies have not really responded well and have lost market share or gone out of business. Other companies have taken advantage of the opportunity and expanded

On the Line   *Managing the Risk Inherent in Global Outsourcing*

Many firms see globalization as much more than outsourcing. Additionally, they regard its essence as being to establish a market presence in other regions of the world and to serve as an engine for growth. Globalization in this context thus means leveraging various regions of the world for potential in several areas, which include establishing a presence in the global market for growth, resource access, and cost savings.

Of course, outsourcing is frequently a key component of the globalization strategy. But all too often the risk inherent in outsourcing decisions is not effectively assessed or managed, putting the firm's business in jeopardy.

Unfortunately, many firms have not placed their outsourcing strategy within the context of a complete global strategic plan. Invariably, pressure is exerted from the top to reduce direct, visible cost. This quickly evolves into an outsourcing strategy to take advantage of the incredible pool of low-cost labor in other regions of the world, particularly in Asia, Latin America, and Eastern Europe.

When pursuing an outsourcing strategy, it is hard for many companies to stop and consider risks because they are blinded by the huge savings potential. A couple of years ago, on a tour of seven factories in South China, the authors saw some shocking examples of where these savings are coming from (and the long-term risk therein embodied), including the following:

- Factory workers routinely working 11 hours per day, six days per week for roughly $100 per month
- An extremely intense work pace
- Competent engineers earning a maximum of $12,000 per year

In a typical financial analysis, this incredible labor cost savings is balanced with higher inventory and transportation costs. But many companies are just now realizing that risk might be the greatest potential cost.

What are the risks associated with global outsourcing? A few examples include catastrophic delays in delivery due to force majeure or even terrorism, quality and damage problems hidden by a long supply line, highly inaccurate forecasts over a long supply line, currency swings, and intellectual property issues.

Are these risks causing an outsourcing backlash? There's no clear trend. For example, one company discussed withdrawing from China, while another firm described taking everything to China. What makes the difference between success and failure? We would argue that the difference is in having a rigorous approach to analyzing and managing outsourcing risk.

Source: J. Paul Dittmann, Ph.D., University of Tennessee, *World Trade Magazine* (January 1, 2007).

aggressively into global markets, e.g., General Electric, IBM, Wal-Mart, McDonald's, P&G, Kimberly-Clark, etc. Many *Fortune* 500 companies experience 50 percent or more of their sales in global markets. Such sales have helped these companies stabilize their revenues and buffet them against turbulent times in the U.S. marketplace, such as occurred in 2007.[11] Small- and medium-sized companies have also been able to be players in global markets, even a company like Red Fish, Blue Fish, LLP.

Success in the global marketplace, obviously, requires developing a cohesive set of strategies including product development, technology, marketing, manufacturing, and supply chains. Global companies tend to be more successful when their strategies help them to simultaneously achieve their business objectives at their various global locations. From a supply chain perspective, this means strategically sourcing materials and components worldwide, selecting global locations for key supply depots and distribution centers, evaluating transportation alternatives and channel intermediaries, providing customer service, understanding governmental influences on global supply chain flows, examining opportunities for collaboration with third- or fourth-party logistics companies, and other supply chain issues. We will discuss some of these topics in this chapter, and the remainder will be covered in subsequent chapters. A topic that merits special consideration is supply chain security, which will be discussed subsequently in this chapter.

From a customer service perspective, global markets and strategy have four important characteristics. First, companies want to standardize to reduce complexity, but they recognize that global markets need some customization. For example, in contrast to the U.S. market where large retail stores buy in volume quantities for delivery to their large warehouses, third-world countries have tiny retail stores that may only be 80 to 100 square feet. This means deliveries of small quantities, more frequent deliveries, different packaging, etc. P&G recently has made changes in its customer service strategy and related areas to customize for these markets. P&G recognizes that the population base is such in these countries that the total volume of sales will offset some of the lower economies of scale at the tiny stores. Customer service levels have to be adjusted for these markets in terms of delivery schedules, volumes, order fulfillment, and other areas.

Second, global competition reduces the product life cycle, as previously mentioned, since products can be copied or reengineered quickly by competitors. Technology companies are faced with this phenomenon even in the U.S. market, but other products are faced with similar experiences. Technology companies counteract with continual upgrades and new products. Apple, for example, had great success with its iPod, but it quickly followed this with the iPhone to maintain financial momentum. Shorter product life cycles present challenges for inventory management with respect to obsolete items. Customer service levels are also impacted because changes have to be made as the product matures in terms of sales volume and then declines, which reduces product profitability. Usually, companies cannot afford to provide the same level of customer service when the product volume declines.

Third, traditional organizational structures and related business models frequently change since companies get more involved in outsourcing manufacturing and some logistical activities such as transportation, warehousing, and order fulfillment. All of this impacts the supply chain and its related customer service activities. The collaboration indicated requires effective coordination among the various parties to ensure that customer service levels (on-time delivery, complete orders, reliability, etc.) are maintained. There are many challenges for supply chain managers.

Fourth, globalization introduces more volatility, as noted in Chapter 1. It is much more likely that supply chains will experience challenges with weather, terrorism, strikes, etc. The need for flexibility and responsiveness is a requisite for customer service through the supply chain. The expanded networks cover long distances and are complex.

In addition to the four areas indicated above, some of the customary strategies used in the domestic market are also challenged. Reduced order cycle time, for example, has become an important part of supply chain management since it can lead to lower inventory levels for customers, improved cash flow, and lower current assets/accounts receivable. The increased length and complexity of the supply chain make it more difficult to achieve shorter lead times.

Also, demand-driven supply or pull systems that can lower inventory levels significantly are challenged by the longer distance and complexity of multi-layered supply chains. Other strategies such as compression and "lean" supply chains are also more difficult to achieve in the global environment. None of this discussion is meant to imply that companies should not be involved in globalization. Rather it is meant to provide understanding of the challenges necessary to improve the likelihood of success. Without a doubt, globalizing has helped many U.S. companies as previously noted. Much higher sales and profits and more revenue stability are some of the advantages that have been pointed out thus far, but globalization is a two-edged sword that requires a company to be nimble and continually proactive in managing and responding to change. The topic of the next section, global supply chain security, ties in directly with this discussion of global supply chain strategy.

Supply Chain Security: A Balancing Act

Global commerce between the United States and the rest of the world came to a halt on September 11, 2001, when terrorists attacked the United States. Air transportation into and out of the United States and even some domestic flights were suspended. Ocean vessels loaded with containers and other freighter ships were prevented from unloading or loading in the major ports. Many had to anchor off the coast for days, waiting to come into the assigned port. Fresh fruits and vegetables rotted, and needed materials did not arrive on time. It was a frightening period but a time when we saw firsthand how global and interdependent with the rest of the world we had become.[12]

Before the events of September 11, 2001, ships would frequently clear U.S. ports in a matter of hours. That scenario has changed because of security measures that have been introduced. More cargo inspections, much more paperwork, and a longer time to clear U.S. borders are now a reality. Ships may be stopped and inspected and cargo inspected and checked. Some ships and items are given very close scrutiny because of their country of origin.[13]

Given the importance of global trade to the United States, a delicate balance exists between security and the efficient flow of global commerce. If security is too tight it could impede the flow of needed goods or materials, causing delays and decreased efficiency. Ports and border gateways can become congested because of security measures. Consequently, clearance time has increased from hours to days in some instances. Steps have been taken to improve the flow through border crossing.[14] This is necessary for our global economy.

Electronic filing of cargo information has helped to improve the border clearance times. The Trade Act of 2002 requires exporters to electronically submit shipping documents to U.S. Customs 24 hours after delivery to a port or 24 hours before vessel departure. For imports, the manifest must be filed by the ocean carrier or the consolidator 24 hours before the U.S.-bound cargo is loaded on the vessel in the foreign port.

Supply Chain Technology

Zara Shows How

Zara, the Spanish fashion leader, is an excellent example of a company that has implemented two different operations models for two different market needs. The industry's fastest growing company, Zara launches more than 11,000 new designs each year. The company has crafted a model in which product development takes three to five weeks, as opposed to the industry average of nine months; new product introductions arrive in stores every two to three weeks on average.

Because short life cycle fashions represent the bulk of Zara's sales and profits, the company deploys an onshore, rapid-response supply model based on quick feedback from stores. Each store manager tracks customer opinion using a handheld device and relays the information to the regional manager, who passes the regional data to the product-development team, which can quickly come up with a new design that meets current trends.

For this core model, the company uses mainly onshore manufacturers in Spain and Portugal, although its number of suppliers in Asia is increasing to serve growing demand in the Far East. The company books manufacturing capacity in advance, committing to make a certain number of blouses before it knows the colors and styles. The combination of instantly relaying customer insights and booking onshore capacity in advance means Zara can have new products on store shelves within weeks of the moment a store manager detects a fashion trend. Stores in Europe, the Americas, and Asia are replenished, on average, twice a week; the average product shelf life is two to three weeks.

However, for basic products like t-shirts and underwear—products that collectively make up less than 30 percent of revenues—Zara relies on low-cost offshore or near-shore manufacturers in countries such as China and Morocco. That basic-product group's larger orders, relatively predictable demand, and long shelf life make it possible to source from those lower-cost locales.

Source: Jaume Ferrer, Johan Karlberg, and Jamie Hintland, "Integration: The Key to Global Success," *Supply Chain Management Review* (March 2007): 29 Copyright © 2007 Reed Business Information, a division of Reed Elsevier. Reproduced by permission.

Because of Canada's importance as a trading partner, an expedited procedure (FAST) has been developed to speed up clearance through the U.S.-Canadian border.[15]

The U.S. Coast Guard was authorized by the U.S. Maritime Transportation Security Act of 2002 to assess the vulnerability of U.S. ports and to deny entry to ships from countries that do not meet U.S. security standards. This act requires the development of standards for container seals and locks, cargo tracking, identification, and screening systems for ocean containers.[16] Some of these requirements have been slow in developing to meet standards.

In addition, the Customs Trade Partnership Against Terrorism (C-TPAT) was established under the direction of the U.S. Department of Homeland Security in November 2001. This voluntary initiative to secure the global supply chain was started with seven companies; by 2007, some 7,400 corporations were involved in this cooperative effort to secure the global supply chain and to facilitate legitimate cargo and conveyance. C-TPAT functions under the U.S. Customs and Border Protection (CBP) Agency, which previously was known as the U.S. Customs Service.

CBP has responsibility for the traditional role of the U.S. Customs Service, namely, preventing illegal entry of people and drugs, protecting agriculture from harmful pests and diseases, protecting the intellectual property of businesses, collecting import duties, and regulating and facilitating global trade. Partner companies in C-TPAT agree to be responsible for keeping their supply chains secure to agreed standards and to implement needed changes. One of the key features of this program is information sharing of best practices for security among members. The goal is to develop a "green lane" to speed goods across the border but also to protect the United States and the global supply chains of the participants.[17]

Ports

As indicated above, ports are a critical part of global supply chains and also a major focus for global security. Every day, thousands of containers from countries all around the world arrive at U.S. seaports. Each shipment is usually for a specific supply chain— for example, porch furniture from Thailand bound for a St. Louis retailer or shoes from China destined for a Chicago distributor.

America's ports are a vital part of its global commerce. Over $2 trillion in trade value per year passes through U.S. ports, and over $18 billion is collected in industry fees and taxes. The 50 states utilize 15 ports to handle their imports and exports; a total of about $5.5 billion worth of goods moves in and out every day. About 99 percent of the international cargo of the United States moves through its ports, or about 2.5 billion tons annually. In 1960, international trade accounted for about 9 percent of U.S. gross domestic product (GDP). Today, it is over 25 percent.[18]

U.S. ports also play a vital role for the cruise industry. In 2005, it was estimated that there were 8.6 million embarkations through U.S. ports, which was an increase of 21 percent from 2003. This flow of passenger traffic has a very positive economic impact on the U.S. economy because of the expenditures to support the cruise industry.[19]

The ports also play a vital role in national defense and security. The ports are bases of operation to deploy troops and equipment. In 2003, the Surface Deployment and Distribution Command loaded 1.6 million tons of equipment and cargo to support the war effort in Iraq. Port security is very important for military and civilian purposes, and it is a shared responsibility between the public and private sectors. C-TPAT is an excellent example of this shared responsibility.

As indicated previously in this chapter, Canada and Mexico are very important trade partners for the United States; they ranked number 1 and 3, respectively, in 2006. These two countries account for about 30 percent of the total U.S. global trade.[20] Given their importance, the next section of this chapter will discuss the **North American Free Trade Agreement (NAFTA).**

North American Free Trade Agreement

The North American Free Trade Agreement was signed by leaders of Canada, the United States, and Mexico in 1993 and was ratified by Congress in early 1994. NAFTA establishes free trade between these three countries and provides the way the agreement is to be interpreted. NAFTA states that the objectives of these three countries is based on the principles of an unimpeded flow of goods, most favored nation (MFN) status, and a commitment to enhance the cross-border movement of goods and services. MFN status provides the lowest duties or customs fees, if any, and simplifies the paperwork required to move goods between the partner countries.

Even though the U.S./Canada Free Trade Agreement has been in effect for some time, certain trade barriers still remain. For example, many U.S. companies do not recognize certain French/English requirements for packaging and ingredient labeling. Trade with Mexico also poses some trade constraints that NAFTA did not eliminate. The supply chain barriers include a poor transportation infrastructure, restrictive foreign capital rules, and customs rules. The Mexican highway system is poor when compared to that existing in the United States and Canada. Mexico only has one railroad, which is owned and operated by the government. There are no national less-than-truckload (LTL) trucking companies, and air transportation is limited to the few airports. Foreign trucking companies are restricted from hauling intracountry shipments in all three countries; these are known as **cabotage restrictions.**

Figure 3.1 shows the procedure usually required to move a truck shipment from the United States into Mexico. The U.S. trucking company moves the shipment to the border, where a Mexican cartage carrier hauls the shipment across the border to Mexican customs and to the Mexican carrier after shipment clearance. The U.S. domestic freight forwarder submits shipment documents to the Mexican customs broker, who submits them to Mexican customs. Mexican customs inspects the documents, collects duties, inspects the goods, and clears the shipment. The Mexican cartage carrier delivers the shipment to a Mexican trucking company, which delivers it to the consignee.

The supply chain constraints will eventually be eliminated as NAFTA experience grows. Computerized customs information systems are currently operating in the United States and Canada, with Mexico a few years behind. The electronic transfer of information for NAFTA shipments into Mexico will speed the border crossing and improve logistics service.

In the long run, the goal of NAFTA is to create a better trading environment; but, in the short run, it has created some confusion due to the record keeping required to prove the origin of the product to obtain favorable tariff treatment. NAFTA's goals involve making the needed structural changes to operate a borderless logistics network in North America. Information systems, procedures, language, labels, and documentation are being redesigned. As new markets and supply sources develop, new transportation and storage facilities as well as intermediaries will need to be developed.

Maquiladora Operations

A concept that has become popular among U.S.-based firms is to use Mexican manufacturing/production facilities for subassembly or component manufacturing, or for final assembly of products such as electronic devices or television sets. While this has been occurring for some time, U.S. firms have begun to include such **Maquiladora operations** (named for the region of Mexico in which many of these plant operations are located) as formal components of their manufacturing and supply chain systems.

Essentially, in a Maquiladora operation, a U.S. manufacturer either operates or subcontracts for a manufacturing, processing, or assembly activity to be performed in Mexico. Mexican production and labor costs are lower than those in the United States, and the operations involve no local content issues. U.S. firms often send semifinished product to Mexico for final assembly, for example, and then have the finished product shipped to the United States. This concept appeals to many companies: U.S. manufacturers operate more than 2,000 Maquiladora facilities in Mexico.

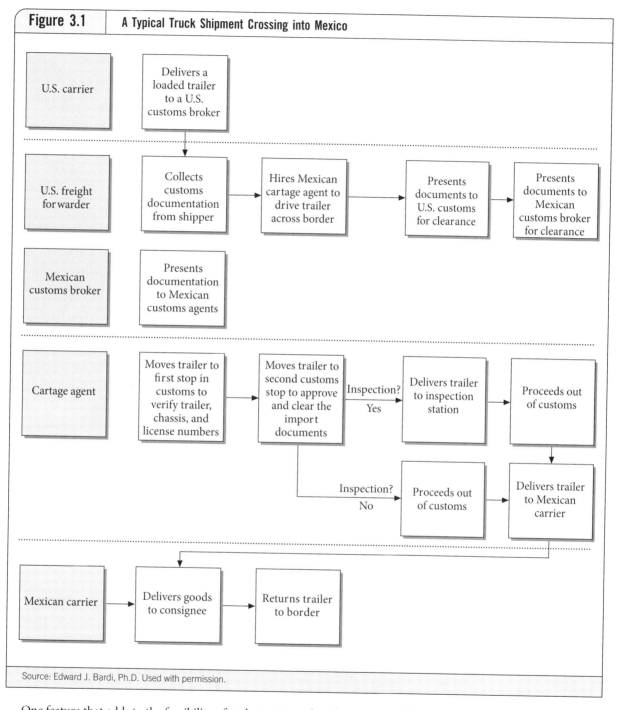

Figure 3.1 | A Typical Truck Shipment Crossing into Mexico

Source: Edward J. Bardi, Ph.D. Used with permission.

One feature that adds to the feasibility of such an approach is the limited tariff duties. The importing, storing, manufacturing, and subsequent export of goods have virtually no net payment of customs duties or import charges. The duties are limited to the value-added portion of the goods, primarily labor, returning from Mexico. Effectively, this contributes to the economic efficiency of supply chain alternatives such as Maquiladora operations.

Successful Mexican Maquiladora operations have served as role models for this concept's further exploitation in Central and South American countries. Coupled with the prospect of closer trade relations between the United States and Mexico, these alternatives offer advantages to the firms utilizing them. There are some constraints in South America because of less than amicable relations with some countries.

Asian Emergence

In perhaps the most significant trend of the past 25 years, Pacific Rim countries have emerged as important players in the global business environment. While Japan has achieved a dominant position in global financial markets, other Asian countries account for significant portions of global trade growth. Hong Kong, South Korea, Singapore, and Taiwan have all assumed leadership positions in certain markets and product types, and they are among the top 10 trading partners of the United States (see Table 3.1). This trend is likely to accelerate in the future.

Many Asian countries have become preferred sources for many raw materials and components. These countries have become trusted suppliers of finished goods such as apparel, furniture, consumer electronics, and automobiles. The advantages many of these countries offer are low labor cost and high quality.

New Directions

Aside from establishing product sources in other countries, global companies are locating plants and key logistics facilities in countries that use or consume their output. For example, Japanese-based firms such as Toyota have located plants in the United States. Similarly, U.S. automobile manufacturers such as Ford and General Motors have located plants in other countries.

Some global manufacturers are using a strategy known as **focus production** in which a given plant produces one or two items of the company's total product line. The plants are typically located in different countries, requiring a global logistics system to tie the focused plant to the customer, who may be located within the producing country or a different country.

An important dimension of any supply chain is transportation links. Transportation can be depicted as the glue that holds the supply chain together. Global supply chains are very dependent upon efficient and effective transportation and the related services of channel intermediaries discussed next.

Global Transportation Options

Global transportation is usually much more complex than domestic U.S. transportation. The distances involved are greater, and the number of parties involved is typically more extensive. Because of the large expanses of water separating most regions of the world, the major modes of global transport are ocean and air. Land modes also carry freight between contiguous countries, particularly in Europe, where land routes are short.

Ocean

Transport by ship is by far the most pervasive and important global shipment method, accounting for two-thirds of all international movements. Ocean transportation's major advantages are low rates and the ability to transport a wide variety of products and shipment sizes. The primary disadvantages include long transit times (slow

Table 3.2	Top 10 Ocean Carriers Ranked by Capacity	
OCEAN CARRIER	**2000**	**2006**
A. P. Moller	1	1
Mediterrian Shipping Co. (MSC)	5	2
CMA CGM Group	12	3
Evergreen Group	2	4
Hapag-Lloyd	14	5
China Shipping (CSCL)	18	6
APL	6	7
Hanji/Senator	4	8
COSCO Container Line	7	9
NYK	8	10
Source: http://www.supplychainbrain.com.		

speed), low accessibility, and higher potential for shipment damage. The pervasive use of containers has reduced damage and increased accessibility via connections with other modes (rail and truck) for inland origins and destinations.

Ocean shipping comprises three major categories. One is **liner service**, which offers scheduled service on regular routes. Another is **charter vessels,** which firms usually hire on a contract basis and which travel no set routes. Finally, **private carriers** can be part of a firm's own supply chain. Table 3.2 contains the top 10 ocean carriers. Note the changes that occurred between 2000 and 2006 in ocean carrier rankings.

Liner carriers offer set schedules over specific routes. They also offer set tariffs and accept certain standards of liability. Liners usually carry break-bulk shipments of less-than-shipload size. Most container and roll-on, roll-off (RO-RO) ships are liners.

Liners are operated by large steamship companies, which usually belong to **shipping conferences**. These conferences are voluntary associations of ocean carriers that operate over common trade routes and use a common tariff for setting rates on the commodities they handle. Conferences also work together to attract customers and to utilize member ships as effectively as possible.

In general, conferences provide good service with frequent and reliable schedules, published daily in the *Journal of Commerce*. Additionally, conferences help to standardize shipping on many routes by stabilizing prices and offering uniform contract rates.

Firms contract charter ships for specific voyages and/or for specified time periods. **Voyage charters** are contracts covering one voyage. The carrier agrees to carry a certain cargo from an origin port to a destination. The price the carrier quotes includes all of the expenses of the sea voyage. **Time charters** allow the use of a ship for an agreed-upon time period. The carrier usually supplies a crew as part of the contract. The charterer has exclusive use of the vessel to carry any cargo that the contract does not prohibit and assumes all expenses for the ship's operation during the charter period. **Bareboat** or **demise charter** transfers full control of the vessel to the charterer. The charterer is then responsible for the ship and all expenses necessary for the vessel's operation, including hiring the crew.

Chartering usually takes place through **ship brokers,** who track the location and status of ships that are open for hire. When a shipper needs to contract for a ship, the shipper contacts a broker, who then negotiates the price with the ship owner. The ship owner pays the broker a commission on the charter's cost.

In a logistics system, **private ocean carriers** play the same role as private carriage in general. In other words, companies utilize private ocean vessels to lower their overall costs and/or to improve their control over transportation service. The major differences between domestic and international private ocean transportation are the scale of investment, the complexity of regulations, and the greater risk international transport entails. In international operations, chartering often provides a very viable substitute for private carriage.

Air

The fast transit times that air transport provides have had an impact on global distribution. The speed of airplanes combined with a frequency of scheduled flights has reduced some global transit times from as many as 30 days to 1 or 2 days. These transit times have spurred the development of global freight services. These carriers offer door-to-door, next-day services for packages between most large American cities and a growing number of overseas points.

The world's air carriers have usually focused on passenger service, and air cargo accounts for a small percentage of international freight by weight. However, the nature of the cargo, mostly high-value, low-density items, causes the total value of airfreight cargo to be a greater proportion of the world total. Air cargoes include high-value items such as computers and electronic equipment, perishables such as cut flowers and live seafood, time-sensitive documents and spare parts, and even whole planeloads of cattle for breeding stock. Table 3.3 provides a list of major international cargo air carriers.

Table 3.3	Major International Cargo Air Carriers
Airborne Express	
British Airways	
BAX Global	
DHL Worldwide Express	
Emery Worldwide	
Federal Express	
Japan Airlines	
KLM Royal Dutch Airlines	
Lufthansa	
Singapore Airlines	
United Airlines	
United Parcel Service	

Most airfreight travels as **belly cargo** in the baggage holds of scheduled passenger flights. Only a few major airlines have all-freight aircraft.

In addition to short transit time, air transportation offers an advantage in packaging. This mode requires less stringent packaging than ocean transport, since air transport will not expose the shipment to rough handling at a port, to a rough ride on the oceans, or to the weather. A firm using air transportation may also be able to use the same packaging for international shipping as for domestic shipping. In addition, shippers have developed special containers for air transport. These containers reduce handling costs and provide protection, but they also make intermodal shipments difficult. Their odd shapes usually require shippers to repack the shipment before transporting it by another mode. Recent container-handling innovations have made it possible to load standard 20-foot containers onto large freight aircraft.

A disadvantage of air carriage is high rates, which have precluded many shippers from transporting international shipments by air. Generally, only highly valuable, highly perishable, or urgently needed commodities can bear the higher cost of airfreight.

Motor

Companies will often use motor transport when shipping goods to an adjacent country—between the United States and Mexico or Canada, for example. It is very common in Europe, where transport distances are relatively short. Motor also plays a large part in intermodal shipments.

The advantages of international motor transport are basically the same as those for domestic shipments: speed, safety, reliability, and accessibility to the delivery site. However, motor shipment across multiple national boundaries involves a number of different import regulations. To minimize paperwork, these shipments are often made **in bond**—the carrier seals the trailer at its origin and does not open it again until it reaches its destination country.

Rail

International railroad use is also highly similar to domestic rail use, but rail's accessibility is much more limited internationally because border crossing points are scarce. Differing track gauges in various countries also prevent long-distance shipments.

Intermodal container shipments by rail are increasing. Various **maritime bridge** concepts involve railroads both for transcontinental shipments and to and from inland points. For example, a shipper using a **land bridge** substitutes land transportation for part of a container's ocean voyage, taking several days off the transit time and saving in-transit inventory costs. A prime example of a land bridge occurs on the trade route between Japan and Europe. The all-water route takes anywhere from 28 to 31 days. If the shipment travels by water from Japan to Seattle (10 days), then by rail to New York (five days), and by water from New York to Europe (seven days), the total shipping time is approximately 22 days.

Strategic Channel Intermediaries

Intermediaries play a much larger role in global supply chain operations than in the domestic United States. The scope of services that intermediaries offer is very comprehensive. Intermediaries play a strategic role in helping new and established companies venture into the global arena. Some companies require assistance in comprehending complex operations involving sources and destinations in other countries.

Foreign Freight Forwarders

For a company with little international shipping expertise, the **foreign freight forwarder** may be the answer. The foreign freight forwarder, which employs individuals who are knowledgeable in all aspects of international shipping, supplies its experts to small international shippers that find employing such individuals in their shipping departments uneconomical. Foreign freight forwarders are regulated by the Federal Maritime Commission.

Foreign freight forwarders, like their domestic counterparts, consolidate small shipments into more economical sizes. In the international arena, these larger sizes range from containers up to entire ships. Foreign freight forwarders also perform the routine actions that shipments require.

Since no two international sales are exactly alike and since shippers have varying international traffic capabilities, the forwarder usually performs the export work that the shipper cannot handle. The supply chain manager must weigh the forwarder's cost against the cost of hiring personnel to perform the same tasks.

The forwarder derives income from different sources. One source is the fees charged for preparing export documentation. Another source is the commissions the forwarder receives from carriers. These commissions are based on the amount of revenue the forwarder generates for the carrier. The third type of income comes from the price difference between the rate the forwarder charges a shipper and the lower rate per pound it pays for the consolidated shipments. The final two sources are from the provision of inland transportation and warehousing functions.

Airfreight Forwarders

Airfreight forwarders perform the same functions as surface freight forwarders, but for air shipments only. They do not require a license from the federal government as foreign freight forwarders do. Airfreight forwarders primarily consolidate small shipments, which they present to the air carrier for movement to the destination.

Like the foreign freight forwarder, the airfreight forwarder generates income from fees charged for services provided and the difference between the rate charged the shipper and that paid to the air carrier. The major competitors of airfreight forwarders are the air carriers, who can go directly to the shipper and eliminate the forwarder. For small shipments, air express carriers, such as Federal Express, Emery, UPS Air, and DHL, compete directly with the forwarders.

Non-Vessel-Operating Common Carriers

The **non-vessel-operating common carrier (NVOCC)** consolidates and dispenses containers that originate at or are bound to inland points. The need for these firms arose from the inability of shippers to find outbound turnaround traffic after unloading inbound containers at inland points. Rail and truck carriers often charge the same rate to move containers, whether they are loaded or empty. NVOCCs are regulated by the Federal Maritime Commission.

To reduce these costs, the NVOCC disperses inbound containers and then seeks outbound shipments in the same containers. It will consolidate many containers for multiple-piggyback-car or whole-train movement back to the port for export. It also provides scheduled container service to foreign destinations.

Shippers and receivers of international shipments gain from the shipping expertise that NVOCCs possess and from the expanded and simplified import and export opportunities. The ocean carrier gains from the increased market area made possible by NVOCCs' solicitation services.

Export Management Companies

Often, a firm wishes to sell its products in a foreign market but lacks the resources to conduct the foreign business itself. An **export management company (EMC)** can supply the expertise such firms need to operate in foreign environments.

EMCs act as agents for domestic firms in the international arena. Their primary function is to obtain orders for their clients' products by selecting appropriate markets, distribution channels, and promotional campaigns. The EMC collects and analyzes credit data for foreign customers and advises exporters on payment terms. It also usually collects payments from foreign customers. EMCs may also supply documentation, arrange transportation, provide warehouse facilities, maintain a foreign inventory, and handle break-bulk operations.

A firm can contract with an export management company to provide its exclusive representation in a defined territory. The EMC may either purchase the goods or sell them on commission. In order to present a complete product line to importers, an EMC will usually specialize in a particular product type or in complementary products.

Using an export management company has several advantages. First, EMCs usually specialize in specific markets, so they understand in detail what an area requires. They will have up-to-date information on consumer preferences and will help the exporter to target its products most effectively. Second, EMCs will usually strive to maintain good relations with the governments of importing countries. This enables them to receive favorable customs treatment when introducing new products. EMCs also remain current on documentation requirements. This helps the goods they are importing to enter with few holdups.

Export Trading Companies

An **export trading company (ETC)** exports goods and services. The ETC locates overseas buyers and handles most of the export arrangements, including documentation, inland and overseas transportation, and the meeting of foreign government requirements. The ETC may or may not take title to the goods.

A trading company may also engage in other aspects of foreign trade, in which case it becomes a **general trading company**. One reason Japan has been successful in international trade is because of its large general trading companies, the **sogo shosha**. These firms, which consolidate all aspects of overseas trade into one entity, may include banks, steamship lines, warehouse facilities, insurance companies, sales forces, and communications networks.

A trading company allows small- to medium-size firms, which do not in and of themselves possess the resources, to engage in foreign trade. The trading company purchases their goods and sells them on the international market, taking care of all the intermediate steps. Having all the functional areas under one control makes coordination easy and speeds response time when markets fluctuate.

Customs House Brokers

Customs house brokers oversee the movement of goods through customs and ensure that the documentation accompanying a shipment is complete and accurate for entry into the country. U.S. customs house brokers are licensed by the Department of the Treasury.

Customs house brokers operate under power of attorney from the shipper to pay all import duties due on the shipment. The importer is ultimately liable for any unpaid duties. The brokers keep abreast of the latest import regulations and of the specific requirements of individual products. The next section discusses storage facilities and packaging from a global perspective.

Storage Facilities and Packaging

Storage Facilities

At several points during an international shipment, the goods being shipped may require storage. Storage may be necessary while the shipment waits for loading on an ocean vessel, after it has arrived at the destination port and is awaiting further transportation, or while customs clearance is being arranged for the merchandise. When packaged in a container, goods are protected from the weather, theft, and pilferage. A carrier or shipper can store containers outside between a journey's stages with little effect on the contents.

Noncontainerized cargo, on the other hand, requires protection if it is to arrive in good order. Ports supply several types of storage facilities to fill this need. **Transit sheds,** located next to the piers or at the airport, provide temporary storage while the goods await the next portion of the journey. Usually, the port usage fee includes a fixed number of days of free storage. After this time expires, the user pays a daily charge. **In-transit storage areas** allow the shipper to perform some required operation on the cargo before embarkation. These actions may include carrier negotiations and waiting for documentation, packing, crating, and labeling to be completed. The carrier usually provides **hold-on-dock storage** free of charge until the vessel's next departure date, allowing the shipper to consolidate goods and to save storage costs.

When goods require long-term storage, the shipper uses a warehouse. **Public warehouses** are available for extended storage periods. The services and charges offered by these facilities are similar to those of public warehouses in the domestic sphere, which are discussed in a later chapter.

Bonded warehouses, operated under customs supervision, are designated by the U.S. secretary of the treasury for the purpose of storing, repacking, sorting, or cleaning imported merchandise entered for warehousing without paying import duties while the goods are in storage. Only bonded carriers may move goods into and out of bonded warehouses. Bonded warehouses are very important in global commerce.

One purpose of bonded warehouses is to hold imported goods for reshipment out of the United States. The owner can store items in a bonded warehouse for up to three years, allowing time to decide on the goods' ultimate disposition without having to pay import duties or taxes on them. If the owner does not reexport the goods before the three years elapse, they are considered imports and are subject to all appropriate duties and taxes.

Packaging

Export shipments moving by ocean transportation require more stringent packaging than domestic shipments normally do. An export shipment undergoes more handling: it is loaded at the origin, unloaded at the dock, loaded onto a ship, unloaded from the ship at port, loaded onto a delivery vehicle, and unloaded at the destination. This handling usually occurs under unfavorable conditions—in inclement weather or with antiquated handling equipment, for example. If storage facilities are inadequate, the goods may remain exposed to the elements for a long time.

The shipper may find settling liability claims for damage to export goods very difficult. Usually, the freight handling involves many firms, and these firms are located in different countries. Stringent packaging is the key to claims prevention for export shipments.

SUMMARY

- Companies competing in global supply chains need to address some important questions for their global networks to ensure their efficiency and effectiveness.
- There have been three phases of globalization: the first was driven by countries, the second by large companies, and the third by individuals and small organizations.
- Successful global companies have transformed their supply chains on an ongoing basis to enable them to deliver low cost and high value to the ultimate customer.
- The scope and magnitude of trade flows between the United States and other countries have grown considerably in the last several decades. One interesting development has been the growth in importance of trade with China and several other Asian countries.
- Success in the global marketplace requires developing a cohesive set of strategies with respect to customer service, product development, business model, and overall supply chains.
- Supply chain security has taken on increased importance since September 11, 2001. Companies individually, jointly, and in cooperation with the various levels of government need to be actively involved. The federal government, in particular, has expanded the scope of its regulations and policies for global security.
- U.S. ports play a critical role in global supply chains since over 90 percent of global trade passes through them. Ports are also an important focus for security.
- Canada and Mexico are ranked number 1 and 3, respectively, on the list of most important trading partners with the United States. That relationship is enhanced by the North American Free Trade Agreement ratified by Congress in 1994. While the treaty had lofty goals, it still is experiencing problems with full implementation of its objectives. Nevertheless, it has fostered trade in North America.
- Global supply chains have a number of transportation and related service options available to managers. Each of the options has advantages and disadvantages that need to be analyzed.

STUDY QUESTIONS

1. Globalization has developed in three phases or eras. What are the major differences between today's third phase and the previous two phases? Do you think that there will be a fourth phase? Why or why not?

2. It has been alleged that the world has become flat. What does this description mean from a global economic perspective? What factors have contributed to this phenomenon?

3. A number of authors have observed that traditional, hierarchical organizations have changed in the current global economy. How have organizations changed? Why have they changed?

4. Wal-Mart has frequently been cited for being a successful supply chain company. Why?

5. What special role do supply chains play in the globalization of organizations? Will supply chains continue to be important in the future?

6. What is meant by the current description of the global economy that "time and distance have been collapsed or compressed"? Do you agree? Do you think that our trading relationships will be affected in the future by this phenomenon?

7. Why are customer service and its related strategy so important for companies operating global supply chains?

8. What is meant by the phrase "that supply chain security, especially on a global basis," is a balancing act?

9. Why are ports so important for global supply chains?

10. Discuss the major alternatives for global transportation.

NOTES

1. "China, India Lure Global Investors with Booming Economics and Robust Trade," *T. Rowe Price Report*, Issue 96 (Summer 2007): 1–10.

2. Thomas L. Friedman, *The World Is Flat* (New York: Farrar, Strauss and Giroux, 2005): 6–11.

3. Ibid.

4. Ibid.

5. Ibid.

6. Charles Fishman, *The Wal-Mart Effect* (New York: Penguin Press, 2006): 1–22.

7. *The Wall Street Journal* (August 9, 2007): 1.

8. Adam Smith, *Wealth of Nations*.

9. Edward Iwata, "Infosys Kicks up Growth Mode," *USA TODAY* (August 4, 2006): 1B.

10. Bob Fernandez, "U.S. Research Making Great Leap," *Philadelphia Inquirer* (November 5, 2006): E-1.

11. Timothy Aeppel, "Overseas Profits Help U.S. Firms Through the Tumult," *The Wall Street Journal* (August 9, 2007): A10.

12. J. J. Coyle, E. J. Bardi, and R. A. Novack, *Transportation*, 6th ed. (Mason, Ohio: Thomson South-Western, 2006): 232–240.

13. Ibid.

14. Ibid.

15. Ibid.

16. Ibid.

17. "Securing the Global Supply Chain," U.S. Customs and Border Protection (Washington, DC: Office of Field Operations, November 2004): 1–25.

18. "America's Ports Today," American Association of Port Authorities (Alexandria, VA: 2007): 1–8.

19. Ibid.

20. "Measurement of Commercial Motor Vehicle Travel Time and Delay at U.S. International Border Stations," U.S. Federal Highway Administration, 2002.

CASE 3.1

Red Fish, Blue Fish, LLP: A Sequel

Fran Fisher, CEO of Red Fish, Blue Fish, was meeting with Eric Lynch who now was vice president for global supply chain management for Red Fish, Blue Fish. Fran started the meeting by praising Eric for his management of their growing global enterprise. "Eric, I can hardly believe how far we have come during the last three years. Our sales have quadrupled and there is every reason to believe that we can double our current sales in more years. Our consulting sales business appears to be stabilizing, and we have to decide if we want to extend our sales area eastward into the Philadelphia, Baltimore, and DC markets. Our Internet sales have been growing geometrically not only in the United States and Canada but also in Western Europe. Interestingly, we have also had some sales in several South American countries during the last year."

"China is still our principal source for the fish that we sell, and Liu-Sheng Trading Company has become almost an extension of our company. Connie Que, COO of Liu-Sheng, and I met in Hong Kong recently to discuss our long-term needs. She assured me that they could handle our continued growth and wanted to be a 'partner' with Red Fish, Blue Fish."

Fran told Eric that he was concerned, for the long run, in depending on one source of supply, that is, Liu-Sheng Trading Company. Also, he was unsure about South American countries as a future growth market. Finally, he told Eric that the complexity of the supply chain needed to be considered.

CASE QUESTIONS

1. What are the advantages and potential disadvantages to Red Fish, Blue Fish of having China (Liu-Sheng Trading Company) as its sole source of supply? What would you recommend?

2. What supply challenge would Red Fish, Blue Fish face in expanding into South America? Do you recommend expanding aggressively into South America? Why or why not?

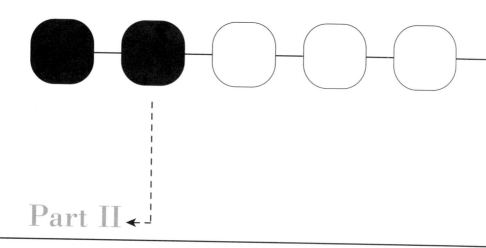

Part II

The first three chapters made frequent reference to the strategic importance of supply chain management and its role in the competitive success of private and public organizations in today's global environment. The strategic role of supply chains cannot be overemphasized along with the need to align supply chain strategy with overall organizational strategy. While there are many strategic dimensions of supply chains, we have selected three topics to include in Part II, which is devoted to strategic factors for supply chains, namely supply chain relationships, performance measurement and financial analysis, and managing information flows.

Chapter 4 addresses the overall topic of collaboration and relationships in supply chains. The types of relationships and their importance are discussed with special emphasis on third- and fourth-party logistics and supply chain providers. Special attention is devoted to the types of services, the role of information technology, and customer satisfaction with these service providers.

Performance measurement and financial analysis are the focus of **Chapter 5**. The scope and complexity of global supply chains require the development and use of effective measures to evaluate the performance of the managers involved in the supply chain and the extent to which the supply chain outcomes are contributing to top-level measurements and strategies of the organization.

Chapter 6 addresses the very important topic of supply chain information technology. Information is "power" in managing a supply chain for efficiency and effectiveness. The key issues and importance of technology in supply chains are discussed as well as the need for quality and integrity in information systems for managing material flows and driving cash flows for financial success.

Chapter 4

SUPPLY CHAIN RELATIONSHIPS

Learning Objectives

After reading this chapter, you should be able to do the following:

- Understand the types of supply chain relationships and their importance.
- Describe a process model that will facilitate the development and implementation of successful supply chain relationships.
- Recognize the importance of "collaborative" supply chain relationships.
- Define what is meant by *third-party logistics* (3PL) and know what types of firms provide 3PL services.
- Know what types of 3PL services are used by client/customer firms and what types of 3PL providers are used.
- Discuss the role and relevance of information technology-based services to 3PLs and their clients/customers.
- Know the extent to which customers are satisfied with 3PL services and identify where improvement may be needed.
- Understand some of the likely future directions for outsourced logistics services.

Supply Chain Profile   *Supply Chain Relationships— There Is No "Magic Bullet"*

One of the most fundamental yet more challenging requirements for supply chain integration is changing the nature of traditional relationships between suppliers and customers in the supply chain. Relationship management affects all areas of the supply chain and has a dramatic impact on performance. In many cases, the information systems, technology, inventory, and transportation management systems required for the supply chain management (SCM) effort are available and ready to be implemented, but the initiatives fail due to poor communication of expectations and the resulting behaviors. Managers often assume that the personal relationships important to the supply chain will fall into place; however, managing relationships among organizations can be the most difficult part of the SCM initiative.

Moreover, the single most important ingredient for successful SCM may be trusting relationships among partners in the supply chain, where each party has confidence in the other members' capabilities and actions. And trust building is characterized as an ongoing process that must be continually managed. One materials management vice president at a *Fortune* 500 manufacturer expressed this feeling as follows:

> *Supply chain management is one of the most emotional experiences I've ever witnessed. There have been so many mythologies that have developed over the years, people blaming other people for their problems, based on some incident that may or may not have occurred sometime in the past. Once you get everyone together into the same room, you begin to realize the number of false perceptions that exist. People are still very reluctant to let someone else make decisions within their area.*

In the early stages of supply chain development, organizations often eliminate suppliers or customers that are unsuitable, because they lack the capabilities to serve the organization, they are not well aligned with the company, or they are simply not interested in developing a more collaborative relationship. Then, organizations may concentrate on supply chain members who are willing to contribute the time and effort required to create a strong relationship. Firms may consider developing a strategy with this supplier to share confidential information, invest assets in joint projects, and pursue significant joint improvements.

However, many firms lack the guidelines to develop, implement, and maintain supply chain alliances. In creating new value systems, companies must rethink how they view their customers and suppliers. They must concentrate not just on maximizing their own profits, but on maximizing the success of all organizations in the supply chain. Strategic priorities must consider other key alliance partners that contribute value for the end customer. Instead of encouraging companies to hold their information close, trust-building processes promote the sharing of all forms of information possible that will allow supply chain members to make better, aligned decisions. Whereas traditional accounting, measurement, and reward systems tend to focus on individual organizations, a unified set of supply chain performance metrics should be utilized as well.

Strategic alliances can occur in any number of different markets and with different combinations of suppliers and customers. A typical supplier-customer alliance involves a single supplier and a single customer. A good example is the relationship between Procter & Gamble and Wal-Mart, which have worked together to establish long-term electronic data interchange (EDI) linkages, shared forecasts, and pricing agreements. Alliances also can develop between two horizontal suppliers in an industry, such as the relationship between Dell and Microsoft—organizations that collaborate to ensure that the technology road map for Dell computers (in terms of memory, speed, etc.) will be aligned with Microsoft's software requirements. Finally, a vertical supplier-supplier alliance may involve multiple parties, such as trucking companies that must work with railroads and ocean freighters to ensure proper timing of deliveries for multimodal transshipments.

Overall, creating and managing a strategic alliance means committing a dedicated team of people to answering these questions, and working through all of the details involved in managing the relationship. Unfortunately, there is no "magic bullet" to ensure that alliances will always work. However, it is reasonable to assume that, like a marriage, the more you work at it, the more successful it is likely to be!

Source: Adapted from Robert Handfield, "Managing Supply Chain Relationships," North Carolina State University. http://www.scrc.ncsu.edu/public/APICS/APICSoct03.html. Reproduced by permission.

Introduction

As indicated throughout this book, many firms have directed significant attention toward working more closely with supply chain partners, including not only customers and suppliers but also various types of logistics suppliers. Considering that one of the fundamental objectives of effective supply chain management is to achieve coordination and integration among participating organizations, the development of more meaningful "relationships" through the supply chain has become a high priority.

This chapter focuses on two highly related topics. The first is that of supply chain relationships in general, with an emphasis on the types of relationships, the processes for developing and implementing successful relationships, and the need for firms to collaborate to achieve supply chain objectives. The second is that of the third-party logistics (3PL) industry in general and how firms in this industry create value for their commercial clients. The 3PL industry has grown significantly over recent years and is recognized as a valuable type of supplier of logistics services.

As suggested by the late Robert V. Delaney in his 11th Annual State of Logistics Report,[1] relationships are what will carry the logistics industry into the future. In commenting on the current rise of interest in e-commerce and the development of electronic markets and exchanges, he states, "We recognize and appreciate the power of the new technology and the power it will deliver, but, in the frantic search for space, it is still about relationships." This message not only captures the importance of developing logistics relationships but also suggests that the ability to form relationships is a prerequisite to future success. Also, the essence of this priority is captured in a quote from noted management guru Rosabeth Moss Kanter[2] who stated that, "being a good partner has become a key corporate asset; in the global economy, a well-developed ability to create and sustain fruitful collaborations gives companies a significant leg up."

Logistics Relationships

Types of Relationships

Generally, there are two types of logistics relationships. The first is what may be termed **vertical relationships;** these refer to the traditional linkages between firms in the supply chain such as retailers, distributors, manufacturers, and parts and materials suppliers. These firms relate to one another in the ways that buyers and sellers do in all industries, and significant attention is directed toward making sure that these relationships help to achieve individual firm and supply chain objectives. Logistics service providers are involved on a day-to-day basis as they serve their customers in this traditional, vertical form of relationship.

The second type of logistics relationship is horizontal in nature and includes those business agreements between firms that have "parallel" or cooperating positions in the logistics process. To be precise, a horizontal relationship may be thought of as a service agreement between two or more independent logistics provider firms based on trust, cooperation, shared risk and investments, and following mutually agreeable goals. Each firm is expected to contribute to the specific logistics services in which it specializes, and each exercises control of those tasks while striving to integrate its services with those of the other logistics providers. An example of this may be a transportation firm that finds itself working along with a contract warehousing firm to satisfy the needs of the same customer. Also, cooperation between a third-party logistics provider and a firm in the software or information technology business would be an example of this type of relationship. Thus, these parties have parallel or equal relationships in the logistics process and likely need to work together in appropriate and useful ways to see that the customer's logistics objectives are met.

Intensity of Involvement

As suggested by Figure 4.1, the range of relationship types extends from that of a vendor to that of a strategic alliance. In the context of the more traditional "vertical" context, a vendor is represented simply by a seller or provider of a product or service, such that there is little or no integration or collaboration with the buyer or purchaser. In essence, the relationship with a vendor is "transactional," and parties to a vendor relationship are said to be at "arm's length" (i.e., at a significant distance). The analogy of such a relationship to that experienced by one who uses a "vending" machine is not inappropriate. While this form of relationship suggests a relatively low or nonexistent level of involvement between the parties, there are certain types of transactions for which this option is desirable. One-time or even multiple purchases of standard products and/or services, for example, may suggest that an "arm's length" relationship would be appropriate.

Figure 4.1	Relationship Perspectives

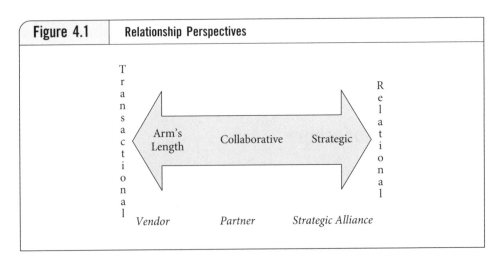

Alternatively, the relationship suggested by a strategic alliance is one in which two or more business organizations cooperate and willingly modify their business objectives and practices to help achieve long-term goals and objectives. The strategic alliance by definition is more strategic in nature and is highly relational in terms of the firms involved. This form of relationship typically benefits the involved parties by reducing uncertainty and improving communication, increasing loyalty and establishing a common vision, and helping to enhance global performance. Alternatively, the challenges with this form of relationship include the fact that it implies heavy resource commitments by the participating organizations, significant opportunity costs, and high switching costs.

Leaning more toward the strategic alliance end of the scale, a partnership represents a customized business relationship that produces results for all parties that are more acceptable than would be achieved individually. Partnerships are frequently described as being "collaborative," which is discussed further at a later point in this chapter.

Note that the range of alternatives suggested in Figure 4.1 is limited to those that do not represent the ownership of one firm by another (i.e., vertical integration) or the formation of a joint venture, which is a unique legal entity to reflect the combined operations of two or more parties. As such, each represents an alternative that may imply even greater involvement than the partnership or strategic alliance. Considering that they represent alternative legal forms of ownership, however, they are not discussed in detail at this time.

Regardless of form, relationships may differ in numerous ways. A partial list of these differences follows:

- Duration
- Obligations
- Expectations
- Interaction/Communication
- Cooperation
- Planning
- Goals
- Performance analysis
- Benefits and burdens

In general terms, most companies feel that there is significant room for improvement in terms of the relationships they have developed with their supply chain partners. The content of this chapter should help to understand some key ways in which firms may improve and enhance the quality of relationships they experience with other members of their supply chains.

Model for Developing and Implementing Successful Supply Chain Relationships

Figure 4.2 outlines the steps in a process model for forming and sustaining supply chain relationships. For purposes of illustration, let us assume that the model is being applied from the perspective of a manufacturing firm, as it considers the possibility of forming a relationship with a supplier of logistics services (e.g., transport firm, warehouseman, etc.).

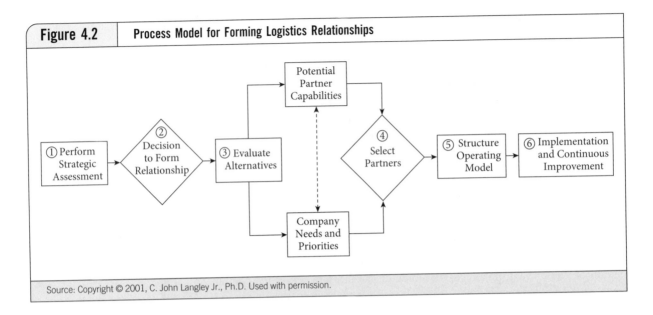

Figure 4.2 | **Process Model for Forming Logistics Relationships**

Source: Copyright © 2001, C. John Langley Jr., Ph.D. Used with permission.

Step 1: Perform Strategic Assessment

This first stage involves the process by which the manufacturer becomes fully aware of its logistics and supply chain needs and the overall strategies that will guide its operations. Essentially, this is what is involved in the conduct of a logistics audit, which is discussed in detail in Chapter 12. The audit provides a perspective on the firm's logistics and supply chain activities, as well as developing a wide range of useful information that will be helpful as the opportunity to form a supply chain relationship is contemplated. The types of information that may become available as a result of the audit include the following:

- Overall business goals and objectives, including those from a corporate, divisional, or logistics perspective
- Needs assessment to include requirements of customers, suppliers, and key logistics providers
- Identification and analysis of strategic environmental factors and industry trends
- Profile of current logistics network and the firm's positioning in respective supply chains
- Benchmark, or target, values for logistics costs and key performance measurements
- Identification of "gaps" between current and desired measures of logistics performance (qualitative and quantitative)

Given the significance of most logistics and supply chain relationship decisions, and the potential complexity of the overall process, any time taken at the outset to gain an understanding of one's needs is well spent.

Step 2: Decision to Form Relationship

Depending on the type of relationship being considered by the manufacturing firm under consideration, this step may take on a slightly different decision context. When

Figure 4.3	What Does It Take to Have an Area of Core Competency?

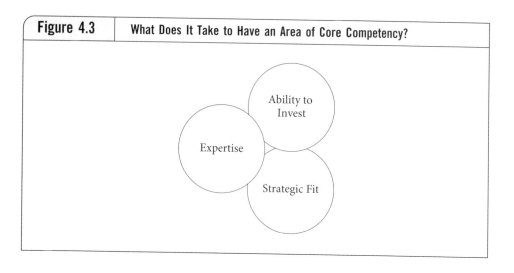

the decision relates to using an external provider of logistics services (e.g., trucking firm, express logistics provider, third-party logistics provider), the first question is whether or not the provider's services will be needed. A suggested approach to making this decision is to make a careful assessment of the areas in which the manufacturing firm appears to have core competency. As indicated in Figure 4.3, for a firm to have core competency in any given area, it is necessary to have expertise, strategic fit, and ability to invest. The absence of any one or more of these may suggest that the services of an external provider are appropriate.

If the relationship decision involves a channel partner such as a supplier or customer, the focus is not so much on whether or not to have a relationship but on what type of relationship will work best. In either case, the question as to what type of relationship is most appropriate is one that is very important to answer.

Lambert, Emmelhainz, and Gardner have conducted significant research into the topic of how to determine whether a partnership is warranted and, if so, what kind of partnership should be considered.[3] Their partnership model incorporates the identification of "drivers" and "facilitators" of a relationship; it indicates that for a relationship to have a high likelihood of success, the right drivers and facilitators should be present.

Drivers are defined as "compelling reasons to partner." For a relationship to be successful, the theory of the model is that all parties "must believe that they will receive significant benefits in one or more areas and that these benefits would not be possible without a partnership." Drivers are strategic factors that may result in a competitive advantage and may help to determine the appropriate type of business relationship. Although other factors may certainly be considered, the primary drivers include the following:

- Asset/Cost efficiency
- Customer service
- Marketing advantage
- Profit stability/Growth

Facilitators are defined as "supportive corporate environmental factors that enhance partnership growth and development." As such, they are the factors that, if present, can help to ensure the success of the relationship. Included among the main types of facilitators are the following:

- Corporate compatibility
- Management philosophy and techniques
- Mutuality of commitment to relationship formation
- Symmetry on key factors such as relative size, financial strength, and so on

In addition, a number of additional factors have been identified as keys to successful relationships. Included are factors such as exclusivity, shared competitors, physical proximity, prior history of working with a partner or the partner, and a shared high-value end user.

Step 3: Evaluate Alternatives

Although the details are not included here, Lambert and his colleagues suggest a method for measuring and weighting the drivers and facilitators that we have discussed.[4] Then, they discuss a methodology by which the apparent levels of drivers and facilitators may suggest the most appropriate type of relationship to consider. If neither the drivers nor the facilitators seem to be present, then the recommendation would be for the relationship to be more transactional, or "arm's length" in nature. Alternatively, when all parties to the relationship share common drivers, and when the facilitating factors seem to be present, then a more structured, formal relationship may be justified.

In addition to utilization of the partnership formation process, it is important to conduct a thorough assessment of the manufacturing company's needs and priorities in comparison with the capabilities of each potential partner. This task should be supported with not only the availability of critical measurements and so on, but also the results of personal interviews and discussions with the most likely potential partners.

Although logistics executives and managers usually have significant involvement in the decision to form logistics and supply chain relationships, it is frequently advantageous to involve other corporate managers in the overall selection process. Representatives of marketing, finance, manufacturing, human resources, and information systems, for example, frequently have valuable perspectives to contribute to the discussion and analysis. Thus, it is important to ensure a broad representation and involvement of people throughout the company in the partnership formation and partner selection decisions.

Step 4: Select Partners

While this stage is of critical concern to the customer, the selection of a logistics or supply chain partner should be made only following very close consideration of the credentials of the most likely candidates. Also, it is highly advisable to interact with and get to know the final candidates on a professionally intimate basis.

As was indicated in the discussion of Step 3, a number of executives will likely play key roles in the relationship formation process. It is important to achieve consensus on the final selection decision to create a significant degree of "buy-in" and agreement among those involved. Due to the strategic significance of the decision to form a logistics or supply chain relationship, it is essential to ensure that everyone has a consistent understanding of the decision that has been made and a consistent expectation of what to expect from the firm that has been selected.

Step 5: Structure Operating Model

The structure of the relationship refers to the activities, processes, and priorities that will be used to build and sustain the relationship. As suggested by Lambert and his colleagues, components "make the relationship operational and help managers create the benefits of partnering."[5] Components of the operating model may include the following:[6]

- Planning
- Joint operating controls
- Communication
- Risk/Reward sharing
- Trust and commitment
- Contract style
- Scope of the relationship
- Financial investment

Step 6: Implementation and Continuous Improvement

Once the decision to form a relationship has been made and the structural elements of the relationship identified, it is important to recognize that the most challenging step in the relationship process has just begun. Depending on the complexity of the new relationship, the overall implementation process may be relatively short, or it may be extended over a longer period of time. If the situation involves significant change to and restructuring of the manufacturing firm's logistics or supply chain network, for example, full implementation may take longer to accomplish. In a situation where the degree of change is more modest, the time needed for successful implementation may be abbreviated.

Finally, the future success of the relationship will be a direct function of the ability of the involved organizations to achieve both continuous and breakthrough improvement. As indicated in Figure 4.4, a number of steps should be considered in the continuous improvement process. In addition, efforts should be directed to creating the breakthrough, or "paradigm-shifting," type of improvement that is essential to enhance the functioning of the relationship and the market positioning of the organizations involved.

Need for Collaborative Relationships[7]

Whether the relationship may or may not be with a provider of logistics services, today's supply chain relationships are most effective when collaboration occurs among the participants who are involved. Collaboration may be thought of as a "business practice that encourages individual organizations to share information and resources for the benefit of all."[8] According to Dr. Michael Hammer, collaboration allows companies to "leverage each other on an operational basis so that together they perform better than they did separately."[9] He continues by suggesting that collaboration becomes a reality when the power of the Internet facilitates the ability of supply chain participants to readily transact with each other and to access each other's information.

While this approach creates a synergistic business environment in which the sum of the parts is greater than the whole, it is not one that comes naturally to most organizations, particularly those offering similar or competing products or services. In terms of a logistics example, consider that consumer products manufacturers sometimes go to great

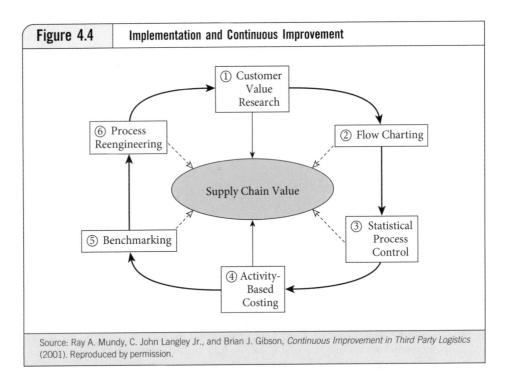

Figure 4.4 | **Implementation and Continuous Improvement**

Source: Ray A. Mundy, C. John Langley Jr., and Brian J. Gibson, *Continuous Improvement in Third Party Logistics* (2001). Reproduced by permission.

lengths to make sure that their products are not transported from plants to customers' distribution centers with products of competing firms. While this practice does have a certain logic, a willingness of the involved parties to collaborate and share resources can create significant logistical efficiencies. Also, it makes sense, considering that retailers routinely commingle competing products as they are transported from distribution centers to retail stores. When organizations refuse to collaborate, real losses may easily outweigh perceived gains.

The contemporary topic of importance is "collaboration." Most simply, collaboration occurs when companies work together for mutual benefit. Since it is difficult to imagine very many logistics or supply chain improvements that involve only one firm, the need for effective relationships is obvious. Collaboration goes well beyond vague expressions of partnership and aligned interests. It means that companies leverage each other on an operational basis so that together they perform better than they did separately. It creates a synergistic business environment in which the sum of the parts is greater than the whole. It is a business practice that requires the following:

- Parties involved to dynamically share and interchange information
- Benefits experienced by parties to exceed individual benefits
- All parties to modify their business practices
- All parties to conduct business in a new and visibly different way
- All parties to provide a mechanism and process for collaboration to occur

Figure 4.5 provides illustrations of three important types of collaboration: vertical, horizontal, and full. Descriptions of these are as follows:

- **Vertical collaboration** (see Figure 4.5a) refers to collaboration typically among buyers and sellers in the supply chain. This refers to the traditional linkages

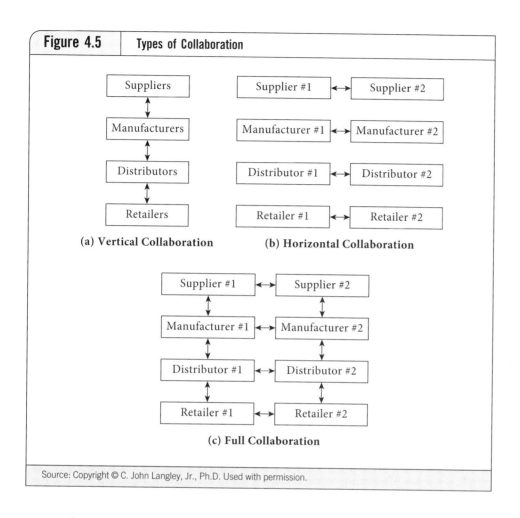

Figure 4.5 | **Types of Collaboration**

(a) Vertical Collaboration

(b) Horizontal Collaboration

(c) Full Collaboration

between firms in the supply chain such as retailers, distributors, manufacturers, and parts and materials suppliers. Transactions between buyers and sellers can be automated, and efficiencies can be significantly improved. Companies can share plans and provide mutual visibility that causes them to change behavior. A contemporary example of vertical collaboration is collaborative planning, forecasting, and replenishment (CPFR®), an approach that helps buyers and sellers to better align supply and demand by directly sharing critical information such as sales forecasts.

- **Horizontal collaboration** (see Figure 4.5b) refers to a relationship that is buyer to buyer and/or seller to seller, and in some cases even between competitors. Essentially, this type of collaboration refers to business arrangements between firms that have *parallel* or cooperating positions in the logistics or supply chain process. Horizontal collaboration can help find and eliminate *hidden* costs in the supply chain that everyone pays for by allowing joint product design, sourcing, manufacturing, and logistics.

- **Full collaboration** (see Figure 4.5c) is the dynamic combination of both vertical and horizontal collaboration. Only with full collaboration do dramatic efficiency gains begin to occur. With full collaboration, it is intended that benefits accrue to all members of the collaboration. The development of agreed-upon methods for sharing gains and losses is essential to the success of the collaboration.

Table 4.1	Seven Immutable Laws of Collaborative Logistics

Collaborative logistics networks must support:

- Real and recognized benefits to all members
- Dynamic creation, measurement, and evolution of collaborative partnerships
- Co-buyer and co-seller relationships
- Flexibility and security
- Collaboration across all stages of business process integration
- Open integration with other services
- Collaboration around essential logistics flows

Source: Copyright © 2000, C. John Langley Jr., Ph.D., used with permission.

While there are numerous sources of suggestion and insight as to how to most effectively create successful, collaborative relationships, Table 4.1 lists each of the "Seven Immutable Laws of Collaborative Logistics." The collective impact of these principles is that they represent a course of action that, if followed, should enhance the success and benefits to be derived from truly collaborative relationships.

Third-Party Logistics—Industry Overview

As indicated throughout this book, firms have directed considerable attention toward working more closely with other supply chain participants, including customers, suppliers, and various providers of logistics services. In essence, this has resulted in the development of more meaningful relationships among the companies involved in overall supply chain activity. As a result, many companies have been in the process of extending their logistics organizations into those of other supply chain participants and facilitators.

One way of extending the logistics organization beyond the boundaries of the company is through the use of a supplier of third-party or contract logistics services.[10] The following section provides some background information on how best to define this type of logistics provider and what services might be included.

Definition of Third-Party Logistics

Essentially, a **third-party logistics firm** may be defined as an external supplier that performs all or part of a company's logistics functions. This definition is purposely broad and is intended to encompass suppliers of services such as transportation, warehousing, distribution, financial services, and so on. As is discussed later, there are other desirable characteristics of a "true" 3PL. Among these, multiple logistics activities are included, those that are included are "integrated" or managed together, and they provide "solutions" to logistics/supply chain problems.

Recently, there have been significant increases in the number of firms offering such services, and this trend is expected to continue. While many of these firms are small, niche players, the industry has a number of large firms as well. Examples of the latter include UPS Supply Chain Solutions, FedEx Supply Chain Services, IBM Supply Chain

On the Line

Don't Underestimate the Importance of Guanxi

"Guanxi" is the Chinese term for the reliance on trust and partnership within a web of relationships to achieve certain advantages. To do business in China successfully, a foreigner needs to understand and respect this ancient social system.

Guanxi provides an entrée into Chinese society that no other form of introduction can rival. During the early years of the 20th century, when Chinese markets were opening up to international competition, some foreign companies were able to use the guanxi of their Chinese partners to build fast and reliable distribution networks of considerable scope. Yet guanxi can also be a formidable constraint to geographic expansion if relationships run out of energy before market space does. Furthermore, because relationships are innately personal, guanxi only gets you so far: It does not globalize easily, nor is it readily transferable. Further, guanxi is not "owned" by an organization but by the individual, and consequently, its influence can apply only to a very particular circumstance and time.

But isn't guanxi being superseded by an age of Web and e-mail connections? Aren't today's Chinese managers much more attuned to merit and objective performance than to kinship, referrals, and shared experience? It is true that the mindset is changing, but there are many enduring cultural reasons why we should expect guanxi to be around for a long time. Author Francis Fukuyama has argued that in societies where people cannot trust "the system" for fairness, they put their trust in relationships they know they can depend upon.* This is as true for business leaders in many parts of the Western world as it is for business people in China.

Source: Adapted from Robert Handfield and Kevin McCormack, "What You Need to Know About Sourcing from China," *Supply Chain Management Review* (September 2005): 35. Reproduced by permission of Robert Handfield.

---

*Francis Fukuyama, *Trust: The Social Virtues and the Creation of Prosperity* (New York, NY: The Free Press, 1995).

Management Services, Ryder, DHL-Exel, Menlo Logistics, Penske Logistics, Schneider Logistics, Caterpillar Logistics, UTi Worldwide, Inc., and Agility, Inc.

Depending on the firm and its positioning in the industry, the terms **contract logistics** and **outsourcing** are sometimes used in place of third-party logistics. While some industry executives take care to distinguish among terms such as these, each of these terms refers to the use of external suppliers of logistics services. Except for the suggestion that the term *contract logistics* generally includes some form of contract, or formal agreement, this text does not suggest any unique definitional differences between these terms. Although most customers who use 3PLs choose to have some formal contract to define the terms of the agreement, it is interesting to note that a small number of companies choose not to have formal contracts with their suppliers of logistics services.

Types of 3PL Providers

Although most 3PL firms promote themselves as providers of a comprehensive range of logistics services, it is useful to categorize them in one of several ways. Included are transportation-based, warehouse/distribution-based, forwarder-based, financial-based, and information-based firms. Each of these is discussed briefly in the following paragraphs.

Transportation Based

Included among the transportation-based suppliers are firms such as UPS Supply Chain Solutions, FedEx Supply Chain Services, DHL, Ryder, Menlo Logistics, and Schneider Logistics; most of these are subsidiaries or major divisions of large transportation firms. Some of the services provided by these firms are leveraged in that they utilize the assets of other companies; some are nonleveraged, where the principal emphasis is on utilizing the transportation-based assets of the parent organization. In all instances, these firms extend beyond the transportation activity to provide a more comprehensive set of logistics offerings.

In early 2000, Transplace was formed through the merger of the logistics business units of several of the largest publicly held truckload carriers in the United States. While this company is transportation based in that major elements of its corporate heritage do involve the commercial transportation industry, its approaches to operations, management, and planning significantly utilize and leverage information technologies. For this reason, a more comprehensive description of this company is found later in this section under the topic of information-based providers.

Warehouse/Distribution Based

Traditionally, most warehouse/distribution-based logistics suppliers have been in the public or contract warehousing business and have expanded into a broader range of logistics services. Examples of such firms include Ozburn-Hessey Logistics, DSC Logistics, Saddle Creek Corporation, and Standard Corporation (now operating as UTi Integrated Logistics). Based on their traditional orientation, these types of organizations already have been involved in logistics activities such as inventory management, warehousing, distribution, and so on. Experience has indicated that these facility-based operators have found the transition to integrated logistics services to be less complex than have the transportation providers.

This category also should include a number of 3PL firms that have emerged from larger corporate logistics organizations. Prominent among these are Caterpillar Logistics Services (Caterpillar, Inc.), Intral Corporation (Gillette), and IBM Supply Chain Management Services (IBM Corporation). These providers have significant experience in managing the logistics operations of the parent firm and, as a result, prove to be very capable providers of such services to external customers. While the idea that a 3PL firm may emerge from a corporate logistics organization is an interesting one, not all of these conversions have been commercially successful as a 3PL.

Forwarder Based

This category includes companies such as Kuehne & Nagel, Fritz, C. H. Robinson, Hub Group, and UTi Worldwide that have extended their middleman roles as forwarders and/or brokers into the broader range of 3PL services. Essentially, these firms are nonasset owners, are very independent, and deal with a wide range of suppliers of logistics services. They have proven quite capable of putting together packages of logistics services that meet customers' needs.

Financial Based

This category of 3PL provider includes firms such as Cass Information Systems (a division of Cass Commercial Corporation), CTC (Commercial Traffic Corporation), GE Information Services (General Electric), AIMS Logistics, and FleetBoston Financial

Corporation. These firms provide services such as freight payment and auditing; cost accounting and control; and logistics management tools for monitoring, booking, tracking, tracing, and managing inventory.

Information Based

At the time of the writing of this text, growth and development of Internet-based, business-to-business, electronic markets for transportation and logistics services was significant. Since these resources effectively represent alternative sources for those in need of purchasing transportation and logistics services, they may be thought of as a newer, innovative type of third-party provider. Examples of two firms that would be representative of this category are Transplace and Nistevo.

- Transplace is an Internet-based company that represents the merger of the 3PL business units from six of the largest publicly held truckload carriers in the United States. The founding carriers are Covenant Transport, Inc.; J.B. Hunt Transport Services, Inc.; M. S. Carriers, Inc. (since merged with Swift Transportation Co., Inc.); Swift Transportation Co., Inc.; U.S. Xpress Enterprises, Inc.; and Werner Enterprises, Inc. Transplace offers a Web-enabled platform to bring together shippers and carriers worldwide to collaborate on their transportation logistics planning and execution in the most efficient and effective manner.

- Nistevo is a recognized provider of an Internet-based, collaborative logistics network. Nistevo's collaborative network is an Internet service that allows shippers and carriers to collaborate to improve profitability and performance. Among the results experienced by both shippers and carriers through use of Nistevo's capabilities are improved operating performance through online, real-time network visibility; management of the entire procurement, service, and delivery cycle from a single application; and improved contract and relationship management. As of this writing, Nistevo was purchased by Sterling Commerce.[11]

Further details concerning information technologies and their applicability to logistics and supply chain management are discussed in Chapter 6: Supply Chain Technology—Managing Information Flows.

3PL Market Size and Scope

Table 4.2 contains an excerpt from a summary of specific shippers who were identified by Armstrong & Associates, Inc., as utilizing multiple 3PLs. Based on Table 4.2, General Motors was ranked highest with 43 third-party providers of logistics services. Other representative shippers using multiple 3PLs are also indicated.

Indicated in Table 4.3 are estimates of the global 3PL industry revenues for the year 2005. As can be seen, the total revenues for North America of US $119 billion represents about one-third of the total estimated global spending of US $370 billion. Figure 4.6 provides a look at growth of the 3PL logistics market in the United States, where turnover growth has risen from US $30.8 billion in 1996 to an estimated US $103.7 billion in 2005. Since many 3PL providers are "non-asset-based," another relevant figure is "net" revenue, which is calculated as "gross" revenue minus the expense of purchased transportation and logistics services. Generally speaking, estimated net third-party logistics revenues would be approximately 55 to 60 percent of the totals indicated in Table 4.3 and Figure 4.6.

Table 4.2	Top Buyers of 3PL Services	
RANK	**SHIPPERS**	**NUMBER OF 3PLS USED**
1	General Motors	43
2	DaimlerChrysler	32
3	Ford Motor Company, Wal-Mart	30
4	Volkswagen	28
5	Hewlett-Packard	26
6	Unilever	24
7	Procter & Gamble	22
8	General Electric	21
9	Siemens	19
10	BMW	17
11	Georgia-Pacific, IBM, Nestle, Royal Philips Electronics, Toyota Motor	16
12	Home Depot, Sara Lee	15

Source: *3PL Market Overview* (Stoughton, WI: Armstrong & Associates, Inc., 2006). Copyright © 2006. Reproduced by permission.

Table 4.3	General 3PL Market—2005
REGION	**YEAR 2005 US $BILUON**
United States	104
Canada and Mexico	15
Total North America	**119**
17 "Old Europe" Countries	133
"New Europe," Russia, and Turkey	9
Total Europe	**142**
Pacific Rim & Asia	85
South America	8
Africa, Middle East & Others	16
Total Global 3PL Market	**370**

Source: *3PL Market Overview* (Stoughton, WI: Armstrong & Associates, Inc., 2006). Copyright © 2006. Reproduced by permission.

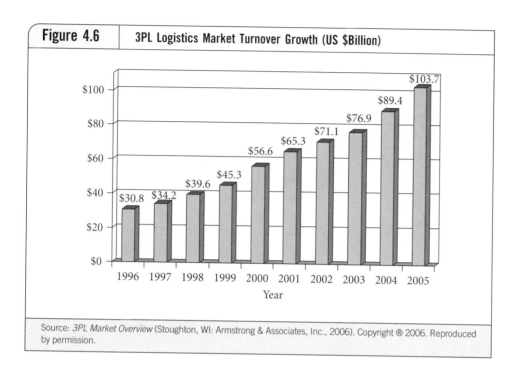

Figure 4.6 | **3PL Logistics Market Turnover Growth (US $Billion)**

Source: *3PL Market Overview* (Stoughton, WI: Armstrong & Associates, Inc., 2006). Copyright ® 2006. Reproduced by permission.

Third-Party Logistics Research Study—Industry Details

One significant research study, "Third-Party Logistics Study: Views from the Customers," is conducted on an annual basis by Dr. C. John Langley Jr. and Capgemini, LLC. The most recent of these, the *2006 Eleventh Annual Third-Party Logistics Study*, was sponsored by Georgia Tech, Capgemini LLC, DHL, and SAP; it provides a comprehensive look at the third-party logistics industry from the perspectives of customers and users of third-party logistics services.[12] Specific study objectives are as follows:

- Measure the development and growth of the 3PL industry across major industry segments and across several diverse regions of the world.
- Summarize the current use of 3PL services.
- Identify customer needs and how well 3PL providers are responding to those needs.
- Understand how customers select and manage 3PL providers.
- Examine why customers outsource or elect not to outsource to 3PL providers.
- Investigate leading topics, including 3PL service offerings and capabilities, technology enablement, structuring and managing effective 3PL relationships, and how customers view success and value from 3PL relationships.
- Understand contemporary issues relating to relationships between 3PLs and customers and look into key issues relating to how 3PL services may be an effective component of a well-functioning supply chain.
- Provide a strategic assessment of the future of the 3PL industry.

The principal vehicle for gathering customer perspectives was a survey sent via the Internet to the chief logistics executives at prominent companies in the following

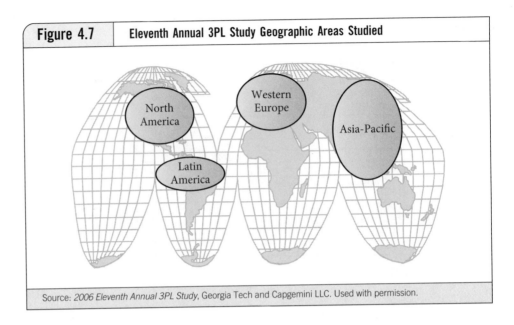

Figure 4.7 | Eleventh Annual 3PL Study Geographic Areas Studied

Source: *2006 Eleventh Annual 3PL Study*, Georgia Tech and Capgemini LLC. Used with permission.

industries: automotive, chemical, consumer products, food and beverage, high-tech and electronics, industrial manufacturing/defense industry, life sciences and healthcare, retail, and telecommunications. These industries were selected because they view logistics as strategically important and are making purposeful moves toward integrated supply chain management. Figure 4.7 provides a map indicating the major geographies in which the study was conducted. Included were North America, Europe, Asia-Pacific, and Latin America. Last, a key element of the study methodology included holding workshops with customers of 3PLs at Accelerated Solutions Environment (ASE) facilities operated by Capgemini in Chicago, Illinois, and Paris, France.[13] An additional customer workshop was held with key logistics executives in Shanghai, China.

Profile of Logistics Outsourcing Activities
Overall Use of 3PLS

The use of 3PL services is significant in the regions of the world that were studied. Figure 4.8 provides a 10-year profile of the firms using 3PL services.[14] Between 1996 and 2001, the percentage of 3PL users remained relatively constant among North American respondents (between 68% and 73%). Between 2002 and 2005, the percentage of North American users showed modest growth coupled with some stability. In the three most recent years of survey data, the percentage of firms using 3PL services in Western Europe has been between 76 percent and 79 percent. In Asia-Pacific, 3PL use for the past two years has been 84 percent in 2004 and 83 percent in 2005. Based on two years of 3PL usage data from Latin America, outsourced logistics services here are less prevalent than in the other regions.

Logistics Activities Outsourced

Table 4.4 summarizes the use of specific logistics services that were reported as being outsourced by respondents in the various regions studied in 2006. Based on this information, the logistics services most frequently outsourced are those that are more

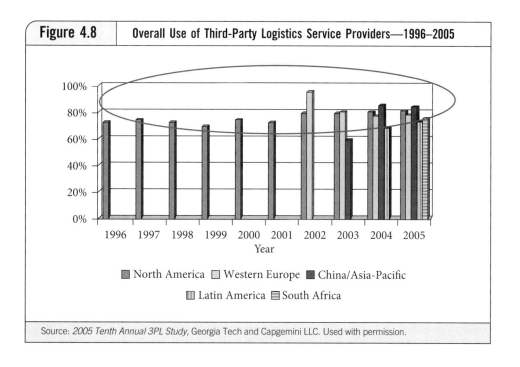

| Figure 4.8 | Overall Use of Third-Party Logistics Service Providers—1996–2005 |

Source: *2005 Tenth Annual 3PL Study,* Georgia Tech and Capgemini LLC. Used with permission.

| Table 4.4 | Outsourced Logistics Services |

	NORTH AMERICA	EUROPE	ASIA-PACIFIC	LATIN AMERICA
Transportation	83%	95%	95%	90%
Warehousing	74	74	74	54
Customs Clearance and Brokerage	74	54	84	64
Forwarding	54	54	64	14
Freight Bill Audit and Payment	54	24	14	14
Shipment Consolidation	44	54	54	34
Cross-Docking	34	44	34	14
Reverse Logistics	24	44	34	34
Transportation Management	24	34	44	14
Product Labeling, Packaging, Assembly, Kitting	24	44	34	24
Supply Chain Consulting Services Provided by 3PLs	24	14	14	14
Order Entry, Processing, and Fulfillment	14	14	14	14
Fleet Management	14	24	24	34
LLP/4PL Services	14	14	4	14
Customer Service	4	4	14	14

Source: *2006 Eleventh Annual 3PL Study,* Georgia Tech and Capgemini LLC. Used with permission.

operational, transactional, and repetitive in nature. Looking at the results over all of the regions studied, the most frequently outsourced services include transportation (90%), warehousing (74%), customs clearance and brokerage (70%), and forwarding (54%). The responses to this question provide support that the services that are outsourced less frequently tend to be customer related, involve the use of information technology, and are more strategic in nature.

A strategic issue is how customers feel that 3PLs should position themselves in terms of depth and breadth of service offerings. Based on findings reported over recent years of the study, users of 3PL services indicate significant agreement with the statement that "third-party suppliers should provide a broad, comprehensive set of service offerings" and disagreement with the statement that "third-party suppliers should focus on a limited range of service offerings." This suggests the continued relevance of customer preferences in certain situations for a single-source solution or a "lead logistics manager" role to the provision of integrated logistics services.

Views of Noncustomers

To help better understand those who were not among the users of 3PL services, the study asked a number of questions regarding their choice not to be so involved. Table 4.5 profiles their responses. Based on these figures, the most important reason that organizations have elected not to outsource logistics services is the belief that logistics is a "core competency" at those organizations. Other reasons include the belief and/or expectations that cost reductions would not be realized, control over outsourced function(s) would diminish, service level commitments would not be realized, and they have more logistics expertise than the 3PL providers.

Interestingly, and as reported in earlier years, many existing customers of 3PLs have been satisfied with such relationships because they help to improve (rather than

Table 4.5	Non-user Respondents' Rationale for Not Using 3PL Services*			
	OVERALL	**NORTH AMERICA**	**EUROPE**	**ASIA-PACIFIC**
Logistics is a core competency at our firm	38%	51%	30%	42%
Cost reductions would not be experienced	34	34	24	24
Control over outsourced function(s) would diminish	24	44	14	24
Service level commitments would not be realized	24	24	14	24
We have more logistics expertise than 3PL providers	24	24	14	34
Logistics too important to consider outsourcing	14	14	24	14
Corporate philosophy excludes outsourcing logistics	14	14	14	14
Global capabilities of 3PLs need improvement	4	14	14	4
Inability of 3PL providers to form meaningful and trusting relationships	4	4	14	4
Issues relating to security of shipments	4	4	4	4

Source: *2006 Eleventh Annual 3PL Study*, Georgia Tech and Capgemini LLC. Used with permission.
*Latin America results insufficient for meaningful analysis.

diminish) control over certain outsourced activities. Also prevalent among the reasons not to outsource is the belief that firms can perform internally at least as effectively as would be expected of a 3PL. If this assertion is true, then the choice of not using a 3PL is understandable. The results from user firms, however, document that, although there is room for improvement, users historically have been satisfied with 3PLs, both from a cost and from a service viewpoint.

Strategic Role of Information Technology

A major objective of the 2006 study was to gain further insight into customer needs for information technology-based services, as well as evaluating how 3PLs are responding. Considering the importance of information technology to supply chain management in general, this topic also is of great relevance to the topic of supply chain relationships and the use of 3PLs.

Table 4.6 provides a look at the currently used and future needs for IT-based services among 3PL users in North America. As indicated, the most currently used services include warehouse/distribution center management (WMS), web-enabled communications, visibility tools (e.g., tracking/tracing, event management), and transportation management—execution (TMS). Looking at the future requirements for technology-based services, the ones in greatest need for enhanced availability are RFID (i.e., radio-frequency identification and asset tracking), collaboration tools (e.g., inventory levels,

Table 4.6	Current-Future IT-Based Services (North America Results)	
FUNCTIONALITY	**CURRENTLY USED**	**FUTURE NEEDS**
Warehouse/Distribution Center Management	65%	17%
Web-Enabled Communications (3PL—User)	61	28
Visibility Tools (e.g., tracking/tracing; event management)	60	29
Transportation Management (Execution)	55	21
Transportation Management (Planning)	31	32
Supplier Relationship Management (e.g., procurement; payables)	30	26
Customer Order Management	25	21
Collaboration Tools (e.g., inventory levels; production schedules)	25	35
Internet-Based Transportation/Logistics Exchanges	23	31
Yard Management	22	16
Supply Chain Planning (e.g., forecasting; inventory planning)	19	30
Customer Relationship Management	17	25
RFID (radio-frequency identification and asset tracking)	13	57

Source: *2006 Eleventh Annual 3PL Study*, Georgia Tech and Capgemini LLC. Used with permission.

production schedules), supply chain planning (e.g., forecasting, inventory planning), and visibility tools (e.g., tracking/tracing, event management).

Although the results of recent studies suggest that customers would like to look to their 3PLs for leadership in information technology, any existing shortcoming may be due to the fact that they do not perceive the 3PL sector to be as involved or as strong in this area as the technology providers themselves. While this may be true in certain instances, many 3PLs are using the technology area to distinguish themselves from their competitors. For example, the availability of competent transportation management software and/or warehouse management software from 3PLs is something that may be expected. This is particularly relevant, considering a finding of recent years' studies that "having the 'right' software" is a major competitive advantage for a 3PL. When asked about their overall satisfaction with the software and IT support available from 3PLs, most users indicate that improvement is needed.

Management and Relationship Issues

The need for competency as it relates to the formation and continuation of successful relationships has become critical in today's 3PL industry. Although both providers and users of 3PL services have been improving in their ability to create more productive, effective, and satisfying business relationships, the media is replete with examples of failed relationships. Then, the important question is "what can we do to improve in this area?"

An interesting finding from one of the earlier year's studies[15] was that the chief executive in the logistics area is the one who clearly is most aware of the need for 3PL services. While available evidence supported the fact that the president or CEO and the finance executive are many times involved with the identification of the need for such services, executives from other areas such as manufacturing, human resources, marketing, and information systems are also aware of such needs but to a lesser degree. Looking specifically at the task of implementing a 3PL relationship, however, it was apparent that information systems executives are becoming increasingly involved. This is not surprising, considering the key role of IT in many of today's logistics and supply chain processes.

A very insightful topic is that of the "selection" factors that are important to customers as they choose 3PLs which they want to work. Based on the results of the *2006 Eleventh Annual 3PL Study,* the two most prevalent 3PL selection factors were price of 3PL services and quality of tactical, operational logistics services. Based on all of the 2006 study responses, 87 percent of respondents indicated that price was a factor, and 85 percent indicated that quality of service was a factor. Looking beyond these two selection criteria, others that were of greater importance included geographic presence in required regions (75%), expected capability to improve service levels (67%), range of available value-added logistics services (63%), and capable information technologies (60%).

Also, successful 3PL relationships establish appropriate roles and responsibilities for both 3PLs and client firms. While sometimes the use of a 3PL is interpreted simply as "turning over all logistics activities" to an outsourced provider, respondents to recent years' studies suggested that a "hybrid" management structure represents a highly effective way to manage 3PL relationships. Essentially, this reflects a desire on the part of the client firm to have sufficient power over operations for a track record of performance or "trust" factor to be built up. Although most client firms (appropriately) retain control over strategy formulation and direction setting for the logistics areas of responsibility, this hybrid approach to the management of operations is an innovative response to the

Supply Chain Technology

3PLs Need to Fill an Expanded Role in Today's Supply Chains

Those who manage logistics and supply chain services are increasingly asking about what the right 3PL service would be for outsourcing certain supply chain processes or functions. Interestingly, many of these concerns relate less to traditional logistics needs such as transportation and warehousing, and more to key changes such as the following:

- Supply chains are increasingly global in scope.
- Inventory optimization strategies have stretched beyond single corporation boundaries to include partners and customers working in cooperation.
- Business process outsourcing (BPO) of noncore functions has executive acceptance.

Last year's global trade management research indicated that more than 90 percent of companies surveyed relied on outsourced logistics providers to execute their global logistics needs. Their high degree of outsourcing reliance for deep competency and capable technologies to manage more complex logistics problems will likely spread to adoption of outsourcing in other areas of supply chain management. Also, companies reporting "far-shore" outsourcing want to make sure that "total landed costs" continue to be attractive. As an example, consider the popular high-end consumer electronics company that regularly expedites a particular high-selling product from Asia because of inaccurate forecasting and the long lead times of its Asian supply chain. The rub? The product cost is $100 per unit, and the expediting costs are $80 per unit.

For more than a decade, companies have been using advanced supply chain planning techniques and technologies to reduce inventory. Today, the best performing companies are able to sense and respond to demand much more frequently, with just the right amount of inventory across a multi-tier supply chain network. As a result, 3PLs are being called upon more frequently to help customers respond to these challenges.

Also, it is reasonable to expect that the increasing prevalence of business process outsourcing should make logistics an even more attractive candidate for outsourcing. By studying the positioning that other BPO companies use and modifying the pitch, 3PLs should be able to form stronger, higher-level strategic relationships with their corporate customers.

Many companies are transforming their logistics departments into a global corporate logistics services function. But international logistics over the next five to seven years is set to explode, with global logistics dramatically increasing compared to what is predominantly domestic today. Global logistics outsourcing should remain high or possibly even increase as companies are not eager to take over the detailed management of logistics from or to all stretches of the globe. With the steady growth of outsourcing, corporate logistics departments will have to change to manage increased outside parties and global processes without losing control and while increasing visibility. This will involve use of technological advances and more seamless integration between companies and their suppliers, and customers and their providers.

Source: Adapted from Greg Aimi, "3PLs Need to Fill an Expanded Role in Today's Supply Chains," *AMR Research*, November 9, 2006. Reproduced by permission of AMR Research.

Table 4.7	Expectation Setting Relative to 3PL Relationship Management
CUSTOMERS' EXPECTATIONS OF 3PL PROVIDERS	**3PL PROVIDERS' EXPECTATIONS OF CUSTOMERS**
• Superior service and execution (proven results and performance)	• Mutually beneficial, long-term relationship with company
• Trust, openness, and information sharing	• Trust, openness, and information sharing
• Solution innovation and relationship reinvention	• Dedicating the right resources at the right levels, including executives
• Ongoing executive-level support	• Clearly defined service-level agreements
• Service offering aligned with customer strategy and deep industry knowledge	• Fiduciary responsibility and overall fairness relative to pricing

Source: *2005 Tenth Annual 3PL Study*, Georgia Tech and Capgemini LLC. Used with permission.

challenge of successfully managing 3PL-client relationships. Table 4.7 provides a useful summary of some of the expectations that 3PLs and their customers have of each other.

Last, an important issue relates to how customers think of their 3PLs. Based on results from the 2006 study and as shown in Figure 4.9, approximately two-thirds of the customers think of their 3PLs as providers of tactical or operational services, while approximately one-third think of them as strategic or integrative. While there may be a temptation to think that the strategic or integrative relationships are superior to or more advanced than the former, the fact is that the best relationships are ones that come closest to meeting the logistics and supply chain needs of the customer and of the provider. While there are some very excellent relationships that are strategic or integrative in nature, there also are some very excellent examples of relationships that are tactical or operational, and that conform very closely to the stated needs and requirements of the customer.

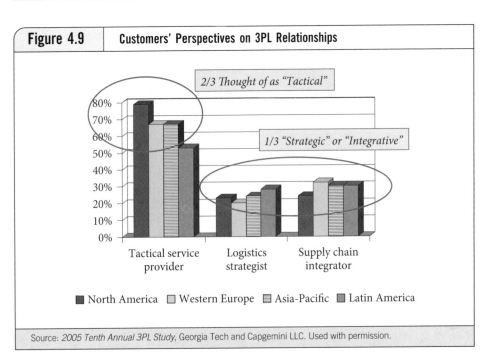

Figure 4.9	Customers' Perspectives on 3PL Relationships

Source: *2005 Tenth Annual 3PL Study*, Georgia Tech and Capgemini LLC. Used with permission.

Customer Value Framework

Generally, 3PL users across the several regions studied characterized their outsourcing efforts as having been successful. This is supported by the information contained in Figure 4.10 that provides a 10-year perspective on the percentages of 3PL users in various regions that rated their 3PL services as being either "extremely" or "somewhat" successful.

In addition, participating executives provided continuing evidence of logistics and supply chain metrics that provide tangible documentation of the benefits they have experienced from the use of 3PL services. Examples of these metrics are included in Table 4.8. Again in 2006, however, the survey respondents highlighted a number of areas where improvement in their 3PL relationships would be desirable. These topics were discussed in further detail in the section entitled "Management and Relationship Issues."

Respondents in recent studies reported experiencing a number of problems. Categorically, their responses tended to focus on several key areas of concern as follows:

- Service-level commitments not realized
- Time and effort spent on logistics not reduced
- Cost reductions have not been realized
- Cost "creep" and price increases once relationship has commenced
- Unsatisfactory transition during implementation stage
- Inability to form meaningful and trusting relationships
- Lack of ongoing improvements and achievements in offerings
- Lack of strategic management and/or consultative/knowledge-based skills
- Lack of global capabilities

This list should be viewed as a starting point for continuous improvement by 3PL providers. Overall, it suggests a need to meet service-level and cost objectives and to

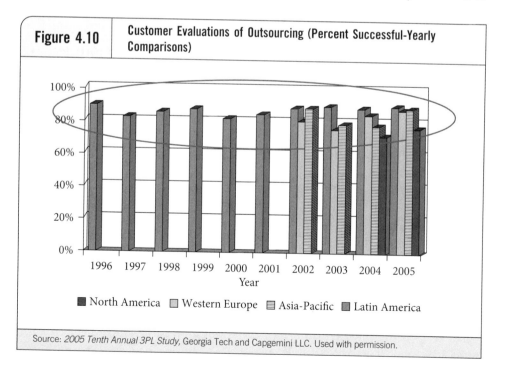

| Figure 4.10 | Customer Evaluations of Outsourcing (Percent Successful-Yearly Comparisons) |

North America   Western Europe   Asia-Pacific   Latin America

Source: *2005 Tenth Annual 3PL Study*, Georgia Tech and Capgemini LLC. Used with permission.

Table 4.8	Average Customer Results from Use of Third-Party Logistics Providers			
COST/BENEFIT	NORTH AMERICA	WESTERN EUROPE	ASIA-PACIFIC	LATIN AMERICA
Logistics cost reduction	10%	11%	14%	12%
Fixed logistics asset reduction	13%	22%	22%	37%
Average order-cycle length change (days)	From 11.0 to 8.4	From 10.1 to 6.5	From 15.7 to 13.9	From 14.9 to 10.0
Service level improvement (percent "yes")	62%	67%	64%	77%

Source: *2006 Eleventh Annual 3PL Study*, Georgia Tech and Capgemini LLC. Used with permission. Service-level improvement figures taken from *2005 Tenth Annual 3PL Study*, Georgia Tech and Capgemini LLC. Used with permission.

avoid unnecessary increases in price to the customer once the relationship has commenced. Also, it appears that some 3PLs need to improve in the areas of strategic management, technology, and knowledge-based skills. These suggest expectations by the customers that currently are not being met. Finally, some users of 3PL services feel that the time and effort spent on logistics have not decreased and that their control over the outsourced function may have lessened. In the latter instance, the previously discussed move to "hybrid" management of the 3PL's responsibilities may be a useful alternative.

Logistics Strategic View and the Role of 3PLs

One major accomplishment of the past 10–15 years has been establishing the validity of the logistics outsourcing model and specifically of the 3PL provider. As we look to the future, we already see increasing acceptance of the 4PL model, likely growth in expenditures by current users of 3PL services, and a growing sophistication in the outsourced business approaches that respond to a dynamic set of customer logistics and supply chain needs.

Fourth-Party Relationships

Although it has been around for some time, the concept a **"fourth-party logistics" (4PL) provider** is becoming more evident in the business world.[16] Essentially a supply chain integrator, a 4PL may be thought of as a firm that "assembles and manages the resources, capabilities, and technology of its own organization with those of complementary service providers to deliver a comprehensive supply chain solution."[17] As suggested by Figure 4.11, a 4PL leverages the capabilities of 3PLs and suppliers of technology-based services through a centralized point of contact. In one sense, an important role of the 4PL is to manage and direct the activities of multiple 3PLs. In another, more strategic role, the 4PL serves as the integrator that brings together the needs of the client and the resources available through 3PL providers, the IT providers, and the elements of business process management.

Expected Growth in Customers' Use of 3PL Services

One way to look at the future plans for outsourcing is to ask users of 3PL services to estimate the expected three-to five-year growth rate of outsourcing expenditures as a percent of overall logistics expenditures. Based on the results for 2006 as shown in Figure 4.12, the average percentage increases expected in the next three to five years would be 17 percent in North America, 11 percent in Western Europe, 11 percent in Asia-Pacific, and 20 percent in Latin America.

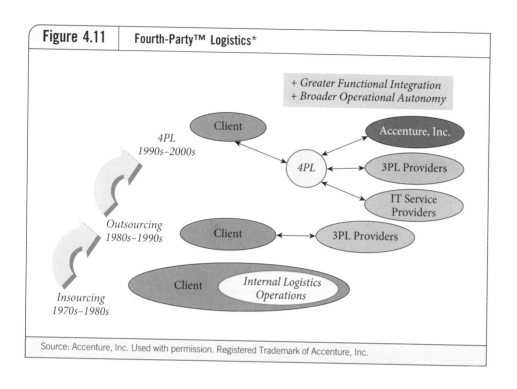

Figure 4.11 | Fourth-Party™ Logistics*

+ *Greater Functional Integration*
+ *Broader Operational Autonomy*

4PL
1990s–2000s

Client

Accenture, Inc.

4PL

3PL Providers

IT Service Providers

Outsourcing
1980s–1990s

Client

3PL Providers

Insourcing
1970s–1980s

Client

Internal Logistics Operations

Source: Accenture, Inc. Used with permission. Registered Trademark of Accenture, Inc.

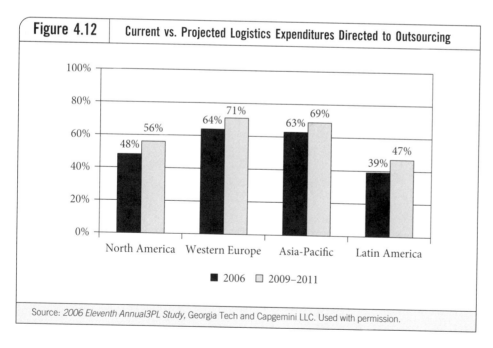

Figure 4.12 | Current vs. Projected Logistics Expenditures Directed to Outsourcing

North America: 48% (2006), 56% (2009–2011)
Western Europe: 64% (2006), 71% (2009–2011)
Asia-Pacific: 63% (2006), 69% (2009–2011)
Latin America: 39% (2006), 47% (2009–2011)

■ 2006 □ 2009–2011

Source: *2006 Eleventh Annual 3PL Study,* Georgia Tech and Capgemini LLC. Used with permission.

Logistics Outsourcing Model for the Future

Figure 4.13 suggests a possible future direction for the further development of logistics outsourcing models. Starting with the proprietary provision of logistics services, or insourcing, at the bottom of the diagram, the model evolves through several successive stages. Included are basic services (e.g., transportation, warehousing, etc.), value-added or

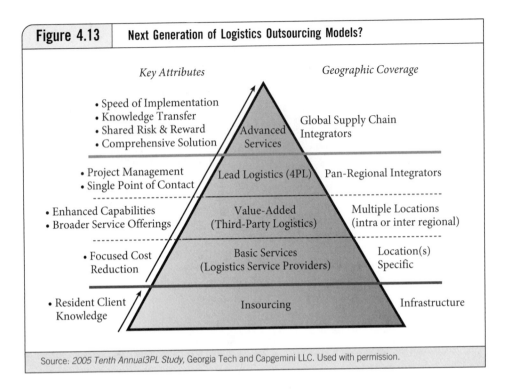

Figure 4.13	Next Generation of Logistics Outsourcing Models?

Source: *2005 Tenth Annual 3PL Study*, Georgia Tech and Capgemini LLC. Used with permission.

third-party logistics services, lead logistics or 4PL services, and advanced services. The diagram also identifies key attributes for each of these stages and specifies a typical geographical coverage for each of the stages.

To conclude the discussion of outsourced logistics services as a key element of supply chain relationships, Table 4.9 identifies a number of trends that seem to characterize the future direction of the 3PL sector. Regardless of how quickly these trends become apparent, the topic of logistics outsourcing is likely to be central and critical to the future successes of logistics and supply chain management.

Table 4.9	Future 3PL Industry Trends

- Continued expansion, acquisition, and consolidation of 3PL industry
- Expansion of global markets and needed services
- Continued broadening of service offerings across supply chain, and broad-based business process outsourcing
- Two-tiered relationship models (strategic and tactical)
- Growing range of "strategic" services offered by 3PLs and 4PLs

- IT capabilities to become an even greater differentiator
- Increased efforts to update, enhance, and improve 3PL provider-user relationships
- Emphasis on relationship reinvention, mechanisms for continual improvement, and solution innovation

Source: *2005 Tenth Annual 3PL Study*, Georgia Tech and Capgemini LLC. Used with permission.

SUMMARY

- The two most basic types of supply chain relationships are "vertical" (e.g., buyer-seller) and "horizontal" (e.g., parallel or cooperating).

- In terms of intensity of involvement, interfirm relationships may span from transactional to relational and may take the form of vendor, partner, and strategic alliances.

- There are six steps in the development and implementation of successful relationships. These six steps are critical to the formation and success of supply chain relationships.

- Collaborative relationships, both vertical and horizontal, have been identified as highly useful to the achievement of long-term supply chain objectives. The "Seven Immutable Laws of Collaborative Logistics" provide a framework for the development of effective supply chain relationships.

- Third-party logistics providers may be thought of as an "external supplier that performs all or part of a company's logistics functions." It is desirable that these suppliers provide multiple services and that these services are integrated in the way they are managed and delivered.

- The several types of 3PLs are transportation-based, warehouse/distribution-based, forwarder-based, financial-based, and information-based suppliers.

- Based on the results of a comprehensive study of users of 3PL services in the United States, over 70 percent of the firms studied are, to some extent, users of 3PL services.

- User experience suggests a broad range of 3PL services utilized; the most prevalent are transportation, warehousing, customs clearance and brokerage, and forwarding.

- While nonusers of 3PL services have their reasons to justify their decision, these same reasons are sometimes cited by users as justification for using a 3PL.

- Customers have significant IT-based requirements of their 3PL providers, and they feel that the 3PLs are attaching a priority to respond to these requirements.

- Approximately two-thirds of the customers suggest 3PL involvement in their global supply chain activities.

- Although most customers indicate satisfaction with existing 3PL services, there is no shortage of suggestions for improvement.

- Customers generally have high aspirations for their strategic use of 3PLs and consider their 3PLs as keys to their supply chain success.

- There is a growing need for fourth-party logistics[18] relationships that provide a wide range of integrative supply chain services.

STUDY QUESTIONS

1. What are the basic types of supply chain relationships, and how do they differ?

2. How would you distinguish between a vendor, a partner, and a strategic alliance? What conditions would favor the use of each?

3. What does it take to have an area of "core competency"? Provide an example.

4. Describe the steps in the process model for forming and implementing successful supply chain relationships. What step(s) do you feel is (are) most critical?

5. What are some of the more common "drivers" and "facilitators" of successful supply chain relationships?

6. What is meant by "collaboration" between supply chain organizations? What are the different types of collaboration?

7. What are the basic types of 3PL firms, and which are in most prevalent use?

8. What are some of the more frequently outsourced logistics activities? Less frequently outsourced?

9. Why do some firms choose not to use the services of 3PL firms?

10. In what ways are clients/customers counting on 3PLs for involvement with information technology-based services?

11. To what extent are clients/customers satisfied with 3PL services? What is the relative importance of cost, performance, and value creation as determining factors for evaluating and selecting 3PLs?

12. To what extent do clients/customers think of their 3PL providers in a strategic sense? What evidence suggests that this may change in the future, and what kind of change may be expected?

NOTES

1. Robert V. Delaney, *11th Annual State of Logistics Report* (St. Louis, MO: Cass Information Systems, June 5, 2000).

2. Rosabeth Moss Kanter, "Collaborative Advantage: The Art of Alliances," *Harvard Business Review* (July–August 1994).

3. Douglas M. Lambert, Margaret A. Emmelhainz, and John T. Gardner, "Developing and Implementing Supply Chain Partnerships," *The International Journal of Logistics Management* 7, No. 2 (1996): 1–17. The content of this section relating to drivers and facilitators has been quoted from this excellent research article.

4. Ibid., 4–10.

5. Ibid., 10.

6. Ibid., 10–13.

7. For an overview of collaborative logistics, see C. John Langley Jr., "Seven Immutable Laws of Collaborative Logistics," 2000 (white paper published by Nistevo, Inc.).

8. Ibid., 4.

9. Ibid., 2.

10. For further information, see Armstrong & Associates, Inc., *Who's Who in International Logistics: Armstrong's Guide to Global Supply Chain Management*, 13th ed. (2005); C. John Langley Jr., et al., *Eleventh Annual Third Party Logistics Study: Views from the Customers* (Georgia Tech and Capgemini LLC, 2006); Robert Lieb, Brooks Bentz, and Richard O'Meara, "Insights, Innovations in Third-Party Logistics from Accenture, Northeastern University," *Global Logistics & Supply Chain Strategies* (January 2006): 16–21; Robert Lieb, "The 3PL Industry: Where It's Been and Where It's Going," *Supply Chain Management Review* 9, No. 2 (September 2005) 20–27; Robert Lieb and Brooks Bentz, "The Use of Third-Party Logistics Services by Large American Manufacturers: The 2004 Survey," *Transportation Journal* 44, No. 2 (2005): 5–15; Bryan Ashenbaum, Arnold Maltz, and Elliot Rabinovich, "Studies of Trends in Third-Party Logistics Usage: What Can We Conclude?" *Transportation Journal* 44, No. 2 (Summer 2005): 39–50; Thomas A. Foster, "The Trends Changing the Face of Logistics Outsourcing Worldwide," *Global Logistics & Supply Chain Strategies* (June 2004); Yemisi A. Bolumole, "Evaluating the Supply Chain Role of Logistics Service Providers," *International Journal of Logistics Management* 14, No. 2 (2003): 93–107; Harry L. Sink and C. John Langley Jr., "A Managerial Framework for the Acquisition of Third-Party Logistics Services," *Journal of Business Logistics* 18, No. 2 (1997): 163–190; and C. John Langley Jr., Brian F. Newton, and Gene R. Tyndall, "Third-Party Logistics: Has the Future Already Arrived?" *Supply Chain Management Review* 3, No. 3 (Fall 1999): 85–94.

11. See http://www.sterlingcommerce.com.

12. C. John Langley Jr., Capgemini LLC, DHL, and SAP, *2006 Eleventh Annual Third-Party Logistics Study*. Information concerning this study and a download of the final report is available at http://www.3plstudy.com. This report provides

details concerning the results and findings from the eleventh annual study. Certain items of relevant information from earlier versions of the same study are also included from time to time.

13. Additional information concerning the Accelerated Solutions Environment (ASE) operated by Capgemini may be found in the *2006 Eleventh Annual Third-Party Logistics Study*, available at http://www.3plstudy.com.

14. Results shown in Figure 4.8 are from *2005 Tenth Annual 3PL Study*, Georgia Tech, Capgemini LLC, DHL, and SAP.

15. C. John Langley Jr., Brian F. Newton, and Gary R. Allen, *Third-Party Logistics Services: Views from the Customers* (Knoxville, TN: University of Tennessee, 2000). This report includes the results and findings from the fifth annual version of this comprehensive study.

16. 4PL and fourth-party logistics are registered trademarks of Accenture, Inc.

17. Accenture, Inc., by permission.

18. Trademark, Accenture, Inc.

CASE 4.1

CoLinx, LLC[1]

CoLinx, LLC is a manufacturer-owned provider of shared e-commerce and logistics services in North America. Founded in 2001, CoLinx was formed by four competing manufacturers in the power transmission industry, when they agreed to create a jointly owned, not-for-profit corporation to handle their logistics and electronic commerce operations to gain efficiencies of scale. CoLinx has since helped to improve service levels for its manufacturers by handling everything from system-to-system transactions with distributors, Web site hosting, warehousing, light assembly, shipping, freight auditing, and import-export operations through its designation as a foreign trade zone. The companies involved have seen remarkable performance improvements, and CoLinx has ambitious plans for further growth.[2]

CoLinx has the following three constituencies:[3]

- **Manufacturers.** The manufacturers who seek the lowest cost Web solutions while maintaining individual control and brand identity.

- **Industrial distributors.** CoLinx's foundation is in enabling distributors to do business with multiple manufacturers through one site, allowing them to respond quickly to their own customers. The founding manufacturers go to market through an open distribution network. Each manufacturer can authorize multiple distributors, and each distributor can represent multiple manufacturers.

- **Employee groups.** CoLinx's strong, mission-driven team is dedicated to using the Web site to build the businesses of the manufacturers.

Although CoLinx operates warehouses in the Reno, Dallas, Philadelphia, Toronto, and Edmonton metro areas, the cornerstone of its warehousing and logistics operations is its 670,000 square feet of warehouse space in Crossville, Tennessee. In the outbound shipping lanes, CoLinx's main value is in freight consolidation. Working with several manufacturers selling through the same distributor base allows it to send like-shipments to like-destinations, meaning fewer trucks in the yard for the distributor, fewer receipts, and a consolidated bill of lading with multiple packing lists, making it easier for the distributor on the receiving end. When shipments are made more frequently, customer service improves, cost per pound declines, and less inventory is needed in the supply chain. When several companies share a distribution center, common areas and support staff are shared, shared frontline specialists better accommodate peaks and valleys, and investments in high fixed cost technologies such as WMS, conveyance, timekeeping, voice-directed activity, and engineered standards become justifiable.

CoLinx provides members with e-commerce capabilities through a Web site hosting service that passes transaction data from customers to manufacturers (PTplace.com) using a standardized format. Also, CoLinx builds direct system-to-system connections between its manufacturers and their distributors, and between manufacturers and freight carriers as well.[4] When many companies are supporting basic e-commerce Web services

---

[1]Portions of this case have been adapted from materials available at http://www.colinx.com. Reproduced by permission.

[2]Douglas Chandler, "CoLinx and the Power of Partnership," *Modern Distribution Management* 34, No. 21 (November 10, 2004).

[3]Surgency, *CoLinx: A Shared Service Portal in Manufacturing* (Cambridge, MA: Surgency, Inc., 2001)

[4]Chandler, "CoLinx and the Power of Partnership."

to the same group of distributors or carriers, a common gateway reduces technical complexity and simplifies life for users.

Services are offered to manufacturers who undergo a formal application process, pay a membership fee, and make a commitment to use CoLinx services to a substantial extent in both e-commerce and logistics. Members have access to any or all services offered by the company and are assessed fees based on proprietary cost-sharing methodology.

To be clear, CoLinx is a different kind of company that is hard to comprehend. CoLinx is not an exchange or marketplace; does not own, plan, release, or insure any inventory; and does not sell directly to distributors or other customers—only the manufacturers do. Manufacturer-members of CoLinx just indicate how many bin locations or pallet locations they want and provide instructions to CoLinx as to what needs to move and when. The company does not operate as a profit center, but all benefits accrued by the company are directly passed back to the members in the form of reduced costs. The company does not promote itself to try to build a brand image. The company's only mission is to "be the best choice" for the member manufacturers it serves and the employees of CoLinx.

CASE QUESTIONS

1. Describe the elements of the value proposition for the manufacturer-members of CoLinx. What would be the elements of the value proposition for the distributors of products that are shipped from CoLinx?

2. What are the major sources of savings for manufacturer-members of CoLinx?

3. What are the keys to long-term sustainability of a relationship such as CoLinx?

CASE 4.2

Ocean Spray Cranberries, Inc.

August is typically a challenging month for Ocean Spray Cranberries, Inc., when the Lakeville, Massachusetts-based firm has to pump up volume to meet the surge in demand for the upcoming holiday season. Ocean Spray is an agricultural co-op owned by more than 750 citrus growers in the United States and Canada. The company produces canned and bottled juice, juice drinks, and food products at distribution centers in Bordentown, New Jersey; Kenosha, Wisconsin; Sulphur Springs, Texas; and Henderson, Nevada.

Ocean Spray was managing its transportation operations internally, but the company decided it wanted to focus on its core competency, which, according to its director of logistics, was "maintaining our leadership in the shelf-stable juice drink category." The company also wanted to centralize its transportation operations. Looking carefully at the issue of overall performance in the logistics and transportation areas, a significant amount of variability was found in its operations. For purposes of uniformity and control, a major priority was attached to centralization of its logistics operations.

In addition, Ocean Spray wanted to be able to reach markets for which it did not already have access, which would require expansion of its logistics network. According to the director of logistics, an analysis was undertaken to study how long it would take and what it would cost to build up Ocean Spray's transportation capabilities to be able to support such a network. As a result, a recommendation was made to seriously investigate the use of a third-party logistics (3PL) provider.

CASE QUESTIONS

1. What rationale is offered by Ocean Spray in support of the idea of using a 3PL? Do you agree with the reasons cited for the interest in a 3PL?

2. Based on your understanding of Ocean Spray and its business needs, what type of 3PL firm do you feel might be of greatest potential value in terms of a relationship?

3. What steps would you suggest be considered by Ocean Spray as it begins to analyze the feasibility of forming a relationship with individual 3PL providers?

4. Once the selection process is complete, what kind of relationship do you feel would be most appropriate: vendor, partner, strategic alliance, or some other option?

Source: Adapted from Adrienne Breiner, "Outsourcing Helps to Take Squeeze Out of Surge," *Food Logistics* (April 15, 1999): 62

Chapter 5

SUPPLY CHAIN PERFORMANCE MEASUREMENT AND FINANCIAL ANALYSIS

Learning Objectives

After reading this chapter, you should be able to do the following:

- Understand the scope and importance of supply chain performance measurement.
- Explain the characteristics of good performance measures.
- Discuss the various methods used to measure supply chain costs, service, profit, and revenue.
- Understand the basics of an income statement and a balance sheet.
- Demonstrate the impacts of supply chain strategies on the income statement, balance sheet, profitability, and return on investment.
- Understand the use of the strategic profit model.
- Analyze the financial impacts of supply chain service failures.
- Utilize spreadsheet computer software to analyze the financial implications of supply chain decisions.

Supply Chain Profile CLGN Book Distributors.com

CLGN Book Distributors.com (CLGN) is a new Internet company that began operation in 2001 for the sale and distribution of college textbooks and supplies. During the first few years, CLGN struggled with the normal technical glitches associated with an Internet-based company, but the concept of online purchasing of college textbooks proved immensely popular with college students. After obtaining information as to the textbook(s) required for a course, the students would use their computers to place their orders, avoiding the dreaded long lines at the campus bookstore.

CLGN's original mission was to be a low-price seller of college textbooks and instructional materials in the United States. The typical textbook price at CLGN averaged 15 percent below that of the local bookstore, and supplies averaged 20 percent lower. When the cost of shipping was included, the landed cost of the textbook was about 10 percent lower and materials 15 percent lower than purchases at the local bookstore. This lower cost and the convenience of online purchasing resulted in double-digit sales increases every year.

Beginning in 2002, CLGN made a profit and has done so every year since then. In 2007, CLGN had sales of $150 million with a net income of $10.5 million. This net profit margin of 7 percent was above average for business-to-consumer (B2C) Internet companies. However, net income as a percent of sales, or net profit margin, was lower than in the previous years. In 2005, net profit margin was 10.3 percent, and in 2006, it was 9.1 percent. This decreasing profit margin trend was causing considerable concern with top management and CLGN's stockholders.

Following release of the 2007 financial data, Ed Bardi, CEO, held a meeting with the executive committee consisting of the vice presidents of marketing, finance, information systems, and supply chain management. After reviewing the 2007 financial results and discussing the underlying causes for the lower net profit margin, each vice president was given the assignment of examining his/her respective area for process changes that would remove costs while maintaining the same level of service customers expected.

Particular attention was given to the supply chain area because supply chain cost increases exceeded those in other areas of the company. Dr. Bardi also pointed out that during the past year he had been receiving complaints from irate customers regarding late deliveries of orders and receipt of improperly filled orders (wrong items or not all items ordered). Lauren Fishbay, vice president of supply chain management, said she was aware of these problems and was working on solutions for order fulfillment problems as well as the escalating shipping costs. She said her area was developing plans to transition from measuring orders shipped on time and orders shipped complete to measuring the perfect order (orders received on time, orders received complete, and accurate documentation).

Following the executive committee meeting, Ms. Fishbay gathered her operating managers to review the situation and explore alternatives. She asked Tracie Shannon, supply chain analyst, to prepare financial data measuring the supply chain process. Sharon Cox, warehouse manager, was asked to examine the nature and cause of the order fulfillment problems and to suggest solutions. Finally, Sue Purdum, transportation manager, was charged with examining the rising transportation costs and longer, and less reliable, delivery times.

Prior to the supply chain operating managers' meeting, Ms. Fishbay received the following 2007 financial information from Tracie Shannon:

CLGN BOOK DISTRIBUTORS.COM
INCOME STATEMENT 2007

Sales		$150,000,000
Cost of goods sold		80,000,000
Gross margin		$ 70,000,000
Transportation	$ 6,000,000	
Warehousing	1,500,000	
Inventory carrying	3,000,000	
Other operating cost	30,000,000	
Total operating cost		40,500,000
Earnings before interest and taxes		$ 29,500,000
Interest		12,000,000
Taxes		7,000,000
Net income		$ 10,500,000

CLGN BOOK DISTRIBUTORS.COM
BALANCE SHEET 2007

Assets	
Cash	$ 15,000,000
Accounts receivable	30,000,000
Inventory	10,000,000
Total current assets	$ 55,000,000
Net fixed assets	90,000,000
Total assets	$145,000,000
Liabilities	
Current liabilities	$ 65,000,000
Long-term debt	35,000,000
Total liabilities	$100,000,000
Stockholders' equity	45,000,000
Total liabilities and equity	$145,000,000

Ms. Shannon determined that the inventory carrying cost rate was 30 percent of the value of the average inventory held per year. The corporate tax rate was 40 percent. Total orders in 2007 amounted to 1.5 million ($150 million in sales at an average sale per order of $100). She estimated the lost sales rate to be 10 percent of the service failures caused by late transportation delivery and 20 percent of the service failures caused by improper order fulfillment. The cost of a lost sale per order is the gross profit per order, or $46.67 ($70 million gross margin divided by 1.5 million orders).

Sharon Cox concluded that the cost of a service failure, whether caused by order fulfillment or delivery problems, resulted in an invoice reduction of $10 per order (to appease the customer) and a rehandling cost of $20 per order (to reship the order). Currently CLGN's order fill rate is 97 percent. The causes of the improper order fulfillment could be attributed to the lack of warehouse personnel training. In the current economic environment, it is very difficult to obtain experienced warehouse workers, and many of the current warehouse employees do not have a high school diploma. Other problems could be traced to a lack of discipline regarding order-picking procedures and the computer-generated pick slip. At least $100,000 was required annually for ongoing training.

Sue Purdum traced the escalating transportation costs to the 35 percent increase in residential delivery rates charged by CLGN's ground delivery carrier for standard service (three to five days transit time). The residential delivery rates charged by other ground express carriers were comparable or higher. An alternative to reducing transportation costs was to switch to the U.S. Postal Service, but delivery times would increase and become less reliable. However, CLGN's current on-time delivery performance is only 95 percent because of the longer order processing times at the warehouse and longer transit times via the ground package carrier to residential delivery locations. By using the carrier's expedited ground service, CLGN could improve service and on-time delivery to 96 percent and increase transportation costs by 10 percent.

Given this information, Lauren Fishbay was pondering what actions she should explore with the operating managers in preparation for the next executive committee meeting. She knew whatever course of action she proposed had to be financially sound and provide the greatest benefit to CLGN's stockholders.

Introduction

The CLGN Book Distributors.com case highlights the need for all organizations to be able to measure supply chain performance and link that performance to its impacts on financial performance. Many organizations today have realized that performance metrics are critical to managing the business and achieving desired results. Many organizations want to do the "right things" (effectiveness) and do them "right" (efficiency). However, simply stating those two objectives is not adequate unless they have specific, measurable metrics that enable the organization to gauge whether or not these objectives are achieved.

The purpose of this chapter is to (1) introduce the dimensions of supply chain performance metrics, (2) discuss how supply chain metrics are developed, (3) offer some methods for classifying supply chain metrics, and (4) use quantitative tools to show how these metrics can be linked to the financial performance of the organization.

Dimensions of Supply Chain Performance Metrics

Before beginning a discussion of the dimensions of supply chain metrics, it is important to answer two questions. First, what is the difference between a measure and a metric? Traditionally, the term *measure* was used to denote any quantitative

Figure 5.1	Characteristics of Good Measures

A GOOD MEASURE	DESCRIPTION
• Is quantitative	• The measure can be expressed as an objective value.
• Is easy to understand	• The measure conveys at a glance what it is measuring and how it is derived.
• Encourages appropriate behavior	• The measure is balanced to reward productive behavior and discourage "game playing."
• Is visible	• The effects of the measure are readily apparent to all involved in the process being measured.
• Is defined and mutually understood	• The measure has been defined by and/ or agreed to by all key process participants (internally and externally).
• Encompasses both outputs and inputs	• The measure integrates factors from all aspects of the process measured.
• Measures only what is important	• The measure focuses on a key performance indicator that is of real value to managing the process.
• Is multidimensional	• The measure is properly balanced between utilization, productivity, and performance and shows the tradeoffs.
• Uses economies of effort	• The benefits of the measure outweigh the costs of collection and analysis.
• Facilitates trust	• The measure validates the participation among the various parties.

Source: J. S. Keebler, D. A. Durtsche, K. B. Manrodt, and D. M. Ledyard, *Keeping Score: Measuring the Business Value of Logistics in the Supply Chain* (University of Tennessee, Council of Logistics Management, 1999), p. 8. Reproduced with permission from Council of Supply Chain Management Professionals.

output of an activity or process. Today, the term *metric* is being used more often in place of the term *measure*. What is the difference? A **measure** is easily defined with no calculations and with simple dimensions. Supply chain examples would include units of inventory and backorder dollars. A **metric** needs definition, involves a calculation or is a combination of measurements, and is often a ratio. Supply chain examples would include inventory future days of supply, inventory turns, and sales dollars per stock-keeping unit.[1]

Second, what are the characteristics of a good metric? Figure 5.1 is an excellent framework that can be used to determine the characteristic of a good metric. Several questions need to be asked to determine if a metric is appropriate for its intended use. A short discussion of the 10 characteristics in Figure 5.1 is necessary here to lay the foundation for the remainder of this chapter.

The first question to be asked about a metric is, "Is it quantitative?" While not all metrics are quantitative, this is usually a requirement when measuring the outputs of processes or functions. Qualitative performance metrics are better suited for measuring perceptions or assigning products or people to categories (e.g., excellent, good, poor). Qualitative metrics are backed up with quantitative data. For example, a transportation carrier might be rated "excellent" if it has only one late delivery for every 100 attempts.

The second question to be asked about a metric is, "Is it easy to understand?" This question is directly related to the fifth question, "Is it defined and mutually understood?" Experience has shown that individuals will understand a metric if they are involved in its definition and calculation.[2] For example, one of the most commonly used metrics in the supply chain is on-time delivery. This is also one of the most commonly misunderstood metrics in the supply chain. Disagreements can occur between shippers and customers or between marketing and transportation. Research has shown that if all parties affected by the metric are involved in its definition and calculation, it will be easy to understand.[3]

The third question to be asked about a metric is, "Does it encourage appropriate behavior?" A basic principle of management is that metrics will drive behavior. A well-intentioned metric could very well drive inappropriate behavior. For example, if a warehouse manager is measured by cubic space utilization, he will try to keep the warehouse filled, which could lower inventory turns, drive up inventory costs, and result in product obsolescence.

The fourth question to be asked is, "Is the metric visible?" Good metrics should be readily available to those who use them. A distinction can be made here between a *reactive* metric and a *proactive* metric. Some firms state that metrics are available in the system for employees to see and use. However, this means that they must attempt to find them. These are *reactive* metrics. Leading firms, however, "push" metrics to metrics owners so they can react immediately. These are called *proactive* metrics. In both cases, metrics are visible. However, proactive metrics will be acted upon quicker because employees need little or no effort to see them.[4]

The sixth question to be asked is, "Does the metric encompass both outputs and inputs?" Process metrics, such as on-time delivery, need to incorporate causes and effects into their calculation and evaluation. For example, a decreasing on-time delivery rate might be caused by late pickups, shipments not being ready on time, or even by production shutdowns. So, the outputs must be somehow related to the inputs.

The seventh question to be asked is, "Does it measure only what is important?" The supply chain operation generates huge volumes of transactional data on a daily basis. Many times, firms will measure those activities or processes for which large amounts of data are available. Just because data are available to calculate a metric does not mean the metric is important. In some cases, data are hard to generate for important metrics. For example, data for on-time delivery must be generated by either the carrier or receiving location. Matching arrival data in a timely and accurate manner with bills of lading can be a cumbersome process. So, it is important to decide what is important and then gather the data rather than identifying what data are available and then generating metrics.

The eighth question to be asked about a good metric is, "Is it multidimensional?" Although a single metric will not be multidimensional, a firm's metric program will be.

This is where the terms **scorecard** and **key performance indicators (KPIs)** will apply. Many organizations will have a few strategic metrics to manage their supply chains. These metrics will represent productivity, utilization, and performance in a balanced approach to managing their supply chain processes.[5]

The ninth question to be asked is, "Does the process use economies of effort?" Another way to ask this question is, "Do we get more benefits from the metric than we incur costs to generate it?" In many cases, much time and effort are devoted to collecting data to generate a specific metric, while the resulting actions from the metric are minimal. Some firms find this to be the case when they first develop a metric. However, the longer a firm has a metric in place, the more likely there is to be economies of effort.[6]

The last question to be asked about a good metric is probably the most important: "Does it facilitate trust?" If it does not, complying with the other nine characteristics makes little or no difference for the effectiveness of the metric. However, if the first nine characteristics are present for a supply chain metric, trust should be an expected conclusion.

On the Line *Measuring Supply Chain Success*

A food manufacturing company finds the perfect recipe for increasing profit growth and cost savings. And a hand and power tool manufacturer nails its targets for improving year-over-year return on net assets.

What helped these companies achieve amplified success in their supply chains—and ultimately throughout their organizations? "World-class purchasing/sourcing measurement systems are the key," says Philip Carter, a professor and executive director of the Center for Strategic Supply Research at Arizona State University's W. P. Carey School of Business.

Comprehensive measuring systems allow organizations to clearly set priorities for purchasing and strategic sourcing, measure accomplishments, and effectively demonstrate purchasing/strategic sourcing's contribution to the company's overall goals, according to Carter's research.

"Corporations today rely on outside suppliers more than ever, and consequently, need measurements to determine if their supplier relationships are effective," Carter says.

"It is vitally important that companies use metrics to measure the performance of both purchasing/supply activities within the company, and the performance of the supplier base," he explains.

BEST PRACTICES

Carter's findings—gleaned from extensive research at 15 *Fortune* 500 organizations in a multitude of industries—show several best practices prevalent among companies with world-class purchasing/supply measuring systems. To succeed, Carter says, these measuring systems should be:

- Aligned with other strategic business units within the company and with overall corporate goals;
- Comprehensive, dynamic, and aggressive;
- Communicated efficiently throughout the organization;
- Tied to performance-based initiatives;
- Backed by organizational resources;
- Supported by technology systems; and
- Championed by C-level executives.

Cutting costs, naturally, is the primary driver for many companies implementing measuring systems. But companies are also starting to gauge how efficient operations are by measuring such benchmarks as dollars spent per employee in purchasing, number of suppliers per buyer, percentage of sourcing done through electronic systems, and number of suppliers being used, among others.

Strategic measures, while harder to quantify, are also gaining attention.

"These measurements can be subjective, but they are vital," Carter says. "Chief purchasing officers need to know whether or not their purchasing department has an impact on new product/new service development, brings good ideas from the supplier base back to the company, and impacts revenue generation."

WORLD-CLASS METRICS

Companies that look at cost, efficiency, and strategic measures together gain a greater understanding of their supply chain and its overall impact on the organization. But they are uncommon.

"Only 10 percent of *Fortune* 500 companies have a world-class measurement system," says Carter. "Most companies employ some type of system, but outside of leading companies, the systems are usually random—they measure a little of this and a little of that.

"Poor metrics make it difficult for organizations to make decisions and allocate resources," he continues. "How can you gauge the number of people to add to a department, for example, if you don't track that department's efficiency?"

"It's not that companies with sub-par measuring systems don't care," Carter explains; "rather they lack available financial and/or technological resources. Such measuring systems can be cumbersome, time-consuming, and expensive to develop and maintain."

THE NEXT PHASE

"Going forward, the importance of efficient measurement systems will increase," Carter predicts.

Improvements in technology will enhance current systems, improve workflow and data sharing, and reduce the time it takes to produce measurement.

"The next phase is Web technology allowing companies to access the right tools and see metric information in a more comprehensive way," says Carter. He also predicts an increase in Web portals, used internally as well as between companies and their supply base.

"Web portals are a better way of collecting information. They help establish standards and data definition models for supply/purchasing measurements," he says.

Over-extensive measuring, however, can be detrimental. With lean staffs the norm at most companies these days, measurement systems can place a burden on the workforce. The key is moderation.

"Companies have to be careful; they can get lost in the forest of measure," says Carter. "The pros outweigh the cons overall, but companies must shoot for the sweet spot—the amount of measuring that makes sense to them."

Source: Inbound Logistics (January 2006): 26–27. Reprinted with permission, http://www.inboundlogistics.com/subscribe.

Evaluating current or potential supply chain metrics is critical to a sound metrics program. Also important to note is that metrics need to change over time; not only the performance standard, for example, 85 percent, but also the individual metric, for example, percentage of orders shipped on time. With regard to the first example, the standard might change to 90 percent as new processes and/or technologies are introduced that enable the organization to consistently exceed the old standard. Advocates of the Six Sigma concept have stressed the focus on continuous improvement, which should result in increasing performance expectations over time.

The second example, indicated previously, regarding changing metrics is also very important. Orders shipped on time and orders shipped complete were frequently used as performance metrics in logistics. These could be considered "internal" metrics because they focus on the performance of the shipping firm. However, as customer service receives more attention in industry, the metrics have changed to "orders delivered on time" and "orders delivered complete." These are more "external" metrics because they measure the experience of the customer. Both "internal" and "external" metrics are essential components to a balanced approach to supply chain performance measurement. Figure 5.2 shows the results of a recent survey conducted by the Aberdeen group asking shippers what supplier performance metrics they use. As can be seen from the results, on-time delivery is once again the most often used metric to measure supplier service performance.

Figure 5.3 explains how the dimensions and importance of performance measurement have expanded. This figure clearly indicates that expectations have increased since the 1960s and 1970s and that in each of the decades identified there have been important drivers for better performance. Each new decade, however, built upon the improvements in the previous decade(s).

A question might be raised as to whether or not the focus on performance measurement is a recent event in industry. The answer to that question is a definite "no." Recall

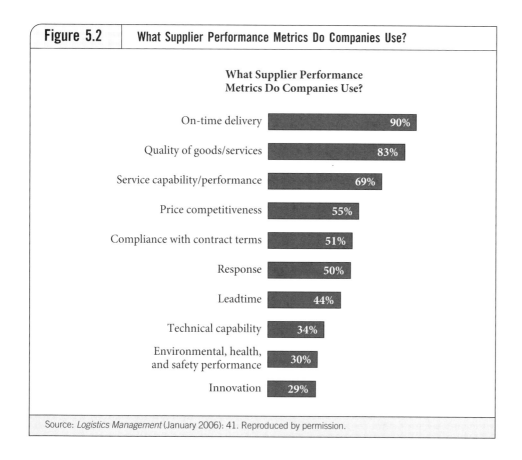

Figure 5.2 | **What Supplier Performance Metrics Do Companies Use?**

What Supplier Performance
Metrics Do Companies Use?

On-time delivery — 90%
Quality of goods/services — 83%
Service capability/performance — 69%
Price competitiveness — 55%
Compliance with contract terms — 51%
Response — 50%
Leadtime — 44%
Technical capability — 34%
Environmental, health, and safety performance — 30%
Innovation — 29%

Source: *Logistics Management* (January 2006): 41. Reproduced by permission.

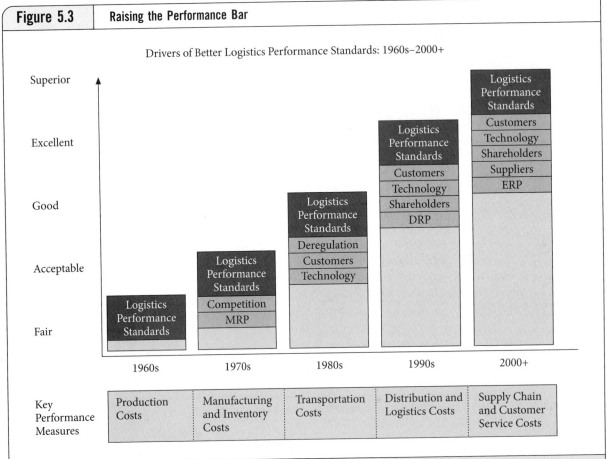

Figure 5.3 | **Raising the Performance Bar**

Drivers of Better Logistics Performance Standards: 1960s–2000+

Key Performance Measures	Production Costs	Manufacturing and Inventory Costs	Transportation Costs	Distribution and Logistics Costs	Supply Chain and Customer Service Costs

Source: J. S. Keebler, D. A. Durtsche, K. B. Manrodt, and D. M. Ledyard, *Keeping Score: Measuring the Business Value of Logistics in the Supply Chain* (University of Tennessee, Council of Logistics Management, 1999). Reproduced with permission from Council of Supply Chain Management Professionals.

from Chapter 2 that the development of the physical distribution and logistics concepts was based upon systems theory with the specific application focused upon least total cost analysis. Total cost is a measure of efficiency and was the rationale supporting physical distribution management. Least total cost was later used to support the logistics management approach.

The focus upon a least total cost system required measuring the tradeoff costs when a suggested change was made in one of the components or elements of the system. For example, this could include switching from rail to motor transportation or adding a distribution center to the distribution network. Cost has long been recognized as an important metric for determining efficiency. This is still true today. However, we have evolved from measuring functional cost to supply chain cost. This means the relevant point of measurement has changed from totally internal to a firm to the collective costs of many firms involved in the supply chain.

The important point to remember is that successful supply chain performance measurement relies on appropriate metrics that capture the entire essence of the supply chain process. Supply chain metrics must also be reviewed to assure that they are relevant and focusing on what is important. A sound, comprehensive set of supply chain performance metrics is critical for an organization to manage its business and identify opportunities to increase profit and market share.

Developing Supply Chain Performance Metrics[7]

The implementation of new technologies, for example, enterprise resource planning (ERP) systems, and the changing business environment have prompted many firms to reexamine their supply chain metrics programs. Another driving influence for this reexamination has been the desire of organizations to change their supply chain focus from a "cost" center to an "investment" center. In other words, how can organizations justify investments in supply chain processes? This will be discussed in a later section in this chapter. This section will offer some suggestions concerning the successful development of a supply chain metrics program.

First, the development of a metrics program should be the result of a team effort. Successful metrics implementations involve development teams comprised of individuals representing functional areas within the firm that will be impacted by the metrics. Because this phase of development requires metric identification and definition, it is critical that all impacted areas agree on the appropriate metrics and their definitions. This agreement will lead to a more successful implementation and use of the metrics to manage the business.

Second, involve customers and suppliers, where appropriate, in the metrics development process. Because customers feel the impact of metrics and suppliers are actively involved in the execution of the metrics, their involvement is also critical to successful implementation.

Third, develop a tiered structure for the metrics. Many organizations develop a small number (usually less than five) of KPIs or "executive dashboard" metrics that are viewed at the executive level for strategic decision making. Tied to each strategic KPI are tactical and operational metrics. In this hierarchy, operating unit metrics are tied directly to corporate strategic metrics.

Fourth, identify metric "owners" and tie metric goal achievement to an individual's or division's performance evaluation. This provides the motivation to achieve metric goals and use metrics to manage the business.

Fifth, establish a procedure to mitigate conflicts arising from metric development and implementation. A true process metric might require a functional area within an organization to suboptimize its performance to benefit the organization as a whole. This might result in conflict from the suboptimized function. For example, achieving the desired on-time delivery metric might require transportation to increase its expenditures, resulting in an unfavorable freight expense. A resolution process must be established to allow the transportation manager to realize the desired on-time delivery goal without being penalized for excess freight expense.

Sixth, the supply chain metrics must be consistent with corporate strategy. If the overall corporate strategy is based upon effectiveness in serving customers, a supply chain metrics program that emphasizes low cost or efficiency could be in conflict with expected corporate outcomes.

Finally, establish top management support for the development of a supply chain metrics program. Successful metrics programs cost more than expected, take longer to implement than desirable, and impact many areas inside and outside the organization. Top management support is necessary to see the development and implementation of the metrics program to its successful conclusion.

Performance Categories

A number of approaches can be used to classify supply chain performance metrics. Figure 5.4 is one method to use for this type of classification. This figure identifies four major categories with examples that provide a useful way for examining logistics and supply chain performance: time, quality, cost, and supporting metrics.

Time has traditionally been given attention as an important indicator of logistics performance, especially with regard to measuring effectiveness. Figure 5.4 lists five widely used metrics for time. The metrics capture two elements of time: the elapsed time for the activity and the reliability (variability) for the activity. For example, order cycle time might be 10 days, plus or minus 4 days, or 10 days, plus or minus 2 days. Both cycle

Figure 5.4	Process Measure Categories

Time

On-time delivery/Receipt
Order cycle time
Order cycle time variability
Response time
Forecasting/Planning cycle time

Quality

Overall customer satisfaction
Processing accuracy
Perfect order fulfillment*

- On-time delivery
- Complete order
- Accurate product selection
- Damage-free
- Accurate invoice

Forecast accuracy
Planning accuracy
- Budgets and operating plans

Schedule adherence

Cost

Finished goods inventory turns
Days sales outstanding
Cost to serve
Cash-to-cash cycle time
Total delivered cost

- Cost of goods
- Transportation costs
- Inventory carrying costs
- Material handling costs

All other costs
- Information systems
- Administrative

Cost of excess capacity
Cost of capacity shortfall

Other/Supporting

Approval exceptions to standard
- Minimum order quantity
- Change order timing

Availability of information

Source: J. S. Keebler, D. A. Durtsche, K. B. Manrodt, and D. M. Ledyard, *Keeping Score: Measuring the Business Value of Logistics in the Supply Chain* (University of Tennessee, Council of Logistics Management, 1999). Reproduced with permission from Council of Supply Chain Management.

times have the same absolute length but have different variability. The difference in variability will have an impact on safely stocks in the supply chain (this will be covered further in Chapter 9: Managing Inventory in the Supply Chain). The important point is that metrics should measure both absolute time and its variability.

The second category indicated in Figure 5.4 is cost, which is the measurement for efficiency. Most organizations focus on cost since it is critical to their ability to compete in the market and make adequate profit and returns on assets and/or investments. A number of cost metrics related to logistics and supply chain management are important to organizations.

Some of the cost metrics shown in Figure 5.4 are obvious and easy to understand. For example, total delivered cost or landed cost will have an impact on the prices that will have to be charged in the market. Total delivered cost is multidimensional and includes the cost of goods, transportation, inventory carrying costs, and warehousing. Inventory turns and days sales outstanding are not as obvious. Inventory turns reflect how long an organization holds inventory and its resulting impact on inventory carrying cost (this will be discussed further in Chapter 9). Days sales outstanding impacts service levels to customers and can affect the rate of order fill. The cash-to-cash cycle is receiving increased attention in organizations because it measures cash flow. Organizations are interested in getting their money back as quickly as possible in order to enhance their financial viability.

Quality is the third category of metrics identified in Figure 5.4. Several dimensions in the Quality category are important to logistics and supply chain management. The perfect order concept is a good example of the increased emphasis being placed upon customer service because it simultaneously measures multiple metrics that must be achieved to get a positive metric.[8] The fourth category indicated in Figure 5.4 offers some supporting metrics such as approval of exceptions to standards.

Another metric classification scheme that has been receiving increased attention is that developed by the Supply Chain Council and contained in the Supply Chain Operations and Reference (SCOR) model. Figure 5.5 is an example of the metrics categories used to measure the performance of Process Dl: Deliver Stocked Product. This figure identifies five major categories of metrics that need to be used to measure the performance of Process Dl: reliability, responsiveness, flexibility, cost, and assets. **Reliability** is the performance of the supply chain in delivering the correct product, to the correct place, at the correct time, in the correct condition and packaging, in the correct quantity, with the correct documentation, to the correct customer. **Responsiveness** is the speed at which the supply chain provides products to the customer. **Flexibility** is the agility of the supply chain in responding to marketplace changes to gain or maintain competitive advantage. **Costs** are the costs associated with operating the supply chain. **Asset management** is the effectiveness of an organization in managing assets to support demand satisfaction; this includes the management of all assets and fixed and working capital.[9] Figure 5.6 identifies metrics in the same categories for the single activity of D1.3, Reserve Inventory and Determine Delivery Date.

Finally, another perspective (see Figure 5.7) suggests that performance metrics for logistics and supply chain management should include logistics operations costs, logistics service metrics, transaction cost and revenue quantification, and channel satisfaction metrics.

Figure 5.5	SCOR Model: Process D1 Metrics

Process Category: Deliver Stocked Product	**Process Number: D1**
Process Category Definition	
The process of delivering product that is maintained in a finished goods state prior to the receipt of a firm customer order.	

Performance Attibutes	**Metric**
Reliability	Perfect Order Fulfillment
Responsiveness	Order Fulfillment Cycle Time
Flexibility	Upside Deliver Flexibility Downside Deliver Adaptability Upside Deliver Adaptability
Cost	Order Management Costs as % of Deliver Costs
Assets	Cash to Cash Cycle Time Return on Supply Chain Fixed Assets

Best Practices	**Features**
Rapid replenishment, VMI, EDI	None Identified
Electronic Catalogues/Malls	None Identified
Internet Ordering	None Identified
Efficient Consumer Response (ECR); Quick Response	Demand Planning, Deployment, Scheduling
Ventor Managed Inventory (VMI)	See Glossary

Source: Supply Chain Council (2007). Reproduced by permission.

In terms of logistics operations costs, a good example is transportation costs. By calculating the tradeoffs between using less expensive (slower and less reliable) and more expensive (faster and more reliable) transportation service, an organization could quantify the total cost impact on transportation and inventory costs. Using faster and more reliable transportation would result in higher transportation costs but lower inventory costs, usually resulting in an increase in cash flow for the organization.

Logistics service can fall into any one of five categories. These categories can be seen in Figure 5.8. Product availability is a logistics metric that is used frequently because it is a good indicator of supply chain performance and its influence on customer inventory requirements, order fill rates, and seller revenue.

Order *cycle time (OCT)* is another very important logistics service metric. OCT influences product availability, customer inventories, and the seller's cash flow and profit. Once an expected order cycle time is established for customers, service failures can be measured. One such measure is the number of late deliveries per 100 shipments. From a revenue or cash flow perspective, an organization can calculate the impact of a late delivery on revenue, profit, and cash flow (this will be discussed further in Chapter 8: Order Management and Customer Service).

All of the logistics outputs listed in Figure 5.8 can be utilized in some form to develop metrics for service performance. As indicated previously, the service output metrics reflect the quality of service being provided to customers, which is important to sustain and, hopefully, increase revenue and cash flow.

Transaction cost and revenue relates to the value added by logistics. In other words, what is the service and price relationship, and what specifically is the customer's

Figure 5.6	SCOR Model: Process D1.3 Metrics

Process Element: Reserve Inventory and Determine Delivery Date	Process Element Number: D1.3

Process Element Definition

Inventory and/or planned capacity (both on and scheduled) is identified and reserved for specific orders and a delivery date is committed and scheduled.

Performance Attributes	Metric
Reliability	Delivery Performance To Customer Commit Date
Responsiveness	Reserve Inventory and Determine Delivery Date Cycle Time
Flexibility	None Identified
Cost	Finished Goods Inventory Days of Supply
Assets	Finished Goods Inventory Carry Cost

Best Practices	Features
EDI links between manufacturing and distributor to achieve visibility of complete finished goods inventory and expected shipment	None Identified
Automatic reservation of inventory and dynamic sourcing of product for single shipment to customer	Integrated order management system that treats each order line as a separate order with integration to inventory source and status; Real-time inventory management
ATP and Product Reservation	Integration with scheduling and inventory management
Priority-based inventory reservstions, for key customers, with FIFO allocation for all others	None Identified
Inventory allocation exception process is clearly defined and jointly owned by manufacturing and sales	None Identified

Inputs	Plan	Source	Make	Deliver	Return
Sourcing Plans	P2.4				
Production Plans	P3.4				
Delivery Plans	P4.4				
Inventory Availability		S	M		
Production Schedule			M1.1		

Outputs	Plan	Source	Make	Deliver	Return
Order Backlog	P1.1, P4.1				
Inventory Availability/Delivery Date	P4.2				
Replenishment Signal		S 1.1			
Available to Promise Date			M		
Inventory Status	P	S	M	D	

perception of service quality? To add logistics value from the seller's perspective, there are three basic alternatives as follows:

- Increased service with a constant price to the customer
- Constant service with a reduced price
- Increased service with a reduced price

All of these alternatives result in the customers receiving more service per dollar for the price they are paying for the service.

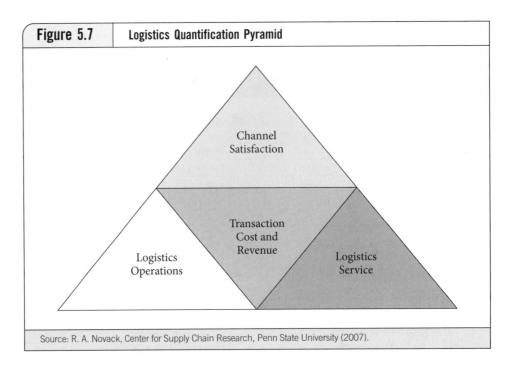

Figure 5.7 | Logistics Quantification Pyramid

Channel Satisfaction

Transaction Cost and Revenue

Logistics Operations

Logistics Service

Source: R. A. Novack, Center for Supply Chain Research, Penn State University (2007).

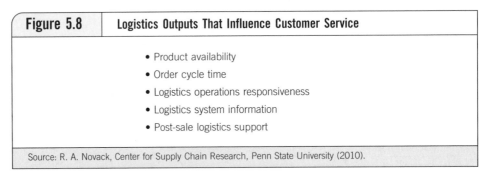

Figure 5.8 | Logistics Outputs That Influence Customer Service

- Product availability
- Order cycle time
- Logistics operations responsiveness
- Logistics system information
- Post-sale logistics support

Source: R. A. Novack, Center for Supply Chain Research, Penn State University (2010).

Another perspective on transaction cost and revenue focuses on how a seller's cost influences a customer's profit and on how a seller's service impacts a customer's revenue. If the cost of a seller's logistics service allows a customer to make more profit from the seller's product, the customer should be willing to buy more products from the seller. For example, a manufacturer is able to deliver its product to the buyer's retail store for $0.25 cheaper per case than the competitor can deliver its product to the same store. By keeping the price constant at the shelf, the buyer can realize an additional $0.25 per case profit. Similarly, a manufacturer's logistics service level will have an impact on the retailer's revenues. For example, the same manufacturer in the previous example has an in-stock rate at the buyer's store of 98 percent, compared to 90 percent for the competition. This higher in-stock service level allows the buyer to realize higher revenues from the higher product availability. So, transaction cost and revenue highlight the need to emphasize the impacts of logistics cost and service on supply chain profits and revenues.

The final category, shown in Figure 5.7, is channel satisfaction. This essentially looks at how logistics cost and service are perceived by channel members. The research in this area is limited. Most of the focus on measurement has been on the perceptions of supply chain members of how well suppliers are performing on logistics cost and service. Leading-edge organizations are beginning to identify the impacts of customer satisfaction on revenues and market share.

Overall, much progress has been made during the last few years towards developing appropriate metrics and using them proactively to measure performance in terms of the impacts upon the financial results of the organization and its customers. However, as this discussion has highlighted, there is much more to be accomplished. The next section will introduce the supply chain-finance connection, which will be used in the appropriate chapters throughout the remainder of this book.

The Supply Chain-Finance Connection

As noted in the Supply Chain Profile at the beginning of this chapter, CLGN Book Dis-tributors.com is focusing its attention on the supply chain process as a means to improving its financial performance. CLGN recognizes the impact supply chain performance has on customer satisfaction and future sales. In addition, the effectiveness of the supply chain process impacts the cost of fulfilling customer orders and transporting these orders to the customer, both of which impact the overall landed cost of the product.

More specifically, the supply chain process influences the flow of products from the supplier to the final point of consumption. The resources utilized to accomplish this flow process determine, in part, the cost of making the product available to the consumer at the consumer's location. This landed cost, then, impacts the buyer's decision to purchase a seller's product.

The cost of providing logistics service not only affects the marketability of the product (via the landed cost, or price), but it also impacts profitability. For a given price, level of sales, and level of service, the higher the logistics cost the lower the organization's profit. Conversely, the lower the logistics costs, the higher the profits.

The decision to alter the supply chain process is essentially an optimization issue. Management must view the supply chain alternatives as to their ability to optimize the corporate goal of profit maximization. Some alternatives might minimize costs but reduce revenue, and possibly, profits. By implementing supply chain alternatives that optimize profits, the decision maker is taking the systems approach and trading off revenue and costs for optimum profit.

Supply chain management involves the control of raw material, in-process, and finished goods inventories. The financing implication of inventory management is the amount of capital required to fund the inventory. In many organizations, capital is in short supply but is required to fund critical projects, such as new plants or new warehouses. The higher the inventory level, the more capital is constrained and the less capital is available for other investments.

The recent focus on inventory minimization is a direct response to the competing needs for capital and the difficulty some organizations have in raising additional capital. Logistics techniques such as just-in-time and vendor-managed inventories are directed toward reducing an organization's inventory levels and making more capital available for other projects

As indicated previously, the level of logistics service provided has a direct impact on customer satisfaction. Providing consistent and short lead times helps manage supply chain inventories and can build customer satisfaction and loyally. However, the cost of providing this service must also be examined for its results on a firm's profit and revenues.

Finally, **efficiency** of the supply chain impacts the time required to process a customer's order. Order processing time has a direct bearing on an organization's **order-to-cash cycle.** The order-to-cash cycle includes all of the activities that occur from the time an order is received by a seller until the seller receives payment for the shipment. Typically, the invoice is sent to the customer after the order is shipped. If the terms of sale are net 30 days, the seller will receive payment in 30 days plus the time needed to process the order. The longer the order-to-cash cycle, the longer it takes for the seller to get its payment. The longer the order-to-cash cycle, the higher the accounts receivable and the higher the investment in "sold" finished goods. So, the length of the order-to-cash cycle directly relates to the amount of capital tied up and not available for other investments.

The Revenue-Cost Savings Connection

Throughout this text, attention is given to supply chain efficiency and cost reduction. While process efficiency and cost savings are worthy goals, top management generally refers to corporate improvements in terms of increases in revenue and profit. The apparent conflict between the goals of top management and supply chain management can be readily resolved by converting cost savings into equivalent revenue increases. To improve communications effectiveness with top management, it behooves the supply chain manager to relate efficiencies and cost savings in a language that top management uses—that is, revenue and profit.

Logistics and supply chain managers find it advantageous to transform cost reductions into equivalent revenue increases to explain to top management the effects of improved supply chain cost performance. To accomplish this, the following equations can be used:

$$\text{Profit} = \text{Revenue} - \text{Costs}$$

where

$$\text{Cost} = (X\%)(\text{Revenue})$$

then

$$\text{Profit} = \text{Revenue} - (X\%)(\text{Revenue}) = \text{Revenue}(1 - X\%)$$

where

$$(1 - X\%) = \text{Profit margin}$$

$$\text{Sales} = \text{Profit}/\text{Profit Margin}$$

Assuming that everything else remains unchanged, a logistics cost saving will directly increase pre-tax profits by the amount of the cost saving. If a logistics cost saving increases profit by the same amount, the revenue equivalent of this cost saving is found by dividing the cost saving by the profit margin as shown in the preceding equations.

Table 5.1	Sales Equivalent of Supply Chain Cost Savings				
	CLGN 2007		SALES EQUIVALENT FOR COST SAVINGS OF		
	(000)	%	$200,000	$500,000	$1,000,000
Sales	$150,000	100.0%	$2,857,143*	$7,142,857**	$14,285,714†
Total cost	139,500	93.0	2,657,143	6,642,857	13,285,714
Net profit	10,500	7.0	200,000	500,000	1,000,000

*$200,000 cost saving 4 ÷ 0.07 profit margin
**$500,000 cost saving 4 ÷ 0.07 profit margin
†$1,000,000 cost saving 4 ÷ 0.07 profit margin

Table 5.2	Equivalent Sales with Varying Profit Margins			
	PROFIT MARGINS			
	20%	10%	5%	1%
Sales	$50,000	$100,000	$200,000	$1,000,000
Total cost	40,000	90,000	190,000	990,000
Cost saving/Profit	10,000	10,000	10,000	10,000

For example, if cost is 90 percent of revenue and the profit margin is 10 percent of revenue, a $100 cost saving is equivalent to additional revenue of $1,000:

$$\text{Revenue} = \text{Cost Saving (or Profit)}/\text{Profit Margin}$$
$$\text{Revenue} = \$100/0.10$$
$$\text{Revenue} = \$1,000$$

Table 5.1 provides examples of equivalent revenue for different logistics cost savings using the data found in the Supply Chain Profile for CLGN. As shown in the table,

CLGN has a profit margin of 7 percent. Given this profit margin, a $200,000 logistics cost saving has the same effect as increasing revenue by $2,857,143, a 1.9 percent increase in revenue. Likewise, a $500,000 and $1 million logistics cost savings have equivalent revenue equal to $7,142,857 (4.76 percent revenue increase) and $14,285,714 (9.52 percent revenue increase), respectively.

The lower the profit margin, the higher the revenue equivalent for a given logistics cost because it takes a greater revenue volume to produce a given profit. Table 5.2 shows the equivalent revenue of a given logistics cost saving with varying profit margins. For a $10,000 logistics cost saving, the equivalent revenue equals $1 million for an organization with a 1 percent profit margin but only $50,000 for an organization with a 20 percent profit margin. Logistics cost savings have a much greater revenue impact for organizations with low profit margins.

In the following section, the financial implications of supply chain strategies are discussed. Following that section, statements contained in the Supply Chain Profile for CLGN Book Distributors.com are analyzed.

The Supply Chain Financial Impact

A major financial objective for any organization is to produce a satisfactory return for stockholders. This requires the generation of sufficient profit in relation to the size of the stockholders' investment to assure that inventors will maintain confidence in the organization's ability to manage its investments. Low returns over time will see investors seek alternative uses for their capital. High returns over time, however, will buoy investor confidence to maintain their investments with the organization.

The absolute size of the profit must be considered in relation to the stockholders' net investment, or net worth. For example, if Company A makes a profit of $1 million and Company B makes a profit of $100 million, it would appear that Company B would be a better investment. However, if A has a net worth of $10 million and B $10 billion, the **return on net worth** for a stockholder in Company A is 10 percent ($1 million/$10 million) and for Company B it is 1 percent ($100 million/$10 billion).

An organization's financial performance is also judged by the profit it generates in relationship to the assets utilized, or **return on assets (ROA).** An organization's return on assets is a financial performance metric that is used as a benchmark to compare management and organization performance to that of other organizations in the same industry or similar industries. As with return on net worth, return on assets is dependent on the level of profits for the organization.

The supply chain plays a critical role in determining the level of profitability in an organization. The more efficient and productive the supply chain, the greater is the profit potential of the organization. Conversely, the less efficient and less productive, the higher is the supply chain costs and the lower the profitability.

Figure 5.9 shows the financial relationship between supply chain management and return on assets. The effectiveness of supply chain service impacts the level of revenue, and the efficiency affects the organization's total costs. As noted earlier, revenue minus cost equals profit, a major component in determining ROA.

The level of inventory owned by an organization in its supply chain determines the assets, or capital, devoted to inventory. The order-to-cash cycle affects the time required to receive payment from a sale, thereby impacting the accounts receivable and cash assets. Finally, the supply chain decisions regarding the type and number of warehouses utilized impacts fixed assets.

Lastly, Figure 5.9 shows that the calculation of ROA is the division of the profit realized by the capital (assets) employed (profit/capital employed). As noted earlier, the higher the profits for a given level of assets (capital) utilized, the higher is the ROA.

Another way to examine the impacts of supply chain services and costs can be seen in Figure 5.10. As shown in this figure, cash and receivables for an organization are influenced by supply chain time (order cycle time/order-to-cash), supply chain reliability (order completion rate and on-time delivery), and information accuracy (invoice accuracy). All of these supply chain services will determine when the customer begins processing the shipment delivery for payment. Inventory investment for an organization is influenced by required service levels and stockout rates for the organization. Property, plant, and equipment investment is impacted by decisions regarding private warehouses and transportation fleets. Decisions regarding the outsourcing activities such as warehousing and transportation will influence current liability levels (accounts payable). Finally, decisions regarding financing for inventories and infrastructure will determine debt and equity levels.

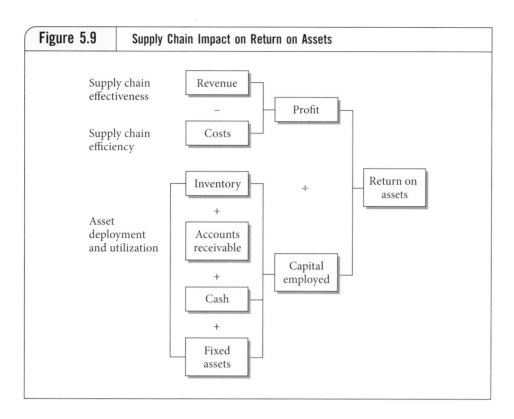

Figure 5.9 | Supply Chain Impact on Return on Assets

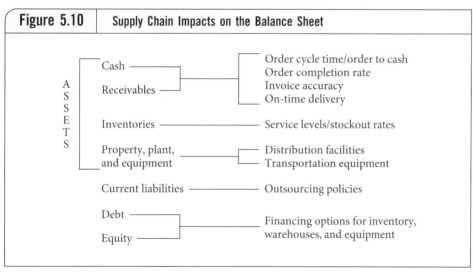

Figure 5.10 | Supply Chain Impacts on the Balance Sheet

Figure 5.11 summarizes the supply chain strategic areas affecting return on assets. The decisions made by the supply chain manager with regard to channel structure, inventory management, order management, and transportation management all have an effect on the level of assets employed or the level of profitability the organization will realize.

Channel structure management includes decisions regarding the use of outsourcing, channel inventories, information systems, and channel structure. By outsourcing supply chain activities, the organization might realize lower supply chain costs (outsourcing firms possess greater functional expertise and efficiencies), a reduction in assets (use of

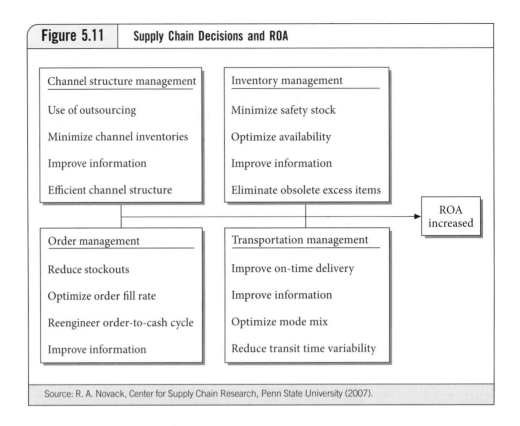

Figure 5.11 | **Supply Chain Decisions and ROA**

Channel structure management

Use of outsourcing

Minimize channel inventories

Improve information

Efficient channel structure

Inventory management

Minimize safety stock

Optimize availability

Improve information

Eliminate obsolete excess items

Order management

Reduce stockouts

Optimize order fill rate

Reengineer order-to-cash cycle

Improve information

Transportation management

Improve on-time delivery

Improve information

Optimize mode mix

Reduce transit time variability

ROA increased

Source: R. A. Novack, Center for Supply Chain Research, Penn State University (2007).

On the Line   *What Drives CEOs?*

CEOs have a lot on their minds, particularly revenue growth and responsiveness. Logistics can support both those goals, according to *Communicating the Value of Supply Chain Management to Your CEO,* a newly released report published by the Council of Supply Chain Management Professionals (CSCMP).

Logistics supports revenue growth by improving speed to market, reducing cost to market, and increasing customer service without adding cost. Companies can achieve revenue growth through differentiated supply chain processes, even when products are viewed as commodities, according to the report. Success in global markets and the ability to efficiently source materials or sell products globally depend largely on supply chain capabilities and processes.

Logistics supports responsiveness by affecting speed to market, increasing turns, accelerating the cash-to cash cycle, increasing ROI, reducing the risk of inventory obsolescence, creating leaner supply chains, and enabling companies to enter and exit markets faster.

Senior managers today are more exposed to logistics and supply chain management terminology, the report notes, supporting a growing awareness that wasn't there even five years ago.

"Leaders invest in their supply chains, but what's scary is that some current market leaders won't be leaders in three to five years," says Karl Manrodt, associate professor, Georgia Southern University, and coauthor of the CSCMP report, along with Brian Gibson of Auburn University and Stephen Rutner of Georgia Southern University.

"If my competitor is investing to be more efficient and build in greater flexibility and I am not, how long do you think I can run the race? I'll be reduced to competing on price, and I will be overtaken," Manrodt says. "Smart CEOs look at logistics and supply chain as a way to compete."

CEOs have become more interested in supply chain management because they see it as a strategic advantage, agrees John T. (Tom) Mentzer, professor of marketing, logistics, and transportation, University of Tennessee.

CEOs, however, are driven by Wall Street to perform this month, this quarter, Mentzer notes. Many advantages that come from effective supply chain management take several business cycles to accomplish and may actually hurt a company's stock in the short term.

"If I form a strategic partnership with one of my retail customers for a vendor-managed inventory program that will take 40 percent of inventory out of the supply chain, for example, during the first quarter it will look like sales went down," Mentzer says. "Wall Street will see this as a poor performance, and downgrade the stock."

"On the other hand, say I'm on the board of a clothing retailer whose stock was trading at $18 two years ago, but is trading at $40 today," he continues. "This clothing company bought another profitable retailer, and in due diligence discovered it could cut $4 million in supply chain costs. These cuts mean the company, which earns $56 million annually, increased earnings by eight percent. That makes Wall Street analysts believers."

Poor supply chain management can lead to huge global mistakes. Take a company that moves production to Southeast Asia as an example, says Mentzer. It does this because it can save $1 million in labor costs. But, as a result of that decision, the supply chain is now five months long, so the company has to carry more inventory in the United States—a fact the management team forgot to account for.

"This costs the company $1.5 million more in inventory, plus another $1 million in transportation," says Mentzer. "So the company spent $2.5 million to make $1 million."

Mistakes of this magnitude certainly get the attention of CEOs.

Source: Inbound Logistics, June 2005: 44. Reprinted with permission, http:// www.inboundlogistics.com/ subscribe.

an outsourcing firm's facilities), and increased revenue (from improved supply chain service). Decisions that lower supply chain assets and/or improve revenue through supply chain service improvements result in a higher ROA.

Minimization of channel inventories results in a direct reduction in an organization's assets. The use of improved information systems enables the organization to better monitor inventory levels, production schedules, and demand forecasts to meet current levels of demand. Streamlining the channel structure through the elimination of unnecessary channel intermediaries—for example, dealing directly with the retailer and bypassing the wholesaler—might eliminate inventory from the channel, as well as reduce the channel cost of transportation and warehousing. The reduction in inventory results in a direct increase in ROA.

Inventory management decisions that reduce inventory (safety stock, obsolete and/or excess stock) and optimize inventory location (in relation to sales or use patterns) reduce the investment in inventory. These decisions require analysis of sales data and inventory levels by channel location, which is readily available with current information systems.

Effective order management not only reduces supply chain costs but also supports increased revenue, the combined effect resulting in a higher ROA. Reducing stockouts implies that sufficient inventories are available to meet demand. Optimizing the order fill rate implies a reduction in the order-to-cash cycle, which reduces the accounts receivable collection time. Reductions in the order processing times, coupled with a reduction in the length of credit period extended to customers, reduce accounts payable and the cost of capital required to fund accounts payable. All of these reductions in time improve the ROA.

Finally, reducing transportation transit time and the variability of transit time will have a positive impact on revenues as well as on inventory levels. By providing short, consistent transit time, a seller can differentiate its product in the market by lowering the buyer's inventories and stockout costs. This product differentiation should produce increased revenues and a potential for increased profits. Modal optimization affords the opportunity to lower transportation cost by utilizing a lower-cost method of transportation that does not increase other costs above the transportation cost savings. Transportation management decisions, then, offer the opportunity to increase revenues and lower inventories and costs, resulting in a higher ROA.

Financial Statements

Attention must now be given to two very important financial statements: the income statement and the balance sheet. The data contained in the Supply Chain Profile for CLGN Book Distributors.com will be used in this section. Figure 5.12 contains the CLGN income statement, and Figure 5.13 shows the balance sheet for CLGN. Both

Figure 5.12	CLGN Book Distributors.com Income Statement: 2007		
	SYMBOL	**(000)**	**(000)**
Sales	S		$150,000
Cost of goods sold	CGS		80,000
Gross margin	$GM = S - CGS$		$ 70,000
Transportation	TC	$ 6,000	
Warehousing	WC	1,500	
Inventory carrying	$IC = IN \times W$	3,000	
Other operating cost	OOC	30,000	
Total operating cost	$TOC = TC + WC + IC + OOC$		40,500
Earnings before interest and taxes	$EBIT = GM - TOC$		$ 29,500
Interest	INT		12,000
Taxes	$TX = (EBIT - INT) \times QA$		7,000
Net income	NI		$ 10,500

Figure 5.13	CLGN Book Distributors.com Balance Sheet: December 31, 2007	
	SYMBOL	(000)
Assets		
Cash	CA	$ 15,000
Accounts receivable	AR	30,000
Inventory	IN	10,000
Total current assets	TCA = CA + AR + IN	$ 55,000
Net fixed assets	FA	90,000
Total assets	TA = FA + TCA	$145,000
Liabilities		
Current liabilities	CL	$ 65,000
Long-term debt	LTD	35,000
Total liabilities	TD = CL + LTD	$100,000
Stockholders' equity	SE	45,000
Total liabilities and equity	TLE = TD + SE	$145,000

financial statements have been prepared using a spreadsheet software program, and the symbol column indicates the symbol and/or equation used for each of the entries.

CLGN's **income statement** shows a net income (NI) of $10.5 million on sales (S) of $150 million, a profit margin of 7 percent. Gross margin (GM) is found by subtracting cost of goods sold (CGS) from sales (S). Earnings before interest and taxes (EBIT) are gross margin minus total operating cost (TOC). Net income (NI) is EBIT minus interest cost (INT) and taxes (TX). The supply chain costs include transportation (TC), warehousing (WC), and inventory carrying cost (IC). Inventory carrying cost is equal to average inventory (IN) times the inventory carrying cost rate (W).

The **balance sheet** in Figure 5.13 indicates CLGN utilized total assets (TA) of $145 million to generate $150 million in sales. Total assets (TA) consist of $15 million of cash (CA), $30 million of accounts receivable (AR), $10 million of inventory (IN), and $90 million of net fixed assets (FA). These assets were financed by debt (liabilities) and stockholders' equity; that is, the $100 million of total debt (TD), consisting of $65 million of current liabilities (CL) and $35 million of long-term debt (LTD), plus $45 million of stockholders' equity (SE), paid for these assets.

Financial Impact of Supply Chain Decisions

Based on the financial data given in Figure 5.12 and 5.13, an analysis can be undertaken to determine the impacts of alternative supply chain actions available to Lauren Fishbay to improve CLGN's profitability. The basic supply chain alternatives are reductions in the areas of transportation, warehousing, and inventory costs. To determine the supply chain area that affords the largest financial impact and then the focus of initial profit improvement efforts, an analysis is undertaken of the effect of a 10 percent reduction in transportation and warehousing costs and a 10 percent reduction in inventory.

Figure 5.14 shows the financial impact of a 10 percent reduction in transportation costs. First, for 2007, CLGN had a net income of $10.5 million on sales of $150 million, or a profit margin of 7.0 percent. CLGN utilized $145 million in assets to produce this profit, thereby generating a return on assets of 7.24 percent. The inventory turn rate for 2007 was 8.0, transportation costs were 4.0 percent of sales, warehousing costs were 1.0 percent of sales, and inventory carrying costs were 2.0 percent of sales.

If CLGN can reduce transportation costs by 10 percent, net income will increase $360,000 to $10,860,000, and the profit margin will increase to 7.24 percent. ROA will increase from 7.24 percent to 7.49 percent. Transportation costs as a percent of sales will decrease from 4.0 percent to 3.6 percent. Warehousing and inventory carrying costs as a percent of sales will not change (assuming the transportation changes do not result in longer or undependable transit times that would cause inventory levels to increase).

Figures 5.15 and 5.16 show the results of a similar analysis of a 10 percent reduction in warehousing costs and a 10 percent reduction in inventory. In each case, the comparison is made to the 2007 CLGN performance; that is, transportation cost and inventory are computed at the 2007 level when the 10 percent warehouse cost reduction is analyzed. As would be expected, the reduction in warehousing cost and inventory results in increases in profits, profit margin, and ROA.

The analyses contained in Figures 5.14 to 5.16 provide the input data necessary to answer the question regarding which of the basic supply chain alternatives will provide the greatest potential for increased profitability. Figure 5.17 contains a comparison of the financial results of the alternative supply chain strategies just examined.

From Figure 5.17, it is evident that CLGN's profit margin will be increased the greatest amount by utilizing a supply chain alternative that reduces transportation costs. This is to be expected, because transportation cost is a larger percentage of sales than the other two supply chain functional areas: 4.00 percent of sales versus 1.0 percent and 2.0 percent for warehousing and inventory, respectively. If the cost to CLGN to realize a 10 percent reduction in these functional areas is the same, it is prudent for Lauren Fishbay to dedicate her resources and efforts to realizing a reduction in transportation costs.

The largest increase in ROA was generated by the transportation alternative. However, the inventory reduction alternative increased ROA by almost the same amount: 7.49 percent versus 7.42 percent. The financial benefit of an inventory reduction is twofold: (1) a reduction in the inventory carrying cost and (2) a reduction in assets. Annual inventory turns are increased with the inventory reduction strategy, requiring CLGN to utilize less capital for inventory and making more capital available for other uses in the organization. Thus, an inventory reduction strategy has a double effect on ROA by increasing profits and reducing assets deployed.

Another methodology available to perform the same financial analysis is the **strategic profit model (SPM).** The SPM makes the same calculations that were made in the spreadsheet analysis. Figure 5.18 contains the SPM for CLGN for 2007 operations and the 10 percent transportation cost reduction.

| Figure 5.14 | Financial Impact of a 10 Percent Reduction in Transportation Cost |

	SYMBOL	CLGN, 2007 $(000)	TRANSPORTATION COST REDUCED 10 PERCENT
Sales	S	$150,000	$150,000
Cost of goods sold	CGS	80,000	80,000
Gross margin	GM = S − CGS	$ 70,000	$ 70,000
Transportation	TC	$ 6,000	$ 5,400
Warehousing	WC	1,500	1,500
Inventory carrying	IC = IN × W	3,000	3,000
Other operating cost	OOC	30,000	30,000
Total operating cost	TOC	$ 40,500	$ 39,900
Earnings before interest and taxes	EBIT	$ 29,500	$ 30,100
Interest	INT	$ 12,000	$ 12,000
Taxes	TX	7,000	7,240
Net income	NI	$ 10,500	$ 10,860
Asset Deployment			
Inventory	IN	$ 10,000	$ 10,000
Accounts receivable	AR	30,000	30,000
Cash	CA	15,000	15,000
Fixed assets	FA	90,000	90,000
Total assets	TA	$145,000	$145,000
Ratio Analysis			
Profit margin	NI/S	7.00%	7.24%
Return on assets	NI/TA	7.24%	7.49%
Inventory turns/year	CGS/IN	8.00	8.00
Transportation as percentage of sales	TC/S	4.00%	3.60%
Warehousing as percentage of sales	WC/S	1.00%	1.00%
Inventory carrying as percentage of sales	IC/S	2.00%	2.00%

The SPM shows the same results as those calculated in Figure 5.14. Two ratios were added to the SPM—asset turnover and return on equity. **Asset turnover** is the ratio of sales to total assets and indicates how the organization is utilizing its assets in relation to sales. **Return on equity** indicates the return the stockholders are realizing on their

Figure 5.15	Financial Impact of a 10 Percent Reduction in Warehousing Costs

	SYMBOL	CLGN, 2007 $(000)	WAREHOUSING COST REDUCED 10 PERCENT
Sales	S	$150,000	$150,000
Cost of goods sold	CGS	80,000	80,000
Gross margin	GM = S – CGS	$ 70,000	$ 70,000
Transportation	TC	$ 6,000	$ 6,000
Warehousing	WC	1,500	1,350
Inventory carrying	IC = IN × W	3,000	3,000
Other operating cost	OOC	30,000	30,000
Total operating cost	TOC	$ 40,500	$ 40,350
Earnings before interest and taxes	EBIT	$ 29,500	$ 29,650
Interest	INT	$ 12,000	$ 12,000
Taxes	TX	7,000	7,060
Net income	NI	$ 10,500	$ 10,590
Asset Deployment			
Inventory	IN	$ 10,000	$ 10,000
Accounts receivable	AR	30,000	30,000
Cash	CA	15,000	15,000
Fixed assets	FA	90,000	90,000
Total assets	TA	$145,000	$145,000
Ratio Analysis			
Profit margin	NI/S	7.00%	7.06%
Return on assets	NI/TA	7.24%	7.30%
Inventory turns/year	CGS/IN	8.00	8.00
Transportation as percentage of sales	TC/S	4.00%	4.00%
Warehousing as percentage of sales	WC/S	1.00%	0.90%
Inventory carrying as percentage of sales	IC/S	2.00%	2.00%

equity in the organization. Asset turnover was 103 percent for both scenarios, but return on equity increased from 23.33 percent ($10,500/$45,000) for the CLGN 2007 scenario to 24.13 percent ($10,860/$45,000) with the reduced transportation cost scenario.

Figure 5.16	Financial Impact of a 10 Percent Reduction in Inventory

	SYMBOL	CLGN, 2007 $(000)	AVERAGE INVENTORY REDUCED BY 10 PERCENT
Sales	S	$150,000	$150,000
Cost of goods sold	CGS	80,000	80,000
Gross margin	$GM = S - CGS$	$ 70,000	$ 70,000
Transportation	TC	$ 6,000	$ 6,000
Warehousing	WC	1,500	1,500
Inventory carrying	$IC = IN \times W$	3,000	2,700
Other operating cost	OOC	30,000	30,000
Total operating cost	TOC	$ 40,500	$ 40,200
Earnings before interest and taxes	$EBIT$	$ 29,500	$ 29,800
Interest	INT	$ 12,000	$ 12,000
Taxes	TX	7,000	7,120
Net income	NI	$ 10,500	$ 10,680
Asset Deployment			
Inventory	IN	$ 10,000	$ 9,000
Accounts receivable	AR	30,000	30,000
Cash	CA	15,000	15,000
Fixed assets	FA	90,000	90,000
Total assets	TA	$145,000	$144,000
Ratio Analysis			
Profit margin	NI/S	7.00%	7.12%
Return on assets	NI/TA	7.24%	7.42%
Inventory turns/year	CGS/IN	8.00	8.89
Transportation as percentage of sales	TC/S	4.00%	4.00%
Warehousing as percentage of sales	WC/S	1.00%	1.00%
Inventory carrying as percentage of sales	IC/S	2.00%	1.80%

| Figure 5.17 | Comparison of Supply Chain Alternatives | | | |

RATIO ANALYSIS	CLGN, 2007 $(000)	TRANSPORTATION COST REDUCED 10 PERCENT	WAREHOUSING COST REDUCED 10 PERCENT	INVENTORY REDUCED 10 PERCENT
Profit margin	7.00%	7.24%	7.06%	7.12%
Return on assets	7.24%	7.49%	7.30%	7.42%
Inventory turns/year	8.00	8.00	8.00	8.89
Transportation as percentage of sales	4.00%	3.60%	4.00%	4.00%
Warehousing as percentage of sales	1.00%	1.00%	0.90%	1.00%
Inventory carrying as percentage of sales	2.00%	2.00%	2.00%	1.80%

The preceding analysis and its conclusion examine only the returns from the alternative actions. The risks associated with each must also be considered. The conclusions that *cannot* be made from the preceding analysis are those regarding the risks associated with the added cost necessary to realize the functional cost reductions, the additional capital required to achieve the reduction, and the service implications accompanying the changes. For example, to accomplish the transportation cost reduction, CLGN might have to revert to a mode of transportation that is slower. This could have a negative impact on customer satisfaction and result in lower sales. Or, the warehouse cost reduction might require the expenditure of $500,000 for automated materials handling equipment that increases the assets deployed and reduces the ROA.

The preceding issues can be added to the financial analysis presented. For example, the added cost associated with reengineering the warehouse or any additional investment in fixed warehouse assets such as facilities or equipment can be added to the financial analysis along with the resulting warehouse cost savings.

Given the financial analysis and the preceding caveats, CLGN has a better insight into the supply chain areas that will result in the greatest improvement in profitability and the accompanying risks (costs). The next section addresses the financial implications of CLGN's supply chain service failures.

Supply Chain Service Financial Implications

As noted in the Supply Chain Profile, CLGN Book Distributors.com has experienced service failures in the areas of **on-time deliveries** and **order fill rates.** The 95 percent on-time delivery rate means that only 95 percent of CLGN orders are delivered when promised (on-time delivery). Also, only 97 percent of the orders are filled correctly. The alternative view of this service is that 5 percent of the orders are delivered after the promised delivery date and 3 percent of the orders are filled incorrectly.

The results of these supply chain service failures are added to the cost to correct the problem and lost sales. Figure 5.19 shows the methodology for determining the cost of service failures. When supply chain service failures occur, a portion of the customers

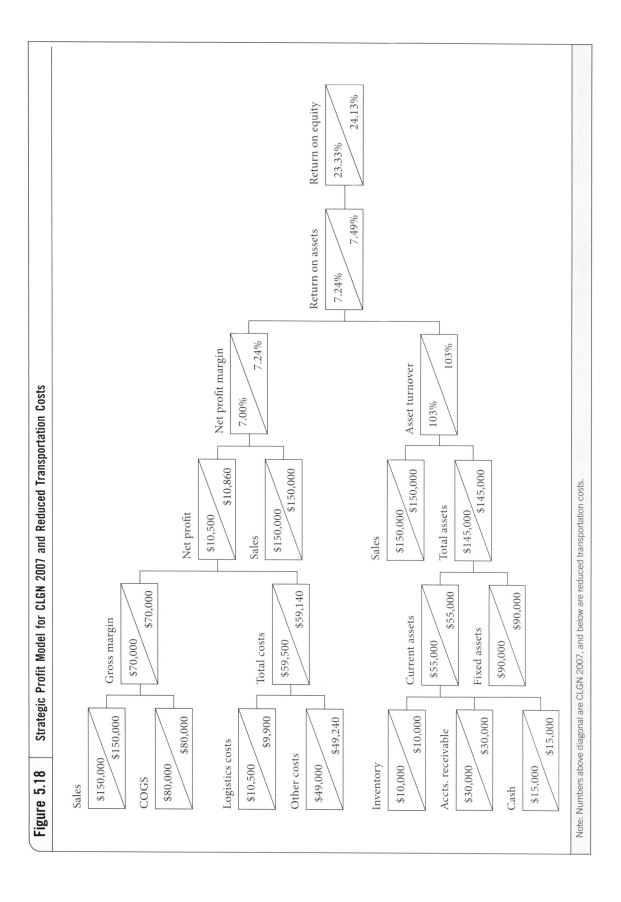

Figure 5.18   Strategic Profit Model for CLGN 2007 and Reduced Transportation Costs

Note: Numbers above diagonal are CLGN 2007, and below are reduced transportation costs.

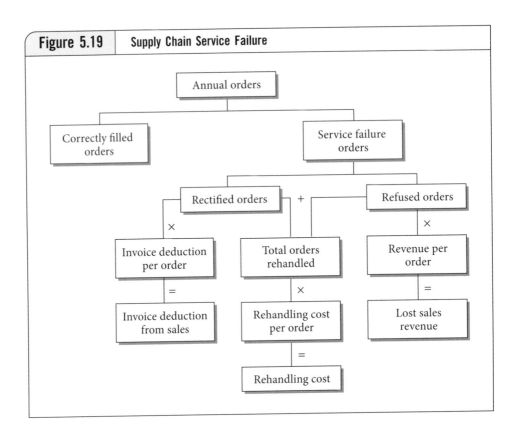

Figure 5.19 | **Supply Chain Service Failure**

experiencing the service failure will request that the orders be corrected and the others will refuse the orders. The refused orders represent lost sales revenue (refused orders times revenue per order) that must be deducted from total sales. For the rectified orders, the customers might request an invoice deduction to compensate them for any inconvenience or added costs. Finally, the seller incurs a rehandling cost associated with correcting the order such as reshipping the correct items and returning the incorrect and refused items (rectified orders plus refused orders times rehandling cost per order).

Referring to the data provided in the Supply Chain Profile for CLGN's on-time delivery and order fill rates, the financial impact of improving these two supply chain service metrics is given in Figures 5.20 and 5.21. Assume that there are 1.5 million orders for the year, the average revenue per order is $100, and the cost of goods per order is $53.33. Also, the lost sales rate for on-time delivery failure is 10 percent and, for order fill failures, 20 percent. The rehandling charge is $20 per rectified and refused order, and the invoice deduction is $10 per rectified order. The costs and assets are those provided in the Supply Chain Profile and used in the previous section. This pertinent information is contained within the boxed area of the spreadsheets in Figures 5.20 and 5.21.

Examining Figure 5.20, note that the upper portion of the spreadsheet analysis determines the number of service failure orders, lost sales orders, rectified orders, and net orders sold. (The symbols provided in the second column are to assist the reader in creating the spreadsheet analysis.) At the 95 percent on-time delivery rate, 1,425,000 are delivered on time (0.95 × 1,500,000 total orders) and 75,000 orders are delivered late (service failures). Of the 75,000 late orders, the customers will decline 7,500 (10%) and CLGN will lose sales on these orders, or $750,000 ($100 revenue per order × 7,500 lost

Figure 5.20 — Financial Impact of Improving On-Time Delivery

	SYMBOL	ON-TIME RATE 55%	ON-TIME RATE 96%	INPUT DATA		95%	96%
Annual orders	AO	1,500,000	1,500,000	%CF		95%	96%
Orders filled correctly	OFC = AO × %CF	1,425,000	1,440,000	Annual orders		1,500,000	1,500,000
Service failure orders	SF = AO − OFC	75,000	60,000	SP = Revenue/order	$ 100	$ 100
Lost sales orders	LS = SF × LSR	7,500	6,000	CG = Cost of goods/order	$ 53.33	$ 53.33
Rectified orders	RO = SF − LS	67,500	54,000	Lost sales rate		10%	10%
Net orders sold	NOS = AO − LS	1,492,500	1,494,000	RCO = Rehandling cost/order	$ 20	$ 20
Sales	S = SP × AO	$150,000,000	$150,000,000	IDR = Invoice deduction rate	$ 10	$ 10
Less: Invoice deduction	ID = IDR × RO	$ 675,000	$ 540,000	Transportation cost	$ 6,000,000	$ 6,600,000
Lost sales revenue	LSR = LS × SP	$ 750,000	$ 600,000	Warehousing cost	$ 1,500,000	$ 1,500,000
Net sales	NS = S − ID − LSR	$148,575,000	$148,860,000	Interest cost	$ 3,000,000	$ 3,000,000
Cost of goods sold	CGS = CG × (NOS)	$ 79,595,025	$ 79,675,020	Other operating cost	$30,000,000	$30,000,000
Gross margin (GM)	GM = NS − CGS	$ 68,979,975	$ 69,184,980	Inventory	$10,000,000	$10,000,000
Rehandling cost	RC = RCO × SF	$ 1,500,000	$ 1,200,000	Cash	$15,000,000	$15,000,000
Transportation	TC	$ 6,000,000	$ 6,600,000	Accounts receivable	$30,000,000	$30,000,000
Warehousing	WC	$ 1,500,000	$ 1,500,000	Fixed assets	$90,000,000	$90,000,000
Inventory carrying	IC = IN × W	$ 3,000,000	$ 3,000,000	W = Inventory carrying rate		30%	30%
Other operating cost	OOC	$ 30,000,000	$ 30,000,000				
Total operating cost	TOC	$ 42,000,000	$ 42,300				
Earnings before interest and taxes	EBIT = GM − TOC	$ 26,979,975	$ 26,884,980				
Interest	INT	$ 3,000,000	$ 3,000,000				
Tax (40% × (EBIT − INT))	TX	$ 9,591,990	$ 9,553,992				
Net income	NI = EBIT − INT − TX	$ 14,387,985	$ 14,330,988				
Profit increase of 1% improvement			($56,997)				

Figure 5.21 Financial Impact of Improving Order Fill Rate

	SYMBOL	ORDER FILL RATE 97%	ORDER FILL RATE 98%	INPUT DATA	97%	98%
Annual orders	AO	1,500,000	1,500,000	%CF	97%	98%
Orders filled correctly	$OFC = AO \times \%CF$	1,455,000	1,470,000	Annual orders	1,500,000	1,500,000
Service failure orders	$SF = AO - OFC$	45,000	30,000	SP = Revenue/order	$ 100	$ 100
Lost sales orders	$LS = SF \times LSR$	9,000	6,000	CG = Cost of goods/order	$ 53.33	$ 53.33
Rectified orders	$RO = SF - LS$	36,000	24,000	Lost sales rate	20%	20%
Net orders sold	$NOS = AO - LS$	1,491,000	1,494,000	RCO = Rehandling cost/order	$ 20	$ 20
Sales	$S = SP \times AO$	$150,000,000	$150,000,000	IDR = Invoice deduction rate	$ 10	$ 10
Less: Invoice deduction	$ID = IDR \times RO$	$ 360,000	$ 240,000	Transportation cost	$ 6,000,000	$ 6,000,000
Lost sales revenue	$LSR = LS \times SP$	$ 900,000	$ 600,000	Warehousing cost	$ 1,500,000	$ 1,600,000
Net sales	$NS = S - ID - LSR$	$148,740,000	$149,160,000	Interest cost	$ 3,000,000	$ 3,000,000
Cost of goods sold	$CGS = CG \times (NOS)$	$ 79,515,030	$ 79,675,020	Other operating cost	$30,000,000	$30,000,000
Gross margin (GM)	$GM = NS - CGS$	$ 69,224,970	$ 69,484,980	Inventory	$10,000,000	$10,000,000
Rehandling cost	$RC = RCO \times SF$	$ 900,000	$ 600,000	Cash	$15,000,000	$15,000,000
Transportation	TC	$ 6,000,000	$ 6,000,000	Accounts receivable	$30,000,000	$30,000,000
Warehousing	WC	$ 1,500,000	$ 1,600,000	Fixed assets	$90,000,000	$90,000,000
Inventory carrying	$IC = IN \times W$	$ 3,000,000	$ 3,000,000	W = Inventory carrying rate	30%	30%
Other operating cost	OOC	$ 30,000,000	$ 30,000,000			
Total operating cost	TOC	$ 41,400,000	$ 41,200,000			
Earnings before interest and taxes	$EBIT = GM - TOC$	$ 27,824,970	$ 28,284,980			
Interest	INT	$ 3,000,000	$ 3,000,000			
Tax (40% × (EBIT − INT))	TX	$ 9,929,988	$ 10,113,992			
Net income	$NI = EBIT - INT - TX$	$ 14,894,982	$ 15,170,988			
Profit increase of 1% improvement			$ 276,006			

Supply Chain Technology	*Metrics for Measuring Your Software's Success*

Metrics are not only keeping tabs on internal and supplier performance, but they are also proving useful for tracking performance of the transportation management systems (TMS) and warehouse management systems (WMS) software itself. "An example of this trend," says Adrian Gonzalez, director of ARC Advisory Group's Logistics Executive Council, "is Descartes Systems Group's "Descartes Challenge" offer for potential customers to "test drive" its software."

"Customers who take the Descartes Challenge pay only for the implementation, then pay for the solution itself later, once its value has been proven," explains Gonzalez. "The measurements used to evaluate the software's performance are different than those for supplier performance, but the analogy is valid," he says.

"Software vendors are saying, 'Here are certain metrics that we're going to put in place to prove our value,'" says Gonzalez, who points to cost reduction and delivery improvements as two areas where vendors are vying to prove themselves. Some vendors also are including payment-for-performance "milestones" in their customer agreements. When those predetermined improvements, which are tracked and monitored via a metrics-based system, have been attained, the customer shells out another installment payment.

"Expect to see more vendors using these metrics-based models in the future," forecasts Gonzalez, who believes the pay-for-performance approach will gain popularity among shippers. "The metrics help paint the 'before and after' picture and assist the vendor and the user in getting to that goal," he says. "That in turn triggers the customer's decision on whether they want to implement the system or not."

Source: Bridget McRea, "Metrics Take Center Stage," *Logistics Management* (January 2006): p. 42. Reproduced by permission.

orders). The rehandling cost is $1,500,000 [$20 per order × 75,000 orders (rectified plus refused)], and invoice deduction is $675,000 ($10 per order × 67,500 orders).

In this example, the 1 percent improvement in on-time delivery (from 95% to 96%) results in net income falling by $56,997. The improved on-time delivery reduces invoice deductions by $135,000 and rehandling cost by $300,000, or a total cost saving of $535,000. However, to realize this cost saving of $535,000, a transportation cost increase of 10 percent or $600,000 is necessary. Since the net income is reduced by $56,997 with the proposed strategy to switch to second-day ground delivery service, CLGN will probably not consider this on-time delivery improvement option.

Examination of Figure 5.21 shows that the $100,000 cost to provide training to the warehouse personnel will improve the order fill rate from 97 percent to 98 percent and result in an increase in net income of $276,006. The combined savings of $420,000 (rehandling cost saving of $300,000 and invoice deductions saving of $120,000) are greater than the additional training cost of $100,000.

Given the two options—improve on-time delivery or order fill rate—CLGN would be advised to implement the order fill improvement strategy.

Figure 5.22 | **Strategic Profit Model for On-Time Delivery Improvement**

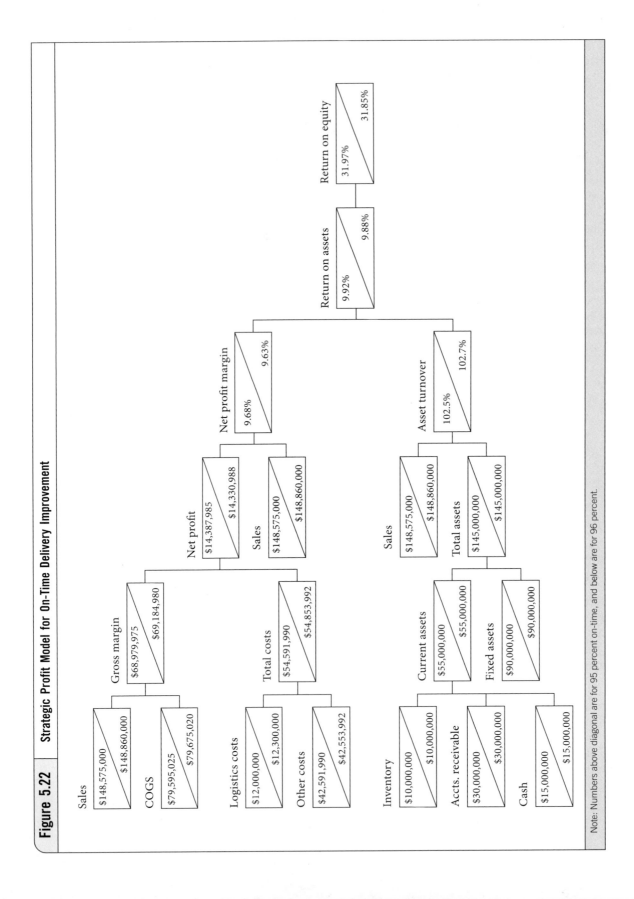

Note: Numbers above diagonal are for 95 percent on-time, and below are for 96 percent.

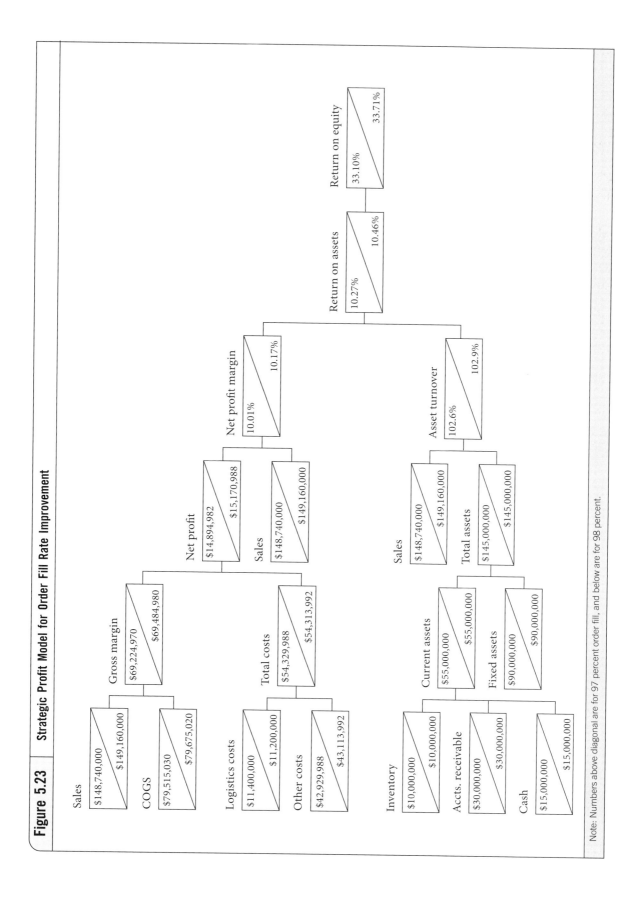

Figure 5.23   Strategic Profit Model for Order Fill Rate Improvement

Note: Numbers above diagonal are for 97 percent order fill, and below are for 98 percent.

The SPM for these two alternatives are given in Figures 5.22 and 5.23. The profit margin, ROA, and return on stockholders' equity are greater with the order fill rate improvement strategy than with the on-time delivery improvement strategy. For the order fill rate improvement from 97 percent to 98 percent, the ROE increases to 33.71 percent from 33.10 percent, the profit margin increases to 10.17 percent from 10.01 percent, and the ROA increases to 10.46 percent from 10.27 percent.

The financial goal for supply chain management is to increase return to stockholders. Examining alternative courses of action in light of the bottom-line impact (net income) and resultant ROE accomplishes this goal.

SUMMARY

- Performance measurement for logistics systems and, especially, for supply chains is necessary but challenging because of their complexity and scope.

- Certain characteristics should be incorporated into good metrics—be quantitative, be easy to understand, involve employee input, and have economies of effort.

- Important guidelines for metric development for logistics and supply chains include consistency with corporate strategy, focus on customer needs, careful selection and prioritization of metrics, focus on processes, use of a balanced approach, and use of technology to improve measurement effectiveness.

- There are four principal categories for performance metrics: time, quality, cost, and miscellaneous or support. Another classification for logistics and supply chains suggests the following categories for metrics: operations cost, service, revenue or value, and channel satisfaction.

- The equivalent sales increase for supply chain cost saving is found by dividing the cost saving by the organization's profit margin.

- Supply chain management impacts ROA via decisions regarding channel structure management, inventory management, order management, and transportation management.

- Alternative supply chain decisions should be made in light of the financial implications to net income, ROA, and ROE.

- The SPM shows the relationship of sales, costs, assets, and equity; it can trace the financial impact of a change in any one of these financial elements.

- Supply chain service failures result in lost sales and rehandling costs. The financial impact of modifications to supply chain service can be analyzed using the SPM.

STUDY QUESTIONS

1. "Performance measurement for logistics managers is relatively recent. Their focus was previously directed toward other managerial activities." Do you agree or disagree with these statements? Explain your position.

2. What role should employees, in general, play in the development of performance metrics? Why is this role important?

3. "Metrics must focus upon customer needs and expectations." Explain the meaning of this statement. Why have customers become more important for performance measurement? What role, if any, should customers play in developing supply chain metrics?

4. It is generally recognized that organizations go through several phases on the path to developing appropriate supply chain metrics. Discuss the stages of supply development for supply chain metrics. Choose which of the stages of evolution you think would be most challenging for an organization. Explain your choice.

5. Using a spreadsheet computer software program, construct a supply chain finance model and calculate the profit margin; ROA; inventory turns; and transportation, warehousing, and inventory costs as a percentage of revenue for the following:

   Sales = $200,000,000

   Transportation cost = $7,000,000

   Warehousing cost = $1,600,000

Inventory carrying cost = 28%

Cost of goods sold = $70,000,000

Other operating costs = $65,000,000

Average inventory = $10,000,000

Accounts receivable = $30,000,000

Cash = $15,000,000

Net fixed assets = $90,000,000

Interest = $10,000,000

Taxes = 40% of (EBIT – Interest)

Current liabilities = $65,000,000

Long-term liabilities = $35,000,000

Stockholders' equity = $45,000,000

6. Using the supply chain finance model developed for Study Question 5, calculate the impact on profit margin; ROA; inventory turns; and transportation, warehousing, and inventory costs as a percentage of revenue for the following scenarios:

Transportation costs increase = 15%

Warehousing costs increase = 15%

Average inventory increase = 15%

Warehousing is outsourced with:

Net fixed assets reduced = 15%

Inventory reduced = 5%

Warehousing costs = $0

Outsourcing provider costs = $1,200,000

7. Develop a strategic model to depict the scenarios given in Study Questions 5 and 6.

8. Construct a financial model to determine the redelivery/rehandling cost, lost sales, invoice deduction cost, and net income for the following:

a. On-time delivery increases from 98 percent to 99 percent with a 2 percent increase in transportation cost.
b. Order fill rate decreases from 99 percent to 98 percent with operating cost remaining constant.

Selling price/order = $150/order

Gross profit/order = $35/order

Lost sales rate:

On-time delivery failure = 20%

Order fill failure = 25%

Annual orders = 200,000

Rehandling cost $=$ \$100/order

Invoice deduction/service failure $=$ \$75/order

Transportation cost $=$ \$1,000,000

Average inventory $=$ \$1,000,000

Interest cost $=$ \$1,500,000

Inventory carrying cost rate $=$ 25%/\$/yr.

Warehousing cost $=$ \$750,000

Other operating cost $=$ \$500,000

Cash $=$ \$3,000,000

Accounts receivable $=$ \$4,000,000

Fixed assets $=$ \$30,000,000

NOTES

1. Thomas S. Davis, Center for Supply Chain Research, Penn State University (2007).

2. Robert A. Novack and Thomas S. Davis, "Developing a Supply Chain Performance Metrics Program," unpublished research, Center for Supply Chain Research, Penn State University (2007).

3. Ibid.

4. Ibid.

5. Ibid.

6. Ibid.

7. Ibid.

8. Robert A. Novack and Douglas J. Thomas, "The Challenges of Implementing the Perfect Order Concept," *Transportation Journal*, Vol. 43, No. 1 (Winter 2004): 5–16.

9. SCOR Model (Pittsburgh, PA: The Supply Chain Council, 2005): 297.

CASE 5.1

CPDW

Harry Groves, CEO of Central PA Distribution and Warehouse (CPDW), had just called the monthly meeting of the board of directors of CPDW to order. Harry looked tired and grim, thought Joe Zimmerman (a local entrepreneur and board member). Harry's opening statement gave reason for the body language. CPDW had another dismal month that was delineated in the monthly financial statements and Harry's description of monthly activities.

Company Background

CPDW is located in Milroy, Pennsylvania, adjacent to an interchange on a major east-west roadway in central Pennsylvania. The company was founded five years ago by a group of individuals who owned local businesses or held management positions in local companies. The board members were all limited partners in the venture so they had a very special interest in the financial viability of the organization.

The partners, under the leadership of Harry Groves, had purchased a building (120,000 square feet) and parcel of land (32.6 acres) from the Sanyo Corporation. The building had been used primarily as a manufacturing facility by Sanyo. The partners purchased the building with the express purpose of utilizing it as a distribution facility for providing logistics services for companies within central Pennsylvania. While the building was not ideal for storage because of the ceiling height, the partners believed that it was versatile enough to be used for various logistics activities including repackaging, order fulfillment, reverse logistics, etc.

The paradox of the situation was that the facility was completely filled with pallet loads of glass from a local glass manufacturer. In fact, the original estimate on useable storage space, excluding aisles, offices, restrooms, etc., was 99,500 square feet. However, Jon Parton, COO of the company, had pushed and squeezed until they were utilizing 110,000 square feet.

Board Meeting

After reviewing the usage rate, Jay Lenard asked Harry for some additional insight into their situation. He prefaced his question with the comment, "I thought that we wanted to fill the facility and in doing so, we would be profitable. When I look at square foot utilization, which I thought was our best performance metric, I'm pleased, but you are telling us that this is a problem. I just don't understand our financial situation based on this metric."

Harry let out a sigh and said, "Jay, I really wish it was that easy. I have come to realize that our base metric for pricing square feet of space utilized is too narrow. With our current situation, even though we are using more square feet than I thought we had available, thanks to Jon, we are not breaking even. When the building is full and nothing is moving in or out, we are in trouble. We need to change our metrics and align them with a new pricing strategy."

CASE QUESTIONS

1. Describe the nature of CPDW's problem.

2. What metrics would you recommend that CPDW use to enhance its pricing strategy? Provide a rationale for your recommendations.

CASE 5.2

DVD4LESS.com

DVD4LESS.com is one of the many new firms that have a presence on the Web. It specializes in manufacturing and selling one type of high-end DVD player. By purchasing large volumes from a small number of suppliers, it receives a significant quantity discount. This reduced cost is passed on to its customer. DVD4LESS.com manages to sell its DVD player for $200 less than all of its high-end competitors, thereby creating its competitive advantage.

DVD4LESS.com receives 112,000 orders for DVD players annually. Each DVD player sells for $500, of which $200 is retained as gross profit. Last year, it filled 97 percent of all orders correctly. Of the orders filled incorrectly, DVD4LESS.com estimates that 20 percent of the customers cancel the order and the remainder will accept a second shipment, which results in a rehandling cost of $20 per order. To maintain customer goodwill, the firm gives a $35 invoice reduction for all units rehandled.

DVD4LESS.com pays $1,950,000 annually for the transportation of its materials and delivery of its products. Its warehousing costs average $1,460,000 annually for the storage of its materials. DVD4LESS.com has $30 million of debt outstanding at an annual interest rate of 10 percent. The total cost for all selling and general administrative expenses (other operating costs) comes to $750,000, and $50,000 is held in cash at all times.

DVD4LESS.com has an average inventory of $5 million. This large inventory is partially attributed to its purchasing policy and also to its inventory management system. The inventory carrying cost rate is estimated at 25 percent of the average inventory value per year. Its accounts receivable averages $250,000 throughout the year primarily due to sales to medium-sized retailers. DVD4LESS.com has a large fixed asset base. It is comprised of land, the manufacturing facility, machinery, and various administrative offices that are valued at $64 million.

DVD4LESS.com has explored a variety of options to improve its correct order fill rate. It is also interested in lowering its average inventory to improve its overall profitability. After weeks of presentations and heated debates, the decision is made to outsource its warehousing operations and inventory management. Many third-party logistics providers bid for the contract; in the end, it is awarded to Basileo Logistics for an annual cost of $500,000 (this is classified as other operating cost). By outsourcing, DVD4LESS.com manages to save $760,000 in warehousing expenses, reduces its average inventory by 30 percent, and now meets its 99 percent correct order fill rate. All other costs remain the same. The tax rate is 40 percent.

CASE QUESTIONS

As the supply chain management analyst at DVD4LESS.com:

1. Calculate the net savings of the outsourcing of the warehousing and inventory management to Basileo Logistics.

2. Develop a strategic profit model of both the old system and the modified system of reflecting the required adjustments. DVD4LESS.corn's net worth is $30 million.

APPENDIX 5A
Financial Terms

Account receivable A current asset showing the amount of sales currently owed by a customer.

Balance sheet A snapshot of everything the company owes and owns at the end of the financial year in question.

Cash cycle Time between payment of inventory and collection of cash from receivables.

Cash flow statement Shows cash receipts and payments from all company financial activities; earnings before interest, taxes, depreciation, and amortization (EBITDA).

Cost of goods sold Total cost of the goods sold to customers during the period.

Cost of lost sales The short-run forgone profit associated with a stockout.

Current assets Cash and other assets that will be converted into cash during one operating cycle.

Current liabilities An obligation that must be paid during the normal operating cycle, usually one year.

Current ratio Current assets divided by current liabilities; measures company's ability to pay short-term debt with assets easily converted to cash.

Debt-to-equity ratio Long-term debt divided by shareholders' equity.

Earnings before interest and taxes (EBIT) Sales minus cost of goods sold and operating costs.

Earnings per share Net earnings divided by average number of shares outstanding.

Gross margin Sales minus cost of goods sold.

Income statement Summarizes revenues and expenses, reporting the net income or loss for a specific accounting period.

Inventory carrying cost The annual cost of holding inventory; the value of the average inventory times the inventory carrying cost rate (W).

Inventory carrying cost rate (W) The cost of holding $1 of inventory for one year, usually expressed as a percentage; includes cost of capital, risk, item servicing, and storage space.

Inventory turns Cost of goods sold divided by average inventory.

Liquidity ratio Cash flow from operations divided by current liabilities; measures short-term cash available to pay current liabilities.

Net income (or loss) Final result of all revenue and expense items for a period; sales minus cost of goods sold, operating costs, interest, and taxes.

Operating expense Every expense other than cost of goods sold, depreciation, interest, and income tax.

Operating ratio Percentage of revenues used for operations; operating expenses divided by operating income.

Order-to-cash cycle Time between receiving customer orders and collection of receivables.

Profit margin Net income divided by sales.

Return on assets Net income divided by total assets.

Return on equity Net income divided by average stockholders' equity.

Shareholder's equity The difference between the value of all the things owned by the company and the value of all the things owed by the company; the investment made by the stockholders at the time the stock was originally issued plus all past earnings that have not been paid out in dividends; sum total of shareholders' investment in a company since it was formed, minus its liabilities.

Working capital Current assets minus current liabilities; working capital finances the business by converting goods and services to cash.

Chapter 6

SUPPLY CHAIN TECHNOLOGY—MANAGING INFORMATION FLOWS

Learning Objectives

After reading this chapter, you should be able to do the following:

- Appreciate the overall importance of information to supply chain management.
- Understand the role of information technology in the supply chain.
- Explain the key components of an integrated supply chain information system.
- Describe and differentiate between the primary types of supply chain solutions and their capabilities.
- Discuss the critical issues in technology selection and implementation processes.
- Recognize the role of emerging technologies for improving supply chain information management.

Supply Chain Profile   *Respect the Bottom Line*

Fast-food retail chain Wendy's International, Inc., is implementing new technology tools that allow inventory managers to look at individual restaurants.

"We're trying to get as granular as possible," states Tony Scherer, director of supply chain management with Wendy's, "but mostly we're looking at tools to forecast demand in an area of 40 to 50 stores. Overall, our total volume might be predictable, but different regions vary greatly. For example, while ski season heats up in the Rockies, eastern markets tend to slow down in colder weather. Regional volume differences make it difficult to do a general forecast, but we can predict seasonality and note different patterns for different locations."

To date, Scherer's team has rolled out a restaurant forecasting tool to about 20 percent of the chain's 6,000 stores. The tool allows individual stores to receive a weekly forecast based on historic sales data. It forecasts volume of sales per product every half hour throughout each day. While the original purpose of the forecasting tool was to better plan labor needs, it has allowed the fast-food chain to also reduce safety stock in the store and the warehouse.

Stores receive three deliveries per week and those on the new system typically maintain eight hours of safety stock on perishable items. However, the majority of stores do not have the automated ordering system. Those stores tend to hold two to three days safety stock on perishables.

"Too much inventory costs us money. We try to operate restaurants as tightly as manufacturers operate under just-in-time programs," Scherer states. "By implementing the technology across our network, we can greatly reduce safety stock."

To minimize safety stock, the forecasting program generates a suggested order for the manager that, 90 percent of the time, the manager uses as is. However, if an individual store manager knows that, say, a local high school football game will mean a surge in business, they can alter the order.

Another piece of Wendy's' technology tool—a collaborative program—is in the testing stage. It supplies certain supply chain metrics upstream to suppliers and distributors. "We take sales data from our 6,000 restaurants and load them into a database to create 18-month forecasts for suppliers. The forecast can be to the individual store level but more commonly it's for all stores served by a distributor," says Scherer.

Wendy's' marketing group plugs factors into the forecast such as promotions past and future, holidays, and seasonality. In the pilot, forecast accuracy is running about 96 percent in the shorter time frames, a major improvement over the 60–65 percent accuracy suppliers and distributors were forecasting on their own. On some items, inventory forecasts are 80 percent accurate as far as 18 months out.

"With a more accurate forecast, suppliers and distributors can plan inventory more closely. Those in the pilot can plan several months in the future to avoid out of stocks," Scherer adds. "To avoid stock outs, suppliers not in the system now carry a month worth of inventory. With our new collaborative program, they could reduce that to a week or even a half week on many items. This investment should allow us to remove enough supply chain cost to give us a competitive edge," he concludes.

Source: Adapted from Helen Richardson, "Respect the Bottom Line," *Logistics Today* (February 2006): 23–24. Reprinted with permission.

Introduction

Knowledge is essential for supply chain success. Information, along with materials and money, must readily flow across the supply chain to enable the planning, execution, and evaluation of key functions. Each participant in the supply chain needs relevant information to make effective forecasts and operational decisions as highlighted by the Supply Chain Profile. For example, timely, accurate information regarding the demand for Apple iPods is needed by retailers to order more products, by Apple to schedule more production and purchase needed components from suppliers, and by contract manufacturers to assemble additional iPods. If each organization in the supply chain had to operate without this sales information, it would be very difficult to maintain a proper flow of the right quantities of the right components and models. A shortage of hot sellers and overage of unwanted models would be the consequence of such poor information flows.

Fortunately, existing supply chain information technologies support timely, cost-efficient sharing of information between suppliers, manufacturers, intermediaries, logistics services providers, and customers. Organizations recognize the potential value of these tools and are investing vast sums of money to collect, analyze, and make more effective use of supply chain information. ARC Advisory Group estimates that global spending on supply chain management (SCM) software applications exceeded $5.5 billion in 2005 and will grow to $8.3 billion by 2010.[1] Additional investments are being made in radio-frequency identification (RFID) and other hardware.

The changing nature of supply chains underlies the need for information and the investment in technology. As supply chains become more global, complex, and demand driven, information technologies must evolve. Staying ahead of the evolutionary curve requires companies to continually pursue the next level of supply chain performance and adopt relevant information technologies.[2] "Supply chain organizations are under intense pressure to meet demands for greater customer intimacy, lower cost of goods sold, and increased global business processes," says Beth Enslow, senior vice president of research for Aberdeen Group. "To succeed, these organizations are identifying that they need to change their supply chain technology footprints."[3]

This chapter focuses on the role of information and technology in the supply chain. It is intended to introduce key information issues and tools that will be addressed in further detail throughout the book. We have divided the chapter into five sections that address the following topics: the role of information in SCM, a supply chain information system framework, software solutions, technology selection, and emerging information tools. As you will learn, effective technology for the management of information flows is vital for synchronizing supply chain processes that span companies and countries, meet customer requirements, and create responsive supply chains.

The Role of Information in the Supply Chain

It has been said that information is the lifeline of business, driving effective decisions and actions. It is especially critical to supply chain managers because their direct line of sight to supply chain processes is very limited. Information provides them with insights and visibility into the supply chain activities taking place at distant supplier and customer locations. This visibility of demand, customer orders, delivery status, inventory stock levels, and production schedules provides managers with the knowledge needed to

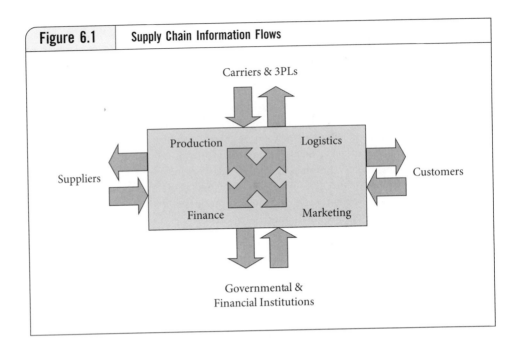

Figure 6.1   Supply Chain Information Flows

make effective situational assessments and develop appropriate responses. In contrast, limited awareness of external activity would leave the supply chain manager blind to the true situation and unable to make knowledge-driven decisions. Actions would be based on educated guesses with no guarantee of effective outcomes.

A wide variety of information is needed for a supply chain to perform as anticipated. As you read through this book, it will become evident just how important information is for both long-range and day-to-day decision making. Supply chain professionals require information from across the channel for strategic planning issues such as network design, tactical planning and collaboration with supply chain partners, and execution of key processes. This information must effectively flow within the organization and between key participants, as outlined in Figure 6.1, to ensure the timely flow and control of materials and money in the supply chain.

Information Requirements

Information quality is a critical characteristic of the knowledge flowing across the supply chain. If you think about it, the seven R's definition of logistics applies to information as much as products with some slight alterations—getting the right *information* to the right *partners,* in the right quantity, in the right *format,* at the right place, at the right time, and at the right cost. Change any "right" to "wrong" and the capabilities of the decision maker will decline. Thus, information quality is paramount to effective management of the supply chain.

To ensure that valuable, actionable knowledge readily flows across the supply chain, information must be accessible, relevant, accurate, timely, and transferable.

Accessible

Information must be available to supply chain managers who have a legitimate need for it, regardless of their location or employer. For example, Whirlpool supply chain managers need access to daily sales information at Lowe's stores to schedule delivery and installation of appliances. Obtaining needed information can be difficult because supply chain data often are dispersed among multiple locations on different information systems that are owned by external organizations. Technical issues must be addressed and trust built between the organizations sharing information.

Relevant

Supply chain managers must have pertinent information to make decisions. They must know what information is needed and be able to quickly acquire only that which is applicable to their current situation. The goal is to avoid being overwhelmed by extraneous data that are not useful to decision makers and waste their time. When a Toyota expeditor logs on to the FedEx Web site to track a critical delivery, he doesn't need to know about every Toyota shipment handled by FedEx that day. He wants to quickly assess the status of the one shipment in question and react accordingly.

Accurate

The information must be correct and depict reality; otherwise, it will be difficult to make appropriate decisions. Information inaccuracies can lead to inventory shortages, transportation delays, governmental penalties, and dissatisfied customers. For example, major retailers rely upon their checkout clerks to accurately scan each item sold because these scans drive the replenishment system. If a clerk scans one bottle of soda four times when a customer actually purchases four different flavors, the store-level inventory loses accuracy and eventually the wrong product will be replenished.

Timely

The information must be up to date and available in a reasonable timeframe. As supply chain managers attempt to synchronize activities, become leaner, and address problems before they become crises, they need the knowledge embedded in realtime data. Envision that a computer hardware manufacturer is experiencing quality problems and must postpone shipments of 200-gigabyte hard drives. If informed in a timely fashion, Dell could update its Web site so that customers could not configure computers with that model. The result would be no backlog of orders or unhappy customers.

Transferable

The final characteristic of information has multiple meanings. Just as we need translators to convert words from one language to another, supply chain managers need the ability to transfer supply chain data from one format to another to make it understandable and useful. Information also needs to be transferred quickly from one location to another to facilitate accessibility and timeliness. A paper-based supply chain cannot support these requirements or a demand-driven supply chain. Hence, information must reside in electronic formats that can be readily transmitted and converted via supply chain information technology.

Information Technology Capabilities

The value and importance of supply chain information technology is not lost on supply chain leaders. Study after study of executives reveals that organizations are putting more emphasis on information technology to help them become more competitive,

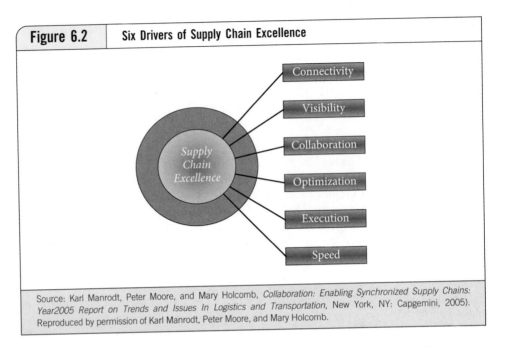

Figure 6.2 | **Six Drivers of Supply Chain Excellence**

Supply Chain Excellence

- Connectivity
- Visibility
- Collaboration
- Optimization
- Execution
- Speed

Source: Karl Manrodt, Peter Moore, and Mary Holcomb, *Collaboration: Enabling Synchronized Supply Chains: Year2005 Report on Trends and Issues In Logistics and Transportation*, New York, NY: Capgemini, 2005). Reproduced by permission of Karl Manrodt, Peter Moore, and Mary Holcomb.

innovative, and adaptive. Their efforts are not only well intended, but they also have a positive influence on supply chain performance. Recent research by Sanders and Premus found that information technology has a direct and positive impact on organizational performance, internal collaboration, and external collaboration.[4]

In their ongoing research regarding trends and issues in supply chain management, Capgemini, Georgia Southern University, and the University of Tennessee have identified six drivers of excellence that are found in adaptive enterprises. These drivers are identified in Figure 6.2. Information technology supports the pursuit of these six drivers, facilitating the evolution to highly coordinated, dynamically responsive supply chains. In their 2005 report, the authors recognize the link between information technology and excellence, stating: "firms that have real-time (or near real-time) information about products, customers, and order fulfillment across the supply chain are more effective and deliver customer service that surpasses their competition."[5]

Connectivity

Information technology is the primary focus of this driver. Geographically dispersed supply chain partners and facilities are linked electronically via the Internet, extranets, and other means. These connections facilitate seamless information sharing through the use of supply chain solutions and processes that are integrated and synchronized.

Visibility

The critical ability to monitor what is happening across the supply chain is achieved via technology. Supply chain tools generate actionable information by collecting vast amounts of data regarding demand, inventory flows, and orders; filtering the data; and presenting it in a form that can be readily used. That is, these sophisticated technology tools allow users to "see" product as it flows through the supply chain.

Collaboration

By virtue of providing connectivity and visibility, technology facilitates real-time data sharing between supply chain participants. They can use this information to make collaborative decisions regarding processes standardization and strategy development.

Optimization

A variety of software is available to help organizations maximize the performance of supply chain activities. Optimization tools analyze all possible options to find the best solution to a supply chain problem, such as finding the most cost efficient delivery routes within a set of delivery requirement constraints.

Execution

Supply chain technology promotes efficient execution and integration of key activities on an hourly and a daily basis to achieve operational excellence. These tools help organizations manage inventory, transportation, and other key supply chain functions more effectively than could be accomplished manually. Operational success in terms of customer service and cost control goals can also be monitored through performance measurement software.

Speed

Properly implemented technologies help organizations rapidly respond to customer requirements for faster, more consistent flows of materials and information. Supply chains are dynamic, and managers need tools to help them adapt to change, resolve problems, and avoid disruptions. New categories of software are emerging with the capability to manage events dynamically, provide recommendations, and automatically resolve some problems.

So what exactly do these technology-assisted drivers of excellence do for an organization? When executed properly, they generate adaptive capabilities, help synchronize high-velocity supply chains, and serve as valuable weapons in the ongoing battle for competitive advantage. AMR Research concurs in its annual identification of the Supply Chain Top 25, the world's best manufacturers and retailers in terms of supply chain capabilities and performance. By embracing supply chain best practices and technologies, "these supply chain leaders are able to shape demand, instantly respond to market changes, and crush their competitors."[6]

Information Technology Challenges

As the previous section indicates, information technology holds great promise for enhancing supply chain performance and organizational competitiveness. However, the implementation of new technologies and software does not guarantee success. Technology is only an enabler. Many organizations have spent lavishly on supply chain technologies only to achieve limited results. Too often, organizations view information technology as the solution to specific problems rather than as a facilitating tool in the quest for supply chain excellence. The problem is that technology cannot make ill-conceived supply chains productive, prompt adversarial organizations to collaborate, or make use of poor quality data (as discussed earlier). In the next few paragraphs, we will discuss some of the major barriers and challenges that must be addressed to make supply chain technology work as intended.

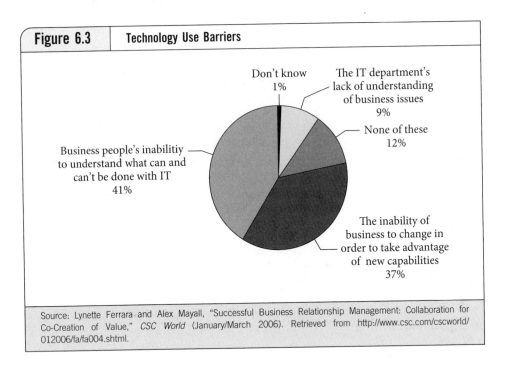

Figure 6.3 | **Technology Use Barriers**

Don't know
1%

The IT department's lack of understanding of business issues
9%

None of these
12%

Business people's inabilitiy to understand what can and can't be done with IT
41%

The inability of business to change in order to take advantage of new capabilities
37%

Source: Lynette Ferrara and Alex Mayall, "Successful Business Relationship Management: Collaboration for Co-Creation of Value," *CSC World* (January/March 2006). Retrieved from http://www.csc.com/cscworld/ 012006/fa/fa004.shtml.

A recent study by Computer Sciences Corporation (CSC) reveals that people are a major barrier to the effective use of information technology. As Figure 6.3 reveals, half of the study's interviewees blame a lack of understanding as the primary issue. Most often, the business executives are to blame as their expectations of technology capabilities tend to be too high. That is, they purchase technology based on the hype and promised benefits without real knowledge regarding how it would impact their business. Information technology executives also shoulder some of the blame as they do not always understand the business processes for which technology is being purchased. Not knowing the key needs and requirements of the business unit can lead to poor technology selection and inefficient implementation.

The CSC study points to another technology use challenge that has been widely reported. Often, organizations do not change their supply chain processes concurrent with the adoption of new information technology tools. They automate existing activities that may well be outdated rather than improve processes or streamline the supply chain network to take full advantage of the technology's capabilities. While incremental productivity improvements are made, the failure to address process issues and root-cause problems will limit the impact of the technology and reduce the return on investment.

Another challenge facing supply chain professionals is the wide variety of software solutions that are promoted as being "supply chain" tools. Often, these software solutions support the automation of individual activities to ensure optimal efficiency but are inadequate for managing supply chain processes across multiple organizations.[7] Also, supply chain technology may be implemented in piecemeal fashion, leading to a "patchwork quilt" of technologies. Both issues can result in the creation of dysfunctional information systems that do not seamlessly share information or foster demand-responsive capabilities.

Poor planning and preparation for technology implementation is also problematic. Some organizations do not take the time to create a change management plan with a staged, logical approach to adopting new technologies. This can cause supply chain disruptions and problems. For example, a furniture manufacturer's software installation was problematic due to implementation miscues, not technical challenges. The resulting manufacturing problems and shipping delays led to the first quarterly loss in company history.[8] Other organizations fail to prepare employees for the new technology. Limited training may lead to suboptimal use of technology as employees do not understand the full array of software features and capabilities. Finally, some organizations do not establish adequate budgets for technology installation and implementation.

The good news is that these challenges are not insurmountable if the organization views technology implementation as a business improvement project rather than an information technology project. Supply chain leaders must take an active role in the planning, implementation, and evaluation of the new tools. They would do well to follow these 10 golden rules for success compiled by Favilla and Fearne.

1. Secure the commitment of senior management.
2. Remember that it is not just an information technology project.
3. Align the project with business goals.
4. Understand the software capabilities.
5. Select partners carefully.
6. Follow a proven implementation methodology.
7. Take a step-by-step approach for incremental value gains.
8. Be prepared to change business processes.
9. Keep end users informed and involved.
10. Measure success with key performance indicators (KPIs).[9]

A Framework for Managing Supply Chain Information[10]

The term **supply chain information system (SCIS)** is widely used, although few formal definitions exist. One such attempt describes SCIS as "information systems that automate the flow of information between a firm and its suppliers to optimize the planning, sourcing, manufacturing, and delivery of products and services."[11] While the definition provides a general idea of the needed links between key supply chain functions, additional issues must be addressed. SCIS should also have the capacity to collect and synchronize data, manage exceptions, and help streamline key processes, among other capabilities.

These additional issues are effectively encapsulated in a model created by Capgemini to link the traditional functional areas of the supply chain to promote visibility of actionable information and enhanced decision making. This master model for achieving excellence in SCM is depicted in Figure 6.4. Although it is not specifically a conceptual model of SCIS, it does identify key capabilities of a well-integrated technology platform. Thus, it will serve as our framework for the effective management of supply chain information.

Foundation Elements

The ability to capture and manage supply chain information depends upon a strong, well-integrated foundation of people, processes, and technology. All three elements must be considered in the development of a SCIS or problems will occur, as highlighted in our discussion of technology use barriers.

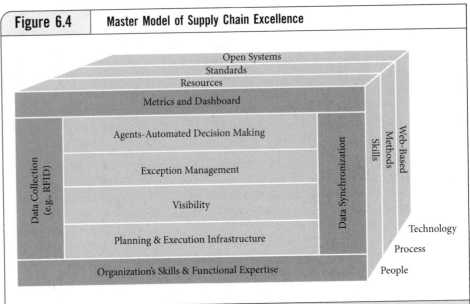

| Figure 6.4 | Master Model of Supply Chain Excellence |

Source: Adapted from Jeff Abott, Karl Manrodt, and Peter Moore, *Visibility to Action: Year 2004 Report on Trends and Issues in Logistics and Transportation* (New York, NY: Capgemini, 2004) and Peter Moore, Karl Manrodt, and Mary Holcomb, *Collaboration: Enabling Synchronized Supply Chains: Year 2005 Report on Trends and Issues in Logistics and Transportation* (New York, NY: Capgemini, 2005). Reproduced by permission of the authors.

People ultimately determine the success or failure of a SCIS. Today, technological capabilities are not usually the problem when it comes to improving supply chain visibility and performance. The sheer computing power and speed of information transfer capabilities available today adequately meet the needs of most supply chains. The problem more commonly lies with the competence of the people involved with the technology. Individuals making information technology selection decisions must have reasonable expectations regarding the technology being considered and access to team members with operational expertise in its functionality. The people tasked with implementing and integrating technology need the requisite skills, as well as adequate staff and financial resources to complete the work. Finally, the day-to-day technology users must be properly trained in the appropriate, accurate use of the tools.

Process management also plays a role in SCIS performance. Organizations should review existing methods in light of the new technology adoption. The risk of not doing this is that inefficient, outdated, or unnecessary processes will be automated, providing little benefit to the organization. Supply chain professionals and their technology counterparts must also determine how the SCIS tools can be used to enhance internal procedures and streamline information flows to supply chain partners. Standard operating procedures and goals regarding supply chain productivity, accuracy, timeliness, and cost also must be established for technology-enhanced processes. Without them, it would be impossible to ensure that processes are being performed correctly across the supply chain or generating the desired outcomes.

Technologies used in SCIS have the greatest impact when they are based on the open systems concept and take advantage of the Internet. Software applications that are based on well-defined, widely used, nonproprietary open standards require minimal changes to interoperate with other SCIS tools and interact with users in a style that facilitates portability (i.e., is easy to transfer). Interoperability can be achieved through enhanced, standardized Web links and simplified protocols that allow different systems to work together in a unified manner. Data transfer becomes seamless, and there is a reduced need for data manipulation by each organization. As a result, you have a handy, easy-to-use package that works like a Swiss Army knife, rather than a random gathering of the latest gadgets that may not work well together.[12]

The Internet provides the platform for supply chain activities to be carried out in a synchronized, instantaneous manner to maximum performance. Just as we leverage the speed and efficiency of the Web to place orders, track shipments, and communicate, organizations are dramatically increasing their use of the Internet to manage their supply chain strategies and processes. Information can be shared among collaborating companies quickly and at low cost using Internet tools as an alternative to or as the platform for electronic data interchange (EDI). Supply chain activities like procurement can be conducted via the Web, and process performance can be monitored. Organizations can even access supply chain software over the Internet as a cost-saving alternative to purchasing, installing, and maintaining it on their own networks. These are just a few examples of the ways that Internet-enhanced SCIS promote efficient, responsive supply chains.

Key Requirements

By themselves, software and other SCIS components cannot provide actionable knowledge for supply chain managers. Data must be collected and synchronized so that it can be used by skilled individuals in the planning and execution of supply chain processes. Scorecards and dashboards are also needed to monitor performance and make necessary adjustments. With these requirements satisfied, managers are able to take full advantage of SCIS data analysis and decision support capabilities. They are also properly positioned to pursue supply chain excellence.

Data collection of relevant information is needed at every point in the supply chain. Whether it is captured via bar codes, radio-frequency identification, or other technology, the information must be relevant, accurate, and accessible to users in real time. A lack of timely information leads to dysfunctional decisions that spread across the supply chain.

Data synchronization focuses on the timely and accurate updating of item information within and across enterprises to ensure dependable, consistent product information within a company's systems and between business partners. It is critical for every organization in the supply chain to have standardized, complete, accurate, and consistently aligned data in their SCIS to perform at peak effectiveness. It is impossible for supply chain partners to effectively collaborate, utilize RFID, or leverage demand-driven replenishment techniques if the product, price, or invoice data being transferred are inaccurate. Thus, organizations must clean and align data internally before sharing it with partners.

Furthermore, processes have to be in place to maintain high-data quality. This requirement has both technology and organizational structure implications. First, the organization must be willing to make data management processes a priority. Second, there must be strong business ownership of product data and aligned SCIS that enables access to timely, accurate data. Those who succeed will achieve inventory and logistics cost reductions, as well as fewer out-of-stock situations.

Functional expertise in each organization will be enhanced by access to the synchronized data. Managers must be able to leverage information from the SCIS to support planning and decision making across all supply chain operations—procurement, production, delivery, and returns. For example, timely point-of-sale (POS) data are needed to initiate the replenishment cycle in a retail supply chain. This sales information is used to build store orders, initiate order preparation at the distribution center, alert the buyer to purchase additional units, and signal the manufacturer to make additional units.

Metrics, as discussed in Chapter 5, help organizations articulate their impact on the supply chain. Just as a baseball manager reviews the standings, statistics, and box scores to assess the team's strengths and weaknesses, so do supply chain managers need score-cards and dashboards to help them evaluate performance and make necessary adjust-ments when things aren't going as planned. These metrics must be defined and understood by all parties, measure service issues that are critical to the customer, and provide actionable information. Given the importance of time, accuracy, and cost in the supply chain, valuable metrics include order cycle time, proportion of perfect orders, and cash-to-cash cycle time.

Differentiating Capabilities

To state that all SCIS are not created equal may be the greatest understatement of fact in this textbook. While leveraging technology for more adaptive capabilities is a widely desired goal, the process of transforming the organization and its SCIS is a complex, multilayered effort. After the foundation has been built and the key requirements attained, supply chain partners must integrate processes and achieve SCIS connectivity to support cross-chain visibility, event management, and automated decision making.

The planning and execution infrastructure consists of the software tools that are utilized to provide supply chain speed, optimization, and connectivity. In the past, the infrastructure was largely comprised of narrowly focused functional applications that tar-geted automation and efficiency. The focus has shifted to applications that promote process effectiveness and the creation of actionable information. Major categories of SCIS software applications are identified and explored in the next section of this chapter.

Visibility tools focus on providing a seamless flow of timely, important information across the supply chain. Accurate knowledge of what is occurring outside the organiza-tion via Web-enabled SCIS allows managers to monitor sourcing, transportation, and inventory data at the order and item level. As the supply chain becomes more transpar-ent, managerial vision and control extend beyond internal activities and facilities. This enhanced intelligence propels supply chain managers from a reactive to a predictive mode, which promotes proactive strategic planning, collaboration, and decision making. Ultimately, the objective is to have the right information available so that action can be taken when needed, not after the fact.

Exception management capabilities take the next logical step beyond visibility. As one industry pundit explains it: "Think of a guy walking on a sidewalk where a piano is about to hit. A visibility solution tells him that the piano is falling. An intelligent excep-tion management solution tells him to get out of the way."[13] Thus, SCIS should support the detection of performance problems and signal exception alerts to the affected organi-zations. Immediate corrective action can be taken to resolve the situation before it impacts the supply chain, and efforts can be made to eliminate the root cause of the problem. Such SCIS capabilities promote supply chain agility and enhance customer service.

Automated decision making is the pinnacle of differentiating capabilities but remains a future prospect for many SCIS. Software tools are rapidly being developed to recognize exception alerts, assess the problem, evaluate alternatives, and recommend solutions. In some cases, these supply chain event management tools will dynamically replan activities and take corrective action without human intervention, and then notify stakeholders that the exception has been resolved.

It is important to remember that the foundation, requirements, and capabilities must be developed in a logical, sequential fashion. Wilson provides the following recommendations for pursuing SCIS capabilities: "Before pursuing extended supply chain optimization, a company's own system needs to be functioning properly. Implementation should be done in segments, company data needs to be accurate, objectives need to be clearly defined, recommendations need to be reliable, and personnel using the system must believe in the system and its results."[14]

Also, organizations cannot expect to quickly activate this world-class supply chain management framework or the supporting SCIS. Integrating systems, synchronizing data, institutionalizing collaboration, and adopting the other drivers of supply chain excellence require more than a one- or two-year effort. Achieving supply chain excellence is a long-term goal that demands dedication and hard work to reach the desired end state, according to the study authors.[15]

SCM Software

One of the key components of a strong SCIS is the software that is used to manage the supply chain. The supply chain software market space includes technologies that address virtually every function and task that occurs in the supply chain. Whether you need to develop a sales and operations forecast, analyze facility relocation options, optimize the delivery of goods, maintain visibility of inventory, or monitor order fulfillment performance, there is software available (or under rapid development) to assist your efforts. These tools attempt to harness the computational power and communication abilities of today's technology to help organizations plan, execute, and control supply chain activities in real time.

Following the dot.com implosion and subsequent years of spending declines, organizations are investing more money on software solutions according to a recent study by Aberdeen Group. Of the 208 companies included in the research, over 90 percent planned to spend the same amount or more in the upcoming year. The amounts are not trivial, as over half the respondents plan six-figure expenditures on new technology projects.[16] Organizations are looking beyond efficiency-focused applications to systems that provide the ability to react quickly to marketing and demand changes, communicate decisions clearly and quickly to everyone affected, and flexibly manage multiple types of supply chains. In short, they are looking to establish the "sense and respond" capabilities of agile, adaptive organizations.

As you might expect, it takes a wide array of tools to accomplish these goals. Not only is it difficult for managers to understand the functionality of these different types of software tools, but it can also be challenging to categorize them. This task is made harder by an inconsistent technology lexicon, a changing software vendor landscape, and the fact that supply chain software is possibly the most fractured group of applications on the planet, according to *CIO* magazine.[17] With these challenges in mind, Figure 6.5 provides an overview of the generally recognized supply chain solutions categories. We use a puzzle analogy to highlight the critical need for linkages and information sharing

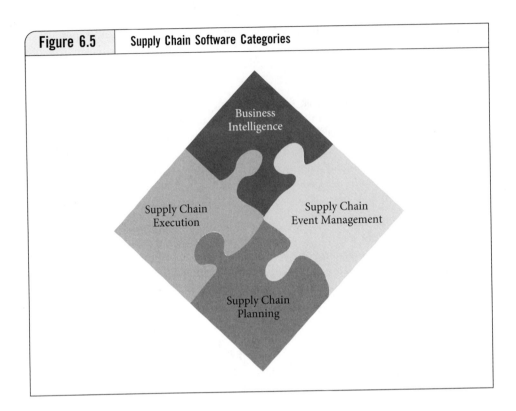

Figure 6.5 | **Supply Chain Software Categories**

between each software category. The more integrated the tools are in a SCIS, the better support they will provide for effective management of the supply chain—from planning to execution, event response, and performance evaluation. This discussion will focus on the general purpose and issues in each category while the details regarding specific software applications will be handled in upcoming chapters.

Planning

Supply chain planning applications and suites help organizations evaluate demand for materials, capacity, and services so that effective fulfillment plans and schedules can be developed. These planning tools are employed across supply chain processes, assisting with decisions regarding the number and location of facilities (network design), where to purchase materials (strategic sourcing), when to build goods (production planning and scheduling), and how to deliver the goods (routing and scheduling), just to name a few tasks. This category encompasses a comprehensive set of software tools designed to help managers gain more accurate, detailed insight into issues that affect their development and planning of supply chain activities.

These tools address a range of longer-term planning horizons (weeks, months, or years) and important issues like demand forecasting. Moving from manual, independent processes to software that leverages real-time data and enables collaboration across departments, suppliers, and customers has a positive effect on forecast speed and enhances accuracy. Shorter-range planning tools that support sales and operations, production, and distribution planning can leverage these accurate forecasts. Supply chain managers will ultimately be able to make better operational and tactical decisions, leading to more efficient process execution, reduced waste and stockouts, and improved profitability.

Can better planning make that much of a difference? In the case of Welch's, the answer is yes. The maker of juice products implemented a demand planning system to coordinate information from marketing, sales, finance, and production to create a single, accurate, companywide forecast and better coordinate trade promotions, production, and distribution. Welch's expects the new planning system will help the organization trim its inventory by 15 percent, cut inbound raw material expediting by 30 percent, and reduce product obsolescence by 30 percent.[18]

Execution

Supply chain execution tools and suites carry out key tasks from the time an order is placed until it is fulfilled. This order-driven category of software focuses on the day-today activities required to buy, make, and deliver the materials that flow through the supply chain. Traditionally, execution tools have focused on a company's internal logistics activities—order management, warehouse management, inventory management, labor optimization, and transportation management. As attention shifts to integrated supply chain capabilities, the category is encompassing a broader array of functionality including procurement and supplier relationship management, manufacturing execution and shop floor control, and customer relationship management.

Supply chain execution doesn't rely upon a single software program. Instead, it consists of a group of tightly integrated tools that link well with supply chain partners' systems to share relevant data and provide visibility. Interest and investment in execution tools is growing because of the strong capabilities being developed, cost savings, and return on investment being achieved. Successful implementation can provide users with improved inventory visibility, improved data accuracy, faster throughput and higher inventory turns, better control of transportation costs, and improved customer service.[19] The tools also support supply chain planning, event management, and performance metrics. "The secret of execution, the reason it's so important," notes a software executive, "is that the data generated is what drives the rest of the business."[20]

Individually, we also rely upon these supply chain execution tools to carry out order fulfillment. When you want to purchase a digital camera from Photo-Op.com, you interact with its order management system via the Internet to prepare and transmit your request. This system checks the availability of inventory through its link to the warehouse management system. If the inventory is available, your order is processed and transmitted to the warehouse management system, which schedules the picking and packing of your camera. When it is ready to be shipped, the transportation management system selects a carrier, optimizing delivery cost within your transit time requirement. You can also use the carrier's transportation management system to monitor the delivery status of your order until it arrives at your front door. Without these execution capabilities, the order to delivery process could take weeks instead of days and you would have little visibility into the process.

Event Management

Supply chain event management tools collect data in real time from multiple sources across the supply chain and convert them into information that gives business managers a clear picture of how their supply chain is performing. These systems track the inventory as it flows through the supply chain, providing graphical displays of expected and actual inventory levels and other key data at each location. An important feature is their ability to define business rules that trigger alerts when specified events occur, or when they fail to occur. This capability allows supply chain managers to focus their attention on managing exceptions rather than having to monitor every movement and compare it against plan.[21]

As the geographic scope and number of companies involved in a supply chain grow, the ability to monitor activities exceeds manual capabilities. Hence, supply chain event management tools are becoming more important, and more organizations are turning toward these solutions to help them detect, evaluate, and resolve issues before they snowball into major problems. The newest tools use optimization techniques to evaluate the severity of the situation and propose alternative solutions to decision makers or initiate action based on established guidelines. Interest in these capabilities is so high that Wintergreen Research predicts spending on these tools will grow from $1.7 billion in 2005 to $7.1 billion in 2012.[22]

A U.S.-based retailer uses an event management system to monitor on-time supply delivery status and received an alert when a late delivery occurs or is likely to occur. By having early visibility into delayed shipments, the company can automatically identify an alternative source of supply to avoid stock-outs. It also has taken steps to reduce safety stock levels. With the new system, the company has increased its confidence in product availability, visibility, and control over its inbound supply chain. It has been able to reduce in-transit inventory by 50 percent (valued at over $20 million) in the first year.[23] Additional examples of supply chain event management opportunities are provided in Table 6.1.

Table 6.1	Supply Chain Event Management Opportunities		
	1. DECIDE WHAT YOU WANT TO KNOW AND MEASURE.	**2. DECIDE WHAT ACTIVITIES AND INFORMATION YOU NEED TO BE TOLD ABOUT.**	**3. DRIVE TOWARD RESOLUTION OF PROBLEMS TO THE APPROPRIATE SYSTEMS.**
	MEASURE	**MONITOR/NOTIFY**	**SIMULATE/CONTROL**
Orders	• Customer-satisfaction levels across products	• Late deliveries or notifications of past-due dates	• Choose alternative transportation modes or alternative suppliers
Shipments	• On-time shipments • Carrier pick-up performance levels	• Late arrivals of shipments • Projected carrier pick-up behind schedule	• Notify carrier of lateness • Choose alternative carriers or alternative modes of transportation
Inventory	• Inventory levels and adherence to safety-stock levels	• Stock-outs • Inventory below safety levels	• Determine alternative source of inventory • Increase orders to suppliers
Manufacturing	• WIP levels by family	• Delays in production • WIP build-ups	• Choose alternative manufacturing solution • Push WIP into finished goods
Financial	• Order-to-catch cycle time	• Payments pending • Late payments • Late invoicing	• Remind suppliers of payments • Renegotiate pricing

Source: *Tackling Uncertainly: Improving Responsiveness with Supply Chain Event Management* (Cambridge, MA: Sapient Corporation, 2002).

Business Intelligence

Business intelligence tools build upon the traditional reports and output systems that provided historical accounts of functional performance for internal planning, operations, and control. The newer capabilities are more dynamic, frequently delivering data from transactional systems across the supply chain to a data warehouse. The data can be analyzed and fresh information sent to frontline employees and executives for more effective planning and decision making.

In addition to the data collection and analysis capabilities, business intelligence software supports self-service reporting, performance scorecarding versus goals, development of dashboards and other graphical report displays, and activity monitoring in support of event management. These tools can provide better access to data residing on multiple SCIS without the need for technology department involvement, improve knowledge of decision makers, and support collaboration across the supply chain.

Interest in business intelligence applications is rising, due primarily to a software vendor focus on increasing user-friendliness of the tools. Previous generations of business intelligence software were geared toward trained analysts who had to define specific problems for the software to analyze. However, emerging capabilities make it easier to interpret data via simple dashboard items, such as charts, graphs, and maps that are easier to understand than pages of data. Because these graphics are linked to the data warehouse, it is possible to manipulate them, review the effect of different variables on results, and test alternative scenarios, in addition to monitoring performance.[24] Gartner Research predicted that spending for new licenses for business intelligence software would reach $2.5 billion for the year.[25]

Wyeth Pharmaceuticals uses scorecards to share information regarding its supply chain performance and service problems with its customers (pharmaceuticals distributors). The scorecard combines reporting data on order fill rates and accuracy, delivery performance, return rates, and related supply chain issues in an easy-to-read spreadsheet. Transactional data received each day from transportation companies via EDI are assembled in Wyeth's data warehouse and their business intelligence tools assemble the data into the tables that make up the scorecard. The scorecards are sent to Wyeth's distributors via EDI, and the information is used to diagnose problems. This comprehensive, timely tool has helped move the Wyeth supply chain closer to just-in-time capabilities.[26]

Enterprise Resource Planning (ERP)

Just as the boundaries between supply chain planning and execution tools are blurring, it is becoming more difficult to completely segment SCIS from enterprise resource planning (ERP) systems. Many of the supply chain software applications discussed above are growing increasingly reliant upon the type of information that is stored inside ERP systems. Thus, it is important to briefly discuss ERP systems and their relationship to supply chain software tools.

ERP systems are multimodule application software platforms that help organizations manage the important parts of their businesses. Initially concentrated on manufacturing issues, ERP systems now focus on integrating information and activities across the organization (i.e., the enterprise) via a common software platform and centralized database system. Key business processes linked via ERP include accounting and finance, planning, engineering, human resources, purchasing, production, inventory/materials

| Figure 6.6 | ERP Integration of Supply Chain Technology Capabilities |

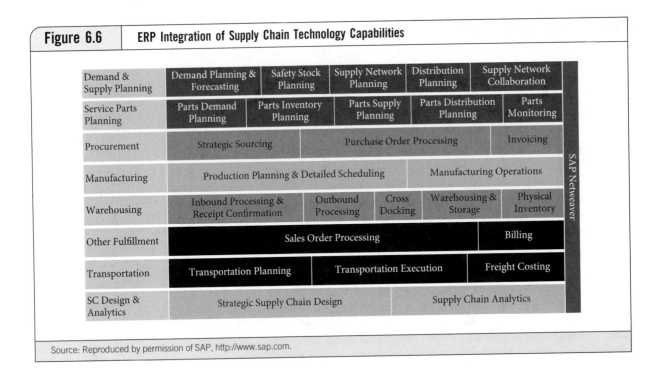

Demand & Supply Planning	Demand Planning & Forecasting	Safety Stock Planning	Supply Network Planning	Distribution Planning	Supply Network Collaboration
Service Parts Planning	Parts Demand Planning	Parts Inventory Planning	Parts Supply Planning	Parts Distribution Planning	Parts Monitoring
Procurement	Strategic Sourcing		Purchase Order Processing		Invoicing
Manufacturing	Production Planning & Detailed Scheduling			Manufacturing Operations	
Warehousing	Inbound Processing & Receipt Confirmation	Outbound Processing	Cross Docking	Warehousing & Storage	Physical Inventory
Other Fulfillment	Sales Order Processing				Billing
Transportation	Transportation Planning		Transportation Execution		Freight Costing
SC Design & Analytics	Strategic Supply Chain Design			Supply Chain Analytics	

SAP Netweaver

management, order processing, and more. The centralized and shared database system ties the entire organization together, allowing information to be entered once and made available to all users. Business processes can also be automated for rapid, accurate execution.

As the ERP systems branch out to include supplier relationship management, customer relationship management, and other supply chain components, the connections between SCIS and ERP grow stronger. Supply chain members can access the organization through the ERP system to assess inventory availability, production schedules, and delivery information. In short, the ERP system provides a mechanism for supply chain members to efficiently share information so that visibility is improved, transactions are completed with more speed and accuracy, and decision making is enhanced.[27] Figure 6.6 reveals the supply chain planning and execution capabilities that SAP, a leading ERP software provider, can integrate with its Net Weaver ERP platform to link the enterprise with its suppliers and customers.

C. R. Bard, a medical device manufacturer, uses a combination of ERP and supply chain execution systems to manage the production and distribution of its catheters and heart stents. A product requisition begins as a work order in the ERP system, which creates a master record that is complete and readily accessible. The ERP system routes the product through various processes (assembly, packaging, and sterilization) at multiple facilities and signals the global distribution center that a delivery is on the way. The warehouse management system receives the signal and prepares for arrival. This system also receives customer orders through the ERP system, fills orders, prepares them for delivery, and updates the ERP system when the order is shipped. These linked tools provide the company with real-time visibility of customer orders, improved fulfillment accuracy and speed, and lot traceability.[28]

Related Tools

While the four categories of supply chain software (plus the ERP tools) cover much of the solutions spectrum, other valuable tools exist. Some fall in between the categories, while other software applications are not supply chain specific. Although difficult to categorize, they help improve the flow and usefulness of supply chain information, support the development and implementation of key strategies, and enhance analysis. These valuable tools include, but are not limited to, the following:

- **Supply chain collaboration tools.** The software helps users integrate their information technology systems with those of trading partners to streamline and automate supply chain processes. These middleware tools provide interoperability between different SCIS to support collaboration initiatives. Leveraging Internet standards, these applications support collaborative planning, forecasting, and replenishment, vendor managed inventory, and other strategic supply chain initiatives.

- **Data synchronization applications.** These tools provide a platform for manufacturers, distributors, and retailers to aggregate and organize item-related data (item number, price, description, weight, etc.). Cleaning up the data so that they are consistent across multiple organizations is required for using RFID technology, streamlining and automating processes, and improving supply chain visibility.

- **Spreadsheets and database software.** You may be surprised to think of these commonly used applications as relevant to this discussion, but Excel has been coined "the most widely used supply chain software" only half jokingly by industry pundits. Spreadsheet software provides managers with handy, portable tools for gathering, consolidating, and analyzing supply chain data. However, it is critical that the planning and analytical work done via these tools be linked to the SCIS so that information does not become fragmented and visibility lost.

Throughout this discussion of the supply chain software categories, we have mentioned some of the individual applications available to supply chain managers. Figure 6.7 provides a diagram of one vendor's software suite that links applications from the four categories. Regardless of the system, tool, or vendor involved, it is important to consider a few factors before moving forward. First, it is important to understand the capabilities of the software—its functionality (making sure to separate the reality from the hype), ease of use, and applicability to your supply chain requirements. Second, the software must work with existing tools, integrating well with your current SCIS and ERP system. Finally, applications must link effectively to supply chain partners, supporting the overall goals of visibility, responsiveness, and cross-enterprise agility.

Supply Chain Technology Implementation

As the preceding section indicates, a wide array of software tools support supply chain planning, execution, and control. Companies spend billions of dollars on these technologies with the goal of making their supply chains more productive and effective. However, spending does not guarantee success. Implementation headaches, systems integration complexities, and training requirements translate into significant spending (often twice the cost of the software) and time (frequently in excess of six months) to achieve software functionality. Thus, gaining a positive return on technology investments can be very challenging.

| Figure 6.7 | Supply Chain Software Suite |

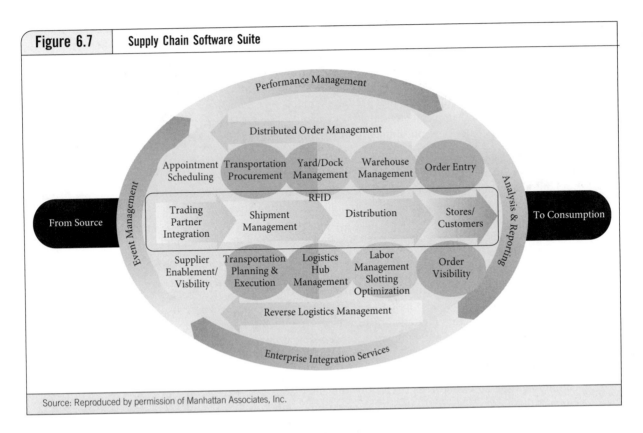

Source: Reproduced by permission of Manhattan Associates, Inc.

The key to overcoming these issues and harnessing the capabilities of supply chain technology within a reasonable timeframe is informed decision making. Supply chain managers must not make rush decisions regarding technology selection. They must take the time to investigate a variety of technology-related issues and base decisions on the specific requirements of their supply chain. It is possible to achieve a 12- to 18-month return on investment if an organization effectively assesses its specific needs, understands software application and delivery options, addresses the technical issues, and asks the right questions before making a purchase decision.

Needs Assessment

The most important step in software selection and implementation is to understand the supply chains that the technology is intended to support. Too often, supply chain managers undertake the software selection process in isolation and without knowledge of the processes to be automated. They may also attempt to use the technology to improve inadequate or outdated processes. Any of these situations will lead to the deployment of technologies that are poorly matched to the true needs of the supply chain; unable to link departments, suppliers, and customers; and/or too narrowly focused to support supply chain visibility and event management.

Organizations must start with a diagnosis of their situation. They should assess their supply chain process capabilities and benchmark them against the needs of their supply chain partners. If the current capabilities are deemed inadequate, improvements and innovations must be developed for relevant processes. Only then should technology be considered, based upon its ability to facilitate the planning and execution of these enhanced processes. Technology can also be used to improve adequate processes but only after deficiencies have been addressed.

This needs assessment sequence highlights the link between effective business processes, appropriate technology, and supply chain performance. Companies like Wal-Mart, Dell, and Zara have generated a competitive advantage in their respective industries because they support innovative supply chain practices with technology. They properly view supply chain software as an enabler of process improvement rather than a "quick fix" solution. This ultimately leads to realistic expectations of the technology, more effective implementation, and greater returns on supply chain software investments.

Software Options

Supply chain managers face a multifaceted decision when selecting supply chain software. As we previously discussed, the manager must determine which type of software—planning, execution, event management, or business intelligence—is appropriate for the given process or situation. Additionally, supply chain managers must compare the advantages of commercial software to in-house solutions, choose between single vendor suites and applications from multiple vendors, and consider licensing versus on-demand purchases, among other issues.

Development Alternatives

The first issue involved in software selection focuses on who will develop the solution. The choices are to develop the tools in house for your organization only or to purchase software from an external vendor. Wal-Mart and Amazon.com are two organizations that largely depend upon their own information technology departments to build supply chain applications. Many third-party logistics firms develop in-house solutions as well. While this requires significant resources and development time, all of the tools are tailored to their specific industries and supply chain processes. They are able to achieve a level of customization and flexibility that is not possible with off-the-shelf tools. Such capabilities can lead to a competitive advantage for their supply chains.[29]

Most organizations, especially small to mid-size companies, are not able to build their own supply chain software. In reality, many supply chain managers struggle just to get supply chain technology on the priority list of the information technology department. Thus, they rely heavily on external software vendors to develop and implement the tools needed to plan and execute supply chain processes. These tools effectively support supply chains that are not overly unique or complex. Because they can be implemented faster than what could be accomplished in house, are built with interoperability as a key focus, and have some ability to be tailored, the vendor-developed tools are the proper choice for most organizations.

Solutions Packages

Should an organization choose to purchase software rather than develop it in house, it has to determine what types of applications are needed and how they should be purchased. Historically, software packages were purchased independently from different vendors and the organization's information technology staff was tasked with making the various tools work together if possible. Today, buyers have another option. Due to mergers and acquisitions in the software industry and ERP vendors moving into the supply chain applications market space, it is possible to purchase supply chain software suites that combine planning, execution, event management, and related capabilities.

The polar options are to work with a single vendor's software or to purchase individual applications from leading providers in each software category, commonly called "best-of-breed" solutions. A food example will highlight the differences. If you have a party catered by one restaurant that offers a main course plus a selection of side items, you're working with a single vendor. This is similar to purchasing an integrated software package that includes an ERP system (the main course) and supply chain applications (the side items). In contrast, if you purchase your party items independently—the main course from a butcher shop, the side items from ethnic restaurants, and the dessert from the local bakery—you're effectively employing specialists that conceivably offer considerably more expertise in their respective areas. This is similar to purchasing an ERP system from one company, a forecasting and planning system from another, and a warehouse management system from a third company. Of course, you could also opt for the middle ground, purchasing the main applications from an organization that provides a supply chain software suite and a few tools obtained from the best-of-breed specialists.

Each strategy has its merits. Single vendor supply chain suites should take less time to implement than a variety of tools from different vendors since there are fewer compatibility and connectivity issues to overcome. Also, there is only one vendor to work with rather than multiple companies, which reduces administrative and coordination effort. Single vendor suites also require less training time and have lower implementation costs as there is only one set of integration requirements to master. Although the best-of-breed tools are more complex and typically take longer to integrate into the SCIS, they are working to streamline the process. Also, they offer more powerful applications for specific functions that provide greater flexibility and can be better tailored to an individual company's supply chain issues. Some suites, especially those from ERP vendors, do not yet contain the advanced functionality or industry-specific capabilities found in specific best-of-breed applications, though they are working to close the gap. The challenge for the supply chain executives choosing between these options is to understand the implementation issues; their organization's need for tailored, advanced capabilities; and the changing vendor landscape (this topic is discussed in the On the Line feature).

Purchase Options

Historically, supply chain software buyers had one option—purchase solutions from software vendors for their own information systems. The licensed software is installed on the buyer's powerful client-server systems, which is a valuable method, given the intense computational activity required by most supply chain processes. The downside of this purchase option is the high capital investment and complex deployment associated with conventional licensed applications. Buyers have to pay for the software upfront; manage the implementation issues; and deal with ongoing issues of software upgrades, fixes, and maintenance costs.

The Internet brought another option—application service providers (ASP)—that offered a new way to buy software. The ASP owns and operates the software application and the servers that run the application. It also employs the staff needed to maintain the application and the information system. Users access the software via the Internet using a Web browser or small software tool. They are billed for the application on a per-use basis or on a monthly/annual fee basis. The benefit of the ASP purchase model is low-cost access to solutions because there are no major upfront license or installation costs. The downside of ASPs is the inefficiency of hosting one copy of the software application

On the Line

Software Gets "Friendlier"

The so-called best-of-breed software vendors, which specialize in specific supply chain applications, are making their products easier to install and use these days. They've adopted ease of use as a selling point—and perhaps a survival strategy—as they confront the growing market presence of the big enterprise resource planning vendors.

Competition has gotten fiercer as the ERP developers have taken a page from the best-of-breed vendors' playbook: industry specialization. Many vendors of transportation management systems (TMS) and warehouse management systems (WMS)—the two most commonly used supply chain execution programs—have focused on niche markets, tailoring their products to the information needs of specific industries.

Now the dominant ERP vendors are doing the same. "SAP and Oracle are augmenting their supply chain software offerings with more vertical competencies," observes James Uchneat, manager director at Benchmarking Partners.

To ward off the ERP developers, makers of supply chain execution software are doing their best to make it easier for logistics managers to pick up their tools and use them. Many TMS vendors, for example, have shifted to an on-demand model for their wares. On-demand TMS players include such companies as LeanLogistics, Descartes, Nistevo, and Cube Route, says Adrian Gonzalez, director of the Logistics Executive Council of ARC Advisory Group.

The on-demand model represents an advance over Web-hosted software. In a typical hosted environment, Gonzalez explains, the application would reside on a computer outside a company's walls, and the user would access the software via the Internet. A drawback of that approach is that every time a vendor made a change to the application, it would have to do so for each individual user. Not so in the on-demand model, he notes. If, for example, a TMS vendor updated a freight-rate data table, it would only have to make the change once, and every user would automatically see the updated information when connected to the network.

EASY INTEGRATION REQUIRED

In the market for warehouse software, however, the on-demand model isn't practical, as that type of application must be heavily customized to meet the user's specific needs. However, WMS vendors are also moving to make their applications easier to use by embracing "service-based architecture," which allows applications to leverage networked resources. That model makes it easier to configure and upgrade their solutions, Gonzalez says.

Many WMS makers are building "adapter sets"—ready-made interfaces that allow their applications to exchange data with ERP systems. This approach makes data mapping easier, says Philip Obal, president of Industrial Data and Information Inc. "It will do more than just map data," he says. "It will treat your WMS like a set of subroutines from (ERP) software."

Adapter sets may soon become a required offering for WMS vendors. "If you don't have an adapter set for a WMS, your days are numbered," predicts John Fontanella, a senior vice president with the Aberdeen Group.

Vendors that are focusing their efforts on making their applications easier to use should also be thinking about how to do that in several languages. That's because North American sales of supply chain software are slowing, and future sales are more likely to come from Europe or Asia, analysts say. "We'll see the stronger players that are multilingual flourish," predicts Obal. "If you have an English-only solution, I would be worried."

Source: Adapted from James A. Cooke, "Software Gets Friendlier," *Logistics Management* (July 2005): 49. Reprinted with permission.

for each client. Also, because these solutions were traditional client-server applications with HTML front ends added as an afterthought, performance was poor and application updates difficult. Hence, the ASP model did not prosper in supply chain management, though some software vendors now provide similar services for their own tools.

Some of the software-as-a-service issues that hampered ASP efforts are being addressed by on-demand solutions providers. These companies provide software that is accessible by multiple parties via the Internet. Because the application is shared, carriers, suppliers, shippers, and customers can all work together using a standard business process and have a common view of supply chain activity. This purchase option is gaining in popularity as more supply chain tools are offered via this method. Faster implementation and return on investment, lower hardware costs, and an ability to manage growth more economically are cited as key reasons for interest in this method.[30] Of course, certain issues must be addressed. On-demand solution providers must prove that they can protect client data, maintain system availability and reliability, and streamline the integration of their tools with licensed software.

Technical Issues

Supply chain managers tend to focus on functionality when considering software, but they also must consider the technical issues related to its operation. Otherwise useful software will become "shelfware" if it is difficult to install, unable to link to other tools in support of visibility and event management, or too cumbersome to use on a daily basis. Hence, upfront effort must be expended to assess implementation challenges before selecting a supply chain software suite or best-of-breed application. We have already identified some of the key considerations such as interoperability and data synchronization. Here, we briefly discuss two additional technical issues in SCIS implementation.

Data Standardization

Given the variety of software vendors, proprietary tools, and legacy systems, coordinating and sharing information across the supply chain can be a significant challenge. Just as different languages, dialects, and alphabets hamper human communication, the variety of systems and programming languages used in SCIS make it difficult to bring data together in an efficient, useful manner. One option is to translate data as they move between software applications, but this can be as cumbersome as two people trying to communicate through a translator. Rather than manually or electronically translating data, a better solution is to use a standardized format to enhance communication between partners. Just as English is the standard language of global business, EDI and extensible markup language (XML) are key elements of data standardization. These tools improve the data flows between applications and organizations.

EDI provides interorganizational, computer-to-computer exchange of structured information in a standard, machine-processable format. It has been the primary method of transaction data sharing between vendors and customers for over two decades, supporting the exchange of trade-related documents, such as purchase orders, invoices, and corporate electronic funds transfer (EFTs) in a standard format. EDI allows the rapid exchange of large amounts of information, reduces errors, and lowers the cost per transaction, allowing supply chain partners to work more efficiently and effectively. EDI does have its drawbacks. Implementation can be complex and value-added network services that provide the company-to-company linkages charge transaction fees, making this standardization method infeasible for smaller organizations.

XML is a robust, logically verifiable text format based on international standards. It provides a flexible way to create structured, common information formats and share both the format and the data via the Internet, intranets, and other networks. XML can be used to define complex documents and data structures such as invoices, inventory descriptions, shipment records, and other supply chain information. The benefits of XML are numerous—it is a simultaneously human- and machine-readable format, it supports multiple languages, its plain text file displays are unencumbered by licenses or restrictions, and it is platform-independent and thus relatively immune to changes in technology. XML is gaining traction in the supply chain because it supports the integration of various information systems, is less complex than EDI, and eliminates the need for value-added networks, which reduces cost while speeding data transmission.

When selecting individual applications, buyers must seek out these data standardization capabilities. Such capabilities will ensure that information is quickly transferred in a format that is usable by the SCIS and key decision makers. Newer tools should provide "out-of-the-box" support for XML-based data exchange standards and/or EDI standards. This will help buyers avoid costly, time-consuming software integration projects and improve SCIS interoperability. Enhanced visibility and faster communication across the supply chain will also be achieved.

Application Integration

Not only is it important to put data into a standardized and common format, but it is also imperative that different tools seamlessly share the data. This can be readily accomplished within a self-contained supply chain software suite, but supply chain partners often rely on different vendors, applications, or software versions. The greater the variety of applications, the more challenging connectivity and information sharing issues become. The problem lies in the fact that these applications tend to present data differently, making communication between them difficult.[31]

Extensive efforts have been made over the last 10 years to improve application integration and foster supply chain information synchronization. The initial work focused on the development of application programming interfaces (API) to allow companies to link their SCIS with supplier and customer applications. ERP vendors like SAP targeted their API efforts on making it easier for third-party vendors to build ERP-compatible supply chain software. Other organizations developed tools to fit between and connect existing applications, such as linking a warehouse management system to an ERP-based order management system. While beneficial, the process can be costly and time consuming as an API needs to be developed for each type of software that will be connected. Also, the connectivity achieved may be temporary, as a change in one application can break the API-created link to other tools.[32]

More recently, the focus has shifted toward adapter sets (see the On the Line feature) and a newer technology model called **service-oriented architecture (SOA).** SOA is the underlying structure supporting communications between services with "plug and play" functionality as a key goal. A service is defined as a unit of work to be performed on behalf of some computing entity, such as a human user or another program. SOA defines how two computing entities interact in such a way as to enable one entity to perform a unit of work on behalf of another entity. For example, when you initiate an online purchase, you are using an order management service that, in turn, communicates with an inventory service to determine product availability. If available, your order and shipping details are submitted to another service that calculates the order cost and furnishes a shipment number that, through another service, allows you to track product delivery. This sequence of software linkages is made possible by the underlying frame-work that SOA provides.[33]

It is anticipated that SOA will standardize the way applications ask for and retrieve information, allowing disparate software systems to talk to each other without forcing companies to scrap or rebuild their existing systems. SOA will allow users to access the functionality and data of many different applications at the same time, thus creating a process that meets the needs of the business, according to the Aberdeen Group. Ultimately, SOA is expected to simplify integration of applications, improve information access, facilitate communication, and increase availability of affordable software packages. SAP's Netweaver and Oracle's Fusion are two examples of SOA-based applications.[34]

Supply chain technology buyers need to understand the challenges of application integration while pursuing improved SCIS connectivity. They must assess and compare integration methods, and then choose those that best fit current needs while providing the flexibility to meet future functionality requirements. Finally, buyers must monitor the development of SOA and its impact on the software applications landscape. If SOA-based applications revolutionize the way applications are built, sold, and distributed, as promised by SOA proponents, buyers will need to alter their supply chain software procurement practices.

Asking the Right Questions[35]

Senior management plays a key role in facilitating the implementation of supply chain technology. Executives must provide the vision, the required resources, and an unshakable commitment to SCIS initiatives if the organization is to achieve its goals. This vision must clearly explain how technology upgrades will facilitate the organization's overall supply chain strategy and improved performance.[36] An intelligent executive will take the time to ask important questions and gather appropriate information in order to establish and refine the vision. Only then should the organization move forward with technology investment and implementation. Some of these key questions include the following:

- **Who will lead our implementation effort?** Senior management has neither the time nor direct knowledge of SCIS to supervise the selection and installation of new applications. Hence, they must identify people who possess the internal expertise regarding current supply chain processes and related software functionality, as well as general technical capabilities of the organization, and assign these experts to direct the process. This person or small team of experts must be given the authority and accountability to make technology decisions that span functions. They must also be given the ability to manage the implementation process without interference.

- **How will technology support our business needs and processes?** As discussed previously, there is a propensity to adopt software without considering the processes that it will support, leading to automation of inefficiencies. Senior management must ensure that their implementation team takes the time to document current processes and identify desired capabilities before embarking upon software reviews. Having a business plan prior to dealing with vendors will ensure that solutions support this plan rather than the business having to adapt to proposed solutions.

- **What is the status of our existing data?** It is critical to assess data quality, relevance, and completeness to ensure that the needed information is available to use with the technology being considered. If the data are lacking in any of these key requirements, the software cannot function as needed and the organization will encounter a garbage in-garbage out scenario. Also, having an accurate data set available is important for testing potential software solutions to determine how well they model reality.

- **How well does our existing system integrate with suppliers and customers?** SCIS fall woefully short on vital capabilities if they are unable to communicate with supply chain partners in an efficient manner. Systems structures and capabilities should be mapped to identify where compatibility challenges exist. Senior management must use this knowledge to support improved linkages of SCIS with key partners. Executive sponsorship of investment in new tools, authorization of supply chain partner access to key data, and support of intercompany systems connectivity will enhance supply chain information integration.

- **What external issues must our systems address?** Given the financial and product flow data contained within most SCIS, they have a major impact on an organization's ability to address government mandates. Because supply chain activities generate expenses and impact revenues, senior management is ultimately responsible for ensuring that the SCIS will feed accurate, complete, and timely information into the organization's financial reporting mechanisms. This is critical to ensure compliance with Sarbanes-Oxley regulations. The SCIS must also provide visibility of orders from suppliers through customer delivery so that the organization can monitor and control its operations, its inventories and other assets, and its financial results. This visibility is also imperative for compliance with governmental security initiatives related to international trade such as the Customs-Trade Partnership Against Terrorism (C-TPAT) and the Advanced Trade Data Initiative.

Supply Chain Technology Innovations

The supply chain industry transformation of the last 20 years has been enabled by technology. Innovations in supply chain and ERP software, automatic identification technologies, communications systems, and Internet functionality have forever changed the way the supply chain works. When effectively deployed, these technical advances improve information speed and access, support process improvement and optimization, and provide product visibility from global supplier to local consumer. Ultimately, these innovative technologies enable fast execution of supply chain strategies, helping organizations to leverage time as a source of competitive advantage.

We have discussed a number of innovations throughout the chapter. Certainly, the Internet provides a critical platform for the development and execution of technologies that can be used in a supply chain context. Innovative tools such as on-demand applications and software-as-a-service, XML, data synchronization, and event management capabilities all leverage the Internet. Increases in raw computing power and data storage facilitate supply chain data mining, visibility, and optimization. And, innovative technology models like SOA support the integration of supply chain applications and may change the software landscape from the current focus on monolithic applications and suites to streamlined functionalities.

The good news is that the technology landscape is not stagnant. Innovations will continue to emerge to address the supply chain technology needs that have been discussed throughout this chapter: connectivity, visibility, collaboration, optimization, execution, and speed. However, the second coming of the Internet or other groundbreaking new tools is not likely to occur anytime soon. We agree with the assessment of one software vendor who states: "Businesses will be disappointed if they expect flashy, new technologies to give them an edge. New technology will definitely play a key role, but the innovation will be more evolutionary than revolutionary. A majority of the emphasis will be on developing better standards to allow for real-time exchange of information and interoperability of systems."[37]

The challenge for supply chain managers is to find and implement the right tools. They must separate the innovations with the potential to positively impact supply chain performance and gain widespread adoption from those that are impractical, ineffective, and/or insignificant. With this challenge in mind, we conclude the chapter with a discussion of technologies that hold significant promise for the future enhancement of supply chain management.

Radio-Frequency Identification (RFID)

No other technology has garnered the attention of the supply chain industry and the media over the last three years than has RFID. While the technology used in RFID has been available for decades and is widely used for aircraft identification, toll collection, and library book tracking, supply chain applications were largely conceptual until major organizations began to develop RFID mandates. As of 2005, Wal-Mart's top 100 suppliers were required to tag shipments with RFID labels and another 200 suppliers were added at the start of 2006. Wal-Mart has deployed RFID at 117 of its warehouses and 500 of its stores and planned to double the RFID-capable store count by the end of 2007.[38] Similar mandates by the U.S. Department of Defense and other retailers (Germany-based Metro Group, United Kingdom-based Tesco, and Target) have driven the intense focus on RFID in supply chain management.

Like barcoding, RFID is an automatic identification method. RFID tags consist of a microchip and a printed antenna that can be packaged into many forms, such as a label or imbedded in between the cardboard layers in a carton or product packaging. Unique product identification information, in the form of a universal electronic product code (EPC) identifying the manufacturer, product category, and individual item, is stored on these 96-bit tags. The tags are affixed to the pallet, case, or individual product and are read when they pass within proximity of an RFID reader. These tags contain unique identifiers not found on barcodes, and direct line of sight is not required to read RFID tags. The collected information is relayed back to the SCIS, updating the location status of the associated product.

Initial results of RFID implementations have been positive. Wal-Mart reports that out-of-stocks decreased 16 percent on RFID-tagged items and that out-of-stocks were replenished three times faster on tagged items than on items with only barcodes.[39] Levi Strauss can complete a storewide inventory in 30 minutes thanks to RFID. It expects to reduce out-of-stocks and enhance customer satisfaction while reducing theft.[40] Despite these success stories, the migration to RFID could slow if key challenges are not addressed. RFID technology costs must continue to decline to make product tagging economically feasible; equipment issues such as reader range, sensitivity, and durability must improve; the case for supplier return on investment of RFID mandates must be made; and consumer privacy issues must be resolved.

As these issues are overcome and future enhancements are made (e.g., the establishment of firm universal standards, sharing of best practices, and integration of emerging wireless and sensor technologies with RFID), adoption will grow and greater results will be achieved. RFID and EPC will provide organizations with an unprecedented real-time view of their inventory, item-level traceability of products, and true event management capabilities. Improvements in inventory management cost and efficiency, in the form of greater product availability, reduced product shrinkage, and improved product integrity will also be realized.

Adaptive Supply Chain Networks[41]

If supply chains are to become more flexible and responsive, the supply chain technologies discussed in this chapter must be effectively connected. Integration of all supply chain and other support systems and processes both within a company and across trading partners is needed to allow true, full supply chain visibility and flexibility. This can be accomplished via the creation of an adaptive supply chain network (ASCN). These integrated, flexible networks of companies, technology tools, and processes focus on customers and their changing requirements. The hallmark of an effective ASCN is its ability to respond to changes in real time, allowing the network to prevent or minimize supply chain problems.

ASCNs help meet the growing need for supply chain connectivity and collaboration, two key information issues identified in an earlier section. Connectivity provides visibility. Collaboration enables a joint response with channel partners to avoid a possible problem identified via the visibility. "Adaptive" in ASCN is the ability to respond to and thrive on unexpected changes as they emerge, not after the fact. The "network" is a dynamic compendium of business partners and their supply chain technology tools working together to provide increased benefit across the supply chain.

When ASCNs are established, companies will move from forecast-driven to demand-driven supply chains. In effect, the ASCN will help them shift from a perspective of "selling what I make" to "making what I sell," which resolves some of the major supply chain forecasting challenges and facilitates lean inventories. The ASCNs also support true collaboration so that buyers and sellers can simultaneously eliminate inefficiencies in their supply chains by synchronizing information flows and activities across the supply chain. Ultimately, the participants will achieve a valuable blend of low-cost, high-quality supply chain performance.

Pervasive Automation

As technology advances and becomes more affordable, we will come closer to the realization of product connectivity where Internet-enabled microprocessors provide digital intelligence and connectivity for almost every commercial and industrial product.[42] Already, manufacturers and service providers are able to communicate with their products and equipment without direct human involvement. Railroad company computer systems monitor refrigerated boxcars and automatically adjust temperature and humidity levels, oil companies remotely examine inventory levels in storage tanks, and trucking company satellite tracking systems can pinpoint the location of en route loads. These applications are made possible by pervasive automation, which is essentially the networking of tiny controllers in ordinary items to make them "smart" devices, capable of real-time assessment and information sharing.[43]

Pervasive automation is viewed by some people as the next big thing in supply chain management. They hypothesize that a convergence of valuable technologies—RFID, ASCNs, wireless communication, and others—that do not require human interaction will support supply chain innovation. Not only will we be able to avoid supply chain disruptions related to equipment breakdowns and inventory shortages, but it will also be possible to fundamentally alter the way items are produced, warehoused, and distributed. Managing product flows across the supply chain will also become much easier as item-level traceability and exception management will be facilitated by RFID, sensors, and automated machine-to-machine communication.[44]

Will any of these three technology innovations gain traction and fundamentally change supply chain management as we know it today? RFID is the most likely to play a major role in the evolution of the supply chain, but the prospects for radical changes via pervasive automation are much less certain. Only time and organizations' investment in these innovations will tell. Of course, the technology landscape is constantly changing. New tools may render existing ones obsolete and supplant emerging innovations. The only way to keep up with the latest advances in supply chain technology is to monitor industry developments. Table 6.2 provides a list of Web sites that focus on information technology innovations and issues.

Table 6.2	Sources of Additional Information: Supply Chain Technology		
NAME	**WEB ADDRESS**	**DESCRIPTION**	**SIMILAR SOURCES**
Achieving Supply Chain Excellence *through* **Technology**	http://www.ascet.com	Addresses timely topics regarding supply chain technology and processes via whitepapers, case studies, and vendor profiles.	
ARC Advisory Group	http://www.arcweb.com	Provides access to ARC'S supply chain technology research studies and industry news summaries.	http://www.aberdeen.com http://www.amrresearch.com http://www.forrester.com
RFID Update	http://www.rfidupdate.com	Newsletter highlighting breaking news and analysis pertinent to RFID technology and implementations.	http://www.aimglobal.org/services http://www.rfidgazette.org http://www.rfidjournal.com
Reed Business Information	http://www.reedbusiness.com	Provides links to a variety of publications that address supply chain strategy, trends, technology, and related topics. Relevant titles include Logistics Management, Purchasing, Supply Chain Management Review, and others.	http://www.cio.com/enterpnse/scm/index.html http://www.inboundlogistics.comhttp://www.logisticstoday.com

SUMMARY

Information is critical to the success of a supply chain and must flow freely between supply chain partners. Without accurate, timely information, it is extremely difficult for supply chain managers to make effective decisions regarding the purchase, production, and distribution of materials. To facilitate the knowledge links and foster supply chain visibility, many organizations are investing heavily in computer hardware, SCIS, and supportive technologies like RFID. They realize that real-time information and the ability to dynamically respond to changing conditions in the supply chain are critical to the success of the organization. Industry leaders are using supply chain information technology to create adaptive supply chain capabilities and substantial competitive advantages in their respective markets.

Harnessing information technology in support of supply chain excellence is an ongoing challenge, given the continuing evolution of SCIS capabilities. Supply chain managers must work diligently to appreciate the growing role of information, understand each type of supply chain software, choose solutions wisely, and overcome key implementation challenges to gain maximum benefit from information technology.

- In order for supply chain managers to utilize information, it must be readily accessible, relevant to their decision-making needs, accurate, timely, and in a format that can be shared.

- When properly implemented, information technology supports critical supply chain capabilities and strategies, including supply chain connectivity, product visibility, partner collaboration, and process optimization.

- A well-designed SCIS framework links people, processes, and technology in a manner that provides actionable information and enhances decision making.

- Timely data collection and synchronization support supply chain visibility, exception management, and effective response to changing customer requirements.

- Supply chain software falls into four general categories: planning tools for forecasting and related activities, execution systems for management of day-to-day processes, event management tools to monitor supply chain flows, and business intelligence applications that help organizations analyze performance.

- Given the potential stumbling blocks, software selection and implementation are not a minor undertaking. Needs must be assessed, software options studied, technical issues addressed, and important questions asked before major SCIS investments are made.

- Change is the norm when it comes to supply chain technologies. It is critical that developments related to RFID and other innovations are understood so that organizations can take full advantage of worthwhile technologies.

STUDY QUESTIONS

1. Discuss the role of information in the supply chain and how it supports supply chain planning and execution.

2. Describe the components of information quality and how they impact supply chain decision making.

3. What are the primary capabilities created by supply chain technology? How can they drive supply chain excellence?

4. Describe a supply chain information system in terms of its key elements, requirements, and capabilities.

5. Identify the four primary categories of supply chain management software and discuss their primary functions.

6. Using the BCRC Web site (http://academic.cengage.com/bcrc/bcrc.html) and company Web sites, develop a profile (types of supply chain software offered, annual sales, and recent news) of the following organizations:

   a. SAP (http://www.sap.com)
   b. Manhattan Associates (http://www.manh.com)
   c. i2 Technologies (http://www.i2.com)

7. What is the role of enterprise resource planning systems in supply chain management?

8. Discuss the relative advantages of best-of-breed software versus supply chain suites.

9. Why would companies choose to use on-demand software versus licensed software?

10. What are XML and service-oriented architecture? Discuss how they are used to support supply chain technology improvement.

11. When preparing to purchase and implement SCIS components, what issues and questions must managers address?

12. Why is there so much interest in radio-frequency identification? What supply chain benefits does RFID facilitate?

NOTES

1. ARC Advisory Group, "The SCM Market Expected to Grow 8.6% Annually: Growth Driven by SCE Segment," http://www.arcweb.com/C12/News/default.aspx, accessed June 22, 2006.

2. David R. Butcher, "Supply Chains Increasing Tech Spending … Subtly," *ThomasNet.com Industrial Market Trends* (April 25, 2006), http://news.thomasnet.com/IMT/archives/2006/, accessed June 22, 2006.

3. "Enterprises Increasing Technology Spending to Drive Supply Chain Innovation, Says New Aberdeen Report," *PR Newswire* (May 23, 2006).

4. Robert Premus and Nada Sanders, "Modeling the Relationship Between Firm IT Capability, Collaboration, and Performance," *Journal of Business Logistics*, Vol. 26, No. 1 (2005): 1–23.

5. Peter Moore, Karl Manrodt, and Mary Holcomb, *Collaboration: Enabling Synchronized Supply Chains, Year 2005 Report on Trends and Issues in Logistics and Transportation* (New York, NY: Capgemini, 2005).

6. Kevin Reilly, "AMR Research Releases Second Annual Supply Chain Top 25," *AMR Research* (November 8, 2005), http://www.amrresearch.com/Content/View.asp?pmillid=18895, accessed June 21, 2006.

7. Mark Smith, "Improving Supply Chain Performance," *Achieving Supply Chain Excellence through Technology*, Vol. 6 (San Francisco, CA: Montgomery Research, Inc., 2004).

8. Marc L. Songini, "Difficult ERP Rollout Slows Furniture Maker, *Computerworld*, Vol. 39, No. 18 (May 2, 2005): 12.

9. Jose Favilla and Andrew Fearne, "Supply Chain Software Implementations: Getting it Right," *Supply Chain Management*, Vol. 10, Issue 3/4 (October 2005): 241–243.

10. Major portions of this section have been adapted from Jeff Abott, Karl Manrodt, and Peter Moore, *From Visibility to Action: Year 2004 Report on Trends and Issues in Logistics and Transportation* (New York, NY: Capgemini, 2004); and Peter Moore, Karl Manrodt, and Mary Holcomb, *Collaboration: Enabling Synchronized Supply Chains, Year 2005 Report on Trends and Issues in Logistics and Transportation* (New York, NY: Capgemini, 2005).

11. Kenneth C. Laudon and Jane P. Laudon, *Essentials of Business Information Systems*, 7th ed. (Upper Saddle River, NJ: Prentice Hall, 2006).

12. Ken Mark, "Technology: Search for Next "Killer App" Replaced by Need to Coordinate Working of Existing Systems," *Canadian Transportation Logistics*, Vol. 108, No. 11 (2005): 58–59.

13. Bob Trebilcock, "How Smart Is Your Software?" *Logistics Management*, Vol. 41, No. 8 (August 2002): 68–70.

14. Scott Wilson, "Extending Visibility?" *Metal Producing and Processing*, Vol. 41, No. 1 (January 2003): 36–37.

15. Peter Moore, Karl Manrodt, and Mary Holcomb, *Collaboration: Enabling Synchronized Supply Chains, Year 2005 Report on Trends and Issues in Logistics and Transportation* (New York, NY: Capgemini, 2005).

16. *The Supply Chain Innovator's Technology Footprint: A Benchmark Report on What Companies Want in Their Next Supply Chain Solution* (Boston, MA: Aberdeen Group, 2006).

17. Ben Worthen, "The ABCs of Supply Chain Management," *CIO Magazine Supply Chain Management Research Center*, http://www.cio.com/research/scm/edit/012202_scm.html#scm_do, accessed June 30, 2006.

18. Ann Bednarz, "Grape Grower Juices Up its Planning Systems," *Network World*, Vol. 21, No. 24 (June 14, 2004): 21–22.

19. David Maloney, "More than Paper Savings," *DC Velocity*, Vol. 4, No. 1 (January 2006): 62–64.

20. Peter Tirschwell, "Planning vs. Execution," *Journal of Commerce* (July 5, 2004): 1.

21. David Taylor, "A Master Plan for Software Selection," *Supply Chain Management Review*, Vol. 8, No. 1 (January 2004): 20–27.

22. Ellen Curtiss and Susan Eustis, *Supply Chain Event Management: Market Opportunities, Strategies, and Forecasts, 2006 to 2012* (Lexington, MA: Wintergreen Research, 2006).

23. *Tackling Uncertainly: Improving Responsiveness with Supply Chain Event Management* (Cambridge, MA: Sapient Corporation, 2002).

24. Michael Totty, "Technology Special Report: Business Intelligence," *The Wall Street Journal* (April 3, 2006): R6.

25. Rick Whiting, "Intelligence Spending," *InformationWeek*, Issue 1079 (March 2, 2006): 63–64.

26. Tony Kontzer, "Wyeth Resolves to Aid its Distributors," *InformationWeek*, Issue 1056 (September 19, 2005): 96–97.

27. For an extensive discussion of Enterprise Resource Planning Systems, see Joel Wisner, G. Keong Leong, and Keah-Choon Tan, *Principles of Supply Chain Management: A Balanced Approach* (Mason, OH: South-Western, 2005): 187–205.

28. Bob Trebilcock, "A Tale of Two ERP Systems," *Modern Materials Handling*, Vol. 60, No. 13 (December 2005): 27–29.

29. William Hoffman, "Doing it Their Way," *Traffic World* (November 21, 2005): 15–16.

30. Bridget McCrea, "Smarter, Faster, Cheaper," *Logistics Management*, Vol. 45, No. 5 (May 2006): 49–51 and John Fontana, "What's Behind On-Demand Software's Rise," *Network World*, Vol. 22, No. 49 (December 12, 2005): 1–2.

31. Michael Levans, "Get More Bang for Your IT Bucks," *Logistics Management*, Vol. 45, No. 4 (April 2006): 32–35.

32. John Dix, "The Three Levels of SOA Maturity," *Network World*, Vol. 23, No. 9 (May 15, 2006): 42.

33. "Service-Oriented Architecture: A Whatis.com Definition," http://searchwebservices.techtarget.com/gDefinition/0,294236, sid26_gci929153,00.htm, accessed July 18, 2006.

34. Bridget McCrea, "Is SOA the Answer to Supply Chain Software Limitations?" *Logistics Management*, Vol. 44, No. 11 (November 2005): 20.

35. This section is adapted from the following presentation: Chris Norek, "Using Evolving Technology to Manage Complex Supply Chains," *Transformation '06: a Business and Logistics Conference* (Las Vegas, NV: February 1, 2006).

36. Jim Welch and Peter Wietfeldt, "How to Leverage Your Systems Investment," *Supply Chain Management Review*, Vol. 9, No. 8 (November 2005): 24–30.

37. "Supply Chain Management—Edgewater Technology," http://www.edgewater.com/Industries/Retail/solutions_supplyChain.htm, accessed July 19, 2006.

38. Anita French, "Wal-Mart Prods Suppliers on RFID," *The Morning News* (January 3, 2006).

39. "Wal-Mart: RFID Reducing Out-of-Stocks," *RFID Update* (October 25, 2005), http://www.rfidupdate.com/articles/index.php?id=977, accessed July 19, 2006.

40. "Gillette, Wal-Mart, Levi, Michelin Share RFID Results," *RFID Update* (May 27, 2005), http://www.rfidgazette.org/2005/05/gillette_walmar.html, accessed July 19, 2006.

41. This section is adapted from the following whitepaper: Chris Norek, "Adaptive Supply Chain Networks: The Next Supply Chain Summit" (Atlanta, GA: Chain Connectors, Inc., 2006).

42. Jim Pinto, "Pervasive Networks," *Automation World* (December 2004), http://www.automationworld.com/articles/Departments/1038.html?ppr_key=12.2004&sky_key=12.2004&term=12.2004, accessed July 19, 2006.

43. Shane Schick, "Expert Warns of Emerging Pervasive Workplace," *Computing Canada*, Vol. 26, No. 21 (October 13, 2000): 36.

44. George Brody, "The Smart, Sensor-Based RFID Network," *Achieving Supply Chain Excellence through Technology*, Vol. 7 (San Francisco, CA: Montgomery Research, Inc., 2005).

CASE 6.1

Catnap Pet Products

Catnap Pet Products (CPP) of Saskatoon, Saskatchewan, in Canada manufactures fancy pet kennels. Unlike traditional wire cage kennels, the Catnappers synthetic wicker kennels are attractive and functional. They are available in six colors and six sizes to accommodate all sizes of cats and dogs. Annual sales have averaged 50,000 units over the past three years. CPP has no sizeable competitors and sells the product directly via the Internet on http://www.catnapping.ca and through five home furnishings mail order catalogs at prices ranging from $99.95 to $279.99 CDN plus shipping and handling.

Catnappers consist of four primary components: the wire frame and door (sourced from Nampa, Idaho), a plastic floor pan (Calgary, Alberta), weaved resin panels (Tijuana, Mexico), and shipping boxes (from nearby Regina, Saskatchewan). The components are assembled, packaged, and warehoused at CPP's Saskatoon facility. CPP management develops quarterly forecasts using Excel macros and shares them via e-mail with each supplier along with the monthly orders for components.

Approximately 35 percent of customer orders are placed through CPP's Web site with the remaining 65 percent coming through its mail order partners. The two largest sellers place daily orders using Internet-based EDI, two others send weekly orders via e-mail, and the smallest catalog company periodically faxes in orders. All customer orders are sent from CPP via small package carriers as no inventory is held by the catalog companies.

Over the years, the company has cobbled together a variety of technology tools to support its efforts. Key components include an e-commerce package to manage the Web site and order taking, a basic warehouse management system that helps CPP monitor inventory levels and manage order picking, and shipment management tools from its primary package carrier to help with routing, documentation, labeling, and tracking. Other processes are managed using a structured query language (SQL) database, spreadsheets, and an accounting software package.

At a recent trade show, CPP executives were approached by two major retailers, PETCO and Target, about carrying the Catnappers product line. The projected volume of these two customers would take annual sales to 250,000 units. While company executives were initially ecstatic, they quickly realized that the current capabilities of the Saskatoon facility and the CPP "information system" could not sustain such volume. Still, they did not want to turn down the business windfall and began working on a plan to handle their new customers.

The first planning meeting generated a basic strategy. The company would continue to serve its current customers through existing facilities and processes. In terms of the additional volume, CPP would manage the sourcing of components and use a contract manufacturer in China to produce the Catnappers for PETCO and Target. The product would be shipped to San Diego, California, via ocean container service and a third-party logistics company would warehouse the inventory and manage final delivery to PETCO and Target stores.

CASE QUESTIONS

1. Given its volume growth and supply chain process changes, what technology challenges will CPP face?

2. As the scope of the CPP supply chain expands, which information technology capabilities will be most important for the company to pursue?

3. From an information sharing standpoint, how will the requirements of PETCO and Target differ from CPP's current customer base? How should CPP respond to these requirements?

4. What type(s) of software will be most beneficial for CPP to adopt? Why?

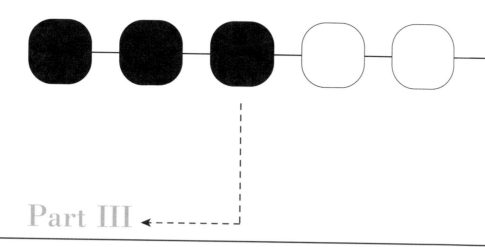

Part III

Up to this point, the topics in this text have provided a basic understanding of the supply chain, how it is managed and measured, and the technology used to help manage information flows. Part III will focus on the concept of forecast to cash, i.e., all of the functional activities involved in developing the forecast up to the collection of cash. This section will discuss the planning and execution of the movement of products to the end customer with the goal of minimizing cost and maximizing customer satisfaction.

Chapter 7 begins by discussing the typical imbalance between supply and demand for an organization and how this imbalance can be mitigated by understanding the various factors that affect demand. Following this discussion, an in-depth presentation of various forecasting methods is given in an attempt to help organizations estimate future customer demands. Basic collaborative forecasting techniques, such as the sales and operations planning (S&OP) process and collaborative planning and forecasting requirements (CPFR), are introduced to show how they can be expanded to include other functional areas within an organization as well as other channel partners. Finally, this chapter presents some basic processes that can be used in the fulfillment process.

Chapter 8 focuses on the concepts of customer service and order management and how they are related and managed within organizations. The basic elements of customer service are identified and discussed from the perspective of how they affect both buyers and sellers. The concept of stockout costs is introduced. Finally, this chapter presents the major outputs of order management, how they are measured, and their financial impacts on buyers and sellers.

Chapter 9 offers a detailed examination of the concept of inventory management. This chapter begins with a general discussion of the roles of inventory in the economy, why organizations carry inventory, and the various types of inventory held in the supply chain. Next, an in-depth discussion is offered on the various techniques for managing inventory, with a special focus on the economic order quantity (EOQ). Other inventory management techniques, such as just-in-time (JIT), materials requirement planning (MRP), distribution requirements planning (DRP), and vendor-managed inventory (VMI), are also discussed. Also covered in this chapter are methods used to classify inventory and the impact on inventory when changing the number of stocking points. Finally, the chapter appendix offers several derivations on the basic EOQ model.

The final two chapters present a detailed discussion on the two logistics areas critical to supply chain fulfillment—transportation and distribution. **Chapter 10** first discusses the importance of transportation to the economy followed by a general analysis of the transportation market and the various modes of transportation. Next, this chapter offers a perspective on transportation planning, execution, and control. Finally, transportation metrics and technology are covered. The focus of **Chapter 11** is on the roles of distribution operations in the supply chain. Special attention is given to distribution planning, strategy, and execution. The chapter ends with a description of the roles of metrics and technology in distribution.

Chapter 7

DEMAND MANAGEMENT

Learning Objectives

After reading this chapter, you should be able to do the following:

- Understand the critical importance of outbound-to-customer logistics systems.

- Appreciate the growing need for effective demand management as part of an organization's overall logistics and supply chain expertise.

- Know the types of forecasts that might be needed and understand how collaboration among trading partners will help the overall forecasting and demand management processes.

- Understand the basic principles underlying the sales and operations planning process.

- Identify the key steps in the order fulfillment process and appreciate the various channel structures that might be used in the fulfillment process.

Supply Chain Profile   *LuAnn's Chocolates*

LuAnn's Chocolates (LC) was founded by LuAnn Jaworski and her husband Denny in 1975. Located in Bellefonte, Pennsylvania, LC produced a relatively small number of chocolate products that catered to normal consumer demand (e.g., chocolate bars) as well as specialty consumer markets (e.g., special boxed assortments). With current annual revenues hovering around $3 million, LC has seen growing revenues, and the seasonal demand for chocolates is beginning to cause some problems in inventory levels and production scheduling.

CURRENT PLANNING PROCESS

Traditionally, LC relied on keeping its only manufacturing plant operating at a steady level throughout the year. Forecasting was done manually with small annual increases in volume applied to demand evenly throughout the year. Forecasts of demand were supplied by the two sales representatives LC employed to call on local retailers. The sales reps' compensation consisted of a base salary plus commission. Manufacturing would then change these forecasts to allow the plant to run smoothly while minimizing changeovers. The plant manager was measured on total manufactured cost per pound. Although the plant kept running at a steady rate, inventory levels would fluctuate wildly throughout the year. To complicate matters, LC often had high levels of the wrong inventory in place in its distribution center, resulting in stockouts. Although finance was concerned about "making the numbers" every quarter, it had little or no input to the forecasting and production scheduling processes.

CURRENT DISTRIBUTION PROCESS

LC makes its chocolate and stores it in its distribution center (DC), also located in Bellefonte. When orders arrive from retail customers, the DC fills them and adjusts the inventory levels in the inventory tracking system. When the inventory level for a product in the DC reaches a predetermined level, the DC places an order on the plant for replenishment. If the plant has inventory for that product on site or if it is currently making that product, a replenishment order is sent to the DC. If neither of these two situations exists, the DC waits for its order until the plant is scheduled to make that product. No advance information is provided to LC by its customers of anticipated demand.

THE MEETING

Every Monday morning, LC holds an executive staff meeting with representatives from sales, logistics, manufacturing, and finance to review the activity from the previous week. This morning's meeting turned into a rather contentious debate about the company's inventory levels and resulting stockouts. Beth Bower, one of the sales reps, voiced her concern over the lack of proper inventory to satisfy the demands of her customers. "I took a beating from my customers last week. Every order I took was cut short or not filled at all because the DC did not have the right inventory." Teresa Lehman, DC manager, had a hasty reply to Beth: "I ship what I have. Don't blame me if I don't have the inventory. My DC is full. Why can't you sell what I have in inventory? That's your job. I take what manufacturing gives me. If you want to blame someone, blame the plant." Vinny Coglianese, plant manager, was upset at this finger-pointing. "If I would make what you ordered when you ordered it, my costs would go through the roof. I get the production schedule and I run it." Jean Beierlein, vice president of finance, was quick to add her comments: "We did not hit our revenue numbers last quarter and the way things are going now, we are going to miss them this quarter. Somebody needs to assess what we are doing or we are going to lose money this year."

Needless to say, LuAnn was perplexed by this conversation. When the company was first started, things were a lot simpler. However, growth has brought with it a wide variety of operating problems she had not anticipated. The reality of losing money for the first time in company history was a situation for which LuAnn was not ready. If you were LuAnn, what would you do to fix the problems at LC?

Introduction

In an effort to better serve their customers, many organizations place significant emphasis on what might be termed their **outbound-to-customer logistics systems**. Also referred to as *physical distribution*, this essentially refers to the processes, systems, and capabilities that enhance an organization's ability to serve its customers. For example, the ways in which retailers such as Wal-Mart, Target, and L.L.Bean fulfill their customers' orders are examples of outbound logistics. This topic has been of significant historical interest in the study of logistics and supply chain management. This chapter will highlight key areas of concern related to this general topic.

Correspondingly, the topic of **inbound-to-operations logistics systems** refers to the activities and processes that precede and facilitate value-adding activities such as procurement (Chapter 13), manufacturing (Chapter 14), and assembly. Other terms that focus on these elements of the supply chain include **materials management** and **physical supply**. A typical example would be movements of automotive parts and accessories that need to move from supplier locations to automotive assembly plants. Although many of the principles of inbound logistics are conceptually similar to those of outbound logistics, some important differences must be recognized. Thus, the topic of inbound logistics systems will be the focus of Chapter 13, which is titled "Sourcing Materials and Services."

Considering the complexity of the topic at hand, this chapter has a relatively aggressive agenda of topics to be discussed. First, a discussion of demand management provides an overview of the importance of effectively managing outbound-to-customer processes. Second, the topic of forecasting is addressed. Third, an introduction to the sales and operations planning (S&OP) process is provided. Fourth, the recent emphasis on collaborative forecasting approaches is covered. Finally, attention is focused on the fulfillment process and the processes and methods used to effectively distribute goods in outbound-to-customer logistics systems.

Demand Management

According to Blackwell and Blackwell, **demand management** might be thought of as "focused efforts to estimate and manage customers' demand, with the intention of using this information to shape operating decisions."[1] Traditional supply chains typically begin at the point of manufacture or assembly and end with the sale of product to consumers or business buyers. Much of the focus and attention has been related to the topic of product flow, with significant concern for matters such as technology, information exchange, inventory turnover, delivery speed and consistency, and transportation. This notwithstanding, it is the manufacturers—who are many times far removed from the end user or consumer market—who determine what will be available for sale, where, when, and how many. If this seems to reflect a disconnect between manufacturing and demand at the point of consumption, that is exactly what it is. Thus, any attention paid to demand management will produce benefits throughout the supply chain.

The essence of demand management is to further the ability of firms throughout the supply chain—particularly manufacturing through the customer—to collaborate on activities related to the flow of product, services, information, and capital. The desired end result should be to create greater value for the end user or consumer. The following list suggests a number of ways in which effective demand management will help to unify channel members with the common goals of satisfying customers and solving customer problems:[2]

- Gathering and analyzing knowledge about consumers, their problems, and their unmet needs
- Identifying partners to perform the functions needed in the demand chain
- Moving the functions that need to be done to the channel member that can perform them most effectively and efficiently
- Sharing with other supply chain members knowledge about consumers and customers, available technology, and logistics challenges and opportunities
- Developing products and services that solve customers' problems
- Developing and executing the best logistics, transportation, and distribution methods to deliver products and services to consumers in the desired format

As organizations identify the need for improved demand management, several problems occur. First, the lack of coordination between departments (i.e., the existence of "functional silos") results in little or no coordinated response to demand information. Second, too much emphasis is placed on forecasts of demand, with less attention on the collaborative efforts and the strategic and operational plans that need to be developed from the forecasts. Third, demand information is used more for tactical and operational than for strategic purposes. In essence, since in many cases historical performance is not a very good predictor of the future, demand information should be used to create collective and realistic scenarios for the future. Primary emphasis should be on understanding likely demand scenarios and mapping their relationships to product supply alternatives. The end result will be to better match demand as it occurs with appropriate availability of needed product in the marketplace.

Figure 7.1 provides an overview of how supply and demand misalignment might impact overall supply chain effectiveness. Using the personal computer (PC) industry as an example, this figure charts production, channel orders, and true end-user demand over the life cycle of a product. Ignoring the early adopters, end-user demand for PCs typically is at its highest level at the time new products are launched, which is also the time that availability is most precarious. As new, competing products become available, end-user demand begins to taper off, eventually reaching a modest level, at which time the product, now much more available, is generally phased out.

Looking more closely at Figure 7.1, we see that in the first phase of a new product launch, when end-user demand is at its peak and opportunities for profit margins are greatest, PC assemblers are not able to supply product in quantities sufficient to meet demand—thus creating true product shortages. Also during this time, distributors and resellers tend to "over-order," often creating substantial "phantom" demand. In the next phase, as production begins to increase, assemblers ship product against this inflated order situation and book sales at the premium, high-level launch price. As channel inventories begin to grow, price competition sets in, as do product overages and returns. This further depresses demand for the PC product, and the PC assemblers are the hardest hit.

In the final phase noted in Figure 7.1, as end-user demand begins to decline, the situation clearly has shifted to one of over-supply. This is largely due to the industry's planning processes and systems, which are primarily designed to use previous period demand as a gauge. Since much of the previous period's demand was represented by the previously mentioned "phantom" demand, forecasts are distorted. The net result of

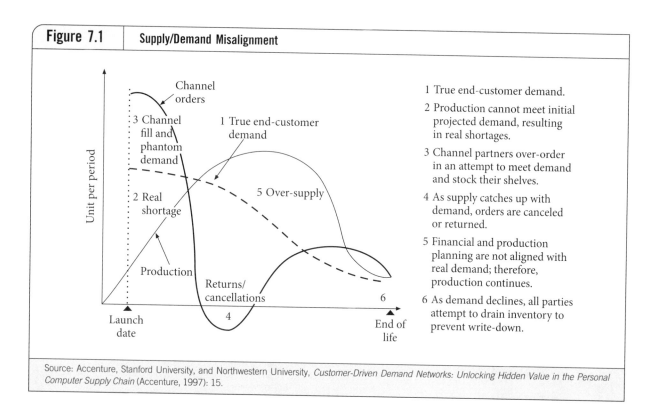

Figure 7.1 | **Supply/Demand Misalignment**

1 True end-customer demand.

2 Production cannot meet initial projected demand, resulting in real shortages.

3 Channel partners over-order in an attempt to meet demand and stock their shelves.

4 As supply catches up with demand, orders are canceled or returned.

5 Financial and production planning are not aligned with real demand; therefore, production continues.

6 As demand declines, all parties attempt to drain inventory to prevent write-down.

Source: Accenture, Stanford University, and Northwestern University, *Customer-Driven Demand Networks: Unlocking Hidden Value in the Personal Computer Supply Chain* (Accenture, 1997): 15.

aligning supply and demand is that a large majority of product is sold during the declining period of profit opportunity, thereby diminishing substantial value creation opportunities for industry participants. Adding insult to injury, substantial amounts of inventory are held throughout the supply chain as a hedge against supply uncertainty.

According to Langabeer, there is growing and persuasive evidence that understanding and managing market demand are central determinants of business success.[3] Aside from this observation, relatively few companies have successfully linked demand management with strategy. Table 7.1 provides a view of how demand data might be used strategically to enhance an organization's growth, portfolio, positioning, and investment strategies. As suggested, effective use of demand data can help organizations to guide strategic resources in a number of important ways.

Balancing Supply and Demand

The essence of demand management, as previously stated, is to estimate and manage customer demand and use this information to make operating decisions. However, demand and supply in an organization will more than likely never be balanced to allow for zero stockouts and zero safely stocks. Many methods to manage this imbalance exist. However, there are four methods that are commonly used across many industries. Two of those, price and lead time, are referred to as **external balancing methods**. The other two, inventory and production flexibility, are called **internal balancing methods**.

External balancing methods are used in an attempt to change the manner in which the customer orders in an attempt to balance the supply-demand gap. Dell has found

Table 7.1	How Demand Management Supports Business Strategy
STRATEGY	**EXAMPLES OF HOW TO USE DEMAND MANAGEMENT**
Growth strategy	• Perform "what if" analyses on total industry volume to gauge how specific mergers and acquisitions might leverage market share. • Analyze industry supply/demand to predict changes in product pricing structure and market economics based on mergers and acquisitions. • Build staffing models for merged company using demand data.
Portfolio strategy	• Manage maturity of products in current portfolio to optimally time overlapping life cycles. • Create new product development/introduction plans based on life cycle. • Balance combination of demand and risk for consistent "cash cows" with demand for new products. • Ensure diversification of product portfolio through demand forecasts.
Positioning strategy	• Manage product sales through each channel based on demand and product economics. • Manage positioning of finished goods at appropriate distribution centers, to reduce working capital, based on demand. • Define capability to supply for each channel.
Investment strategy	• Manage capital investments, marketing expenditures, and research and development budgets based on demand forecasts of potential products and maturity of current products. • Determine whether to add manufacturing capacity.

Source: Jim R. Langabeer II, "Aligning Demand Management with Human Strategy," *Supply Chain Management Review* (May/June 2000): 58. Copyright © 2000 Reed Business Information, a division of Reed Elsevier. Reproduced by permission.

these methods to be relatively effective in smoothing demand to meet supply. For example, Dell frequently refreshes its Web site with price changes and availability changes based on the demand for an item and its supply. If customer demand exceeds the current supply, Dell can increase the lead time for that item for customer delivery. By doing so, one of two results can occur. First, if the customer finds the increased lead time unacceptable, she or he might decide to specify an alternative item from Dell for which there is sufficient inventory. Second, if the customer decides the increased lead time is acceptable, Dell now has the opportunity to wait for the next delivery of that item from suppliers. If customer demand is less than current inventory levels for a particular item, a price reduction for that item will appear on the Web site, hopefully increasing demand for the item. Using both methods allows Dell to manage stockouts while minimizing safety stock inventories.

Internal balancing methods utilize an organization's internal processes to manage the supply-demand gap. Production flexibility allows an organization to quickly and efficiently change its production lines from one product to another. This is one principle of lean manufacturing. Being able to react quickly to changing demand by altering production schedules will allow for a minimum of safely stocks while reducing the possibility of a stockout. The tradeoff here is between production changeover costs and safely stock costs. Inventory is probably the most common, and maybe the most expensive, method used to manage the imbalance between supply and demand. Many organizations produce product to a forecast that includes safely stock to smooth the effects of both demand and lead time variability. This allows an organization to minimize the number of changeovers it needs to make in production but also results in high inventory levels. In these cases, stockout costs are usually high as are production changeover costs.

These four methods are not mutually exclusive in most organizations. Some combination of all of them is used to manage safety stocks and stockouts. Their use and level of implementation will be determined by the nature of the product and the cost of stocking out. Also affecting their use will be the organization's ability to properly forecast customer demand. Forecasting will be the topic of the next section.

Traditional Forecasting

A major component of demand management is **forecasting** the amount of product that will be purchased, when it will be purchased, and where it will be purchased by customers. Although various statistical techniques exist to forecast demand, the common thread for all forecasts is that they will ultimately be wrong. The key to successful forecasting is to minimize the error between actual demand and forecasted demand. Although this sounds simple, many factors can arise in the marketplace that will change demand contrary to the forecast. However, forecasts are necessary because they serve as a plan for both marketing and operations to set goals and develop execution strategies. These goals and strategies are developed through the sales and operations planning (S&OP) process. This concept will be covered in a later section in this chapter. The remainder of this section will focus on the various basic types of forecasting techniques used throughout industry.

Factors Affecting Demand

Two types of demand exist: independent and dependent. **Independent demand** is the demand for the primary item. **Dependent demand** is directly influenced by the demand for the independent item. For example, the demand for bicycles would be called *independent*. It is the demand for the primary, or finished, product and is directly created by the customer. The demand for bicycle tires would be called *dependent*, because the number of tires demanded is determined by the number of bicycles demanded. Most forecasting techniques focus on independent demand. For example, a bicycle manufacturer will forecast the demand for bicycles during a given period. Given that level of demand, the manufacturer knows that two tires will be required for each bicycle demanded. As such, there is no need for the bicycle manufacturer to forecast the demand for tires. From a different perspective, the tire manufacturer will need to forecast the demand for tires, because these are its independent demand items. However, the tire manufacturer will not need to forecast the demand for rims since each tire requires one rim. So, each organization in a particular supply chain will have different definitions for independent and dependent demand items. Forecasting, however, will still usually be done at the independent demand item level.

Normally, the demand for independent demand items is known as **base demand**, that is, *normal demand*. However, all demand is subject to certain fluctuations. One type of demand fluctuation is caused by **random variation**. Random variation cannot be anticipated and is usually the cause to hold safety stocks to avoid stockouts. For example, the hurricanes that devastated parts of Louisiana caused an unexpected surge in the demand for building supplies in that region. A second type of demand fluctuation is caused by **trend**. Trend is the gradual increase or decrease in demand over time for an organization. The demand for advanced electronic components in the consumer market (for example iPods and DVD players) is trending upwards. The demand for VCR players is trending downwards. A third type of demand fluctuation is caused by **seasonal patterns**. Seasonal patterns will normally repeat themselves during a year for most organizations. For example, chocolate manufacturers are normally faced with several seasonal patterns during the year, such as Valentine's Day, Easter, and Halloween. Finally, demand fluctuations can be caused by normal **business cycles**. These are usually driven by the nation's economy and can be growing, stagnant, or declining. These patterns usually occur over periods of more than one year. Almost every firm is subject to all of these demand influences, making forecasting an even more challenging task. The next section will briefly examine some of the more popular forecasting methods and will show how some of these demand variations can be included in an organization's forecasts.

Simple Moving Average

The **simple moving average** is probably the simplest to develop method in basic time series forecasting. It makes forecasts based on recent demand history and allows for the removal of random effects. The simple moving average method does not accommodate seasonal, trend, or business cycle influences. This method simply averages a predetermined number of periods and uses this average as the demand for the next period. Each time the average is computed, the oldest demand is dropped and the most recent demand is included. A weakness of this method is that it forgets the past quickly. A strength is that it is quick and easy to use.

Refer to Table 7.2 for an example of using the simple moving average technique on the demand for chocolate candy made by LuAnn's Chocolates (LC). Table 7.2 shows the average demand in cases per month for LC's most popular candy bar in Column 2. This example will use a three-period moving average. To determine the forecast for April's demand, the demand for January, February, and March is averaged. This calculation is shown in Formula 7.1.

$$A_t = \frac{\text{Sum of last } n \text{ demands}}{n}$$
$$= D_t + D_{t-1} + D_{t-2} + \ldots D_{t-n+1} \qquad 7.1$$

where

$$D_t = \text{Actual demand in period } t$$
$$n = \text{Total number of periods in the average}$$
$$A_t = \text{Average for period } t$$

This would result in the following calculation:

$$(560 + 1{,}300 + 750)/3 = 870 \text{ cases}$$

The demand for May drops the demand for January from its calculation and adds the demand for April. The calculation is as follows:

$$(1{,}300 + 750 + 1{,}465)/3 = 1{,}171.7 \text{ cases}$$

This process repeats itself until all forecasts are made. The three-period moving average is shown in Column 3, and the forecast is shown in Column 4. The error term is simply the difference between the forecast and the actual demand and can be seen in Column 5. Adding together the error terms for the forecasts results in what can be called

Table 7.2	Simple Moving Average Forecast			
(1) t PERIOD	(2) D_t DEMAND	(3) A_t THREE-PERIOD MOVING AVERAGE	(4) F_t THREE-PERIOD FORECAST	(5) E_t $D_t - F_t$ ERROR
January	560			
February	1,300			
March	750	870.0		
April	1,465	1,171.7	870.0	+595.0
May	725	980.0	1,171.7	−446.7
June	675	955.0	980.0	−305.0
July	575	658.3	955.0	−380.0
August	815	688.3	658.3	+156.7
September	1,275	888.3	688.3	+586.7
October	1,385	1,158.3	888.3	+496.7
November	950	1,203.3	1,158.3	−208.3
December	1,425	1,253.3	1,203.3	+221.7
Total	11,900			
$\bar{x}$	991.7			
Bias	$\Sigma(D_t - F_t)$			+716.8
Bias $\bar{x}$	$\Sigma(D_t - F_t)/n$			+79.6
Absolute Deviation $\Sigma|D_t - F_t|$				3,396.8
Absolute Deviation $\bar{x}$ $\Sigma|D_t - F_t|/n$				377.4

bias. Bias measures how accurate the forecast is compared to actual demand. A positive bias means that the demand was higher than forecast during the forecast period, resulting in stockouts; a negative bias means the demand was lower than the forecast, resulting in excess inventories. The closer the bias term is to zero, the better the forecast. In this example, the bias is +716.8 units or +79.6 units per forecast period (+716.8/9 periods). This means that this forecast was lower than actual demand by 716.8 cases in total and lower than actual demand per month by 79.6 cases. Absolute deviation removes the positive and negative signs from the error terms and is a measure of how accurate the overall forecast is. The closer to zero, the better the forecast is at estimating demand. This measure will be used later when the concept of mean absolute deviation is discussed. Recall that the simple moving average technique does not incorporate seasonal influences into its forecasts. As previously mentioned, the chocolate candy industry is subject to dramatic seasonal influences. As such, this method might not be appropriate for this type of demand data. The next technique will attempt to improve on this forecast accuracy.

Weighted Moving Average

In the simple moving average method, each previous demand period was given an equal weight. The **weighted moving average** method assigns a weight to each previous period with higher weights usually given to more recent demand. The weights must equal to one. The weighted moving average method allows emphasis to be placed on more recent demand as a predictor of future demand. For example, Table 7.3 shows the monthly demand for LuAnn's candy bar. Assume that the weights to be used will be 0.60 for the most recent period, 0.25 for the second most recent, and 0.15 for the third most recent. The average for the next period will be calculated using Formula 7.2.

$$A_t = 0.60D_t + 0.25D_{t-1} + 0.15D_{t-2} \qquad 7.2$$

Table 7.3	Weighted Moving Average Forecast			
(1) t PERIOD	(2) D_t DEMAND	(3) A_t THREE-PERIOD MOVING AVERAGE	(4) F_t THREE-PERIOD FORECAST	(5) E_t $D_t - F_t$ ERROR
January	560			
February	1,300			
March	750	859.0		
April	1,465	1,261.5	859.0	+606.0
May	725	913.75	1,261.5	−536.5
June	675	806.0	913.75	−238.75
July	575	622.5	806.0	−231.0
August	815	734.0	622.5	+192.5
September	1,275	1,055.0	734.0	+541.0
October	1,385	1,272.0	1,055.0	+330.0
November	950	1,107.5	1,272.0	−322.0
December	1,425	1,300.25	1,107.5	+317.5
Total	11,900			
$\bar{x}$	991.7			
Bias	$\Sigma(D_t - F_t)$			+658.75
Bias $\bar{x}$	$\Sigma(D_t - F_t)/n$			+73.2
Absolute Deviation $\Sigma|D_t - F_t|$				3,315.3
Absolute Deviation $\bar{x}$ $\Sigma|D_t - F_t|/n$				368.4
$\alpha\, D_t = 0.60,\ \alpha\, D_{t-1} = 0.25,\ \alpha\, D_{t-2} = 0.15$				

Column 3 in Table 7.3 shows the results of this formula. The weighted moving average for period 3 would be calculated as follows:

$$(0.60 \times 750) + (0.25 \times 1{,}300) + (0.15 \times 560) = 859.0 \text{ cases}$$

This becomes the forecast for period 4. These forecasts can be seen in Column 4. Once again, the error term is calculated and shown in Column 5. The bias term for this method is $+658.75$ cases with an average bias per period of $+73.2$ cases. The results shown for this method are better than those found by using the simple moving average method. This is primarily because the weighted moving average method does not assume equal weights for each period in the calculation. However, the results from the weighted moving average method are still not very good forecasts of demand. There are three possible causes for this. First, the weights assigned to the three periods might not accurately reflect the patterns in demand. Second, using three periods to develop the forecast might not be the appropriate number of periods. Finally, the weighted moving average technique does not easily accommodate demand patterns with seasonal influences. In an attempt to improve on this forecast, another technique will be applied to LuAnn's demand data.

Exponential Smoothing

Exponential smoothing is one of the most commonly used techniques because of its simplicity and its limited requirements for data. Exponential smoothing needs three types of data: an average of previous demand, the most recent demand, and a smoothing constant. The smoothing constant must be between 0 and 1. Using a higher constant assumes that the most recent demand is a better predictor of future demand. Formula 7.3 is used to calculate the forecast.

$$A_t = \alpha(\text{Demand this period}) + (1 - \alpha)(\text{Forecast calculated last period})$$
$$= \alpha D_t + (1 - \alpha)A_{t-1} \qquad 7.3$$

Using the data contained in Table 7.2, the forecast using exponential smoothing is generated and can be seen in Table 7.4. Assume that the average for the previous period (the average of the 12 periods was used for convenience) is 992 cases. Table 7.4 shows the forecasts and the bias for two scenarios, one with a constant of 0.1 and the other with a constant of 0.3. The forecast for January is simply the average from the previous period (992 cases). The forecast for February is calculated as follows:

$$\text{Forecast} = (0.1 \times 560) + (0.9 \times 992) = 948.8 \text{ cases}$$

The forecast for March follows the same calculation.

$$\text{Forecast} = (0.1 \times 1{,}300) + (0.9 \times 948.8) = 983.9 \text{ cases}$$

This same methodology is used to calculate the forecasts using 0.3 as the constant, except 0.3 is used in the formula instead of 0.1. The resulting bias terms show that using 0.1 results in a better forecast than using 0.3 as a smoothing constant. The resulting average bias per period (12 periods were used here) shows that using exponential smoothing with a constant of 0.1 has so far produced the best forecast. However, exponential smoothing forecasts will lag actual demand. If demand is relatively constant, exponential smoothing will produce a relatively accurate forecast. However, highly seasonal demand patterns or patterns with trends can cause inaccurate forecasts using exponential smoothing. The next method will attempt to introduce the concept of trend into the forecast.

Table 7.4		Exponential Smoothing Forecast[*]				
(1) t PERIOD	(2) D_t DEMAND	(3) F_t $\alpha = 0.1$ FORECAST	(4) E_t $D_t - F_t$ ERROR	(5) F_t $\alpha = 0.3$ FORECAST	(6) E_t $D_t - F_t$ ERROR
January	560	992.0	−432.0	992.0	−432.0
February	1,300	948.8	+351.2	862.4	+437.6
March	750	983.9	−233.9	993.7	−243.7
April	1,465	960.5	+504.5	920.6	+544.4
May	725	1,010.95	−285.95	1,083.9	−358.9
June	675	982.4	−307.4	976.2	−301.2
July	575	951.7	−376.7	885.8	−310.8
August	815	914.0	−99.0	792.6	+22.4
September	1,275	904.1	+370.9	799.3	+475.7
October	1,385	941.2	+443.8	942.0	+443.0
November	950	985.6	−35.6	1,074.9	−124.9
December	1,425	982.0	−443.0	1,037.4	+387.6
Total	11,900				
x̄	991.7				
Bias	$\Sigma(D_t - F_t)$		+342.85		+539.2
Bias x̄	$\Sigma(D_t - F_t)/n$		+28.6		+44.9
Absolute Deviation $\Sigma|D_t - F_t|$			3,883.95		4,082.2
Absolute Deviation x̄ $\Sigma|D_t - F_t|/n$			323.7		340.2

[*]Assume F1 = 992

Adjusting Exponential Smoothing for Trend

As previously mentioned, exponential smoothing will tend to cause severe lags in forecasts for demand patterns that contain trends. As such, exponential smoothing can be adjusted to accommodate trends by estimating the magnitude of the trend. This is done by computing the average of the series in the previous period to the average computed last period.[4] To adjust the forecast for trend, the estimates for both the average and the trend are smoothed by constants. Formula 7.4 calculates the average demand for a period.

$$A_t = \alpha(\text{Demand this period}) + (1 - \alpha)$$
$$(\text{Average} + \text{Trend estimate last period})$$
$$= \alpha D_t + (1 - \alpha)(A_{t-1} + T_{t-1}) \qquad 7.4$$

(1) t PERIOD	(2) D_t DEMAND	(3) A_t SMOOTHED FORECAST	(4) T_t TREND ESTIMATE	(5) F_t $A_t + T_t$ FORECAST	(6) E_t $D_t - F_t$ ERROR
Table 7.5 Trend-Adjusted Exponential Smoothing Forecast					
January	560	560.0	50.0	0	0
February	1,300	748.0	77.6	825.6	+474.4
March	750	810.5	74.6	885.1	−135.1
April	1,465	1,001.1	97.8	1,098.9	+366.1
May	725	1,024.1	82.8	1,106.9	−381.9
June	675	1,020.5	67.0	1,087.5	−412.5
July	575	985.0	46.5	1,031.5	−456.5
August	815	988.2	37.8	1,026.0	−211.0
September	1,275	1,075.8	47.8	1,123.6	+151.4
October	1,385	1,175.9	58.3	1,234.2	+150.8
November	950	1,177.4	46.9	1,224.3	−274.3
December	1,425	1,264.4	54.9	1,319.3	+105.7
Total	11,900				
$\bar{x}$	991.7				
Bias	$\Sigma(D_t - F_t)$				−622.9
Bias $\bar{x}$	$\Sigma(D_t - F_t)/n$				−56.6
Absolute Deviation $\Sigma|D_t - F_t|$					3,119.7
Absolute Deviation $\bar{x}$ $\Sigma|D_t - F_t|/n$					283.6
$\alpha = 0.20$, $\beta = 0.20$					

Formula 7.5 calculates the average trend for a period.

$$T_t = \beta(\text{Average this period} - \text{Average last period})$$
$$+ (1 - \beta)(\text{Trend estimate last period})$$
$$= \beta(A_t - A_{t-1}) + (1 - \beta)T_{t-1} \qquad 7.5$$

where:

A_t = Exponentially smoothed average of the series in period t
T_t = Exponentially smoothed average of the trend in period t
α = Smoothing parameter for the average
β = Smoothing parameter for the trend

The smoothing parameters for both average demand and average trend must be between 0 and 1. Estimates for average demand and the trend can be made from historical data. Refer to Table 7.5 for an application of this method to the LuAnn's Chocolates data. Column 1 shows the month, and Column 2 shows the demand. This example starts with the smoothed average equaling the demand for period 1. A trend estimate of 50 cases will be used. A smoothing parameter for both the average and trend of 0.2 will be used. To calculate the smoothed average for February, the following calculation is used (see above formula):

$$\text{Smoothed Average} = (0.2 \times 1{,}300) + (0.8)(560 + 50) = 748 \text{ units}$$

The trend estimate is also calculated using the above formula as follows:

$$\text{Smoothed Trend} = (0.2)(748 - 560) + 0.8(50) = 77.6$$

With these calculations and similar ones for the remaining periods, values for Columns 3 and 4 can be estimated. The forecast is simply calculated by adding the smoothed average and the smoothed trend. The results can be seen in Column 5. Column 6 contains the error figure, which is the difference between the forecast and actual demand. The results of applying this technique to the data for LuAnn's Chocolates show a total bias of -622.9 cases or -56.6 cases per forecast period. Whereas the previous techniques resulted in positive bias figures, the trend-adjusted exponential smoothing method resulted in a negative. Normally, the smoothing constant can be adjusted in numerous trials in an attempt to reduce the bias of the forecast. With a positive bias, stockouts will occur. Management must decide whether or not this is acceptable based on the cost of a stockout. One more technique will be examined that will incorporate the concept of seasonality into the forecast.

Seasonal Influences on Forecasts

Many organizations are faced with seasons that repeat themselves during a particular period. These seasons might be by time of day (for example, demand for hamburgers at a fast-food outlet), by day of the week (for example, the demand for gasoline), by week, by the month, or by some combination of these. Adjusting a forecast for seasons basically uses a combination of seasonal factors and average demand to arrive at an adjusted forecast. Assume that LuAnn's Chocolates experiences five separate seasons per year: Valentine's Day, Easter, Summer, Halloween, and Christmas. Table 7.6 shows that each season is defined by several months: (1) Valentine's Day includes January and February; (2) Easter includes March and April; (3) Summer includes May, June, July, and August; (4) Halloween includes September and October; and (5) Christmas includes November and December. Three years' worth of data will be used to calculate the forecast using this technique.[5] To calculate the forecast, a four-step process will be used.[5] The first step is to calculate the average demand for each season for each year. For example, Column 2 in Table 7.6 shows the demand for year 1. Total demand for year 1 is 11,900 cases. Since there are five seasons, divide total demand per year (11,900) by the number of seasons (5) to arrive at the average demand per season for that year. For year 1, the average demand per season is 2,380 cases. Table 7.6 shows the results of Step 1 for the three years' worth of data. The second step requires that the total demand for a season in a year is divided by the average demand per season for that year. For example, for year 1, the Valentine's Day actual demand is 1,860 cases. This is divided by the average demand per season for year 1 (2,380 cases) and results in an index of 0.7815 for season 1 (Valentine's Day) for year 1. Step 2 results for all three years, worth of data can be seen in Table 7.7. The third step requires that an average seasonal index is calculated for all of the years in the data. For season 1 (Valentine's Day), the three-year average seasonal index is 0.7836. This is calculated by adding together the three indices for this season (0.7815, 0.7869, and 0.7824) and dividing by three (the number of years of data).

Table 7.6	Seasonal Influenced Forecast: Step 1			
STEP 1 (1) t PERIOD	(2) D₁ YEAR 1 DEMAND	(3) D₂ YEAR 2 DEMAND	(4) D₃ YEAR 3 DEMAND	(5) TOTAL DEMAND
January	560	588	600	1,748
February	1,300	1,365	1,392	4,057
Total	1,860	1,953	1,992	5,805
March	750	795	819	2,364
April	1,465	1,553	1,600	4,618
Total	2,215	2,348	2,419	6,982
May	725	740	733	2,198
June	675	689	682	2,046
July	575	587	581	1,743
August	815	831	823	2,469
Total	2,790	2,847	2,819	8,456
September	1,275	1,326	1,392	3,993
October	1,385	1,440	1,512	4,337
Total	2,660	2,766	2,904	8,330
November	950	998	1,038	2,986
December	1,425	1,496	1,556	4,477
Total	2,375	2,494	2,594	7,463
Total Demand	11,900	12,408	12,728	37,036
Demand per Season	2,380	2,482	2,546	7,407

The resulting seasonal index for Valentine's Day is 0.7836. The results of this step can be seen in Table 7.7. The final step estimates the average demand per season for the next period (year 4) by multiplying each season by its seasonal index. The results of this step can be seen in Table 7.8. For example, total demand for year 4 has been estimated to be 13,237 cases. The average demand per season is then 13,237 cases divided by five seasons, resulting in an average demand per season of 2,647.4 cases. Multiplying this seasonal average by the seasonal index for season 1 (Valentine's Day) of 0.7836 results in a forecast of 2,075 cases. The actual demand for this season is 2,012 (Column 4) cases resulting in an error of −63.0 cases. As can be seen, this method results in a bias value of −398.0 for the year and an average bias per season of −79.6. This means that each season will have excess inventories using this forecasting technique. Again, management must decide if this inventory policy is acceptable based on the cost of a stockout versus the cost of holding excess inventory.

Table 7.7	Seasonal Influenced Forecast: Steps 2 and 3		
STEP 2 t SEASON	(2) YEAR 1	(3) YEAR 2	(4) YEAR 3
1	1,860/2,380 = 0.7815	1,953/2,482 = 0.7869	1,992/2,546 = 0.7824
2	2,215/2,380 = 0.9307	2,348/2,482 = 0.9460	2,419/2,546 = 0.9501
3	2,790/2,380 = 1.1723	2,847/2,482 = 1.1471	2,819/2,546 = 1.1072
4	2,660/2,380 = 1.1176	2,766/2,482 = 1.1144	2,904/2,546 = 1.1406
5	2,375/2,380 = 0.9979	2,494/2,482 = 1.0048	2,594/2,546 = 1.0189
Step 3 Season	Average Seasonal Index		
1	(0.7815 + 0.7869 + 0.7824)/3 = 0.7836		
2	(0.9307 + 0.9460 + 0.9501)/3 = 0.9423		
3	(1.1723 + 1.1471 + 1.1072)/3 = 1.1422	4	
4	(1.1176 + 1.1144 + 1.1406)/3 = 1.1242		
5	(0.9979 + 1.0048 + 1.0189)/3 = 1.0072		

Table 7.8	Seasonal Influenced Forecast: Step 4				
STEP 4 (1) SEASON	(2) YEAR 4 AVERAGE DEMAND	(3) SEASONAL INDEX	(4) D_t ACTUAL DEMAND	(5) F_t FORECAST	(6) E_t $D_t - F_t$ ERROR
1	2,647.4	0.7836	2,012	2,075	−63.0
2	2,647.4	0.9423	2,420	2,495	−75.0
3	2,647.4	1.1422	2,931	3,024	−93.0
4	2,647.4	1.1242	2,888	2,976	−88.0
5	2,647.4	1.0072	2,587	2,666	−79.0
Total Demand	13,237				
Bias	$\Sigma(D_t - F_t)$				−398.0
Bias $\bar{x}$	$\Sigma(D_t - F_t)/n$				−79.6
Absolute Deviation $\Sigma|D_t - F_t|$					398.0
Absolute Deviation $\bar{x}$ $\Sigma|D_t - F_t|/n$					79.6

This section provided several examples of forecasting techniques commonly used in industry. As can be seen from these examples, none of them were perfectly accurate. This is the nature of forecasting: all forecasts are wrong. What these examples did show is that different techniques will provide different results. Organizations must decide which technique and what level of data best fit their business demands. The idea here is that management must choose the method that minimizes forecast error, either positively or negatively. Measuring forecast error is the focus of the next section.

Forecast Errors

As previously mentioned, almost all forecasts will be wrong. Some forecasts will be higher than demand, and some will be lower. Managing the forecasting process requires minimizing the errors between actual demand and forecasted demand. The key to successful forecasting is to choose the technique that provides the least amount of forecast error. To determine which forecasting technique is best for a set of data, the forecast error must be measured.

Four types of forecast error measures can be used. The first is called the **cumulative sum of forecast errors (CFE)** and can be calculated using Formula 7.6.

$$\text{CFE} = \sum_{t-1}^{n} e_t \qquad\qquad 7.6$$

CFE calculates the total forecast error for a set of data, taking into consideration both negative and positive errors. This is also referred to as *bias* and was used in Tables 7.2 through 7.8. This gives an overall measure of forecast error. However, taking into consideration both negative and positive errors, this method can produce an overall low error total although individual period forecasts can either be much higher or much lower than actual demand.

The second measure of forecast error is **mean squared error (MSE)**. This measure is introduced in Table 7.9 and can be calculated using Formula 7.7.

$$\text{MSE} = \frac{\Sigma E_t^2}{n} \qquad\qquad 7.7$$

This measure squares each period error so the negative and positive errors do not cancel each other out. MSE also provides a good indication of the average error per period over a set of demand data. Closely related to MSE is the third type of forecast error measure: **mean absolute deviation (MAD)**. It can be calculated using Formula 7.8.

$$\text{MAD} = \frac{\Sigma |E_t|}{n} \qquad\qquad 7.8$$

This measure is also calculated in Table 7.9. By taking the absolute value of each error, the negative and positive signs are removed and a good indication of average error per period is calculated. This measure is popular because it is easy to understand and provides a good indication of the accuracy of the forecast.

The final measure of forecast error is **mean absolute percent error (MAPE)**. MAPE can be calculated using Formula 7.9.

$$\text{MAPE} = \frac{\Sigma (|E_t|/D_t)100}{n} \qquad\qquad 7.9$$

Table 7.9 shows the MAPE as well. MAPE relates the forecast error to the level of demand so different types of forecasts can be compared.

Table 7.9	Forecast Error*					
(1) t PERIOD	(2) D_t DEMAND	(3) F_t FORECAST	(4) E_t ERROR	(5) E_t^2 ERROR^2	(6) $|E_t|$ ABSOLUTE ERROR	(7) $(|E_t|/D_t)100$ ABSOLUTE % ERROR
January	560	992	−432.0	186,624	432.0	77.1
February	1,300	948.8	+351.2	123,341.4	351.2	27.0
March	750	983.9	−233.9	54,709.2	233.9	31.2
April	1,465	960.5	+504.5	254,520.3	504.5	34.4
May	725	1,010.95	−285.95	81,767.4	285.95	39.4
June	675	982.4	−307.4	94,494.8	307.4	45.5
July	575	951.7	−376.7	141,902.9	376.7	65.5
August	815	914.0	−99.0	9,801.0	99.0	12.1
September	1,275	904.1	+370.9	137,566.8	370.9	29.1
October	1,385	941.2	+443.8	196,958.4	443.8	32.0
November	950	985.6	−35.6	1,267.4	35.6	3.7
December	1,425	982.0	+443.0	196,249.0	443.0	31.1
Total	11,900			1,479,202.6	3,883.95	428.1%
$\bar{x}$	991.7					
CFE			+342.85			
CFE$_{\bar{x}}$			+28.6			

Mean Squared Error: $\text{MSE} = \dfrac{\Sigma E_t^2}{n} = \dfrac{1,479,202.6}{12} = 123,266.9$

Standard Deviation: $\sigma = \sqrt{\text{MSE}} = \sqrt{123,266.9} = 351.1$

Mean Absolute Deviation: $\text{MAD} = \dfrac{\Sigma |E_t|}{n} = \dfrac{3,883.95}{12} = 323.7$

Mean Absolute Percent Error: $\text{MAPE} = \dfrac{\Sigma(|E_t|/D_t)100}{n} = \dfrac{428.1}{12} = 35.7\%$

*Uses exponential smoothing forecast ($\alpha = 0.1$) from Table 7.4.

Table 7.10 provides a summary of the five types of forecasts used on LC's data and resulting forecast error measures for each. For the most part, the forecasts became more accurate as they progressed from using simple moving average in the first example to the seasonal influenced forecast in the last example. This is to be expected because each technique became more sophisticated by including trends and seasons in forecasts. Using MAPE as the forecast measure, Table 7.10 shows that the forecast became more accurate as it moved from using simple moving average to seasonal influenced (if the

Table 7.10	Forecast Accuracy Summary					
	(1) n	(2) CFE $\Sigma(D_t - F_t)$ BIAS	(3) $\Sigma(D_t - F_t)/n$ BIAS $\bar{x}$	(4) $\Sigma|D_t - F_t|$ ABSOLUTE DEVIATION	(5) $\Sigma|D_t - F_t|/n$ ABSOLUTE DEVIATION $\bar{x}$	(6) MAPE
1. Simple Moving Average	9	+716.8	+79.6	3,396.8	377.4	39.1%
2. Weighted Moving Average	9	+658.75	+73.2	3,315.3	368.4	37.4%
3. Exponential Smoothing						
$\alpha = 0.1$	12	+342.85	+28.6	3,883.95	323.7	35.7%
$\alpha = 0.3$	12	+539.2	+44.9	4,082.2	340.2	36.8%
4. Trend-Adjusted Exponential Smoothing	11	−622.9	−56.6	3,119.7	283.6	32.5%
5. Seasonal Influenced	5	−398.0	−79.6	398.0	79.6	3.1%

exponential smoothing method using $\alpha = 0.3$ is ignored). This would also be true if MAD was used as the forecast error measure.

Forecasting demand is a highly scientific art. Rigorous quantitative techniques exist to manipulate historical data to predict the future. However, the assumption made here is that the future will repeat the past. This is normally not the case. As such, it is important to choose the technique that best fits the data in order to minimize the forecast error. Minimizing this error will result in the most accurate forecast.

Sales and Operations Planning

The previous section discussed statistical methods for arriving at a preliminary demand forecast for an organization. Historically, many organizations developed several functional forecasts for the same products during the same time period. It would not be unusual for a manufacturer to have a financial forecast, a manufacturing forecast, a marketing forecast, and a distribution forecast. What compounds the complexity of having multiple forecasts is that most times these functional forecasts did not agree. Marketing would forecast higher demands that neither manufacturing nor distribution could execute. Finance forecasts would be higher than marketing would be able to meet. It is necessary for an organization to arrive at a forecast internally that all functional areas agree upon and can execute. A process that can be used to arrive at this consensus forecast is called the **sales and operations planning process**. The S&OP Benchmarking Consortium in the Center for Supply Chain Research adopted a five-step process in arriving at this consensus forecast.[6] The five-step S&OP process can be seen in Figure 7.2. Step 1 (Run sales forecast reports) requires the development of a statistical forecast of future sales. This would be done using one or more of the forecasting techniques discussed in the previous section. Step 2 (Demand planning phase) requires the sales and/or marketing departments to review the forecast and make adjustments based on promotions of existing products, the introductions of new products, or the elimination of products. This

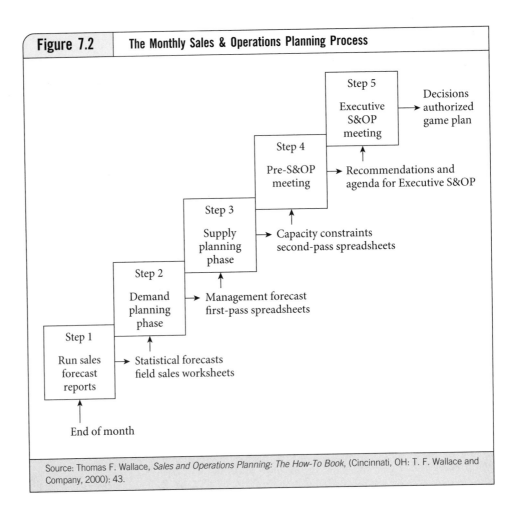

Figure 7.2 | **The Monthly Sales & Operations Planning Process**

Step 5

Executive S&OP meeting → Decisions authorized game plan

Step 4

Pre-S&OP meeting → Recommendations and agenda for Executive S&OP

Step 3

Supply planning phase → Capacity constraints second-pass spreadsheets

Step 2

Demand planning phase → Management forecast first-pass spreadsheets

Step 1

Run sales forecast reports → Statistical forecasts field sales worksheets

End of month

Source: Thomas F. Wallace, *Sales and Operations Planning: The How-To Book*, (Cincinnati, OH: T. F. Wallace and Company, 2000): 43.

---

revised forecast is usually stated in terms of both units and dollars since operations are concerned with units and finance is concerned with dollars.

Step 3 (Supply planning phase) requires operations (manufacturing, warehousing, and transportation) to analyze the sales forecast to determine if existing capacity is adequate to handle the forecasted volumes. This requires analyzing not only the total volumes but also the timing of those volumes. For example, existing manufacturing capacity might be adequate if demand is stable over the forecast period. However, heavy promotions might produce a "spike" in demand that might exceed existing capacity. Two options to solve this capacity constraint are available. First, the promotional activity could be curtailed to bring demand to a more stable level. This could result in lost revenue. Second, additional manufacturing could be secured either by investing in more manufacturing capacity internally or securing contract manufacturing capacity externally. This would result in additional costs. The same types of capacity issues would need to be considered for both warehousing space and transportation vehicle capacity with similar resulting options if capacity does not meet demand: either curtail demand or invest in additional capacity. The decisions to these capacity issues are addressed in Step 4.

Step 4 (Pre-S&OP meeting) involves individuals from sales, marketing, operations, and finance. This meeting will review the initial forecast and any capacity issues that might have emerged during Step 3. Initial attempts will be made during this meeting to solve capacity issues by attempting to balance supply and demand. Alternative scenarios are usually developed to present at the executive S&OP meeting (Step 5) for consideration. These alternatives would identify potential lost sales and increased costs associated with balancing supply and demand. The sales forecast is also converted to dollars to see if the demand/supply plan meets the financial plan of the organization.

Finally, Step 5 (Executive S&OP meeting) is where final decisions are made regarding sales forecasts and capacity issues. This is where the top executives from the various functional areas agree to the forecast and convert it into the operating plan for the organization. Consensus among the various functional areas is critical in this meeting. Decisions regarding tradeoffs between revenue and costs are made in this meeting. Once the final plan is approved, it is important that the appropriate metrics are in place for each functional area to encourage compliance to the plan. For example, assume that the traditional operating metric for manufacturing is cost per pound manufactured. The lower the cost per pound, the better is the performance of the manufacturing group. However, the S&OP plan requires additional investment in capacity for manufacturing, which raises the cost per manufactured pound. This would make manufacturing performance unacceptable. While low cost is important, manufacturing has little or no control over the increased cost. A revised metric of compliance to schedule might be more appropriate. This new metric would reward manufacturing for making the planned quantities at the planned times. The point here is that the appropriate metrics must be in place for each functional area so it is encouraged and rewarded for achieving the business plan.

Collaborative Planning, Forecasting, and Replenishment

The S&OP process described how organizations are structuring their planning processes to arrive at a consensus forecast internally. The next logical step would be for members of a supply chain to also agree upon a consensus forecast. Many industry initiatives have attempted to create efficiency and effectiveness through the integration of supply chain activities and processes. They have been identified by such names as quick response (QR), vendor-managed inventory (VMI), continuous replenishment planning (CRP), and efficient consumer response (ECR). All of these have had some success at integrating replenishment between supply chain members. However, they were all somewhat deficient in that they did not include a strong incentive for collaborative planning among supply chain members.

One of the most recent initiatives aimed at achieving true supply chain integration is **collaborative planning, forecasting, and replenishment (CPFR)**.[7] CPFR has become recognized as a breakthrough business model for planning, forecasting, and replenishment. Using this approach, retailers, distributors, and manufacturers can utilize available Internet-based technologies to collaborate on operational planning through execution. Transportation providers have now been included with the concept of **collaborative transportation management (CTM)**. Simply put, CPFR allows trading partners to agree to a single forecast for an item where each partner translates this forecast into a

With revenues 10 times those of West Marine, it seems unlikely that ITT Industries would have much to learn about business processes from a boating supplies customer of its pump division. After all, ITT led *Forbes* magazine's December 2005 list of the seven best-managed conglomerates in five-year total return.

Yet ITT's Jabsco division has incorporated West Marine's CPFR approach, coupling it with a lean Six Sigma framework, to develop an adaptive, high-performance organization that collaborates across the extended supply chain. The results of Jabsco's initiative have been dramatic. In 2004, manufacturing cycle time fell from 25 days to 3 days, overall sales increased by 11 percent, labor hours were cut by 17 percent, and on-time deliveries increased from 74 percent to 94 percent.

West Marine is Jabsco's largest customer. But in 2002, the pump maker was in danger of losing the business. Its on-time delivery was a dismal 10 percent, and it was struggling to comply with West Marine's EDI program. Our in-stocks of Jabsco products were always low, and the supplier didn't seem to be able to manage its capacity requirements predictably. Given ITT's emphasis on business process, observers could be excused for thinking there should not have been a problem. ITT had invested more than $35 million on Six Sigma training and had 350 certified Six Sigma Black Belts and 10,000 certified Green Belts.

The change began after Nick Hill, then Jabsco's president, attended West Marine's first "breakthrough" meeting. Hill learned that his company seemed to be missing a central tenet: the voice of the customer. Although Jabsco was using lean manufacturing to emphasize efficiency—cutting costs, controlling resources consumed, and reducing rework—it was not highlighting effectiveness issues such as on-time delivery and customer satisfaction. Jabsco lacked the processes to capture demand information, let alone use it; managers didn't understand why customer-responsive processes were needed.

Hill appointed Jabsco Six Sigma Master Black Belt Mike Feeney to improve performance—and the relationship with West Marine. Learning about CPFR from us, Feeney absolutely "got" what West Marine was trying to do. He championed the idea that CPFR and Six Sigma are symbiotic, and he knew that Jabsco had to go further than just putting in place cross-functional sales and operations planning processes. Instead, Jabsco needed to move by stages toward advanced process implementations (see Table 7.11). Today, Jabsco's commitment to supply chain improvement is evident in its investments in enabling technology, the largest of which is a Web-based supply chain performance management application. Used throughout Jabsco and by its own supplier base, the system provides current demand and production visibility and decision support.

Table 7.11	ITT's Stages of CPFR Progress		
PROCESS AREA	**BASIC**	**DEVELOPING**	**ADVANCED**
Collaborative Processes	Limited one-way communication	Standardized and integrated collaboration	Computer-assisted integrated collaboration
Planning and Forecasting Processes	Manual nonstandard forecasting and planning	Standardized demand data creation and input	Integrated planning, forecasting, and collaboration
Replenishment Processes	Pre-DC limited or no retail visibility	DC replenishment focus	Computer-assisted retail ordering flow-through
Supply Chain Management	No supply chain focus or plan	Internal enterprise optimization	Supply chain optimization

Source: Larry Smith, "West Marine: A CPFR Success Story," *Supply Chain Management Review* (March 2006): p. 35 Copyright © 2006 Reed Business Information, a division of Reed Elsevier. Reproduced by permission.

single execution plan. This replaces the traditional method of forecasting where each trading partner developed its own forecast for an item and each forecast was different for each partner.

The first attempt at CPFR was between Wal-Mart and Warner-Lambert (now a part of Johnson & Johnson) in 1995 for its Listerine product line. In addition to rationalizing inventories of specific line items and addressing out-of-stock occurrences, these two organizations collaborated to increase their forecast accuracy, so as to have the right amount of inventory where it was needed, when it was needed. The three-month pilot produced significant results and improvements for both organizations. This resulted in the adoption of CPFR by both Wal-Mart and many of its other suppliers to manage inventories through collaborative plans and forecasts.

Figure 7.3 shows the CPFR model as a sequence of several business processes that include the consumer, retailer, and manufacturer. The four major processes are strategy

| Figure 7.3 | The CPFR Model |

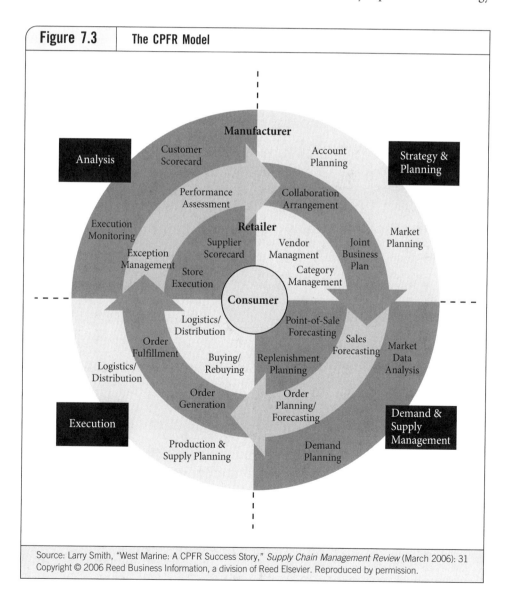

Source: Larry Smith, "West Marine: A CPFR Success Story," *Supply Chain Management Review* (March 2006): 31
Copyright © 2006 Reed Business Information, a division of Reed Elsevier. Reproduced by permission.

and planning, demand and supply management, execution, and analysis. Two aspects of this model are important to note. First, it includes the cooperation and exchange of data among business partners. Second, it is a continuous, closed-loop process that uses feedback (analysis) as input for strategy and planning.

Figure 7.4 demonstrates how the process shown in Figure 7.3 is executed. As shown in Figure 7.4, CPFR emphasizes a sharing of consumer purchasing data (or point-of-sale data) as well as forecasts at retail among and between trading partners for the purpose of helping to manage supply chain activities. From these data, the manufacturer analyzes its ability to meet the forecasted demand. If it cannot meet the demand, a collaborative effort is undertaken between the retailer and manufacturer to arrive at a mutually agreed-upon forecast from which execution plans are developed. The strength of CPFR is that it provides a single forecast from which trading partners can develop manufacturing strategies, replenishment strategies, and merchandising strategies.

The CPFR process begins with the sharing of marketing plans between trading partners. Once an agreement is reached on the timing and planned sales of specific products, and a commitment is made to follow that plan closely, the plan is then used to create a forecast, by stock-keeping unit (SKU), by week, and by quantity. The planning period can be for 13, 26, or 52 weeks. A typical forecast is for seasonal or promotional items that represent approximately 15 percent of sales in each category. The regular turn items, or the remainder of the products in the category, are forecast statistically. Then the forecast is entered into a system that is accessible through the Internet by either trading partner. Either partner may change the forecast within established parameters.

Theoretically, an accurate CPFR forecast could be translated directly into a production and replenishment schedule by the manufacturer since both quantity and timing are included in the CPFR forecast. This would allow the manufacturer to make the products to order (based on the quantity and timing of demand) rather than making them to inventory, thus reducing total inventories for the manufacturer. The retailer would enjoy fewer out-of-stocks at the retail shelf. Although CPFR has not yet fully developed into a make-to-order environment, it has enjoyed the benefits of reduced supply chain inventories and out-of-stocks. West Marine employed the CPFR model with its suppliers and reaped some amazing results. More than 70 of its top suppliers are loading West Marine order forecasts directly into their production planning systems. In-stock rates at stores are close to 96 percent, forecast accuracy has risen to 85 percent, and on-time shipments are better than 80 percent.[8] So, the use of collaborative efforts among supply chain partners can have positive results on the service and cost performance of these partners.

Fulfillment Models

The beginning of this chapter emphasized the planning and forecasting aspects of demand management. Once these elements of demand management are agreed upon, the plan needs to be executed. This will be done through the fulfillment process. Chapter 8 will discuss in more depth the concept of order management. The remainder of this chapter, however, will highlight the various distribution channel strategies that can be used to deliver on the demand forecast.

Figure 7.4	CPFR Business Model

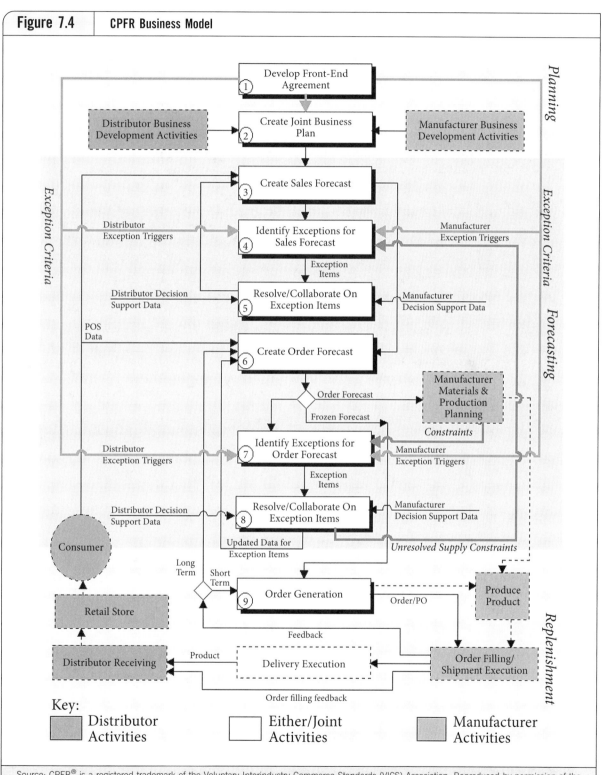

Channels of Distribution

A **channel of distribution** consists of one or more organizations or individuals who participate in the flow of goods, services, information, and finances from the production point to the final point of consumption. A channel of distribution can also be thought of as the physical structures and intermediaries through which these flows travel. These channels encompass a variety of intermediary firms, including those that can be classified as distributors, wholesalers, retailers, transportation providers, and brokers. Some of these intermediary firms take physical possession of the goods, some take title to the goods, and some take both. Thus, it is critical in the design of a distribution channel to take into consideration both the logistics channel and the marketing channel.

The **logistics channel** refers to the means by which products flow physically from where they are available to where they are needed. The **marketing channel** refers to the means by which necessary transactional elements are managed (for example, customer orders, billing, accounts receivable, etc.). These two channels are illustrated in Figure 7.5.

Effective channel management requires a good grasp of the different alternatives available to deliver a product and the resulting benefits of each. The four basic functions of the logistics channel are sorting out, accumulating, allocating, and assorting. Channel systems can be classified as either direct or indirect and can be further subdivided into traditional and vertical marketing systems (VMS). With the VMS, some degree of implicit or explicit relationship exists among the organizations in the channel and channel members have considerable opportunities to coordinate their activities.

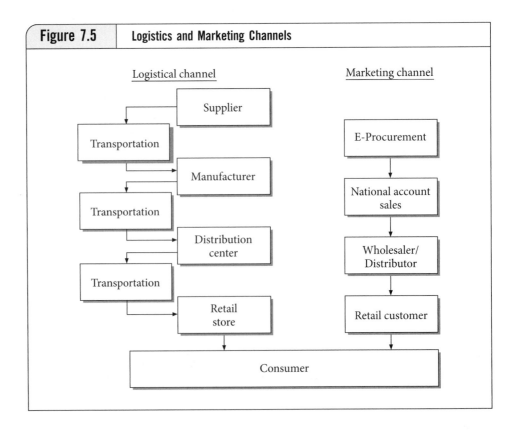

| Figure 7.5 | Logistics and Marketing Channels |

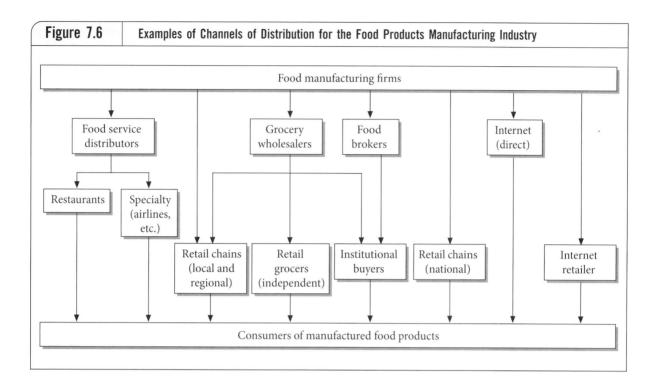

Figure 7.6 | Examples of Channels of Distribution for the Food Products Manufacturing Industry

Using the grocery industry as an example, Figure 7.6 shows the numerous channels of distribution that are responsible for delivering products to consumers. While it is true that several of these channels might compete with one another, collectively they provide the consumer with a significant number of choices as to where and how to purchase grocery products. Each individual channel represents a unique path from grocery manufacturer to consumer, and a set of effective logistics strategies must be developed for each channel.

An important observation to note about channel structure involves the elements of fixed costs versus variable costs. Using Figure 7.6 as an example, assume that a food manufacturer uses a traditional channel to deliver its product to a retail store. One channel would include the manufacturer, the manufacturer's distribution center, the retailer's distribution center, and the retailer's store. This channel involves a significant amount of fixed costs in the form of distribution centers and stores. However, variable costs, in the form of transportation, are relatively low since most shipments would be made in large volume quantities between channel members. Assume that the food manufacturer decided to begin Internet fulfillment direct to the consumer (this is the second channel from the right in Figure 7.6). While much of the fixed cost in this channel is significantly reduced (eliminate the need for the retailer's distribution center and stores), the variable transportation costs will increase significantly. This occurs because the origin (food manufacturer) and ultimate destination (consumer) in both channels are the same, resulting in approximately the same distance to move product, but the shipment size is reduced significantly. The lower the shipment size the higher the transportation cost per pound, holding constant commodity and distance. So, a rule of thumb in channel design is, given the origin and destination remain the same, the more intermediaries used to deliver the product the higher the fixed cost and the lower the variable cost, and vice versa.

Figure 7.7	Direct-to-Customer (DTC) Fulfillment

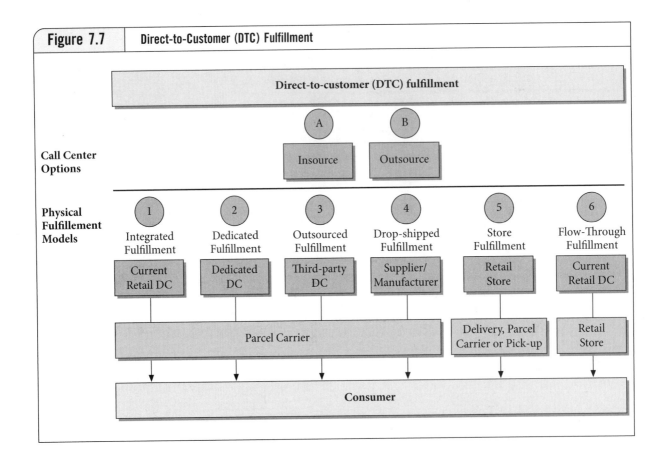

Direct-to-Customer (DTC) Fulfillment

As previously mentioned, many different types of channel structures are available in an industry to deliver product to the point of consumption. This section will offer a brief discussion of several models that can and are being used in the retail industry. Figure 7.7 shows several of these channels and will provide the basis for discussion in the remainder of this section.

Integrated Fulfillment

Many retailers today maintain both a "bricks-and-mortar" and "clicks-and-mortar" presence to the consumer. That is, retailers have both retail stores as well as Internet sites where consumers can buy direct. One example would be Wal-Mart with its large number of retail outlets as well as its presence with Wal-Mart.com. **Integrated fulfillment** means the retailer operates one distribution network to service both channels. This fulfillment model can be seen in Figure 7.8. In a typical distribution center for this model, both store orders and consumer orders are received, picked, packed, and shipped. One advantage to this model is low start-up costs. If the retailer has an established distribution network that handles store orders and then decides to develop an Internet presence, the existing network can service both. In other words, new distribution centers need not be built. This would also eliminate the need to have a duplicate inventory to handle the Internet orders. Another advantage to this model is workforce efficiency because of consolidated operations. The existing workforce now has an opportunity to move more volume through a fixed-cost facility. However, this model has

Figure 7.8	Integrated Fulfillment

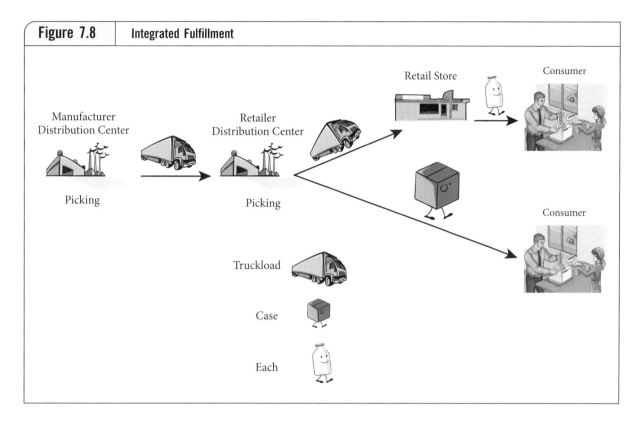

several challenges. First, the order profile will change with the addition of consumer Internet orders. While store orders would probably be picked in case and/or pallet quantities, consumer orders would require eaches in smaller order quantities. Second, products might not be available in consumer units (eaches). While cases and inner-packs might be the minimum order quantity for a store, an individual unit (each) might be required for a consumer order. Third, the addition of unit pick (each pick) would require a "fast pick," or broken case, operation to be added to the distribution center. Case pick operations are usually very efficient because of the use of automation in the form of conveyors to move a large volume very quickly. Unit picks are very labor intensive and will not be able to move very much volume. Finally, a conflict might arise between a store order and an Internet order. If both orders want the same item and there is not sufficient inventory to fill both, which gets priority? Some would argue that the Internet order should be filled because the retailer has already received the money for the items. Others might argue that the store should get the inventory since it is also a customer of the distribution center and each store is a separate profit and loss center. So, this model presents some economies because it can use existing resources to satisfy the needs of two channels. However, it presents some operating challenges that must be addressed.

Dedicated Fulfillment

Another option for the retailer that desires to have both a store and an Internet presence is called **dedicated fulfillment**. Dedicated fulfillment achieves the same delivery goals as integrated fulfillment but with two separate distribution networks. This model can be seen in Figure 7.9. Having a separate distribution network for store delivery and consumer delivery eliminates most of the disadvantages of integrated fulfillment. However, now the retailer is faced with duplicate facilities and duplicate inventories. This assumes that the

Figure 7.9	Dedicated Fulfillment

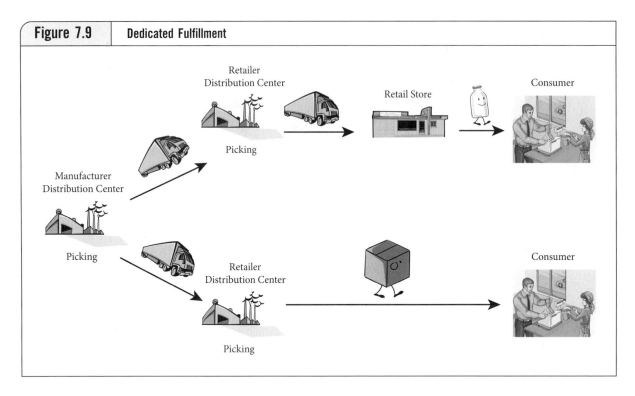

retailer offers exactly the same product offering through both channels. However, many retailers offer many more products on their Internet sites than they offer in their stores. This makes dedicated fulfillment a more logical choice.

Outsourced Fulfillment

While both integrated and dedicated fulfillment assume that the retailer will perform the fulfillment itself, outsourced fulfillment assumes that another firm will perform the fulfillment. Many retailers, such as Toys R' Us and Eddie Bauer, will maintain internal control of store fulfillment and outsource Internet fulfillment to a third party. This can be seen in Figure 7.10. One advantage of this outsourcing is low start-up costs for the retailer to service the Internet channel. Toys R' Us outsourced its direct-to-consumer fulfillment to Amazon.com as did Eddie Bauer. Amazon.com has an established Internet fulfillment network for books and CDs and is very efficient at picking, packing, and shipping consumer units. Also, possible transportation economies could result from using outsourced fulfillment for Internet orders. Amazon.com could easily add products from Eddie Bauer and Toys R' Us to its existing Web site. Consumers, then, would have more choices of products when creating their orders, resulting in more items per order and possibly lower transportation costs. A major disadvantage often cited with outsourcing fulfillment is the loss of control the retailer might experience over service levels. This topic was covered in Chapter 4, entitled "Supply Chain Relationships." So, the major benefit of outsourced fulfillment is the ability to use existing external expertise in fulfillment. The major disadvantage of this model is the potential loss of control.

Drop-Shipped Fulfillment

Drop-shipped fulfillment is also referred to as **direct store delivery**. In this model, the manufacturer delivers its product directly to a retailer's stores, bypassing the retailer's distribution network. This model is seen in Figure 7.11. The distribution practices of Frito-Lay are a good example of this type of fulfillment. Frito-Lay manufactures its

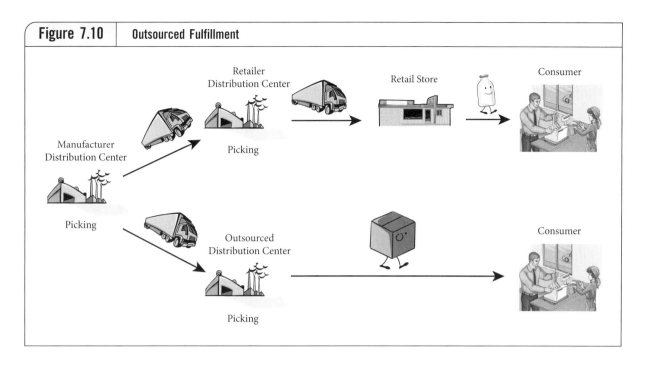

Figure 7.10 | **Outsourced Fulfillment**

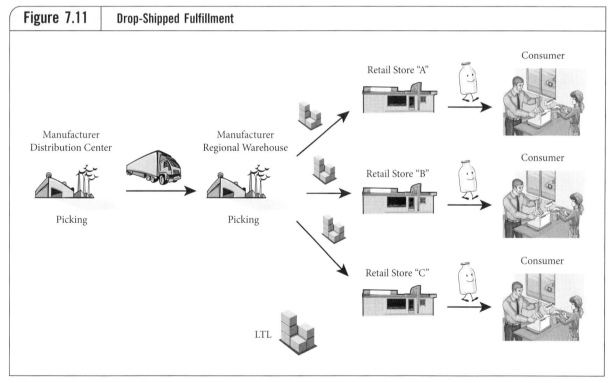

Figure 7.11 | **Drop-Shipped Fulfillment**

products and stores them in its distribution network. From this central distribution network, products flow to regional storage locations where Frito-Lay delivery vehicles are stocked and then make direct store deliveries in a small geographic area. The driver of the vehicle will restock the retailer's shelves, rotate stock, merchandise the inventory, and gather competitive pricing and slotting information at the store level. A major advantage

Supply Chain Technology

An S&OP Success Story

In the mid-1990s, one of the largest telecommunications and data services providers in the United States realized that its business would benefit significantly from improved collaboration between suppliers and internal operations. The company was challenged with balancing supply and demand because of the extremely short life cycle of its cell phone products. Additionally, order lead times for handset accessories were as long as 16–18 weeks, making it difficult to achieve forecast accuracy and supply chain responsiveness.

The repercussions of this environment were significant. Limited product availability meant that the company lost customers to competitors with little hope of recapturing them in the future. Excess inventory produced lower margins as incentives were used to sell product or disposal costs were accrued for obsolete product. The company recognized that the challenging nature of phone supply, short product life cycles, and the competitive market pressures made it critical to collaborate better with suppliers and internal stakeholders to improve forecast accuracy while maintaining supplier fill rates.

What the company needed was a way to understand its demand drivers and supply risk so that it could make sourcing decisions that ensured product availability while minimizing inventory. Good decision making was especially critical at the end of the product's life cycle. Inventory varied significantly because constant changes in pricing and promotions made demand unpredictable. However, rather than allow the market to dictate demand, the company decided it would adjust its promotion strategies to increase consumer interest in products at the end of life that were slow to sell or that were in short supply.

The company implemented a multistep process to initiate and drive S&OP across the organization. A formal, monthly S&OP meeting was conducted with the stakeholders to review demand patterns and supply risks and to establish the supply plan for the next quarter. Participants of these regular meetings included executive staff and key stakeholders from operations, marketing, and finance.

The S&OP team meetings were organized around a "stoplight" system (green = okay, yellow = warning, red = problem) where all products were reviewed to identify the opportunities, risks, and areas that needed the most attention. Once the supply chain plan had been developed during the S&OP process, the marketing organization committed to making sure that pricing and promotion programs consistently supported the supply plan.

Between monthly S&OP meetings, a portion of the S&OP team began to hold weekly meetings to analyze the current sales pace. The goal of these meetings was to determine what was working and what was not and to project performance eight weeks into the future. A second meeting involved suppliers in order to complete weekly collaborative planning, forecasting, and replenishment.

A critical success factor for this company's S&OP process was uniting the key stakeholders. For this reason, suppliers were engaged in the formal process. This resulted in improvements in the supply base in the areas of cost, product availability, and capability.

As part of the S&OP process, the telecommunications leader created unconstrained demand plans using a demand planning software. This functionality enabled marketing to manage changes to the current product forecast, the introduction of new products, and the retirement of selected current products. Then a constrained plan was created and utilized, acknowledging supplier shortages and taking into account the need to drive unfulfilled demand to other suppliers. The company used price and promotion changes to manipulate demand. Finally, an advanced supply chain planning solution was leveraged to create planned orders, drop requisitions, and plan the final packaging.

Relying on the demand planning software, the telecommunications company was able to sustain S&OP best practices in a high-volume, data-intensive environment. The solution served as an S&OP "demand hub" data repository, which alleviated the burden of data collection. All relevant sources of critical information were consolidated, enabling data transfer and validation.

As a result of implementing S&OP, the telecommunications company realized substantial benefits. First, the company demonstrated the ability to triple the number of products offered. Through the course of an eight-year period, forecast accuracy was improved by 36 percent, and inventory-related working capital was reduced by 25 percent. Finally, store service levels increased to 98 percent or better.

Sources: This case study is based on material appearing in the Aberdeen Group's Sales & Operations Planning Benchmark, 2004 and Maha Muzumdar and John Fontanella, "The Secrets to S&OP Success," *Supply Chain Management Review* (April 2006): 40 Copyright © 2006 Reed Business Information, a division of Reed Elsevier. Reproduced by permission.

of this model is the reduction of inventory in the distribution network. This occurs because the retailer does not need to stock Frito-Lay's inventory in its distribution centers. Another major advantage to Frito-Lay is the direct control of its inventories at the store level. A disadvantage to the retailer is the possible reduction of inventory visibility of Frito-Lay's products since the retailer does not "touch" these products in its distribution network. This type of model requires close collaboration and agreement between the manufacturer and retailer for several reasons. First, not every retailer supplier can do drop-shipped fulfillment. From a practical perspective, if every supplier to a store delivered direct on a daily basis, the number of delivery vehicles and manufacturer personnel in a store would cause overwhelming congestion at the store. Second, the retailer and manufacturer need to agree on the types and timing of information shared on inventory levels to provide the retailer with the proper level of inventory visibility. Finally, drop-shipped fulfillment works best for products that have a short shelf life and/or where freshness is a requirement. As such, this model makes sense for a limited number of products sold in a retail store.

Store Fulfillment

For a retailer that has both a storefront as well as an Internet presence, **store fulfillment** can offer several opportunities. In this model, shown in Figure 7.12, the order is placed through the Internet site. The order is sent to the nearest retail store where it is picked and put aside for the customer to pick up. This works well for large electronic appliances (such as plasma screen televisions) and is used by firms such as Best Buy and Circuit City. Several advantages exist for this type of fulfillment. First, there is a short lead time to the customer, if the item is in stock. Second, there are low start-up costs for the retailer. Inventory is already in place in close proximity to the consumer. Third, returns can be handled in the usual manner through the retail store. Finally, the product will be available in consumer units.

Several disadvantages exist for this type of fulfillment. First, there might be reduced control and consistency over order fill since each store will be responsible for its own order picking. Second, conflict may arise between inventories. Stores hold inventories for the shopper, which can result in impulse buys. Now the store is required to remove the item from the shelf for an Internet order, resulting in a possible out-of-stock at the shelf. One method to alleviate this conflict is to adjust the profit of the store so it also

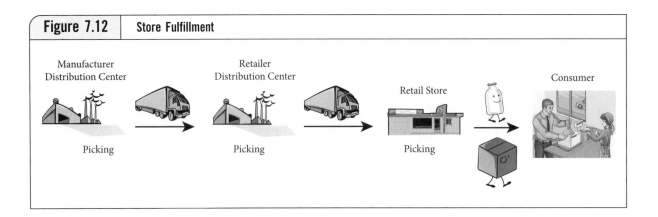

Figure 7.12 | **Store Fulfillment**

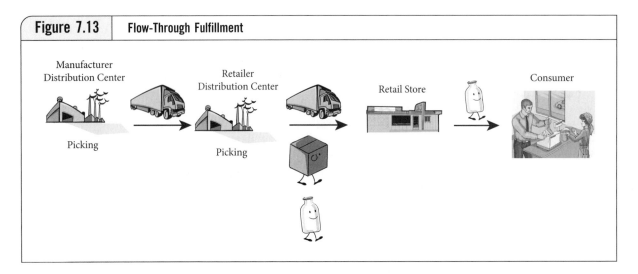

Figure 7.13 | **Flow-Through Fulfillment**

gets credit for the Internet sale. Third, the retailer must have real-time visibility to in-store inventories in order to satisfy the Internet order. Finally, stores lack sufficient space to store product. Staging products for customer pickups in any area of the store takes space away to generate additional sales for the store.

Flow-Through Fulfillment

The **flow-through fulfillment** method is very similar to store fulfillment and can be seen in Figure 7.13. The main difference between the two is that in flow-through fulfillment the product is picked and packed at the retailer's distribution center and then sent to the store for customer pickup. Again, this is a common method used in the consumer electronics retailing industry. The flow-through model eliminates the inventory conflict the store might realize between store sales and Internet sales. Because the consumer is providing the pickup service, the retailer avoids the cost of the "last mile." The retailer also does not need store level inventory status in the flow-through model. Returns can be handled through the existing store network, as in store fulfillment. Storage space at the store for pickup items remains an issue.

In conclusion, the retailing industry offers many models of fulfillment to get product into consumers' hands. Each one has advantages and disadvantages. The choice of the proper model(s) will depend on both cost considerations and market influences.

SUMMARY

- Outbound-to-customer logistics systems have received the most attention in many companies; but, even in today's customer service environment, outbound and inbound logistics systems must be coordinated.

- Demand management may be thought of as "focused efforts to estimate and manage customers' demand, with the intention of using this information to shape operating decisions.

- Although many forecasts are made throughout the supply chain, the forecast of primary demand from the end user or consumer will be the most important. It is essential that this demand information be shared with trading partners throughout the supply chain and be the basis for collaborative decision making.

- Various approaches to forecasting are available, each serving different purposes.

- The S&OP process has gained much attention in industry today. It serves the purpose of allowing a firm to operate from a single forecast.

- The S&OP process is a continual loop involving participation from sales, operations, and finance to arrive at an internal consensus forecast.

- CPFR is a method to allow trading partners in the supply chain to collaboratively develop and agree upon a forecast of sales. This allows for the elimination of inventories held because of uncertainty in the supply chain.

- A number of distribution channel alternatives might be considered by organizations today. Effective management of the various choices requires coordination and integration of marketing, logistics, and finance within the firm, as well as coordination of overall channel-wide activities across the organizations in the channel.

STUDY QUESTIONS

1. Explain why outbound logistics systems in some organizations are viewed as being more important than inbound logistics systems.

2. How do outbound logistics systems relate directly to the needs of the customer?

3. How can demand management help to unify channel members, satisfy customers, and solve customer problems?

4. What are some of the logistics problems that might arise when supply and demand for a product are not aligned properly? What are some of the methods used to soften the effects of this imbalance?

5. What are the basic types of forecasts? What are their strengths and weaknesses?

6. What are the basic elements of the S&OP process? How do marketing, logistics, finance, and manufacturing contribute to each element?

7. What are the critical elements of collaborative planning? What benefits do they provide for the supply chain?

8. What are the various retail fulfillment models? What are the strengths and weakness of each?

NOTES

1. Roger D. Blackwell and Kristina Blackwell, "The Century of the Consumer: Converting Supply Chains into Demand Chains," *Supply Chain Management Review*, No. 3 (Fall 1999): 22–32.

2. Ibid., 32.

3. Jim R. Langabeer, "Aligning Demand Management with Business Strategy," *Supply Chain Management Review* (May/June 2000): 66–72.

4. Lee J. Krajewski and Larry P. Ritzman, *Operations Management: Strategy and Analysis*, 4th ed. (Reading, MA: Addison-Wesley Publishing Company, 1996): 474.

5. This section was adapted from Krajewski and Ritzman (1996): 477–478.

6. Adapted from Tom Wallace, *Sales and Operations Planning: The "How-To" Handbook* (Cincinnati, OH: T. F. Wallace & Co., 1999): 43–50. This process will be briefly described in this section.

7. CPFR® is a registered trademark of the Voluntary Interindustry Commerce Standards (VICS) Association.

8. Larry Smith, "West Marine: A CPFR Success Story," *Supply Chain Management Review* (March 2006): 20–36.

CASE 7.1

Tires for You, Inc.

Tires for You, Inc. (TFY), founded in 1987, is an automotive repair shop specializing in replacement tires. Located in Altoona, Pennsylvania, TFY has grown successfully over the past few years because of the addition of a new general manager, Katie McMullen. Since tire replacement is a major portion of TFY's business (it also performs oil changes, small mechanical repairs, etc.), Katie was surprised at the lack of forecasts for tire consumption for the company. Her senior mechanic, Skip Grenoble, told her that they usually stocked for this year what they sold last year. He readily admitted that several times throughout the season stockouts occurred and customers had to go elsewhere for tires.

Although many tire replacements were for defective or destroyed tires, most tires were installed on cars whose original tires had worn out. Most often, four tires were installed at the same time. Katie was determined to get a better idea of how many tires to hold in stock during the various months of the year. Listed below is a summary of last year's individual tire sales by month:

MONTH	TIRES USED
January	510
February	383
March	1,403
April	1,913
May	1,148
June	893
July	829
August	638
September	2,168
October	1,530
November	701
December	636
Total	**12,752**

CASE QUESTIONS

Katie has hired you to determine the best technique for forecasting TFY demand based on the given data.

1. Calculate a forecast using a simple three-month moving average.

2. Calculate a forecast using a three-period weighted moving average. Use weights of 0.60, 0.25, and 0.15 for the most recent period, the second most recent period, and the third most recent period, respectively.

3. Calculate a forecast using the exponential smoothing method. Assume the forecast for period 1 is 1,063.

4. Calculate a forecast using the trend-adjusted exponential smoothing method. Use 0.20 for both alpha and beta.

In an effort to determine if there is a seasonal pattern in the demand for tires, Katie has provided you with tire consumption data for the past three years. The table below gives the demand for two years ago (year 2) and three years ago (year 3).

MONTH	YEAR 3 DEMAND	YEAR 2 DEMAND
January	501	526
February	376	394
March	1,377	1,446
April	1,878	1,972
May	1,127	1,183
June	876	920
July	814	854
August	626	657
September	2,128	2,235
October	1,502	1,578
November	689	723
December	626	658
Total	12,520	13,146

5. Calculate a seasonal influenced forecast.

6. Based on the various methods used to calculate a forecast for TFY, which method produced the best forecast? Why? How could you improve upon this forecast?

Chapter 8

ORDER MANAGEMENT AND CUSTOMER SERVICE

Learning Objectives

After reading this chapter, you should be able to do the following:

- Understand the relationships between order management and customer service.

- Appreciate how organizations influence customers' ordering patterns as well as how they execute customers' orders.

- Realize that activity-based costing (ABC) plays a critical role in order management and customer service.

- Identify the various activities in the SCOR process D1 (deliver stocked product) and how it relates to the order-to-cash cycle.

- Know the various elements of customer service and how they impact both buyers and sellers.

- Calculate the cost of a stockout.

- Understand the major outputs of order management, how they are measured, and how their financial impacts on buyers and sellers are calculated.

- Be familiar with the concept of service recovery and how it is being implemented in organizations today.

Introduction

Chapter 7 (Demand Management) discussed how organizations develop forecasts from which marketing, production, finance, and logistics plans are created. These plans are used to align the resources of the organization to meet organization and market goals. Chapter 8 will discuss the concepts of order management and customer service, which serve as the mechanisms to *execute* the plans. Order management defines and sets in motion the logistics infrastructure of the organization. In other words, how an organization receives an order (electronically versus manually), how it fills an order (inventory policy and number and location of warehouses), and how it ships an order (mode choice and its impacts on delivery times) are all dictated by how an organization manages an order. This chapter will present two phases of order management. First, the concept of **influencing the order** will be presented. This is the phase where an organization attempts to change the manner by which its customers place orders. Second, the concept of **order execution** will be discussed. This phase occurs after the organization receives the order.

Customer service, on the other hand, is *anything that touches the customer.* This includes all activities that impact information flow, product flow, and cash flow between the organization and its customers. Customer service can be described as a *philosophy, as performance measures,* or as an *activity.*[1] Customer service as *a philosophy* elevates customer service to an organization-wide commitment to providing customer satisfaction through superior customer service. This view of customer service is entirely consistent with many organizations' emphasis on value management, elevates it to the strategic level within an organization, and makes it visible to top executives. Customer service as *performance measures* emphasizes customer service as specific performance measures, such as on-time delivery and percentage of orders filled complete. These customer service measures pervade all three definitions of customer service and address strategic, tactical, and operational aspects of order management. Finally, customer service as an *activity* treats customer service as a particular task that an organization must perform to satisfy a customer's order requirements. Order processing, invoicing, product returns, and claims handling are all typical examples of this definition of customer service.

Most organizations employ all three definitions of customer service in their order management process. Figure 8.1 shows one way in which order management and customer service are related. As this figure shows, customer service is involved in both influencing a customer's order as well as in executing the customer's order. The topics in this figure will be discussed in more detail in this chapter.

The remainder of this chapter will be organized as follows. First, the concept of **customer relationship management (CRM)** will be explored. Second, the concepts of **activity-based costing** and **customer profitability** will be discussed. Third, **customer**

| Figure 8.1 | Relationship Between Order Management and Customer Service |

		As a Philosophy	As Performance Measures	As an Activity
Order Management	Influence the Order	Customer Relationship Management (CRM)	Determine Performance Measures/Levels	Provide Pretransaction Order Information
	Execute the Order	Service Recovery	Manage to/Measure Performance Levels	Order Execution

Customer Service

segmentation will be introduced. Fourth, the **order execution process** will be presented. Fifth, **customer service** will be discussed. Finally, the concept of **service recovery** will be explained.

Influencing the Order—Customer Relationship Management

Customer relationship management is the art and science of strategically positioning customers to improve the profitability of the organization and enhance its relationships with its customer base. CRM is not a new concept. It has been used for many years in service industries, such as banking, credit cards, hotels, and airline travel. Frequent-flier programs, used by the airline industry, are typical examples of the use of CRM to segment and reward an airline's best customers based on number of miles traveled. Similarly, the hotel industry segments its customers by the number of nights stayed and the amount of money spent at a particular hotel. Both CRM strategies target customers that are low in cost to service and who are very profitable. Normally, business travelers would earn a "best" rating in both industries because of the amount of travel and hotel stays involved.

The concept of CRM, however, has not been widely used in the business-to-business environment until lately. Traditionally, manufacturers and distributors are more adept at and actively involved in order execution, which involves filling and shipping *what* their customers order. Today, more manufacturers and distributors are becoming adept at and actively involved in influencing *how* their customers order. This shift in philosophy comes from the realization that not all customers are equally profitable for an organization. *How* customers order, *how much* customers order, *what* customers order, and *when* customers order all impact an organization's cost of executing an order. Customers whose ordering patterns maximize the efficiencies of the shipping organization's logistics network will be the most profitable customers. Using the CRM philosophy allows an organization to identify and reward those customers.

There are four basic steps in the implementation of the CRM process in a business-to-business environment.[2]

Step 1: Segment the Customer Base by Profitability

Most firms allocate direct materials, labor, and overhead costs to customers using a single allocation criterion, e.g., pounds of product purchased during a particular time period. However, firms today are beginning to use techniques such as activity-based costing (to be discussed in the next section) to more accurately allocate costs to customers based on the specific costs of servicing a customer's orders based on how, how much, what, and when a customer orders. Normally, a **cost-to-serve (CTS) model** is developed for each customer. These CTS models are very much like an income statement for the customer.

Step 2: Identify the Product/Service Package for Each Customer Segment

This step presents one of the most challenging activities in the CRM process. The goal of this step is to determine what each customer segment values in its relationship with the supplier. This decision is usually based on feedback from customers and sales

Table 8.1	Hypothetical Product/Service Offerings: Option A		
PRODUCT/SERVICE OFFERING	CUSTOMER SEGMENT A	CUSTOMER SEGMENT B	CUSTOMER SEGMENT C
Product quality (% defects)	Less than 1%	5%–10%	10%–15%
Order fill	98%	92%	88%
Lead time	3 days	7 days	14 days
Delivery time	Within 1 hour of request	On day requested	During week requested
Payment terms	4/10 net 30	3/10 net 30	2/10 net 30
Customer service support	Dedicated rep	Next available rep	Through Web site

representatives. The challenge here is how to "package" the value-adding products and services for each customer segment. One solution is to offer the same product/service offering to each customer segment, while varying the product quality or service levels. For example, Table 8.1 presents a scenario where the offerings for each customer segment do not change, but the level of the offering does. In this table, assume that Customer Segment A is the most profitable and Customer Segment C is the least profitable. As is shown, Customer Segment A receives the best product and the best service, while the other two customer segments receive less quality in product and service. This type of "package" assumes that all customer segments value the same types of supplier offerings. This could be a disadvantage for this approach. The advantage to this approach is that it is easy for the supplier to manage.

Another solution to this part of the CRM process is to vary the service offerings for each customer segment. An example of this approach can be seen in Table 8.2. In Table 8.2, the offerings for each segment are different, with the top customer segment (A) receiving the most differentiation. The basis for this package is that each segment values different services. The advantage to this method is that it meets the needs of each segment. The disadvantage is that it is much more difficult for the supplier to manage. Of the two methods shown in Tables 8.1 and 8.2, Option A (Table 8.1) is most commonly found in industry today.

Step 3: Develop and Execute the Best Processes

In Step 2, customer expectations were determined and set. Step 3 delivers on those expectations. Organizations many times go through elaborate processes to determine customer needs and set target performance levels, only to fail when it comes to executing on those customer promises. One cause for this might be that organizations fail to recognize that process reengineering might be necessary to meet expected performance targets. For example, the order fill rate promised to Customer Segment A in Table 8.1 might not be possible given the current inventory policy of the supplier's organization. So, inventory levels and locations might have to be reconsidered given a target performance rate for order fill of 98 percent. The higher the expectations of the customer are, the more the dissatisfaction if they are not achieved.

Table 8.2	Hypothetical Product/Service Offerings: Option B
Customer Segment A	
Product quality (% defects)	Less than 1%
Order fill	98%
Lead time	3 days
Delivery time	Within 1 hour of request
Payment terms	4/10 net 30
Customer service support	Dedicated rep
Customer Segment B	
Product quality (% defects)	5%–10%
Credit hold	Less than 48 hours
Return policy	Up to 10 days after delivery
Customer Segment C	
Order fill	88%
Ordering process	Through Web site

Step 4: Measure Performance and Continuously Improve

The goal of CRM is to better serve the different customer segments of the supplier organization, while at the same time improving the profitability of the supplier. Once the CRM program has been implemented, it must be evaluated to determine if (1) the different customer segments are satisfied and (2) the supplier's overall profitability has improved. Remember, the goal of CRM is to identify those customers who provide the most profit by ordering product in a manner that minimizes the supplier's costs. So, another measure of the CRM program might be the number of customers who have moved from one customer segment to another by changing their ordering patterns. The goal of CRM is not to eliminate customers; rather, it is to satisfy the customer while maximizing profits for the supplier. If the CRM program is not achieving these goals, it must be reevaluated and/or repositioned to bring it into alignment with performance targets.

The concept behind CRM is simple: align the supplier's resources with its customers in a manner that increases both customer satisfaction and supplier profits. The execution of a CRM program presents many challenges. CRM implementation is not so much of a destination as it is a journey. CRM is a strategic initiative by a supplier organization that requires changes in resource allocation, organizational structure, and market perception.

This section presented a general overview of CRM. The next section will delve deeper into the details of how customers are segmented using activity-based costing and customer profitability.

Activity-Based Costing and Customer Profitability

Traditional cost accounting is well suited to situations where an output and an allocation process are highly correlated. Take, for example, a warehouse that receives product in pallet quantities, stores product in pallets, picks product in pallets, and ships product in pallets. Also, assume that the same amount of labor expense, machine expense, and space expense are consumed for each pallet regardless of the type of product on the pallet. In this scenario, cost accounts such as direct labor, direct machine expense, and direct overhead (space) can be allocated to each product based on the number of pallets moved through the warehouse for a particular time period.

On the other hand, traditional cost accounting is not very effective in situations where the output is not correlated with the allocation base. This is the more likely scenario in logistics. For example, assume that the warehouse just described will need to start picking and shipping in case quantities and in inner-pack quantities as well as in pallet quantities. Using an allocation base of pallets, products shipped in pallets will burden a majority of the direct costs incurred in the warehouse. However, the case pick and inner-pack pick, being very labor intensive, are driving most of the costs in the warehouse. As such, traditional cost accounting in this case would be penalizing the most cost effective method of moving product through the warehouse and subsidizing the least cost effective method of moving product. This is where activity-based costing can be effective. ABC can be defined as, "A methodology that measures the cost and performance of activities, resources, and cost objects. Resources are assigned to activities, then activities are assigned to cost objects based on their use. ABC recognizes the causal relationships of cost drivers to activities."[3] Using the ABC methodology in the warehouse example previously discussed would more accurately assign costs to those activities that absorbed the most resources. In other words, ABC would identify that picking and shipping inner-packs is more expensive that picking and shipping pallets.

Another way to look at the difference between traditional cost accounting and ABC can be seen in Figure 8.2. As this figure shows, conventional accounting assigns resources to department cost centers (for example, warehouse labor is assigned to the warehousing department), then allocates a particular cost to a product (for example, labor dollars per pallet). ABC assigns resources to an activity (for example, labor cost for picking product), identifies the cost drivers (for example, labor cost for picking a pallet versus picking an inner-pack), and then allocates those costs to products, customers, markets, or business units. ABC more accurately reflects the actual cost of performing an activity than does traditional cost accounting.

An example of how ABC works might be beneficial here. Assume that a consumer goods distribution center (DC) always receives and stores product in pallet quantities but picks and ships in pallets, tiers, cases, and eaches (individual consumer units). The product flow can be seen in Figure 8.3. The DC receives pallets for both storage and returns from customers. The returns process is separate and will not be discussed here. Once the pallet is received, it is put away (stored) until product is ready to be picked. Customers are allowed to order in quantities from eaches to full pallets. Shipping can be done from eaches to full pallets. After the pallet is stored, ten separate processes can be used to pick and ship product to comply with the customer's order. Intuitively, the most cost efficient method in this figure is obviously pallet pick and pallet ship. The most expensive method in this figure is each pick and each ship. Tier picking means a customer orders a product in "tier" quantities. "Tier" is the number of cases of a product that fits onto a single layer on a pallet. "High" is the number of layers of products on a pallet. Usually, tier picking results in a "rainbow" pallet, which is a pallet that contains

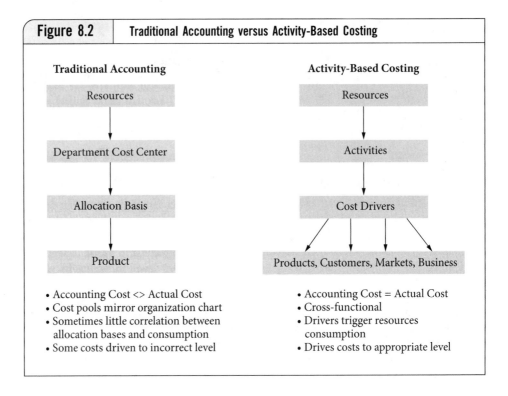

Figure 8.2 | **Traditional Accounting versus Activity-Based Costing**

Traditional Accounting

Resources

Department Cost Center

Allocation Basis

Product

- Accounting Cost <> Actual Cost
- Cost pools mirror organization chart
- Sometimes little correlation between allocation bases and consumption
- Some costs driven to incorrect level

Activity-Based Costing

Resources

Activities

Cost Drivers

Products, Customers, Markets, Business

- Accounting Cost = Actual Cost
- Cross-functional
- Drivers trigger resources consumption
- Drives costs to appropriate level

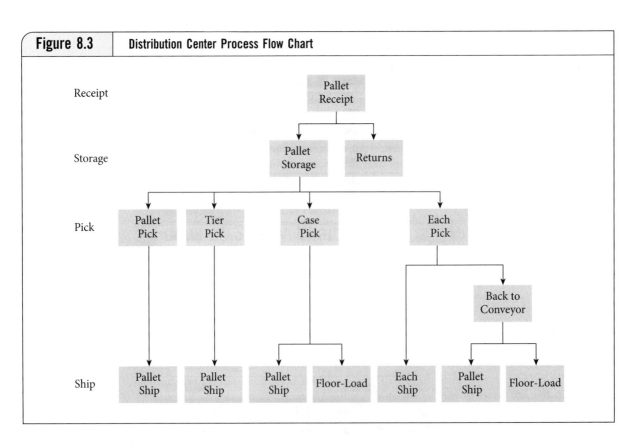

Figure 8.3 | **Distribution Center Process Flow Chart**

Receipt — Pallet Receipt

Storage — Pallet Storage, Returns

Pick — Pallet Pick, Tier Pick, Case Pick, Each Pick → Back to Conveyor

Ship — Pallet Ship, Pallet Ship, Pallet Ship, Floor-Load, Each Ship, Pallet Ship, Floor-Load

Table 8.3	Distribution Center Space Allocation
ACTIVITY	PERCENT OF TOTAL NET SQUARE FEET
Storage	73.0
Case pick	10.0
Receiving	5.0
Each pick	4.0
Test location	3.0
Staging	3.0
Returns	2.0
Total	100.0

several layers of different products. In case picking, the case can be picked and assembled onto a pallet for shipping or the case can put onto the conveyor system and eventually floor-loaded (each case loaded separately) in the trailer. In each picking, the each can be combined with other eaches into a reusable shipping case, put back onto the conveyor with other cases, and either floor-loaded or palletized. Each picks can also be shipped as eaches.

With the numerous methods that product can flow through the DC identified, the next step is to identify the activities that absorb the two main costs in a DC: space and labor. Space consumption by activity can be seen in Table 8.3. This table shows that storage absorbs 73 percent of the DC overhead cost. So, products that require excess storage space will be allocated more of the direct overhead (facility) costs. Table 8.4 shows the number of full-time equivalent employees (FTEs) required to perform the different types of activities shown in Figure 8.3. Picking cases to be placed onto the conveyor requires the most FTEs (19.54).

Combining the costs from these two tables with the product flows identified in Figure 8.3 results in the costs to perform these activities and can be seen in Figure 8.4. Using equivalent case quantities as the allocation basis, it is easy to understand that receiving, storing, picking, and shipping products in pallets results in the lowest cost per case for the DC. Alternatively, receiving and storing products in pallets and picking and shipping eaches results in the highest cost per case. This ABC methodology, then, can be used to determine the costs of the various customer ordering policies and may be used to influence how the customer orders.

Distribution center costs are but one cost that a shipper incurs in dealing with a customer. Traditional customer profitability analyses would start with gross sales less returns and allowances (net sales) and subtract the cost of goods sold to arrive at a gross margin figure. Although this number might provide a general guideline for the profitability of a customer, it falls short on capturing the real costs of serving a customer. A broader approach to determining customer profitability can be seen in Table 8.5. This is an actual example from a company that shall remain anonymous. This example identifies many other cost drivers that are impacted by customers and how they interact with the shipper. Notice that the DC example just covered falls under the "Operations"

Table 8.4   Distribution Center Labor Allocation

ACTIVITY	FTEs[*]
Receiving	17.73
Storage	6.90
Case pick	19.54
Floor-loading	6.90
Test area	6.90
Each pick	6.90
Back to conveyor	1.28
Courier delivery	1.28
Pallet pick	5.49
Returns	9.71
Total FTEs	82.63

*Full-time equivalent employees.

Figure 8.4   Flow-Through Costing for a Distribution Center

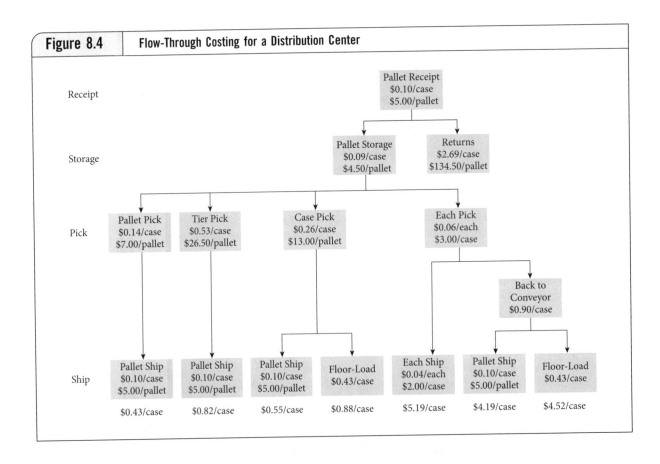

Table 8.5	Customer Profitability Analysis

CUSTOMER P&L STATEMENT — **CUSTOMER A TOTAL U.S. CONSOLIDATED**

MAC CODE: 123456	1997 ACTUALS	% TO SALES	1998 QUARTER 1	1998 QUARTER 2	1998 QUARTER 3	1998 QUARTER 4	1998 YTD ACTUALS	% TO SALES
Gross Sales			$17,439,088	$15,488,645	$17,382,277	$16,632,060	$66,942,069	102.6%
Returns			78,383	60,150	66,828	143,225	348,587	100.5%
Cash Discounts			348,782	309,773	347,646	332,641	1,338,841	102.1%
Net Sales			$17,011,923	$15,118,722	$16,967,803	$16,156,194	$65,254,641	100.0%
Cost of Goods Sold:			$ 4,392,341	$ 3,686,569	$ 4,170,382	$ 3,959,373	$16,208,665	24.8%
Standard Costs			$ 4,279,660	$ 3,615,837	$ 4,070,518	$ 3,830,855	$15,796,870	24.2%
Royalties			$ 112,681	$ 70,732	$ 99,864	$ 128,518	$ 411,795	0.6%
Gross Margin			$12,619,582	$11,432,153	$12,797,421	$12,196,820	$49,045,976	75.2%
Promotional Costs:			$ 1,366,220	$ 1,476,337	$ 1,624,152	$ 2,210,575	$ 6,677,284	10.2%
Allowances			$ 299,893	$ 85,025	$ 110,627	$ 0	$ 495,544	0.8%
Off Invoice			$ 957,617	$ 885,877	$ 1,054,432	$ 1,115,520	$ 4,013,447	6.2%
Trade Promotion Funds			$ 108,710	$ 505,435	$ 459,093	$ 1,095,055	$ 2,168,293	3.3%
Racks			$ 0	$ 0	$ 0	$ 0	$ 0	0.0%
Other			$ 0	$ 0	$ 0	$ 0	$ 0	0.0%
Advertising:			$ 0	$ 0	$ 0	$ 0	$ 0	0.0%
Market Research			$ 0	$ 0	$ 0	$ 0	$ 0	0.0%
Other Variable Expenses:			$ 576,922	$ 396,040	$ 464,740	$ 474,752	$ 1,912,454	2.9%
Bracket Pricing			$ 373,099	$ 256,242	$ 300,028	$ 320,522	$ 1,249,892	1.9%
Freight			$ 203,822	$ 139,798	$ 164,712	$ 154,229	$ 662,562	1.0%
Direct Profit Contribution			$10,676,440	$ 9,559,776	$10,708,529	$ 9,511,494	$40,456,238	62.0%
Selling Expenses:			$ 277,303	$ 288,458	$ 320,217	$ 377,591	$ 1,263,569	1.9%
Headquarters Selling			$ 59,690	$ 59,690	$ 59,690	$ 59,690	$ 238,762	0.4%
Retail Selling			$ 45,481	$ 45,481	$ 46,843	$ 75,246	$ 213,052	0.3%
Category Management			$ 50,238	$ 50,238	$ 50,238	$ 50,238	$ 200,953	0.3%
CBT's			$ 121,893	$ 133,048	$ 163,446	$ 192,416	$ 610,802	0.9%

(continued)

| Table 8.5 | Continued |

CUSTOMER P&L STATEMENT   **CUSTOMER A TOTAL U.S. CONSOLIDATED**

MAC CODE: 123456	1997 ACTUALS	% TO SALES	1998 QUARTER 1	1998 QUARTER 2	1998 QUARTER 3	1998 QUARTER 4	1998 YTD ACTUALS	% TO SALES
Operations:			$ 192,555	$ 266,837	$ 269,382	$ 269,673	$ 998,447	1.5%
Warehousing			$ 100,632	$ 145,456	$ 142,890	$ 153,564	$ 542,541	0.8%
Order Processing			$ 91,923	$ 121,381	$ 126,492	$ 116,109	$ 455,905	0.7%
Operating Profit			$10,206,582	$ 9,004,481	$10,118,929	$ 8,864,230	$38,194,223	58.5%
Write Offs:			$ 15,791	$ 4,701	$ (820)	$ 18,433	$ 38,105	0.1%
Allowance Reserve			$ 310	$ 2,939	$ (88)	$ 7,792	$ 10,953	0.0%
Claims Reserve			$ 15,481	$ 2,688	$ 1,365	$ 6,641	$ 26,175	0.0%
Handling Charges			$ 0	$ (926)	$ (2,097)	$ 4,000	$ 977	0.0%
Adjusted Operating Profit			$10,190,791	$ 8,999,780	$10,119,749	$ 8,845,797	$38,156,118	58.5%
Footnotes:								
Items Journaled Requiring Further Investigation			$ 1,034	$ 2,223	$ 2,492	$ 9,125	$ 14,875	0.0%
Unearned Cash Discounts Written Off			$ 0	$ 809	$ 0	$ 30,213	$ 31,022	0.0%

section of this customer profitability formula. As can be seen with this example, using gross margin alone as the indicator of profitability understates the costs incurred with serving this customer. Every line item under gross margin is represented by a process model as shown in Figure 8.4. With this information on how a customer's interaction drives a shippers costs, the shipper can then segment its customers by profitability.

Figure 8.5 shows one method to classify customers by profitability. The vertical axis measures the net sales value of the customer, while the horizontal axis represents the cost to serve. Those customers who fall into the "Protect" segment are the most profitable. Their interactions with the shipper provide the shipper with the most cost efficiencies. Those customers who are in the "Danger Zone" segment are the least profitable and are more than likely incurring a loss for the shipper. For these customers, the shipper has three alternatives: (1) change the manner in which the customer interacts with the shipper so the customer can move to another segment; (2) charge the customer the actual cost of doing business (this would more than likely make the customer stop doing business with the shipper—this is usually not an acceptable strategy employed by most shippers); or (3) switch the customer to an alternative distribution channel (for example, the shipper might encourage the customer to order through a distributor or wholesaler rather than buying direct from the shipper). The customers who fall into the "Build" segment have a low cost to serve and a low net sales value. The strategy here is to maintain the cost to serve but build net sales value to help drive the customer into the "Protect" segment. Finally, the customers who are in the "Cost Engineer" segment have a high net sales value and a high cost to serve. The strategy here is to find more efficient ways for the customer to interact with the shipper. This might include encouraging the customer to order in tier quantities rather than in case quantities. This switch in ordering policy

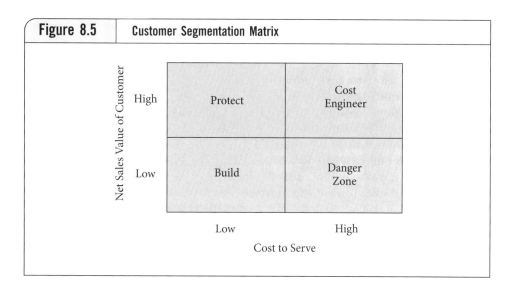

Figure 8.5 | **Customer Segmentation Matrix**

	Low Cost to Serve	High Cost to Serve
High Net Sales Value of Customer	Protect	Cost Engineer
Low Net Sales Value of Customer	Build	Danger Zone

would reduce the operating cost of the shipper and possibly move the customer into the "Protect" segment.

Combining ABC, customer profitability, and customer segmentation to build profitable revenue is a strategy being utilized by an increasing number of organizations today. This strategy helps define the true cost of dealing with customers and helps the shipper influence how the customer interacts with the shipper to provide the highest level of cost efficiency for the shipper. Combining these three tools with CRM allows the shipper to differentiate its offerings to its different customer segments, resulting in maximum profit for the shipper and maximum satisfaction for the customer.

This section discussed the methods organizations use to influence how a customer orders. The next section will discuss the methods used by shippers to execute the order once it is received.

Executing the Order—Order Management and Order Fulfillment

The order management system represents the principal means by which buyers and sellers communicate information relating to individual orders of product. Effective order management is a key to operational efficiency and customer satisfaction. To the extent that an organization conducts all activities relating to order management in a timely, accurate, and thorough manner, it follows that other areas of company activity can be similarly coordinated. In addition, both present and potential customers will take a positive view of consistent and predictable order cycle length and acceptable response times. By starting the process with an understanding of customer needs, organizations can design order management systems that will be viewed as superior to competitor firms.

The logistics area needs timely and accurate information relating to individual customer orders; thus, more and more organizations are placing the corporate order management function within the logistics area. The move is good not only from the perspective of the logistics process but also from that of the overall organization.

Order-to-Cash (OTC) and Replenishment Cycles

When referring to outbound-to-customer shipments, the term **order to cash** (or **order cycle**) is typically used. The difference between these two terms will be discussed shortly. The term **replenishment cycle** is used more frequently when referring to the acquisition of additional inventory, as in materials management. Basically, one organization's order cycle is another's replenishment cycle. For the remainder of this discussion, the term *order to cash* (OTC) will be used. Traditionally, organizations viewed order management as all of those activities that occur from when an order is received by a seller until the product is received by the buyer. This is called the *order cycle*. The OTC cycle is all of those activities included in the order cycle plus the flow of funds back to the seller based on the invoice. The OTC concept is being adopted by many organizations today and more accurately reflects the effectiveness of the order management process.

Figure 8.6 is a representation of the OTC cycle. This figure is also referred to as Process Dl: Deliver Stocked Product in the Supply Chain Council's SCOR Model. It will be

Figure 8.6	SCOR Model Process D1: Deliver Stocked Product

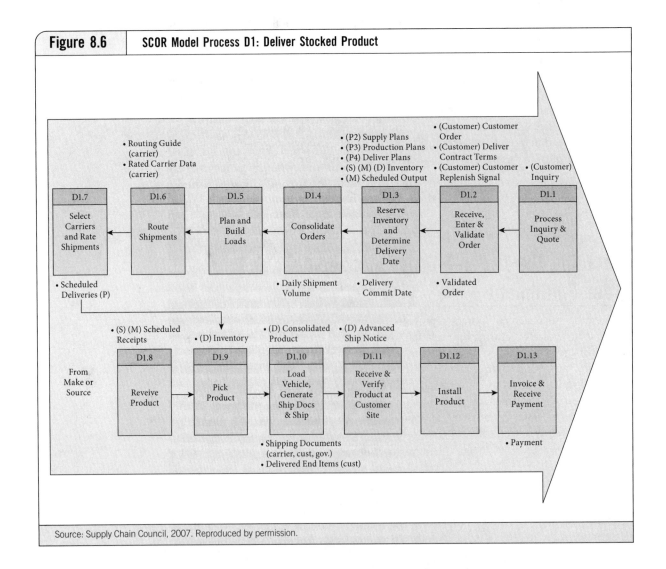

Source: Supply Chain Council, 2007. Reproduced by permission.

used as the basis of discussion for this session. This process represents not only the lead time for delivery of product to the customer but also the flow of funds back to the seller. Thirteen principal activities constitute the OTC cycle. The first seven (D1.1 through D1.7) represent information flows; the next five (D1.8 through D1.12) represent product flows; and the last activity (D1.13) represents cash flow. Each of these will be discussed in the following section.

D1.1: Process Inquiry and Quote

This step in the process precedes the actual placement of the order by the customer. In D1.1, the customer is looking for product, pricing, or availability information from the supplier to determine whether or not to place an order. This step in the process requires that the seller have up-to-date information in a single location to provide quickly and accurately to the prospective buyer. Information availability is critical in this step.

D1.2: Receive, Enter, and Validate Order

This step involves the placement and receipt of the order. In many organizations, this step is accomplished through the application of technology such as electronic data interchange (EDI) or the Internet. In some organizations, the order is called in to a customer service representative (CSR) who then enters the order into the seller's order management system. The application of technology to this step has significantly reduced order errors as well as the OTC cycle. Step D1.2 "captures" the order and prepares it for the next step, order processing.

D1.3: Reserve Inventory and Determine Delivery Date

This step in the process has traditionally been referred to as order processing. In the buyer/seller relationship, this might be the most critical step because it sets delivery expectations for the customer. Once the order has been "captured" in the seller's order management system, current inventory levels are checked to determine availability and location. If inventory is available in the seller's distribution network, it is reserved for the order and a delivery date is given to the customer. In the case where the seller has inventory to fill the order, the delivery date is based on the concept of **available to deliver (ATD)**. This means that the seller has the inventory and can promise a delivery date.

In some instances, the seller does not have the inventory but knows when it will be produced internally or delivered from a supplier to the seller's distribution centers. In this case, the delivery date is based on the concept of **available to promise (ATP)**. This means that even though the seller does not have physical possession of the inventory to fill the order, it can still promise a delivery date. In either case, the customer has no need to know whether the delivery date is based on ATD or ATP. Implementing the ATP concept requires upstream coordination of information systems between the seller and its manufacturing facilities and/or the seller and its supplier's manufacturing facilities or distribution centers. For example, assume that an order for 40 cases of Product A is ordered from the seller. The seller currently has 20 cases of this product in inventory but knows that its manufacturing facility will be producing another 20 cases tomorrow. The seller can now set an ATP delivery date because it knows that by tomorrow, 40 cases of Product A will be available for the order. Similarly, if the seller has only 20 cases of Product A in inventory but knows that its supplier will deliver another 20 cases this afternoon, it can still set an ATP delivery date. Critical to the success of the ATP concept is the assurance that the upstream suppliers (internal manufacturing facilities or supplier facilities) will keep their promise of delivery of the additional 20 cases. If they cannot meet this promise, either order fill or on-time delivery performance for the seller will suffer.

Once the delivery date is set with the customer, this step will usually transmit the order to the warehouse management system (WMS) for pick scheduling and to the financial system for invoice generation. So this step determines the order execution plan that the seller has determined and communicated to the customer. Its successful completion is critical to internal efficiencies for the supplier (e.g., order fill rate and on-time delivery rate) and external effectiveness for the customer (customer satisfaction).

D1.4: Consolidate Orders

This step examines customer orders to determine opportunities for both freight consolidation as well as for batch warehouse picking schedules. Both of these consolidation opportunities offer cost efficiencies for the seller. However, consolidation plans will normally add time to the delivery cycle of the order to the customer. These opportunities, then, need to be examined taking into consideration the ATD or ATP delivery dates specified in the previous step.

D1.5: Plan and Build Loads

This step takes the freight consolidation opportunities identified in D1.4 and the delivery date given in D1.3 and develops a transportation plan. Many times, this step is used with less-than-truckload (LTL), small package, stop-off, or pool freight operations. The concept is to designate the order to a specific carrier or transportation vehicle to optimize transportation efficiencies while maintaining customer delivery requirements. Many organizations use transportation management systems (TMS) to build loads for customer deliveries.

D1.6: Route Shipments

This step can follow or be concurrent with D1.5. Here, the "load" (usually a transportation vehicle) is assigned to a specific route for delivery to the customer. Again, many organizations use a TMS to complete this step.

D1.7: Select Carriers and Rate Shipments

Following or concurrent with D1.5 and D1.6, this step will assign a specific carrier to deliver an order or a consolidation of orders. This is usually based on the seller's routing guide that is many times contained in the TMS. For example, a seller has 2,000 pounds of freight to be delivered from its distribution center to a destination 1,500 miles away with a two-day delivery window. The routing guide might suggest that a small package air freight carrier (e.g., UPS, FedEx, or DHL) handle this load. If the delivery window is five days, the routing guide might suggest an LTL carrier (e.g., Yellow/Roadway, FedEx Ground). Once the carrier has been designated, the seller predetermines the freight costs for the shipment based on agreements with the individual carrier. In any situation, this step takes into consideration size of shipment (load), destination (route), and delivery (ATD or ATP) to determine the appropriate carrier and freight costs.

D1.8: Receive Product at Warehouse

This step gains importance when an ATP has been given to a customer's order. In this step, product is received at the distribution center and the order management system is checked to see if there are any orders outstanding that need this particular product. If so, the product is immediately combined with the on-hand inventory in preparation to be picked for the order. If the product is not immediately needed to fill an open order, it is put to storage to await the picking process.

D1.9: Pick Product

This step uses the outputs from D1.3, D1.4, and D1.5 to determine the order picking schedules in the distribution center. With the many order picking strategies that can be used at distribution centers, this step is critical to route orders through the distribution center to optimize order picking efficiency while maintaining delivery schedules.

D1.10: Load Vehicle, Generate Shipping Documents, Verify Credit, and Ship

Based on the output from D1.5 and D1.6, the transportation vehicle is loaded in this step. In some cases, the sequencing of the order or orders in a transportation vehicle might not be important. For example, in a full truckload shipment where there is one order with one destination, the sequencing of the products in the vehicle takes on less importance. However, in an LTL or stop-off transportation vehicle where there are multiple orders with multiple destinations, the sequence is important. In this case, the last delivery would be loaded in the "nose" or front of the vehicle, while the first delivery is located on the rear of the vehicle. The proper loading sequence is critical in delivery efficiencies as well as in meeting delivery requirements.

Although some organizations do a credit check on the buyer in this step, credit checks are normally done in D1.2. "Ability to pay" on the part of the buyer is required by many organizations to set the order fulfillment process in motion.

Finally, this step will generate shipment documents to provide to the carrier to execute the shipment. These documents might include bills of lading, freight bills, waybills, and manifests for domestic shipments as well as customs clearance documents for international shipments. When the shipment is legally turned over to the carrier, the shipment process can begin. This is also the step where sellers will officially invoice the customer.

D1.11: Receive and Verify Product at Customer Site

Once the shipment is delivered to the customer location, the receiving location will determine whether or not the delivered product is what was ordered. This verification is important because it is at this point in the process where the buyer will begin processing the seller's invoice if the delivered order is correct. If it is not correct, the buyer and seller need to agree on how to solve any discrepancies. This step also concludes the traditional order cycle. So the seller's success in completing all steps in the process up to this point determines the speed at which the seller will receive payment for the order.

D1.12: Install Product

If an order involves a product that must be installed at the customer location, it is at this point in the OTC cycle where installation takes place. An example might be where a buyer ordered a palletizing machine from a seller that required the seller to provide for installation. The success of the installation could also have an impact on the speed of cash flow back to the seller.

D1.13: Invoice

This step is the culmination of the OTC cycle for the buyer and seller. This is where the buyer is satisfied with the order cycle performance and has initiated payment to the seller. This cash flow represents the final flow of the three critical flows in the supply chain: information, product, and cash.

Process D1, the OTC cycle, represents those activities necessary in both order management and order fulfillment. The absolute time and reliability of the OTC cycle have implications on both the buyer and seller. This will be discussed in the next section.

Length and Variability of the Order-to-Cash Cycle

While interest has traditionally focused more on the overall length of the OTC cycle, recent attention has been centered on the variability or consistency of this process. Industry practices have shown that while the absolute length of time is important, variability is more important. A driving force behind the attention to OTC cycle variability is safety stock. The absolute length of the order cycle will influence demand inventory. The concept of the order cycle is used here because the focus is on the delivery of product to the buyer and not on the flow of cash to the supplier. For example, assume that the order cycle (time from order placement to order receipt) takes 10 days to complete and the buyer needs five units per day for its manufacturing process. Assuming the basic economic order quantity (EOQ) (this will be discussed at length in the next chapter) model is being used by the buyer, the buyer will place an order when it has 50 units of demand inventory on hand. Assuming that the supplier has been able to reduce the order cycle to eight days, the buyer will now place an order when it has 40 units of demand inventory on hand. This is a reduction of 10 units of demand inventory on hand during lead time for the buyer.

Now assume that the 10-day order cycle time has a variability of +/−3 days, producing a range of 7–13 days for the order cycle. If the buyer wants to ensure that no stockouts occur for its manufacturing process, it must place an order when it has 65 units of inventory on hand (5 units per day × 13 days). So, the variability of this order cycle has added 15 units of inventory at the buyer's location when compared to the specific 10-day order cycle time. Figure 8.7 is a good representation of how the variability of the order cycle components impacts inventories. In the "Before System Change," the average order cycle time is 13 days with a range of 4–22 days. If the supplier is to guarantee delivery to the buyer in 13 days every time, the buyer would need to have 65 units of demand inventory on hand when placing an order (5 units per day × 13 days). The 18-day variability (4–22 days) now requires that the buyer maintain 45 units of safety stock on hand if it wants to avoid any stockouts [5 units per day × 22 days − (65 units)], resulting in a total inventory of 110 units. In the "After System Change," the buyer would order when it had 55 units of demand inventory on hand if the supplier could guarantee an 11-day order cycle time (5 units per day × 11 days). The variability of 10 days (6–16 days) would require the buyer to maintain 25 units of safety stock if it wants to avoid any stockouts [5 units per day × 16 days −(55 units)]. This is a reduction of 10 units of demand inventory and 25 units of safety stock resulting from a reduction in order cycle time length and variability.

Figure 8.7 | Order Cycle Length and Variability

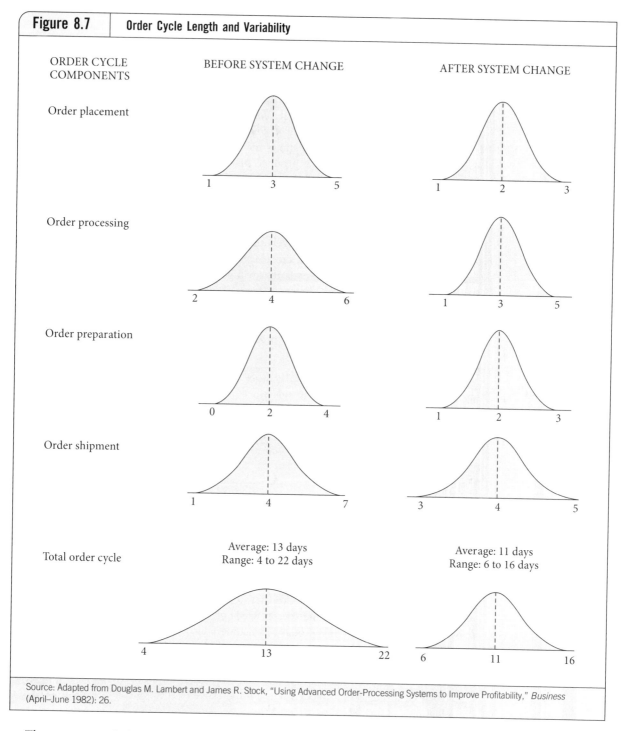

ORDER CYCLE COMPONENTS — BEFORE SYSTEM CHANGE — AFTER SYSTEM CHANGE

Order placement

Order processing

Order preparation

Order shipment

Total order cycle

Before System Change — Average: 13 days, Range: 4 to 22 days

After System Change — Average: 11 days, Range: 6 to 16 days

Source: Adapted from Douglas M. Lambert and James R. Stock, "Using Advanced Order-Processing Systems to Improve Profitability," *Business* (April–June 1982): 26.

The concepts of absolute time and variability of time will be covered more in depth in Chapter 9 (Inventory Management). However, it is important to note here that the time and variability associated with order management affects not only customer satisfaction but also a customer's inventories. These cost and service implications of order management are critical to a seller's competitive advantage in the marketplace.

E-Commerce Order Fulfillment Strategies

This discussion on order management would not be complete without a brief discussion on how the Internet has affected how the OTC cycle is designed and managed. Many organizations are using Internet technology as a means to capture order information and transmit it to their "back end" systems for picking, packing, and shipping. What the Internet is now allowing is the faster collection of cash by the seller organizations. As can be seen in the D1 process shown in Figure 8.6, cash is collected by the seller in the last step of the process. This figure shows the traditional "buy-make-sell" business model used by many organizations that produce product to inventory to wait for an order. Obviously, the longer it takes the selling organization to complete the order management process, the longer it takes to collect its cash. Probably, the most notable example of an organization managing its cash flow is Dell. Dell employs the "sell-buy-make" business model. A large percentage of orders (both consumer and business) received by Dell for its products are placed through its Web site. Once the order is received and confirmed (sell), Dell will process the buyer's credit card or purchasing card to begin the flow of funds before it owns the components that will go into building the customer's order. So Dell has the customer's money before it owns the components for the final product. If we use Process D1 from Figure 8.6 as an example, Step D1.13 now comes after D1.3. Dell estimates that it has a +40-day negative working capital balance. In other words, it has its customers' cash for an average of 40 days before it must pay its suppliers for the components.

Applying Internet technology to the order management process has allowed organizations to not only take time out of the process but also to increase the velocity of cash back to the selling organization. These two benefits have added strategic importance to the order management process.

Customer Service

No discussion of outbound logistics systems would be complete without the inclusion of customer service, since customer service is the output of the logistics engine. Having the right product, at the right time, in the right quantity, without damage or loss, to the right customer are underlying principles of logistics systems that recognize the importance of customer service.

Another aspect of customer service that deserves mention is the consumer awareness of the price/quality ratio and the special needs of today's consumers, who are time conscious and demand flexibility. Today's consumers also have high standards for quality, and brand loyalty is not necessarily something they always support. Essentially, they want products at the best price, with the best levels of service, and at times convenient to their schedules. Successful companies, such as Wal-Mart and Dell, have adopted customer service strategies that recognize the importance of speed, flexibility, customization, and reliability.

The Logistics/Marketing Interface

Customer service is often the key link between logistics and marketing within an organization. If the logistics system, particularly outbound logistics, is not functioning properly and a customer does not receive a delivery as promised, the organization could lose both current and future revenue. Manufacturing can produce a quality product at the right cost and marketing can sell it, but if logistics does not deliver it when and where promised, the customer will not be satisfied.

Figure 8.8 represents the traditional role of customer service at the interface between marketing and logistics. This relationship manifests itself in this perspective through the "place" dimension of the marketing mix, which is often used synonymously with channel-of-distribution decisions and the associated customer service levels provided. In this context, logistics plays a static role that is based upon minimizing the total cost of the various logistics activities within a given set of service levels, most likely determined by marketing.

However, as Chapter 5 and examples in this chapter illustrate, logistics today is taking on a more dynamic role in influencing customer service levels as well as in impacting an organization's financial position. Again, appropriate examples here would include both Dell and Wal-Mart that have both used logistics and customer service to reduce product prices, increase product availability, and reduce lead times to customers. These two organizations have gained an appreciation for the impact of dynamic logistics systems on their financial positions.

Defining Customer Service

Attempting to define the concept of customer service can be a difficult task. The beginning of this chapter offered three different perspectives on customer service: (1) as a philosophy, (2) as a set of performance measures, and (3) as an activity. However, customer service needs to be put into perspective as including *anything that touches the customer*. From a marketing perspective, there are three levels of a product that an organization provides to its customers: (1) the core benefit or service, which constitutes what the buyer is really buying; (2) the tangible product, or the physical product or service itself; and (3) the augmented product, which includes benefits that are secondary, but an integral enhancement to, the tangible product the customer is purchasing. In this context, logistics customer service can be thought of as a feature of the augmented product that adds value for the customer.[4] However, the product and logistics customer service are not the only outputs by which a seller "touches" the customer. Customer service also includes how a seller interfaces with a customer and provides information about the product. This would include providing information about product availability, pricing, delivery dates, product tracking, installation, postsale support, and so on. Customer service is really an all-encompassing strategy for how a seller interacts with its customers. Customer service is an activity, a set of performance measures, a philosophy, a core benefit, a tangible product, and an augmented product. Customer service focuses on how a seller interacts with its customers on information flows, product flows, and cash flows.

Elements of Customer Service

Customer service is an important reason for incurring logistics costs. Economic advantages generally accrue to the customer through better supplier service. As an example, a supplier can lower customer inventories by utilizing air transportation rather than motor carrier transportation. Lower inventory costs result from air transportation's lower and more reliable transit time, which will decrease order cycle time but result in higher transportation costs than those incurred by using motor carriage. The supplier's logistics analysis must balance the improved service level the customer desires and the benefits the supplier might gain from possible increased revenue versus

Figure 8.8	The Traditional Logistics/Marketing Interface

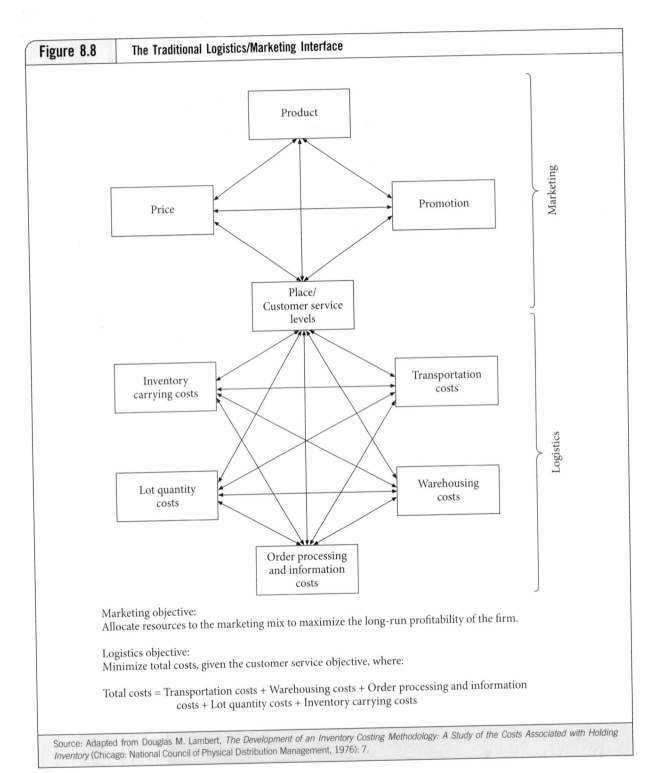

Marketing objective:
Allocate resources to the marketing mix to maximize the long-run profitability of the firm.

Logistics objective:
Minimize total costs, given the customer service objective, where:

Total costs = Transportation costs + Warehousing costs + Order processing and information costs + Lot quantity costs + Inventory carrying costs

Source: Adapted from Douglas M. Lambert, *The Development of an Inventory Costing Methodology: A Study of the Costs Associated with Holding Inventory* (Chicago: National Council of Physical Distribution Management, 1976): 7.

the cost of providing that service. Figure 8.9 is an attempt to show the relationship between service levels and the cost of providing that service. Every incremental improvement in service (e.g., on-time delivery) will require some incremental level of investment from the supplier. This investment could be in faster and more reliable

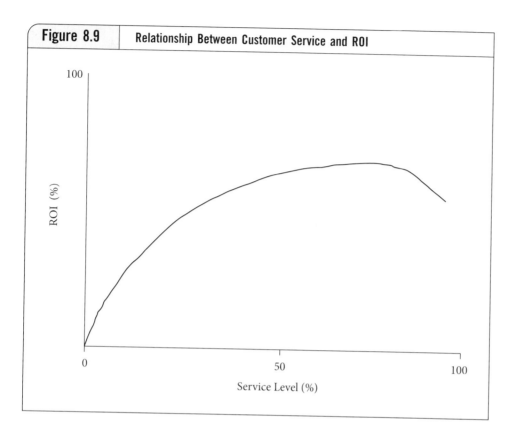

| Figure 8.9 | Relationship Between Customer Service and ROI |

transportation or in additional inventories. An assumption is that for every incremental improvement in service there is an incremental increase in revenue for the supplier from the customer. With the cost and revenue parameters identified, a return on investment (ROI) can be calculated. Figure 8.9 attempts to illustrate that the ROI from service improvement increases at a decreasing rate. In other words, as service continues to improve, the marginal cost of providing the improved service increases, while the marginal increase in revenue decreases. At some point, the cost of service will far outweigh the incremental revenue gained from that service, providing a negative ROI. This is why it is impractical for most firms to provide 100 percent service levels. Therefore, suppliers must recognize the importance of balancing the tradeoffs between service and cost.

As previously discussed, customer service is an all-encompassing concept for an organization. From the perspective of logistics, however, customer service can be viewed as having four distinct dimensions: time, dependability, communications, and convenience. The next section will discuss ways in which these elements affect the cost centers of both buying and selling organizations.

Time

The *time* factor is usually order to cash, particularly from the seller's perspective. On the other hand, the buyer usually refers to the time dimension as the order cycle time, lead time, or replenishment time. Regardless of the perspective or the terminology, several basic components or variables affect the time factor.

Successful logistics operations today have a high degree of control over most, if not all, of the basic elements of lead time including order processing, order picking, and order shipping. By effectively managing activities such as these, thus ensuring that order cycles will be of reasonable length and consistent duration, seller organizations have improved the customer service levels that they provide to buyers. Remember, inconsistent and long order cycle times adversely impact buyer inventories.

Modifying all of the elements that contribute to lead time might be too costly. The seller organization might therefore make modifications in one area and permit others to operate at existing levels. For example, investing in an Internet-based ordering system for buyers would allow the seller to reduce order receipt and order processing time as well as reduce the number of errors on manually generated orders. This would permit the seller to offset the investment in technology with a reduction in the cost of human "touches" to the order.

Being able to guarantee a given lead time is an important advancement in order management. Efficiencies might accrue to both the buyer (lower inventories) and the seller (productivity improvements) with consistent lead times. However, the concept of time, by itself, means little without dependability.

Dependability

To many buyers, *dependability* can be more important than the absolute length of lead time. The buyer can minimize its inventory levels if lead time is constant. That is, a buyer who knows with 100 percent assurance that lead time is 10 days could adjust its inventory levels to correspond to the average demand during the 10 days and would have no need for safety stock to guard against stockouts resulting from inconsistent lead times.

Cycle Time

Lead time dependability, then, directly affects the buyer's inventory levels and stockout costs. Providing a dependable lead time reduces some of the uncertainty faced by the buyer. A seller who can assure the buyer of a given level of lead time, plus some tolerance, distinctly differentiates its product from that of its competitors.

Figure 8.10 graphs a frequency distribution pertaining to overall lead time, measured in days. The graph is bimodal and indicates that lead time tends to be in the vicinity of either four days or 12 days. The buyer typically receives within four days orders that the seller can fill from existing inventory. Orders that the seller cannot fill from available inventory, and for which the buyer must place a back order, typically result in a total order cycle time of approximately 12 days.

Inconsistent lead times can result in stockouts, delays, and lost production for the buyer. The seller might incur the costs of claims, lost revenue, and expedited delivery for missing promised delivery dates. These possible outcomes reinforce the importance of dependable order cycle times between buyers and sellers.

Safe Delivery

The safe delivery of an order is the ultimate goal of any logistics system. As was noted earlier, the logistics process is the culmination of the selling process. If product arrives damaged or is lost in transit, the buyer cannot use the product as intended. A shipment containing damaged product impacts several buyer cost centers—inventory, production, and marketing.

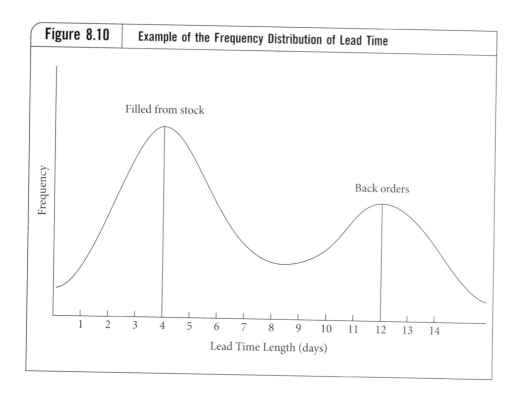

Figure 8.10 | **Example of the Frequency Distribution of Lead Time**

Filled from stock

Back orders

Frequency

1 2 3 4 5 6 7 8 9 10 11 12 13 14

Lead Time Length (days)

Receiving damaged product deprives the buyer of items for sale, production, or personal consumption. This might increase stockout costs in the form of foregone profits or production. To guard against these costs, the buyer must increase safety stock inventory levels. Thus, unsafe delivery would be unacceptable for a buyer interested in minimizing or eliminating inventories through some form of just-in-time program.

Correct Orders

Finally, dependability embraces filling orders correctly. A buyer who is awaiting the arrival of an urgently needed shipment might discover upon receiving the shipment that the seller made an error in filling the order. The buyer who has not received what was requested might face potential lost sales, production, or satisfaction. An incorrectly filled order might force the buyer to reorder, if the buyer is not dissatisfied enough to buy from another seller.

Communications

Three types of communication exist between the buyer and the seller: pretransaction, transaction, and posttransaction. Pretransaction communication includes current product availability and the determination of delivery dates. These can be communicated either electronically or manually. In either case, pretransaction communication provides the buyer with information upon which the buying decision is made.

Transaction information has both a buyer-seller component as well as what can be called a seller-seller component. The seller-seller component involves the communication of customer order information to the seller's order filling area and the actual process of picking the items ordered out of inventory. If during this process the seller discovers that the promised inventory is not available, then buyer-seller communication is necessary to inform the buyer of the situation. Another buyer-seller communication here involves shipment status and tracking. Many times, buyers need to know if the order is proceeding as planned and will contact the seller for status information.

Finally, posttransaction communication involves repair, assembly, or returns. After a shipment is delivered, the buyer might have questions about its use or assembly. Being able to provide this information quickly and accurately to the buyer allows the seller to differentiate its product from that of its competitors. Buyers might also want to return part of, or the entire, shipment. The returns process, especially for Internet-based operations, is critical. Allowing a dissatisfied buyer to return product to the seller in an easy manner is another differentiating factor for the seller.

Convenience

Convenience is another way of saying that the logistics service level must be flexible. From the logistics operation perspective, having one or a few standard service levels that applies to all buyers would be ideal; but this assumes that all buyers' logistics requirements are alike. In reality, this is not the situation. For example, one buyer might require the seller to palletize and ship all shipments by rail; another might require motor carrier delivery only, with no palletization; still others might request special delivery times. Basically, logistics requirements differ with regard to packaging, the mode of transportation and carrier the buyer requires, routing, and delivery times.

The need for convenience in logistics service levels can be attributed to the different consequences these service levels have for different buyers. More specifically, the cost of lost sales will differ among the buyer groups. For example, a buyer purchasing 30 percent of a seller's output loses more revenue for the seller than a buyer purchasing less than 0.01 percent of the seller's output does. Also, the degree of competitiveness in market areas will differ; highly competitive market areas will require a higher service level than less-competitive markets will. The profitability of different product lines in a seller's product portfolio will influence the service levels the seller can offer; that is, a seller might provide a lower service level for low-profit product lines.

However, the logistics manager must place the convenience factor in proper operational perspective. At the extreme, meeting the convenience needs of buyers would mean providing a specific service level policy for each buyer. Such a situation would set the stage for operational chaos; the unlimited offerings of service-level policies would prevent the logistics manager from optimizing the logistics process. The need for flexibility in service-level policies is warranted and is a factor in determining how the buyer perceives the "ease of doing business" with the seller. However, the logistics manager should carefully restrict this flexibility to easily identifiable buyer groups and must examine the tradeoffs between the benefits (improved revenue and profits or elimination of lost profits) and the costs associated with unique service levels in each specific situation.

Performance Measures for Customer Service

The four traditional dimensions of customer service from a logistics perspective—time, dependability, convenience, and communications—are essential considerations in developing a sound and effective customer service program. These dimensions of customer service also provide the underlying basis for establishing standards of performance for customer service in the logistics area.

Table 8.6	Elements and Measurement of Customer Service	
ELEMENT	**DEFINITION**	**TYPICAL METRIC**
Product Availability	Usually defined as percent of times product is available to fill first request orders	• order fill rate • case fill rate
Order cycle time	Activities and time that elapses between when an order is placed and when the shipment is received.	• order cycle time in days • % orders received within × days • on-time delivery
Logistics operations Responsiveness	• Ability of the supply chain to meet special customer requests • Ability of the supply chain to adapt to sudden changes in volume	• Response time to special request (hours, days) • Time required (days) to respond to ×% increase in unanticipated demand
Logistics System Information	Ability of an information system to supply timely and accurate information	• Response time (hours, days) to requests for information • % compliance to EDI standards
Postsale Product Support	Ability to provide customer support after product delivery, including technical information, spare (replacement) parts, or product return.	• Response time to service request • Cost to return product • Spare part availability

Source: Adapted from James F. Robeson and Robert G. House, eds., *The Distribution Handbook*, The Free Press, a division of Simon & Schuster, Inc.

Table 8.6 expands these four elements into a format that has been used by organizations in developing customer service policy and performance measurement standards. The traditional performance metrics that have been used are stated in the right-hand column. Typically, such metrics were stated from the perspective of the seller, for example, orders shipped on time, orders shipped complete, product availability when an order was received, order preparation time, and so on. Using Figure 8.6 as a reference, traditional logistics metrics would measure performance after the completion of Step D1.10.

The new supply chain environment for customer service has resulted in much more rigorous standards of performance. Logistics performance metrics today are now stated from the buyer's point of view:

• Orders received on time
• Orders received complete
• Orders received damage free
• Orders filled accurately
• Orders billed accurately

Again, using Figure 8.6, the supply chain perspective would measure performance after the completion of Step D1.12. If the seller is concerned only with customer service prior to shipping, as per traditional metrics, the buyer might not be satisfied and the seller might not know it, because of problems occurring during the delivery process. Furthermore, the seller using traditional metrics would have no basis upon which to evaluate the extent and magnitude of the problem. The supply chain approach, focusing on measurement at the delivery level, not only provides the database to make an evaluation, but it also, and perhaps more importantly, provides an early warning of problems as they are developing. For example, if the standard for on-time delivery is 98 percent and it

Figure 8.11	SCOR Process Model D1: Performance Metrics

PROCESS CATEGORY: DELIVER STOCKED PRODUCT	PROCESS NUMBER: D1

Process Category Definition

The process of delivering product that is maintained in a finished goods state priorto the receipt of a firm customer order.

Performance Attributes	Metric
Reliability	Perfect Order Fulfillment
Responsiveness	Order Fulfillment Cycle Time
Flexibility	Upside Deliver Flexibility Downside Deliver Adaptability Upside Deliver Adaptability
Responsiveness	Order Fulfillment Cycle Time
Cost	Order Management Costs as % of Deliver Costs
Assets	Cash-to-Cash Cycle Time Return on Supply Chain Fixed Assets

Best Practices	Features
Rapid replenishment, VMI, EDI	None identified
Electronic Catalogs/Malls	None identified
Internet Ordering	None identified
Efficient Consumer Response (ECR); Quick Response	Demand Planning, Deployment, Scheduling
Vendor-Managed Inventory (VMI)	See Glossary

Source: Supply Chain Council, 2007. Reproduced by permission.

decreases during a given month to 95 percent, an investigation might show that a carrier is not following instructions or even that the buyer is at fault by not being ready to accept shipments.

Another perspective on supply chain metrics can be seen in Figure 8.11 (this was also referenced in Figure 8.5). The SCOR model provides suggested metrics across multiple dimensions for each of the five Level One processes in the model. Figure 8.11 contains the suggested metrics for Process D1 as shown in Figure 8.6. Notice that "reliability," "responsiveness," and "flexibility" are all customer service dimensions. In other words, these three dimensions measure the impact of a seller's service on the buyer. "Cost" and "assets" are internally focused dimensions and provide the seller with an indication of the resources it is expending to provide service to its buyers.

Figure 8.11 suggests the concept of "perfect order fulfillment" as the metric for reliability. Many organizations today are using multiple metrics simultaneously to measure how well they are serving their customers. The concept of the perfect order combines multiple metrics into an index that attempts to capture the entire customer experience. For example, a simple perfect order index might include percent of orders delivered on time, percent of orders filled complete, and percent of correct invoices. Assume that the current performance by a seller on each of the three metrics is 90 percent, 90 percent, and 90 percent, respectively. Given that each metric is normally distributed and that none of the metrics are correlated, the perfect order index for this level of performance is 73 percent (90% × 90% × 90%). Therefore, what traditionally might be thought of as an average 90 percent service level is actually a 73 percent service level. However, the 73 percent perfect order index is a more accurate reflection of the true service level experienced by the customer. The number and determination of which metrics to be included in the perfect order index will depend on the seller and its market requirements. However, the development and management of the perfect order index can be challenging for the seller, yet rewarding for the buyer.[5]

Expected Cost of Stockouts

A principal benefit of inventory availability is to reduce the number of stockouts. Once a convenient method is determined to calculate the cost of a stockout, stockout probability information can be used to determine the total expected stockout cost. Finally, alternative customer service levels can be analyzed by directly comparing the expected cost of stockouts with the revenue-producing benefits of improved customer service.

This section examines stockout issues that relate more to finished goods inventories than to inventories of raw materials or component parts. Calculating stockout costs for finished goods is generally more challenging than calculating these costs for raw material stockouts. The main reason for this is that finished goods stockouts might result in lost current and/or future customer revenue. Raw material stockouts might result in production shutdowns. Both types of stockouts need to be addressed when determining inventory levels.

A **stockout** occurs when desired quantities of finished goods are not available when or where a customer needs them. When a seller is unable to satisfy demand with available inventory, one of four possible events might occur: (1) the buyer waits until the product is available; (2) the buyer back-orders the product; (3) the seller loses current revenue; or (4) the seller loses a buyer and future revenue. From the perspective of most organizations, these four outcomes are ranked from best to worst in terms of desirability and cost impact. Theoretically, scenario 1 (customer waits) should cost nothing; this situation is more likely to occur where product substitutability is very low. Scenario 2 would increase the seller's variable costs. Scenario 3 would result in the buyer canceling a portion of or the entire order, thus negatively impacting the current revenue of the seller. Scenario 4 is the worst situation for the seller and the most difficult to calculate because it results in the loss of future revenue from the buyer.

Back Orders

As previously mentioned, a **back order** occurs when a seller has only a portion of the products ordered by the buyer. The back order is created to secure the portion of the inventory that is currently not available. For example, a buyer orders 100 units of Product A from the seller. However, the seller has only 60 units of Product A available to send to the buyer. A back order for 40 units of Product A is created so when the additional 40 units become available, they are shipped to the buyer. In this simple example, there is usually no major cost disadvantage to the buyer. By placing the back order, the buyer is indicating that it is willing to wait for the additional inventory. However, after experiencing multiple back orders with a seller, a buyer might decide to switch to another seller. This example will assume that switching sellers is not an option for the buyer. Although the buyer incurs minimal or no cost in this situation, the seller experiences an increase in its variable costs (this concept was introduced in Chapter 5). A back order creates a second order document internal to the seller's order management system. It also requires the generation of another pick list for the distribution center. Labor costs in the seller's distribution center will also increase for that order. For example, had the 100 units of Product A been available to fill the original order, the order picker would have made one trip to the location of Product A to pick 100 units. With the back order situation, the order picker needs to make two trips to the same location: the first trip to pick 60 units and the second trip to pick the remaining 40 units. Transportation costs might also increase for the seller. The complete order of 100 units might have qualified for standard transportation service (e.g., three-day delivery). While the original 60 units still might qualify for standard transportation, the back-ordered 40 units might need more expensive expedited transportation (e.g., next day). For every incremental increase of variable expense for a seller on a particular order, there is a corresponding incremental decrease in operating profit for that order. As such, a seller can estimate the cost of a back order by calculating the incremental variable expenses it incurs for each back order and then compare it with the cost of preventing a back order (e.g., an increase in inventories).

Lost Sales

Most organizations find that although some customers might prefer a back order, others will turn to alternative supply sources. Much of the decision here is based on the level of substitutability for the product. In such a case, the buyer has decided that if the entire order cannot be delivered at the same time, it will cancel the order and place it with another seller. As such, the stockout has resulted in a lost sale for the seller. The seller's direct loss is either the revenue or profit (depending on how the seller wants to account for a lost sale) on the items(s) that was not available when the buyer wanted it. With this information, the seller can calculate the cost of a lost sale. For example, assume that the seller accounts for lost sales with a resulting loss in profit. The buyer orders 100 units of Product A, but the seller has only 60 units available. Operating profit (pretax) for each unit is $10. If the buyer accepts the 60 units and cancels the remaining 40 units, the lost sale cost to the seller is $400. If the buyer decides to cancel the entire order, the lost sale cost to the seller is $1,000.

In the likely event that the seller will sustain lost sales with inventory stockouts, the seller will have to assign a cost to these stockouts as suggested earlier. Then the seller should analyze the number of stockouts it could expect with different inventory levels. The seller should then multiply the expected number of lost sales by the profit (revenue) lost and compare the result with the cost of carrying additional inventory.

Lost Customer

The third possible event that can occur because of a stockout is the loss of a customer; that is, the customer permanently switches to another supplier. A supplier who loses a customer loses a future stream of income. Estimating the profit (revenue) loss that stockouts can cause is difficult. Marketing researchers have attempted to analyze brand switching for some time. Such analysis often uses management science techniques along with more qualitative marketing research methods. This is usually the most difficult loss to estimate because of the need to estimate the number of units the customer might have purchased in the future.

Determining the Expected Cost of Stockouts

To make an informed decision as to how much inventory to carry, an organization must determine the expected cost it will incur due to a stockout. That is, how much money will an organization lose if a stockout occurs?

The first step is to identify a stockout's potential consequences. These include a back order, a lost sale, and a lost customer. The second step is to calculate each result's expense or lost profit (revenue) and then to estimate the cost of a single stockout. For the purposes of this discussion, assume the following: 70 percent of all stockouts result in a back order, and a back order requires the seller to spend an additional $75; 20 percent result in a lost sale for the order, and this loss equals $400 in lost profit; and 10 percent result in a lost customer, or a loss of $20,000.

Calculate the overall impact as follows:

70% of $75 = $52.50

20% of $400 = $80.00

10% of $20,000 = $2,000.00

Total estimated cost per stockout = $2,132.50

Since $2,132.50 is the average dollar amount the organization can save (or avoid losing) by averting a stockout, it should carry additional inventory to protect against stockouts only as long as carrying the additional inventory costs are equal to or less than $2,132.50.

An organization can easily use this information when formally evaluating two or more logistics system alternatives. For each alternative, the organization would need to estimate the potential number of stockouts and multiply those numbers by the estimated cost of a single stockout. This would represent a way to include stockout costs in the overall decision-making process. This concept will be demonstrated more fully in the next section.

Order Management Influences on Customer Service

A major portion of this chapter has discussed the concepts of order management and customer service as somewhat mutually exclusive. However, the beginning of this chapter explained that these two concepts are, in fact, related to one another. This section of the chapter will introduce and explain the five major outputs of order management that influence customer service: product availability, order cycle time, logistics operations responsiveness, logistics system information, and postsale logistics support. Each of these outputs impacts customer service/satisfaction, and the performance of each is determined by the seller's order management and logistics systems. When examining these five outputs, the question might arise as to which is most important to the buyer and the seller. The answer is that they are all important because they are all related. For

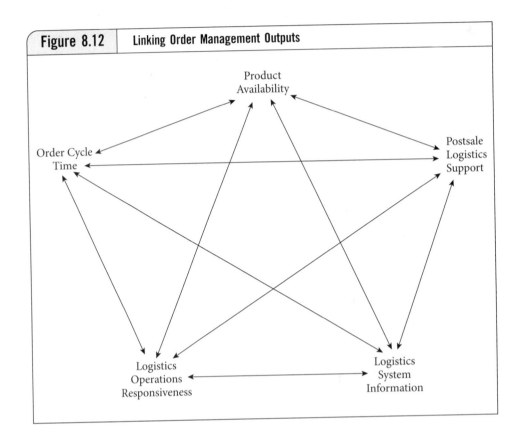

Figure 8.12 | **Linking Order Management Outputs**

example, product availability will impact order cycle time; order cycle time will influence postsale product support; logistics system information will impact logistics operations responsiveness. Figure 8.12 is an attempt to highlight how interrelated these outputs really are. They cannot be managed as single outputs. Synchronizing the order management and logistics systems provides the seller the opportunity to achieve acceptable performance in all of these outputs. As previously mentioned, however, there are costs associated with delivering these outputs. These costs must be weighed against the benefits of providing acceptable levels of performance to the customer.

Product Availability

As Figure 8.12 shows, *product availability* is at the top of the outputs. Although not the most important, product availability is usually the most basic output of an organization's order management and logistics systems. This is true because product availability can be measured by asking the simple question: Did I get what I wanted, when I wanted it, and in the quantity I wanted? As such, product availability is the ultimate measure of logistics and supply chain performance. Product availability influences both the seller's and buyer's inventories. Sellers will normally hold more inventory to increase product availability. Buyers will hold more inventory to reduce stockouts, thus increasing product availability. Product availability can also influence seller and buyer revenues and profits. If a seller fails to make a product available to a buyer, the buyer might cancel the order and thus reduce revenue to the buyer. If the buyer, for example a retailer, fails to have product on its store shelves, consumers will not have the opportunity to purchase the item.

On the Line

Cat Sees Big Growth in Services

Caterpillar, Inc., (Cat) is a master of the service game. The manufacturer has an inventory of more than half a million spare part numbers and a huge worldwide installed base of earthmovers, engines, excavators, and other equipment, some of which need service for 40 years or more. Yet Cat can ship its customers exactly what they want inside 24 hours, 99.7 percent of the time.

Indeed, Cat has done so well on the service front that it has extended its capabilities in service parts management and logistics to external customers. Forming Cat Logistics in 1987, the company set out to build a global growth business and to capture much more of the available market for service parts management. Today, Cat Logistics counts among its customers such companies as DaimlerChrysler, Ford, Toshiba, and Honeywell. It employs more than 9,000 logistics professionals across six continents, managing more than 18 million stock-keeping units (SKUs) and shipping more than 160 million orders and 16 billion pounds of freight a year. The opportunities are significant. Cat chairman and CEO Jim Owens says: "Cat Logistics has been generating growth of 25 percent annually in revenues from external customers, and massive opportunities remain for creative third-party logistics providers in this $170 billion industry."

Companies such as Caterpillar show that service excellence depends on processes and systems that create visibility across the supply and distribution network. As early as the 1970s, Cat built a central global database for tracking inventory across its network, initially focusing on parts that originated from Caterpillar's central distribution centers. In 2002, the system was extended to include parts obtained locally to ensure global visibility into all parts in the distribution network. One outcome: Since the late 1980s, the equipment maker has halved its service parts inventories while improving its already highly regarded customer service. For Caterpillar, top-notch customer service levels are the primary driver of repeat business. At the same time, these improvements are saving the company more than $460 million a year compared to the late 1980s.

Cat is not complacent about its wins to date. Knowing that its core competency is in supply chain management and logistics and not in software development, the company is developing its next-generation global service and parts management system in collaboration with SAP, Ford Motor Company, and Deloitte Consulting.

Source: Jeffrey J. Glueck, Peter Koudal, and Wim Vaessen, "Putting a Premium on Service," *Supply Chain Management Review* (April 2006): 31. Copyright © 2006 Reed Business Information, a division of Reed Elsevier. Reproduced by permission.

An important aspect of product availability is defining where in the supply chain it is being measured. As an example to demonstrate this point, the consumer market for processed peanuts will be used. Most peanuts are purchased by consumers on "impulse." In other words, consumers normally don't go to a store with the specific intention of buying peanuts. Rather, peanuts are purchased as the consumer walks through the salted snack food aisle to get to where the "destination" items (e.g., meat, milk, eggs) are located. If the peanuts are not available on the store shelf, the sale is missed. So, in the case of peanuts, product availability is critical to all members of this supply chain. Assume that the peanut farmer makes raw peanuts available to the processing plant 90 percent of the time; the processing plant makes packaged peanuts available to its distribution center 90 percent of the time; the distribution center makes cases of peanuts available to the retailer's distribution center 90 percent of the time; and the retailer's distribution center makes peanuts available to the store 90 percent of the time. While a 90 percent product availability for each segment of this supply chain might be acceptable, the cumulative effect at the shelf is not. Assuming statistical normality, the probability of having peanuts available at the store shelf is only 65.6 percent ($0.9 \times 0.9 \times 0.9 \times 09$), resulting in a stockout and lost sale 34.4 percent of the time. Hence, it is important to understand and identify where in the supply chain product availability should be measured.

Another important aspect of product availability is determining whether or not all products should be made available at the same level. Some organizations strive to have 100 percent product availability across all products. The cost associated with achieving this goal would be prohibitive and unnecessary as discussed previously in this chapter. Product availability levels for products can be determined by examining the level of substitutability and related stockout costs for a product as well as the demand profile for that product. If a product has a high level of substitutability, and therefore a high stockout cost, inventory levels must be adequate to provide high levels of availability, and vice versa. If the demand for a product is low, the decision might be made to minimize inventory levels to maintain some minimally acceptable level of availability. The point here is that not all products require the same level of availability to the buyer. Sellers must examine their product profile and determine the market requirements for each product or product family. Maintaining high levels of inventory where they are not required results in excess costs for the seller and provides little, if no, benefit to the buyer.

Metrics

Many methods exist to measure the efficiency and effectiveness of product availability. However, four metrics are widely used across multiple industries: item fill rate, line fill rate, order fill rate, and perfect order. Item fill rate and line fill rate are considered **internal metrics**; that is, they are designed to measure the efficiency of how well the seller is setting its inventories to fill items or lines on an order. Order fill rates and perfect order rates are **external metrics**; that is, they are designed to capture the buyer experience with product availability. An "item" might be a case of product, an inner-pack, or an "each" on an order. A "line" represents a single product on a multiple product order. Item fill rate is defined as the percent of items in stock available to fill an order. Line fill rate is defined as the percent of total lines filled complete on a multiple line order. Order fill rate is the percent of orders filled complete. Finally, perfect order rate is the percent of orders filled completely, received on time, billed accurately, etc. (the nature and number of items in the perfect order are determined by the organization that is measuring the perfect order). Typically, the item fill rate is higher than the line fill rate, which is higher than the order fill rate, which is greater than the perfect order rate. Table 8.7 represents a hypothetical multiple line order. Each line is a different product that the buyer is ordering from the seller. For example, Line A might be laundry detergent, Line B might be hair shampoo, and so on. This order contains a request for 10 separate lines containing 200 items (an item here might be a case of product). In Scenario 1, the buyer is able to completely fill 9 out of the 10 lines requested (A through I) but has no product available to fill the 10th line (J). The line fill rate is 90 percent (9 divided by 10), the item fill rate is 45 percent (90 items divided by 200 items), the order fill rate is zero, and the perfect order rate is zero (both are zero because the order was not completely filled). In this case, line fill > item fill > order fill and perfect order fill. In Scenario 2, Lines A, D, and J are filled completely, while the other lines have no inventory available. In this scenario, line fill is 30 percent (3 divided by 10), item fill is 65 percent (130 divided by 200), and both order

Table 8.7	Multiple Line Order		
LINE	ITEMS ORDERED	SCENARIO 1 ITEMS FILLED	SCENARIO 2 ITEMS FILLED
A	10	10	10
B	10	10	0
C	10	10	0
D	10	10	10
E	10	10	0
F	10	10	0
G	10	10	0
H	10	10	0
I	10	10	0
J	110	0	110
Total 10	200	90	130

fill and perfect order are zero. In this case, item fill > line fill > order fill and perfect order. Whenever line fill or item fill is less than 100 percent, order fill and perfect order rates will be zero. The selling firm needs to measure item fill and line fill rates to determine inventory policy and where corrections in inventories need to be made. The selling firm also needs to measure order fill and perfect order rates because these directly impact the satisfaction and operations of the buyer. However, increasing fill rates has a direct effect on a seller's inventories. This relationship can be seen in Figure 8.13. As fill rates increase, a seller's inventories will tend to increase at an increasing rate. This will usually result in marginally decreasing profits for the seller as the fill rate increases. Figure 8.13 and 8.9 show the same relationship in different terms. As service levels increase (in this case it would be fill rate), a seller's ROI would decrease because the increase in inventory costs would increase at a rate greater than that of additional revenues. So, it is important to understand the relationship between costs and revenues when determining fill rate goals.

Financial Impact

Calculating the financial impact of fill rates was introduced in Chapter 5. However, it is important to offer another example of the financial impacts of order fill on a seller's firm. Assume that a seller has the following order profile:

- 100 units per order (average)
- 25,000 orders per year
- Pretax profit per unit is $100
- Pretax profit per order is $10,000
- Invoice deduction per order is $250
- Percentage of incomplete orders back-ordered is 70%

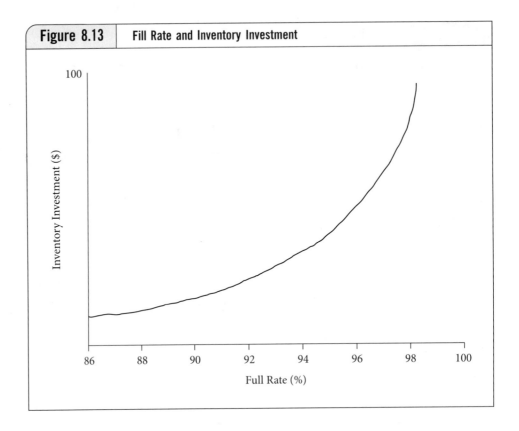

| Figure 8.13 | Fill Rate and Inventory Investment |

- Back order costs per order: administrative = $25.00; rehandling = $50.00; redelivery = $100.00
- Percent of incomplete orders cancelled is 30%

Assume that the seller's current order fill rate is 80 percent, meaning that 80 percent of all orders received are filled completely. The calculation for lost cash flow is as follows:

$$\text{Cash Flow Lost} = (\text{Number of Incomplete Orders Back-Ordered} \\ \times \text{Back Order Cost per Order}) + (\text{Number of} \\ \text{Incomplete Orders Cancelled} \times \text{Lost Pretax} \\ \text{Profit per Order}) + (\text{Number of Incomplete} \\ \text{Back-Ordered} \times \text{Invoice Deduction per Order})$$

This would result in the following calculation:

$$\text{Cash Flow Lost} = [(20\% \times 25{,}000 \times 70\%) \times \$175] + [(20\% \\ \times 25{,}000 \times 30\%) \times \$10{,}000] + [(20\% \times 25{,}000 \\ \times 70\%) \times \$250] = \$16{,}487{,}500$$

Assume that the seller is able to improve its order fill rate to 85 percent. The new cash flow lost calculation would be as follows:

$$\text{Cash Flow Lost} = [(15\% \times 25{,}000 \times 70\%) \times \$175] + [(15\% \\ \times 25{,}000 \times 30\%) \times \$10{,}000] + [(15\% \times 25{,}000 \\ \times 70\%) \times \$250] = \$12{,}365{,}625$$

Table 8.8	Cash Flow Lost and Inventory Investment	
SERVICE LEVEL	CASH FLOW LOST	INVENTORY
50%	$41,218,750	$ 5,000,000
60	32,975,000	6,250,000
70	24,731,250	8,750,000
80	16,487,500	12,500,000
90	8,243,750	17,500,000
95	4,121,875	23,750,000
99	824,375	31,250,000

The result of improving the order fill rate by 5 percent results in a cash flow lost avoidance of **$4,121,875**. In other words, a 5 percent improvement in order fill results in a 25 percent improvement in cash flow. Obviously, increasing the order fill rate might require some type of investment in inventories and/or technology. So, a strategic profit model calculation would be required to determine the change in ROI as a result of the improvement in order fill rate.

The next step would require the seller to determine the break-even point between order fill rates and inventory costs as shown in Figure 8.13. Assume that the stockout costs identified in this example (back order costs per order of $175, cancelled order cost of $10,000, and invoice deduction cost per order of $250) are inclusive of all stockout costs. In other words, no other stockout costs are incurred. Assume that the most minimal service level (product availability) of 50 percent requires an inventory investment of $5 million. Also assume that the seller has calculated approximate inventory investments for various service levels. This can be seen in Table 8.8. Also seen in this table is the resulting cash flow lost for service levels between 50 percent and 99 percent (the assumption here is that a 100 percent service level is not possible in the long run). These cash flow calculations were made using the numbers from the previous paragraph. Figure 8.14 shows the results of plotting the cash flow lost and inventory investment figures for each service level. As can be seen, the break-even point is at a service level of approximately 83 percent with a resulting inventory investment of $14 million. At an 83 percent service level, the cash flow lost is $14,014,375. This figure suggests that the seller should invest no more than $14 million in inventory to provide service to the customer. Investments above this amount would result in decreasing returns in the form of lost cash flow avoided. This is a very simple example and is used to show the basic trade-offs between cost and service. Obviously, additional factors must be taken into consideration when setting service levels. However, it is important to understand every service level and its associated costs and benefits.

Order Cycle Time

As previously discussed, order cycle time is the time that elapses from when a buyer places an order with a seller until the buyer receives the order. The absolute length and reliability of order cycle time influences both seller and buyer inventories and will have resulting impacts on both revenues and profits for both organizations. Normally, the

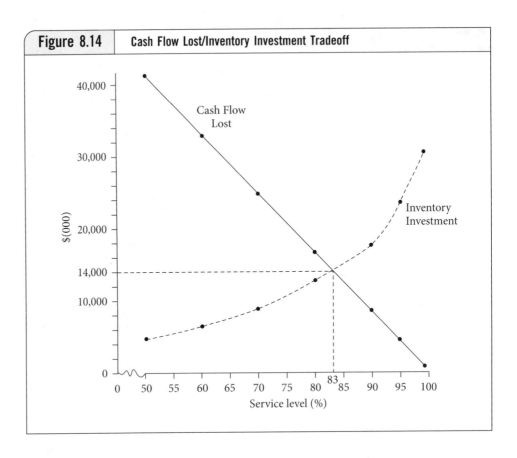

Figure 8.14 | **Cash Flow Lost/Inventory Investment Tradeoff**

shorter the order cycle time the more inventory that must be held by the seller and the less inventory that must be held by the buyer, and vice versa. For example, assume that an appliance retailer maintains floor models of various washing machines in its stores with no additional inventory for consumer pickup or delivery. In a normal situation, a consumer will decide which model of washing machine to buy and place an order with the store. The store will give the consumer an expected delivery date for the appliance. If consumers demand rapid delivery (e.g., one to two days), then the retailer will need to hold demand inventory in its own distribution network. If the consumer is not sensitive to delivery times and allows the retailer to dictate terms (e.g., seven-day or more delivery window), the retailer might not have to carry any demand inventory in its network and could rely on the manufacturer to absorb the inventory. In fact, given enough lead time, the manufacturer might not have to carry any inventory if it can produce the appliance for delivery within the stated service window. In this example, a short order cycle time results in additional inventories for the retailer and vice versa. Hypothetically, it might be stated that order cycle times do not eliminate inventories from the supply chain but rather "shift" them from one supply chain member to the next.

Metrics

As previously mentioned, order cycle time, or lead time, includes all activities and related time from when an order is placed by a buyer until the order is received by the buyer. This definition can be viewed as the buyer's perception of lead time because this time ends when the buyer receives the ordered goods. A seller might look at lead time

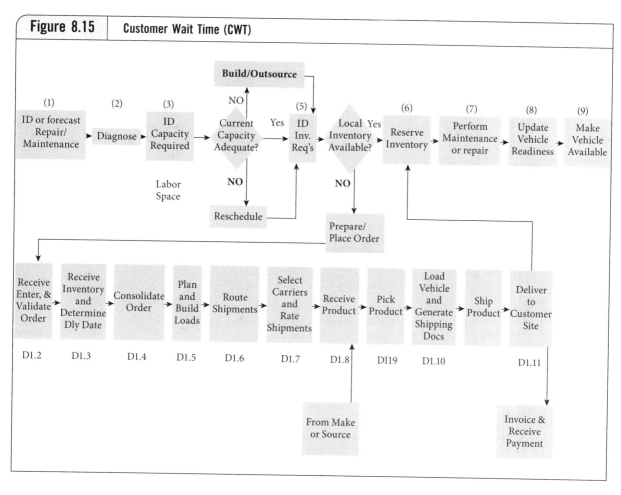

Figure 8.15 | **Customer Wait Time (CWT)**

from the perspective of order-to-cash cycle time. This definition of lead time for the seller is important because the receipt of payment for the shipment ends this process for the seller. Another, often overlooked, definition of order cycle time is **customer wait time** (**CWT**). Used in both the private and public sectors, CWT includes not only order cycle time but also maintenance time. CWT is a popular metric when a customer needs a vehicle repaired. CWT is basically the time that elapses from when a vehicle breaks down until it is ready to be used again. Figure 8.15 is an example of what CWT might look like. CWT can be used for two types of vehicle repair. First, it can be used to measure the time needed for scheduled maintenance, e.g., an oil change. Second, it can be used to measure the time needed for unscheduled maintenance, e.g., a vehicle breakdown. The process shown on top in Figure 8.15 is for maintenance; the bottom process is the order cycle time needed to get parts delivered to be able to conduct the maintenance. (This is Process D1 of the SCOR model, introduced earlier.) Thus, order cycle time can be measured in different ways depending on the perspective of who is providing the measurement.

Financial Impact

Order cycle time can also have an impact on a buyer's or seller's financial position, depending on who owns the inventories in the supply chain. Inventory costs have an impact on both the balance sheet and income statement. Balance sheet impacts reflect ownership of inventory as an asset and liability; income statement impacts reflect the cost of holding inventory as an expense and therefore a reduction in cash flow. This discussion will focus on the income statement impact. Order cycle time influences two types of inventory: demand, or cycle, stock and safety stock. An example is appropriate here. From the data presented below, assume that a buyer and a seller have a current relationship with the stated performance levels and the seller is proposing a shorter, more reliable order cycle time.

	CURRENT	PROPOSED
Average order cycle time	10 days	5 days
Standard deviation of OCT	3 days	1 day
Demand per day (units)	1,377	1,377
Service level	97.7%	97.7%

Also assume that the delivered cost of each unit to the buyer costs the seller $449 and the inventory carrying cost (to be discussed in more detail in the next chapter) is 28 percent. The proposed order cycle time offers not only a reduced absolute length (10 days to 5 days) but also an improved reliability (reduction in standard deviation from 3 days to 1 day). So two inventory cost reduction calculations are necessary. The first calculation will look at the effects of a reduced standard deviation of order cycle time on safety stocks. The formula for this calculation is as follows:

$$\text{Safety Stock} = \{\text{Demand per Day} \times [\text{OCT} + (z \times \text{Standard Deviation of OCT})]\} - (\text{Demand per Day} \times \text{OCT})$$

This formula focuses on safety stocks since the amount of demand stock is included in the first part of the formula (Demand per Day × OCT) and is subtracted out in the second part of the formula. The z is the z-transformation for the required service level. In this case, the service level of 97.7 percent requires a z-transformation of two standard deviations to capture 97.7 percent of all observations under the normal distribution. To calculate the required safety stock levels between the buyer and the seller under the current order cycle time, the calculation is as follows:

$$\begin{aligned} \text{Current Safety Stock} &= \{1{,}377 \times [10 + (2 \times 3)]\} - (1{,}377 \times 10) \\ &= (1{,}377 \times 16) - 13{,}770 \\ &= 8{,}262 \text{ units} \end{aligned}$$

This means that 8,262 units of safety stock need to be held, normally, at the buyer's location to prevent stockouts 97.7 percent of the time. To determine the safety stock levels needed under the proposed order cycle time, the calculation is as follows:

$$\begin{aligned} \text{Proposed Safety Stock} &= \{1{,}377 \times [5 + (2 \times 1)]\} - (1{,}377 \times 5) \\ &= (1{,}377 \times 7) - 6{,}885 \\ &= 2{,}754 \text{ units} \end{aligned}$$

The difference between the two order cycle times is a reduction in safety stock levels of 5,508 units. Given the delivered cost of $449 per unit and a 28 percent inventory carrying cost, the net reduction in safety stock cost is calculated as follows:

$$\text{Safety Stock Cost Reduction} = \text{Reduction in Safety Stock Units} \times \text{Cost per Unit} \times \text{Inventory Carrying Cost Percent}$$

The resulting calculation is as follows:

$$\text{Safety Stock Cost Reduction} = 5{,}508 \times \$449 \times 28\% = \$692{,}465.76$$

This has the impact of reducing the variable expense of holding safety stock inventory, thereby increasing the cash flow of the inventory owner (the buyer in this case) by almost $700,000.

A second calculation is needed to determine the impact of the reduction of absolute order cycle time on demand inventories. The formula here is quite simple:

$$\text{Demand Inventory Cost Reduction} = \text{Difference in Absolute OCT} \\ \times \text{Demand per Day} \times \text{Cost} \\ \text{per Unit} \times \text{Inventory} \\ \text{Carrying Cost Percent}$$

This results in the following calculation:

$$\text{Demand Inventory Cost Reduction} = 5 \text{ days} \times 1{,}377 \text{ units} \times \$449 \\ \times 28\% = \$865{,}582.20$$

Adding together the cost reductions (or in this case a possible cost avoidance) for both safety stock and demand stock results in an improvement in cash flow of **$1,558,047.96**. While this is a simple example, it highlights the dramatic effects of order cycle time on supply chain inventories and their associated costs. The financial impact will be felt by the party that owns the inventories.

Logistics Operations Responsiveness

The concept of **logistics operations responsiveness (LOR)** examines how well a seller can respond to a buyer's needs. This "response" can take two forms. First, LOR can be how well a seller can customize its service offerings to the unique requirements of a buyer. Second, LOR can be how quickly a seller can respond to a sudden change in a buyer's demand pattern. In either case, LOR is a concept that involves value-adding activities that are above and beyond basic logistics services. As such, LOR does not have a specific, generalizable definition that can apply to all buyer-seller interactions. For example, Buyer A might define LOR with a seller as how well the seller can customize end-of-aisle display pallets for in-store delivery. Buyer B might define LOR with the same seller as how long it takes the seller to respond to a rapid increase in demand. As such, developing metrics for LOR will be based on both what to measure and the level of performance required.

Metrics

Usually, LOR metrics will measure performance above and beyond basic on-time delivery or order fill rates. Examples of LOR metrics can be found in Process D1 of the SCOR model (see Figure 8.11) under flexibility. These three metrics are: (1) upside deliver flexibility, (2) downside deliver adaptability, and (3) upside deliver adaptability. These metrics address how well the seller can adapt its deliver capabilities in a situation where buyer demand fluctuates either up or down. Corresponding metrics for manufacturing could also be identified as: (1) upside manufacturing flexibility, (2) downside manufacturing adaptability, and (3) upside manufacturing adaptability.

Another dimension of LOR metrics is one that addresses a seller's ability to customize a product or its packaging. In the consumer-packaged goods (CPG) industry, manufacturers routinely offer special packaging of products through the use of co-packers. So, a metric that could be used to address customization might be one that measures the time it takes the seller to offer a new package for sale in the retailers' stores. Metrics for LOR, then, address both flexibility/adaptability of process and customization of product/ service.

Financial Impact

An excellent example of measuring the financial impacts of LOR activities was first identified and used by Procter & Gamble (P&G) during its implementation of the efficient consumer response (ECR) initiative in the grocery industry.[6] P&G developed a menu of value-adding activities that it was willing to offer to its customers in an attempt to customize its products/services to meet the unique needs of customers. One of these customized products was store-built pallets. P&G was willing to build "rainbow" (multiple-product) pallets for its grocery customers that would flow through, or cross-dock, the customer's distribution center and be delivered directly to a store where they could be taken onto the store floor where shelves could be restocked. This would save the customer money by eliminating "touches" and inventory. Building these pallets would require an investment from P&G. Table 8.9 is an example of the analysis that P&G undertook to determine the savings to the customer as a result of this cross-docking activity. In this table, it can be seen that the customer would incur a one-time savings of $21,747.50 as a result of this cross-docking initiative. So, the financial impact of this LOR activity to the customer is evident. But what about savings for P&G? P&G would partner with the customer to determine a "reinvestment ratio," which is the percentage of the customer's savings that would be reinvested in P&G products. This reinvestment would take one of two forms: (1) buy more P&G products, or 2) lower the price to the consumer on P&G products. For example, assume that in the case of the cross-docked pallets, the reinvestment ratio is 40 percent and the cost to P&G for building the pallets is $15,000. The reinvestment amount would be $8,699 for the customer and assume that the customer will reinvest that amount by buying more P&G products. A simple ROI calculation would show that the return for the $15,000 made by P&G would be approximately 58 percent ($8,699/$15,000). So, the customer saves money

Table 8.9	Logistics Operations Responsiveness Financial Impact		
PROCTER & GAMBLE CROSS-DOCK ANALYSIS SAMPLE CUSTOMER			
Base Service: Normal Warehouse Delivery			
Option Service: Cross-Dock Delivery			
Variables in Calculation	Base	Option	Change
A: Event Cases	50,000	50,000	0
B: Daily Customer Sales A/7	$7,142.90	$7,142.90	0
C: Days in Main Warehouse	20	11	9
D: Days in Outside Warehouse	0	0	0
E: Event WHSE Inventory Cases	50,000	50,000	0

Table 8.9	Continued			
F: Cases per Unit Load	100	100	0	
G: Unit Loads in Inventory E/F	500	500	0	
H: Net Days Credit	10	10	0	
I: Transit Time in Days	2	2	0	
J: Days Inventory Paid C+D+I−H	12	3	9	
Acquisition Cost				
Net Acquisition Cost/case	$50.00	$50.00	$0.00	
× Event Volume	50,000	50,000	0	
= Event Net Acquisition Costs	$2,500,000	$2,500,000	$0	
Main Warehouse Costs				
Handling Cost/case	$0.270	$0.120	$0.150	
+ Occupancy Cost/case	$0.300	$0.200	$0.100	
= Total Cost/case	$0.570	$0.320	$0.250	
× Event Volume	50,000	50,000	0	
= Event Main Warehouse Cost	$28,500	$16,000	$12,500	
Outside Warehouse Costs	$0	$0	$0	
Interest on Inventory				
Event WHSE Inventory Cases	50,000	50,000	0	
× Net Acquisition Cost/case	$50.00	$50.00	$0	
× Daily Interest Rate	.0411%	.0411%	.0411%	
× Days of Inventory Paid (J)	12	3	9	
= Event Interest on Inventory	$12,330	$3,082.50	$9,247.50	
Total Costs				
Net Acquisition Costs	$2,500,000	$2,500,000	$0	
+ Main Warehouse Costs	$28,500	$16,000	$12,500	
+ Outside Warehouse Costs	$0	$0	$0	
+ Interest on Inventory Costs	$12,330	$3,082.50	$9,247.50	
= Total Event Costs of Saving	$2,540,830	$2,519,082.50	$21,747.50	

Source: *Creating Logistics Value: Themes for the Future* (Oak Brook, IL Council of Logistics Management, 1995): 153. Reproduced with permission of Council of Supply Chain Management Professionals. All numbers are disguised.

and P&G revenues increase. In this case, LOR activities require an investment by the seller to create a savings for the buyer. However, both parties enjoy a favorable financial impact from this LOR activity.

Logistics System Information

Logistics system information (LSI) is critical to the logistics and order management processes. It underlies an organization's ability to provide quality product availability, order cycle time, logistics operations responsiveness, and postsale logistics support. Timely and accurate information can reduce inventories in the supply chain and improve cash flow to all supply chain partners. For example, improving forecast accuracy by using point-of-sale data could reduce safety stocks, improve product availability, and increase manufacturing efficiency. Today's technology allows for the accurate capture (barcodes, RFID tags) and transmission (radio frequency, EDI, Internet) of data among trading partners. The challenge is for organizations to determine how they are going to use these data to improve operations.

The beginning of this chapter identified three types of information that must be captured and shared to execute the order management process: pretransaction, transaction, and posttransaction. Pretransaction information includes all information that is needed by the buyer and seller before the order is placed. Transaction information includes all information that is required to execute the order. Posttransaction information includes all information that is needed after the order is delivered. An example of the types of information needed for each category to execute a transportation move can be seen in Table 8.10. All three parties involved in a transportation move need information across all three categories. What is also important here is that the information must be timely and accurate. Pretransaction information is needed before transaction information. Another way to think about these three categories of information might be that pretransaction information is used for planning, transaction information is used for execution, and posttransaction information is used for evaluation. So, LSI is critical to successful order management and customer service.

Table 8.10	**Information Needed to Manage the Transportation Process**		
	INFORMATION USER		
TRANSPORTATION ACTIVITY	**SHIPPER**	**CARRIER**	**RECEIVER**
Pretransaction	P.O. Information	BOL Information	Advance Ship Notice
	Forecasts	Forecasts	Delivery Time
	Equipment Availability	Pickup/Delivery Time	
Transaction	Shipment Status	Shipment Status	Shipment Status
Posttransaction	Freight Bill	Payment	Carrier Performance
	Carrier Performance	Claim Information	Proof of Delivery
	Proof of Delivery		Claim Information
	Claim Information		

Metrics

Most metrics involved with LSI address how accurate and timely the data are to allow a decision to be made or an activity to be performed. For example, forecast accuracy is the result of accurate data on past consumption as well as on good predictions on future consumption. Another example would be inventory accuracy. The accuracy of the inventory counts in a distribution center is the result of capturing consumption data from that facility in an accurate and timely manner. Data integrity is another metric that can be used to measure the quality of outputs from an LSI. Data integrity is a measure of the quality/accuracy of *inputs* to an LSI. Finally, EDI compliance is used by many organizations to measure how well their trading partners are complying with EDI standards when sharing data.

Financial Impact

As previously mentioned, LSI is usually not directly measured. What is measured are the results of how an organization uses the information generated by an LSI. Similarly, the financial impacts of an LSI are usually not measured but its results are. An actual example involved a computer manufacturer that had suppliers and customers all around the world. Most component shipments to their plants and finished goods shipments from their distribution centers were completed using air freight. Because of the high value of this manufacturer's finished products, their global customers required a proof of delivery (POD) to begin processing the invoice. The old procedure for generating and delivering the POD was very manual, involving the delivering ground carrier, the air freight company, and the air freight forwarder. This process resulted in an average order-to-cash cycle of 50 days for the manufacturer. The manufacturer analyzed an investment in an electronic global freight tracking system that would use barcodes and EDI for shipment status and well as the generation of electronic advance shipment notices (ASNs) and PODs. Using this new system, the manufacturer could send a POD electronically to a customer, resulting in a reduction of 20 days in the order-to-cash cycle. The new system would cost approximately $1 million to purchase and install. Multiple factors were taken into consideration by the manufacturer when analyzing the investment in this new tracking system. This example will highlight the analysis performed on using information to reduce the order-to-cash cycle. Three months of shipment data over three global trade lanes were used as the basis for the analysis. Obviously, all numbers used here are disguised. Assume that the average invoice value for each shipment during this period was $648,000. Also assume that the cost of capital for the manufacturer was 10 percent. The calculation used to measure the result on cash flow for decreasing the order-to-cash cycle was as follows:

$$\text{Cash Flow Increase} = \text{Invoice Value} \times (\text{Cost of Capital}/365) \\ \times \text{Difference in Days in the Order-to-Cash Cycle}$$

Using the numbers above, a sample calculation is as follows:

$$\text{Cash Flow Increase} = \$648,000 \times (10\%/365) \times 20 \text{ days} \\ = \$3,550.68 \text{ per order}$$

During the three-month time period, the manufacturer shipped 344 of these orders, resulting in a combined cash flow increase of **$1,221,434**. Because the customers began processing the invoice when the POD was received, receiving the POD 20 days sooner using the new system allowed the manufacturer, theoretically, to invest its money at 10 percent for 20 days longer, resulting in an improved cash flow. The ROI for the new system was obviously very favorable. So, while measuring the financial impact of an LSI is challenging, measuring the financial impacts of how it is used is not.

PostSale Logistics Support

Many organizations focus primarily on outbound logistics, i.e., getting the product to the customer. For some organizations, supporting a product after it is delivered is a competitive advantage. **Postsale logistics support (PLS)** can take two forms. First, PLS can be the management of product returns from the customer to the supplier. Organizations such as GENCO have established their core competencies on managing product returns for suppliers. The importance of this form of PLS was discovered too late by many Internet sites during the late 1990s. During the dot.com boom, many Web sites were just "front ends," delivering superior customer interfaces on the computer but having no "back end" or physical delivery capability. Their focus was on taking the order and passing it on to a manufacturer or distributor for delivery. What was not considered successfully was what to do for product returns. This was very evident for some Web sites during the Christmas season of 1999. Because these sites had no physical retail presence or physical distribution capability, consumers found it very difficult to return unwanted products. This proved disastrous for many Web sites. Amazon.com, started as a front end-only Web site, quickly discovered the importance of product returns as a competitive weapon. Today, Amazon.com has a physical distribution network not only to provide initial product delivery but also to allow for the efficient return of unwanted product.

The second form of PLS is product support through the delivery and installation of spare parts. This is critical in the very competitive heavy equipment industry as well as in the U.S. military. Firms such as Caterpillar, New Holland, and Ingersoll-Rand have developed core competencies in making spare parts available for their equipment to keep that equipment running while it is at a job site. For firms such as these, it has become increasingly difficult to compete solely on the quality of their heavy equipment. These pieces of machinery can cost thousands or millions of dollars to purchase and thousands more per hour if they are disabled. As such, the accurate and timely delivery of spare parts to dealers and job sites to keep these machines running has become a competitive advantage.

Metrics

For the most part, the PLS that manages product returns is measured by the ease in which a customer can return a product. A metric such as time to return a product to a seller is usually not important to a customer. Remember, a product return usually involves some level of dissatisfaction by a customer for a seller's product. So, making it easy for a customer to return a product is a critical metric. Wal-Mart, for example, allows a consumer to bring a product back to a store, drop it off at the customer service desk, and get a replacement product with no questions asked. Craftsman Tools allows a 100 percent refund policy at any Sears store for its products. Web sites, such as Easton Sports, allow a customer to receive a replacement product (e.g., a baseball bat), repackage the return product in the replacement shipping package, and send the product back (usually by UPS, DHL, or FedEx) to an Easton facility for disposition. All of these firms have made the returns process easy for the consumer, resulting in a competitive advantage.

Metrics for a PLS that manages spare parts are the same as those used for all products: order fill, inventory availability, order cycle time, and so on. These metrics are used to measure the performance of a manufacturer's ability to deliver a bulldozer as well as its ability to deliver a water pump for that bulldozer. So, the metrics used to measure the performance of spare parts logistics are those usually found in all other industries providing outbound logistics for customers. However, because of the large stockout costs to the customer for a disabled piece of equipment, availability and time become even more critical for spare parts logistics.

Financial Impact

Of the two types of PLS, spare parts logistics provides an easier methodology for calculating financial impacts. As such, the example in this section will focus on spare parts logistics. Assume that a heavy equipment manufacturer knows that its product rebuy life cycle is five years; that is, customers usually will replace a piece of equipment after five years of use. Also assume that the customer bases the rebuy decision on both initial machine quality as well as on spare part availability. The average revenue per machine for the manufacturer is $25,000, with a pretax profit of $5,000. The average support revenue (parts/labor) for each machine for the manufacturer is $2,000 per year, with a pretax profit of $800 per year. Assume that the manufacturer sells 5,000 machines per year. The current level of spare parts support is 70 percent (the part is available 70 percent of the time). The manufacturer also knows that 80 percent of the time when a spare part is not available, a customer will not switch brands when the rebuy decision is made and 20 percent of the time the customer will buy another brand. When a spare part is not available, the expediting costs per machine per year are $1,000 for the manufacturer. The calculation to determine the spare part service cost is as follows:

$$\text{Service Cost} = \text{Penalty Cost} + \text{Lost Purchase Margin} + \text{Lost Support Margin}$$

As in the previous example examining the cost of not filling an order, not having spare parts inventory available when a customer wants it has two components: (1) a penalty, or expediting cost and (2) a lost profit cost. At a 70 percent service level, spare parts were not available for 1,500 machines (30% × 5,000 machines). For those customers who would still rebuy from the manufacturer, the manufacturer would incur an expediting cost of $1,000 per year of machine life (5 years) for each of the 1,500 machines. For those customers who switch to another manufacturer because of the lack of spare part support, the manufacturer would lose the initial purchase pretax profit on those machines ($5,000) and the support pretax profit on those machines ($800 per year for five years). At a 70 percent service level, then, the calculation would be as follows:

70 percent service level

$$\begin{aligned}
\text{Service Cost} = \ &(80\% \times 1{,}500 \text{ units} \times \$1{,}000 \times 5 \text{ years}) + (20\% \\
&\times 1{,}500 \text{ units} \times \$5{,}000) + (20\% \times 1{,}500 \text{ units} \times \$800 \\
&\times 5 \text{ years}) = \$8{,}700{,}000
\end{aligned}$$

At a 70 percent service level, then, the manufacturer would incur an expediting cost of $6,000,000, a lost initial pretax profit of $1,500,000, plus a lost support pretax profit of $1,200,000.

Assume that the manufacturer was able to increase spare parts availability to 85 percent. The resulting calculation would be as follows (remember, now only 750 machines will not have spare parts available):

85 percent service level

$$\begin{aligned}
\text{Service Cost} = \ &(80\% \times 750 \text{ units} \times \$1{,}000 \times 5 \text{ years}) + (20\% \times 750 \\
&\text{units} \times \$5{,}000) + (20\% \times 750 \text{ units} \times \$800 \times 5 \text{ years}) \\
&= \$4{,}350{,}000
\end{aligned}$$

Supply Chain Technology

Connecting with Big Customers

Rohm and Haas, a specialty chemicals company, touts its ability to improve the lives of consumers by doing everything from extending the freshness of fruits and vegetables to purifying antibiotics, according to the company. However, with service completely removed at the end, the company was having trouble properly connecting with its customers. In particular, Rohm and Haas had run into difficulties creating and maintaining customer relationships online.

The number of people involved in the purchasing process, as well as the size of the orders, had made online transactions and lead generation nearly impossible. "You're not going to buy two tanker cars of emulsion on the Web," says Eric Soll, the company's sales and marketing business process manager.

By implementing SAP CRM 3.0 in 2002 (the company later implemented the Internet Sales components in 2003 and upgraded to SAP CRM 4.0 in 2006), Rohm and Haas has been able to use its Web site to truly engage with its customers. Today, interested visitors who would have only gotten an e-mail are registered as prospects in a database. Rohm and Haas will soon be rolling out lead management solutions to work with these prospective buyers.

SAP's solution enables customers to view order status, various shipping documents, and the most accurate numbers in real time. This is most important in manufacturing, as many departments of a business customer need access to such information. "When you're dealing with a customer who's not the same person all the time, having that ease of doing business makes a big difference," Soll says. "It's going to lower their want to look elsewhere."

Source: Jessica Sebor, "Money for Future Muscle," *CRM Magazine [AA]*, Vol. II, No. 1 (January 2007): 17. Reproduced by permission.

So, a 15 percent increase in spare parts availability would improve the pretax cash flow to the manufacturer by $4,350,000, or a 50 percent increase in cash flow. While this is a simple example, it shows that the lack of spare parts, as in the lack of original product for order fill rates, can have a significant impact on an organization's cash flow. Also, remember that the investment needed by the manufacturer to provide this increase in spare parts availability must be taken into consideration in light of the resulting improvement in cash flow to determine an ROI.

Service Recovery[7]

No matter how well an organization plans to provide excellent service, mistakes will occur. Even in a Six Sigma statistical environment, 100 percent performance will not happen. High performance organizations today realize this and are using the concept of *service recovery*. Basically, service recovery requires an organization to realize that mistakes will occur and to have plans in place to fix them. Although many ways for an organization to practice service recovery are available, a few warrant discussion here.

A major portion of this chapter has focused on *measuring the costs* of poor service. Not being able to fill an order completely or delivering an order late can result in back orders, lost sales, and/or lost revenue for the selling firm. Understanding the costs of poor service is critical for an organization because it dictates investment in resources, such as inventories. If there is no cost associated with poor service, then little or no additional investment is necessary. However, this is hardly ever the case. Most organizations will suffer financially for not meeting customer expectations.

Another aspect of service recovery is *anticipating the needs for recovery*. In any organization, certain areas of operations will present higher than normal opportunities for failures to occur. These areas need to be identified, and corrective action plans need to be developed *before* the error occurs. A good example of this can be seen in the passenger airline industry. Delayed and/or cancelled flights leave many passengers stranded at airports throughout the United States every day. Airlines have developed plans to accommodate these passengers either through rebooking on another flight or through providing a hotel room until the next flight is available. In this chapter, the concept of the order-to-cash cycle was introduced through SCOR model Dl. This model provides an excellent framework for an organization to identify where service failures might occur and to develop plans to mitigate those failures, subject to the cost of failure.

Another principle of service recovery requires an organization to *act fast*. The longer a dissatisfied customer waits for a problem to be solved, the higher the level of dissatisfaction will grow. Being able to fix service failures quickly relies on the ability of the organization to know where a failure is likely to occur and have plans in place to fix them. Included in this concept is the need to communicate with the dissatisfied customer as to how and when the failure will be fixed. For example, a seller has determined that it does not have adequate inventory to fill a buyer's order. This is a common occurrence for which a seller needs to have alternative plans because of the potential high stockout costs. In a service recovery mode, the seller notifies the buyer immediately (usually by phone or e-mail) that current inventory levels are not adequate but additional inventory will become available within, say, two days to fill the order completely. With this action, the seller has acted fast to identify the problem as well as taken steps to communicate with the buyer the actions that will be taken to remedy the situation.

Finally, service recovery requires that *employees be trained and empowered* to be able to identify potential service failure areas and take actions to satisfy the customer. Remember, however, that this must be done considering the cost of a service failure. Frontline employees, usually customer service representatives, need to understand the cost of failure to the entire organization, must be given the appropriate tools for addressing the failure, and must be given a sense of ownership of the failure and the resulting loss of customer satisfaction. Nothing can be more frustrating to a dissatisfied customer than to wait for resolution while recovery actions are being discussed through multiple echelons of an organization's management structure. Granted, some failures will be so large as to require upper management intervention. However, customer contact personnel need to be given the authority to handle service failures quickly and appropriately.

SUMMARY

- Order management and customer service are not mutually exclusive; there is a direct and critical relationship between these two concepts.
- There are two distinct, yet related, aspects of order management: influencing the customer's order and executing the customer's order.
- Customer relationship management (CRM) is a concept being used today by organizations to help them better understand their customers' requirements and understand how these requirements integrate back into their internal operations processes.
- Activity-based costing (ABC) is being used today to help organizations develop customer profitability profiles which allow for customer segmentation strategies.
- Order management, or order execution, is the interface between buyers and sellers in the market and directly influences customer service.
- Order management can be measured in various ways. Traditionally, however, buyers will assess the effectiveness of order management using order cycle time and dependability as the metric, while sellers will use the order-to-cash cycle as their metric.
- Customer service is considered the interface between logistics and marketing in seller organizations.
- The three definitions of customer service are: (1) as an activity, (2) as a set of performance metrics, and (3) as a philosophy.
- The major elements of customer service are time, dependability, communications, and convenience.
- Stockout costs can be calculated as back order costs, the cost of lost sales, and/or the cost of a lost customer.
- The five outputs from order management that influence customer service, customer satisfaction, and profitability are: (1) product availability, (2) order cycle time, (3) logistics operations responsiveness, (4) logistics system information, and (5) postsale logistics support.
- The concept of service recovery is being used by organizations today to help identify service failure areas in their order management process and to develop plans to address them quickly and accurately.

STUDY QUESTIONS

1. Explain how order management and customer service are related.

2. Describe the two approaches to order management. How are they different? How are they related?

3. What is the role of activity-based costing in customer relationship management? In customer segmentation?

4. Compare and contrast the concepts of order-to-cash cycle time and order cycle time.

5. Explain the impacts of order cycle time length and variability on both buyers and sellers.

6. Customer service is often viewed as the primary interface between logistics and marketing. Discuss the nature of this interface and how it might be changing.

7. Organizations can have three levels of involvement with respect to customer service. What are these, and what is the importance of each?

8. Explain the relationship between customer service levels and the costs associated with providing those service levels.

9. Discuss the nature and importance of the four logistics-related elements of customer service.

10. Effective management of customer service requires measurement. Discuss the nature of performance measurement in the customer service area.

11. What events might occur when an organization is out of stock of a needed product? How might the cost of a stockout be calculated?

12. Assume an organization's current service level on order fill is as follows:

> Current order fill = 70%
> Number of orders per year = 10,000
> Percent of unfilled orders back-ordered = 85%
> Percent of unfilled orders cancelled = 15%
> Back order costs per order = $100
> Lost pretax profit per cancelled order = $15,000

 a. What is the lost cash flow to the seller at this 70 percent service level?
 b. What would be the resulting increase in cash flow if the seller improved order fill to 85 percent?
 c. If the seller invested $2 million to produce this increased service level, would the investment be justified financially?

NOTES

1. Bernard J. LaLonde, "Customer Service," Chapter 11 in the *Distribution Handbook* (New York, NY: The Free Press, 1985): 243.

2. The steps discussed in the process were adapted from a real CRM implementation by a large, global manufacturer during 2005–2006.

3. Norm Raffish and Peter B. Turney, "Glossary of Activity-Based Management," *Journal of Cost Management*, Vol. 5, No. 3 (1991): 53–64.

4. Philip Kotler, *Marketing Management*, 5th ed. (Englewood Cliffs, NJ: Prentice-Hall, 1990): 225–226.

5. For a further discussion of the perfect order concept, see Robert A. Novack and Douglas J. Thomas, "The Challenges of Implementing the Perfect Order Concept," *Transportation Journal*, Vol. 43, No. 1 (Winter 2004): 5–16.

6. For a full discussion of this analysis, see Robert A. Novack, C. John Langley, Jr., and Lloyd M. Rinehart, *Creating Logistics Value: Themes for the Future* (Oak Brook, IL: Council of Logistics Management, 1995): 148–153.

7. This discussion is adapted from Christopher W. L. Hart, James L. Heskett, and W. Earl Sasser, Jr., "The Profitable Art of Service Recovery," *Harvard Business Review* (July–August 1990): 148–154.

CASE 8.1

Telco Corporation

Telco Corporation (Telco) is a $25 billion global manufacturer of industrial products, with its global headquarters located in Bloomington, Indiana. Telco is comprised of six major divisions: electrical generators, turbines, industrial air conditioners, machine tools (e.g., drill presses and lathes), fork trucks and skid loaders, and air compressors. Each division is managed as a separate profit center, and each has its own sales force, manufacturing facilities, and logistics network. Telco has approximately 15,000 customers worldwide, with 40 percent buying from more than one Telco division.

At a recent operating council meeting, Jean Beierlein, CFO, was lamenting to the other council members the fact that pretax profits were falling even though revenues were growing. "We're in a perplexing situation. The stock market likes us because revenues are growing. However, I don't see how we are going to make our dividend objectives this year because our operating profits are decreasing from last quarter. Our service levels to customers are at an all-time high and our sales forces are consistently meeting their revenue objectives." Troy Landry, vice president of supply chain for the compressor division, added his observation on this dilemma. "I'll tell you what the problem is. We are constantly exceeding our logistics budget to provide this outstanding service for customers who shouldn't be getting it. Sales is constantly promising expedited delivery or special production runs for customers who generate very little revenue for us. One of these customers, Byline Industries, only spends $1 million per year with us and yet our logistics costs as a percent of revenue for them is 25 percent. Compare this with our average logistics costs as a percent of revenue across our customer base of 11 percent and you can see where the problem lies." Tom Novack, president of the generator division, disagreed with Troy's observation of Byline. "Wait a minute, Troy. Byline is one of my best customers. They buy 15 percent of my revenue at a logistics cost of 8 percent. We need to make sure they are happy."

Listening to this exchange was the new Telco president, Nick Martin. Nick recently joined Telco after spending 15 years as COO of a global agricultural products manufacturer. This problem was not new to Nick. His former employer was also structured across business lines with common customers across the globe and found that a similar service strategy for all customers was not a viable alternative. Nick added, "I've seen this before. The problem is that we are treating all customers alike and we are not taking into consideration those customers who buy from more than one division. Before the meeting, I asked Jean to run some profitability numbers across our customer base. The results are amazing. Thirty-three percent of all of our customers account for 71 percent of our operating profits. Another 27 percent account for approximately $100 million in losses. Obviously, we have some customers who are more profitable than others. We need to develop a strategy to segment our customers and offer each segment the suite of services they are willing to pay for."

"Wait a minute," exclaimed Chris Sills, vice president of corporate sales. "You're asking us to take some services away from our customers. Who is going to break the news? What about the sales commissions for my reps? This is not going to be received well by the customer base."

You have been hired as an expert on customer relationship management. Telco's current service offerings to its entire customer base include product quality, order fill rates, lead time, delivery time, payment terms, and customer service support. You have been asked to prepare a report outlining how Telco could adopt the CRM approach to its customers. Specifically, this report should address the following:

CASE QUESTIONS

1. How should Telco approach segmenting its customers? That is, on what basis (cost to service, profitability, etc.) should the customers be segmented?

2. How should Telco tailor its service offerings to each customer segment?

3. Should certain customers be asked to take their business elsewhere?

4. How should the revised service packages to each segment be introduced to that segment? By the sales force? Should all segments be done at the same time?

5. Each division has its own sales force, manufacturing facilities, and logistics network. As such, common customers (those who buy from more than one division) place separate orders with each division, receive multiple shipments, and receive multiple invoices. Would it make sense for Telco to organize around customer rather than around product? If so, how would this be done? What would the new organizational metrics look like?

Chapter 9

MANAGING INVENTORY IN THE SUPPLY CHAIN

Learning Objectives

After reading this chapter, you should be able to do the following:

- Appreciate the role and importance of inventory in the economy.
- List the major reasons for carrying inventory.
- Discuss the major types of inventory, their costs, and their relationships to inventory decisions.
- Understand the fundamental differences among approaches to managing inventory.
- Describe the rationale and logic behind the economic order quantity (EOQ) approach to inventory decision making, and be able to solve some problems of a simple nature.
- Understand alternative approaches to managing inventory—just-in-time (JIT), materials requirement planning (MRP), distribution requirements planning (DRP), and vendor-managed inventory (VMI).
- Explain how inventory items can be classified.
- Know how inventory will vary as the number of stocking points changes.
- Make needed adjustments to the basic EOQ approach to respond to several special types of applications.

Supply Chain Profile   *Micros and More*

"Inventory, inventory, inventory …, I am sick and tired of hearing the complaints about our inventory levels and the costs associated with carrying inventory," muttered Ben Finlan, COO and cofounder of Micros and More (Micros). "What am I supposed to do? We need inventory to operate our computer assembly operation, and we need inventory to satisfy our customer service requirements. I know that too much inventory increases our cost of goods sold (COGS), which means higher prices or lower profit margins. Ever since that article was published about Dell Computers, which stated that Dell turned inventory over one hundred times per year and that they expected to reach two hundred turns, some people around here have been giving me a hard time about our inventory. I can't wave a magic wand and make the inventory disappear and reappear when we need it. The first time we are out of components for one of our computers that we are assembling in the plant, or we can't deliver parts in two or less hours to repair the computers that we sold to Penn State or Raytheon, my neck will be on the line. I can't seem to win for losing, and I feel like everybody's scapegoat these days."

Ben was in his office alone, so no one heard the conversation that he was having with himself. Ben was being too sensitive about some comments that had been made at a recent board meeting by several board members when the current financial data were being reviewed by Mac Ross, CFO of Micros. Most vociferous was Dr. Derek Van Horn, a retired professor from Penn State and a major stockholder. He was the one who had distributed the Dell article several months earlier and had been complaining about excess inventory ever since. The problem was that several members of the board, especially Dr. Van Horn, did not really understand the role of inventory in an organization. To them, inventory was an expense that increased the COGS, and it should be minimized and ideally eliminated if Micros was going to continue to grow and be profitable.

COMPANY BACKGROUND

Micros and More was founded in State College, Pennsylvania, in 1995 by two friends who had similar experiences and a common interest in entrepreneurship. Ben Finlan had completed a degree in computer science at Penn State in 1992 and had worked in Fishkill, New York, for IBM in operations. Nick Kiraly had been a finance major at Clarion University and had worked for Mellon Bank in Pittsburgh for several years where he specialized in assisting small businesses with their banking and related financial needs.

Ben and Nick had grown up together and maintained contact throughout their college careers and their first jobs. During the Christmas holidays in 1994, they had met and talked about wanting to work for themselves. They were both fascinated with computer technology and speculated about starting their own computer company in central Pennsylvania. They pooled their resources, borrowed money from a variety of sources, and began operations in an old school building in State College, Pennsylvania. Their business vision was to (1) build customized computers for college students and small businesses; (2) provide software to meet the unique requirements of individual customers; and (3) provide outstanding customer service, which they defined as beyond anyone's expectations.

With a little luck and a lot of hard work, the company grew and prospered at a reasonable rate from 1995 to 2005. The plant in State College had been significantly expanded and now employed almost 200 people. The company went public in 2005 and sold stock through a local brokerage firm. It became a relatively popular stock and attracted numerous local investors. The board included several large stockholders like Dr. Van Horn but also some local business executives such as Alex Novack, president of the Central Region of Nittany Bank, and Ed Friedman, a local real estate developer.

CURRENT SITUATION

Micros had diversified its product line and expanded its customer base to continue to grow its market share. Its sales were expected to reach the $50 million in the 2007 fiscal year. It had floated a large loan in 2006 from Nittany Bank to finance a new plant and warehouse in Clearfield, Pennsylvania, with the hope of selling computers to Wal-Mart, which had a large distribution center near Clearfield. Part of its modified vision statement was to "grow" the business to the next level.

The fall of 2005 was a turning point for Micros. Competition from foreign sources had become very intense, and domestic manufacturers, such as Dell and Hewlett-Packard (HP), were increasing their market shares. Computers were a commodity in a highly price-sensitive market. Micros was facing the possibility of its first financial loss. Costs needed to be cut to maintain sales at competitive prices.

Ben realized that as COO he had a major role to play in whether the company would survive. Inventory was certainly one of the focal points, and an in-depth analysis had to be made of not only its managerial practices with respect to controlling inventory but also its relationships with suppliers and customers who were a part of the company's overall supply chain. As you read this chapter, consider Ben's challenges. Assume that you have to help him understand the role and rationale for inventory as well as the important tradeoffs. He also needs some insight into understanding inventory costs.

Introduction

As discussed in Chapter 1, the effective management of inventories in the supply chain is one of the key factors for success in any organization. Inventory as an asset on the balance sheet and as a variable expense on the income statement has taken on greater importance as organizations attempt to more effectively manage assets and working capital. As discussed in Chapter 8, however, inventory takes on added importance because of its direct impacts on service levels. As such, inventory management has taken a strategic position in many firms today.

Inventories also have an impact on return on investment (ROI) for an organization, which was discussed as return on net worth in Chapter 5. ROI is an important financial metric from both internal and external perspectives. Reducing inventories usually has a short-term improvement in ROI because it reduces assets and increases available working capital. Inventory increases will have the opposite effect on assets and working capital. Important here is the fact that inventory consumes an organization's resources and is also responsible for generating revenues. So, decisions regarding inventories must take into consideration the tradeoffs between costs and service.

The ultimate challenge in managing inventories is balancing the supply of inventory with the demand for inventories. This was presented in Chapter 7. In other words, an organization would ideally want to have enough inventory to satisfy the demands of its customers for its products with no lost revenue because of stockouts. However, the organization does not want to have too much inventory on hand because it consumes valuable working capital. Balancing supply and demand is a constant challenge for organizations to master but is a necessity to compete in the marketplace.

This chapter will offer a comprehensive view of managing inventories in the supply chain. Special importance will be placed on discussing why inventory is important, the nature of inventory costs, and the various approaches to managing inventories. The next section will offer an overview of the importance of inventory in the U.S. economy.

Inventory in the U.S. Economy

The influence of information technology during the late 1990s and its impact on inventories was reflected in the U.S. economy's ability to grow dramatically while holding inflation in check. This exchange of "information for inventory" showed the impact that inventories have on our economy. With information technology advances escalating in the early twenty-first century, organizations are still implementing programs to take inventories out of the supply chain.

The results of this aggressive management of inventories can be seen in Table 9.1, which shows inventory investment as a percent of U.S. gross domestic product (GDP)

Table 9.1	Macro Inventory in Relation to U.S. Gross Domestic Product					
YEAR	**VALUE OF ALL BUSINESS INVENTORY ($ BILLION)**	**INVENTORY CARRYING RATE PERCENT**	**INVENTORY CARRYING COSTS ($ BILLION)**	**NOMINAL GDP ($ TRILLION)**	**INVENTORY CARRYING AS A PERCENT OF GDP**	**INVENTORY COSTS AS A PERCENT OF GDP**
1990	$1,041	27.2%	$283	$ 5.80	4.9%	17.9%
1991	1,030	24.9	256	6.00	4.3	17.2
1992	1,043	22.7	237	6.34	3.7	16.5
1993	1,076	22.2	239	6.66	3.6	16.2
1994	1,127	23.5	265	7.07	3.7	15.9
1995	1,211	24.9	302	7.40	4.1	16.4
1996	1,240	24.4	303	7.82	3.9	15.9
1997	1,280	24.5	314	8.30	3.8	15.4
1998	1,317	24.4	321	8.75	3.7	15.1
1999	1,381	24.1	333	9.27	3.6	14.9
2000	1,478	25.3	374	9.82	3.8	15.1
2001	1,403	22.8	320	10.13	3.2	13.8
2002	1,451	20.7	300	10.49	2.9	13.8
2003	1,510	20.1	304	11.00	2.8	13.6
2004	1,647	20.4	336	11.73	2.9	13.9
2005	1,763	22.3	393	12.49	3.1	14.1
2006	1,857	24.0	446	13.18	3.4	14.1

Source: *18th Annual State of Logistics Report*, http://www.cscmp.org (2007). Reproduced with permission of Council of Supply Chain Management Professionals.

from 1990 through 2006. As would be expected, the level or value of inventory increases with growth in the U.S. economy. However, the important question is whether total inventory in the economy grows at the same rate as GDP. Obviously, it is best for inventory to increase at a slower rate than GDP. This means that the economy is generating more revenue with less assets and working capital investment.

Table 9.1 shows that the nominal GDP grew by 127.2 percent in the time period between 1990 and 2006. Similarly, the value of business inventory increased by 78.4 percent during the same time period. However, inventory costs as a percent of GDP declined from 17.9 percent in 1990 to 14.1 percent in 2006. So, even though the absolute value of inventory increased during this time period, it decreased as a percent of GDP. This declining trend indicates that the economy is producing more revenue with less assets and working capital. While the trend is down, the year-to-year changes indicate the element of volatility faced by many organizations.

The focus of these data should be on the trend, which clearly indicates a relative decline in inventory value and inventory carrying cost as a percent of GDP—a positive metric for the economy and business organizations in general. Inventories represent a cost of doing business and are included in the prices of products and services. Reductions in inventory costs, especially if there is no decline in customer service, are beneficial to both buyers and sellers.

As discussed in Chapter 2, the major cost tradeoff in logistics is between transportation and inventory. That is, the faster and more reliable (and more expensive) the transportation, the less the cost of inventories. Like inventory costs, transportation costs as a percent of GDP declined during the 1990s. However, the cost of fuel today, coupled with capacity constraints in the transportation industry, has escalated the costs of transportation. The economics of this rapid rise in transportation costs have not yet been determined. However, it will be interesting to see if the traditional tradeoffs between transportation and inventory costs will remain the same in this new environment.

Inventory in the Firm: Rationale for Inventory

As indicated previously, inventory plays a dual role in organizations. Inventory impacts the cost of goods sold as well as supporting order fulfillment (customer service). Table 9.2 reports total logistics costs for the economy and shows that inventory carrying costs are on average about 34 percent of total logistics costs for organizations. Transportation costs comprise about 61.4 percent of all logistics costs.

Consumer-packaged goods (CPG) firms and the wholesalers and retailers that are a part of their distribution channels face a special challenge in keeping inventories at acceptable levels because of the difficulty of forecasting demand and increasing expectations from customers concerning product availability. Both of these factors are magnified by these firms increasing the complexity of their product offerings. For example, if Hershey forecasted aggregate demand for Kisses™ for the first quarter next year to be 1 million cases, it would have to break this number down by stock-keeping unit (SKU), packaging, geography, and so on. This could result in hundreds or thousands of SKUs that require some level of inventory and safety stock. Consumer preferences can change quickly, which makes managing inventory levels a special challenge.

To illustrate the cost side of the challenge, assume that Hershey expects to carry an average monthly inventory during the first quarter of the year of 250,000 cases of Kisses.

Table 9.2	Total Logistics Costs—2006	
		$ BILLION
Carrying Costs—$1,857 Trillion All Business Inventory		
Interest		93
Taxes, Obsolescence, Depreciation, Insurance		252
Warehousing		101
	SUBTOTAL	446
Transportation Costs Motor Carriers		
Truck—Intercity		432
Truck—Local		203
	SUBTOTAL	635
Other Carriers		
Railroads		54
Water (international 32, domestic 8)		37
Oil Pipelines		10
Air (international 15, domestic 23)		38
Forwarders		27
	SUBTOTAL	166
Shipper-Related Costs		8
Logistics Administration		50
	TOTAL LOGISTICS COST	1,305

Source: *18th Annual State of Logistics Report,* http://www.cscmp.org (2007). Reproduced with permission of Council of Supply Chain Management Professionals.

If each case is valued at $25, the value of the inventory would be $6.25 million (250,000 cases × $25). If its cost of carrying inventory (to be explained later in this chapter) is 25 percent, its cost of carrying inventory during this period would be $1,562,500. If the average inventory increased to 350,000 cases, this would result in an additional $2.5 million of inventory cost. If the increase in inventory was not accompanied by an equal or greater increase in revenue, Hershey would face a reduction in pretax profit.

Hopefully, the point has been made that managing inventory is a critical factor for success in many organizations. Many organizations have responded to this challenge—as indicated by the macro data presented in the previous section—and have reduced inventory levels while maintaining appropriate customer service levels. Their ability to achieve the twin goals of lower inventory (efficiency) and acceptable customer service levels (effectiveness) is based on a number of factors discussed in this chapter. A good starting point is an understanding of why organizations usually have to carry inventories and the resulting tradeoffs and relationships.

Batching Economies/Cycle Stocks

Batching economies or **cycle stocks** usually arise from three sources—procurement, production, and/or transportation. Scale economies are often associated with all three, which can result in the accumulation of inventory that will not be used or sold immediately—which means some cycle stock or inventory will be used up or sold over some period of time.

In the procurement area, it is not unusual for a seller to have a schedule of prices that reflects the quantity purchased. In other words, larger purchased volumes result in lower prices per unit and vice versa. Purchase discounts are also prevalent for personal consumption items. For example, buying a package of 12 rolls of paper towels at Sam's Club would result in a lower price per roll than if the 12 rolls were bought separately. When the larger package is purchased, cycle stock is created. What is not consumed immediately will have to be stored. When organizations buy raw materials and supplies, particularly in our global economy, they are often offered price discounts for larger quantities. The tradeoff logic that was mentioned earlier suggests that the price discount savings have to be compared to the additional cost of carrying inventory. This is a relatively straightforward analysis, which is discussed later in this chapter. In spite of the analytic framework available for analyzing discount tradeoffs, sometimes organizations just focus on the price savings and do not justify the discount against the additional inventory carrying cost.

A related discount situation occurs with transportation services. Transportation firms usually offer rate/price discounts for shipping larger quantities. In the motor carrier industry, a common example is the lower rate/price per pound for shipping truck-load quantities versus less-than-truckload quantities. The motor carrier saves money in pick-up, handling, and delivery costs with the truckload shipment, and these are reflected in a lower rate/price to the shipper. The larger shipment quantities to justify the discount have the same effect as the purchase quantities—that is, cycle stocks. The tradeoff requirement is the same. Do the costs savings from the larger shipment offset the additional inventory carrying cost?

Note that purchase economies and transportation economies are complementary. That is, when organizations buy larger quantities of raw materials or supplies, they can ship larger quantities, which can result in transportation discounts. Therefore, they are frequently the recipients of two discounts for the same item purchased, which can make the tradeoff evaluation positive. One of the big challenges, discussed later in this chapter, is that many organizations might not calculate their carrying costs accurately.

The third batching economy is associated with production. Many organizations feel that their production costs per unit are substantially lower when they have long production runs of the same product. Long production runs decrease the number of change-overs to a production line but increase the amount of cycle stock that must be stored until they are sold. Traditionally, organizations rationalized long productions runs to lower unit costs without really evaluating the resulting inventory carrying costs, which can be high for finished goods. There is also a related concern about obsolescence of finished goods when high inventories are kept.

Most organizations have cycle stocks, even if they do not purchase products, because of the purchase of supplies. Obviously, cycle stocks can be beneficial as long as the appropriate analysis is done to justify the cost of the inventory.

Uncertainty/Safety Stocks

All organizations are faced with uncertainty. On the demand or customer side, there is usually uncertainty in how much customers will buy and when they will buy it. Forecasting demand (discussed in Chapter 7) is a common approach to resolving demand uncertainty, but it is never completely accurate. On the supply side, there might be uncertainty about obtaining what is needed from suppliers and how long it will take for the fulfillment of the order. Uncertainty can also arise from transportation providers in terms of receiving reliable delivery. The net result of uncertainty is usually the same: organizations accumulate safety stock to buffer themselves against stockouts. The challenge and analysis are different for safety stock than for cycle stock; safety stock is much more complex and challenging to manage because it is redundant inventory.

If a production line shuts down because of a supply shortage or a customer does not receive a delivery, problems will arise. Tradeoff analysis is appropriate and can be accomplished using the appropriate tools to assess the risk and measure the inventory cost. In addition, organizations today are taking a more proactive approach to reducing uncertainty using the power of information to help reduce the need for safety stocks. A previous discussion noted that information can be used to replace inventory. There has literally been an information revolution because of the technology now available to transmit and receive timely and accurate information between trading partners. Collaboration in the sharing of information in some supply chains has yielded significant results in reducing inventories and improving service at the same time. Collaborative planning, forecasting, and replenishment (CPFR) is an excellent example of such an approach. Sophisticated barcodes, RFID tags, electronic data interchange (EDI), the Internet, and so on, have enabled organizations to reduce uncertainty. However, it is not possible to eliminate uncertainty completely so analyses need to be performed to measure the tradeoffs.

Setting safety stock levels for an organization is both an art and a science. As with forecasting, setting safety stock levels assumes that the past will repeat itself in the future. If this assumption holds true, then setting safety stock levels is purely science. However, the future rarely replicates the past exactly. This is when setting safety stock levels becomes an art. And, as with forecasting, it is usually wrong. However, statistical techniques are available to represent the science of setting safety stock levels. This will be discussed in a later section in this chapter.

Time/In-Transit and Work-in-Process Stocks

The time associated with transportation (e.g., supplier to manufacturing plant) and with the manufacture or assembly of a complex product (e.g., automobile) means that even while goods are in motion, an inventory cost is associated with the time period. The longer the time period, the higher the cost.

The time period for in-transit inventory and work-in-process (WIP) inventory should be evaluated in terms of the appropriate tradeoffs. The various transportation modes available for shipping freight have different transit time lengths, transit time variability, and damage rates. The rates/prices charged by carriers in the different modes reflect these differences in service. For example, air freight service is usually the fastest and often the most reliable, but the price charged for this service is considerably higher than that charged by motor carriers, railroads, or ocean carriers. However, air freight should result in less inventory in transit. As an example, assume that ABC Power Tools currently ships 40-foot containers from its manufacturing plant in Europe to a customer's distribution center in California. Currently, ABC uses a mix of motor carrier,

Supply Chain Technology

P&G Shaves Safety Stock with Terra Technology

For Procter & Gamble, supply chain management is a core competency that requires continuous reinvestment to improve performance and achieve competitive advantage. The company recently undertook an initiative to boost its short-term forecasting accuracy as a way to lower safety stocks. Dick Clark, associate director for demand planning at Procter & Gamble, selected Terra Technology's Demand Sensing solution as a bolt-on addition to its SAP system. Terra's so-called "black box" solution takes existing forecast information from the demand plan, combines it with other real-time data like daily shipments and orders, and applies complex pattern recognition algorithms and other formulas to create forecasts on a daily basis for every product at the line-item level.

"Terra essentially reruns the forecast and replaces the first 42 days of the SAP forecast," says Mark Kremblewski, global business expert on demand planning for Procter & Gamble.

The program automatically updates these forecasts daily based on real-time data on orders and shipments as they continually flow into the system. Once the demand plan is created and sent, virtually no human interaction is required.

Since Terra is predicting shipments to customers, capacity constraints are taken into account afterwards through **distribution resource planning (DRP)** and production scheduling. Further, it takes a weekly granular forecast and replaces it with a daily granular forecast.

"It is more than a different 'split by day,'" says Kremblewski. "It will modify the weekly quantity if that is more accurate."

The SAP forecast is still important as it provides one of the inputs to the black box, but Kremblewski points out that forecast error typically accounts for about 90 percent of safety stock.

"If you plan your supply chain using the forecast to set inventory targets, over a zero- to 28-day horizon, I'd say you'll at a minimum reduce inventory by 10 percent. Looking at actual pilot results in some supply chains, we've actually seen examples much higher than that," says Kremblewski.

Procter & Gamble is live on the software in several business segments in Western Europe and North America and is rolling the software out globally over the next few years. Safety stock has decreased by more than 10 percent in businesses where the software is live. Out-of-stocks as a result of incorrect safeties did not increase.

Procter & Gamble anticipates that the greatest benefit from adopting this type of solution may come over the long term, as it shifts its demand planners away from the inevitable fire-fighting and scrambling inherent in focusing on short-term forecasts.

"Our demand planners have more than enough things to do without focusing on the next one, two or three days, or the next week," Kremblewski says. "The 'black box' takes care of all that, which allows our demand planners to focus on the longer term, on the trends, on the business intelligence regarding the marketplace, what our customers are doing, etc. And that's where their real value is added, not watching orders or watching short-term trends. If the box can do it, let the box do it."

Source: Global Logistics and Supply Chain Strategies Magazine (July 2007): 58. Reproduced by permission.

railroad, and ocean carriers to complete this move. What would the cost impact be if ABC replaced the ocean and railroad carriers with an air freight carrier? Figure 9.1 is a summary of the current mode mix, proposed mode mix, and relevant cost data. Table 9.3 shows the analysis of the relevant costs associated with the current mode mix. Inventory value is calculated by multiplying the number of units in the container times the manufactured cost of each item divided by 365 days. The value of the inventory is considered an annual valuation. As such, the value of each day's worth of inventory takes the annual value divided by 365. As Table 9.3 shows, the current mode mix takes 22 days

Figure 9.1	ABC Power Tools—In-Transit Inventory Analysis

ABC ships product in 40-foot containers from Europe to a customer in California
Current mode mix:

- Plant to European port: motor carrier drayage
- European port to U.S port (East Coast): ocean carrier
- Eastern U.S port to rail siding: motor carrier drayage
- Eastern U.S rail siding to California rail siding: rail
- California rail siding to customer DC: motor carrier drayage

Assume that one 40-foot container holds 500 units of Product A:

- Manufactured cost per unit of Product A = $449

Assume ABC owns the inventory to delivery at customer DC
Assume ABC ships 100 containers per year to this customer
Transportation costs (per container):

- Motor carrier drayage: $150
- Ocean: $700
- Rail: $900
- Air: $2,500

Change modes: Replace ocean and rail with air

Table 9.3	ABC Power Tools In-Transit Inventory Analysis—Current

SUPPLY CHAIN MOVE	DAYS	INVENTORY VALUE	TRANSPORTATION MODE	FREIGHT COST
ABC plant to European port	1	$ 615.07	Drayage	$ 150.00
Through European port	2	1,230.14	—	—
European port to East Coast U.S. port	5	3,075.35	Ocean	700.00
Through U.S. port	2	1,230.14	—	—
U.S. port to rail siding	1	615.07	Drayage	150.00
East Coast U.S. to California	10	6,150.70	Rail	900.00
California rail to customer	1	615.07	Drayage	150.00
Total	22	$13,531.54		$2,050.00

Table 9.4	ABC Power Tools—In-Transit Inventory Analysis (Proposed)			
SUPPLY CHAIN MOVE	DAYS	INVENTORY VALUE	TRANSPORTATION MODE	FREIGHT COST
ABC plant to European airport	1	$ 615.07	Drayage	$ 150.00
Through European airport	1	615.07	—	—
European airport to California airport	1	615.07	Air	2,500.00
Through California airport	1	615.07	—	—
California airport to customer	1	615.07	Drayage	150.00
Total	5	$3,075.35		$2,800.00

from origin to destination with an inventory value of $13,531.54 and a freight cost of $2,050. Table 9.4 shows the cost analysis for the proposed mode mix that replaces the ocean and rail moves with an air freight move. As this table shows, the new inventory value decreased by $10,456.19, but the freight cost increased by $750. The reduction in time through the supply chain from the proposed mode mix resulted in a positive variance for ABC Power Tools. Although this is a simple example, it shows the financial impact of reducing transit time on inventory and transportation costs. The cash flow impacts of this example will be discussed further after the introduction to inventory carrying costs in this chapter.

Finally, WIP inventories are associated with manufacturing. Significant amounts of inventory can be accumulated in manufacturing facilities, particularly in assembly operations such as automobiles and computers. The length of time WIP inventory sits in a manufacturing facility waiting to be included in a particular product should be carefully evaluated in relationship to scheduling techniques and the actual manufacturing/assembly technology. Similar to the transportation example above, if an investment in technology reduces the amount of time WIP sits in the facility, a positive variance could result to the manufacturer. As always, a tradeoff analysis of the costs needs to be performed.

Seasonal Stocks

Seasonality can occur in the supply of raw materials, in the demand for finished product, or in both. Organizations that are faced with seasonality issues are constantly challenged when determining how much inventory to accumulate. Organizations that process agriculture products are a good example of supply seasonality. While the supply of the raw material is available during only one part of the year, demand is stable throughout the year. Therefore, the finished product usually has to be stored until it is sold. That is, when the raw material is available, it needs to be converted to finished product. This scenario many times is faced with high storage costs and/or high obsolescence costs. An alternative scenario might be to store the raw material, or some pre-processed version of it, and use it to make the finished product as the demand dictates.

Sometimes seasonality can impact transportation, particularly if domestic water transportation is used. Rivers and lakes can freeze during the winter, which might interrupt the shipment of basic raw materials and cause organizations to accumulate raw materials before the freeze to avoid interruption. Another example would be the seasonality of the construction industry in the United States and its impact on the availability of flatbed tractor trailers. Although construction takes place in many areas of the United States year round, the northern states experience a slowdown in construction activity during the winter months. As spring approaches in the north, construction activity increases dramatically. The peak springtime construction season places a heavy demand on a fixed capacity of flatbed trailers to move construction supplies.

Many organizations are faced with seasonality in their product demand. As noted in the forecasting discussion in Chapter 7, Hershey is one of these organizations. A majority of Hershey's demand falls into five "events" throughout the year: Valentine's Day, Easter, Back-to-School, Halloween, and Christmas. The challenge for an organization like Hershey is multifaceted: meet wide swings in demand, keep production running at a fairly constant level, and avoid excessive inventories. The main tradeoff here is between manufacturing cost per unit and inventory costs.

Anticipatory Stocks

A fifth reason to hold inventory arises when an organization anticipates that an unusual event might occur that will negatively impact its source of supply. Examples of these events would include strikes, significant raw materials or finished goods price increase, a major shortage of supply because of political unrest or weather, and so on. In such situations, organizations might accumulate inventory to "hedge" against the risk associated with the unusual event. Again, an analysis should be undertaken to assess the risk, probability, and cost of inventory. Obviously, the analysis is more challenging because of the degree of uncertainty. However, analytical techniques are available to help mitigate these challenges.

Summary of Inventory Accumulation

Most organizations will accumulate some level of inventory for very good reasons. In many instances, the inventory cost might be more than offset by savings in other areas. The basic principle is that decisions to accumulate inventory need to be evaluated using a tradeoff framework. In addition to the five reasons just discussed, there are other reasons for accumulating inventory such as maintaining suppliers or employees. For example, during periods of low demand, an organization might continue to purchase from some suppliers to maintain the relationship and/or keep employees by producing to inventory. Again, an evaluation of the tradeoffs is necessary.

As already discussed, several functional areas in most organizations have a vested interest in decisions that determine how much inventory should be held and related issues regarding timing and location. The next section examines some of the contrasting viewpoints of these functional areas.

The Importance of Inventory in Other Functional Areas

As discussed in Chapter 2, logistics interfaces with an organization's other functional areas, such as marketing and manufacturing. The interface is usually more prominent in the inventory area. As background for analyzing the importance of inventory in the logistics system, several aspects of how logistics relates to other functional business areas with respect to inventory must be discussed.

Marketing

The primary mission of marketing is to identify, create, and help satisfy demand for an organization's products/services. In a product-oriented environment, the presence of the correct levels and types of inventory is crucial to fulfilling this mission. As such, marketing tends to have a favorable view on holding sufficient, and/or extra, inventory to ensure product availability to meet customer needs. Marketing's desire to hold inventory is also driven by new product offerings and continued market growth objectives.

Manufacturing

In many organizations, manufacturing operations are measured by how efficiently they can produce each unit of output. This situation typically means that manufacturing operations tend to be optimized when they have long production runs of a single product while minimizing the number of changeovers. These long productions runs will result in high inventory levels but low labor and machine costs per unit. Within industries faced with seasonal demand patterns, manufacturing is optimized by producing product even though demand for the product does not exist at the time of production. Adding the complexity of production scheduling to accommodate product line growth and brand extensions to this seasonality can result in significantly high inventories to create low manufacturing costs.

Finance

Inventories impact both the income statement and balance sheet of an organization. Inventories create both an asset and liability on the balance sheet as well as a cash flow impact on the income statement. As such, finance usually looks favorably at low inventories to increase inventory turns, reduce liabilities and assets, and increase cash flow to the organization.

The preceding discussion highlights why other functional areas within an organization are interested in inventory. Objectives of the finance area might obviously conflict with marketing and manufacturing objectives. A more subtle conflict sometimes arises between marketing and manufacturing. The long production runs that manufacturing might desire could cause shortages of some products needed by marketing to satisfy customer demand. For example, manufacturing might want to run 5,000 units of a particular product, while marketing needs another product currently in short supply.

Many companies can make a case for using a formal logistics organization to help resolve these inventory objective conflicts. Inventory is a critical decision area for logistics, and the logistics manager is in an excellent position to analyze inventory tradeoffs, not only within logistics but also with the other functional areas discussed here.

Proper inventory management and control affects customers, suppliers, and an organization's functional areas. In spite of the many possible advantages to holding inventory in a logistics system, the costs of holding this inventory are a major expense. So, in making decisions about inventory levels, an organization needs to assess the tradeoffs between costs and the resulting service.

Inventory Costs

Inventory costs are important for three reasons. First, inventory costs represent a significant component of logistics costs in many organizations. Second, the inventory levels that an organization maintains at nodes in its logistics network will affect the level of service the organization can offer its customers. Third, cost tradeoff decisions in logistics frequently depend on and ultimately impact inventory carrying costs.

The following section provides basic information concerning the costs that logistics managers should consider when making inventory policy decisions. The major types of costs include inventory carrying cost, order/setup costs, expected stockout costs, and inventory in-transit carrying costs.

Inventory Carrying Costs

Inventory carrying costs are those that are incurred by inventory at rest and waiting to be used. From a finished goods inventory perspective, inventory carrying costs represent those costs associated with manufacturing and moving inventory from a plant to a distribution center to await an order. There are four major components of inventory carrying cost: capital cost, storage space cost, inventory service cost, and inventory risk cost.[1]

Capital Cost

Sometimes called the **interest** or **opportunity cost**, this cost type focuses on the cost of capital tied up in inventory and the resulting lost opportunity from investing that capital elsewhere. For example, all organizations borrow money from external sources to fund operations. This money might be in the form of equity (from stock issues) or debt (borrowing from banks). In either case, borrowed money has a cost associated with it. For equity, it is dividends; for debt, it is interest payments. In either case, an organization incurs a cost for borrowing money. If an organization decides to use this money to buy raw materials, build manufacturing plants, and hire labor to produce finished products for storage, then this inventory carries this "borrowed money" cost while sitting waiting to be sold. As such, capital tied up in inventory still requires dividend or interest payments to the funding source. The opportunity cost of this inventory is the return on capital the organization might have realized if it had invested in another opportunity rather than in raw materials, plants, and labor.

The capital cost is frequently the largest component of inventory carrying cost. An organization usually expresses it as a percentage of the dollar value of the inventory held. For example, a capital cost expressed as 20 percent of a product's value of $100 equals a capital cost of $20 ($100 × 20%).

In practice, determining an acceptable number to use for capital cost is not an easy task. One way of calculating capital cost for inventory decision making might use an organization's **hurdle rate**, the minimum rate of return on new investments. In this way, the organization makes inventory decisions in the same way that it does for investing in new facilities, advertising, and so on. Another way of calculating capital cost is for an organization to use its **weighted average cost of capital (WACC)**. WACC is the weighted average percent of debt service of all external sources of funding, including both equity and debt. This method reflects the direct debt service costs of having capital tied up in inventory.

The inventory valuation method used is critical to accurately determining capital cost and is subsequently critical to determining overall inventory carrying cost. According to Stock and Lambert, "the opportunity cost of capital should be applied only to the out-of-pocket investment in inventory.... This is the direct variable expense incurred up to the point at which inventory is held in storage."[2] Thus, the commonly accepted accounting practice of valuing inventory at fully allocated manufacturing cost is unacceptable in inventory decision making because raising or lowering inventory levels financially affects only the variable portion of inventory value and not the fixed portion of allocated cost. So, normally only direct materials, direct labor, and direct plant cost are included in the out-of-pocket investment in inventory. Including inbound transportation costs to a distribution center in inventory value is consistent with this notion of including variable costs in inventory value.

Storage Space Cost

Storage space cost includes handling costs associated with moving products into and out of inventory, as well as storage costs such as rent, heating, and lighting. Such costs might vary considerably from one circumstance to the next. For example, organizations often unload raw materials from rail cars and store them outside, whereas finished goods typically require covered and more sophisticated storage facilities.

Storage space costs are relevant to the extent that they either increase or decrease as inventory levels rise or fall. Thus, organizations should include variable, rather than fixed, expenses when estimating space costs as well as capital costs. This can be illustrated by contrasting the use of public warehousing versus private warehousing. When an organization uses public warehousing, almost all handling and storage costs vary directly with the level of stored inventory. As a result, these variable costs are relevant to decisions regarding inventory. When an organization uses private warehousing, however, many storage space costs (such as depreciation on the building) are fixed and are not relevant to inventory carrying costs. However, the opposite might be the case in the use of private warehousing where the organization is allocating all costs to products based on their activity levels. As such, each product would be allocated a portion of the fixed costs in the inventory carrying cost calculation.

Inventory Service Cost

Another component of inventory carrying cost includes insurance and taxes. Depending on the product value and type, the risk of loss or damage might require high insurance premiums. Also, many states impose a tax on inventory value, sometimes on a monthly basis. High inventory levels resulting in high tax costs can be significant in determining specific locations where organizations store products. Insurance and taxes might vary considerably from product to product, and organizations must consider this when calculating inventory carrying costs.

Inventory Risk Cost

The final major component of inventory carrying cost reflects the very real possibility that inventory dollar value might decline for reasons beyond an organization's control. For example, goods held in storage for long periods of time might become obsolete and thus decrease in value. This situation is commonly found in the computer and electronics industries. Also, fashion apparel might rapidly deteriorate in value once the selling season is over. This situation also occurs with fresh fruits and vegetables when quality deteriorates or the price falls over time. Manufactured products might face similar risks, although typically not to the same degree. A box of breakfast cereal will have a relatively long shelf life with little risk of depreciating in value over a reasonable amount of time.

Any calculation of inventory risk costs should include the costs associated with obsolescence, damage, pilferage, and other risks to stored products. The extent to which inventoried items are subject to such risks will affect the inventory value and thus the carrying cost.

Calculating the Cost of Carrying Inventory

Calculating the cost to carry (or hold) a particular item in inventory involves three steps. First, the value of the item stored in inventory must be determined. Each organization has predetermined accounting practices to determine the value of inventory for balance sheet purposes. The most relevant value measure for determining carrying costs is the cost of goods sold or the direct labor, materials, and overhead consumed by that item plus the direct costs of moving that item from the manufacturing facility into a distribution center for storage.

Second, determine the cost of each individual carrying cost component and add them together to determine the total direct costs consumed by the item while being held in inventory. Two types of costs should be considered here: variable-based costs and value-based costs. Variable-based costs are those that are specifically out-of-pocket expenditures, for example, inbound freight expense to the distribution center. Value-based costs are those that use the total value (or total direct costs consumed) of the item at the location where carrying costs are being determined, for example, taxes. Normally, inventory carrying costs are calculated on an annual basis. This assumes that the item will be held in storage for a one-year time period. These two costs must be adjusted for the actual length of time the item will be in storage. One word of caution when calculating inventory carrying costs: a decision must be made (in accordance with the organization's accounting standards) as to which costs are "one-time" and which costs are "recurring." This will be especially true when the length of time an item is stored will be greater than one year.

Third, divide the total costs calculated in Step 2 by the value of the item determined in Step 1. This will determine the annual inventory carrying cost for that item.

Example

Assume that ABC Power Tools assembles industrial machine tools and hand-held tools for the construction industry. Item 1 is a heavy-duty band saw that is assembled at the plant and shipped to an ABC distribution center for storage, waiting for an order to be placed. Table 9.5 summarizes the cost of holding Item 1 in storage for a one-year time period. The direct materials, labor, and overhead incurred at the plant to assemble this item is $614.65. Moving Item 1 to the distribution center incurs a direct transportation cost of $32.35. Receiving this item into the distribution center and labor used for this item while in storage consumes a direct labor expense of $22.00. Direct space cost allocated to storing Item 1 is $28.80 per year. The direct insurance cost for holding Item 1 in storage for one year is $2.00. Interest, taxes, loss and damage, and obsolescence costs are based on the value of Item 1 ($614.65) and are $61.47, $6.15, $23.97, and $6.15, respectively. The interest is assumed to be an opportunity cost incurred for the investment of $614.65 of capital into Item 1. Therefore, the total cost to hold Item 1 in storage for one year is $182.89, or 29.8 percent of the value of Item 1.

Table 9.5	ABC Power Tools—Inventory Carrying Cost for Item 1	
COST CATEGORY	**COMPUTATION**	**ANNUAL COST**
1. Direct materials, labor, overhead		$614.65
2. Inbound freight to DC		$ 32.35
3. Labor	$10 per unit received plus $1 per unit per month × 2 months	$ 22.00
4. Space	$0.30/sq. ft./month × 8 sq. ft. × 12 months	$ 28.80
5. Insurance	$2.00 per unit per year	$ 2.00
6. Interest	10% @ $614.65	$ 61.47
7. Taxes	$5 per $100 value @ 20%	$ 6.15
8. Loss and damage	3.9% per year @ $614.65	$ 23.97
9. Obsolescence	1% per year @ $614.65	$ 6.15
10. Total inventory carrying costs		$182.89
11. Inventory carrying cost percent	$182.89/$614.65	29.8%

Assume that ABC Power Tools sells this item through a typical home improvement type of retailer like Lowe's or Home Depot. Calculating the cost to hold Item 1 in inventory would be slightly different in this situation compared to the previous example since Item 1 would not be in storage for an entire year before it would be sold to a consumer. Table 9.6 shows how the cost to hold/move Item 1 would be calculated. This example makes two assumptions: (1) inventory carrying costs begin to accrue at the ABC distribution center and (2) all value-based costs must be prorated for each supply chain location based on the days of supply for that location. As can be seen from Line 2, the manufactured cost of Item 1 does not change as it moves through the supply chain. What does change are the cumulative variable-based costs (Line 4) and the cumulative value-based costs (Line 7). This occurs because additional costs are incurred each time Item 1 moves further down the supply chain. Variable-based costs increase every time Item 1 is moved and stored. This increases the value (costs consumed—shown in Line 5) of Item 1. The value-based costs increase because the value of Item 1 increases as it moves further to the point of consumption. Although this is a simple example, it shows that as an item receives multiple "touches" in the supply chain, the cumulative cost of doing so increases dramatically. As Table 9.6 illustrates, the cost of moving/storing Item 1 increases almost three times from the ABC distribution center to the retail store. This is a good example of how adding "touch points" to inventory drastically increases the cost of holding that inventory.

Nature of Carrying Cost

Items with basically similar carrying costs should use the same estimate of carrying cost per dollar value. However, items subject to rapid obsolescence or items that require servicing to prevent deterioration might require separate cost estimates. The estimate of carrying cost per inventory dollar value expressed as a percent of the inventory value carried during the year will reflect how carrying costs change with average inventory

Table 9.6	ABC Power Tools—Inventory Carrying Costs for Item 1 to Customer			
CATEGORY	ABC Plant →	ABC DC →	Retail DC →	Retail Store
1. Days of supply	0	60	45	30
2. Direct manufactured cost	$614.65	$614.65	$614.65	$614.65
3. Variable-based costs:				
a. Freight	$ 0	$ 32.35	$ 32.35	$ 32.35
b. Labor	0	12.00	11.50	11.00
c. Space	0	4.80	3.60	2.40
d. Insurance	0	0.33	0.25	0.17
4. Total variable-based costs (cumulative)	$ 0	$ 49.48	$ 97.18	$143.10
5. Total value Item 1 (L2 + L4)	$614.65	$664.13	$711.83	$757.75
6. Value-based costs (based on L5):				
a. Interest (10% per year)	$ 0	$ 11.07	$ 8.90	$ 6.31
b. Taxes	0	6.64	7.12	7.58
c. Loss and damage	0	4.32	3.47	2.46
d. Obsolescence	0	1.11	0.89	0.63
7. Total value-based costs (cumulative)	$ 0	$ 23.14	$ 43.52	$ 60.50
8. Total costs (L4 + L7)	$ 0	$ 72.62	$140.70	$203.60
9. Carrying cost percent (L8/$614.65)	0	11.8%	22.9%	33.1%

value. Table 9.7 shows that as average inventory increases for ABC Power Tools for Item 1 at its distribution center, annual carrying costs increase, and vice versa. In other words, carrying cost is variable and is directly proportional to the average number of items in inventory or the average inventory value.

Order/Setup Cost

A second cost affecting total inventory cost is **ordering cost** or **setup cost.** Ordering cost refers to the expense of placing an order for additional inventory and does not include the cost or expense of the product itself. Setup cost refers more specifically to the expense of changing or modifying a production or assembly process to facilitate line changeovers.

Order Cost

The costs associated with ordering inventory have both fixed and variable components. The fixed element might refer to the cost of the information system, facilities, and technology available to facilitate order-placement activities. This fixed cost remains constant in relation to the number of orders placed.

Table 9.7	Inventory and Carrying Costs for ABC Power Tools			
ORDER PERIOD	NUMBER OF ORDERS PER YEAR	AVERAGE INVENTORY* UNITS	VALUE**	TOTAL ANNUAL INVENTORY CARRYING COST[†]
1 week	52	25	$ 15,366.25	$ 4,440.85
2 weeks	26	50	30,732.50	8,881.69
4 weeks	13	100	614,650.00	17,763.39
13 weeks	4	325	199,761.25	57,731.00
26 weeks	2	650	399,522.50	115,462.00
52 weeks	1	1,300	799,045.00	230,924.00

*One week's inventory supply is 50 items. Average Inventory = Beginning Inventory (units) – Ending Inventory (assumed to be zero) ÷ 2

**Value per unit is $614.65.

[†]Carrying Cost = 28.9%

There are also a number of costs that vary in relation to the number of orders that are placed to acquire additional inventory. Some types of activities that might be responsible for these costs include (1) reviewing inventory stock levels, (2) preparing and processing order requisitions or purchase orders, (3) preparing and processing receiving reports, (4) checking and inspecting stock prior to placement in inventory, and (5) preparing and processing payment. While the roles played by people and processes might seem trivial, they become very important when considering the total range of activities associated with placing and receiving orders.

Setup Costs

Production setup costs might be more obvious than ordering costs. Setup costs are expenses incurred each time an organization modifies a production or assembly line to produce a different item for inventory. The fixed portion of setup cost might include the use of capital equipment needed to change over production or assembly facilities, while the variable expense might include the personnel costs incurred in the process of modifying or changing the production or assembly line.

Nature of Cost

Separating the fixed and variable portions of order/setup cost is essential. Just as calculations should emphasize the variable components of inventory carrying costs, calculations of order and setup costs should emphasize the variable portion of these expenses. As discussed later in this chapter, this emphasis becomes central to developing meaningful inventory strategies.

When calculating annual ordering costs, organizations usually start with the cost or charge associated with each individual order or setup. Correspondingly, the annual number of orders or setups affects the total order cost per year; this number is inversely related to individual order size or to the number of units manufactured (production run length) within a simple setup or changeover. Table 9.8 shows this general relationship. As can be seen in Table 9.8, more frequent order placement results in customers

Table 9.8	Order Frequency and Order Cost for Computer Hard Disks	
ORDER FREQUENCY	NUMBER OF ORDERS PER YEAR	TOTAL ANNUAL ORDER COST*
1 week	52	$10,400
2 weeks	26	5,200
4 weeks	13	2,600
13 weeks	4	800
26 weeks	2	400
52 weeks	1	200
*Assuming a cost per order of $200.		

placing a larger number of smaller orders per year. Since both small and large orders incur the variable expense of placing an order, total annual order cost will increase in direct proportion to the number of orders placed per year. As long as annual sales and demand remain the same, total annual order or setup cost will relate directly to the number of orders or setups per year and will relate inversely to individual order size or individual production run length.

Future Perspectives

Although an accurate, comprehensive statement of inventory cost must include the portion related to order/setup activities, the magnitude of these costs is likely to decrease in the future. Considering the move to highly automated systems for order management and order processing, and the streamlining of inventory receiving practices, the variable cost of handling individual orders is certain to decrease significantly. In organizations where **vendor-managed inventory (VMI)** programs are being utilized, the concept of placing orders itself loses significance, and therefore the concept of order cost loses relevance.

Carrying Cost versus Order Cost

As shown in Table 9.9, order cost and carrying cost respond in opposite ways to changes in the number of orders or size of individual orders. Total cost also responds to changes in order size. Close examination indicates that order costs initially decrease more rapidly than carrying costs increase, which decreases total costs. In other words, a positive tradeoff occurs, since the marginal savings in order costs exceed the marginal increase in inventory carrying costs. However, at a certain point, this relationship begins to change and total costs start to increase. A negative tradeoff occurs here because the marginal order cost savings are less than the marginal carrying cost increase. Figure 9.2 shows this set of relationships in terms of cost curves.

Expected Stockout Cost

Another critical cost to making inventory decisions is **stockout cost**—the cost associated with not having a product available to meet demand. When a product is unavailable to meet demand, several consequences might occur. First, the customer might be willing to wait and accept a later shipment (back order). This usually results in the shipping firm incurring incremental variable costs associated with processing and making the extra

Table 9.9				Summary of Inventory and Order Cost				
ORDER PERIOD	NUMBER OF ORDERS PER YEAR	AVERAGE INVENTORY* (UNITS)	TOTAL ANNUAL ORDER COST**	CHANGE IN TOTAL ORDER COST	TOTAL ANNUAL INVENTORY CARRYING COST†	CHANGE IN TOTAL CARRYING COST	TOTAL COST
1 week	52	50	$10,400		$1,250		$11,650
				−$5,200		$+1,250	
2 weeks	26	100	5,200		2,500		7,700
				−2,600		+2,500	
4 weeks	13	200	2,600		5,000		7,600
				−1,800		+11,250	
13 weeks	4	650	800		16,250		17,050
				−400		+16,250	
26 weeks	2	1,300	400		32,500		32,900
				−200		+32,500	
52 weeks	1	2,600	200		65,000		65,200

*Assume sales or usage at 100 units per week. Average Inventory = (Beginning Inventory − Ending Inventory) ÷ 2
**Cost per order is $200.
†Value is $100 and carrying cost is 25%.

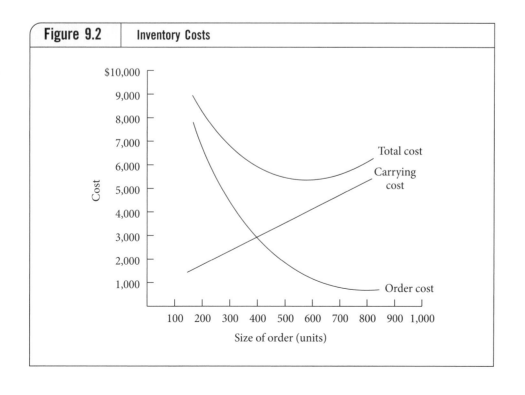

Figure 9.2 Inventory Costs

shipment. This also might result in a less-than-satisfied customer. Second, the customer might decide to purchase a competitor's product in this instance, resulting in a direct loss of profit and revenue for the supplier. Third, the customer might decide to permanently switch to a competitor's product, thus resulting in the loss of future profits and revenues for the supplier. If a stockout occurs on the physical supply side, manufacturing might have to shut down a machine or the entire facility until the material is available.

Stockout costs can be difficult to determine because of the uncertainty of future consequences (e.g., future lost revenue) that might occur. Most organizations will hold safety stock to prevent or minimize product stockouts. However, this increases inventory costs. Therefore, a tradeoff exists between the cost of holding safety stock versus the cost of a stockout. Accurate inventory levels cannot be determined without calculating the cost of a stockout. However, many organizations still set inventory levels without knowing the cost of a stockout because of the challenging nature of identifying true stockout costs. Chapter 8 offers a detailed example of how to determine the tradeoffs between safety stock and stockout costs.

Safety Stock

As previously stated, most organizations will hold **safety stock,** or **buffer stock,** to minimize the possibility of a stockout. Stockouts will occur because of the uncertainties in both demand and lead time. Many techniques exist for setting safety stock levels to accommodate uncertainties in demand and lead time. An example will now be presented.

Assuming that both demand and lead time are normally distributed around the mean, the Formula 9.1 can be used to calculate safety stocks.

$$\sigma_C = \sqrt{R\sigma_S^2 + S^2\sigma_R^2} \qquad\qquad 9.1$$

where:

$\sigma_C =$ Units of safety stock needed to satisfy 68% of all probable observations

$R =$ Average replenishment cycle (days)

$\sigma_R =$ Standard deviation of the replenishment cycle (days)

$S =$ Average daily demand (units)

$\sigma_S =$ Standard deviation of daily demand (units)

Assume that ABC Power Tools has a monthly demand for Item 1 as shown in Table 9.10.

From this table, the average daily demand of 1,315 units and the standard deviation of demand of 271 units can be calculated. Table 9.11 shows the distribution of lead time being anywhere from 7 to 13 days, with a mean of 10 days and a standard deviation of 1.63 days. Given these data, safety stock requirements can be calculated using Formula 9.2.

$$
\begin{aligned}
\sigma_C &= \sqrt{R\sigma_D^2 + D^2\sigma_R^2} \\
&= \sqrt{(10)(271)^2 + (1{,}315)^2(1.63)^2} \qquad\qquad 9.2 \\
&= \sqrt{734{,}410 + 4{,}594{,}378} \\
&= 2{,}308.42 \approx 2{,}308 \ \text{units}
\end{aligned}
$$

Using this safety stock requirement from the calculation, relevant safety stock levels for varying service levels can be calculated and can be seen in Table 9.12. Figure 9.3

Table 9.10	Average Daily Demand for Item 1
DAY	**DEMAND (UNITS)**
1	1,294
2	1,035
3	906
4	777
5	1,035
6	1,165
7	1,563
8	1,424
9	1,424
10	1,424
11	1,682
12	1,553
13	1,682
14	1,035
15	1,165
16	1,165
17	1,294
18	1,812
19	1,424
20	1,553
21	906
22	1,294
23	1,682
24	1,424
25	1,165

Average daily demand (D) = 1,314.92 ≈ 1,315

Standard deviation of daily demand (σ_D) = 270.6 ≈ 271

So,

- 68% of the time, daily demand is between 1,044 and 1,586 units.
- 95% of the time, daily demand is between 773 and 1,857 units.
- 99% of the time, daily demand is between 502 and 2,128 units.

Table 9.11	Lead Time Distribution for Item 1			
LEAD TIME (DAYS)	FREQUENCY (f)	DEVIATION FROM MEAN (d)	DEVIATION SQUARED (d^2)	fd^2
7	1	−3	9	9
8	2	−2	4	8
9	3	−1	1	3
10	4	0	0	0
11	3	+1	1	3
12	2	+2	4	8
13	1	+3	9	9
$\bar{x} = 10$	$n = 16$			$\sum fd^2 = 40$

Average replenishment cycle (R) = 10 days

Standard deviation of replenishment cycle (σ_R) = 1.63 days

$$\sigma_R = \sqrt{\frac{\sum fd^2}{n-1}}$$
$$= 1.63$$

Table 9.12	Safety Stock Levels for Various Service Levels—Item 1	
SERVICE LEVEL	STANDARD DEVIATIONS	SAFETY STOCK (UNITS)
84.1%	1.0	2,308
90.3	1.3	3,000
94.5	1.6	3,693
97.7	2.0	4,616
98.9	2.3	5,308
99.5	2.6	6,001
99.9	3.0	6,924

shows the relationship between service levels and safety stocks graphically. As can be expected, as service level requirements increase, safety stocks increases at an increasing rate. The curve approaches the 100 percent service level but will not statistically reach it, even at three standard deviations from the mean. So, the higher the service level requirement (thus, the lower the stockout rate), the higher the inventory level requirement. As the example in Chapter 8 explained, there is a tradeoff between holding this extra inventory and avoiding the cost of a stockout.

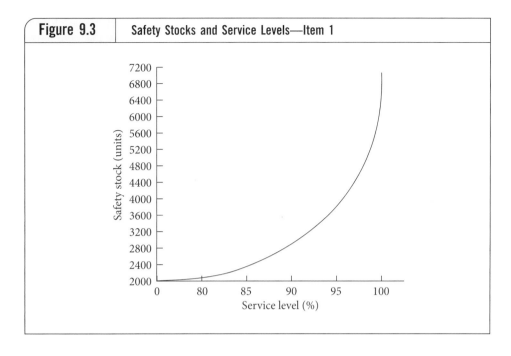

Figure 9.3 | Safety Stocks and Service Levels—Item 1

Cost of Lost Sales

Although this concept was introduced in Chapter 8, a quick review in this chapter is necessary. Determining safety stock levels and the related inventory carrying costs might be relatively straightforward, but not so for determining the cost of a lost sale. Likewise, determining the cost of a production shutdown for lack of raw materials is also a challenge. For example, assume that a manufacturing line has an hourly production rate of 1,000 units and a pretax profit of $100 per unit. Also assume that the total labor costs per hour for that line are $500. If the line is shut down for lack of raw materials for a total of four hours, the cost of the shutdown would be $402,000 [(1,000 units × $100 × 4 hours) + ($500/hr. × 4 hours)]. This figure is probably conservative because it does not include overhead costs or the costs to start the line up again. However, it does give an indication of the out-of-pocket expense of a shutdown and provides a basis for determining raw materials inventory levels.

In-Transit Inventory Carrying Cost

Another inventory carrying cost that many organizations ignore is that of carrying inventory in transit. This cost might be less apparent than those discussed earlier. However, under certain circumstances, it might represent a very significant expense. Remember, someone will own the inventory while it is in transit and will incur the resulting carrying costs. For example, an organization selling its products "free-on board" (FOB) destination is responsible for transporting the products to its customers, since title does not pass until the products reach the customer's facility. Financially, the product remains under the ownership of the shipper until it is unloaded from the transportation vehicle at the customer's location. In-transit inventory carrying cost becomes especially important on global moves since both distance and time from the shipping location both increase.

Since this "moving" inventory is shipper-owned until delivered to the customer, the shipper should consider its delivery time part of its inventory carrying cost. The faster delivery occurs, the sooner the transaction is completed and the faster the shipper receives payment for the shipment. This also means the shipper owns the product in transit for a shorter period of time. Since faster transportation typically means higher transportation cost, the shipper might want to analyze the tradeoff between transportation cost and the cost of carrying inventory in transit. Appendix 9A specifically addresses this situation.

Determining the Cost of In-Transit Inventories

An important question at this point is how to calculate the cost of carrying inventory in transit—that is, what variables should an organization consider? An earlier discussion in this chapter focused on four major components of inventory carrying cost: capital cost, storage space cost, inventory service cost, and inventory risk cost. While these categories are still all valid, they apply differently to the cost of carrying inventory in transit.

First, the capital cost of carrying inventory in transit generally equals that of carrying inventory in a warehouse. If the organization owns the inventory in transit, the capital cost will be the same.

Second, storage space cost generally will not be relevant to inventory in transit since the transportation service provider typically includes equipment (space) and necessary loading and handling costs within its overall transportation price.

Third, while taxes generally would not be relevant to inventory service costs, the need for insurance requires special analysis. For example, liability provisions when using common carriers are specific and shippers might not need to consider additional insurance for their products. However, some transportation providers offer limited liability for the products they carry, thus requiring additional insurance while the products are in transit. This is particularly true for U.S. domestic small package transportation and international ocean transportation.

Fourth, obsolescence or deterioration costs are lesser risks for inventory in transit because the transportation service typically takes only a short time. Also, the fact that inventory is "moving" to the next node in the supply chain assumes that there is a demand for that inventory, lessening the probability that it will not be sold. Thus, this inventory cost is less relevant here than it is for inventory in the warehouse.

Generally, carrying inventory in transit usually costs less than carrying inventory in the warehouse. However, an organization seeking to determine actual cost differences more accurately should examine the details of each inventory cost in depth.

Fundamental Approaches to Managing Inventory

Historically, managing inventory involved two fundamental questions: *how much* to order and *when* to order. By performing a few simple calculations, an inventory manager could easily determine acceptable solutions to these questions. Today, questions regarding *where* inventory should be held and *what* specific line items should be available at specific locations pose more interesting challenges to inventory decision makers.

Today, organizations are faced with product line extensions, new product introductions, global markets, higher service requirements, and a constant pressure to minimize costs. This dynamic operating environment has caused organizations to examine their inventory policies as well as their customer service policies and find the optimal solution

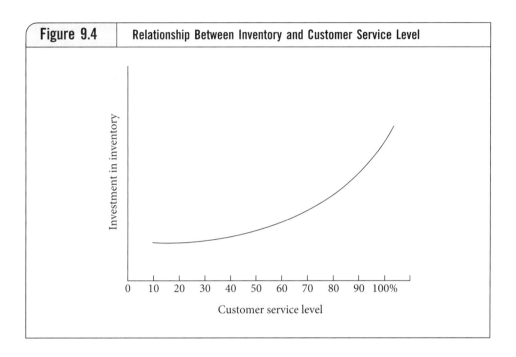

| Figure 9.4 | Relationship Between Inventory and Customer Service Level |

that balances both service and cost. Many approaches exist to identify and analyze this tradeoff. Organizations will choose the approach that serves them the best as defined by their markets and corporate goals.

Regardless of the approach selected, inventory decisions must consider the basic tradeoff between cost and service. Figure 9.4, which illustrates this tradeoff, suggests that increasing investments in inventory will probably result in higher levels of customer service. While there is evidence that this relationship exists in industry, a priority today is on identifying logistics solutions that will result in higher levels of customer service while reducing inventory investments. Several factors make this objective achievable: (1) "real-time" order management systems, (2) improved technologies to manage logistics information, (3) more flexible and reliable transportation resources, and (4) improvements in the ability to position inventories so that they will be available *when* and *where* they are needed. Thus, organizations have been able to avail themselves of these improvements to shift the curve shown in Figure 9.4 to show how less inventory is needed today to drive improvements in customer service.

Key Differences Among Approaches to Managing Inventory

Given the various approaches to managing inventory that are available and used today, it is important to know how they differ. These differences include dependent versus independent demand, pull versus push, and system-wide versus single-facility solutions to inventory management decisions.

Dependent versus Independent Demand

Demand for a given inventory item is termed "independent" when such demand is unrelated to the demand for other items. Conversely, demand is defined as "dependent" when it is directly related, or derives from, the demand for another inventory item or product. For example, the demand for a desktop computer is *independent,* while the demand for its computer chip is dependent. This dependency can be *vertical* (the desktop needs the chip for assembly) or horizontal (the desktop needs an instruction manual for final delivery to customer).

So, for many manufacturing processes, basic demand for raw materials, component parts, and subassemblies depends on the demand for the finished product. In contrast, the demand for the end-use items, which are typically sold to a customer, is independent of the demand for any other higher-order manufactured item.

An important point to remember is that developing inventory policies for items exhibiting independent demand requires that forecasts be developed for these items. Alternatively, forecasting is less relevant for items having dependent demand, since the required quantities for these items depend entirely on the demand for the end-use product. So, once the difficult task of forecasting demand for end-use items is completed, determining the demand for dependent items requires simple calculations based on the bill of materials for that item.

Of the approaches to inventory management that will be discussed, just-in-time (JIT), materials requirement planning (MRP), and manufacturing resource planning (MRP II) are usually associated with items having dependent demand. Alternatively, DRP generally involves the movement of items having independent demand. The economic order quantity (EOQ) and vendor-managed inventory approaches apply to both independent and dependent demand items.

Pull versus Push

The "pull" approach relies on customer orders to move product through a logistics system, while the "push" approach uses inventory replenishment techniques in anticipation of demand to move products. For example, Dell has traditionally used the pull approach for the assembly of its computers. With little or no finished goods inventory for computers, Dell waits for a customer order for a computer before it begins assembly. Recently, however, Dell began selling a limited line of its computers through Wal-Mart retail stores. To do this, Dell employs the push model to anticipate future demand, assemble computers to inventory, and move them through its logistics system into Wal-Mart stores.

A principal attribute of pull systems is that they can respond quickly to sudden or abrupt changes in demand because they produce to an order and have very little, if no, finished goods inventory. This is especially true for products where the final addition of value can be postponed. Alternatively, push systems produce to inventory in anticipation of demand, thus making its ability to adapt to changing demand volumes and preferences limited.

Pull systems usually run on short-term forecasts, allowing them the flexibility to adapt to swings in demand. On the other hand, push systems use longer-term forecasts that allow for scale economies in manufacturing but result in high finished goods inventories. These high levels of finished goods inventories can make shelf life a problem in push systems, while this is not an issue for pull systems.

Characteristically, JIT is a pull system since organizations place orders for more inventory only when the amount on hand reaches a certain minimum level, thus "pulling" inventory through the logistics system as needed. Having established a master production schedule, MRP develops a time-phased approach to inventory scheduling receipt. Because they generate a list of required materials in order to assemble or manufacture a specific amount of finished products, MRP and MRP II approaches are push based. Similar to these, but on the outbound or physical distribution side of logistics, DRP involves the allocation of available inventory to meet market demands. Thus, DRP is also a push-based strategy. VMI uses preset reorder points and economic order quantities along with on-hand inventory levels in customers' warehouses to generate replenishment orders. Because the customer is not placing a replenishment order, VMI can be considered a push approach. Finally, the EOQ approach is generally a pull approach, but applications today include elements of the push approach as well. While this permits the EOQ technique to be reactive when necessary, it also allows the preplanning of certain inventory decisions in a proactive, or push, manner. In fact, many EOQ-based systems in evidence today are hybrid approaches that include elements of both pull- and push-based strategies.

System-Wide versus Single-Facility Solutions

A final inventory management issue is whether the selected approach represents a system-wide solution, or whether it is specific to a single facility, such as a distribution center. Basically, a system-wide approach plans and executes inventory decisions across multiple nodes in the logistics system. MRP and DRP are typically system-wide approaches to managing inventory. Both approaches plan inventory releases and receipts between multiple shipping and receiving points in the network. On the other hand, a single-facility approach plans and executes shipments and receipts between a single shipping point and receiving point. EOQ and JIT are normally considered single-facility solutions. Both release orders from a single facility to a specific supplier for inventory replenishment. Usually, MRP and DRP are employed to plan system inventory movements and EOQ and JIT are used to execute these plans at a single-facility level. VMI can be used to plan system-wide replenishment as well as execute replenishment on a single-facility basis.

Principal Approaches and Techniques for Inventory Management

In many business situations, the variables affecting the decision regarding the approach to inventory management are almost overwhelming. Therefore, models developed to aid in the decision process are frequently abstract or represent a simplified reality. In other words, models generally make simplifying assumptions about the real world they attempt to represent.

The complexity and accuracy of a model relate to the assumptions the model makes. Often, the more the model assumes, the easier the model is to work with and understand; however, simple model output is often less accurate. The model developer or user must decide on the proper balance between simplicity and accuracy.

The next several sections of this chapter contain an in-depth treatment of the inventory approaches previously mentioned: the fixed order quantity under conditions of certain and uncertain demand and lead time (also known as the economic order quantity approach), the fixed order interval approach, JIT, MRP, DRP, and VMI.

Fixed Order Quantity Approach (Condition of Certainty)

As its name implies, the **fixed order quantity** model involves ordering a fixed amount of product each time reordering takes place. The exact amount of product to be ordered depends on the product's cost and demand characteristics and on relevant inventory carrying and reordering costs.

Organizations using this approach generally need to develop a minimum stock level to determine when to reorder the fixed quantity. This is called the **reorder point**. When the number of units of an item in inventory reaches the reorder point, the fixed order quantity (the EOQ) is ordered. The reorder point, then, triggers the next order.

The fixed order quantity model is often referred to as the **two-bin** model. When the first bin is empty, the organization places an order. The amount of inventory in the second bin represents the quantity needed until the new order arrives. Both notions (trigger and bin) imply that an organization will reorder inventory when the amount on hand reaches the reorder point. The reorder point quantity depends on the time it takes to get the new order and on the demand for the item during this lead time. For example, if a new order takes 10 days to arrive and the organization sells or uses 10 units per day, the reorder point will be 100 units (10 days × 10 units/day).

Inventory Cycles

Figure 9.5 shows the fixed order quantity model. It shows three inventory cycles, or periods. Each cycle begins with 4,000 units, the fixed quantity ordered or produced. Reordering

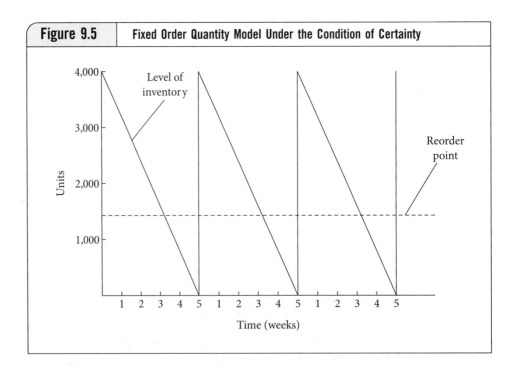

Figure 9.5 Fixed Order Quantity Model Under the Condition of Certainty

occurs when the inventory on hand falls to a level of 1,500 units (reorder point). Assuming that the demand or usage rate and the lead time length are constant and known in advance, the length of each cycle will be a constant five weeks. This is an example of the application of the fixed order quantity model under conditions of certainty.

As suggested earlier, establishing a reorder point provides a trigger or signal for reordering the fixed quantity. For example, many consumers have reorder points for personal purchases such as gasoline. When the fuel gauge reaches a certain level, such as one-eighth of a tank, the driver will pull into a gas station to refill the tank. This reorder point also serves the purpose of guaranteeing that a gasoline stockout (running out) does not occur during a trip.

Business inventory situations base the reorder point on lead time and the demand during lead time. The constant monitoring necessary to determine when inventory has reached the reorder point makes the fixed order quantity model a **perpetual inventory system**. Most inventory management systems today are automated with real-time consumption data to make this potentially time-consuming approach more easily achievable.

Simple EOQ Model

The following are the basic assumptions of the simple EOQ model:

1. A continuous, constant, and known rate of demand
2. A constant and known replenishment or lead time
3. All demand is satisfied
4. A constant price or cost that is independent of the order quantity (i.e., no quantity discounts)
5. No inventory in transit
6. One item of inventory or no interaction between items
7. Infinite planning horizon
8. Unlimited capital

The first three assumptions are closely related and basically mean that conditions of certainty exist. Demand in each relevant time period (daily, weekly, monthly) is known, and the usage rate is linear over time. The organization uses or depletes inventory on hand at a constant rate and knows the time needed to replenish stock. In other words, the lead time between order placement and order receipt is constant with no variability. As a result, the organization has no need to be concerned about stockouts and safety stock.

There is some concern that these three assumptions of certainty make the basic model too simplistic and, consequently, the outputs too inaccurate. Although this might be true in certain situations, several important reasons justify using the simple model. First, in some organizations, demand variation is so small that making the model too complex is too costly for the incremental accuracy achieved. Second, organizations just beginning to develop inventory models frequently find the simple EOQ model convenient and necessary because of the limited data available to them. Third, the simple EOQ model results are somewhat insensitive to changes in input variables. That is, variables such as demand, inventory carrying cost, and ordering cost can change without significantly affecting the calculated value of the economic order quantity.

The fourth assumption (constant costs) essentially means that quantity discounts do not exist. That is, the price of each unit remains the same, regardless of how much is ordered.

Assuming that there is no inventory in transit means that the organization purchases goods on a delivered price basis (purchase price includes transportation costs) and sells the goods FOB origin (the buyer pays the transportation costs). On the inbound side, this means that title to the goods does not pass until the buyer receives them. On the outbound side, title passes when the product leaves the shipping point. Under these assumptions, the organization has no responsibility for inventory in transit.

The sixth assumption means that the simple model is used to order one item of inventory at each order placement. The basic model easily handles the demand for a single, independent demand item with a single price. Introducing the calculation of an economic order quantity for more than one item into the simple model compounds the difficulty of the mathematics.

Assumptions seven and eight are most times decision made outside the logistics area. An infinite planning horizon assumes that constraints are not imposed on the length of the time periods that are included in the basic model. Unlimited capital means that there are no financial reasons to limit the quantity ordered.

Given the assumptions listed, the simple EOQ model considers only two basic types of cost: inventory carrying cost and ordering cost. The simple model arrives at an optimum decision that analyzes the tradeoffs between these two costs. If the model focused only on inventory carrying cost, which varies directly with changes in order quantity, the order quantity would be as small as possible (see Figure 9.6). If the model considered only ordering cost, large orders would decrease total order costs, and small orders would increase total order costs (see Figure 9.7). The lot size decision attempts to minimize total cost by reaching a compromise between these two costs (see Figure 9.8).

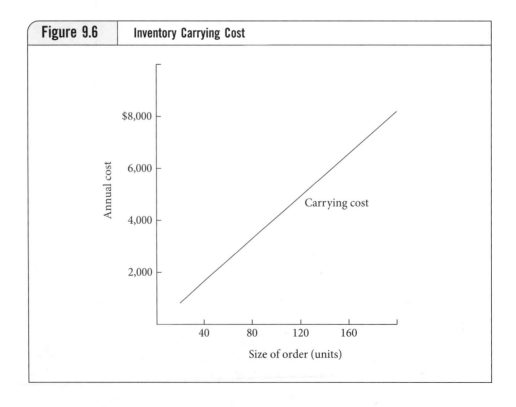

| **Figure 9.6** | **Inventory Carrying Cost** |

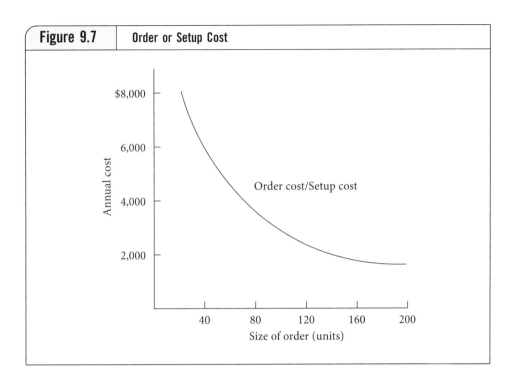

Figure 9.7 | Order or Setup Cost

Figure 9.8 | Inventory Costs

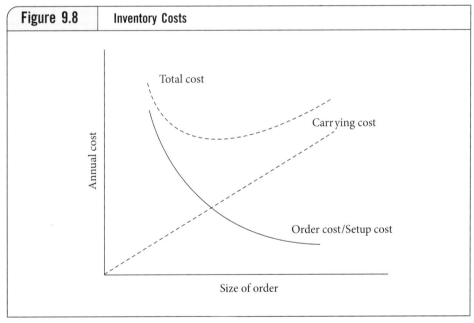

Mathematical Formulation

The EOQ model can be developed in standard mathematical form, using the following variables:

R = Annual rate of demand (units)

Q = Quantity ordered (units)

A = Cost of placing an order ($ per order)

V = Value or cost of one unit of inventory ($ per order)

W = Carrying cost per dollar value of inventory per year (% of product value)

$S = VW$ = Inventory carrying cost per unit per year ($ per unit per year)

t = Time (days)

TAC = Total annual cost ($ per year)

Given these variables, the total annual cost for a specific economic order quantity can be expressed as either Formula 9.3 or Formula 9.4.

$$\text{TAC} = \frac{1}{2}QVW + A\frac{R}{Q} \qquad\qquad 9.3$$

or

$$\text{TAC} = \frac{1}{2}QS + A\frac{R}{Q} \qquad\qquad 9.4$$

The first term on the right-hand side of the equation refers to annual inventory carrying cost; it states that these costs equal the average number of units in the economic order quantity during the order cycle (½Q) multiplied by the value per unit (V) multiplied by the carrying cost percentage (W). In Figure 9.9, called the **sawtooth model,** the equation's logic becomes more apparent. The vertical line labeled Q represents the amount ordered at a given time and the amount of inventory on hand at the beginning of each order cycle. During the order cycle (t), an organization depletes the amount of inventory on hand at a known and constant rate (represented by the slanted line). The average number of units on hand during the order cycle is simply one-half of the economic order quantity (Q). The broken horizontal line in Figure 9.9 represents average inventory. The logic is very simple. Assuming that Q equals 100 units and that daily demand is 10 units, 100 units would last 10 days (t). At the period's midpoint, the end of the fifth day, 50 units would still be left, which is one-half of Q (½ × 100). Another way to examine this is to assume that average inventory during a period is beginning inventory minus ending inventory divided by 2. Since the beginning inventory equals 100 units and the ending inventory equals zero units, 100 minus zero divided by 2 results in 50 units of average inventory.

Determining the average number of units is only part of the equation. Knowing the value per unit and the percentage carrying cost is still necessary. The larger the Q,

Figure 9.9	Sawtooth Model

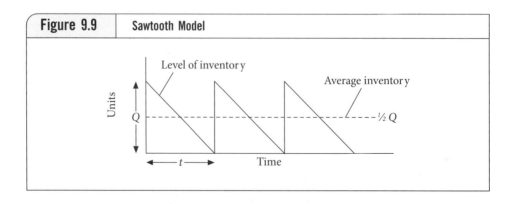

the higher the inventory carrying cost will be. This relationship was described earlier: as the order size increases, inventory carrying costs increase. Given constant demand, average inventory will increase as the economic order quantity increases (see Figures 9.10a and 9.10b).

The second term in Formulas 9.3 and 9.4 refers to annual ordering cost. Again, the cost to place an order is assumed to be constant, regardless of how much is ordered. Therefore, if Q increases, the number of orders placed per year will decrease, since annual demand is known and constant. Larger order quantities, then, will reduce annual ordering costs.

The discussion so far has focused on the general nature of annual inventory cost and annual ordering cost. The next step is to discuss the calculation of Q, the economic order

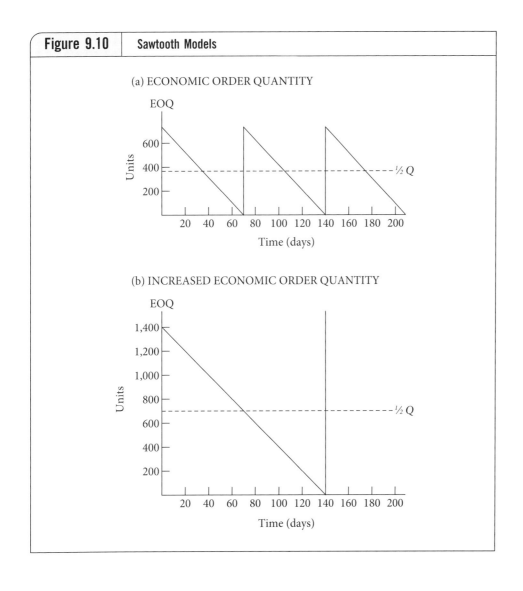

| Figure 9.10 | Sawtooth Models |

(a) ECONOMIC ORDER QUANTITY

(b) INCREASED ECONOMIC ORDER QUANTITY

quantity. As indicated previously, this involves a tradeoff between inventory carrying cost and ordering cost. Determining Q can be accomplished by differentiating the TAC function with respect to Q, as shown in Formula 9.5.

$$\text{TAC} = \frac{1}{2}QVW + A\frac{R}{Q}$$

$$\frac{d(\text{TAC})}{dQ} = \frac{VW}{2} - \frac{AR}{Q^2}$$

9.5

Setting $d(\text{TAC})/dQ$ equal to zero and solving for Q gives:

$$Q^2 = \frac{2RA}{VW}$$

or

$$Q = \sqrt{\frac{2RA}{VW}}$$

or

$$Q = \sqrt{\frac{2RA}{S}}$$

The following example illustrates how Formula 9.5 works:

$\quad V = \$100$ per unit

$\quad W = 25\%$

$\quad S = \$25$ per unit per year

$\quad A = \$200$ per order

$\quad R = 3{,}600$ units

To solve for Q, the example proceeds as shown in Formula 9.6.

$$Q = \sqrt{\frac{2RA}{VW}} \qquad Q = \sqrt{\frac{2RA}{S}}$$

$$Q = \sqrt{\frac{(2)(3{,}600)(\$200)}{(\$100)(25\%)}} \qquad Q = \sqrt{\frac{(2)(3{,}600)(\$200)}{\$25}}$$

9.6

$$Q = 240 \text{ units} \qquad Q = 240 \text{ units}$$

Analysis

Table 9.13 and Figure 9.11 show the proceeding solution's tradeoffs and logic. These illustrations show how inventory carrying cost, ordering cost, and total cost vary as Q ranges from a low of 100 units to a high of 500 units.

As Table 9.13 shows, the lower quantities of Q result in higher annual ordering costs but result in lower annual inventory carrying costs, as expected. As Q increases from 100 to 240 units, annual ordering costs decrease because the numbers of orders placed per year decreases while annual inventory carrying costs increase because of the higher average inventories. Beyond 240 units, the incremental increase in annual inventory carrying cost exceeds the incremental decrease in annual ordering cost, thereby increasing total annual cost.

Table 9.13	Total Costs for Various EOQ Amounts		
Q	ORDER COSTS AR/Q	CARRYING COST ½QVW	TOTAL COST
100	$7,200	$1,250	$8,450
140	5,143	1,750	6,893
180	4,000	2,250	6,250
220	3,273	2,750	6,023
240	3,000	3,000	6,000
260	2,769	3,250	6,019
300	2,400	3,750	6,150
340	2,118	4,250	6,368
400	1,800	5,000	6,800
500	1,440	6,250	7,690

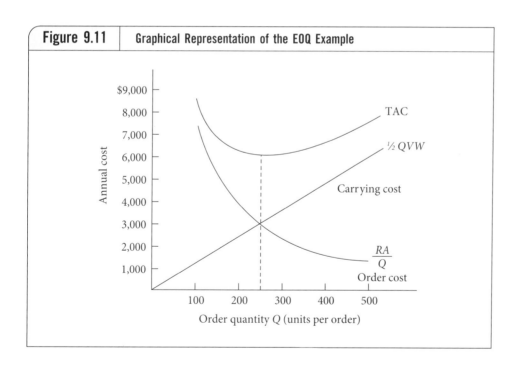

Figure 9.11 | Graphical Representation of the EOQ Example

By defining the optimum Q in total cost terms, the data in Table 9.13 show that a Q of 240 units is optimal (least total cost). Figure 9.11 also demonstrates this optimum level. Note, however, that the TAC curve between EOQ values of 180–200 units and 300–320 units is quite shallow. This means that the inventory manager can alter the EOQ considerably without significantly affecting TAC.

Reorder Point

A previous discussion indicated that knowing when to order was as necessary as knowing how much to order. The *when,* called the reorder point, depends on the inventory level on hand. Under the assumptions of certainty, an organization needs only enough inventory to last during the replenishment time or lead time. Therefore, given a known lead time, multiplying lead time length by daily demand determines the reorder point.

Replenishment time consists of several components: order transmittal, order processing, order preparation, and order delivery. The time for each depends on factors such as the means used to transmit the order (electronic versus manual), the inventory availability at the supplier, and the transportation mode used for delivery. Factors affecting lead time will be discussed later in this chapter.

Using the previous example, assume that order transmittal takes one day, order processing and preparation take two days, and order delivery takes five days. This results in a replenishment or lead time of eight days. Given that demand is 10 units per day (3,600 units/360 days), the reorder point will be 80 units (8 days × 10 units per day).

A Note Concerning the Min-Max Approach

One widely used adaptation of the fixed order quantity approach is the **min-max inventory management approach**. With the traditional approach, inventory will deplete in small increments, allowing an organization to initiate a replenishment order exactly when inventory reaches the reorder point.

The min-max approach applies when demand might be larger and when the amount on hand might fall below the reorder point before the organization initiates a replenishment order. In this case, the min-max approach increments the amount ordered by the difference between the reorder point and the amount on hand. In effect, this technique identifies the minimum amount that an organization should order so that inventory on hand will reach a predetermined maximum level when the organization receives the order. While the min-max approach is very similar to the EOQ approach, individual order amounts will tend to vary under the min-max approach.

Summary and Evaluation of the Fixed Order Quantity Approach

Traditionally, the EOQ approach has been a cornerstone of effective inventory management. While not always the fastest way to respond to customer demand, the fixed order quantity approach has been a widely used technique.

Recently, however, many organizations have become more sophisticated in their use of EOQ-based approaches, adapting them to include a push as well as a pull orientation. As a result, many EOQ-based systems effectively blend both push and pull concepts. As indicated earlier, push, or proactive, inventory management approaches are far more prevalent in organizations having greater logistics sophistication.

One principal shortcoming of the EOQ-based approach is that it suits inventory decision making at a single facility more than it suits decision making at multiple locations in a logistics network. Also, the EOQ approach sometimes encounters problems when parallel points in the same logistics system experience peak demands simultaneously. This happens, for example, when many consumers simultaneously stock up on groceries before a major snowstorm. The EOQ approach alone, reacting to demand levels only as they occur, would respond too slowly to replenish needed inventory.

As stated at the outset, the simple EOQ approach, though somewhat unrealistic because of the number of assumptions it requires, is still useful because it illustrates the logic of inventory models in general. Actually, organizations can adjust the simple model to handle more complex situations. Appendix 9A covers applications of the EOQ approach in four special instances: (1) when an organization must consider the cost of inventory in transit, (2) when volume transportation rates are available, (3) when an organization uses private transportation, and (4) when an organization utilizes in-excess freight rates.

Typically, organizations associate EOQ-based approaches with independent, rather than dependent, demand. However, the EOQ approach can also be used for dependent demand items. The overall approach explicitly involves carrying calculated average inventory amounts; the tradeoffs among inventory, order, and expected stockout costs justify carrying these amounts.

Fixed Order Quantity Approach (Conditions of Uncertainty)

Under the assumptions used until now, the reorder point was based on the amount of inventory on hand and demand was known and constant. When inventory on hand reached zero, a new order was received in an economic order quantity and stockout costs were not incurred. Although assuming such conditions of certainty might be useful to simplify inventory models, these conditions do not represent the normal situations faced by most organizations today.

Most organizations would not operate under conditions of certainty for a variety of reasons. First, consumers usually purchase products somewhat sporadically. The demand rates for many products vary depending on weather, social needs, physical needs, and a whole host of other factors. As a result, the demand for most products varies by day, week, and season.

In addition, several factors can affect lead time. For example, transit times can and do change, particularly over long distances, despite transportation provider efforts. Factors such as weather, highway congestion, port congestion, and border stops can make transit times very unreliable. In fact, transit time reliability is a major factor used by organizations when they are making both mode and carrier decisions.

Other factors that can cause variations in lead time are order transmittal and processing. Although a significant amount of orders today are transmitted electronically, many are still sent through the U.S. Post Office. Mailed orders can be subject to the same unreliability in transit time as mentioned previously. During order processing, factors such as credit blocks and inventory unavailability can cause delays in orders proceeding through the system.

Because of all the potential factors that can influence the reliability of demand and lead time, inventory models need to be adjusted to account for this uncertainty. Figure 9.12 shows the fixed order quantity model adjusted for uncertainty in demand and lead time. This figure varies from the model introduced in Figure 9.5 in three ways. First, demand (affecting on-hand inventory levels) in Figure 9.5 was known and constant. This is why the on-hand inventory line in Figure 9.5 always begins the

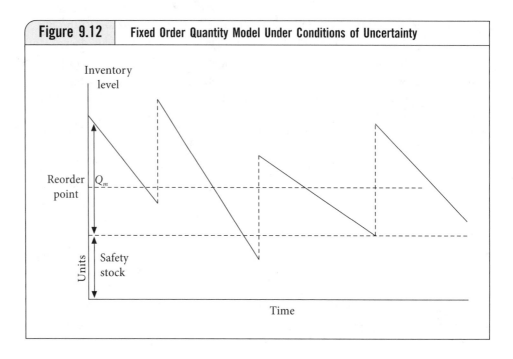

Figure 9.12 | **Fixed Order Quantity Model Under Conditions of Uncertainty**

period at the EOQ amount and ends the period at zero units. This same line in Figure 9.12 fluctuates above the EOQ amount and below zero units because demand is not known or constant. Second, the lead time (or cycle) in Figure 9.5 is known and constant at five weeks, resulting in a very uniform "sawtooth" pattern. When lead time is not known or constant, as shown in Figure 9.12, the length of the period (or lead time) varies resulting in an uneven spacing between orders. Finally, Figure 9.5 makes no allowances for stockouts since its assumptions present conditions of certainty. In Figure 9.12, the uncertainty of demand and lead time makes necessary the addition of safety stock to prevent stockouts. The amount of safety stock to be held will depend on the variability around demand and lead time and the service customers require.

Reorder Point—A Special Note

As noted previously, the reorder point under the basic model is the on-hand inventory level needed to satisfy demand during lead time. Calculating the reorder point is relatively easy since demand and lead time are constant. Under uncertainty, an organization must reformulate the reorder point to allow for safety stock. In effect, the reorder point becomes the average daily demand during lead time plus the safety stock, as Figure 9.12 shows. The following discussion clarifies this recalculation.

Uncertainty of Demand

The first factor that might cause uncertainty deals with demand or usage rate. While focusing on this variable, the following assumptions concerning EOQ still apply:

1. A constant and known replenishment or lead time

2. A constant price or cost that is independent of order quantity or time

3. No inventory in transit

4. One item of inventory or no interaction between items

5. Infinite planning horizon

6. No limit on capital availability

In discussing demand, logistics managers emphasize balancing the cost of carrying safety stock against the cost of a stockout (lost sales).

In a fixed quantity model with an established reorder point, introducing uncertainty into the analysis initially affects the inventory level needed to cover demand during lead time. Recall that in the previous example, conditions of certainty resulted in an EOQ of 240 units and a reorder point of 100 units. In other words, the inventory period began with 240 units on hand, and reordering occurred when inventory reached a level of 100 units.

The fact that demand will vary—and that the time that elapses between a level of 240 units and 100 units might vary—is not critical to the inventory problem when conditions of uncertainty exist. Determining whether 100 units is the best amount to have on hand at the start of the lead time cycle *is* critical. Thus, raising the reorder level accounts for safety stock. However, raising it too high will leave too much stock on hand when the next order arrives. Setting it too low will result in a stockout.

Using the previous problem, assume that the organization's demand during lead time ranges from 100 units to 160 units, with an average of 130 units. Also assume that demand has a discrete distribution varying in 10-unit blocks and that the organization has established probabilities for these demand levels (see Table 9.14).

In effect, the organization must consider seven different reorder points, each corresponding to a possible demand level as shown in Table 9.14. Using these reorder points, the matrix in Table 9.15 can be developed.

While Table 9.15 shows many of the possible situations confronting the organization, it does not use information from the probability distribution of demand. Using the probability of demand would allow the organization with seven possible reorder points to determine the expected units "short" or "in excess" at each point during lead time.

Assume that the organization incurs a stockout cost (k) of $10 per unit whenever a customer demands a unit that is not in inventory. The profit lost on the immediate sale and future sales is an opportunity cost.

Table 9.14	Probability Distribution of Demand During Lead Time

DEMAND (UNITS)	PROBABILITY
100	0.01
110	0.06
120	0.24
130	0.38
140	0.24
150	0.06
160	0.01

Table 9.15	Possible Units of Inventory Short or in Excess During Lead Time with various Reorder Points						
	REORDER POINTS						
ACTUAL DEMAND	100	110	120	130	140	150	160
100	**0**	10	20	30	40	50	60
110	−10	**0**	10	20	30	40	50
120	−20	−10	**0**	10	20	30	40
130	−30	−20	−10	**0**	10	20	30
140	−40	−30	−20	−10	**0**	10	20
150	−50	−40	−30	−20	−10	**0**	10
160	−60	−50	−40	−30	−20	−10	**0**

Inventory carrying cost associated with safety stock is calculated the same way as it was for calculating carrying cost for the simple EOQ model. The value per unit is still assumed to be $100, and the percentage annual inventory carrying cost is still 25 percent. Remember that the percentage figure is for the annual cost of inventory stored in the warehouse. Therefore, the $25 derived by multiplying 25 percent by $100 is the annual cost per unit of inventory in the warehouse. The $25 contrasts with the $10 stock-out cost, which is a unit cost per cycle of order period. Therefore, as Table 9.16 shows, multiplying $10 by the number of cycles or orders per year translates this cost into an annual basis.

Table 9.16 develops expected units short or in excess by multiplying the number of units short or in excess by the probabilities associated with each demand level. The numbers below (shorts) and above (in excess) the horizontal line are added, as the lower portion of Table 9.16 shows, to find the number of units the organization expects to be short or in excess at each of the seven possible reorder points. The variables for this calculation are as follows:

e = Expected excess in units

g = Expected shorts in units

k = Stockout cost in dollars per unit stocked out

$G = gk$ = Expected stockout cost per cycle

$G\left(\dfrac{R}{Q}\right)$ = Expected stockout cost per year

eVW = Expected carrying cost per year for excess inventory

After performing the calculations indicated in Table 9.16, the total cost for each of the seven reorder points may be calculated. In this instance, the lowest total cost corresponds to the reorder point of 140 units. Although this number does not guarantee an excess or shortage in any particular period, it gives the overall lowest total cost per year: $390.

Note that the number of orders used in Step 5 of Table 9.16 came from the preceding problem with conditions of certainty. This number was the only information available at

| Table 9.16 | Expected Number of Units Short or in Excess | | | | | | | |

		REORDER POINTS						
ACTUAL DEMAND	PROBABILITIES	100	110	120	130	140	150	160
100	0.01	**0.0**	0.1	0.2	0.3	0.4	0.5	0.6
110	0.06	−0.6	**0.0**	0.6	1.2	1.8	2.4	3.0
120	0.24	−4.8	−2.4	**0.0**	2.4	4.8	7.2	9.6
130	0.38	−11.4	−7.6	−3.8	**0.0**	3.8	7.6	11.4
140	0.24	−9.6	−7.2	−4.8	−2.4	**0.0**	2.4	4.8
150	0.06	−3.0	−2.4	−1.8	−1.2	−0.6	**0.0**	0.6
160	0.01	−0.6	−0.5	−0.4	−0.3	−0.2	−0.1	**0.0**
CALCULATION OF LOWEST COST REORDER POINT								
1. Expected excess per cycle (of values above diagonal line) (e)		0.0	0.1	0.8	3.9	10.8	20.1	30.0
2. Expected carrying cost per year (VW)		$0	$2.50	$20.00	$97.50	$270	$502.50	$750
3. Expected shorts per cycle (of values below diagonal line) (g)		30.0	20.1	10.8	3.9	0.8	0.1	0.0
4. Expected stockout cost per cycle (gK) = G		$300	$201	$108	$39	$8	$1	$0
5. Expected stockout cost per year (G$\frac{R}{Q}$)		$4,500	$3,015	$1,620	$585	$120	$15	$0
6. Expected total cost per year (2 + 5)		$4,500	$3,017.50	$1,640	$682.50	$390	$517.50	$750

that point. Now the total cost model can be expanded to include the safely stock and stockout cost. Formula 9.7 represents he expanded equation.

$$\text{TAC} = \frac{1}{2}QVW + A\frac{R}{Q} + (eVW) + \left(G\frac{R}{Q}\right) \qquad 9.7$$

Solving for the lowest total cost gives Formula 9.8.

$$\frac{d(\text{TAC})}{dQ} = \left[\frac{1}{2}VW\right] - \left[\frac{R(A + G)}{Q^2}\right] \qquad 9.8$$

Setting this equal to zero and solving for Q results in Formula 9.9.

$$Q = \sqrt{\frac{2R(A + G)}{VW}} \qquad 9.9$$

Using the expanded model and the computed reorder point of 140 units, a new value for Q can be calculated as shown in Formula 9.10.

$$Q = \sqrt{\frac{2 \times 3{,}600 \times (200 + 8)}{\$100 \times 25\%}} \qquad \text{9.10}$$

$$= 245 \text{ units approximately}$$

Note that Q is now 245 units with conditions of uncertainty. Technically, this would change the expected stockout cost for the various reorder points in Table 9.16. However, the change is small enough to ignore in this instance. In other cases, recalculations might be necessary. The optimum solution to the problem with conditions of uncertainty is a fixed order quantity of 245 units, and the organization will reorder this amount when inventory reaches a level of 140 units (the calculated reorder point).

Finally, this situation requires a recalculation of total annual cost as shown in Formula 9.11.

$$\begin{aligned}
\text{TAC} &= \frac{1}{2}QVW + A\frac{R}{Q} + eVW + G\frac{R}{Q} \\
&= \left(\frac{1}{2} \times 245 \times \$100 \times 25\%\right) + \left(200 \times \frac{3{,}600}{245}\right) \\
&\quad + (10.8 \times \$100 \times 25\%) + \left(8 \times \frac{3{,}600}{245}\right) \qquad \text{9.11} \\
&= \$3{,}062.50 + \$2{,}938.78 + \$270 + \$117.55 \\
&= \$6{,}389
\end{aligned}$$

The \$6,389 figure indicated what happens to total annual cost when conditions of uncertainty with respect to demand are introduced into the model. Introducing other factors, such as the lead time factor, would increase costs even more.

Uncertainty of Demand and Lead Time Length

This section considers the possibility that both demand and lead time might vary and builds on the preceding section in attempting to make this inventory approach more realistic. As expected, however, determining how much safety stock to carry will be noticeably more complex now than when only demand varied (the mathematical determination of safety stock when both demand and lead time vary was covered at the beginning of this chapter).

As in the previous section, the critical issue is just how much product customers will demand during the lead time. If demand and lead time are constant and known, calculating the reorder point (as was done in the section covering the case of certainty) would be easy. Now that both demand and lead time might vary, the first step is to identify the likely distribution of demand during the lead time. Specifically, the mean and standard deviation of demand during lead time must be estimated.

Figure 9.13 illustrates two key properties of a normal distribution. These concepts were covered earlier in this chapter, but it is important to revisit them here in the context of the fixed order quantity model under uncertainty. First, the normal distribution is symmetrical, with approximately 68.26 percent of all observations within one standard deviation around the mean, 95.44 percent within two standard

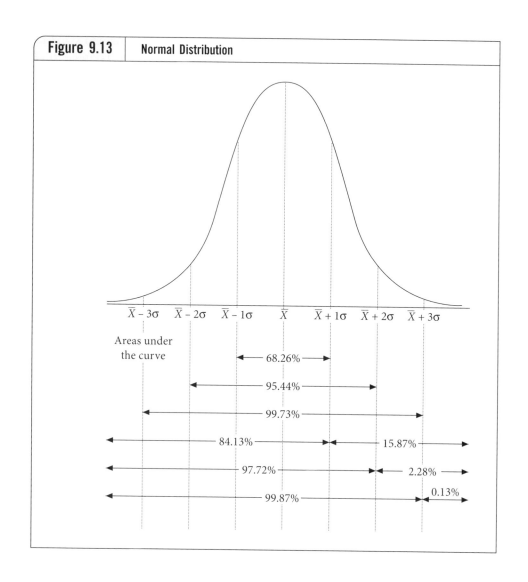

Figure 9.13 | Normal Distribution

deviations, and 99.73 percent within three standard deviations. Second, in the normal distribution, the mode (highest point or most observations) equals the mean (average).

After calculating values for the mean and standard deviation of demand during lead time, the stockout probability for each particular reorder point can be described. For example, assume that Figure 9.13 represents the demand distribution during lead time. Setting the reorder point equal to $\overline{X} + 1\sigma$ will result in an 84.13 percent probability that lead time demand will not exceed the inventory amount available. Increasing the reorder point to $\overline{X} + 2\sigma$ raises the probability of not incurring a stockout to 97.72 percent; reordering at $\overline{X} + 3\sigma$ raises this probability to 99.87 percent. Note that in the case of uncertainty, increasing the reorder point has the same effect as increasing the safely stock commitment. An organization must ultimately find some means to justify carrying this additional inventory.

Borrowing Formula 9.1 previously presented in this chapter, the mean and standard deviation for demand during lead time can be calculated as shown in Formulas 9.12 and 9.13.

$$\overline{X} = SR \qquad\qquad 9.12$$

$$\sigma = \sqrt{R(\sigma_S)^2 + S^2(\sigma_R)^2} \qquad\qquad 9.13$$

where:

$\overline{X}$ = Average demand during lead time (units)

σ = Standard deviation of demand during lead time (units)

R = Average replenishment cycle (days)

σ_R = Standard deviation of replenishment cycle (days)

S = Average daily demand (units)

σ_S = Standard deviation of daily demand (units)

For example, if the mean and standard deviation of daily demand are 20 and four units, respectively, and if the mean and standard deviation of lead time are eight and two days, respectively, then the mean and standard deviation of demand during lead time can be calculated as shown in Formula 9.14.

$$
\begin{aligned}
\overline{X} &= SR \\
&= 20(8) \qquad\qquad 9.14 \\
&= 160 \text{ units}
\end{aligned}
$$

$$
\begin{aligned}
\sigma &= \sqrt{R(\sigma_S)^2 + S^2(\sigma_R)^2} \\
&= \sqrt{(8)(4)^2 + (20)^2(2)^2} \\
&= \sqrt{1{,}728} \\
&= 41.57 \text{ or } 42 \text{ units}
\end{aligned}
$$

Using the procedure suggested earlier, setting the reorder point at $X + 1\sigma$, or 202 units, reveals an 84.13 percent probability that demand during lead time will not exceed the inventory available. Stated differently, the probability of a stockout is only 15.87 percent (100% − 84.13%) when the reorder point is set at one standard deviation from the mean. Table 9.17 shows these figures and the ones computed for setting the reorder point at two and three standard deviations from the mean. An organization should thoroughly compare the financial and customer service benefits of avoiding stockouts with the cost of carrying additional safely stock before choosing a reorder point.

Table 9.17	Reorder Point Alternatives and Stockout Possibilities	
REORDER POINT	**PROBABILITY OF NO STOCKOUT OCCURRING**	**PROBABILITY OF A STOCKOUT SITUATION**
$\overline{X} + 1\alpha = 202$	84.13%	15.87%
$\overline{X} + 2\alpha = 244$	97.72%	2.28%
$\overline{X} + 3\alpha = 286$	99.87%	0.13%

Fixed Order Interval Approach

The second form of the basic approach is the **fixed order interval** approach to inventory management, also called the **fixed period** or **fixed review period** approach. In essence, this technique involves ordering inventory at fixed or regular intervals; generally, the amount ordered depends on how much is in stock and available at the time of review. Organizations usually count inventory near the interval's end and base orders on the amount on hand at that time.

In comparison with the basic EOQ approach, the fixed interval model does not require close surveillance of inventory levels; thus, the monitoring is less expensive. This approach is best used for inventory items that have a relatively stable demand. Using this approach for volatile demand items might quickly result in a stockout since time triggers orders rather than inventory levels.

If demand and lead time are constant and known in advance, then an organization using the fixed order interval approach will periodically reorder exactly the same amount of inventory. If either demand or lead time varies, however, the amount ordered each time will vary, becoming a result of demand as well as lead time length. For example, as Figure 9.14 indicates, an organization starting each period with 4,000 units and selling 2,500 units before its next order will have to reorder 2,500 units plus the units it anticipates selling during the lead time to bring inventory up to the desired beginning level of 4,000 units. Figure 9.14 shows an instance in which the amount ordered differs from one five-week period to the next.

Like the fixed order quantity approach to inventory management, the fixed order interval approach typically combines elements of both the pull and push philosophies. This shows again how organizations, in an effort to anticipate demand rather than simply react to it, are developing systems that incorporate the push philosophy.

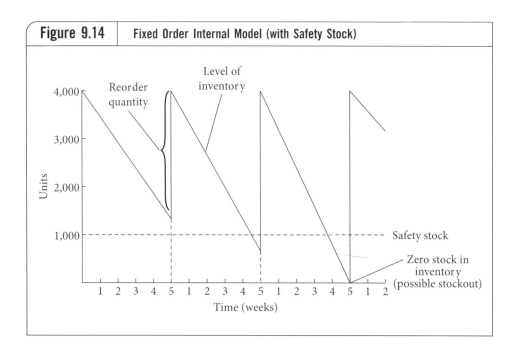

| Figure 9.14 | Fixed Order Internal Model (with Safety Stock) |

Summary and Evaluation of EOQ Approaches to Inventory Management

Arguments exist that there are really four basic forms of the EOQ inventory model: fixed quantity/fixed interval, fixed quantity/irregular interval, irregular quantity/fixed interval, and irregular quantity/irregular interval. In an organization that knows demand and lead time with certainty, either the basic EOQ or the fixed order interval approaches will be the best choices (and would produce the same results). If either demand or lead time varies, however, approach selection must consider the potential consequences of a stockout. In instances involving A (high importance) items, a fixed quantity/irregular interval approach might be the best. The irregular quantity/fixed interval approach might be the best when C (low importance) items are involved. Only under very restrictive circumstances could an organization justify using the irregular quantity/irregular interval approach to inventory management.

The fixed order quantity (EOQ) and fixed order interval approaches have proven to be effective inventory management tools when demand and lead time are relatively stable, as well as when significant variability and uncertainty exist. Most importantly, using these approaches requires that the inherent logistics tradeoffs be considered when making inventory decisions.

Organizations today that are expanding beyond the basic order quantity and order interval approaches have had considerable success with concepts such as JIT, MRP, MRP II, and DRP, which are the next topics of discussion. Keep in mind that all of these techniques for managing inventory incorporate some version of the basic EOQ model into their philosophies.

Additional Approaches to Inventory Management

The management of inventory levels in the supply chain has often been the underlying rationale for the focus on supply chain management. The interest in reducing inventory levels along the supply chain is indicative of the importance of inventory as a cost of doing business. In many organizations, inventory is the first or second largest asset on the balance sheet.

Organizations, therefore, can reduce their costs of doing business and improve their return on investment or assets (ROI/ROA) by decreasing inventory levels. Keep in mind that service levels are important constraints when decreasing inventories. It should also be noted that the investment in inventory can add value by reducing costs in other areas, such as manufacturing and transportation, or enhance revenue through better service levels. Therefore, the cost and benefit tradeoffs of maintaining inventory in the supply chain must be considered when striving to achieve a balanced view of inventory.

In the following sections, several approaches to inventory management that have special relevance to supply chain management will be examined: JIT, MRP, and DRP.

The Just-in-Time Approach

One of the most common approaches to inventory management is the just-in-time approach. In today's business environment, discussions focus on JIT manufacturing processes, JIT inventories, or JIT delivery systems. The underlying theme of the phrase "just-in-time" suggests that inventories should be available when an organization needs them—not any earlier or later. This section emphasizes additional factors that characterize a true just-in-time system.

Definition and Components of JIT Systems

Generally, just-in-time systems are designed to manage lead times and to eliminate waste. Ideally, product should arrive exactly when an organization needs it, with no tolerance for late or early deliveries. Many JIT systems place a high priority on short, consistent lead times. However, in a true JIT system, the length of the lead time is not as important as the reliability of the lead time.

The JIT concept is an Americanized version of the **Kanban** system, which the Toyota Motor Company developed in Japan. *Kanban* refers to the cards attached to carts delivering small amounts of needed components and other materials to locations within manufacturing facilities. Each card precisely details the necessary replenishment quantities and the exact time when the replenishment activity must take place.

Production cards *(kan* cards) establish and authorize the amount of product to be manufactured; requisition cards (ban cards) authorize the withdrawal of needed materials from the supply operation. Given knowledge of daily output volumes, these activities can be accomplished manually, without the need for computer assistance. Finally, an **Andon system,** or light system, is used as a means to notify plant personnel of existing problems—a yellow light for a small problem and a red light for a major problem. Either light can be seen by personnel throughout the plant. In this way, workers are advised of the possibility of an interruption to the manufacturing process, if the problem warrants such action.[3]

Experience indicates that effectively implementing the JIT concept can dramatically reduce parts and materials inventories, work-in-process inventories, and finished product. In addition, the Kanban and JIT concepts rely heavily on the quality of the manufactured product and components and on a capable and precise logistics system to manage materials and physical distribution.

Four major elements underlie the JIT concept: zero inventories; short, consistent lead times; small, frequent replenishment quantities; and high quality, or zero defects. JIT is an operating concept based on delivering materials in exact amounts and at the precise times that organizations need them—thus minimizing inventory costs. JIT can improve quality and minimize waste and completely change the way an organization performs its logistics activities. JIT, as practiced by many organizations, is more comprehensive than an inventory management system. It includes a comprehensive culture of quality, supplier partnerships, and employee teams.

The JIT system operates in a manner very similar to the two-bin or reorder point system. The system uses one bin to fill demand for a part; when that bin is empty (the signal to replenish the part), the second bin supplies the part. Toyota and other organizations have been very successful with this system because of its master production schedule, which aims to schedule every product, every day, in a sequence that intermixes all parts. Manufacturing products in small quantities through short production runs also creates a relatively continuous demand for supplies and component parts. In theory, the ideal lot size or order size for a JIT-based system is one unit. Obviously, this encourages organizations to reduce or eliminate setup costs and incremental ordering costs.

By adhering to extremely small lot sizes and very short lead times, the JIT approach can dramatically reduce lead times. For example, when manufacturing forklift trucks, Toyota experienced a cumulative material lead time of one month, including final assembly, subassembly, fabrication, and procurement. Other manufacturers of forklift trucks cited lead times ranging from six to nine months.[4]

JIT versus EOQ Approaches to Inventory Management

Table 9.18 highlights key ways in which the JIT philosophy differs from customary inventory management in many organizations. The next section discusses these differences.

First, JIT attempts to eliminate excess inventories for both the buyer and the seller. Some feeling exists that the JIT concept simply forces the seller to carry inventory previously held by the buyer. However, successful JIT applications will significantly reduce inventories for both parties.

Second, JIT systems typically involve short production runs and require production activities to change frequently from one product to another. This approach minimizes the economies of scale that are generated from long production runs of a single product. It also will result in higher changeover costs, assuming that the cost of each changeover is constant. However, shorter production runs will result in lower finished goods inventory levels. So, the tradeoff here is between changeover costs and finished goods inventory levels. Many organizations have been successful at reducing changeover costs, thus taking advantage of lower inventory costs.

Third, JIT minimizes wait times by delivering materials and products when and where an organization needs them. Automobile manufacturers, using JIT, have components and parts delivered to the assembly line when needed, where needed, and in the exact quantity.

Fourth, the JIT concept uses short, consistent lead times to satisfy the need for inventory in a timely manner. This is why many suppliers tend to locate their facilities close to their customers who are planning to use the JIT approach. Short lead times reduce cycle stock inventories; consistent lead times reduce safety stock inventories. Of the two components of lead time, consistency is more important. That is, a short lead time for JIT success is not as important as a consistent lead time.

Table 9.18	EOQ versus JIT Attitudes and Behaviors	
FACTOR	**EOQ**	**JIT**
Inventory	Asset	Liability
Safety stock	Yes	No
Production runs	Long	Short
Setup times	Amortize	Minimize
Lot sizes	EOQ	1 for 1
Queues	Eliminate	Necessary
Lead times	Tolerate	Shorter
Quality inspection	Important parts	100% process
Suppliers/customers	Adversaries	Partners
Supply sources	Multiple	Single
Employees	Instruct	Involve

Source: Adapted from William M. Boyst, III, "JIT American Style," *Proceedings of the 1988 Conference of the American Production & Inventory Control Society* (APICS, 1988): 468.

Fifth, JIT-based systems rely on high-quality incoming parts and components and on exceptionally high-quality inbound logistics systems. The fact that JIT systems synchronize manufacturing and assembly with timely, predictable receipt of inbound materials reinforces this need.

Sixth, the JIT concept requires a strong, mutual commitment between the buyer and the seller, one that emphasizes quality and seeks win-win decisions for both parties. JIT success requires a concern for minimizing inventory throughout the distribution channel (or the supply channel); JIT will not succeed if organizations only push inventory back to another channel partner.

Summary and Evaluation of JIT

The just-in-time concept can enable logistics managers to reduce unit costs and to enhance customer service. A close examination of JIT-based approaches shows that they resemble the more reactive systems such as the EOQ and fixed order quantity approaches, since JIT is demand responsive.

The principal difference between JIT and the more traditional approaches is the JIT commitment to short, consistent lead times and to minimizing or eliminating inventories. In effect, JIT saves money on downstream inventories by placing greater reliance on improved responsiveness and flexibility. Ideally, the use of JIT helps to synchronize the logistics system so thoroughly that its operation does not depend on inventories strategically located at points throughout the logistics system.

Successful JIT applications also place a high priority on efficient and dependable manufacturing processes. Since JIT systems require the delivery of parts and materials when and where the demand arises, they rely heavily on the accuracy of the forecasting process used to anticipate finished product demand. In addition, timely JIT system operation demands effective and dependable communications and information systems, as well as high-quality consistent transportation services.

Materials Requirements Planning

Another inventory and scheduling approach that has gained wide acceptance is **materials requirements planning**. Originally popularized by Joseph Orlicky, MRP deals specifically with supplying materials and component parts whose demand depends on the demand for a specific end product. MRP's underlying concepts have existed for many years, but only recently have technology and information systems permitted organizations to benefit fully from MRP and to implement such an approach.

Definition and Operation of MRP Systems

An MRP system consists of a set of logically related procedures, decision rules, and records designed to translate a master production schedule into time-phased net inventory requirements and the planned coverage of such requirements for each component item needed to implement this schedule. An MRP system recalculates net requirements and coverage as a result of changes in the master production schedule, demand, inventory status, or product composition. MRP systems meet their objectives by computing net requirements for each inventory item, time-phasing them, and determining their proper coverage.[5]

The goals of an MRP system are to (1) ensure the availability of materials, components, and products for planned production and for customer delivery; (2) maintain the lowest possible inventory levels that support service objectives; and (3) plan manufacturing activities, delivery schedules, and purchasing activities. In doing so, an MRP system considers

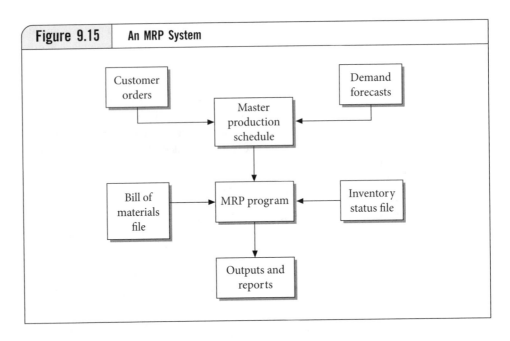

Figure 9.15   An MRP System

current and planned quantities of parts and products in inventory, as well as the timing needed for these parts and products.

MRP begins by determining how much end products (independent demand items) customers desire and when they are needed. Then MRP disaggregates the timing and need for components based on the end-product demand. Figure 9.15 shows how an MRP system operates by using the following key elements:

- **Master production schedule (MPS).** Based on actual customer orders as well as on demand forecasts, the master production schedule drives the entire MRP system. The MPS details exactly what independent demand items an organization must produce and when they are needed. In other words, the MPS provides a detailed schedule of the production timing and quantities for various products.

- **Bill of materials file (BOM).** Just as a recipe specifies the ingredients needed to bake a cake, the bill of materials file specifies the exact amount of raw materials, components, and/or subassemblies needed to produce an independent demand item. Besides identifying gross requirements as needed quantities, the BOM specifies when the individual inputs must be available for the production process. This file also identifies how the various inputs relate to one another and shows their relative importance to producing the end product. Therefore, if several components with different lead times need to be combined as a subassembly, the BOM will indicate this relationship.

- **Inventory status file (ISF).** This file maintains inventory records so that the organization may subtract the amount on hand from the gross requirements, thus identifying the net requirements at any point in time. The inventory status file also contains important information on specifics such as safety stock and lead time requirements. The ISF plays a critical role in maintaining the MPS and helping to minimize inventory.

- **MRP program.** Based on the independent item need specified in the MPS and on information from the BOM, the MRP program first disaggregates the end-product demand into gross requirements for individual parts and/or other materials. Then the program calculates net requirements based on ISF information and places orders for the inputs necessary for the production process. The orders respond to needs for specific quantities of materials and to the timing of those needs. The example in the next section clarifies these MRP program activities.

- **Outputs and reports.** After an organization runs the MRP program, several basic outputs and reports will help managers involved in logistics and manufacturing. Included are records and information related to the following: (1) quantities the organization should order and when they should be ordered, (2) any need to expedite or reschedule arrival dates of needed input quantities, (3) canceled need for product, and (4) MRP system status. These reports are key to controlling the MRP system and in complex environments are reviewed every day to make appropriate modifications and provide information.

Example of an MRP System

To understand the MRP approach more fully, consider an organization that assembles egg timers. Assume that according to the MPS, the organization desires to assemble a single, finished egg timer for delivery to a customer at the end of eight weeks. The MRP application would proceed as follows.

Figure 9.16 shows the BOM for assembling a single egg timer. The gross requirements for one finished product include two ends, one bulb, three supports, and one gram of sand. Figure 9.16 also shows that the organization must add the gram of sand to the bulb before assembling the finished egg timer.

Table 9.19 displays the ISF for the egg timer example and calculates the net requirements as the difference between gross requirements and the amount of inventory on hand. The table also notes the lead time for each component. For example, the lead

| Figure 9.16 | Relationship of Parts to Finished Product: MRP Egg Timer Example |

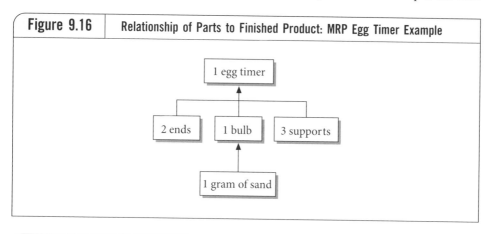

| Table 9.19 | Inventory Status File: MRP Egg Timer Example |

PRODUCT	GROSS REQUIREMENTS	INVENTORY ON HAND	NET REQUIREMENTS	LEAD TIME (IN WEEKS)
Egg timers	1	0	1	1
Ends	2	0	2	5
Supports	3	2	1	1
Bulbs	1	0	1	1
Sand	1	0	1	4

time needed to procure supports and bulbs is one week, whereas sand needs four weeks and ends require five. Once all components are available, the time needed to assemble the finished egg timer is one week.

Finally, Figure 9.17 is the master schedule for all activities relating to ordering and receiving components and assembling the finished egg timer. Because the organization

---

Figure 9.17   Master Schedule: MRP Egg Timer Example

EGG TIMERS (LT=1)	1	2	3	4	5	6	7	8
Quantity needed								1
Production schedule							1	

ENDS (LT=5)	1	2	3	4	5	6	7	8
Gross requirements							2	
Inventory on hand	0	0	0	0	0	0	0	
Scheduled receipts							2	
Planned order releases		2						

SUPPORTS (LT=1)	1	2	3	4	5	6	7	8
Gross requirements							3	
Inventory on hand	2	2	2	2	2	2	2	
Scheduled receipts							1	
Planned order releases						1		

BULBS (LT=1)	1	2	3	4	5	6	7	8
Gross requirements							1	
Inventory on hand	0	0	0	0	0	0	0	
Scheduled receipts							1	
Planned order releases						1		

SAND (LT=4)	1	2	3	4	5	6	7	8
Gross requirements						1		
Inventory on hand	0	0	0	0	0	0		
Scheduled receipts						1		
Planned order releases		1						

must have the single egg timer assembled and ready for customer delivery at the end of eight weeks, appropriate parts quantities must be available in the seventh week. The upper portion of Figure 9.17 shows this requirement.

Working backward from the need for parts in the seventh week, the lower portions of Figure 9.17 identify strategies for ordering and receiving component inventories. For example, for two ends requiring a lead time of five weeks, the organization must place an order in the second week. For the one additional support requiring a lead time of a single week, the organization should release an order during the sixth week. Finally, the organization must order the bulb in the sixth week for delivery in the seventh and order the sand in the second week for delivery in the sixth.

This example illustrates how the MRP-based approach relates to inventory scheduling and inventory control. In effect, the MRP program itself would perform the calculations involved in Figure 9.17. Once the program develops the master schedule, reports present this information in a format suitable for a manager's use.

In practice, MRP is exceptionally suitable for planning and controlling the ordering and receipt of large numbers of parts and products that might interact during assembly or manufacture. Organizations such as Dell and Boeing use the MRP approach to assembling computers and aircraft, respectively. With the exception of very simple problems such as the egg timer example, computer technology is virtually a prerequisite to using MRP-based applications.

Summary and Evaluation of MRP Systems

Having established the MPS, the MRP program develops a time-phased approach to inventory scheduling and inventory receipt. Because it generates a list of required materials in order to assemble or manufacture a specified number of independent demand items, MRP represents a push approach. Correspondingly, this encourages purchase order and production order development. Typically, MRP applies primarily when the demand for parts and materials depends on the demand for some specific end product.

Since actual demand is key to the establishment of production schedules, MRP systems can react quickly to changing demand for finished products. Although some JIT proponents feel that a pull approach is inherently more responsive than a push approach such as MRP, the reverse is sometimes true. MRP systems can also help organizations to achieve other typical JIT objectives, such as those pertaining to lead time management and elimination of waste. In short, MRP can achieve objectives more commonly associated with the JIT-based approaches, while at times decisions made through the pull concept do not reflect the future events for which the JIT policies are intended.

The principal advantages of most MRP-based systems include the following:

- They attempt to maintain reasonable safety stock levels and to minimize or eliminate inventories whenever possible.
- They can identify process problems and potential supply chain disruptions long before they occur and take the necessary corrective actions.
- Production schedules are based on actual demand as well as on forecasts of independent demand items.
- They coordinate materials ordering across multiple points in an organization's logistics network.
- They are more suitable for batch, intermittent assembly, or project processes.

Shortcomings of MRP-based approaches include the following:

- Their application is computer intensive, and making changes is sometimes difficult once the system is in operation.
- Both ordering and transportation costs might rise as an organization reduces inventory levels and possibly moves toward a more coordinated system of ordering product in smaller amounts to arrive when the organization needs it.
- They are not usually as sensitive to short-term fluctuations in demand as are order point approaches (although they are not as inventory intensive, either).
- They frequently become quite complex and sometimes do not work exactly as intended.[6]

A Note Concerning MRPII Systems

Manufacturing resource planning has a far more comprehensive set of tools than MRP alone. Although MRP is a key step in MRPII, MRPII allows an organization to integrate financial planning and operations/logistics.

MRPII serves as an excellent planning tool and helps describe the likely results of implementing strategies in areas such as logistics, manufacturing, marketing, and finance. Thus, it helps an organization to conduct "what if?" analyses and to determine appropriate product movement and storage strategies at and between points in the logistics system.

MRPII is a technique used to plan and manage all of the organization's resources and reaches far beyond inventory or even production control to all planning functions of an organization.[7] MRPII is a holistic planning technique that can draw together all of the corporate functional areas into an integrated whole. The ultimate benefits of MRPII include improved customer service through fewer shortages and stockouts, better delivery performance, and responsiveness to changes in demand. Successfully implementing MRPII should also help to reduce inventory costs, reduce the frequency of production line stoppages, and create more planning flexibility.[8]

Distribution Requirements Planning

Distribution requirements planning is a widely used and potentially powerful technique for outbound logistics systems to help determine the appropriate level of inventory to be held to meet both cost and service objectives. DRP determines replenishment schedules between an organization's manufacturing facilities and its distribution centers. The success stories involving DRP indicate that organizations can improve service (decrease stockouts), reduce the overall level of finished goods inventories, reduce transportation costs, and improve distribution center operations. With this potential, it is no wonder that manufacturers are interested in the capabilities of DRP systems.

DRP is usually coupled with MRP systems in an attempt to manage the flow and timing of both inbound materials and outbound finished goods. This is particularly true in industries where numerous inbound items are needed to produce a finished product, as is the case in the automobile industry. Items that need to be combined and used in the assembly of a finished product usually have varying lead times. Therefore, MRP is tied to the master production schedule, which indicates what items are to be produced each day and the sequence in which they will be produced. This schedule is then used as the basis to forecast the number of parts needed and when they will be needed.

The underlying rationale for DRP is to more accurately forecast demand and to explode that information back for use in developing production schedules. In that way,

Table 9.20	DRP Table for Chicken Noodle Soup								
COLUMBUS DISTRIBUTION CENTER—DISTRIBUTION RESOURCE PLANNING									
WEEK	JAN. 1	2	3	4	FEB. 5	6	7	8	MAR. 9
CHICKEN NOODLE: Current BOH = 4,314; Q = 3,800; SS = 1,956; LT = 1									
Forecast	974	974	974	974	989	1,002	1,002	1,002	1,061
Sched. Receipt	0	0	3,800	0	0	0	3,800	0	0
BOH—ending	3,340	2,366	5,192	4,218	3,229	2,227	5,025	4,023	2,962
Planned order	0	3,800	0	0	0	3,800	0	0	3,800
Actual order	Q = Quantity SS = Safety stock LT = Lead time								

Source: A. J. Stenger, "Distribution Resources Planning," Penn State University, class example.

an organization can minimize inbound inventory by using MRP in conjunction with production schedules. Outbound (finished goods) inventory is minimized through the use of DRP.

DRP develops a projection for each SKU and requires the following:[9]

- Forecast of demand for each SKU
- Current inventory level of the SKU (balance on hand, BOH)
- Target safety stock
- Recommended replenishment quantity
- Lead time for replenishment

This information is used to develop replenishment requirements at each distribution center. One of the key elements of a DRP system is the development of a DRP table, which consists of a variety of elements including the SKU, BOH, scheduled receipt, planned orders, and so on. Table 9.20 illustrates the DRP table for chicken noodle soup at the Columbus distribution center. The table shows only nine weeks, but a DRP table would typically show 52 weeks and be a dynamic document that undergoes continual change as the data, especially demand, changed. Individual tables provide useful information, but combining tables can produce an increased advantage. For example, combining all of the individual SKU tables of items shipped from one source can provide useful information about transportation consolidation opportunities and when to expect orders to arrive at a distribution center. Essentially, the combining of tables helps to develop efficient production plans and shipping plans, as illustrated in Figure 9.18.

Summary and Evaluation of DRP

DRP systems accomplish for outbound shipments what MRP accomplishes for inbound shipments. The focal point for combining these two systems is the manufacturing facility, where the optimum flow of material is critical. DRP is an example of a push approach and can be used for both single-facility and system-wide applications. The key to a successful DRP approach is having accurate demand forecasts by SKU by

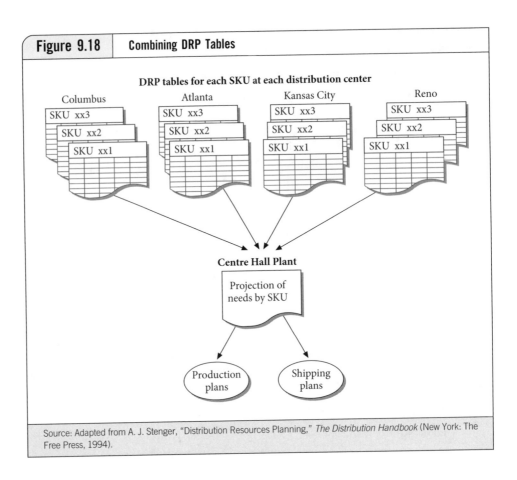

Figure 9.18 | **Combining DRP Tables**

DRP tables for each SKU at each distribution center

Columbus

SKU xx3
SKU xx2
SKU xx1

Atlanta

SKU xx3
SKU xx2
SKU xx1

Kansas City

SKU xx3
SKU xx2
SKU xx1

Reno

SKU xx3
SKU xx2
SKU xx1

Centre Hall Plant

Projection of needs by SKU

Production plans

Shipping plans

Source: Adapted from A. J. Stenger, "Distribution Resources Planning," *The Distribution Handbook* (New York: The Free Press, 1994).

distribution center. Consolidating this demand by SKU and incorporating lead times and safely stock requirements allows the manufacturing facility to determine the master production schedule. Once the MPS is determined, MRP can be used to coordinate the flow and timing of material into the manufacturing facility so it can meet the desired shipments to the distribution centers. So, combining MRP with DRP results in an approach that coordinates the flow of materials from raw materials suppliers through the manufacturing facility (where finished goods are produced) and on to the distribution centers to meet the shipment demands of customers.

Vendor-Managed Inventory

The inventory techniques discussed so far are usually used to manage inventories *within* an organization's logistics network. JIT and MRP manage raw materials and component inventories on the inbound side of a manufacturing facility. DRP manages finished goods inventories between the manufacturing facility and its distribution centers. A relatively new inventory management technique, vendor-managed inventory, manages inventories *outside* an organization's logistics network. In other words, VMI is used by an organization to manage its inventories held in its customer's distribution centers.

The concept of VMI was initiated by Wal-Mart so its suppliers could manage their inventories within Wal-Mart distribution centers. The basis of this concept was that suppliers could manage their inventories better than Wal-Mart. As such, suppliers took responsibility for making sure that their products were always available in Wal-Mart distribution centers when stores demanded them. VMI has since been adopted by many other organizations across multiple industries.

The basic principles underlying the concept of VMI are relatively simple. First, the supplier and its customer agree on which products are to be managed using VMI in the customer's distribution centers. Second, an agreement is made on reorder points and economic order quantities for each of these products. Third, as these products are shipped from the customer's distribution center, the customer notifies the supplier, by SKU, of the volumes shipped on a real-time basis. This notification is also called "pull" data. That is, as the customer "pulls" a product from storage to be shipped to a store or other facility, the supplier is notified that the product has been pulled for shipment, thus diminishing on-hand inventories. Fourth, the supplier monitors on-hand inventories in the customer's distribution center and when the on-hand inventory reaches the agreed-upon reorder point, the supplier creates an order for replenishment, notifies the customer's distribution center of the quantity and time of arrival, and ships the order to replenish the distribution center. So, the customer has no need to place an order for replenishment; through real-time information sharing, the supplier has knowledge of product demand and "pushes" inventory to the customer's location.

VMI was traditionally used for independent demand items between suppliers and retailers. However, organizations like Dell are allowing component suppliers to use VMI to manage their inventories in third-party warehouses located near Dell assembly plants. So, VMI can be used for both independent and dependent demand items.

Many organizations are now using VMI in conjunction with CPFR (discussed in Chapter 7) to manage system-wide inventories. Remember that CPFR is a concept that allows suppliers and their customers to mutually agree upon system-wide demand for products. Since CPFR is used to develop the system-wide plan, organizations need a technique to execute those plans on a system-wide and facility basis. This is where VMI plays a role. VMI can be used to monitor system inventories as well as facility inventories and use these data to help validate the CPFR plan.

The use of VMI to manage inventories is not affected by which organization *owns* those inventories. Traditionally, suppliers using VMI shipped products to customer distribution centers under the FOB destination concept. That is, the supplier owned the inventory in transit, but ownership transferred once the product was received by the customer's distribution center. So, the supplier was managing its inventories, but the customer maintained ownership. Some customers have been investigating the use of what can be called **almost consignment inventory** in their distribution centers. In this scenario, the supplier manages and owns the inventory in the customer's distribution centers until that inventory is pulled for shipment. Under the almost consignment concept, suppliers have the challenge of minimizing their inventory investment in their customer's distribution centers while making sure that a sufficient amount of inventory is available to meet demand.

A major benefit of VMI is the knowledge gained by the supplier of real-time inventory levels of its products at its customer locations. This allows the shipper more time to react to sudden swings in demand to assure that stockouts do not occur. A drawback of VMI is that sometimes suppliers use VMI to push excess inventory to a customer distribution center at the end of the month in order to meet monthly sales quotas. This results in the customer holding extra inventory, adding costs to their operations.

All of the inventory techniques discussed to this point have subtle differences and similarities. However, they all use some form of the EOQ and reorder point techniques. Remember that the EOQ and reorder point techniques answer the questions of *how*

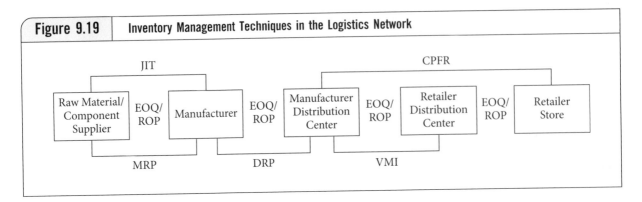

| Figure 9.19 | Inventory Management Techniques in the Logistics Network |

much and *when.* JIT, MRP, DRP, and VMI all strive to ship the proper quantity at the proper time. As such, all use the EOQ and reorder point techniques. Figure 9.19 is an attempt to show where all these inventory techniques fit into the logistics network. In this figure, a retail network is used. As an inventory technique manages inventory closer to the point of real demand (e.g., VMI and CPFR), forecast accuracy increases, forecast cycles decrease, and product availability increases. Many organizations today use all of these techniques in managing inventories in their logistics networks.

The discussion so far has focused on techniques for managing raw materials, component, and finished goods inventories in a logistics network. One assumption that has been made is that all items are held at all stocking points, thus simplifying the use of these techniques. However, demand levels and variability, as well as lead time levels and variability, are not consistent among items produced by an organization. The next section will address the concept of inventory evaluation, which requires an organization to assess not only which items are most important but also where they will be stored to meet demand.

Classifying Inventory

Multiple product lines and inventory control require organizations to focus on more important inventory items and to utilize more sophisticated and effective approaches to inventory management. Inventory classification is usually a first step toward efficient inventory management. Many techniques exist that can be used to classify inventory. However, the discussion in the following section will focus on one of the more basic and popular techniques.

ABC Analysis

The need to rank inventory items in terms of importance was first recognized in 1951 by H. Ford Dicky of General Electric (GE).[10] He suggested that GE classify items according to relative sales volume, cash flows, lead time, or stockout costs. He used what is now referred to as **ABC analysis**. This classification technique assigns inventory items to one of three groups according to the relative impact or value of the items that make up the group. A items are considered to be the most important, with B items being of lesser importance, and C items being the least important. Important to remember here is that the criteria used to evaluate an item will determine the group to which it is assigned. Using revenue per item as the criterion might assign Item 1 to the A group, while using profit per item as the criterion might assign Item 1 to the C group. Determining which criteria to use for inventory classification will depend on the goals the organization is trying to achieve. Also remember that an organization might determine that it needs more or less than three groupings.

Pareto's Law, or the "80–20 Rule"

Actually, ABC analysis is rooted in Pareto's law, which separates the "trivial many" from the "vital few."[11] In inventory terms, this suggests that a relatively small number of items or SKUs might account for a considerable impact or value on the organization. A nineteenth-century Renaissance man, Vilfredo Pareto, suggested that many situations were dominated by a relatively few vital elements and that the relative characteristics of members of a population were not uniform.[12,13] His principle that a relatively small percentage of a population might account for a large percentage of the overall impact or value has been referred to as the "80–20 rule," which has been found to exist in many practical situations.

For example, marketing research might find that 20 percent of an organization's customers account for 80 percent of its revenues; a university might find that 20 percent of its courses generate 80 percent of its student credit hours; or a study might find that 20 percent of a city's population account for 80 percent of its crime. Although the actual percentages might differ somewhat from example to example, some variation of the 80–20 rule usually applies.

Inventory Illustration

Figure 9.20 demonstrates ABC analysis as it applies to inventory management. The diagram indicates that only 20 percent of the items in the product line account for 80 percent of total sales. The items that make up this 20 percent are referred to as A items, because of the significant portion of sales for which they are responsible. The items in the B category account for approximately 50 percent of the items in the product line, yet contribute only an additional 15 percent of total sales. Finally, the C items are represented by the remaining 30 percent of the items which account for approximately 5 percent of total sales.

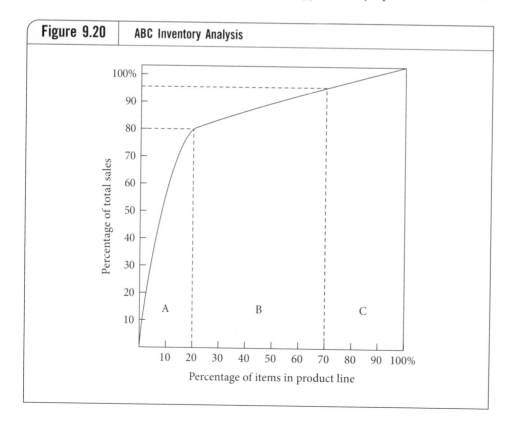

Figure 9.20 | **ABC Inventory Analysis**

In many ABC analyses, a common mistake is to think of the B and C items as being far less important than the A items and, subsequently, to focus most or all of management's attention on the A items. For example, a decision might be made to assure very high in-stock levels for A items and little or no availability for the B and C items. The fallacy here relates to the fact that all items in the A, B, and C categories are important to some extent and that each category of items deserves its own strategy to assure availability at an appropriate level of cost (stockout cost versus inventory carrying cost). This thinking has led some organizations to differentiate inventory stocking policies by ABC category, making sure that the A items are available either immediately or through the use of express logistics services. The B and C items, while perhaps available at an upstream location in the logistics channel, could be available in a timely manner when needed.

The importance of the B and C items should not be overlooked for a number of additional reasons. Sometimes, the use of B and C items might be complementary to the use of A items, meaning the availability of B and C items might be necessary for the sale of A items; or, in some instances, the C items might be new products that are expected to be successful in the future.

Performing an ABC Classification

ABC classification is relatively simple. The first step is to select some criterion, such as revenue, for developing the ranking. The next step is to rank items in descending order of importance according to this criterion and to calculate actual and cumulative total revenue percentages for each item. This calculation will allow the items to be grouped into the ABC categories.

Table 9.21 shows how to base an ABC inventory analysis on revenue generated per line item. The first column identifies the 10 items in the Big Orange product line. The

Table 9.21	ABC Analysis for Big Orange Products, Inc.				
ITEM CODE	ANNUAL REVENUE	PERCENTAGE OF ANNUAL REVENUE	CUMULATIVE REVENUE	PERCENTAGES ITEMS	CLASSIFICATION CATEGORY
64R	$ 6,800	68.0%	68.0%	10.0%	A
89Q	1,200	12.0	80.0	20.0	A
68I	500	5.0	85.0	30.0	B
37S	400	4.0	89.0	40.0	B
12G	200	2.0	91.0	50.0	B
35B	200	2.0	93.0	60.0	B
61P	200	2.0	95.0	70.0	B
94L	200	2.0	97.0	80.0	C
11T	150	1.5	98.5	90.0	C
20G	150	1.5	100.0	100.0	C
	$10,000	100.0%			

second and third columns show the annual revenue and percentage of total annual revenue represented by each item. The fourth and fifth columns show revenue and items, respectively, as percentages of the total. From these columns, it is simple to identify what percentage of items makes up what percentage of revenue. The last column places each item into the ABC classification on the basis of annual revenue.

The last step assigns the items into ABC groups. This step is the most difficult, and no simple technique is available. While the analysis is supported by data inputs, the ultimate decisions will require subjective judgment on the part of the decision maker. As the item rankings are examined, significant natural "breaks" sometimes appear. This is not always the case, and the decision maker will have to consider other variables such as the item's importance and the cost of managing that item.

ABC analysis can also be used in various situations using various criteria to group "items." A warehouse manager might assign inventory items to groups using item velocity as the criterion. A marketing manager might assign customers to groups using customer profitability as the criterion. A sales manager might assign sales representatives to groups using gross revenue generated as the criterion. Other classification schemes using ABC analysis might use multiple criteria to rank items, such as profit per item times item turnover. The point here is that items can be classified in many ways, using various criteria, resulting in various groupings. The use of ABC analysis to rank items will depend on the goals management needs to accomplish.

Quadrant Model

Another technique used to classify inventory is called the **quadrant model**. Typically used to classify raw materials, parts, or components for a manufacturing firm, the quadrant model can also be used to classify finished goods inventories using value and risk to the firm as the criteria. Value is measured as the value contribution to profit; risk is the negative impact of not having the product available when it is needed. Figure 9.21 shows an example of a quadrant model. When needed, items with high value and high risk (critical items) need to be managed carefully to ensure adequate supply. Items with low risk and low value (generic or routine items) can be managed much less carefully. Each

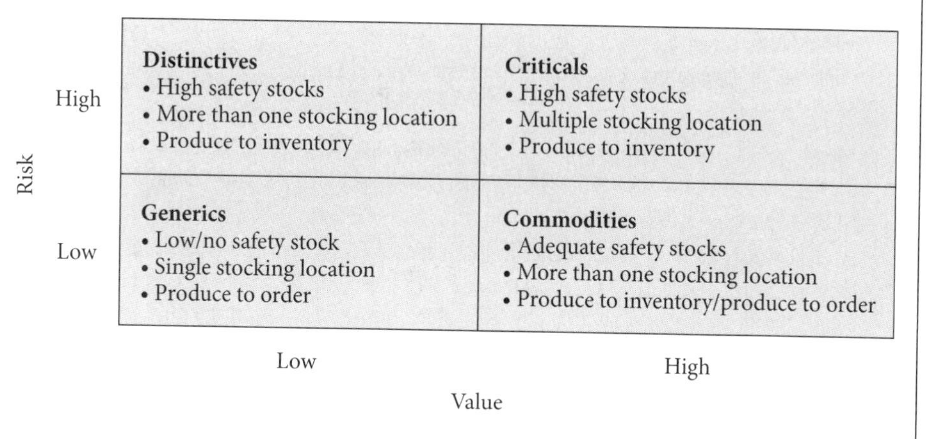

Figure 9.21 Quadrant Model

particular classification in the quadrant model not only suggests stocking policies but also production policies. For example, items in the commodities group (low value/high risk) might be stored in only one location and/or might be produced only when an order exists. Items in the criticals group might have high levels of safety stock and are always produced to inventory. The quadrant model combines more than one criterion to group items into a category. From that grouping, decisions concerning logistics and manufacturing can be made. The impact of inventory classification on stocking decisions will be the topic of the next section.

Inventory at Multiple Locations— The Square-Root Rule

In their aggressive efforts to take costs out of logistics networks, organizations are searching for new ways to reduce inventory levels without adversely affecting customer service. One current approach is to consolidate inventories into fewer stocking locations in order to reduce overall inventories and their associated costs. This strategy requires the involvement of capable transportation and information resources to assure that customer service is held at existing levels and improved whenever possible.

The **square-root rule** helps determine the extent to which inventories might be reduced through such a consolidation strategy. Assuming that total customer demand

---

On the Line   *Procter & Gamble to Cut Inventory Locations by 50%*

Procter & Gamble has seen its profits fall under double digits for the past few years. One move to improve the picture is to reduce its asset base. Calling the move "Distribution Reinvention," the company will reduce its worldwide distribution centers (DCs) from 450 to approximately 225 over the next two years.

Accompanying the slimming down of P&G's physical infrastructure is a reorganization of its logistics operations through a boost in product demand velocity. That means increased shipping frequency for some of the company's faster moving products as well as a new approach in its transport asset management for some other market offerings. For transportation, this will reportedly involve creating a better balance in the management of truckload and less-than-truckload shipments to improve the costs of its transportation and to improve supply chain relationships with retail customers.

Not only is the hope to reduce stockouts for retailers, but P&G is also seeking to create new logistics capabilities for what it deems high-value products with distinctive marketing patterns, most notably in its Gillette products.

In support of its evolving logistics strategy, P&G has increased its production base in developing countries over the past 10 years. It now produces 30 percent of its goods in these countries. The output is both for consumption within these countries as well as for export to P&G's more traditional markets.

Source: Logistics Today (February 2007): 14.

remains the same, the square-root rule estimates the extent to which aggregate inventory need will change as an organization increases or decreases the number of stocking locations. In general, the greater the number of stocking locations, the greater the amount of inventory needed to maintain customer service levels. Conversely, as inventories are consolidated into fewer stocking locations, aggregate inventories will decrease.

The square-root rule states that total safety stock inventories in a future number of facilities can be approximated by multiplying the total amount of inventory in existing facilities by the square root of the number of future facilities divided by the number of existing facilities. Mathematically, this relationship can be stated as shown in Formula 9.15.

$$X_2 = (X_1)\sqrt{n_2/n_1} \qquad\qquad 9.15$$

where:

n_1 = Number of existing facilities

n_2 = Number of future facilities

X_1 = Total inventory in existing facilities

X_2 = Total inventory in future facilities

To illustrate, consider an organization that currently distributes 40,000 units of product to its customers from a total of eight facilities located throughout the United States. Current distribution centers are located in Boston, Chicago, San Francisco, Los Angeles, Dallas, Orlando, Charlotte, and Baltimore. The organization is evaluating an opportunity to consolidate its operations into two facilities, one in Memphis and the other in Reno/Sparks, Nevada. Using the square-root rule, the total amount of inventory in the two future facilities is computed as shown in Formula 9.16.

$n_1 = 8$ existing facilities

$n_2 = 2$ future facilities $\qquad\qquad$ 9.16

$X_1 = 40,000$ total units of product in the 8 existing facilities

thus,

$$\begin{aligned} X_2 &= \text{total units of product in the 2 future facilities} \\ &= (40,000)\sqrt{2/8} \\ &= (40,000)(0.5) \\ &= 20,000 \ \text{units} \end{aligned}$$

Based on the results of this analysis, the two future facilities would carry a total inventory of 20,000 units to satisfy existing demand. If the organization designed these facilities to be of equal size, and if market demand was equal for the geographic areas, each of these distribution centers would carry one-half of this total, or 10,000 units each. Conversely, if the organization considered increasing the number of distribution centers from 8 to, say 32, total inventory needs would double from 40,000 to 80,000 units.

Using data from an actual organization, Table 9.22 shows the total average units of inventory implied by specific numbers of distribution centers in the logistics network. For example, as stocking locations increase from 1 to 25, the total average number of units in inventory increases from 3,885 units to 19,425 units. This is consistent with the rationale underlying the square-root rule. Table 9.22 also shows the percentage change in inventories as the number of distribution centers in the network increases.

Table 9.22	Example Impacts of Square-Root Rule on Logistics Inventories		
NUMBER OF WAREHOUSES (n)	$\sqrt{n}$	TOTAL AVERAGE INVENTORY (UNITS)	PERCENT CHANGE
1	1.0000	3,885	—
2	1.4142	5,494	141%
3	1.7321	6,729	173%
4	2.0000	7,770	200%
5	2.2361	8,687	224%
10	3.1623	12,285	316%
15	3.8730	15,047	387%
20	4.4721	17,374	447%
23	4.7958	18,632	480%
25	5.0000	19,425	500%

Although the square-root rule is simply stated, the model is based on several reasonable assumptions: (1) inventory transfers between stocking locations are not common practice; (2) lead times do not vary, and thus inventory centralization is not affected by inbound supply uncertainty; (3) customer service levels, as measured by inventory availability, are constant regardless of the number of stocking locations; and (4) demand at each location is normally distributed.[14] In addition, it has been shown that the potential for aggregate inventory reduction through consolidation of facilities will be greater when the correlation sales between stocking locations is small to negative and when there is less sales variability at each of the stocking locations.[15]

Combining the square-root rule with ABC analysis further explains why aggregate inventories are reduced when stocking locations are reduced. Using the example above, assume all eight distribution centers carry A, B, and C items with their associated safety stocks. Reducing the number of stocking points to 2 has two results: (1) redundant safety stocks are eliminated because now there are two quantities of safety stocks rather than eight and (2) the organization has the option of further reducing inventories by consolidating C items into one of the two future facilities. In other words, both safety stocks and cycle stocks can be reduced by consolidating facilities as well as by consolidating inventories. So, facility, as well as inventory, consolidation can result in significant reductions in inventories for organizations.

SUMMARY

- Inventory as a percent of overall business activity continues to decline. Explanatory factors include greater expertise in managing inventory, innovations in information technology, greater competitiveness in markets for transportation services, and emphasis on reducing cost through the elimination of non-value-adding activities.

- As product lines proliferate and the number of SKUs increases, the cost of carrying inventory becomes a significant expense of doing business.

- There are a number of principal reasons for carrying inventories. Types of inventory include cycle stock, work-in-process, inventory in transit, safety stock, seasonal stock, and anticipatory stock.

- Principal types of inventory cost are inventory carrying cost, order/setup cost, expected stockout cost, and in-transit inventory carrying cost.

- Inventory carrying cost is composed of capital cost, storage space cost, inventory service cost, and inventory risk cost. There are precise methods to calculate each of these costs.

- Choosing the appropriate inventory model or technique should include an analysis of key differences that affect the inventory decision. These differences are determined by the following questions: (1) Is the demand for the item independent or dependent? (2) Is the distribution system based upon a push or pull approach? (3) Do the inventory decisions apply to one facility or to multiple facilities?

- Traditionally, inventory managers focused on two important questions to improve efficiency, namely, how much to reorder from suppliers and when to reorder.

- The two aforementioned questions were frequently answered using the EOQ model, trading inventory carrying cost against ordering costs, and then calculating a reorder point based on demand or usage rates.

- The two basic forms of the EOQ model are the fixed quantity model and the fixed interval model. The former is the most widely used. Essentially, the relevant costs are analyzed (traded off), and an optimum quantity is decided. This reorder quantity will remain fixed unless costs change, but the intervals between orders will vary depending on demand.

- The basic EOQ model can be varied or adapted to focus more specifically on decisions that are impacted by inventory-related costs, such as shipment quantities where price discounts are involved.

- Just-in-time inventory management captured the attention of many U.S. organizations during the 1970s, especially the automobile industry. As the name implies, the basic goal is to minimize inventory levels with an emphasis on frequent deliveries of smaller quantities and alliances with suppliers or customers. To be most effective, JIT should also include quality management.

- Materials requirements planning and distribution requirements planning are typically used in conjunction with each other. In addition, a master production schedule is utilized to help balance demand and supply of inventory. DRP is used on the outbound side of a logistics system. Demand forecasts of individual SKUs are developed to drive the DRP model. Then, an MPS schedule is developed to meet the scheduled demand replenishment requirements.

- VMI is used to manage an organization's inventories in its customers' distribution centers. Using pull data, suppliers monitor inventory levels and create orders to ship product to bring inventory levels up to an economic order quantity in the customers' distribution centers.

- ABC analysis is a useful tool to improve the effectiveness of inventory management. Another useful tool is the quadrant model.

- When organizations are adding warehouses to their logistics networks, a frequently asked question is, "How much additional inventory will be required?" The square-root rule is a technique that can be used to help answer this question.

STUDY QUESTIONS

1. Explain why inventory costs and inventory levels have declined relative to GDP over the last 20 years. Is this beneficial to the economy? Why or why not?

2. What are the major components of inventory carrying cost? How would you measure capital cost for making inventory policy decisions?

3. How can inventory carrying cost be calculated for a specific product? What suggestions would you offer for determining the measure of product value to be used in this calculation?

4. Explain the differences between inventory carrying costs and ordering costs.

5. Why is it usually more difficult to determine the cost of lost sales for finished goods than it is for raw materials inventories?

6. How does inventory carrying cost for inventory in transit differ from the cost of inventory at rest?

7. What is the difference between independent and dependent demand items? Why is this distinction important to inventory managers?

8. Compare and contrast the fixed quantity version of EOQ with the fixed interval version. In which situations would each be used?

9. Why has the JIT approach to inventory control become popular in some industries? How does the JIT approach compare to the EOQ approach to inventory management? Should JIT be adopted by all inventory managers? Why or why not?

10. Explain the essential characteristics of MRP, DRP, and VMI. How do they operate with each other to provide a systematic approach to managing supply chain inventories?

11. What are the benefits of classifying inventory using ABC analysis? What are the different types of criteria that could be used to classify inventory?

12. What is the underlying principle of the square-root rule? How do inventories change as the number of warehouses in a logistics network changes?

NOTES

1. Douglas M. Lambert, *The Development of an Inventory Costing Methodology: A Study of the Costs Associated with Holding Inventory* (Oak Brook, IL: National Council of Physical Distribution Management, 1976).

2. Douglas M. Lambert and James R. Stock, *Strategic Logistics Management*, 3rd ed. (Homewood, IL: Irwin, 1993): 378–379.

3. Walter E. Goddard, "Kanban or MRPII—Which Is Best for You?" *Modern Materials Handling* (November 5, 1982): 42.

4. Ibid., 45–46.

5. Joseph Orlicky, *Materials Requirements Planning* (New York, NY: McGraw-Hill, 1975): 22.

6. Denis J. Davis, "Transportation and Inventory Management: Bridging the Gap," *Distribution* (June 1985): 11.

7. John Gatorna and Abby Day, "Strategic Issues in Logistics," *International Journal of Physical Distribution and Materials Management* 16 (1986): 29.

8. For additional information regarding MRPII, see Oliver W. Wright, "MRPII," *Modern Materials Handling* (September 12, 1980): 28.

9. Alan J. Stenger, "Materials Resources Planning," *The Distribution Handbook* (New York, NY: The Free Press, 1994): 89–97.

10. Robert Goodell Brown, *Advanced Service Parts Inventory Control*, 2nd ed. (Norwich, VT: Materials Management Systems, 1982): 155.

11. Thomas E. Hendrick and Franklin G. Moore, *Production/Operations Management*, 9th ed. (Homewood, IL: Irwin, 1985): 173.

12. Lambert and Stock, *Strategic Logistics Management*, 426–429.

13. Jay U. Sterling, "Measuring the Performance of Logistics Operations," in James F. Robeson and William C. Copacino, ed., *The Logistics Handbook*, Chapter 10 (New York, NY: The Free Press, 1994): 226–230.

14. Walter Zinn, Michael Levy, and Donald J. Bowersox, "Measuring the Effect of Inventory Centralization/Decentralization on Aggregate Safety Stock: The 'Square Root Law' Revisited," *Journal of Business Logistics* 10, No. 1 (1989): 14.

15. Ibid., 14.

CASE 9.1

MAQ Corporation

MAQ Corporation, a major producer of consumer electronics equipment, is currently faced with a rapidly growing product line and its associated inventory problems. MAQ's president, Mary Semerod, has decided to initiate a program to analyze the company's inventory requirements utilizing different inventory techniques. The first phase of this program consists of an ABC analysis of the company's product line (shown in the following table). Ms. Semerod has encountered difficulties in deciding on the appropriate criteria to use in the classification and in developing appropriate cutoff levels for each class of inventory. To solve her dilemma, Ms. Semerod has contracted the services of a logistics consulting firm to perform the inventory analysis.

SALES DATA (ONE-YEAR PERIOD)

PRODUCT #	UNITS SOLD	PRICE PER UNIT	PROFIT PER UNIT
SR101	12,386	$275	$82.50
SR103	784	1,530	459.00
SR105	1,597	579	173.30
SR201	48	2,500	975.00
SR203	2	3,000	1,200.00
SR205	9,876	450	149.00
SR301	673	600	180.00
SR303	547	725	200.00
SR305	3,437	917	240.00
SR500	78	1,000	312.00

CASE QUESTIONS

1. If you were employed by the consulting firm, how would you construct your method of analysis?

2. What criteria would you use?

3. What would the cutoff levels be? Be sure to provide explanations of the reasoning supporting your decisions.

CASE 9.2

Nittany Fans

Nittany Fans of Lewistown, Pennsylvania, is a distributor of industrial fans used in plants, warehouses, and other industrial facilities. Its market area encompasses most of Pennsylvania, eastern Ohio, and New Jersey. The fans are manufactured in Neenah, Wisconsin, and currently shipped to Lewistown via rail transportation. Kenny Craig, vice president of logistics, has asked his staff to evaluate using motor carrier service to ship the fans.

Nick Gingher, director of distribution, has collected the following information:

- Annual demand: 36,000 fans
- Fan value (price): $4,000 each
- Inventory carrying cost (annual): 25%
- Cost per order to replenish inventory: $200
- In-transit inventory carrying cost: 15%
- Order cycle time using rail: 4 days
- Order cycle time using motor carrier: 2 days
- Rail rate: $1.00 per cwt (100 lbs.)
- Motor carrier rate: $1.25 per cwt
- Unit weight: 250 lbs. per fan

CASE QUESTIONS

1. What is the economic order quantity for Nittany Fans in units? In pounds?

2. What is the total cost (not considering transportation-related costs) of the EOQ?

3. What is the total cost for using rail transportation?

4. What is the total cost for using motor carrier transportation?

5. Which alternative should Nittany Fans use?

APPENDIX 9A

Special Applications of the EOQ Approach

Adjusting the Simple EOQ Model for Modal Choice Decisions—The Cost of Inventory in Transit

Chapter 1 mentioned the tradeoff possibilities between inventory costs and transportation decisions regarding choice of mode. Implied in this discussion was the idea that longer transit times resulted in higher inventory costs. This is because in-transit inventory carrying costs will be incurred by the firms having ownership of the goods while they are being transported. In effect, the carrying costs of inventory in transit will be similar to the carrying costs of inventory in the warehouse. There are differences between inventory in transit and inventory in the warehouse, but basically the company is responsible for inventory in both instances. There is always some cost attached to having inventory, whether it is sitting in a warehouse or plant or moving to another point. Therefore, if modes of transportation have different transit times and different rates (prices) with other variables being equal, the tradeoff between transportation rates and the inventory cost associated with the transit times should be examined. The transportation rates are usually easy to obtain. However, to calculate the cost of carrying inventory in transit, it will be necessary to modify the basic or simple EOQ model.

Recall that the simple EOQ model essentially considered only the tradeoff between order or setup costs and the carrying cost associated with holding inventory in a warehouse. To consider how different transit times affect transportation and its cost, the company must relax one basic assumption of the EOQ model and adapt the model accordingly.

One assumption of the simple EOQ model was that inventory incurred no cost in transit, because the company either purchased inventory on a delivered-price basis or sold it FOB plant. If conditions change so that the company makes purchases FOB origin or sells products on a delivered-price basis, then it will be necessary to consider the cost of carrying inventory in transit. Figure 9A.1 depicts a modified sawtooth inventory model; the lower half shows the inventory in transit.

The Sawtooth Model Adjusted

Comparing the lower half of Figure 9A.1 with the upper half, which depicts inventory in the warehouse, we can see two differences relevant for calculating the appropriate costs. First, inventory is usually in transit for only part of the cycle. Typically, the number of inventory shipping days would be less than the number of days that inventory from the preceding EOQ replenishment would be in the warehouse. Second, inventory in transit is not used up or sold; warehouse inventory may be used up or sold.

Since inventory in transit has these two distinctive characteristics, the cost of carrying inventory in transit will differ from that of storing inventory in the warehouse. We can calculate this cost in several ways. If a daily inventory-in-transit carrying cost were available, we could multiply it by the number of days in transit. We could calculate this daily cost by multiplying the inventory-in-transit value by a daily opportunity cost. After

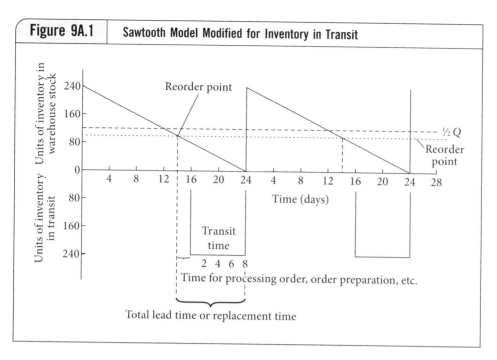

Figure 9A.1 | **Sawtooth Model Modified for Inventory in Transit**

multiplying this cost by the number of transit days, we could multiply it by the number of orders per year or cycles per year. This would give an annual cost of inventory in transit. In effect, this resembles the procedure we followed when calculating the cost of inventory in the warehouse.

Consider the following:

Y = Cost of carrying inventory in transit

V = Value/unit of inventory

t = Order cycle time

t_m = Inventory transit time

M = Average number of units of inventory in transit

We calculate the value of M as follows:

$\dfrac{t_m}{t}$ = Percentage of time inventory is in transit per cycle period

Therefore,

$$M = \frac{t_m}{t}Q$$

We could rewrite this as follows:

$$t(\text{days in cycle}) = \frac{360\,(\text{days in year})}{R/Q\,(\text{cycles per year})}$$

$$t = 360\frac{Q}{R}$$

$$M = \frac{(t_m Q)}{360}\frac{Q}{R}$$

$$M = \frac{t_m}{360}R$$

The two approaches to calculating M give the same result, given the preceding assumptions. The second equation for M, however, is frequently more useful, since the variables are given in the problem.

Now that we have developed a way of calculating the average number of units in transit, all that remains is to multiply this figure by the value per unit and the percentage annual carrying cost of inventory in transit. The result will be a dollar cost for inventory in transit that compares to the dollar cost of inventory in the warehouse:

$$\frac{t_m}{t} QVY$$

We could write the new total inventory cost equation in either of the following forms:

$$\text{TAC} = \frac{1}{2}QVW + A\frac{R}{Q} + \frac{t_m}{t}QVY$$

or

$$\text{TAC} = \frac{1}{2}QVW + A\frac{R}{Q} + \frac{t_m}{360}RVY^*$$

Example Of Modal Selection

We can measure the tradeoff between transit times and transportation cost using the total cost formula developed in the preceding section. First review the information provided in the example in Chapter 9 to demonstrate the simple EOQ model:

$R = 3,600$ units (annual demand)

$A = \$200$ (cost of one order or setup)

$W = 25\%$ (cost of carrying inventory in warehouse)

$V = \$100$ (value per unit)

$Q = 240$ units (this would remain the same)

Now consider that a hypothetical company is choosing between two transportation modes (rail or motor) and that the following information is available:

Rail: 8 days in transit time

$3 per hundred pounds

Motor: 6 days transit time

$4 per hundred pounds

Next assume that the company will ship the same amount, 240 units, regardless of mode. If each unit weighs 100 pounds, this represents 24,000 pounds, or 240 hundredweight (cwt). The cost of carrying inventory in transit (Y) is 10 percent. Given the preceding variables, we may examine the two alternatives using the formula developed previously.

---

*Differentiating this equation and solving for Q with the expanded total cost formula results in the same equation as the previous one, since the last term added is not a function of Q; that is,

$$Q = \sqrt{\frac{2RA}{VW}}$$

The first step is to look at the product's total inventory cost if the company decides to ship by rail:

$$\text{Total Inventory Cost (rail)} = \left(\frac{1}{2} \times 240 \times \$100 \times 25\%\right) + \left(\$200 \times \frac{3,600}{240}\right)$$
$$+ \left(\frac{8}{24} \times 240 \times \$100 \times 10\%\right)$$
$$= \$3,000 + \$3,000 + \$800$$
$$= \$6,800$$

If we add the transportation cost to the inventory cost, the total cost would be as follows:

$$\text{Total Cost (rail)} = \$6,800 + \left(\$3 \times 240 \times \frac{3,600}{240}\right)$$
$$= \$6,800 + \$10,800$$
$$= \$17,600$$

The next step is to determine the total inventory cost if the company ships the items by motor as shown:

$$\text{Total Inventory Cost (motor)} = \left(\frac{1}{2} \times 240 \times \$100 \times 25\%\right) + \left(\$200 \times \frac{3,600}{240}\right)$$
$$+ \left(\frac{6}{24} \times 240 \times \$100 \times 10\%\right)$$
$$= \$3,000 + \$3,000 + \$600$$
$$= \$6,600$$

Once again, we should add the transportation cost to the inventory costs as follows:

$$\text{Total Cost (motor)} = \$6,600 + \left(\$4 \times 240 \times \frac{3,600}{240}\right)$$
$$= \$6,600 + \$14,400$$
$$= \$21,000 \text{ by motor}$$

Given these calculations, the rail alternative would be less costly and thus preferable. Before leaving this section, we should examine the tradeoffs more closely. As you can see, the rail alternative has a higher inventory cost because of the slower transit time, but the transportation cost savings offset this. The net effect is an overall savings by rail.

Finally, we should note that the procedure suggested in this section is based on conditions of certainty. If transit times varied, we would need to establish probabilities and approach the solution in a more sophisticated manner.

Adjusting the Simple EOQ Model for Volume Transportation Rates

The basic EOQ model discussed previously did not consider the possible reductions in transportation rates per hundredweight associated with larger-volume shipments. For example, the hypothetical company in the previous illustration decided that 240 units was the appropriate quantity to order or produce. If we assume again that each unit weighed 100 pounds, this would imply a shipment of 24,000 pounds. If the rate on a shipment of 24,000 pounds (240 cwt) was $3 per hundred pounds (cwt) and the rate for a 40,000-pound shipment was $2 per cwt, knowing whether to ship 400 units (40,000 pounds) instead of the customary 240 units would be worthwhile.

Shippers transport a specified minimum quantity (weight) or more commonly publish volume rates on carload (rail) and truckload (motor carrier)* quantities. Therefore, in inventory situations, the decision maker responsible for transporting goods should consider how the lower-volume rate affects total cost. In other words, in addition to considering storage (holding) cost and order or setup cost, the decision maker should consider how lower transportation costs affect total cost.

Cost Relationships

Sometimes the economic order quantity suggested by the basic model may be less than the quantity necessary for a volume rate. We can adjust the model to consider the following cost relationships associated with shipping a volume larger than the one determined by the basic EOQ approach.

- **Increased inventory carrying cost for inventory in the warehouse.** The larger quantity required for the volume rate means a larger average inventory ($\frac{1}{2}Q$) and consequently an increased inventory carrying cost.
- **Decreased order or setup costs.** The larger quantity will reduce the number of orders placed and the ordinary costs of order placement and/or order setup.
- **Decreased transportation costs.** The larger quantity will reduce the cost per hundredweight of transporting the goods, consequently lowering transportation costs.
- **Decreased in-transit inventory carrying cost.** Carload (CL) and truckload (TL) shipments usually have shorter transit times than less-than-carload (LCL) or less-than-truckload (LTL) shipments, and the faster time generally means a lower cost for inventory in transit.

Figure 9A.2 represents the cost relationships and considers possible transportation rate discounts (volume rates versus less-than-volume rates). The total cost function "breaks," or is discontinuous, at the quantity that permits a company to use the volume rate. Therefore, we cannot use the cost function for the transportation rate discount or discounts in the original EOQ formulation. Rather, we must use sensitivity analysis, or a sensitivity test, to determine whether total annual costs are lower if the company purchases a quantity larger than the basic EOQ amount. Note that although Figure 9A.2 indicates that using the volume rate will lower total cost, this does not necessarily have to be the case. For example, if the inventory dollar value was very high, then the increased storage (holding) costs could more than offset reductions in order and transport cost.

Mathematical Formulation

Although there are several ways to analyze opportunities for using volume transportation rates, a useful method is to calculate and compare the total annual costs of the EOQ-based approach with those of the volume-rate-based approach. The following symbols will be useful in this analysis:

$$\text{TAC} = \text{Inventory Carrying Cost} + \text{Order Cost} + \text{Transportation Cost} + \text{In-Transit Inventory Carrying Cost}$$

$$\text{TAC}_b = \text{Total Annual Cost at Basic EOQ}$$

---

*Motor carriers often publish different LTL rates and TL rates on quantities of 500, 2,000, and 5,000 pounds.

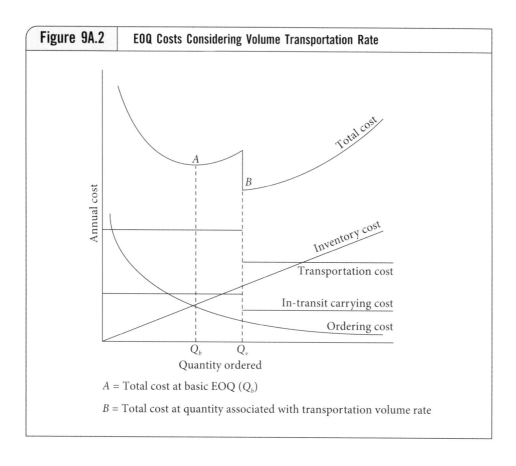

Figure 9A.2 | **EOQ Costs Considering Volume Transportation Rate**

A = Total cost at basic EOQ (Q_b)

B = Total cost at quantity associated with transportation volume rate

TAC_v = Total Annual Cost at Volume Rate Quantity

Q_b = Basic EOQ

Q_v = Volume Rate Quantity

t_m = Time in Transit for Less-Than-Volume Shipment

t_n = Time in Transit for Volume Shipment

H = Less-Than-Volume Rate (high rate)

L = Volume Rate (low rate)

We calculate each total annual cost as follows:

$$\text{TAC}_b = \frac{1}{2}Q_b VW + A\frac{R}{Q_b} + HQ_b\frac{R}{Q_b} + \frac{t_m}{t}Q_b VY$$

$$\text{TAC}_v = \frac{1}{2}Q_v VW + A\frac{R}{Q_v} + LQ_v\frac{R}{Q_v} = \frac{t_m}{t}Q_v VY$$

Noting that $HQ_b\frac{R}{Q_b}$ can be written simply as HR and that $LQ_b\frac{R}{Q_b}$ can be written simply as LR, we can reduce these equations to the following:

$$\text{TAC}_b = \frac{1}{2}Q_b VW + A\frac{R}{Q_b} + HR + \frac{t_m}{t}Q_b VY$$

$$\text{TAC}_v = \frac{1}{2}Q_v VW + A\frac{R}{Q_v}LR + \frac{t_n}{t}Q_v VY$$

Transportation Rate Discount Example

An example that builds on the previous problem will illustrate in this section how transportation rate discounts produce possible annual cost savings.

For this new example, assume the following variables:

H = $3.00/cwt (assume each unit weighs 100 pounds)

L = $2.00/cwt with a minimum of 40,000 pounds
(with each unit weighing 100 pounds, this would be 400 units, or 400 cwt)

t_n = 6 days (time in transit for volume movement)

Y = 10% (carrying cost of inventory while in transit)

Q_v = 400 units

t_v = 40 days (length of a single inventory cycle for Q_v = 400 units)

From the previous problem, we know the following:

R = 3,600 units (3,600 cwt)(annual sales)

A = $200 (cost of placing an order or cost of setup)

V = $100/cwt/unit (value per unit)

W = 25%

Q_b = 240 units (240 cwt, or 240,000 pounds)

t_m = 8 days (time in transit for LTL movement)

t = 24 days (length of a single inventory cycle or period)

Solving for TAC_b and TAC_v, we get the following result:

$$TAC_b = \left[\frac{1}{2} \times 240 \times \$100 \times 25\%\right] + \left[\$200 \times \frac{3,600}{240}\right]$$

$$+ [\$3 \times \$3,600] + \left[\frac{8}{24} \times 240 \times \$100 \times 10\%\right]$$

$$= \$17,600$$

$$TAC_v = \left[\frac{1}{2} \times 400 \times \$100 \times 25\%\right] + \left[\$200 \times \frac{3,600}{500}\right]$$

$$+ [\$2 \times \$3,600] + \left[\frac{6}{40} \times 400 \times \$100 \times 10\%\right]$$

$$= \$14,240$$

Since TAC_b, exceeds TAC_v by $3,360, the most economical solution is to purchase the larger quantity, 400 cwt. Reductions in ordering, transportation, and in-transit inventory carrying costs offset the increased cost of holding the larger quantity.

We may modify this analysis to consider potential volume discounts for purchasing in larger quantities. The same procedure of calculating and comparing total annual costs under the various alternatives applies, providing we make minor modifications to the equations.

Adjusting the Simple EOQ Model for Private Carriage

Many companies that use their own truck fleet or that lease trucks for private use assess a fixed charge per mile or per trip, no matter how much the company ships at any one time. In other words, since operating costs such as driver expense and fuel do not vary significantly with weight, and since fixed costs do not change with weight, many companies charge a flat amount per trip rather than differentiate on a weight basis. Therefore, since additional weight costs nothing extra, it is logical to ask what quantity the company should ship.

The basic EOQ model can handle this analysis, since the fixed trip charge is comparable to the order cost or setup cost. Therefore, the decision maker must trade off the prospect of a smaller number of larger shipments against the increased cost of carrying larger average inventory amounts.

If T_c represents the trip charge, we can write the formula as follows:

$$\text{TAC} = \frac{1}{2}QVW + \frac{R}{Q}A + \frac{R}{Q}T_c$$

We can derive the basic model as follows:

$$\text{EOQ} = \sqrt{\frac{2R(A + T_c)}{VW}}$$

From the previous example, we can add a charge of $100 per trip.

$$\text{EOQ} = \frac{\sqrt{2 \times \$3,600 \times (\$200 + \$100)}}{\$100 \times 25\%}$$

$$= \frac{\sqrt{\$2,160,000}}{\$25}$$

$$= \sqrt{86,400}$$

$$= 293.94$$

The EOQ size has been increased to 293.94 units because of additional fixed charges associated with private trucking costs.

Adjusting the Simple EOQ Model for the Establishment and Application of In-Excess Rates*

We can adjust the basic inventory analysis framework discussed in Chapter 9 to utilize an in-excess rate. Through in-excess rates, carriers encourage heavier shipper loadings. The carrier offers a lower rate for weight shipped in excess of a specified minimum weight. A logistics manager must decide whether the company should use the in-excess rate and, if so, the amount the company should include in each shipment.

Consider the following example: CBL Railroad has just published a new in-excess rate on items that XYZ Company ships quite often. CBL's present rate is $4/cwt with a 40,000-pound minimum (400 cwt). The in-excess rate just published is $3/cwt on shipment weight in excess of 40,000 pounds up to 80,000 pounds. The XYZ logistics manager presently ships in 400-cwt lots. The manager wants to know whether XYZ should use the in-excess rate, and, if so, what quantity the company should ship per shipment.

XYZ supplied the following data:

$R = 3,200,000$ pounds (32,000 cwt)(annual shipments)
$V = \$200$ (value of item per cwt)
$W = 25\%$ of value (inventory carrying cost/unit value/year)

Each item weighs 100 pounds.

*This section is adapted from James L. Heskett, Robert M. Ivie, and Nicholas A. Glaskowsky, *Business Logistics* (New York: Ronald Press, 1964): 516–520.

XYZ should use the in-excess rate as long as the annual transportation cost savings offset the added cost of holding a larger inventory associated with heavier shipments. That is, realizing the transportation cost savings of the in-excess rate will increase XYZ's inventory carrying cost. The optimum shipment size occurs when annual net savings are maximal, that is, when annual transport savings minus the annual added inventory carrying cost are the greatest.

In developing the savings and cost functions, we will use the following symbols:

S_r = Savings per cwt between present rate and new in-excess rate

Q = Optimum shipment quantity in cwt

Q_m = Old minimum shipment quantity in cwt

The annual net savings equals the annual transport savings minus the annual added inventory carrying cost, or $N_s = S_y - C_y$.

The annual transport savings equals the number of shipments per year times the savings per shipment, or:

$$S_y = \frac{R}{Q} S_r (Q - Q_m)$$

where R/Q is the number of shipments per year, $Q - Q_m$ is the amount of shipment weight the company will ship at the lower in-excess rate, and $S_r(Q - Q_m)$ is the transportation savings per shipment. Rewriting the equation for S_r results in the following:

$$S_y = RS_r \left(1 - \frac{Q_m}{Q} \right)$$

The annual added inventory carrying cost, C_y, equals the added inventory carrying costs of the consignor (shipper or seller) and the consignee (receiver or buyer). The calculations must consider the consignee's added inventory, since the seller must pass these savings on as a price discount to encourage the buyer to purchase in larger quantities, or the seller will incur this cost if the shipment goes to the seller's warehouse or distribution center, for example.

We calculate the added average inventory—the difference between the average inventories with the larger shipment quantity and the smaller (present) shipment quantity—as follows:

$$\text{Consignor's added inventory} = \frac{1}{2}Q - \frac{1}{2}Q_m$$

$$\text{Consignee's added inventory} = \frac{1}{2}Q - \frac{1}{2}Q_m$$

$$\text{Total added inventory} = 2\left(\frac{1}{2}Q - \frac{1}{2}Q_m \right) = Q - Q_m$$

$C_y = WV(Q - Q_m)$, where $V(Q - Q_m)$ equals the value of added inventory and W equals the inventory carrying cost per dollar value. Table 9A.1 and Figure 9A.3 show the savings and cost relationships developed here.

The function that maximizes annual net savings is as follows:

$$N_s = S_y - C_y = RS_r \left(1 - \frac{Q_m}{Q} \right) - WV(Q - Q_m)$$

Table 9A.1	Annual Savings, Annual Cost, and Net Savings by Various Quantities Using Incentive Rates		
Q	**SY**	**CY**	**N_s**
400	0	0	0
410	781	500	281
420	1,524	1,000	524
430	2,233	1,500	733
440	2,909	2,000	909
450	3,556	2,500	1,056
460	4,174	3,000	1,174
470	4,766	3,500	1,266
480	5,333	4,000	1,333
490	5,878	4,500	1,378
500	6,400	5,000	1,400
505	6,654	5,250	1,404
510	6,902	5,500	1,402
520	7,385	6,000	1,385
530	7,849	6,500	1,349
540	8,296	7,000	1,296
550	8,727	7,500	1,227
560	9,143	8,000	1,143
570	9,544	8,500	1,044
580	9,931	9,000	931
590	10,305	9,500	805
600	10,667	10,000	667
610	11,017	10,500	517
620	11,355	11,000	355

Taking the first derivative, setting it equal to zero, and solving for Q results in the following:

$$\frac{d(N_s)}{dQ} = RS_r \frac{Q_m}{Q^2} - WV = 0$$

$$WV = \frac{RS_r Q_m}{Q^2}$$

$$Q^2 = \frac{RS_r Q_m}{WV}$$

$$Q = \sqrt{\frac{RS_r Q_m}{WV}}$$

Figure 9A.3	Net Savings Function for Incentive Rate

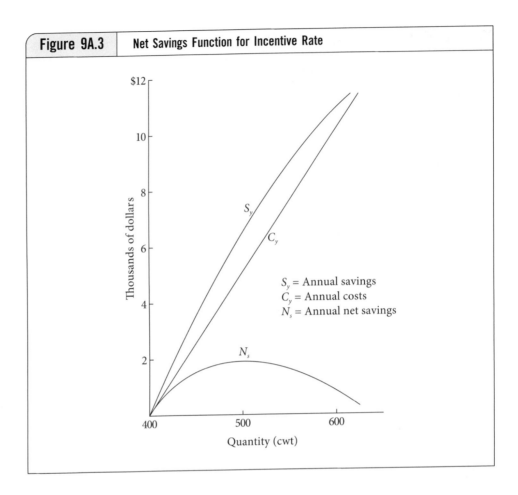

Now, taking the data from the problem posed in this example, we find the solution as follows:

$$Q = \sqrt{\frac{(32,000)(\$1.00)(400)}{(0.25)(\$200)}} = \sqrt{256,000} = 506 \text{ cwt}$$

The conclusion is that XYZ Company should use the in-excess rate and should ship 50,600 pounds in each shipment.

SUMMARY

The four adjustments to the basic EOQ approach discussed in this appendix all relate to decisions important to the logistics manager—modal choice, volume rates, private trucking, and in-excess rates. We could include other adjustments, but these four should be sufficient in most cases. While all of the adjustments discussed here assume a condition of certainty, other adjustments may require modifying the model for conditions for uncertainty.

Chapter 10

TRANSPORTATION—MANAGING THE FLOW OF THE SUPPLY CHAIN

Learning Objectives

After reading this chapter, you should be able to do the following:

- Explain the role transportation plays in the supply chain.
- Discuss the service and cost characteristics of the primary transportation modes.
- Discuss the key activities involved in transportation planning and execution.
- Explain current transportation management strategies used to improve supply chain performance.
- Use service and cost metrics to analyze transportation performance.
- Describe how information technology supports transportation planning and execution.

Supply Chain Profile   *Economic Recovery and Transportation Demand*

The need for transportation is dependent upon the marketplace demand for products. This derived-demand reality was starkly demonstrated during the recent economic crisis as a 12.2 percent decline in worldwide trade led to a reduced need for transportation services. Spending for transportation services in the United States plummeted 20.8 percent from 2008 to 2009. Demand for less-than-truckload (LTL) service fell nearly 30 percent, truckload revenues declined 4.4 percent, and rail carload volume dropped 18 percent. The situation was no better internationally, as air cargo traffic declined 11.3 percent and ocean carriers scrambled to eliminate excess capacity.

The transportation situation took a turn for the better in 2010 as the world began to climb out of the global recession. The World Trade Organization (WTO) indicated that the faster-than-expected recovery in global trade flows would result in 13.5 percent growth of world trade for the year. In turn, the transportation industry began to recover with volume and revenue growth in all modes.

The outlook for 2011 is generally positive. WTO economists project global trade to grow by 6.5 percent. That's good news for transportation companies that survived the economic crisis and streamlined their capacity. With less capacity available for a growing level of freight, transportation companies are now in a better position to raise rates and recover market share. Of course, this translates to higher costs for freight customers.

Transportation experts' predictions for 2011 and beyond include:

- **Higher truckload rates**—Carrier bankruptcies, industry consolidation, new safety regulations, and a driver shortage, coupled with higher demand, will lead to rate increases in the second half of 2011 and 2012.

- **LTL rate increases**—An overall increase in demand for services and a shrinking competitor base will help the industry boost rates and increase revenues.

- **Rail rate battles**—Customers maintain that rates are too high relative to service levels while railroads state that they are earning little more than their cost of capital. Expect customers to push for economic reregulation of the U.S. railroads.

- **Stable rates for ocean transport**—After significant rises in container-load rates during 2010, ocean transportation rates are expected to remain flat in 2011 due to expanded capacity.

- **Flat air cargo rates**—Rates are not expected to grow in the first half of 2011, and future increases hinge upon multiple variables such as oil prices, capacity management, and trade activity in the Pacific Rim.

- **Rising demand for intermodal services**—Intermodal transportation has been on a growth curve, and the trend will continue as freight customers seek the best combination of modes that balance service and costs.

Of course, the recovery of the global economy and the transportation industry is not guaranteed. Rising oil prices, major catastrophes such as the earthquake and tsunami in Japan, and political instability in the Middle East could curtail economic growth. If these types of problems negatively impact industrial and consumer purchase activity, then demand for transportation service will wane and growth of the transportation industry will be short-lived.

Sources: Patrick Burnson, "2010 State of Logistics: Make Your Move," *Logistics Management* (July 2010): 22–32; Patrick Burnson, "Special Report: 2011 State of Air Cargo," *Supply Chain Management Review* (March/April 2011): S58–S61; Dan Goodwill, "Some Key Trends That Will Drive Freight Transportation in 2011," *Canadian Transportation & Logistics* (December 29, 2010), retrieved April 14, 2011, from http://blogdg.ctl.ca/2010/12/some_key_trends_that_will_driv.html; Zacks Equity Research, *Airline Industry Outlook 2011*, retrieved April 14, 2011, from http://www.zacks.com/stock/news/51121/Airline+Industry+Outlook+-+April+2011.

Introduction

Transportation involves the physical movement of people and goods between origin and destination points. As individuals, we rely heavily on transportation to get to work and back home each day, to bring us the products that we need, and to increase our access to society. From a business standpoint, the transportation system links geographically separated partners and facilities in a company's supply chain—customers, suppliers, channel members, plants, warehouses, and retail outlets. Be it by truck, train, plane, ship, pipeline, or fiber optic wire, transportation facilitates the creation of time and place utility in the supply chain.

Transportation also has a major economic impact on the financial performance of businesses. In 2010, more than $760 billion was spent on freight transportation in the United States.[1] This figure represents nearly 63 percent of all expenditures for logistics activities, far exceeding the amount of money spent on warehousing, inventory management, order processing, and other fulfillment system expenses. Thus, transportation costs must be taken into account during the development of supply chain strategies and processes.

This chapter focuses on the role of transportation in logistics management and the supply chain. We focus on the key methods, strategies, and decisions required for the cost-efficient, effective flow of goods between sellers and buyers. As you will learn, proper management of these transportation issues is vital to the fulfillment of customer demand and the ultimate success of an organization.

The Role of Transportation in Supply Chain Management (SCM)

Conceptually, a supply chain is a network of organizations that are separated by distance and time. Transportation provides the critical links between these organizations, permitting goods to flow between their facilities. By bridging these buyer–seller gaps, transportation allows organizations to extend the reach of their supply chains beyond local supplier capabilities and market demand. With efficient, effective transportation capabilities, organizations can build global supply chains that leverage low-cost sourcing opportunities and allow them to compete in new markets.

Transportation service availability is critical to demand fulfillment in the supply chain. As the Supply Chain Profile points out, demand for transportation service is derived from customer demand. It is important to match transportation capacity to demand to avoid customer service failures. Companies like Best Buy must work effectively with financially solvent carriers who can flex capacity up and down to match demand. A transportation capacity shortage would negate Best Buy's efforts to create and fulfill customer demand because the product inventory would not reach the stores in a timely fashion.

Transportation efficiency promotes the competitiveness of a supply chain. In terms of supply management, cost-effective transportation helps companies gain access to higher-quality, lower-priced materials and realize economies of scale in production. Likewise, low-cost transportation improves demand fulfillment opportunities. By keeping transportation expenses reasonable, the total landed cost of a product (its production costs plus transportation costs and related supply chain fulfillment costs) can be competitive in multiple markets. For example, if a Switzerland-based manufacturer sells watches for $105 plus $10 for order processing and delivery versus $120 for a similar-quality domestic watch, the Swiss company can compete effectively in the local market.

Not only must transportation costs be effective, but service capabilities must also be in line with customer requirements. Inexpensive transportation is of little value to a supply chain if the product does not arrive as scheduled and damage-free to the correct location. High-quality, customer-focused transportation has a direct impact on an organization's ability to provide the "Seven Rs of Logistics"—getting the right product to the right customer, in the right quantity, in the right condition, at the right place, at the right time, and at the right cost. Additionally, transportation can create supply chain flexibility. By working with carriers that offer a range of transit times and service options, organizations can satisfy supply chain demands for expedited, next-day service as well as more economical standard delivery requests.

In addition to the linking and customer service roles, transportation plays a key role in supply chain design, strategy development, and total cost management.

- Transportation service availability, capacity, and costs influence decisions regarding the number and location of supply chain facilities. For example, many organizations attempt to avoid locating distribution facilities in the state of Florida due to transportation costs. With little freight originating in the state, carriers compensate for the empty outbound trips by charging higher rates to move freight into Florida.

- Transportation capabilities must align with the company's goals. In its 2009 annual report, Amazon.com states that it seeks to be Earth's most customer-centric company and strives to provide easy-to-use functionality, fast and reliable fulfillment, and timely customer service.[2] To hit these targets, Amazon.com needs to partner with carriers that deliver customer orders consistently and quickly, provide shipment visibility, and charge reasonable shipping rates.

- Intentional tradeoffs should be made between transportation and related activities (e.g., procurement, production, and inventory management) to optimize supply chain efficiency. For example, retailers can hold lower safety stock levels if the cost of more frequent, faster deliveries does not exceed the inventory carrying cost savings. Similarly, manufacturers can employ lean production strategies if lot sizes can be minimized without creating excessive transportation costs.

Given these critical roles, it is clear that proactive management of transportation processes is fundamental to the efficient and economical operation of a company's supply chain. Company leadership must not treat transportation as a "necessary evil" or an afterthought to production and marketing. Instead, they must consider transportation issues when developing organizational plans, integrate transportation into supply chain processes, and optimize total supply chain cost rather than minimize transportation costs. Leading organizations like PepsiCo and Walmart have already moved in this direction. They recognize that supply chains can only achieve time and place utility through effective transportation processes that physically move goods to the place desired at the time required by their key supply chain participants—the customers.

Challenges to Carrying out This Role

While transportation can provide valuable support to an organization's supply chain, it is a mistake to assume that these roles can be accomplished with ease. There are numerous obstacles—supply chain complexity, competing goals among supply chain partners, changing customer requirements, and limited information availability—to synchronizing transportation with other supply chain activities. Further compounding the challenge is a variety of supply chain trends and external issues that must be addressed by the organization.

The growth of outsourcing, particularly offshore manufacturing, creates major transportation challenges. The increasing reliance on global supply chains that extend from China, India, and other countries to your hometown requires more expensive transportation processes to connect buyers and sellers that are thousands of miles apart. Also, the extended transit times and greater potential for supply chain disruptions necessitate higher inventory levels. As a result, some organizations have begun to look closer to home for manufacturing opportunities. This strategy of "near-shoring" provides an opportunity to leverage low labor costs without the risk and expense of transporting goods vast distances.

Customer demands for tailored services and defect-free delivery also impact the transportation function. The shift to smaller, more frequent deliveries limits the ability of organizations to move product in economic truckload or container-load quantities. Shrinking order cycle requirements result in higher costs for faster delivery and longer fulfillment operation hours. Also, the desire for real-time shipment visibility requires technological strength. Organizations must align their operations with high-quality carriers that provide a balanced mix of capacity, speed, and consistency at a reasonable cost.

Transportation capacity constraints pose another challenge to organizations needing to move freight through the supply chain. When transportation demand outstrips the capacity of our infrastructure, major bottlenecks occur. For example, port facilities must grapple with a surge of containers, and highways in major cities suffer from congestion. Carriers also struggle to keep pace with freight growth, whether it be hiring and retaining enough truck drivers or putting enough locomotives into service. The outcomes of a capacity crunch include higher freight rates, shipment delays, and limited negotiating capabilities.

Unstable transportation rates present another major concern for organizations. When demand waned and excess capacity grew during the recent recession, customers enjoyed low freight expenses. As the Supply Chain Profile indicated, rates have been rising due to greater demand for transportation services and industry consolidation from carrier mergers, acquisitions, and bankruptcies. Carriers are now in a strong position to increase rates to cover the rising costs of fuel, labor, and other expenses. They have also built fuel surcharges into contracts with their customers, which add an extra charge to the customer's freight bill. In early 2011, FedEx's fuel surcharges ranged from 10 to 13 percent of transportation rates for air freight services and 6.5 to 7.5 percent for ground service.[3] The goal of the surcharge is to reimburse the carrier for excessive fuel costs that were not built into the original contract price. Surcharges are based on U.S. Department of Energy index price calculations for fuel.

The transportation industry is also impacted by governmental requirements that affect cost structures and service capabilities. Historically, government regulation of transportation has focused on competition and pricing. For decades, these rules limited opportunities and incentives for carriers to develop unique service offerings and tailored pricing. Economic deregulation of most modes by 1980 and ocean shipping in 1998 gave carriers the freedom to operate with little governmental intrusion, sparking much-needed competition based on services, price, and performance. An extended discussion of economic regulation can be found in Appendix 10A.

In contrast, regulation is growing in areas where the transportation industry has the potential to impact the quality of life, the safety of citizens, and the growth of commerce.

Most recently, legislation has been passed to improve the safety of the transportation industry, reduce its impact on the environment, and defend the country against terrorism.

- Protection of the traveling public is a primary driver of transportation safety regulation. Federal and state laws limit the size of transportation equipment, combined freight and equipment weight, and travel speed. Regulations also exist to ensure that commercial vehicle operators are properly qualified. For example, concerns regarding operator fatigue led to revision of the 1935 commercial vehicle driver hours of service (HOS) rules in 2003. The HOS regulations allow 11 hours of driving time within a consecutive 14-hour period, after which drivers must be off duty for 10 hours. Previously, driving time was limited to 10 hours in a 15-hour period that could be interrupted by off-duty breaks, followed by 8 hours off duty. The issue is ongoing, and lawmakers are considering further reduction to the maximum driving time and on-duty hours. Most recently, the Federal Motor Carrier Safety Administration (FMCSA) introduced the Compliance, Safety, Accountability (CSA) initiative. CSA 2010 is designed to provide motor carriers and drivers with attention from FMCSA and state partners about their potential safety problems with an ultimate goal of achieving a greater reduction in large truck and bus crashes, injuries, and fatalities.[4]

- A wide variety of environmental protection issues are also addressed by governmental regulation. Federal and state regulations have been in effect since the 1970s to control aircraft noise pollution. Transportation of hazardous materials—flammable and combustible substances, poisons, and radioactive materials—is highly regulated to minimize the risks to life, property, and the environment. Air pollution is another key issue. Vehicle emission regulations such as the Heavy-Duty Highway Diesel Rule, which took effect in 2007, require lower sulfur levels in fuel as well as cleaner-burning engines.

- The ongoing threat of terrorism has led to security-focused legislation that directly impacts the transportation industry. The Trade Act of 2002 contains requirements mandating the advance electronic filing of all import and export cargo information for all modes of transportation. As part of this regulation, the Bureau of Customs and Border Protection (CBP) enforces the "24 Hour Rule," which requires ocean carriers to provide complete manifest information for all cargo bound for the United States to the CBP 24 hours prior to loading aboard a vessel in a foreign port. More recently CBP has established rules for the Importer Security Filing 10 + 2 program in which the importer must electronically file a 10–data element report with CBP and the carrier must provide a vessel stow plan and container status message for arriving vessels.

When initiating legislation to benefit society, the government makes a significant effort to avoid unnecessary restriction of the flow of legitimate trade. Despite these efforts, it can be expensive for carriers to comply with government mandates. For example, industry experts indicate that that the vehicle emissions regulation has led to higher fuel prices, more costly truck engines, and lower fuel efficiency than previous equipment. Regulation also impacts organizations whose freight flows through the transportation system. Like many other mandates, the HOS regulations have led to rate increases and prompted organizations to revise their shipping strategies.

Ultimately, this variety of external issues makes it difficult to develop transportation processes that mesh well with supply chain requirements. Individual organizations must make a concerted effort to overcome these constraints to move freight in the most cost-efficient, customer-supportive manner possible. Fortunately, a variety of modal options exists to handle the task of moving freight in today's challenging environment.

Modes of Transportation

The primary modes of transportation available to the logistics manager are truck, rail, air, water, and pipeline. Additionally, intermodal transportation combines the use of two or more of the basic modes to move freight from its origin to destination. Each mode has different economic and technical structures, and each can provide different qualities of link service. This section provides an overview of each mode from the perspectives of service characteristics, volume and type of freight handled, cost structure, carrier types and service offerings, equipment variety, and current industry trends. Comparisons of the service capabilities, freight rates, and tradeoffs between the modes are provided in the discussion of modal selection later in the chapter.

Collectively, 12.5 billion tons of goods valued at nearly $11.7 trillion move through the U.S transportation system.[5] Table 10.1 provides key data for each mode of transportation. In terms of **ton-miles** (an output measurement combining weight and distance, or tonnage multiplied by miles transported), truck and rail are similar. However, the trucking industry dominates the U.S. transportation market in terms of the value of goods moved, followed by multimodal transportation.

In terms of freight expense, organizations spent $760 billion for transportation services in 2010. Almost 78 percent of the total was spent on trucking services at $592 billion, an increase of 9.3 percent over the previous year. Rail follows with 7.9 percent; air, 4.3 percent; water, 4.3 percent; forwarders, 4.2 percent, and pipeline, 1.3 percent.[6] The combined levels of freight value, volume, and spending suggest that truck, multimodal, and air transportation are premium-priced services for moving higher-value goods. In contrast, rail, water, and pipelines provide more economically priced services for lower-value commodities.

Motor Carriers

Motor carriage is the most widely used mode of transportation in the domestic supply chain. This mode is very much a part of an organization's supply chain with trucks,

Table 10.1	U.S. Domestic Freight Shipments by Mode: 2007		
MODE OF TRANSPORTATION	**VALUE OF GOODS**	**TONS (MILLIONS)**	**TON-MILES (BILLIONS)**
Truck	71.3%	70.0%	40.1%
Rail	3.7%	14.8%	40.2%
Water	1.0%	3.2%	4.7%
Air	2.2%	<1%	<1%
Pipeline	3.4%	5.2%	*
Multiple modes	16.0%	4.6%	12.5%

*Accurate data unavailable.

Source: Bureau of Transportation Statistics, *Pocket Guide to Transportation* (2011): 32.

ranging from the smallest delivery van to the largest tractor-trailer combinations, moving its freight. The sophisticated U.S. highway network permits trucks to reach all points of the country. Thus, trucking companies have excellent accessibility to virtually all freight shipping and receiving locations. This accessibility, combined with the industry's excellent service capabilities, has made trucking the mode of choice for high-value, time-sensitive goods.

The trucking industry is highly competitive and made up of 502,000 private, for-hire, and other U.S. interstate motor carriers.[7] These companies range in size from single-truck, owner-operator service providers to UPS, a $45.3 billion transportation conglomerate with over 400,000 employees, 78,000 vehicles, and 22,000 trailers. UPS Freight provides regional and interregional trucking services.[8] Of the $592 billion spent on trucking in 2010, 68 percent was spent on intercity transportation service versus 32 percent for local service.[9]

The economic structure of the motor carrier industry contributes to the vast number of carriers in the industry. First, there are no significant cost economies of scale that make it impossible for small carriers to compete. The equipment and licensing costs are not out of reach for most organizations. Second, most expenses are incurred as the result of moving freight; thus, trucking is a high-variable-cost, low-fixed-cost business. Trucking companies typically do not require extensive terminal and equipment investment and do not have to maintain the highway infrastructure. The U.S. government builds and maintains the highways, and motor carriers pay for highway use through fees such as use taxes and licensing charges. Thus, variable operating costs—wages and benefits, fuel, maintenance, and tires—have a greater impact on the economics of trucking companies.

Much of the freight moved by the trucking industry is regional in nature, moving within a 500-mile radius of the origin. Some of the primary commodities handled by this mode include consumer-packaged goods, electronics, electrical machinery, furniture, textiles, automotive parts, and other finished and semifinished goods. Shippers rely on the trucking industry to transport these goods because they are time sensitive and need superior protection while in transit.

The trucking industry is comprised of for-hire and private fleet operations. Private fleets primarily transport freight that is owned by the organization that is operating the trucks. They move over $3.4 trillion worth of goods and 37.5 percent of U.S. freight tonnage.[10] PepsiCo operates the largest private trucking fleet in the U.S. with 13,779 tractors, 50,993 straight trucks and vans, and 21,625 trailers in operation.[11]

For-hire trucking companies move freight for other organizations to the tune of $5 trillion worth of goods and 32.5 percent of U.S. freight tonnage.[12] The three general types of for-hire carriers include the following:

- **Truckload (TL) carriers** handle single large shipments per trailer that exceed 15,000 pounds or use the full cubic capacity of a trailer. TL carriers provide direct service, picking up the load at the origin point and delivering it directly to the destination without stopping at freight-handling terminals.

- **Less-than-truckload (LTL) carriers** move multiple shipments ranging from 150 pounds up to 15,000 pounds in each trailer. National LTL carriers use a hub-and-spoke network of local and regional terminal facilities to sort and consolidate shipments moving to a particular market area. Regional LTL carriers focus their efforts on a particular area of the country.

- **Small package carriers** handle shipments up to 150 pounds and move multiple shipments on a single van or truck. They use networks similar to LTL carriers to move freight efficiently throughout the country. UPS and FedEx Ground are the two largest small package ground carriers in the country.

The lines between these carrier types has blurred over the past few years. Carriers have responded to customer desires for transportation providers with multiple capabilities through acquisition activities. For example, FedEx and UPS transitioned from small package carriers to full service trucking companies over the last decade. Additionally, regional LTL carriers offer some direct TL-like services, and TL carriers are providing multi-stop deliveries for their customers. Suffice it to say that the trend will continue with carriers serving new markets, handling different-sized freight, and meeting unique customer service requirements as long as it is profitable for them to do so.

The flexibility of the trucking industry to handle the varying commodities and shipment sizes discussed above is provided by a wide range of equipment options. No longer are carriers limited to straight trucks and tractors hauling 35-foot trailers. New equipment innovations and less restrictive regulations allow carriers to use single trailers up to 53 feet long and twin 28-foot trailers. In a limited number of states, specially trained truck drivers are allowed to move longer combination vehicles (LCVs) on designated highways. Figure 10.1 highlights the variety of equipment combinations used in the trucking industry.

While motor carriers enjoy an enviable position in the transportation industry, they face daunting challenges in the future—rising costs, labor issues, and competition. Trucking companies are able to pass along rising fuel and insurance costs during economic expansions, but cannot always do so if capacity exceeds demand. A shortage of truck drivers will only become more serious as current drivers retire, and up to 8 percent of drivers may be eliminated through the CSA program. Finally, competition will remain

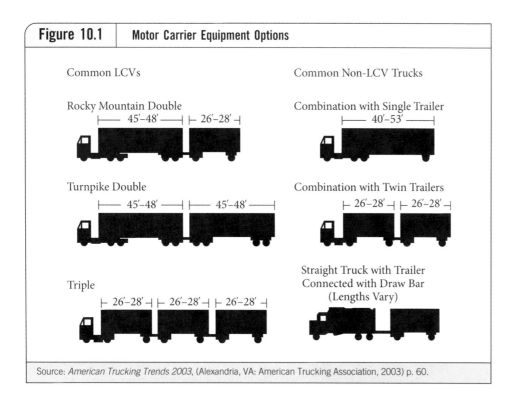

Figure 10.1 | **Motor Carrier Equipment Options**

Common LCVs

Rocky Mountain Double
|—— 45'–48' ——| |– 26'–28' –|

Turnpike Double
|—— 45'–48' ——| |—— 45'–48' ——|

Triple
|– 26'–28' –| |– 26'–28' –| |– 26'–28' –|

Common Non-LCV Trucks

Combination with Single Trailer
|—— 40'–53' ——|

Combination with Twin Trailers
|– 26'–28' –| |– 26'–28' –|

Straight Truck with Trailer
Connected with Draw Bar
(Lengths Vary)

Source: *American Trucking Trends 2003*, (Alexandria, VA: American Trucking Association, 2003) p. 60.

fierce within the trucking industry as well as with other modes of transportation. Customers expect near-perfect performance and will look for different options if service disruptions occur.

Railroads

Railroads transport a significant volume of freight in the United States, moving nearly 1.9 billion tons of freight annually. The combination of volume and the average shipment length of 728 miles make rail the highest ton-mile mode of transportation.[13] These activity levels have been achieved despite a lack of direct accessibility to all parts of the supply chain. Nagging perceptions of rail being a slow, inflexible, and inconsistent mode are challenges that must be overcome if the industry is to compete for higher-value, more profitable freight.

Although there are 563 railroads in the United States, the industry is dominated by seven Class I railroads (linehaul railroads with revenues in excess of $379 million). These Class I carriers generated $46.1 billion of rail industry revenues and handled 26 million carloads and 9.9 million intermodal trailers and containers.[14] Four of these companies—BNSF Railway, CSX Transportation, Norfolk Southern Railway, and Union Pacific Railroad—have evolved as the dominant carriers in the industry. None of these major rail carriers services the entire country by itself; they work together via interline agreements to provide coast-to-coast rail service.

This mode's economic structure partly accounts for the limited number of rail carriers. Railroads, which fall within that infamous group of business undertakings labeled as "natural monopolies," require a large investment in terminals, equipment, and trackage to begin operation; the accompanying huge capacity allows railroads to be a decreasing cost industry. As output (ton-miles) increases, the average per-unit production cost decreases. Thus, having fewer railroads in operation in a given area and permitting those few firms to realize inherent large-scale output economies are economical and beneficial to society.

Railroad transportation is primarily used for the long-distance movement of low-value raw materials and manufactured products. Primary commodities handled include coal, chemicals, farm products, minerals, food, and other basic materials. These products tend to be shipped in large quantities and stockpiled by customers to gain transportation efficiencies. Railroads also handle some high-value goods, primarily automobiles and intermodal containers filled with imported finished goods. In fact, intermodal volume is rising faster on a percentage basis than traditional rail freight.

The rail industry is comprised of the following two carrier types:

- **Linehaul freight carriers** provide service between major markets and customers within those markets. These carriers move freight in container, carload, and unit train quantities. The seven Class I railroads are linehaul carriers that provide a full array of interregional or regional services.

- **Shortline carriers** provide the local and regional links between individual customers and the national rail network of the Class I railroads. They serve smaller markets, handle local delivery service, and facilitate the interline process—activities that the long-haul carriers no longer find profitable. Some shortline railroads have been consolidated via holding companies. An example is RailAmerica, Inc., an operator of 40 shortline and regional railroads with approximately 7,300 miles of tracks in the United States and Canada.

Railroads can move almost any type of freight—liquid or gas, slurry or solid, hazardous or harmless—in very large quantities. From tri-level auto racks capable of holding up to 15 vehicles to tank cars that hold nearly 20,000 gallons of corn syrup, equipment exists to move the customer's freight. Hopper cars, boxcars, intermodal well cars, gondolas, and other specialized equipment are available from railroads, railcar leasing companies, or private owners.

Rail equipment can be organized into loads and transported in one of the three following primary ways:

- Manifest trains contain a mixture of equipment and freight for multiple customers. These mixed trains travel through multiple rail yards where railcars may be added to or removed from the train, depending on their destination and the route of the train. This time-consuming assembling and disassembling of trains, called **classification**, can easily add more than 24 hours to the delivery process.

- Unit trains move an entire block of railcars carrying a single commodity (e.g., coal) from the origin to a single destination. Unit trains use one type of railcar and eliminate the need to stop for the time-consuming rail yard classification activities. These types of trains move directly from origin to destination and operate on priority schedules. Thus, they can provide service that is as fast or faster than trucks, especially on cross-country moves.

- Intermodal trains are special types of unit trains that focus on the long-distance or linehaul movement of intermodal containers and trailers. These trains move products from ports and other high-volume origin points to major market areas where the containers are offloaded and given to trucking companies for final customer delivery.

The rail industry faces a number of challenges moving forward. Capacity is an ongoing concern. Railroad companies have responded by adding staff and locomotives, but the impact on service and capacity has been limited. With the track infrastructure remaining largely unchanged, additional freight, crews, and equipment cannot dramatically impact system delays.

On a positive note, demand for intermodal rail service is growing. Over a five-year period, U.S. intermodal rail traffic grew from 5.2 percent of ton-miles to 7.3 percent of ton-miles.[15] To leverage this opportunity, rail companies must provide consistent service quality. Class I railroads must address their congestion issues and deliver goods on time.

Air Carriers

Historically, air cargo transportation has been viewed as an expensive, "use only in an emergency" mode. The advent of e-commerce, the growth of global supply chains, and initiatives to reduce inventory and order cycle time have changed this outdated perspective and, in doing so, have contributed to a sustained increase in demand for air transportation. While air cargo transportation remains a small and specialized mode in terms of tonnage, U.S. spending was $33 billion in 2010.[16] Worldwide, air cargo industry revenues are approaching $594 billion, and freight traffic is projected to grow at an annual rate of 6.1 percent over the next 20 years.[17]

The Federal Aviation Administration activity report identifies 88 carriers that are engaged in air cargo, 22 of which are considered major carriers. The majors have revenues in excess of $1 billion from freight and/or passenger operations.[18] The majority of air cargo activity is handled by FedEx, UPS, Delta, and United. International air freight movement is handled by a broader range of organizations, with FedEx, UPS, Korean Air Lines, Cathay Pacific, and Lufthansa recording the largest ton-kilometers activity in the industry.[19]

The air carrier cost structure consists of high variable costs in proportion to fixed costs, somewhat akin to the motor carrier cost structure. Like motor and water carriers, air carriers do not invest heavily in facility infrastructure or byways. The government builds terminals and provides traffic control of the airways. Air carriers pay variable lease payments and landing fees for their use. Equipment costs, though quite high, are still a small part of the total cost.

Air transportation is used to ship small quantities of high-value, low-weight semi-finished and finished goods. Primary commodities handled by this mode include computers, precision instruments, electronics, pharmaceuticals, perishable foods, periodicals, and apparel. Companies are willing to pay a high premium to transport these goods because they are very time sensitive and need superior protection while in transit.

The following two primary carrier types dominate this mode:

- **Combination carriers** move freight and passengers, often on the same trip, with cargo loaded in the belly of the aircraft. As demand has grown, some of the larger international carriers have dedicated equipment specifically to cargo movement and provide scheduled service to meet the growing needs of global commerce. Of the major U.S. airlines that are combination carriers, Delta, United, and American handle the most freight ton-kilometers each year.

- **Air cargo carriers** focus exclusively on the movement of letters and envelopes, packages, and freight. Some carriers provide scheduled daily service through a highly coordinated network, while others provide on-demand service for customers who need more immediate, direct transportation or the full capacity of the aircraft. Air carriers can also be separated on the basis of service capabilities.

  - **Integrated carriers** provide door-to-door service, a consistent schedule of pickup and delivery windows, and standard expedited service through their hub-and-spoke networks. Because these carriers make air transportation of time-sensitive goods such a simple, well-controlled process, they dominate the U.S. domestic market for next-day and second-day movement of letters, small packages, and small shipments. Examples include FedEx and UPS.

  - **Nonintegrated carriers** provide on-demand, air-only service from airport to airport. They rely on freight forwarders or the customer to provide delivery service to and from the airport. The advantages of these carriers are the speed and flexibility of unscheduled direct service and the potential for same-day cargo movement.

Air cargo carriers employ a wide variety of aircraft to move freight domestically and around the world. Propeller planes capable of handling only a few thousand pounds are used to move letters and small packages from smaller markets to consolidation points and sort operations. Jets ranging in size up to the largest Boeing 747-400 freighter (capacity of nearly 27,500 cubic feet and 124 tons of freight) are used for long-range domestic and international service. Aircraft like the Anatov 124 can transport unique products of up to 150 tons with dimensions as large as 13 feet high by 19 feet wide. Whatever the shipment requirement may be, an aircraft with an appropriate combination of payload, range, and speed is likely available.

The air cargo industry faces numerous obstacles to profitable growth, including cost issues, competition, and security challenges. First, the rising cost of kerosene-type jet fuel directly impacts the success of the industry. For every $1 increase per barrel of oil, worldwide airline industry costs increase $1.6 billion.[20] Some of these costs may be recouped through fuel surcharges, but the growth of next-day trucking services is putting pressure on the domestic air cargo industry. Air carriers may find it difficult to pass along increased costs in the face of this growing competition. Finally, the industry is under pressure from costly security mandates. Homeland security fees, 100 percent cargo screening costs, training, and related security expenses are estimated to have an annual impact of more than $4 billion on the industry according to the Air Transport Association.

Water Carriers

Water transportation has played a significant role in the development of many countries and is a major facilitator of international trade. In the United States, $115 billion worth of freight and 4.7 percent of the total ton-miles annually is moved via water transportation.[21] The industry generated $33 billion in revenue, $28 billion for the movement of international goods, and $5 billion for domestic coastal, inland, and Great Lakes traffic.[22] Globally, water carriers dominate all other modes, garnering approximately half of the international freight revenue and handling nearly all tonnage.

The 652 carriers in the U.S. domestic water industry use 9,000 vessels and 31,000 barges to move 3.2 percent of the nation's freight. The fleet includes nearly 3,000 dry cargo and passenger vessels, 578 ferries, 5,400 towboats for barges, and 76 tankers to move liquid products. Over half of the vessels and 86 percent of the barges operate in the Mississippi River System and the Gulf Intracoastal Waterway, moving bulk raw materials.[23] Although very slow and limited by the natural infrastructure, domestic water carriers offer tremendous capacity per vessel (e.g., one barge holds as much freight as 15 rail cars or 60 trucks), efficient fuel consumption, and low cost.

The economics of water transportation is similar to that of airlines. To begin operation, these carriers require no investment for the right-of-way—nature provides the "highway," and government entities known as port authorities provide unloading and loading services, storage areas, and freight transfer facilities. The water carriers pay user fees for these port services only when used. Large oceangoing ships require significant capital investments, but cost is spread over a large volume of freight transported during the lengthy lifespan of most ships.

The domestic carriers compete vigorously with railroads for long-distance movement of low-value, high-density, bulk cargoes that mechanical devices can easily load and unload. Like the railroads, water carriers allow customers to cost-effectively move large quantities of raw materials like petroleum, coal, iron ore, chemicals, forest products, and other commodities. However, water carriers handle a wider variety of goods. Every conceivable type of cargo is transported via international water carrier, from low-value commodities to imported automobiles. Many imported consumer goods flow to the United States from the Far East in 20- and 40-foot ocean shipping containers.

Two primary carrier types dominate the for-hire portion of the water industry, as follows:

- **Liner services** employ a wide variety of ships in their fixed-route, published-schedule service. Liner service carriers like AP Moeller-Maersk, Mediterranean Shipping Company, and CMA CGM Group typically handle individual shipments for their customers, including containers, pallets, and other unit loads.

- **Charter services** lease ships to customers on a voyage or time basis and follow routes of the customer's choosing. The charter customer normally uses the entire capacity of the ship for large-volume freight. Charter services operate similarly to taxicab service (customer-specified route, tailored service), while liner service is much like a scheduled bus service (fixed route, standard service).

Ocean transportation of goods ranging from crude oil to electronics is facilitated by a wide range of specialized ships. The most widely used options include the following:

- **Containerships** are critical to the globalization of trade. These ships are specially designed to carry standardized containers, which are commonly rated in TEU (20-foot equivalent units) or FEU (40-foot equivalent units). Containerships vary considerably in size, from small ships capable of holding fewer than 400 containers to post-Panamax ships with capacities exceeding 6,000 TEU. In recent years, Maersk Line launched ships that regularly carry 11,000 TEU and has ordered an 18,000 TEU ship. Containerships have the flexibility to carry a wide variety of cargo, including many products that require special handling, temperature control, and so on.

- **Bulk carriers** carry cargoes with low value-to-weight ratios, such as ores, grain, coal, and scrap metal. Very large openings on these ships' holds allow easy loading and unloading. Watertight walls dividing the holds allow a ship to carry more than one commodity at a time.

- **Tankers** carry the largest amount of cargo by tonnage, usually on a charter basis. These ships range in size from World War II–era tankers of 18,000 tons to very large crude carriers (VLCCs), some of which top 500,000 tons. Tankers are constructed in much the same way as bulk carriers but with smaller deck openings. New tankers are required to be double-hulled to protect the environment in case of a collision.

- **General cargo ships** are usually engaged to transport shipload cargoes on a charter basis and have large cargo holds and freight-handling equipment to facilitate the loading and unloading of a large variety of freight. The self-sufficiency of these ships allows them to load and discharge cargo at ports that lack up-to-date cargo-handling equipment. This feature is very important for ships transporting goods to less-developed portions of the world.

- **Roll-on, roll-off (RO–RO) vessels** are another type of ship proving its value in international trade. RO–ROs are basically large ferry ships. The carrier drives the cargo directly onto the ship using built-in ramps and drives or tows it off at its destination. Larger RO–ROs can transport 2,000 or more automobiles, as well as freight trailers, containers, farm and construction equipment, and other wheeled vehicles.

The major challenges faced by carriers in international water transportation relate to capacity, trade imbalances, environmental concerns, and security. Capacity shortages can be a problem when the global economy is growing, but the problem shifted to excess capacity during the global recession. Also, the imbalance of international trade between export-dominant Asian countries and import-dominant North America can create equipment availability problems at the origin and port congestion problems at the destination. Both problems result in supply chain delays that impact demand fulfillment. The industry must also work to reduce carbon dioxide emissions as ships burning low-grade fuel account for 4.5 percent of all global emissions of this greenhouse gas. Security is a multifaceted challenge that must be addressed. The On the Line feature highlights the growing problem of piracy.

On the Line   *Piracy: A Modern Day Problem*

Though the Pirates of the Caribbean movies portray piracy as an adventurous relic of the 17th century, the 21st century version is anything but fun. The growing criminal enterprise of the high seas focuses on cargo theft, multi-million dollar ransoms, and terrorism rather than treasure seeking adventure.

The International Maritime Bureau (IMB) reported that 266 pirate attacks occurred in the first six months of 2011 versus 196 during the same period in 2010. The attacks are highly coordinated, violent, and involve the use of heavy weaponry including automatic machine guns and rocket propelled grenade launchers. Also of great concern is the increasingly violent nature of these attacks. Worldwide, pirates murdered seven sailors, injured another 39, and took 495 hostages during the first half of 2011.

The epicenter of the problem is in the Gulf of Aden off the coast of Somalia where 163 attacks resulted in the hijacking of 21 ships during this six month time frame, notes the IMB. With potential ransoms of up to $10 million, these pirates are getting more daring with coordinated, swarming attacks and one incident that took place in the territorial waters of Oman. The chemical tanker was boarded while at anchor and the crew forced to set course for Somalia. Other maritime piracy hot spots include the Strait of Malacca, South China Sea, and the Red Sea.

Ocean carriers and government agencies are taking decisive steps to combat the modern day piracy problem. Ship captains have been instructed to move vessels at faster speeds, take routes that are longer but safer, and train their crews to detect and defend against attacks. Governments are developing stronger anti-piracy laws, using their navies to patrol dangerous waters, and working together to combat pirates. Warships from the European Union, the United States, China, Japan, Russia, India and other nations have thwarted numerous pirate attacks in the Gulf of Aden. These efforts are aimed at combating a growing piracy problem, estimated to cost the global shipping industry between $3.5 billion and $8 billion.

Sources: David Rosenberg, "Somali Pirates Grow More Daring," *The Jerusalem Post*, August 30, 2011; Fleming Emil Hansen, "Piracy Spurs Maersk to Raise Fee," *The Wall Street Journal*, May 9, 2011; Katerina Kerr, "First Quarter 2011 the Worst Ever for Piracy," *IFW*, April 15, 2011, "Piracy at Sea," The New York Times, February 24, 2011, "Pirate Attacks at Sea Getting Bigger and Bolder, Says IMB Report, July 14, 2011, retrieved from http://www.icc-ccs.org/news/450-pirate-attacks-at-sea-getting-bigger-and-bolder-says-imb-report.

Pipelines

Pipelines are the "hidden giant" of the transportation modes, quietly handling 5.2 percent of U.S. freight tonnage. This is a unique mode of transportation as the equipment is fixed in place and the product moves through it in high volume. Pipelines effectively protect the product from contamination and also provide a warehousing function. Pipelines provide the most economical form of transportation with the lowest cost per ton of any mode.

The United States has the largest network of energy pipelines of any nation in the world. The oil pipeline network alone in the United States is more than 10 times larger than that in Europe. There are 339 operators of hazardous liquid pipelines that primarily carry crude oil and petroleum products. Some organizations focus strictly on transportation, while large oil companies like ExxonMobil, BP, and Shell produce and transport products via individually or jointly owned pipelines. The natural gas pipeline industry is much less concentrated with 967 organizations involved in the transmission of product and another 1,285 involved in the final distribution of natural gas.[24]

Pipeline costs are predominantly fixed. Pipeline operators must build their own right-of-way, which is a rather expensive proposition. Variable costs in the industry are very low as little labor is required to operate the pipelines and limited fuel is needed to run pumps. The construction of a pipeline becomes cost effective when product flows continuously, allowing the fixed costs to be spread over a high volume of goods.

The vast majority of products moved by pipeline are liquids and gases, the economically feasible products to flow via this mode. Common liquid products include crude oil and petroleum-based fuels for transportation and home heating. Widely distributed gaseous products include natural gas for home heating and propane, anhydrous ammonia, and carbon dioxide used in agricultural and industrial applications. In the past, attempts have been made to move solid product in a slurry form, but this has not proved to be competitive with water and rail transportation.

The pipeline industry is comprised of for-hire and private carriers that maintain their own infrastructures. For-hire carriers of liquid products can move different products through their system at the same time, separated by a batching plug that maintains the integrity of individual products. Private carriers include petroleum and natural gas companies that use pipelines to move product to and from their refineries, processing plants, and storage facilities. Companies, like a power plant or a chemical plant, may operate a small pipeline system to bring fuel to the plant or to move feed-stocks from one plant to another.

The oil system is made up of the following three primary types of pipelines:

- **Gathering lines** are very small pipelines, usually from 2 to 8 inches in diameter. They are used together and move oil from both onshore and offshore oil wells to trunk lines. It is estimated that between 30,000 to 40,000 miles of gathering lines exist, primarily in the larger oil-producing states.
- **Trunk lines**, measuring from 8 to 24 inches in diameter, bring crude oil from extraction points to refineries. There are approximately 55,000 miles of crude oil trunk lines in the United States, including the well-known Trans-Alaska Pipeline System. This 800-mile long, 48-inch diameter pipeline connects Prudhoe Bay on Alaska's North Slope to Valdez, the northernmost ice-free port in North America.
- **Refined product pipelines** carry petroleum products—gasoline, jet fuel, home heating oil, and diesel fuel—from refineries to large fuel terminals with storage tanks in almost every state in the country. These pipelines vary in size from relatively small 8- to 12-inch diameter lines up to 42-inch diameter lines. The total mileage nationwide of refined products pipelines is approximately 95,000 miles. These pipelines deliver petroleum products to large fuel terminals with storage tanks. Major industries, airports, and electrical power generation plants can be supplied directly by pipeline.[25]

Natural gas pipelines use similar networks of gathering lines, transmission lines, and main distribution lines to move product closer to the market. The major difference is the direct delivery of natural gas to homes and businesses using local distribution lines. These distribution lines, found below street level in almost every city and town, account for the vast majority of pipeline mileage in the United States—1.8 million miles.

The ongoing issues for the pipeline industry are safety and security. Compared to other modes, pipelines have enviable safety and environmental records with spills amounting to only one gallon per million barrel-miles. However, vigilance is critical because pipeline accidents can quickly become catastrophic events. For example, a September 2010 natural gas pipeline explosion in San Bruno, California, killed eight people and destroyed 38 homes.[26] Pipeline operators must also be cognizant of security risks that pipelines present and take actions to protect their assets and the flow of vital petroleum products through the supply chain. Contingency plans to deal with disruptive events like hurricanes or a terrorist attack on pipeline operations must also be maintained.

Intermodal Transportation

While the five primary modes give supply chain managers numerous transportation options, another group of alternatives exists. **Intermodal transportation service** refers to the use of two or more carriers of different modes in the origin-to-destination movement of freight. Shifting freight between modes may seem inefficient and time consuming, but the improved reach and combined service advantages created by intermodal transportation offset these issues. These primary benefits of intermodalism include the following:

- Greater accessibility is created by linking the individual modes. The road infrastructure allows trucks to reach locations that are inaccessible to other modes, especially air transportation, water transportation, and pipelines. For example, air transportation can only move freight between airport facilities. Trucks provide the flow between the origin and the departure airport as well as the arrival airport and the customer destination. Railroads can also facilitate the use of domestic river transportation and international ocean transportation. Getting low-sulfur coal from a Wyoming mine to a utility company in Japan would be best accomplished through a combination of rail and water transportation.

- Overall cost efficiency can be achieved without sacrificing service quality or accessibility. In other words, intermodal transportation allows supply chains to utilize the inherent capabilities of multiple modes to control cost and fulfill customer requirements. If a furniture manufacturer needed to move 20 loads of furniture from North Carolina to California, a combination of truck and rail transportation would improve upon truck-only service. The speed and accessibility of trucks would be used for the initial pickup and final delivery, while the cross-country transportation would be handled by the cost-efficient railroads.

- Intermodal transportation facilitates global trade. The capacity and efficiency of ocean transportation allow large-volume shipments to be transported between continents at relatively low per-unit costs. The speed of air transportation allows perishable goods to flow quickly between countries. The final domestic leg of the delivery can take place via truck. The ocean–truck combination makes product competitive across global markets by keeping the landed cost in check. The air–truck combination facilitates expedited distribution of "hot commodities" like fashion and rapid replenishment of products that are in high demand.

Although no universal statistics are kept on intermodal transportation, there is strong evidence that intermodal transportation has grown in importance and volume. The number of containers flowing from around the world through U.S. ports has increased from 15.5 million TEUs in 1990 to 37.2 million TEUs in 2009.[27] Experts predict that this trend will continue as the global economy recovers. Domestic flows of intermodal freight have also risen over the same 20-year period. For example, the U.S. rail system moved 8.2 million containers and 1.6 million trailers in 2009.[28]

Much of this intermodal growth can be attributed to the development of standardized containers that are compatible with multiple modes. A standard dry box container looks much like a truck trailer without the chassis; can be lifted, stacked, and moved from one piece of equipment to another; and is built to standard dimensional height and width specifications in a variety of lengths (10-, 20-, and 40-foot marine containers for international transportation and 40-, 48-, and 53-foot containers for domestic truck and rail transportation). Specialized containers are also available for handling temperature-sensitive goods (refrigerated containers), commodities (tank and dry bulk cargo containers), and other unique cargoes.

Other factors have contributed to the growth of intermodal transportation. They include better information systems to track freight as it moves through the supply chain and the development of intermodal terminals to facilitate efficient freight transfers between modes. In addition, new generations of ocean vessels, railcars, and truck trailers are being built specifically to handle intermodal freight in greater quantity and with greater ease.

Ocean carriers are continually developing larger containerships to handle international intermodal traffic, improve fuel efficiency, and reduce carbon emissions per container transported. Importantly, the Panama Canal Authority is in the midst of an eight-year, $5.25 billion expansion project to handle these ships. More than half the funds—$3.35 billion—will be spent on new single-lane, three-step locks at the Atlantic and Pacific entrances, as well as on new channels. The project, scheduled to be completed in 2014, will augment existing locks and allow the canal to handle 12,000 TEU ships.

The rail industry also offers a variety of equipment for moving intermodal shipments. Initial efforts focused on moving standard truck trailers on flatbed rail cars. This was called "piggy-back" service or trailer-on-flatcar (TOFC) service. This type of service is shrinking in favor of container-on-flatcar (COFC) service and double-stack container services. These methods allow rail companies to carry a wider variety of containers—everything from 10-foot ocean containers to 53-foot domestic freight containers—in nearly any combination. Double-stack service is especially efficient.

The freight services provided by intermodal transportation can be viewed in terms of product-handling characteristics as follows:

- **Containerized freight** is loaded into or onto storage equipment (a container or pallet) at the origin and delivered to the destination in or on that same piece of equipment with no additional handling. For example, if a load of DVD players needed to be shipped from the factory to the market, the players would be loaded into a 40-foot container at the factory in Taiwan, transferred to the port via truck, and then loaded on a containership bound for Los Angeles. Upon arrival, the container would be moved from the ship onto another truck and delivered to the retailer's distribution center.

- **Transload freight** involves goods that are handled and transferred between transportation equipment multiple times. Transload freight primarily consists of bulk-oriented raw materials that must be scooped, pumped, lifted, or conveyed from one container to another when transferred from one mode to another. For example, orange juice concentrate may be picked up using a rail tank car, pumped into the hold of a cargo ship for the linehaul move, and then pumped into a tank truck for final delivery.

Figure 10.2	Widely Used Intermodal Transportation Combinations

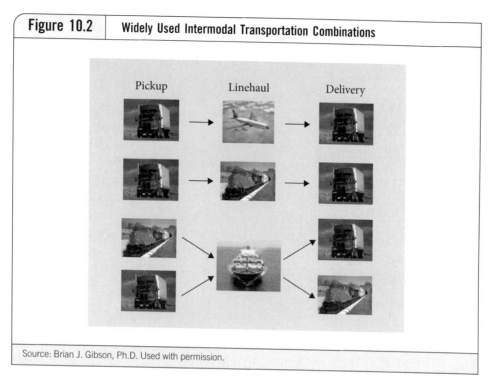

Source: Brian J. Gibson, Ph.D. Used with permission.

Another way to look at the intermodal option is based on the type of service used. Figure 10.2 depicts the most prevalent forms of intermodal transportation, including truck–rail, truck–air, and truck–water, although other combinations are also used. Some carriers (e.g., CSX, Maersk Sealand, and FedEx) have multimodal capabilities, allowing them to utilize the most efficient and economical combinations of intermodal transportation for their customers. In the majority of cases, the carrier makes the determination of what mode or modal combinations to use. After all, when customers drop overnight letters in the express delivery box, they are not concerned about the combination of modes used as long as the letters arrive on time!

A recurring issue in the intermodal transportation market is congestion. While ocean carriers can add or reduce capacity to meet demand levels, transfer points are not as flexible and can get clogged with freight. During peak economic growth, the U.S. seaport facilities along the Pacific coast have struggled to keep product flowing through their facilities in a timely fashion during critical seasons. Intermodal capacity problems in the rail industry also surface from time to time. Equipment shortages, transfer facility congestion, and labor issues create delivery delays and supply chain disruptions. Infrastructure investment, equipment purchases, and operator hiring will be needed to prepare for the anticipated growth of intermodal transportation.

Transportation Planning and Strategy

Understanding the modal options is an important aspect of transportation management. However, before the freight begins to flow, other vital issues must also be addressed. Supply chain professionals must make a series of interrelated transportation decisions and design processes that properly align with the organization's supply chain strategies. These planning issues, highlighted in Figure 10.3, are discussed next.

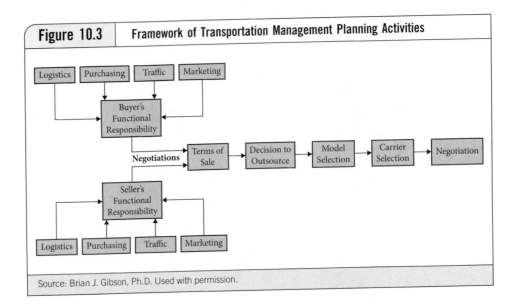

Figure 10.3 | **Framework of Transportation Management Planning Activities**

Source: Brian J. Gibson, Ph.D. Used with permission.

Functional Control of Transportation

The initial decision for any organization is straightforward but important—determining which department(s) will be responsible for each part of the transportation process. Whenever you buy goods, sell goods, or do both, somebody has to be responsible for making key decisions and managing the process. Even in a simple purchase over the Internet, you have to select a carrier (UPS, FedEx, U.S. Postal Service, etc.), service level (next-day, second-day, etc.), insurance coverage, and a related price. A failure on your part to take responsibility can result in the seller making decisions that do not fit your budget or service needs.

In most organizations, responsibility for transportation decisions falls to one or more of the following departments: logistics, procurement, and marketing. Historically, transportation was divided into two separate issues, inbound transportation of goods purchased and outbound transportation of goods sold. In this structure, the purchasing department controls inbound transportation decisions, while marketing has responsibility for outbound transportation control. Often, this decision-making structure leads to a secondary focus on transportation in lieu of procurement costs or customer demands. In the worst-case scenario, these departments arbitrarily relegate decision making to suppliers and customers. The outcome is limited opportunity to leverage transportation efficiencies and services for the benefit of all supply chain partners.

Today, savvy organizations assign transportation decision-making responsibility to a single department (e.g., logistics, distribution, operations, transportation). This department strives to coordinate inbound and outbound transportation, develop common goals, leverage purchasing power, and procure quality service in support of supply chain excellence. The results of single-department control and coordination can be impressive. Many companies have been able to bolster capacity, improve freight visibility and control, enhance customer service, and reduce empty miles, all while better managing their transportation spending.

Terms of Sale

Free-on-board (FOB) terms of sale specify when the ownership and title of the goods pass from a seller to a buyer in a domestic transaction. International terms of sale are covered by International Commercial Terms (Incoterms). Wise selection of FOB terms or Incoterms is critical as your decision determines control over mode and carrier selection, transportation rate negotiation, and other key decisions.

Another important aspect of terms of sale is the determination of in-transit freight accountability. FOB terms and Incoterms determine where the buyer's responsibilities begin and where the seller's responsibilities end.

FOB Terms

Domestically, if the terms are FOB origin, title (ownership) to the goods changes hands at the origin—usually the shipping point or seller's distribution center loading dock. From that point on, the goods belong to the buyer, and any loss or damage is the responsibility of the buyer. If the terms are FOB destination, the title transfers at the destination—typically the buyer's unloading dock. The seller has total responsibility for the goods until they are delivered to the buyer.

A related issue is the responsibility for carrier payment. In general, the seller pays the carrier for the transportation service cost under FOB destination terms, while the buyer pays the carrier under FOB origin terms. However, exceptions to these guidelines do occur. The option for Freight Prepaid or Freight Collect should be specified with the FOB terms. In cases where the seller has more clout with carriers, it is wise to have the seller negotiate transportation rates under the Freight Prepaid option. Freight Collect is typically used when the buyer has more power with carriers. Table 10.2 highlights the six different FOB payment responsibility options with their respective buyer and seller duties.

Table 10.2	Key Responsibilities Under FOB and Freight Payment Terms				
FOB TERM AND FREIGHT PAYMENT RESPONSIBILITY	**WHO OWNS GOODS IN TRANSIT?**	**WHO HANDLES FREIGHT CLAIMS?**	**WHO SELECTS AND PAYS CARRIER?**	**WHO ULTIMATELY BEARS FREIGHT COSTS?**	**BEST USED WHEN _____ HAS GREATER INFLUENCE WITH CARRIER**
FOB Origin, Freight Collect	Buyer	Buyer	Buyer	Buyer	Buyer
FOB Origin, Freight Prepaid	Buyer	Buyer	Seller	Seller	Seller
FOB Origin, Freight Prepaid & Charged Back	Buyer	Buyer	Seller	Buyer The seller adds freight costs to goods invoice.	Seller
FOB Destination, Freight Prepaid	Seller	Seller	Seller	Seller	Seller
FOB Destination, Freight Collect	Seller	Seller	Buyer	Buyer	Buyer
FOB Destination, Freight Collect & Allowed	Seller	Seller	Buyer	Seller The buyer deducts freight cost from goods payment.	Buyer

Source: Adapted from Bruce J. Riggs, "The Traffic Manager in Physical Distribution Management," *Transportation and Distribution Management*, June 1968, p. 45.

Incoterms

International transactions often present greater challenges, and parties to the transaction must understand how these terms of sale can impact transportation decision making. Even a relatively straightforward international transaction involves long distances, multiple modes of transportation and logistics intermediaries, duties and tariffs, government inspections, and significant opportunity for damage or delay. Thus, transportation managers must be extremely concerned about when and where the title to the goods will change hands.

Incoterms facilitate efficient freight flows between countries. As described by the International Chamber of Commerce, Incoterms are international rules that are accepted by governments, legal authorities, and practitioners worldwide for the interpretation of the most commonly used terms in international trade. They address matters relating to the rights and obligations of the parties to the contract of sale with respect to the delivery of goods sold.[29]

These terms of sale decisions help to clarify the following questions:

- Who will be responsible for control and care of the goods while in transit?
- Who will be responsible for carrier selection, transfers, and related product "flow" issues?
- Who will bear various costs—freight, insurance, taxes, duties, and forwarding fees?
- Who will handle documentation, problem resolution, and other related issues?

Since 1936, Incoterms have been revised and refined seven times. The most recent update, known as Incoterms 2010, is an effort to simplify these trade terms. The number of Incoterms options has been reduced from 13 to 11, seven of which apply to all modes of transportation and four of which apply only to water transportation. Among other changes, Incoterms 2010 have been clarified so that they can apply to both international and domestic freight.

The 11 options range from the buyer taking all transportation responsibilities at the seller's location to the seller taking responsibility all the way through delivery to the buyer's location (and numerous locations in between). It is easiest to think of these 11 options in terms of their groupings – E terms where the buyer takes full responsibility from point of departure, F terms in which the main carriage is not paid by the seller, C terms in which the main carrier is paid by the seller, and D terms where the seller takes full responsibility to an arrival point. Figure 10.4 highlights the respective roles of the seller and buyer under each of the 11 Incoterms.

Taking control of freight through FOB terms or Incoterms can be very beneficial for organizations with the expertise, volume, and time to manage the process. Having this control allows you to leverage your purchasing power with specific carriers to achieve lower rates, coordinate inbound and outbound flows, and consolidate freight to achieve greater efficiencies. Other potential benefits include the ability to manage risk, achieve greater freight visibility, and ensure available equipment capacity. Hence, companies with well-organized, integrated logistics functions should view terms of sale as a strategic opportunity to improve transportation and supply chain performance.

Decision to Outsource Transportation

The organization with FOB freight control and procurement responsibility must analyze the transportation "make or buy" decision. Firms must choose between transporting goods using a private fleet (the "make" option) and using external service providers to

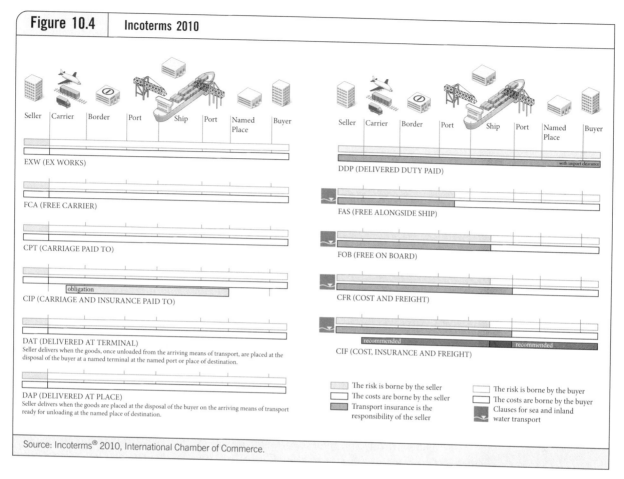

Figure 10.4 | Incoterms 2010

EXW (EX WORKS)

FCA (FREE CARRIER)

CPT (CARRIAGE PAID TO)

CIP (CARRIAGE AND INSURANCE PAID TO)

DAT (DELIVERED AT TERMINAL)
Seller delivers when the goods, once unloaded from the arriving means of transport, are placed at the disposal of the buyer at a named terminal at the named port or place of destination.

DAP (DELIVERED AT PLACE)
Seller delivers when the goods are placed at the disposal of the buyer on the arriving means of transport ready for unloading at the named place of destination.

DDP (DELIVERED DUTY PAID)

FAS (FREE ALONGSIDE SHIP)

FOB (FREE ON BOARD)

CFR (COST AND FREIGHT)

CIF (COST, INSURANCE AND FREIGHT)

The risk is borne by the seller
The costs are borne by the seller
Transport insurance is the responsibility of the seller

The risk is borne by the buyer
The costs are borne by the buyer
Clauses for sea and inland water transport

Source: Incoterms® 2010, International Chamber of Commerce.

move freight (the "buy" option). The decision involves multiple considerations and can be difficult. The primary options are discussed next.

Private fleets account for nearly half of all U.S. freight transportation spending and more than half the miles traveled. Companies like PepsiCo, Walmart, and DuPont move freight (primarily finished goods) on company-owned or company-operated equipment. These companies use private fleets for a variety of economic, customer service, and marketing reasons. They have proven that a well-run private fleet can operate at costs competitive with for-hire carriers while providing greater scheduling flexibility and control over transit time. Intangible benefits such as the promotional impact and prestige of having highly visible company trucks on the road can also be gained. Many organizations have turned their trailers into 48- to 53-foot rolling billboards.

On the other hand, some organizations have decided that it is best to have external experts move the freight or manage the transportation process. For-hire carriers in all modes (e.g., Schneider National, Lufthansa, Canadian Pacific Railway, Hapag-Lloyd) have the expertise, flexibility, and capacity to move freight for a wide variety of customers. External service providers also offer a variable-cost, simplified, headache-free alternative to private transportation.

By using for-hire carriers, the customers do not have to incur the large capital cost of starting a private fleet, invest the time needed to build transportation expertise, or take on the potential risks (liability for accidents, compliance with government regulations, dealing with unions, etc.) inherent in operating a private fleet. As a result, the for-hire transportation industry is huge. More than $697 billion is spent on for-hire freight transportation each year in the United States.

Another alternative to a private fleet is third-party logistics (3PL), discussed in Chapter 4. Third-party firms provide a wide array of transportation services. Dedicated contract carriage is one such service of 3PLs (e.g., Exel and Transfreight) and truckload carriers (e.g., Werner Enterprises and J. B. Hunt). Under this arrangement, the 3PL serves as the organization's private fleet and devotes a management team, drivers, and equipment to the relationship.

Another service is traffic management where the 3PL provides transportation planning and tactical decision making, handles administrative functions like freight bill auditing, and coordinates supply chain activities. Finally, some 3PLs provide international transportation assistance in the areas of documentation, carrier and route selection, Customs clearance, and other tasks that impact the timely, cost-effective flow of goods across borders.

Modal Selection

A critical transportation management issue is modal selection; it affects how quickly and efficiently products will flow across portions of the supply chain. If an organization has determined that controlling the transportation process and using external service providers (for-hire carriers or 3PLs) are in its best interest, it must then determine which mode(s) of transportation to use. Choosing among the six modal options is a function of three factors—modal capabilities, product characteristics, and modal freight pricing.

All modes provide the same basic service of moving freight from point to point in the supply chain. However, a review of Table 10.1 reveals that the modes serve different customer requirements and goods in terms of value, tonnage, and ton-miles. The reason for the different uses is that each mode has unique attributes and capabilities that affect its ability to serve specific customer requirements. Many of these unique attributes are summarized in Table 10.3.

Numerous studies have been conducted over the years to identify the most important performance capabilities in modal selection. These studies commonly identify accessibility, transit time, reliability, and product safety as the key determinants in choosing a mode. Of course, cost is another critical consideration in modal selection. A discussion of each capability and relevant modal performance is provided next.

Accessibility

Accessibility determines whether a particular mode can physically perform the transport service required. Accessibility considers the mode's ability to reach origin and destination facilities and provide service over the specified route in question. The geographic limits of a mode's infrastructure or network and the operating scope that governmental regulatory agencies authorize also affect accessibility. Accessibility problems often eliminate a mode from consideration during the selection process.

- **Accessibility advantage:** Motor carriage, because of its inherent ability to provide service to virtually any location. Given the road networks in most countries, motor carriage is more accessible to sellers and buyers than any other mode for domestic transportation.

Table 10.3	Comparison of Modal Capabilities				
MODE	**STRENGTHS**	**LIMITATIONS**	**PRIMARY ROLE**	**PRIMARY PRODUCT CHARACTERISTICS**	**EXAMPLE PRODUCTS**
Truck	• Accessible • Fast and versatile • Customer service	• Limited capacity • High cost	• Move smaller shipments in local, regional, and national markets	• High value • Finished goods • Low volume	• Food • Clothing • Electronics • Furniture
Rail	• High capacity • Low cost	• Accessibility • Inconsistent service • Damage rates	• Move large shipments of domestic freight long distances	• Low value • Raw materials • High volume	• Coal/coke • Lumber/paper • Grain • Chemicals
Air	• Speed • Freight protection • Flexibility	• Accessibility • High cost • Low capacity	• Move urgent shipments of domestic freight and smaller shipments of international freight	• High value • Finished goods • Low volume • Time sensitive	• Computers • Periodicals • Pharmaceuticals • Business to consumer (B2C) deliveries
Water	• High capacity • Low cost • International capabilities	• Slow • Accessibility	• Move large domestic shipments via rivers and canals • Move large shipments of international freight via oceans	• Low value • Raw materials • Bulk commodities • Containerized finished goods	• Crude oil • Ores/minerals • Farm products • Clothing • Electronics • Toys
Pipeline	• In-transit storage • Efficiency • Low cost	• Slow • Limited network	• Move large volumes of domestic freight long distances	• Low value • Liquid commodities • Not time sensitive	• Crude oil • Petroleum • Gasoline • Natural gas

Source: Brian J. Gibson, Ph.D. Used with permission.

- **Accessibility disadvantage:** Air, rail, and water. All face accessibility limitations due to infrastructure issues. Air transportation is affected by the number and location of airports. Rail transportation can directly serve only those customers that are adjacent to rail tracks. Water transportation is limited by the availability and depth of waterways. Still, all three modes serve virtually every major market thanks to intermodalism. These modes provide the long-distance linehaul service, while motor carriers provide pickup and delivery activities that occur away from the air, water, or rail terminals.

Transit Time

Transit time is critical in supply chain management because of its impact on inventory availability, stockout costs, and customer satisfaction. Transit time is the total elapsed time that it takes to move goods from the point of origin to the destination (i.e., door to door). This includes the time required for pickup activities, terminal handling, linehaul movement, and customer delivery. Companies typically monitor average transit time for their service providers. Transit time is impacted by the speed of the mode and the ability of the mode to handle pickup and delivery responsibilities.

- **Transit time advantage:** Air transportation is very fast for the linehaul move but loses some velocity as pickup and delivery activities must be handled by truck. Motor carriage is also relatively fast because it can provide more direct movement from origin to destination far more often than any other mode.
- **Transit time disadvantage:** Rail, water, and pipeline are extremely slow with average transit speeds of 22 miles per hour, 5–9 miles per hour, and 3–4 miles per hour, respectively.

Reliability

Reliability is a critical issue. Many companies feel that transit time reliability is more important than speed as it impacts their ability to plan supply chain activities. Reliability refers to the consistency of the transit time provided by a transportation mode. It is easier to forecast inventory needs, schedule production, and determine safety stock levels if it is known with some certainty when goods will arrive. Reliability is measured by the statistical variation in transit time.

Modal reliability is affected by a variety of factors including equipment and labor availability, weather, traffic congestion, freight-handling requirements, number of terminal stops involved, and other factors. Internationally, reliability is impacted by distance, port congestion issues, security requirements, and border crossings, especially when the two countries do not have a proactive trade agreement.

- **Reliability advantage:** Motor carriers and air carriers, as they are the most reliable (variability relevant to average transit time). Numerous carriers in both modes achieve on-time delivery performance in the 98 percent or greater level.
- **Reliability disadvantage:** Water carriers and rail carriers. Historically, they have been slow and consistent, but with the capacity and congestion challenges, they have become less consistent. As a result, some customers have reduced their use of these modes when possible.

Product Safety

Safety is critical to the achievement of customer service, cost control, and supply chain effectiveness. From a safety standpoint, goods must arrive at the destination in the same condition they were in when tendered for shipment at the origin. Proper precautions must be taken to protect freight from loss due to external theft, internal pilferage, and misplacement, as well as damage due to poor freight-handling techniques, poor ride quality, and accidents. Safety is often pursued through substantial protective packing.

- **Safety advantage:** Air transportation and motor carriage have the best reputations for product security. Their equipment provides excellent ride quality and protection from the elements. Faster transit times also reduce the opportunity for theft and other mishaps.
- **Safety disadvantage:** Rail and water face significant challenges to maintaining product integrity. Goods moving via rail encounter a great deal of vibration created by steel wheels on steel track, swaying, and jarring from freight cars being coupled at speeds of up to 10 miles per hour. Water transportation often exposes goods to the elements (corrosive salt water, heat, etc.), excessive movement (sway, pitch, roll, etc.), and rough handling during the loading and unloading processes.

Cost

The cost of transportation is an important consideration in the modal selection decision, especially when a low-value commodity needs to be moved. Transportation costs include the rate for moving freight from origin to destination plus any accessorial and terminal fees for additional services provided. Examples of these additional costs include inside delivery to a retailer located inside a mall, packing freight in crates for international delivery, or setting up a delivery of furniture in a residential location. A number of factors are taken into consideration when freight rates are developed, including weight of the shipment, distance from origin to destination, nature and value of the product, and the speed required. A detailed discussion of freight ratemaking is provided in Appendix 10B.

- **Cost advantage:** The cost of transportation service varies greatly between and within the modes. In general, pipeline, water, and rail service are low-cost transportation methods. They move large quantities of product over extremely long distances at very reasonable rates, creating a very low cost per ton-mile for their customers. The tradeoff, of course, is slow speed, which forces a company to hold a greater level of inventory to meet demand during these longer transit times.

- **Cost disadvantage:** Motor carriage and air transportation are high-cost modes compared to the others. On average, motor carriage is about 10 times more expensive than rail, and air service is more than twice the cost of motor carriage. It is important to note that while these average costs can be used for general comparisons, each transportation situation is unique, and these higher cost modes are appropriate options.

Given the varying capabilities and cost of each transportation mode, it is obvious that modal selection is not a quick and easy process. Table 10.4 provides a comparative summary of the relevant modal capabilities. These factors must be considered in conjunction with freight costs. The total supply chain cost and service quality of moving, storing, and fulfilling demand for a product must be considered in the modal selection decision. Also, care must be taken to choose the mode with the greatest feasibility and desirability for the supply chain being served. Feasibility of a mode is determined in large part by the product being transported and the capability of the mode to effectively move the

Table 10.4	**Performance Rating of Modes**				
	MODE OF TRANSPORTATION				
CRITERIA	**TRUCK**	**AIR**	**RAIL**	**WATER**	**PIPELINE**
Accessibility*	1	3	2	4	5
Transit time*	2	1	3	4	5
Reliability*	2	3	4	5	1
Security*	3	2	4	5	1
Cost**	4	5	3	2	1

*1 = Best to 5 = Worst
**1 = Lowest cost to 5 = Highest cost
Source: Edward J. Bardi, Ph.D. Used with permission.

product. Desirability focuses on the mode or combination of modes with the ability to meet supply chain requirements.

The nature of a product—size, durability, and value—may eliminate some modes from consideration as they cannot physically, legally, or safely handle the goods. Product size considerations of weight, cube, density, and shape greatly impact modal selection. Lightweight small electronics and apparel are more suitable to air and motor transportation, while larger, longer products (e.g., lumber) gravitate toward rail and water transportation. Heavy goods, especially when moved in large quantity, also tend to be moved by rail and water. Low-density products such as pillows, plastic plates, and ping pong balls are poor candidates for air transportation as they absorb valuable capacity that could be used for other revenue-generating freight. They tend to be moved by truck or intermodal container. Shape is another factor that must be considered. If your product exceeds certain dimensions, air and motor carriage may not be a cost-effective option.

Durability is another key consideration in the modal selection process. Fragile products (glass, computers, etc.) must be shipped via modes with the best ride quality. Temperature-sensitive goods (food, pharmaceuticals, some hazardous chemicals, etc.) must move via modes with consistent warming or cooling capabilities. Perishable goods (magazines, newspapers, flowers, etc.) require modes with the fastest transit times. The superior speed and freight protection capabilities of air and motor carriage serve these types of low durability, high time-sensitivity products well.

Product value is a critical factor in modal selection. If a company spends too much on transportation relative to the value of a product, it will not be able to sell the product at a competitive price. Generally, an inverse relationship exists between product value and the impact of transportation on its value. Transportation is a major cost in low-value products but a minor cost in high-value products. For example, transportation costs comprise 27 percent of stone, glass, and clay product costs but only 4 percent of clothing costs. Thus, water, rail, and pipeline are generally more suitable for low-value, bulk commodities, while truck and air costs can be more readily absorbed by higher-value finished goods. However, incurring higher transportation costs in proportion to product value may be warranted in some supply chains. If a company can generate a customer service advantage, hold less inventory, reduce warehouse space, or eliminate protective packaging by using a faster, more reliable mode of transportation, the additional cost can be justified.

Shipment characteristics—size, route, and required speed—cannot be ignored in modal selection. The product size issue discussed earlier can be extended to shipments in that modal capacities must be matched to the total weight and dimensions of shipments. Origin points, destination points, and specified routes affect modal accessibility and must be factored into selection decisions. Infrastructure availability, geographic distance, natural challenges like oceans and mountains, and man-made obstacles such as borders and development tend to limit modal selection to two or three realistic options. Finally, the shipment-related requirements of speed, reliability, and safety must be matched to the modal customer service capabilities discussed earlier.

The general strategy regarding modal selection focuses on determining which mode or combination of modes best suits the requirements of the freight buyer. This long-range decision requires an analysis of the best fit and balance between modal capabilities, product characteristics, supply chain requirements for speed and service, and freight transportation cost. Short of major price, infrastructure, service quality, or technological changes in the modes, the decision does not need to be revisited frequently.

Carrier Selection

Carrier selection is a specialized purchasing decision that typically will be made by a logistics, transportation, or traffic manager who has expertise and experience in the purchase of transportation services. After the modal decision has been made, attention turns to selecting the individual transportation service providers within the mode. Like the modal decision, carrier selection is based on a variety of shipment criteria and carrier capabilities: transit time average and reliability, equipment availability and capacity, geographic coverage, product protection, and freight rates.

A major difference between modal and carrier selection is the number of options. Modal selection involves six primary options, but the carrier selection may involve fewer or many more alternatives. In the case of rail transportation, many markets are only served by a single carrier. The choice is limited—either use that carrier or find another mode. At the other extreme is truckload transportation where dozens of carriers serve a particular market. Time and effort must be expended in evaluating potential carrier capability, service quality, and price.

Another difference is the frequency of the decision. Carrier selection requires more active and frequent engagement of the transportation buyer than does the more long-range modal selection decision. This engagement does not focus on choosing a new carrier for each freight move; it focuses more on the transportation buyer remaining vigilant and managing the performance of chosen carriers. It is critical to monitor each carrier's service level and freight rates on an ongoing basis. Should carrier performance deteriorate, it may be necessary to select new service providers.

The type of service provided within a mode affects carrier selection. Most carriers have their roots in one of two types of service—direct service or indirect service—between which customers must choose. Direct service provides immediate point-to-point flows of goods. Indirect service requires interim stops or transfer of freight between equipment. Direct service provides the advantage of speed and safety because freight is handled less and moves without detour to the destination. Indirect service gives up speed and subjects the freight to additional handling but offers lower cost because carriers can consolidate the freight for more efficient transportation. A passenger example of these alternatives is limousine service versus bus service. You will pay more for limo service to take you directly to your destination because you have exclusive use of the vehicle. In contrast, you save money by taking a bus but may have to take a slower, less direct route.

Within a mode, most carriers have the capabilities to provide a similar level of service, but these service levels can and do vary greatly from one transportation company to another. Also, since the cost structures are essentially the same for carriers in a given mode, their rates tend to be aligned for a given movement. Given this similarity, transportation rates tend not to be the most important criterion in carrier selection. Service performance is the key determinant for this decision. Carrier selection research suggests that reliability of on-time delivery and on-time pickup, technical capabilities, carrier response to emergencies, information sharing, freight damage experience, carrier financial stability, and total transit time are among the most important criteria to transportation service buyers.[30] Of course, the relative importance of these selection criteria will be influenced by an individual organization's supply chain structure and freight requirements.

Carrier selection strategy commonly focuses on concentrating the transportation buy with a limited number of carriers. Using a small group of carriers helps the organization leverage its purchasing dollars for lower overall rates, build relationships with service providers who gain a better understanding of freight flows and requirements over time, and effectively monitor performance of the carrier base. A core carrier strategy takes this concentration focus to a greater depth with the organization narrowing its carrier base to a select few service providers that have proven to be the best carriers in terms of service quality and cost efficiency. These core carriers ultimately handle the vast majority of an organization's freight, sometimes in a dedicated fleet capacity. In many cases, the core carriers become an indispensable extension of the organization's transportation management team; they are able to manage freight flows across the supply chain with limited direction or oversight. The ability to rely on the transportation expertise of trusted core carriers also allows the organization to focus its attention on other supply chain issues.

Rate Negotiations

Following the significant economic deregulation of most transportation modes, transportation buyers focused on carrier competition to reduce transportation expenses. Buyers would pit carriers against each other for freight and ultimately award the business to the carrier offering the greatest discount from published rates. This led to destructive competition within the trucking industry, and bankruptcies were a common result. Many decentralized organizations ended up with a hodgepodge of carriers, often numbering in the hundreds, as individual facilities negotiated independent deals with carriers. Not only was it difficult to manage such a large number of carriers, but it was also impossible for organizations to leverage their freight volume with carriers for better rates.

Over time, organizations have shifted from decentralized transportation purchases based on published rate discounts to centralized freight rate negotiations with carriers. These negotiations focus on developing contracts with carriers for a tailored set of transportation services at a specific price. Key negotiation issues for the buyer include equipment availability, delivery speed and consistency, freight protection and problem resolution, billing accuracy, and the cost of service. Transportation companies focus on volume commitments, shipment frequencies, origin–destination combinations, freight characteristics, and related cost issues that impact their ability to serve the buyer profitably. When the parties successfully complete a mutually desirable negotiation, a contract for transportation services is developed and signed. It is estimated that more than 80 percent of commercial freight moves under contractual rates today.

The strategy of centralized, contract-based rate negotiation aligns well with the core carrier concept described previously. Leveraging volume with a small set of carriers whose capacity and capabilities to provide tailored services align well with the buyer's needs makes great sense and benefits both organizations. The buyer only contracts and pays for services that are needed, gains a commitment for scarce capacity, and locks into competitive rates for a specified period of time. The carrier receives a relatively stable volume of business across a set of geographic lanes which allows it to plan for greater labor and equipment utilization efficiency and reduce the cost of operations. The contracts also promote the creation of a mutually beneficial, long-term relationship in which the parties collaborate to create greater supply chain value beyond transportation savings.

Transportation Execution and Control

When a shipment needs to be moved across the supply chain, transportation planning efforts culminate and execution processes take center stage. Decisions must be made regarding shipment size, route, and delivery method; freight documents must be prepared; in-transit problems must be resolved; and service quality must be monitored.

Shipment Preparation

When the need for transportation service is generated by a customer request, replenishment signal, or prescheduled order, the delivery process is set in motion. All of the prior work to identify the correct modes and carriers, secure capacity, and control transportation spending culminates in shipment preparation and handoff to a carrier for delivery. Given the size, service requirements, and destination of a particular shipment, the transportation managers must choose the most appropriate carrier. Steps can also be taken to minimize transportation cost and protect the shipment.

To ensure maximum effectiveness in the shipment–carrier matching process, many organizations maintain a corporate transportation routing guide. These documents specify the carriers to be used by internal personnel and vendors for freight moves that are controlled by the organization. The routing guides commonly provide instructions for carton and shipment labeling, insurance and billing requirements, advanced shipping notification, and other pertinent information.

Some routing guides are simple one- or two-page documents that plainly state shipment requirements. For example, Hallmark's routing guide is easy to read and leaves no room for misinterpretation. It instructs vendors to use FedEx ground and limit parcel shipments to 200 pounds, 10 cartons, and cubic size of 130 inches per carton.[31] Other companies create more detailed routing guides with specific sections for inbound, outbound, and returns freight; regional routing information; origin–destination tables and matrices; and related shipping requirements.

The strategy behind routing guides is to promote supply chain excellence through transportation. Genentech, a biotechnology company, states at the top of its routing guide: "The objective is to provide suppliers with detailed instructions that will aid in streamlining the processes of receiving, stocking and consuming materials while reducing freight and handling costs."[32] Routing guides also help organizations maintain centralized control over the number of carriers used and avoid off-contract or "maverick" buying of transportation services. Another goal is to ensure that contractual volume commitments to specific carriers are achieved, as a failure to meet these commitments can result in higher transportation rates or penalty fees.

In preparing freight for delivery, transportation managers have the ability to make last-minute, cost-saving decisions. As the individual orders and delivery requests are received, efforts should be made to consolidate freight, coordinate shipment deliveries, and take full advantage of container capacity. Multiple orders destined for a single location can be combined into a single shipment with one set of documentation. This can be especially cost effective for small package and parcel shipments. For example, the cost of shipping 10 items that weigh five pounds apiece in 10 separate shipments to a destination is more than twice the cost of sending those same 10 items in a single 50-pound shipment. Consolidation of LTL shipments into TL deliveries or creating TL stop-off deliveries of multi-destination LTL shipments can also generate cost savings. The key to reducing cost is giving the transportation manager advance knowledge of freight volume, destinations, and service requirements, as well as the lead time, to develop efficient delivery decisions.

The transportation operation is the last line of defense in protecting product integrity and value. Prior to loading the shipment, an accurate freight count should be taken to ensure that the invoice and related documents are correct, packaging should be inspected to ensure that the contents are not likely to be damaged en route, and the freight container should be examined for safety and product protection problems (e.g., obvious signs of leakage and other freight exposure issues). During the loading process, the freight must be stacked properly and stabilized to withstand vibration, swaying, and other ride quality issues. Of course, it is imperative to use carriers with an effective track record of damage- and shortage-free delivery service.

Freight Documentation

Freight does not move by itself.[33] Shipments are accompanied by related documents that spell out the details of the shipment—the product, destination, ownership, and more. The type and variety of documents required depend on the origin and destination points, characteristics of the freight, mode(s) being used, and carrier handling the freight. A simple truckload delivery of dry groceries from the Opelika, Alabama, Walmart distribution center to the Walmart store in Auburn, Alabama, via the company's private fleet, will require only a basic bill of lading. In contrast, a shipment of fireworks moving from Liuyang City, China, to Las Vegas, Nevada, will require extensive paperwork. Suffice it to say that the more complex the transportation requirements, the more documents are needed to facilitate the uninterrupted flow of goods through the supply chain. The most prevalent documents include the bill of lading, freight bill, and claims form.

The **bill of lading** is probably the single most important transportation document. It originates the shipment, provides all the information the carrier needs to accomplish the move, stipulates the transportation contract terms including the scope of the carrier's liability for loss and damage, acts as a receipt for the goods the shipper tenders to the carrier, and in some cases shows certificate of title to the goods. Figure 10.5 shows a typical bill of lading with the essential types of shipment information contained in the document.

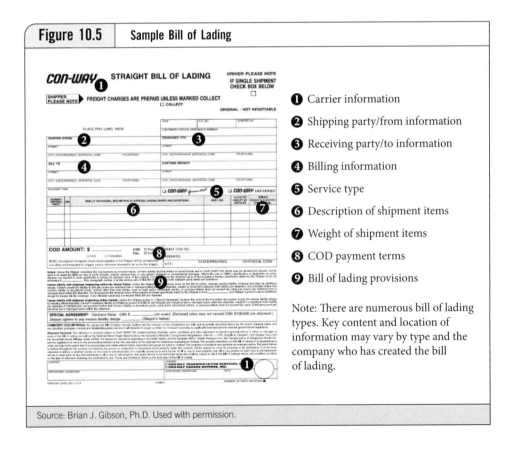

Figure 10.5   Sample Bill of Lading

❶ Carrier information

❷ Shipping party/from information

❸ Receiving party/to information

❹ Billing information

❺ Service type

❻ Description of shipment items

❼ Weight of shipment items

❽ COD payment terms

❾ Bill of lading provisions

Note: There are numerous bill of lading types. Key content and location of information may vary by type and the company who has created the bill of lading.

Source: Brian J. Gibson, Ph.D. Used with permission.

The bill of lading is created by the shipper of the goods and is either negotiable or nonnegotiable. A straight bill of lading is nonnegotiable, and the carrier must deliver the goods only to the specific receiving organization and destination in return for freight charge payment. An order bill of lading is negotiable and serves as a title to the goods listed on the document. The owner of the goods has the right to transfer title to the goods to another party and reroute the shipment to a location other than the one listed on the bill of lading.

Bills of lading also differ by type of move. An inland bill of lading is used for overland transportation and provides the required information for the domestic movement of goods by truck, rail, water, or combinations of these modes. An ocean bill of lading is a "contract of carriage" between an exporter and an ocean carrier to transport goods to a specified market overseas. A through bill of lading covers both the domestic and international transport of export goods between specified points for a specified charge. An air waybill is a bill of lading that covers both domestic and international flights transporting goods to a specified destination. It establishes the terms between a shipper and an air transportation company for the transport of goods.

The **freight bill** is the carrier's invoice for the fees the carrier charges to move a given shipment. The freight bill lists the shipment, origin and destination, consignee, items, total weight, and total charges. The freight bill differs from the bill of lading in that the freight bill sets forth the charges applicable to the shipment while the bill of lading sets forth the terms of the shipment and is a document of title.

The total charges specified in the freight bill are based on the rate negotiated by the freight buyer and carrier, the size of the shipment, and supplementary fees for accessorial services. Freight bills are submitted by the carrier when the freight is picked up by carrier (prepaid basis) or when the freight is delivered (collect basis). In most contracts, the freight buyer has a specified number of days to pay the bill after carrier submission and may receive a discount for early payment.

A **freight claims form** is a document that the transportation buyer files with the carrier to recoup monetary losses resulting from the carrier's failure to properly protect the freight. The shipper must file in writing freight claims with the carrier within a timeframe specified in the contract. Freight claims can be filed for visible damage or shortages that are detected when the product is received and inspected, for concealed losses that are not discovered until packages are opened, or for financial losses due to unreasonable delays. Claims can be supported by photographs of the damage, notations of problems on the delivery receipt, and proof of the damaged goods' monetary value (e.g., the invoice or price catalog).

Freight claims are intended to compensate the transportation buyer an amount equal to the value of the goods had the carrier safely delivered them. Carrier liability is limited if the shipper elected to send the goods under a released value (i.e., valuing the freight at less than its full worth) in exchange for lower freight rates. Carriers are not liable for freight claims if the damage is attributable to some uncontrollable factor such as the following:

- Natural disaster or some other "act of God"
- Military attack or similar "act of public enemy"
- Government seizure of freight or "act of public authority"
- Failure to adequately package the freight or other negligent "act of the shipper"
- Extreme fragility, perishability, or similarly problematic "inherent nature of the goods"

A number of other documents may also be required to move freight efficiently through the supply chain. These include critical transaction documents like the commercial invoice that provides a record or evidence of a transaction between an exporter and importer or the certificate of origin that authenticates the country of origin for the goods being shipped. Both are used for commodity control and duty valuation by the country of import. In addition to the transportation documents described earlier, valuable and sometimes necessary paperwork includes a shipper's letter of instructions, dock receipts, shipment manifests, dangerous goods declaration forms, and insurance certificates.

Documentation-based freight delays and disruptions can be minimized with attention to detail. Accurate and thorough information is a straightforward yet critical issue. Carriers and governmental authorities may halt the flow of goods if documents appear to be inaccurate, incomplete, or fraudulent. Availability of documents prior to the tendering of goods to carriers is also critical. Most carriers will not accept freight without the necessary paperwork. For international freight, the U.S. Customs 24-Hour Advance Vessel Manifest Rule requires carriers to submit cargo information a full day before it is loaded onto vessels with a port of call in the United States. Transportation buyers must factor this rule into their plans for delivering freight and paperwork to carriers or risk denial of loading, missed voyages, and supply chain disruptions.

Maintain In-Transit Visibility

Management of the transportation process does not end when the documents and freight are given to the carrier. It is important to control the freight and manage key events as product moves across the supply chain. Visibility of in-transit freight is a key facilitator of this control as it prevents freight from temporarily "falling off the radar screen." The goal of visibility is to provide the location and status of the shipments regardless of the position in the supply chain, enabling transportation buyers to make decisions on the fly in the interest of better meeting customer needs. These accurate and up-to-the-minute shipment data make it possible for organizations to respond to problems as they are developing and to manage the supply chain as a single entity rather than disjointed functions.

Technology facilitates the ability to monitor product flowing across the supply chain. Time-definite carriers and truckload carriers are using satellite tracking capabilities to maintain constant visibility of equipment. Equipment operators are increasingly equipped with smartphones, onboard computers with satellite uplinks, and tablet computers, which allow frequent and timely contact. Leading integrated carriers like FedEx and UPS offer extensive tracking capabilities that are accessible to transportation buyers at no cost via the Internet and smartphones. Such tools encourage carriers and their customers to proactively manage issues and exceptions as they become apparent rather than after they become major supply chain disruptions.

By itself, in-transit visibility of product adds little value to the supply chain. This information is not valuable unless it is somehow put to use. Thus, visibility tools must be linked to other capabilities and processes to have an impact on supply chain event management. These additional pieces of an event management solution include a clear supply chain strategy, ongoing collaboration with key customers and suppliers, appropriate business processes that can be used to act upon visibility information, and integrated communications systems through the supply chain.

Monitor Service Quality

Upon completion of freight delivery, transportation managers must take the time to analyze the outcome of all their transportation strategy, planning, and decision-making efforts. This is accomplished through a coordinated, ongoing effort to monitor carrier performance. The focal point of this monitoring effort should be the commitments made by the carriers during contract negotiation. Service and cost issues with the greatest potential impact on the supply chain warrant the constant attention of the transportation buyer as well as the carrier.

A key requirement for service quality monitoring is information. The transportation manager must have information regarding the customer service demands and the service level that current carriers provide. Without it, the transportation manager cannot make a rational evaluation of performance. This information must be compiled from multiple sources—shipment date and cost from the freight bill, arrival date from the delivery receipt, and shipment damage information from the receiving party—to gain a full picture of delivery performance and carrier service quality. Numerous transportation metrics are used to consolidate all of the information from various sources and shipments into useful knowledge.

A popular strategy for developing an objective, holistic view of carrier service quality is to develop standardized scorecards or evaluation reports. Most scorecards use a weighted point plan to emphasize key criteria for each carrier used. The transportation manager assigns weight factors to the criteria, measures carrier performance, and multiplies the results by the weighting factor or percentage. An overall carrier score is obtained by summing the weighted scores for the criteria. The scores are shared with carriers to identify service quality issues and performance improvement opportunities. Some organizations use the results to make future purchase decisions or streamline their carrier base.[34] Table 10.5 provides an example scorecard that emphasizes delivery timeliness and freight protection, two key service quality issues discussed next. In this example, a carrier providing 96.6 percent on-time deliveries would receive 32 points for the category (weight factor of 8 multiplied by the performance evaluation score of 4).

Transportation Metrics

The quality of transportation services is tangible—the key service requirements are generally observable and quantifiable. This allows organizations to monitor activities through transportation metrics or key performance indicators (KPIs). Transportation KPIs are objective measures of carrier or private fleet performance that are critical to the success of the organization. KPIs can be used to evaluate current performance versus historical results, internal goals, and carrier commitments. They can also be used to benchmark results against those achieved by competitors, world-class organizations, and other links in the supply chain.

Many aspects of transportation performance can be evaluated. Important issues include transportation spending efficiency, freight protection, delivery service quality, and customer satisfaction, among others. The challenge lies in narrowing down the vast array of metrics available to monitor transportation performance to a limited, manageable number of KPIs that reflect the transportation needs and objectives of a supply chain. Properly chosen KPIs provide numerous benefits: They signal to carriers an organization's transportation priorities, they keep score of carrier performance, and they maintain organizational focus on the ever-rising expectations of supply chain partners and customers.

Table 10.5	Transportation Performance Scorecard			
PERFORMANCE CRITERIA	**WEIGHT FACTOR**	**PERFORMANCE EVALUATION**	**POTENTIAL SCORE**	**CRITERIA SCORE**
On-time delivery	8	>98% = 5 96.01–98% = 4 94.01–96% = 3 92.01–94% = 2 <92% = 0	40	
Loss and damage rate	5	<0.5% = 5 0.5–1% = 4 1–1.5% = 3 1.5–2% = 2 >2% = 0	25	
Billing accuracy	3	>99% = 5 97–99% = 3 95–96% = 1 <95% = 0	15	
Equipment condition	2	Safe; clean; correct type = 5 Poor condition; incorrect = 0	10	
Customer service	2	Superior = 5 Good = 4 Average = 3 Fair = 2 Unacceptable = 0	10	
		Total Score	100	

Source: Brian J. Gibson, Ph.D. Used with permission.

The two primary categories of transportation KPIs include service quality and efficiency. Service quality means doing things right the first time according to customer-defined requirements and expectations. The "Seven Rs" effectively identify the focus and scope of transportation service quality KPIs—"at the right time" targets transit time, "in the right condition" concentrates on freight protection, and "at the right cost" pertains to billing accuracy issues. While there are other, more qualitative aspects of service, these three issues are fundamental to the success of supply chains as described in the following discussion.

The focus on lean supply chains and just-in-time operations makes consistent, on-time delivery a critical requirement. Multiple studies suggest that on-time delivery is the most important KPI used by transportation buyers to evaluate their carriers. Timely service facilitates inventory rationalization through lower safety stock levels, provides consistent replenishment to reduce out-of-stock problems, and reduces supply chain uncertainty and the resulting bullwhip effect.

- On-time delivery KPIs measure the ratio of shipments delivered in a timely fashion (i.e., the date and time promised by the carrier) to the total shipments delivered by the carrier. Most transportation buyers set 95 percent as a minimum acceptable level of performance from their motor carriers, with goals of 98 percent or above.

- Delivery consistency metrics compare the average origin–destination transit time of shipments to the transit time promises made by carriers. Sizable deviations from these promises and significant variation from the transit time average suggest that carriers are not providing adequate service and corrective action should be taken.

Freight protection is another key element of transportation service quality. It's not enough to get the shipment to its destination quickly: It has to get there safely and completely. Time and money are sacrificed when freight is damaged or lost. Supply chains supporting just-in-time operations and continuous replenishment retail distribution systems are especially vulnerable to delivery disruptions, as they keep little to no safety stock on hand to replace the unavailable goods.

- Claims-free delivery is a primary freight protection KPI. The ratio of claims-free deliveries (no need for a freight claim due to loss, damage, or any other reason) to the total number of deliveries is evaluated by the transportation buyer. Perfection is the goal—most organizations will accept nothing less than 99 percent claims-free deliveries. A high level of claims indicates that carriers are not taking adequate steps to protect the freight or that the freight packaging is insufficient. Service failures must be diagnosed and corrected immediately to prevent future claims.

Since transportation rates and service requirements are tailored to a specific customer's requirements, it is imperative that carriers apply the correct shipment data, rate structures, and charges to each customer. Billing accuracy KPIs measure a carrier's ability to properly translate customer bill of lading information and instructions to the freight bills. Incorrect data entry or application of contract provisions can lead to overstatement of rates and accessorial service charges, improper deliveries, misrouted freight, and incorrect payment due dates.

- Freight bill accuracy KPIs measure the ratio of accurate freight bills to the total number of freight bills. The minimum acceptable accuracy level is 95 percent for most organizations, with a goal of 100 percent accuracy. Billing errors create administrative correction costs, and continued problems lead to the use of third-party firms to audit freight bills, a non-value-adding inspection activity that adds expense to the supply chain.

The ultimate service quality KPI is the execution of perfect deliveries, the ratio of defect-free deliveries to the total number of deliveries made. Transportation buyers should seek out high-quality carriers that are capable of consistently providing flawless service that is on time, damage free, accurate, responsive, and cost effective. Defect-free transportation eliminates the need for rework, reduces administrative intervention, and tempers the use of premium service, as well as promoting customer satisfaction, inventory reduction, and reduced variation in the supply chain.

While service quality is critically important for customer satisfaction, transportation service efficiency cannot be ignored. Organizations need to balance their service requirements and the expenses related to moving freight. Transportation costs must be kept low in proportion to the value of the goods or they will not have a competitive landed cost. If cost didn't matter, many more shipments would move via air express to minimize transit time. Proper and effective use of equipment is another efficiency issue, as is the productive use of transportation labor. Transportation efficiency KPIs help keep organizations focused on these goals.

Transportation is the single largest logistics expense, and it is imperative that organizations get the greatest "bang for their buck" when buying transportation services. Aggregate efficiency measures focus on the total transportation spending versus goal or budget. Item-level KPIs focus on the transportation expense per unit of measure (e.g., pound, case, selling unit). It is a simple calculation of total freight cost divided by the number of units shipped. Understanding what is spent to move each unit highlights transportation's impact on the overall cost of goods. This KPI also provides a baseline from which improvement efforts can be made.

Asset utilization is a critical aspect of transportation cost control. Moving empty or partially loaded equipment is inefficient and expensive. It is estimated that 18 to 28 percent of all truck movement involves empty equipment, at a multibillion-dollar cost. This is not only a carrier challenge; customers ultimately pay for these empty miles in the form of higher rates, wasted natural resources, and higher carbon emissions.

Equipment utilization KPIs help buyers work toward more effective freight deployment. Comparisons of shipment weight or cube to the available equipment capacity identify opportunities to improve capacity utilization. As more capacity of a container is used, the freight cost is spread across a greater number of units and the transportation cost per unit is reduced. Technology is also being used to address this efficiency problem, as noted in the Supply Chain Sustainability feature.

Efficiency measures can also be used to evaluate and improve the performance of carriers and private fleets. Labor productivity KPIs ensure that equipment operators, freight handlers, and other personnel are performing at acceptable levels. Minimization of loading and unloading time improves carrier employee and equipment turnaround time, keeping both in productive use. These and similar KPIs directly benefit carriers by focusing on cost control. Freight buyers that contribute to efficient carrier operations reduce their exposure to equipment detention and accessorial charges, as well as put themselves in a solid position to negotiate more advantageous freight rates.

Systematic measurement of KPIs in transportation brings substantial benefits. KPIs can help organizations take a proactive, knowledge-based approach to transportation decision making. Transportation KPIs are instrumental for monitoring quality and dealing with service issues in a timely fashion before they have a major impact on the supply chain. KPIs also help organizations pinpoint inefficiencies and develop strategies for supply chain cost reduction. Finally, KPI data can be used to analyze cost–service level tradeoffs. This knowledge can be used to make better carrier selection and assignment decisions. A failure to identify, measure, and monitor relevant KPIs puts the organization in a reactive mode and limits the transportation manager's ability to make informed, timely decisions.

Transportation Technology

The dynamic nature of transportation combined with the wide array of delivery requirements and options create a complex environment for transportation buyers and managers. Multiple factors must be considered when developing strategies and making operational decisions if appropriate and economical decisions are to be made. Fortunately, software and information technology tools have been developed to support transportation planning, execution, and performance evaluation. In this final section of the chapter, the primary technologies are presented.

Supply Chain Sustainability	*Reducing Empty Miles*

As fuel costs rise and sustainability gains attention, transportation companies and their customers are seeking ways to improve equipment utilization. A major focal point is to reduce empty backhauls caused by trucks returning to their origin points without freight after making a delivery. The empty trip costs are typically borne by the customer.

In an effort to reduce empty backhauls, a major department store retailer and its dedicated carrier have enrolled in an inexpensive Internet-based system that matches loads with empty vehicles. The matching service was created by the Voluntary Interindustry Commerce Solutions Association (VICS), an organization that seeks to improve supply chain performance. Using the system, Macy's and Schneider National cut 30 empty loads each week, which helped Schneider reduce diesel use by more than 5,500 gallons and cut carbon dioxide emissions by 62 tons. Macy's also benefits from a $25,000 reduction in annual transportation expenses.

The VICS Empty Miles solution focuses on routes over which companies repeatedly move freight outbound but have few return loads to offer to the transportation provider. The system searches for complimentary recurring loads to fill the equipment for the return trip. When a match is found, the companies contact each other and negotiate offline using tools provided by VICS. The return trip loads are moved at a discount and the shipper shares part of the revenue with the original customer as a refund. All parties benefit from the arrangement, negative environmental impacts are reduced, and equipment utilization is vastly improved.

Kraft Foods has attacked the empty miles problem with other solutions. One effort involves using transportation management software from Oracle to reduce 500,000 empty miles from its private fleet trips last year and boost trailer capacity utilization (which reduces the number of trips needed). Kraft has also streamlined distribution operations and realigned facilities to reduce the number of trucks it needs and the number of miles they travel. Finally, the company is lobbying Congress to allow heavier trucks on the roads with the hope of cutting trips, fuel use, and emissions.

Similar initiatives are underway at PepsiCo. The company's Pepsi Bottling Group uses advanced routing software to cut mileage by about 12 percent and reduce costs. Also, the company and its carriers are members of the SmartWay Transport Partnership. Finally, G&J Pepsi-Cola Bottlers of Columbus, Ohio, installed shut-off equipment on trailers to prevent idling for more than five minutes, saving about 17,500 gallons of fuel annually. Each of these initiatives is an example of PepsiCo's "performance with purpose" focus on sustainability where the company and society gain measurable benefits from more efficient transportation operations.

Sources: David Biederman, "Sustainability Proves Sustainable," *Journal of Commerce* (January 4, 2010); John Kerr, "Macy's Maneuver to Fill Empty Miles," *Logistics Management* (March 2010): 26–28; "Kraft Foods Cuts 50 Million Truck Miles," *Journal of Commerce* (December 11, 2009).

Transportation Management Systems

Software tools related to the movement of goods across the supply chain are lumped together in a general category called **transportation management systems (TMS)**. TMS is defined as information technologies used to plan, optimize, and execute transportation operations. This simple definition captures the essence of TMS, presenting it as a melting pot of applications used to assist managers in nearly every aspect of transportation from basic load configuration to complex transportation network optimization.

The planning capabilities of TMS assist transportation buyers and managers with the key pre-shipment decisions discussed earlier. These individuals cannot adequately evaluate the thousands of potential lane/mode/carrier/service/price combinations in their supply chains without technological help. TMS tools allow organizations to consider a vast array of transportation options in a matter of minutes versus hours or days of manual design activity. In addition, freight planning tools can be linked to order management systems, warehouse management systems, and supply chain planning tools to gain timelier, more comprehensive information. With this knowledge, better supply chain decisions and tradeoffs can be made. Critical TMS planning applications include the following:

- **Routing and scheduling**—Proper planning of delivery routes has a major impact on customer satisfaction, supply chain performance, and organizational success. Thus, this is a critical TMS capability sought by transportation decision makers. TMS software uses mathematical methods and optimization routines to evaluate possible combinations in which routes could be run and chooses the most economical one. Only those feasible routes that satisfy relevant constraints (container capacity, delivery windows, transit speed, and operator restrictions) are considered. Typical TMS output includes a detailed schedule of the routes, cost analysis, and route maps.

- **Load planning**—Effective preparation of safe, efficient deliveries can be accomplished via TMS load optimization programs. These programs help transportation managers build a database of package dimensions, loading requirements (e.g., top load, keep upright), and equipment capacity. Then, the specifics of a shipment or multiple shipments traveling together, such as weight, cube, and number of cartons, are entered into the TMS. In a matter of seconds or minutes, the TMS software optimizes how product should be stacked on pallets or arranged in the container. The optimization results in more efficient use of cargo space, fewer loads being shipped, and less damage to the product.

TMS execution tools help transportation managers streamline some of their shipment activities. With multiple shipments needing delivery each day, manual processes are susceptible to errors, missed deadlines, and customer service failures. Various TMS capabilities automate repetitive activities to reduce labor costs and accuracy problems. For example, standardized templates can be used to ensure that complete and accurate shipment data are provided in transportation documents. Other tools post detailed shipment information to a shared network or a Web site to promote shipment visibility and provide greater freight control. Three of the key execution tools include the following:

- **Load tendering**—Organizations may have a number of approved carriers that could be used for a particular shipment. However, their rates may differ slightly based on the origin–destination locations and shipment size. Rather than subjectively assigning loads to carriers, a TMS database determines which carriers are eligible to move the freight and then tenders the freight to the best carrier. The tendering decision takes into consideration routing guide requirements, carrier cost, transit time, and required service capabilities contained in the database. As a result, contract compliance is improved and freight costs are optimized.

- **Status tracking**—Maintaining visibility of shipments as they move across the supply chain through delivery confirmation can be a time-consuming task. The in-transit progress of shipments can be monitored using TMS in conjunction with satellite capabilities and other visibility tools. Shipment status information, especially notifications regarding problems and shipments at risk of late delivery, can be shared with key stakeholders. The goal of this TMS tool is to provide timely information regarding potential delivery exceptions so that corrective actions can be taken. The Supply Chain Technology feature highlights the efforts of American Railcar to maintain visibility of in-transit goods.

- **Appointment scheduling**—To avoid facility congestion, equipment delays, and operator inefficiency, organizations are using TMS capabilities to automate the scheduling function. TMS tools provide the real-time visibility necessary to make appointment scheduling easier and more accurate. Many systems support Internet-based access to the scheduling system where carriers can schedule pickup and delivery times at specific dock locations. These systems help carriers avoid time-intensive phone calls, interim stops, and wait time.

Supply Chain Technology

TMS Shines Light on Inbound Supply Chain

A black hole in their supply chain. That's how the purchasing team at American Railcar Inc. (ARI) described the issue that led them to select and implement a transportation management system last year. And that decision is reaping benefits both expected and unexpected.

Like a lot of manufacturing companies, ARI was having particular difficulty tracking its inbound shipments from suppliers. "We had visibility when the product was ready at suppliers, but then it went into a black hole once it left our vendors' docks until it arrived at our location, " says Brent Roever, purchasing agent at St. Charles, Mo.-based ARI, which manufactures and services rail-cars and parts.

In some respects, ARI was better off than some other manufacturers because it has a smaller supply base than a typical manufacturer, so there were fewer inbound shipments disappearing into the black hole. As a railcar manufacturer with two primary manufacturing locations in Arkansas, its supply base is limited to companies that can meet the rigorous specifications and certifications required by the American Association of Railroads. As a result its relatively short supplier list is based primarily in the U.S.

According to Richard Armbruster, ARI's vice president of purchasing, about 80% of its inbound shipments come via flatbed truckload. Only about 5% come in by truckload van and the rest come from suppliers via less-than-truckload. And, of course, the majority of its outbound shipments go out on rail—literally.

But as a Lean organization, ARI was always looking for ways to streamline its just-in-time manufacturing model and reduce its inventories. In its previous logistics model, ARI provided its suppliers with lists of preferred carriers and routing guides, but "it was on the honor system" according to Roever.

So under Ambruster's direction, ARI's Senior Director of Purchasing Scott Smith worked with Roever to investigate what the solution to the black hole problem was. And while they knew it would require some outside help, the first question they needed to answer was TMS vs. 3PL?

"We reviewed both 3PLs and TMS providers and decided a mix of both would suit us best," says Roever. When it came to the TMS, ARI was sure it wanted to go with a web-based TMS that would integrate easily with its in-house ERP system.

With those priorities set, ARI decided that St. Louis-based Logistics Management Solutions (LMS) was the right choice for its TMS provider. In early 2009, the team began working with LMS to incorporate its TMS system into ARI's purchasing and logistics processes.

The key to effectively streamlining the inbound freight flows was getting ARI's suppliers on board with the program. And it had to be a simple, straightforward process for the suppliers if it were going to be embraced.

In the new process all of ARI's orders flow from the ERP system into the LMS TMS system where suppliers can view those orders. Suppliers respond to those orders and indicate that their shipment is ready either by providing a form or by logging into the LMS system depending on their frequency of shipments and can include notes on how that product needs to be shipped. Some shipments may require a tarp or a flatbed truck, for example, all of which can be indicated on the notification.

With those details in place, LMS can then tender the load to one of ARI's carriers in that given lane. Carriers are only dispatched when the shipment is ready, which avoids costly carrier delays.

But most importantly, the system indicates to Roever and the ARI team when the shipment was picked up at the supplier and when it can be expected at ARI's facility based on established delivery times. Black hole averted.

"This allows us to control early and late shipments and ultimately this helps us reduce our on-hand inventory," says Roever. "It's our goal to have just enough inventory to build our railcars while taking into account transit times. We measure inventory month over month and it is improving from a host of activities, including our work with LMS."

The TMS system also lets the purchasing team at ARI track which suppliers ship on time and which are late. That data is then included in the supplier's scorecard and also lets ARI perform root-cause analysis on those that are consistently late. "We're using Lean to become world-class so being able to use reporting tools to identify and fix problems is very valuable," says Roever. "These tools give us more data to analyze in these areas."

While there was some pushback from suppliers early in the process, currently ARI has 99% of its suppliers on the system. Roever says one thing that made the transition smoother was LMS-assigned dedicated reps to the ARI contract, so all of ARI's suppliers are interfacing with the same people at LMS each time.

"Communication at every stage is crucial," says Roever. "Bring suppliers in early when you're looking at the change and ask them how it would impact their business."

Source: David Hannon, "American Railcar Uses TMS to Shine Light on Inbound Supply Chain," *Purchasing* (March 11, 2010): 13–14. Reproduced by permission.

TMS analytical tools provide organizations with the ability to make postshipment evaluations of carrier performance, customer service, and network cost. The data required for analysis can be spread across the entire supply chain in a variety of documents and information systems. It is critical to collect these data in a timely fashion so that the KPIs can be measured, performance assessed and benchmarked, and corrective action taken. TMS help organizations assemble and make sense of the vast array of transportation data that are generated by freight movement. Two useful analytical applications are as follows:

- **Performance reporting and scorecarding**—Managing carrier performance requires extensive data collection and calculation as discussed earlier in the section on transportation metrics. TMS tools can automate the collection of data, measurement of KPIs, and dissemination of periodic reports. These reports can provide information on overall performance as well as the results in specific segments of the transportation operation. Customized reports like monthly carrier performance scorecards and benchmarking analyses can also be generated. These tools provide transportation managers with timely, objective information upon which future decisions can be made.

- **Freight bill auditing**—Payments made to carriers must reflect the agreed-upon contractual rates and the services rendered. To ensure that they are neither being over- nor undercharged for freight services, many organizations are turning to TMS software to reconcile invoices with their contracts. These tools automate a manual process that did not always catch discrepancies in a timely, accurate manner.

The wide range of planning, execution, and analytical capabilities will help the TMS market grow. Industry experts predict the TMS market to grow for several years, with double-digit growth emerging in 2011 and a projected five-year compound annual growth rate of 9.4 percent.[35] Organizations seeking shipment visibility, collaboration with supply chain partners, and operational efficiency are purchasing the software with the expectation that TMS tools will help them address the variety of transportation challenges discussed throughout the chapter.

The challenge of technology is that it is forever changing and expanding. While the TMS capabilities and emerging tools discussed above represent the leading edge of technology for managing supply chain flows, they may soon be yesterday's news. Thus, the most important idea to take away from this section is the importance of information technology in transportation. Simply stated, technology helps us manage the vast volume of data and options in transportation in order to make better decisions regarding modal and carrier selection, routing, packaging, loading, and many other activities. These decisions lead to greater customer service, tighter cost control, and competitive advantage in the supply chain.

SUMMARY

- Transportation is a dynamic activity and a critical supply chain process. It is the largest logistics cost component in most supply chains, and it also directly impacts fulfillment speed and service quality. By providing the physical links between key participants across domestic and global supply chains, transportation facilitates the creation of time and place utilities.

- Managing the transportation process for maximum supply chain impact requires considerable knowledge of transportation options, planning, decision making, analytical skills, and information sharing capabilities.

- Transportation is a key supply chain process and must be included in supply chain strategy development, network design, and total cost management.

- Numerous obstacles—global expansion of supply chains, rising costs, limited capacity, and government regulation—must be overcome to synchronize transportation with other supply chain processes.

- Fulfillment of supply chain demand can be accomplished through five modal options or the intermodal use of truck, rail, air, water, and pipeline transportation.

- Multiple planning activities occur prior to carrier and mode selection: Who will be responsible for managing the transportation function within the organization, what terms of sale and payment will be used, and how goods will be transported must all be determined with a strategic supply chain focus.

- Mode selection is based on the relative strengths of each modal or intermodal option in terms of accessibility, transit time, reliability, safety and security, transportation cost, and the nature of the product being transported.

- Carrier selection focuses on the type of service required (direct or indirect), geographic coverage, service levels, and carrier willingness to negotiate reasonable rates.

- Most commercial freight moves under contractual rates that are negotiated directly between freight buyers and transportation companies for specific volumes of tailored services at mutually agreed-upon prices.

- Shipment routing guides help organizations ensure internal compliance with service contracts and maintain centralized control over freight tendering decisions.

- Freight documentation provides the details of each shipment, sharing critical information that promotes uninterrupted flows of goods through the supply chain.

- Organizations must continue to manage freight after it has been tendered to carriers by maintaining in-transit visibility of shipments and monitoring carrier performance.

- Numerous metrics are available to evaluate transportation service quality in terms of carrier timeliness, freight protection, accuracy, and perfect deliveries. Service efficiency measures focus on spending proficiency, asset utilization, and labor productivity.

- Transportation management systems are widely used information technologies that support the effective planning, execution, and analysis of transportation processes.

STUDY QUESTIONS

1. Discuss the role of transportation in the supply chain. Provide examples of how transportation can positively and negatively impact supply chain performance.

2. Describe the major challenges faced by transportation managers in the current environment.

3. What are the primary capabilities, advantages, and disadvantages of each of the basic modes?

4. Using financial Web sites, company Web sites, and search engines, develop a basic overview report (primary service offerings, annual sales, current stock price, and recent news) for one domestic or international transportation company from each SIC code:

    a. SIC 4011—Railroads, Linehaul Operating

    b. SIC 4213—Trucking, Except Local

    c. SIC 4513—Air Courier Services

    d. SIC 4412—Deep Sea Foreign Transportation of Freight

5. Discuss the primary considerations and issues that must be factored into modal and carrier selection.

6. Identify and discuss appropriate modes of transportation for the following items:

    a. Apple iPads

    b. True Religion jeans

    c. Pressure treated lumber

    d. Coal

7. Using company Web sites, compare the service offerings for the following transportation companies:

    a. J. B. Hunt (http://www.jbhunt.com) and New Penn (http://www.newpenn.com)

    b. FedEx (http://www.fedex.com) and Polar Air Cargo Worldwide, Inc. (http://www.polaraircargo.com)

    c. Maersk Line (http://www.maerskline.com) and Wallenius Wilhelmsen Logistics (http://www.2wglobal.com)

    d. Canadian National Railway Company (http://www.cn.ca) and Alaska Railroad (http://www.akrr.com)

8. Describe the purpose and value of freight documentation. Discuss the function of the following documents: bill of lading, freight bill, and freight claim.

9. How would a transportation manager monitor the quality of service provided by the carriers used? What types of metrics would be used?

10. What role does information technology play in the management of transportation planning, execution, and analysis?

NOTES

1. Rosalyn Wilson, *22nd Annual State of Logistics Report* (Oak Brook, IL: Council of Supply Chain Management Professionals, 2011).

2. *Amazon.com Annual Report* (2009): 11. Retrieved April 14, 2011 from http://phx.corporate-ir.net/phoenix.zhtml?c=97664&p=irol-reportsannual

3. *FedEx Fuel Surcharge.* Retrieved April 19, 2011 from http://fedex.com/cgi-bin/fuelsurcharge.cgi?link=4&cc=ca_english&language=english&region=us

4. *About CSA: What Is It?* Retrieved April 19, 2011 from http://csa.fmcsa.dot.gov/about/default.aspx

5. Bureau of Transportation Statistics and U.S. Census Bureau, *2007 Economic Census: Transportation–Commodity Flow Survey* (April 2010): 15. Available from http://www.bts.gov/publications/commodity_flow_survey/final_tables_december_2009/pdf/entire.pdf

6. Rosalyn Wilson, *22nd Annual State of Logistics Report* (Oak Brook, IL: Council of Supply Chain Management Professionals, 2011).

7. Federal Motor Carrier Safety Administration, *Commercial Motor Vehicle Facts* (December 2010): 2. Retrieved April 19, 2011 from http://www.fmcsa.dot.gov/documents/facts-research/CMV-Facts.pdf

8. "The Transport Topics Top 100 For-Hire Carriers," *Transport Topics* (2010): 4.

9. Rosalyn Wilson, *22nd Annual State of Logistics Report* (Oak Brook, IL: Council of Supply Chain Management Professionals, 2011).

10. Bureau of Transportation Statistics and U.S. Census Bureau, *2007 Economic Census: Transportation—Commodity Flow Survey* (April 2010): 15. Available from http://www.bts.gov/publications/commodity_flow_survey/final_tables_december_2009/pdf/entire.pdf

11. "The Transport Topics Top 100 Private Carriers," *Transport Topics* (2010): 4.

12. Bureau of Transportation Statistics and U.S. Census Bureau, *2007 Economic Census: Transportation—Commodity Flow Survey* (April 2010): 15. Available from http://www.bts.gov/publications/commodity_flow_survey/final_tables_december_2009/pdf/entire.pdf

13. Ibid.

14. Association of American Railroads, *U.S. Freight Railroad Statistics* (November 23, 2010). Retrieved April 19, 2011 from http://www.aar.org/~/media/aar/Industry%20Info/AAR%20Stats%202010%201123.ashx

15. Bureau of Transportation Statistics and U.S. Census Bureau, *2007 Economic Census: Transportation—Commodity Flow. Survey* (April 2010): 16. Available from http://www.bts.gov/publications/commodity_flow_survey/final_tables_december_2009/pdf/entire.pdf

16. Rosalyn Wilson, *22nd Annual State of Logistics Report* (Oak Brook, IL: Council of Supply Chain Management Professionals, 2011).

17. Damian Brett, "IATA Has Gloomier Outlook for Air Freight," *IFW* (March 3, 2011). Retrieved April 20, 2011 from http://www.cargosystems.net/freightpubs/ifw/index/iata-has-gloomier-outlook-for-air-freight/20017854002.htm

18. Research and Innovative Technology Administration, *Transportation Statistics Annual Report* (Washington, DC: Bureau of Transportation Statistics, 2009). Retrieved April 19, 2011 from http://www.bts.gov/publications/transportation_statistics_annual_report/2009/html/chapter_02/table_02_01_02.html

19. *World Air Transport Statistics*, 54th ed. (Montreal, Quebec: International Air Transport Association, 2010). Retrieved April 20, 2011 from http://www.iata.org/ps/publications/Pages/wats-freight-km.aspx

20. Hugo Martin, "Airfares Are Rising Along with Oil Prices," *Los Angeles Times* (March 7, 2011). Retrieved April 20, 2011 from http://articles.latimes.com/2011/mar/07/business/la-fi-0307-travel-briefcase-20110307

21. Bureau of Transportation Statistics and U.S. Census Bureau, *2007 Economic Census: Transportation—Commodity Flow Survey* (April 2010): 15. Available from http://www.bts.gov/publications/commodity_flow_survey/final_tables_december_2009/pdf/entire.pdf

22. Rosalyn Wilson, *22nd Annual State of Logistics Report* (Oak Brook, IL: Council of Supply Chain Management Professionals, 2011).

23. Institute for Water Resources, *Waterborne Transportation Lines of the United States* (Alexandria, VA: U.S. Army Corps of Engineers, 2008): 3. Available from http://www.ndc.iwr.usace.army.mil/veslchar/pdf/wtlusvl1_08.pdf

24. Research and Innovative Technology Administration, *Transportation Statistics Annual Report* (Washington, DC: Bureau of Transportation Statistics, 2009). Retrieved April 19, 2011 from http://www.bts.gov/publications/transportation_statistics_annual_report/2009/html/chapter_02/table_02_01_02.html

25. American Petroleum Institute and the Association of Oil Pipe Lines, *How Many Pipelines Are There?* Retrieved April 19, 2011 from http://www.pipeline101.com/Overview/energy-pl.html

26. Matthew L. Wald, "Panel Seeking Answers in Fatal Pipeline Blast," *The New York Times* (February 28, 2011). Retrieved April 19, 2011 from http://www.nytimes.com/2011/03/01/us/01sanbruno.html

27. American Association of Port Authorities, *Port Industry Statistics: North American Port Container Traffic*. Retrieved April 19, 2011 from http://www.aapa-ports.org/industry/content.cfm?ItemNumber=900&navItemNumber=551#Statistics

28. Association of American Railroads, *U.S. Freight Railroad Statistics* (November 23, 2010). Retrieved April 19, 2011 from http://www.aar.org/~/media/aar/Industry%20Info/AAR%20Stats%202010%201123.ashx

29. International Chamber of Commerce, *Incoterms 2010*. Retrieved April 20, 2011 from http://www.iccwbo.org/incoterms/

30. Shane R. Premeaux, "Motor Carrier Selection Criteria: Perceptual Differences between Shippers and Motor Carriers," *Transportation Journal* (Winter 2002).

31. Shipment Routing Guide for Hallmark's Corporate Store Group, retrieved April 20, 2011 from http://corporate.hallmark.com/Vendors/Transportation-Overview.

32. Genentech: Supplier Transportation, retrieved March 20, 2011 from http://www.gene.com/gene/contact/transportation.html

33. For an extensive discussion of freight documentation, see John J. Coyle, Robert A. Novack, Brian J. Gibson, and Edward J. Bardi, *Transportation*, 7th ed. (South-Western, 2011), Chapter 10: 338–44.

34. Brian J. Gibson and Jerry W. Wilson, "Carrier Scorecarding: Purposes, Processes, and Benefits," *Journal of Transportation Management*, Vol. 15, No. 1 (2004).

35. Bridget McCrea, "TMS: The Key Enabler," *Logistics Management* (January 14, 2011).

CASE 10.1

Supreme Sound Explosion

Supreme Sound Explosion (SSE), located in Memphis, Tennessee, produces concert-quality sound systems for rock, rap, and country musicians. Recently, the company partnered with two new suppliers to create an innovative line of speakers called Blasters. Blasters provide 100 decibels more sound versus competitors' speakers. Interest in the product is great as potential buyers want to reduce the number of sound system components that need to be taken on tour. This is no small matter when you consider that groups like the Rolling Stones and U2 regularly use dozens of tractor trailers to move equipment during their stadium tours. Tour costs can be reduced if equipment is streamlined and fewer trucks are needed to haul the equipment between tour stops. Also, more tour stops can be scheduled as loading, unloading, setup, and tear-down time is reduced.

One of the key suppliers makes woofers in Athens, Georgia, while the other makes tweeters in Portland, Oregon. Two tweeters are inserted into each woofer to make a Blaster. SSE assembles Blasters and uses existing suppliers for other required components. While SSE has negotiated per-unit purchasing costs with the two suppliers, decisions regarding delivery of the components remain. Each supplier has proposed two different delivery options. The proposals are now in the hands of SSE's operations manager, who has limited experience with transportation issues. Demand for Blasters is expected to be 400 units per month, and production is scheduled to begin in less than a month.

Product and delivery characteristics are shown in the following table:

	WOOFERS	TWEETERS
Manufactured in	Athens, GA	Portland, OR
SSE purchase price	$740 each	$2,380 per pair
Weight	48 pounds	6 pounds
Dimensions	36" (L) × 24" (W) × 24" (H)	12" (L) × 8" (W) × 6" (H)
Characteristics	Sturdy, bulky, not easily damaged, supplier maintains sizeable inventory	Compact, vibration and moisture sensitive, supplier builds to order
Delivery options	W1—delivery via LTL once per week with FOB origin, Freight Collect terms. The freight cost per delivery is $832 with an expected transit time of two days.	T1—delivery via LTL once per week with FOB destination, Freight Collect and Allowed. The freight cost per delivery is $689 with an expected transit time of five days.
	W2—delivery via TL every other week with FOB destination, Freight Collect terms. The freight cost per delivery is $932 with an expected transit time of one day.	T2—delivery via airfreight two times per week with FOB origin, Freight Collect terms. The freight cost per delivery is $669 with an expected transit time of two days.

CASE QUESTIONS

1. What is the delivery cost per unit of woofers and tweeters for each option?

2. Why do the delivery costs of woofers and tweeters vary among the four options?

3. Which option do you recommend for the delivery of woofers and tweeters? Why?

4. What responsibilities will SSE have under your recommendation in Question 3?

5. What other supply chain issues and costs must SSE take into consideration when making these transportation decisions?

Source: Brian J. Gibson, Ph.D. Used with permission.

CASE 10.2

Bob's Custom BBQs

Bob's Custom BBQs, a manufacturer of outdoor grills, uses three primary carriers to move grills from its Texas factory to major home improvement retailers in the United States and Canada. The owner, Bob Flame, wants to evaluate the performance of the three carriers and collected data for the following metrics over a three-month period.

PERFORMANCE CRITERIA	ALLIED TRANSPORT	BESTWAY FREIGHT	CERTAINT CARRIERS
On-time delivery	99.5%	98.7%	98.2%
Billing accuracy	99.3%	99.6%	98.2%
Loads with damage claims	0.9%	1.6%	0.4%
Loads rejected	1.3%	2.1%	0.9%
Customer satisfaction ratings	4.6	4.2	3.9

Bob asked his transportation manager to develop a scorecard to help compare the carriers on these five metrics. The manager came up with the following chart:

PERFORMANCE CRITERIA	WEIGHT FACTOR	PERFORMANCE EVALUATION	POTENTIAL SCORE	ACTUAL SCORE
On-time delivery	8	>98.5% = 5 96.1–98.5% = 4 93–96% = 2 <93% = 0	40	
Billing accuracy	3	>99% = 5 97–99% = 3 95–96% = 1 <95% = 0	20	
Loads with damage claims	5	<0.5% = 5 0.5–1% = 4 1.1–2% = 2 >2% = 0	20	

PERFORMANCE CRITERIA	WEIGHT FACTOR	PERFORMANCE EVALUATION	POTENTIAL SCORE	ACTUAL SCORE
Loads rejected		<1% = 5	10	
		1%–2% = 4		
		2.1–3% = 2		
		>3% = 0		
Customer satisfaction ratings	2	>4.5 = 5	10	
		4–4.5 =4		
		3–3.9 = 2		
		<3 = 0		
		Total Score	100	

CASE QUESTIONS

1. Calculate the performance score for each of the three carriers.

2. Which carrier would you recommend that Bob consider for elimination? Why?

3. If Bob decides to keep all three carriers, what should each of them work to improve?

Source: Brian J. Gibson, Ph.D. Used with permission.

APPENDIX 10A

Federal Regulation of the Transportation Industry

Federal regulation of transportation has been with us since the Act to Regulate Commerce passed in 1887. The years immediately preceding the enactment of this law were full of turmoil for both shippers and carriers. Inland transportation was basically by railroad, and the carriers charged high rates when possible and discriminated against small shippers. Control over the transportation industry was important to U.S. economic growth, and a stable transportation service supply that would be compatible with the needs of an expanding society was essential.

Regulatory initiatives initially focused on economic issues to ensure competition and fair pricing for freight customers. In the twenty-first century, efforts to regulate the transportation industry have concentrated more on national security, safety of the traveling public, and protection of the environment.

Economic Regulation[1]

The need for federal economic regulation of transportation is rooted in the significance of transportation to the overall U.S. economy. Transportation enables business to accomplish the very foundation of economic activity—the exchange of commodities from areas of oversupply to areas of undersupply. The transportation activity benefits all citizens; thus, it can be argued that the government should provide transportation just as it provides public interest functions such as the court system and national defense.

Traditionally, however, private enterprise has provided freight transportation. Fueled by the dollars that shippers spend, transportation companies commit to various transportation services; such resource allocation is more efficient than what a political allocation could produce. Since the free enterprise marketplace has imperfections that may allow monopolies to develop, government control of transportation attempts to allocate resources in the public's interest by maintaining and enforcing the competitive market structure.

Despite arguments for economic regulation of the transportation industry, the regulatory cycle has come full circle to the point where most of the regulation adopted between 1887 and 1973 has been eliminated or reduced. Table 10A.1 highlights the major legislative efforts to regulate, and later deregulate, economic aspects of the transportation industry. Current federal economic regulation of transportation is very minimal, and marketplace forces are the major controls used to enforce a competitive market structure.

The lessening of federal economic regulatory controls over transportation began with the passage of the **Airline Deregulation Act** in 1978. This act effectively returned the airline industry to a free marketplace by eliminating most economic regulation. The **Staggers Rail Act of 1980** and the **Motor Carrier Act of 1980** soon followed. These two acts eliminated most of the economic regulation for the railroad and trucking industries. The **Shipping Act of 1984** granted antitrust immunity to ocean shipping conferences in

Table 10A.1	Chronology of Major Transportation Regulation	
DATE	**ACT**	**NATURE OF REGULATION**
Initiation Era		
1887	Act to Regulate Commerce	Regulated railroads and established Interstate Commerce Commission (ICC); rates must be reasonable; discrimination prohibited
1903	Elkins Act	Prohibited rebates and created filed rate doctrine
1906	Hepburn Act	Established maximum and joint rate controls
1910	Mann-Elkins Act	Shipper given right to route shipments
1912	Panama Canal Act	Prohibited railroads from owning water carriers
Positive Era		
1920	Transportation Act of 1920	Established rule of ratemaking; pooling and joint use of terminals allowed; began recapture clause
1933	Emergency Transportation Act	Financial assistance to railroads
Intermodal Era		
1935	Motor Carrier Act	Federal regulation of trucking similar to railroads
1938	Civil Aeronautics Act	Federal regulation of air carriers; established Civil Aeronautics Board (CAB)
1940	Transportation Act	Provided for federal regulation of water carriers; declaration of national transportation policy
1942	Freight Forwarder Act	Federal regulation of surface freight forwarders
1948	Reed-Bulwinkle Act	Antitrust immunity for joint ratemaking
1958	Transportation Act	Eliminated umbrella (protective) ratemaking; provided financial aid to railroads
1966	Department of Transportation Act	Established U.S. Department of Transportation
1970	Rail Passenger Service Act	Established Amtrak
1973	Regional Rail Reorganization Act	Established Consolidated Rail Corporation
Deregulation Era		
1976	Railroad Revitalization and Regulatory Reform Act	Rate freedom; ICC could exempt railroad operations; abandonment and merger controls began
1977	Airline Deregulation Act	Deregulated air transportation; sunset CAB
1980	Motor Carrier Act	Eased entry restrictions; permitted rate negotiation
1980	Staggers Rail Act	Permitted railroads to negotiate contracts; allowed rate flexibility; defined maximum rates
1984	Ocean Shipping Reform Act	Permitted greater tariff and contracting flexibility for ocean carriers and conferences

(continued)

	Table 10A.1	Continued	
DATE	**ACT**	**NATURE OF REGULATION**
1993	Negotiated Rates Act	Provided for settlement options for motor carrier undercharges
1994	Trucking Industry Regulatory Reform Act	Eliminated motor carrier filing of individual tariffs; ICC empowered to deregulate categories of traffic
1994	FAA Reauthorization Act	Prohibited states from regulating interstate trucking
1995	ICC Termination Act	Abolished ICC; established Surface Transportation Board (STB); eliminated most economic regulation of trucking
1996	Maritime Security Act	Authorized a program to assist an active, privately owned U.S.-flagged and U.S.-crewed merchant shipping fleet
1998	Ocean Shipping Reform Act	Eliminated authority of shipping conferences over contracts; modified contract filing requirements
1998	Transportation Equity Act for the 21st Century	Allocated over $216 billion for the maintenance and safety of surface transportation
2001	Aviation and Transportation Security Act	Established the Transportation Security Administration
2002	Homeland Security Act	Moved Coast Guard and TSA into Department of Homeland Security

Source: John J. Coyle, Robert A. Novack, and Edward J. Bardi, *Transportation: A Supply Chain Perspective*, 7th ed. (Mason, Ohio: South-Western Cengage Learning, 2011), Chapter 3. Reproduced by permission.

U.S. foreign commerce. These conferences were allowed to set prices and control the capacity available for the transportation.

Further reduction of federal power over the transportation industry occurred in the 1990s. The enactment of the **ICC Termination Act of 1995** eliminated the Interstate Commerce Commission, reduced or eliminated most economic regulation over motor and water carriers, and established the Surface Transportation Board to administer the remaining railroad regulations. The **Ocean Shipping Reform Act** of 1998 modernized and deregulated international ocean shipping. It transformed the industry from a common carriage focus with required rate filings to a contract-based system in which pricing is kept confidential.

The current status of federal regulation of the transportation modes is as follows:

- **Motor carriers**—All rate and tariff-filing regulations are eliminated except for household goods and noncontiguous trade (continental United States and Alaska, for example). The common carrier concept is eliminated, but the carriers are held liable for damage. All carriers may contract with shippers. Antitrust immunity is granted to carriers for collective ratemaking (for example, joint publishing of a freight classification), and the carriers must provide tariffs (containing rates and rules) to shippers upon request. In essence, little federal economic control is exercised over these modes.

- **Railroads**—In theory, rail economic regulation still exists. The STB has jurisdiction over rail rates and rules as well as routes, services, facilities, and mergers. The railroads are subject to the common carrier obligations to provide service to all shippers; to not discriminate against persons, places, or commodities; to charge reasonable rates; and to be liable for damage to the goods. The filing of rail tariffs and contracts is not required. The railroad industry remains the most highly regulated transportation mode, but complete rate deregulation exists over certain types of rail traffic—intermodal freight, for example.

- **Air transportation**—In 1977, economic regulation of air transportation was eliminated; the marketplace determines rates and services. Safety regulation, however, remains a major thrust of federal controls over air carriers. Such safety regulations as the controls over the number of landings and takeoffs permitted at an airport indirectly determine the level of service provided by an air carrier and whether an air carrier can provide service to a particular airport (availability of landing slots).

- **Ocean transportation**—The Shipping Act of 1984 initiated the economic deregulation of the ocean shipping industry, removing the requirement for Federal Maritime Commission (FMC) approval of rates and conference agreements (ocean conferences are groups of carriers that band together to set common prices). This act expanded antitrust immunity to conference members and allowed independent contracting by conference members but required contracts to be filed with the FMC for public dissemination. The Ocean Shipping Reform Act of 1998 greatly diminished the power of the conferences by eliminating their authority over conference members' participation in service contracts with customers. OSRA also changed tariff-filing rules in that contract rates are not made public (though basic information—port ranges, commodities, and minimum commitments—still must be published). These revisions have hastened the economic deregulation of ocean shipping, with greatly expanded use of contracts and a significant reduction in the number of ocean conferences.

- **Freight forwarders and brokers**—Both forms of transportation are required to register with the STB, and the broker must post a $10,000 surety bond to ensure the carrier used will receive payment from the broker. However, there are no federal economic controls over the rates or services provided by these two intermediaries. A freight forwarder is considered a carrier and is held liable for freight damage, whereas the broker is not considered a carrier and is not liable for freight damage.

Safety Regulation[2]

Noneconomic regulation primarily focuses on transportation safety, promotion, and research issues. Established in 1966, the U.S. Department of Transportation (DOT) was charged with providing the United States with a national transportation policy aimed at improving the safety and efficiency of the transportation system.[3] The DOT is now partitioned into 13 administrations and bureaus, each charged with specific responsibilities.[4] The primary DOT agency for each major mode of transportation is identified in the following paragraphs.

The Federal Highway Administration (FHWA) primarily affects the motor carrier industry. The FHWA is charged with the broad responsibility of ensuring that U.S. roads and highways continue to be the safest and most technologically up to date. The agency conducts safety research, technology, and outreach projects aimed at reducing the frequency and severity of crashes, mitigating congestion, and protecting the environment. The FHWA provides financial and technical support to states for constructing, improving, and preserving the U.S. highway system.

The Federal Motor Carrier Safety Administration (FMCSA) was established as a separate entity from FHWA in the Motor Carrier Safety Improvement Act of 1999. The goals of this agency are to improve the safety of commercial motor vehicles and to reduce crashes, injuries, and fatalities involving large trucks and buses. This agency develops, maintains, and enforces federal regulations; administers the commercial driver's license program; and regulates hazardous materials transportation. One of the most contentious activities has been the revision of the hours of service regulation that altered the amount of time that truck drivers can work each day. Most recently, the FMCSA initiated the **Compliance, Safety, Accountability (CSA)** initiative to reduce commercial motor vehicle crashes, fatalities, and injuries on U.S. highways. CSA introduces a new enforcement and compliance model that allows FMCSA and its state partners to contact a larger number of carriers earlier in order to address safety problems before crashes occur.[5]

The Federal Aviation Administration (FAA) primarily affects the airline industry. The major responsibilities of the FAA include regulation of air safety, promotion of air commerce, and monitoring of air space. The agency's aviation safety office controls the certification, production approval, and continued airworthiness of aircraft and certifies pilots, mechanics, and others in safety-related positions. The FAA also provides federal grant money to plan and develop public airports and to improve technical capabilities at airport facilities.

The Federal Railroad Administration (FRA) affects rail companies. This agency's responsibilities focus on the enforcement of railroad safety issues. The FRA Operations Practices Division examines and ensures that carrier operating rules, employee qualification guidelines, and carrier training and testing programs are in compliance with the Railroad Safety Act of 1970, railroad occupational safety and health standards, the Hours of Service Act, and accident and personal injury reporting requirements. The FRA also administers federal assistance to some carriers to ensure the continuation of freight and passenger rail service.

The Maritime Administration (MARAD) is responsible for promoting and operating the U.S. merchant marine. The agency's mission is to strengthen the U.S. maritime transportation system—including infrastructure, industry, and labor—to meet the economic and security needs of the country.[6] During times of war, the United States relies heavily on water carriage for overseas shipments of troops and materials. To keep U.S. ships properly maintained and in seaworthy condition, the federal government offers water carriers subsidies. These subsidies are administered by MARAD. Given the importance of maritime vessels in national defense, the federal government has also granted the maritime industry an antitrust exemption. The exemption allows carriers to form shippers' conferences and to discuss specific rates. Some large customers oppose shippers' conferences because they allow carriers to monopolize certain trade routes. Some industry experts expect antitrust immunity to disappear, ending shippers' conferences and deregulating the industry much like the other transportation modes.

While the U.S. Coast Guard (USCG) is a branch of the armed forces, it also works with the DOT to promote marine safety and environmental protection. The USCG is responsible for enforcing maritime law, developing and enforcing safety regulations, assisting in rescue efforts, and protecting U.S. borders. Its mission is to protect the public, the environment, and U.S. economic interests—in the nation's ports and waterways, along the coast, on international waters, or in any maritime region to support national security.[7]

SUMMARY

Regulation is a dynamic component of the transportation process that is always subject to change. While we are currently in a time of limited economic regulation, governments actively develop transportation policies and regulations to address safety, security, and environmental challenges; meet societal requirements; and adapt to technological change. The intention of such regulation is positive but can have a major impact on the cost, time, and ease with which product flows across the supply chain. Thus, transportation managers must remain vigilant and factor current and pending legislation into their planning processes.

NOTES

1. For an extensive discussion of economic regulation, see John J. Coyle, Robert A. Novack, Brian J. Gibson, and Edward J. Bardi, *Transportation: A Supply Chain Perspective*, 7th ed. (Mason, Ohio: South-Western Cengage Learning, 2011), Chapter 2.

2. Adapted from David J. Bloomberg, Stephen LeMay, and Joe B. Hanna, *Logistics* (Upper Saddle River, NJ: Prentice-Hall, Inc., 2002): 95–96.

3. DOT Act of 1966, Public Law 89-670, Sec. 2(b)(1).

4. For more information regarding these U.S. DOT agencies, see http://www.dot.gov/DOTagencies.htm.

5. "About CSA: What Is It?" retrieved July 22, 2011 from http://csa.fmcsa.dot.gov/about/.

6. "MARAD Mission, Goals, and Vision," retrieved July 22, 2011, from http://www.marad.dot.gov/about_us_landing_page/administrators_office_home/administrators_office_home.htm.

7. "United States Coast Guard Overview," retrieved July 22, 2011, from http://www.uscg.mil/top/about/.

APPENDIX 10B

Basis of Transportation Rates

Transportation ratemaking would be a simple process if carriers sold all transportation services on a ton-mile basis, charging customers X dollars to move each ton of a product each mile. However, carriers do not operate in such a simplistic manner. Multiple factors must be considered by carriers and their customers when determining how much it costs to move a product from origin to destination. With 33,000 major shipping points in the United States alone, a countless array of commodities with unique characteristics, varying shipment sizes, and specific service requirements, the challenge of ratemaking becomes clear.

Ratemaking has become a sophisticated activity with tremendous efforts being made to optimize the negotiated price of transportation services. Customers recognize the need for carriers to charge rates that earn a reasonable profit margin, or the carrier will not be in business over the long run. This section briefly discusses primary factors that are incorporated into the transportation rate development process. To ensure that transportation rates are fair and reasonable for both parties, the following issues must be considered: (1) the cost and value of service, which affect the different rates the carrier establishes for different commodities; (2) the distance between origin and destination; (3) the weight of the shipment; (4) the characteristics of the commodity being transported; and (5) the level of service required.

Cost of Service

Basing rates on the **cost of service** considers the supply side of pricing. The cost of supplying the service establishes the floor for a rate; that is, the supply cost permits the carrier's viability by providing the rate's lower limit (see Figure 10B.1).

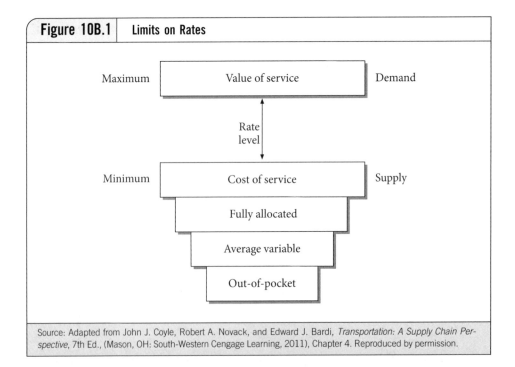

Figure 10B.1	Limits on Rates

Maximum — Value of service — Demand

Rate level

Minimum — Cost of service — Supply

Fully allocated

Average variable

Out-of-pocket

Source: Adapted from John J. Coyle, Robert A. Novack, and Edward J. Bardi, *Transportation: A Supply Chain Perspective*, 7th Ed., (Mason, OH: South-Western Cengage Learning, 2011), Chapter 4. Reproduced by permission.

The continual problem of what cost basis to use has plagued this area. Carriers have used fully allocated (average total) costs as well as average variable costs and out-of-pocket (marginal) costs. In essence, this problem sets up subfloors to the lower rate limit: the carrier will base the higher limit on fully allocated costs and the lower limit on out-of-pocket costs.

Common and **joint costs** also increase the problem of using service cost as a basis for rates. The carrier incurs common and joint costs when producing multiple units of output; the carrier cannot directly allocate such costs to a particular production unit. A joint cost is a particular type of common cost in which the costs a carrier incurs in producing one unit unavoidably produce another product. For example, moving a commodity from A to B unavoidably produces the movement capacity and cost from B to A—the backhaul. The procedure the carrier uses to assign these common and joint costs determines the cost basis, permitting latitude for cost variations and, consequently, for rate variations.

Value of Service

Value of service pricing considers the demand side of pricing. We may define value of service pricing as "charging what the traffic will bear." This basis considers the transported product's ability to withstand transportation costs. For example, in Figure 10B.2, the highest rate a carrier can charge to move producer A's product to point B is $0.50 per unit. If the carrier assesses a higher rate, producer A's product will not be competitive in the B market area. Thus, value of service pricing places the upper limit on the rate.

Generally, rates vary by transported product. The cost difference associated with various commodity movements may explain this, but this difference also contains the value of service pricing concept. For higher-value commodities, transportation charges are a small portion of the total selling price. From Table 10B.1, we can see that the transportation rate for diamonds, for a given distance and weight, is 100 times greater than that for coal; but

---

Figure 10B.2	Example of Value of Service Pricing

Maximum rate = $0.50

A ——————————————————————— B

A's production cost = $2.00   B's production cost = $2.50

Source: Edward J. Bardi, Ph.D. Used with permission.

Table 10B.1	Transportation Rates and Commodity Value

	COAL	DIAMONDS
Production value per ton*	$30.00	$10,000,000.00
Transportation charge per ton*	10.00	1,000.00
Total selling price	$40.00	$10,001,000.00
Transportation cost as a percentage of selling price	25%	0.01%

*Assumed.
Source: Edward J. Bardi, Ph.D. Used with permission.

transportation charges amount to only 0.01 percent of the selling price for diamonds, as opposed to 25 percent for coal. Thus, high-value commodities can sustain higher transportation charges, and carriers price the transport services accordingly—a specific application of demand pricing.

Distance

Rates usually vary with respect to **distance**; that is, the greater the distance the commodity moves, the greater the cost to the carrier and the greater the transportation rate. However, certain rates do not relate to exact point-to-point distance. One example of these is a **blanket rate** or **zone rate**.

A blanket rate does not increase as distance increases; the rate remains the same for all points in the blanket area the carrier designates. The postage stamp rate is an extreme example of a blanket rate. No matter what distance you ship a first-class letter domestically, your cost as the shipper (sender) is the same. In freight transportation, carriers develop zones that contain a particular area such as a city's commercial zone, a given state, a region, or a number of states, for example. In each case, the transportation rate is the same regardless of the particular freight pickup or delivery location within the zone. This simplifies the ratemaking process as multiple locations are assigned to the same zone rather than treating every origin and destination point as a unique location for pricing purposes. UPS, FedEx, and other small package carriers use zone rates extensively.

While transportation rates increase as distance increases, the increase is not directly proportional to distance. This relationship of rates to distance is known as the **tapering rate principle**. As Figure 10B.3 shows, the rate increases as distance increases, but not linearly. The rate structure tapers because carriers spread terminal costs (cargo handling, clerical, and billing) over a greater mileage base. These terminal costs do not vary with

| **Figure 10B.3** | **Example of the Tapering Rate Principle** |

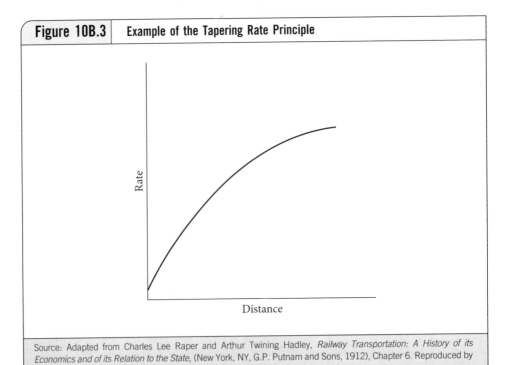

Source: Adapted from Charles Lee Raper and Arthur Twining Hadley, *Railway Transportation: A History of its Economics and of its Relation to the State*, (New York, NY, G.P. Putnam and Sons, 1912), Chapter 6. Reproduced by permission.

distance; as the shipment's movement distance increases, the terminal cost per mile decreases. The intercept point in Figure 10B.3 corresponds to the terminal costs.

Weight of Shipment

Carriers quote freight rates in cents per hundredweight (actual weight in pounds divided by 100 = hundredweight, or cwt) and determine the total transportation charge by the total weight of the shipment in cwt and the appropriate rate per cwt. The rate per cwt relates to the shipped volume: Carriers charge a lower rate for volume shipments and a higher rate for less-than-volume quantities. In essence, carriers offer a quantity discount for shipping large volumes (buying service in a large quantity). This is partly due to the fact that some of the basic shipment costs like document preparation, shipment pickup, and shipment delivery are spread over a larger amount of freight.

Railroads term these quantity discounts **carload (CL)** and **less-than-carload (LCL)**; motor carriers call them **truckload (TL)** and **less-than-truckload (LTL)**. The CL and TL rates represent the lower, volume rates; and the LCL and LTL rates denote the higher, less-than-volume rates.

One noteworthy exception to the rate–volume relationship is the **any-quantity (AQ) rate**, which bears no relationship to volume shipped. The rate per cwt remains constant regardless of the volume a firm tenders to the carrier for shipment; that is, no quantity discount is available.

Commodity Characteristics

Another ratemaking consideration is the type of product being moved. If carriers must take out-of-the-ordinary steps to protect freight, devote extra capacity to lightweight freight, or have specialized equipment to handle certain commodities, the cost of providing transportation service increases. The freight price must reflect the increased cost of the additional service to maintain carrier profitability. Hence, carriers consider commodity density, stowability, ease or difficulty of handling, and liability issues when developing freight rates.

Freight density reflects the weight *and* volume of freight. If a carrier developed rates on weight alone, bulky and lightweight products (e.g., potato chips) would move very inexpensively versus compact and heavy products (e.g., canned soups) even though the potato chips would take up far more space in the container. To adjust for density issues, carriers charge higher rates per cwt for low-density products than they do for higher-density products. For example, air carriers compare the true weight of the freight and the dimensional weight of the freight (package length × width × height/166), using the higher of the two weights in the calculation of freight rates. This prevents low-density freight from commandeering critical capacity at unreasonably low rates.

Stowability refers to how the product being shipped will affect the space utilization in the container. Certain products ship well and waste little space (e.g., a computer monitor in a narrow box), while other products stow poorly and force a carrier to haul air (e.g., a fully assembled bicycle). Products resulting in wasted space are typically charged a higher price per unit.

Ease of handling is another ratemaking consideration. The more that goods must be handled, the greater the cost to the carrier. Handling requirements may include repalletizing or repacking goods, ordinary cross-docking of LTL shipments, the use of specially trained labor, and the need for special handling equipment. Logically, products with more specialized handling requirements are charged higher rates by carriers to offset the costs involved in providing the services.

Carriers must also assess their potential liabilities when developing rates. The more susceptible a shipment is to loss, damage, or theft, the greater the carrier's risk. Fragile or easily damaged freight results in more liability claims from shippers. Hence, carriers develop higher rates for valuable products (e.g., liquid-crystal-display TVs) and delicate products (e.g., light bulbs) to offset the financial risk of moving such products. Lower rates are afforded to sturdy products (e.g., wood flooring) that aren't likely to be stolen or damaged.

Efforts have been made to simplify these product characteristic issues. Rather than evaluating every commodity independently, classification systems have been developed to group together products with similar transportation characteristics for the purpose of ratemaking. For example, the trucking industry has long relied on the National Motor Freight Classification (NMFC) as a pricing tool that provides a comparison of commodities moving in interstate, intrastate, and foreign commerce. The NMFC groups commodities into one of 18 classes based on an evaluation of the four transportation characteristics discussed earlier. Together, these characteristics establish a commodity's "transportability."[1]

While the NMFC provides some simplification of pricing, there is still a great deal of complexity to manage. The challenge is compounded by the widespread discounting by carriers against these class rates. To reduce the complexity, some industry experts are advocating a product density–based pricing system similar to those used in Europe. Other experts suggest using freight all kinds (FAK) rates that consolidate freight under one class.

Level of Service

Another critical factor in transportation ratemaking is the service requirements of the freight buyer. The demand for faster and time-definite service is increasing in all modes of transportation. When a customer requires faster-than-normal service or guaranteed delivery times, carriers often need to break from their standard processes to accommodate the requirement. This could involve dispatching trailers before they are full, putting an additional operator and piece of equipment into service, deviating from normal routes, or a number of other exceptions. Any of these steps will likely reduce the efficiency of the carrier's operations and cause it to incur additional expenses. Thus, customers are charged premium rates to offset the additional costs created by their more demanding service requirements.

UPS (and many other carriers) offers numerous service-level options and charges accordingly. The current nondiscounted rates obtained from the company's Web site for moving a single carton weighing 10 pounds from Atlanta to New York are as follows:

- $136.54 for "Next Day Air Early A.M." service with delivery by 8:00 AM
- $101.05 for "Next Day Air" service with delivery by 10:30 AM
- $92.17 for "Next Day Air Saver" service with delivery by 3:00 PM
- $42.48 for "2nd Day Air" service by end of the second business day
- $13.23 for "UPS Ground" service nonguaranteed service by the end of the second day with delivery by 4:30 PM

As this example reveals, the rates vary significantly even for a few hours time difference. Freight buyers must objectively evaluate their need for extremely fast service because they will pay a major premium for it.

SUMMARY

This appendix provides a primer on transportation ratemaking. It addresses the key factors that should be included in all rate development initiatives—cost and value of service, shipment distance and size, commodity characteristics, and service characteristics. While no ratemaking initiative can ignore these considerations, other factors may be added to the analysis, depending on the situation. An extensive discussion of these additional factors, mode specific rate issues, and rate types (e.g., released value rates, deferred rates, and incentive rates) can be found in freight transportation textbooks.

NOTE

1. For more information on freight classification, visit http://www.nmfta.org.

Chapter 11

DISTRIBUTION—MANAGING FULFILLMENT OPERATIONS

Learning Objectives

After reading this chapter, you should be able to do the following:

- Discuss the strategic value-adding role distribution plays in the supply chain.
- Recognize the tradeoffs between distribution and other supply chain functions.
- Understand the analytical framework for distribution planning decisions.
- Evaluate fulfillment strategies and distribution methods.
- Describe the primary fulfillment processes and support functions in distribution center (DC) operations.
- Use productivity and quality metrics to analyze fulfillment performance.
- Describe how information technology supports distribution operations.
- Discuss materials-handling objectives, principles, and equipment uses.

Supply Chain Profile   *Kroger: Grocery Giant Changes the Game*

Eight years ago, Kroger created a new design for grocery distribution. Today, the grocer is building store-ready mixed pallets in an automated environment.

In the not so distant past, most grocery distribution centers made do with labor-intensive, traditional materials-handling technologies and processes. Pallets were moved by lift trucks and stored in racks. Mixed pallets were built the old fashioned way, with manual labor.

For some leading grocers, those days are history. The same industry that led the way in the adoption of warehouse management and labor management systems, wireless barcode scanning, and voice technology is now adopting automated materials handling in a big way.

The Kroger Company is one of those industry leaders. About eight years ago, it began working with Witron Integrated Logistics Corporation, a systems integrator, to create a new design to automate its grocery DCs. The end result was a system that can receive and put away full pallets then break them down and rebuild them into store-ready mixed pallets according to how they will be stocked on the shelves in a store aisle. It all happens with almost no human intervention: Operators typically touch a product once when lift truck operators unload pallets at the receiving dock and once again when they are loaded at the shipping dock for delivery to stores. The system involves a complex array of equipment and processes:

- Automatic pallet exchange and depalletizing machines;
- A 10-crane unit load automated storage and retrieval system (AS/RS) with approximately 21,000 pallet positions for reserve storage;
- A 32-aisle miniload AS/RS with nearly 400,000 tray positions for temporary storage of cartons prior to order fulfillment;
- Transfer vehicles that deliver pallets from the system induction area in receiving to a pallet exchange station and from the conveyor system to the AS/RS crane selected for putaway; and
- A unique system that automatically builds mixed pallets in the sequence they will be stocked on shelves in a specific store aisle; the system uses a separate miniload system for buffer storage, a custom-designed palletizer to place the cartons on the right spot on the pallet, and an automatic stretch wrapper.

In all, Kroger processes about 110,000 cases per day with a peak capacity of 160,000 cases in the first facility built with the new design in Arizona.

"When we began working with our system integrator to create this design, we were looking for a paradigm change in grocery warehousing," says John Winkels, Kroger's senior director of logistics engineering and network strategy. As Winkels' title suggests, the design was part of a long-term supply chain strategy. After going live with the Arizona facility, Kroger built a second facility in Colorado and is in the process of building a third using the same design in southern California.

Founded 126 years ago, Kroger is one of the best-known names in American business. Like most of its competitors, for many years it had been a traditional grocery logistics and distribution company. The grocery industry, however, is incredibly competitive, operating on razor-thin margins. Any reductions in operating costs in warehousing, order fulfillment, and transportation go right to the bottom line. For that reason, Kroger set out to reengineer the way it distributes product to its stores.

"The philosophy that most of our industry has taken is that you need to be close to your store base with your facilities," says Winkels. "We wanted to look at our network and rethink that" Surprisingly, cycle times and throughput were not major issues for the new design. Kroger was able to meet its throughput requirements in its traditional warehouses by adding labor. Instead, Kroger wanted a solution that would address some of the major long-term challenges of operating a grocery distribution center.

The first was to deal with SKU proliferation efficiently. The second was to build a mixed case pallet for individual stores efficiently. Finally, Kroger wanted a system that would address the changing warehouse industry workforce. After Kroger identified its high-level supply chain priorities and the operational challenges it wanted to address, Winkels says it was clear that materials-handling automation was the way to go. The solution incorporates a number of familiar automated materials-handling technologies.

What's unique is how those familiar technologies come together to build aisle-aligned pallets. The case order machine, for instance, takes cases from the miniload and places them in a buffer storage system that then delivers them in sequence to the palletizer; that machine uses a unique series of arms to maneuver a carton into the right position on a pallet before delivering the finished pallet to an automatic stretch wrapper. "The trick isn't to build an AS/RS or a miniload," says Winkels. "The trick is to seamlessly connect the pieces. What's special about this solution is the way the software coordinates pulling the pallets out of the AS/RS, dictates how much product needs to be placed in a miniload tray, and sequences the delivery of the cartons to the palletizer."

Kroger measures its success in several ways. "Our orders are more accurate and we have reduced product damage, which means we're getting more of the product our customers want to the store in a sellable condition," says Winkels. "What's more, it has provided us with significant logistics efficiency. We're not just more efficient in the warehouse, we're making better utilization of the cube of the trailer and making our stores more efficient. The impact can be felt across our supply chain."

Source: "Kroger: Grocery Giant Changes the Game," *Modern Materials Handling* (February 2010). Reproduced by permission.

Introduction

Distribution in the twenty-first century focuses on the continuous flows of product to fulfill customer requirements at the lowest possible cost. No longer focused on long-term storage of inventory in static warehouses, distribution operations provide a variety of capabilities for the supply chain. Whether the facility fulfills Internet orders, cross-docks production parts for an automobile assembly plant, or mixes high-volume products for a grocery retailer as outlined in the Supply Chain Profile, the goal is to serve the supply chain quickly and accurately.

While speed is of the essence, running efficient distribution facilities and networks is also critical. With U.S. warehousing and distribution-related expenses accounting for $119 billion of the $357 billion in inventory carrying costs, there is a great need to focus on fulfillment costs in the supply chain.[1] Cost-reducing opportunities such as limiting product handling, consolidating facilities, and streamlining inventories must be leveraged for supply chains to be competitive.

This chapter focuses on the importance of distribution in meeting customer needs across the supply chain. We will discuss the planning and development of distribution capabilities, as well as the operations, processes, and technologies involved in efficient demand fulfillment. Throughout the chapter, you will gain an understanding of the roles that distribution strategies, facilities, and tools play in the effective management of inventory and the creation of customer value through improved product availability.

The Role of Distribution Operations in SCM

In a perfect world, supply and demand would be balanced, with desired products being assembled when needed and delivered directly to the point of use. However, this goal is not feasible for most consumer products because production and consumption are not perfectly synchronized, transportation of individual units is too costly, and coordination of activities between such a large number of origin and destination points is very complex. To overcome such issues, distribution operations—distribution centers, warehouses, cross-docks, and retail stores—are established within the supply chain.

These inventory handling, storage, and processing facilities help supply chains create time and place utility. By positioning raw materials, components, and finished goods in production- and market-facing positions, goods are available when and where they are needed. Shorter lead times can be achieved, product availability increased, and delivery costs reduced, increasing both the effectiveness and efficiency of the distribution operations. In highly contested markets, these responsive capabilities can help a supply chain enhance its competitive position.

Enhanced customer service is not the sole rationale for inserting distribution operations into the supply chain. Such facilities also help organizations overcome challenges, support other processes, and take advantage of economies of scale. These roles involve several factors:

- **Balancing supply and demand**—Whether seasonal production must service year-round demand (e.g., corn) or year-round production is needed to meet seasonal demand (e.g., holiday wrapping paper), distribution facilities can stockpile inventory to buffer supply and demand.

- **Protecting against uncertainty**—Distribution facilities can hold inventory for protection against forecast errors, supply disruptions, and demand spikes.

- **Allowing quantity purchase discounts**—Suppliers often provide incentives to purchase product in larger quantities. Distribution facilities can hold the additional quantities until needed, reducing the purchase cost per unit.

- **Supporting production requirements**—If a manufacturing operation can reduce costs via long production runs or if outputs need to age or ripen (e.g., wine, cheese, fruit), the output can be warehoused prior to distribution.

- **Promoting transportation economies**—Fully utilizing container capacity and moving product in larger quantities is less expensive per unit than shipping "air" and moving small quantities at a time. Distribution facilities can be used to receive and hold the larger deliveries of inventory for future requirements.

Distribution Facility Functionality

Distribution facilities can provide numerous services, depending on the requirements of the supply chain. In traditional distribution operations, four primary functions are carried out: (1) accumulation, (2) sortation, (3) allocation, and (4) assortment.[2]

Figure 11.1 | **The Distribution Center's Accumulation Role**

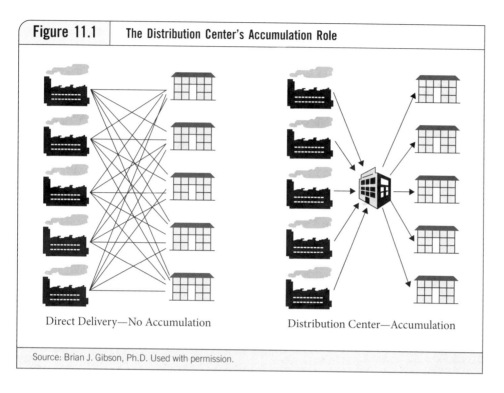

Direct Delivery—No Accumulation   Distribution Center—Accumulation

Source: Brian J. Gibson, Ph.D. Used with permission.

Accumulation involves the receipt of goods from a variety of sources. The DC serves as a collection point for product coming from multiple origins and provides required transfer, storage, or processing services. The accumulation function allows organizations to consolidate orders and shipments for production and fulfillment processes. As Figure 11.1 demonstrates, with accumulation there are fewer deliveries to schedule and manage. Also, significant transportation cost savings are achieved through larger, more cost-efficient deliveries.

Sortation focuses on assembling like products together for storage in the distribution facility or for transfer to customers. During the receiving process, goods are segmented according to their key characteristics—production lot number, stock-keeping unit (SKU) number, case pack size, expiration date, etc.—and prepared for safe storage in the facility or immediate distribution. Proper sortation is essential for the effective management of inventory and fulfillment of customer orders. For example, mixing cases of fresh chicken with two different expiration dates on a single pallet can lead to improper inventory rotation and some product spoilage. Likewise, improper sortation of SKUs may result in shipping the wrong products to customers.

Allocation focuses on matching available inventory to customer orders for a SKU. The order is compared to inventory levels, and available units are retrieved from storage according to the quantity requested by the customer. This break-bulk capacity promotes product availability for multiple customers and allows them to purchase needed quantities rather than excess volume that is not desired. For example, rather than distributing chewing gum only by the pallet (36 cases × 12 display boxes × 24 selling units = 10,368 packs of gum), a DC can allocate product on a case or individual display box basis.

Assortment involves the assembly of customer orders for multiple SKUs held in the distribution facility. As Figure 11.2 highlights, the facility provides a product mixing capability, allowing customers to quickly order a variety of items from a single location. This avoids the expenses related to placing numerous orders and having them shipped

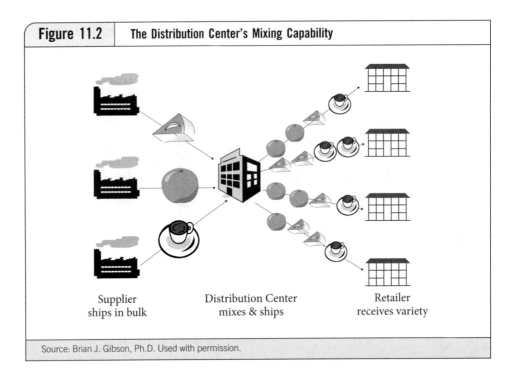

| Figure 11.2 | The Distribution Center's Mixing Capability |

Supplier
ships in bulk

Distribution Center
mixes & ships

Retailer
receives variety

Source: Brian J. Gibson, Ph.D. Used with permission.

from a variety of locations. Just as companies benefit from the assortment function, individuals gain from the assortment/product mixing concept when shopping for food. Rather than traveling to the butcher shop, bakery, dairy store, and produce market, we make a single trip to the grocery store, saving us time and transportation costs. Given the congestion, capacity, and fuel costs faced by industry today, this product mixing role is a key distribution facility capability.

While these four roles are key to the success of a distribution facility, other functions and capabilities are needed. Many distribution facilities are taking on a number of value-adding roles to complement their basic functionality and to support evolving supply chain needs. Most distribution facilities are no longer viewed as places to store products but as activity centers with flexible space and labor that can be leveraged for a variety of customer needs ranging from product labeling to light manufacturing. The value-added activities highlighted in Table 11.1 help organizations handle special customer requirements, create supply chain efficiencies, and differentiate themselves from their competition.

Distribution Tradeoffs

To this point, we have focused on the value-adding roles and functionality of distribution operations. Although many organizations tout the importance of distribution operations, others do not see it the same way. They view distribution facilities as costly operations that interrupt the flow of goods. Both perspectives are realistic, and it is up to supply chain professionals to determine how to best balance customer service and costs. This requires an understanding of the tradeoffs highlighted in Figure 11.3.

One important interaction that must be considered is the tradeoff between distribution and transportation operations. When a supply chain has no market-facing DCs or warehouses (product is sent directly from plants to individual customers), transportation costs will be very high. Organizations may benefit substantially from the establishment of

Table 11.1	Value-Adding Roles of Distribution Operations

- **Assembly services**—Handle limited/light assembly of products such as building and filling in-store display units.

- **Inventory management and visibility**—Provide consignment and vendor-managed inventory programs.

- **Product kitting, bundling, and unbundling**—Build customized combinations of products to meet specific customer requirements such as all components needed for the assembly of a desktop computer or repacking a combination of goods for retail promotion (gift with purchase or multi-pack goods).

- **Product postponement**—Conduct specific activities (assembly, sizing, packaging, and/or labeling) that have been delayed until customer places order.

- **Production sequencing**—Prepare inventory for just-in-time line-side delivery to manufacturing facilities. Components are picked, loaded, and delivered in the precise sequence needed for assembly.

- **Recycling, repair, and returns management**—Provide services related to reverse flows of products from customers such as inspection, disposal, refurbishment, or credit.

Source: Brian J. Gibson, Ph.D. Used with permission.

Figure 11.3	Functional Tradeoffs

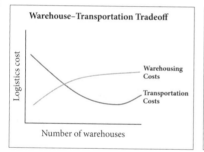

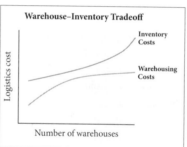

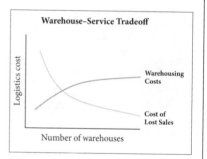

Source: Brian J. Gibson, Ph.D. Used with permission.

one or several warehouses to reduce transportation costs. Why? Large shipments can be transported over long distances from plants to distribution facilities via truckload carriers; then the smaller shipments are delivered to nearby customers. However, there comes a point where you build too many warehouses and total costs increase. Why is this so? With so many facilities, operating costs will increase and transportation expenses will rise (inbound shipments will become less-than-truckload shipments, which are more expensive than shipping full truckloads).

Another key tradeoff must be made between distribution and inventory. Generally, the more DCs and warehouses, the higher the total inventory carrying costs will be. As facilities are added to a fulfillment system, the amount of inventory will increase in total, but at a decreasing rate. This move toward decentralized inventory inhibits the ability to adopt a **risk pooling** strategy as each facility must hold additional safety stock. Supply chain leaders must be mindful of this interaction and regularly evaluate the tradeoff between smaller inventories versus more facilities.

A common fulfillment strategy of many firms is to use the normal distribution network for most items and maintain one centralized facility for their low-velocity items. These slow movers may be replacement parts, items that are critical to important customers, or high-profit margin products. Maintaining just one central inventory rather than holding the goods in multiple facilities creates inventory carrying cost savings that offset the increased cost associated with longer delivery distances.

The tradeoff between distribution operations and customer service is another important issue. More distribution facilities in the supply chain create better service for customers. Buyers are more comfortable if they know the supplier has a DC within a day's drive from their operations. They don't feel so comfortable if the facility is a thousand miles away. Decision makers must balance the value of better service levels with the additional costs of operating facilities and carrying inventory.

Tradeoffs must also be made at the facility level between the primary resources available to distribution managers—space, equipment, and people. Space allows for the storage of goods when supply and demand are imbalanced. Warehouse equipment, including materials-handling devices ranging from racks to conveyor lines, supports the efficient movement and storage of product within the distribution facility. People are the most critical distribution resource, playing multiple roles in the facility over different schedules. Their capabilities can be increased through training, while their numbers can be quickly increased to handle demand surges.

For internal efficiency targets to be met, it is necessary to make conscientious financial and performance tradeoffs between resources. The primary tradeoffs and relationships include the following:

- **Space vs. equipment**—The larger the facility and the more space used for distribution operations, the more equipment will be needed in the facility. Proper equipment allows organizations to leverage space by using the vertical capacity in the facility and improving the speed by which products travel through the facility.

- **Equipment vs. people**—The greater the use of equipment to automate materials handling and distribution activity, the lower the labor requirements of a facility. Conversely, the more manual the operation, the more people are needed to complete distribution activities.

- **People vs. space**—The larger the facility workforce, the larger the facility size and operation possible. It is difficult for a small team to operate a sizable facility unless there is significant use of materials handling and flow automation. Thus, it is critical to hire and schedule enough labor to effectively use the facility and serve customers.

Distribution goals also impact resource requirements. Demands for faster order cycle times or increased facility throughput will require a larger workforce or use of more materials-handling equipment. High safety stock requirements will require more facility capacity to handle the additional inventory. Increased order accuracy requirements will promote the use of equipment, as automated systems are not prone to the errors commonly found in labor-focused operations. Finally, increased demand will necessitate more space, people, and/or equipment.

While there are other tradeoffs to consider in distribution, these cross-organizational and cross-functional tradeoffs are among the most important. They highlight the need for advanced planning, communication, and collaboration among supply chain partners and within organizations. A failure to plan, communicate, and collaborate will lead to ineffective decision making and poor utilization of resources.

Distribution Challenges

Distribution is a dynamic component of the supply chain. Each day in a distribution facility brings new challenges, additional customer orders, and expectations for perfect order fulfillment. Chief among these challenges are labor availability issues, demand variation, and increasing customer requirements. DC management must be flexible and creative in addressing these issues, which often impact each other. Failure to do so leads to higher costs and service problems for the organization, as well as disruptions of the supply chain.

In most organizations, distribution is a people-intensive activity. Unfortunately, it is growing increasingly difficult to find and train high-quality personnel for DC operations. From an hourly position perspective, DC work is physically demanding and often occurs around the clock, seven days a week. Wages are typically competitive with other hourly positions, but there is limited opportunity for salary growth. Add this all up, and the result is an industry with an ongoing turnover challenge. Compounding the problem is the demographic trend toward the graying of America. U.S. Census Bureau projections reveal that the number of retirement-age Americans (65 and older) will grow at a much faster rate than the age groups that will be needed to replace them. The result of this aging population will be a smaller labor pool from which to find quality employees. Finding capable employees, training them to be productive, and retaining them requires great effort and investment on the part of the organization.

Demand variation is another supply chain challenge that affects distribution operations. Many products are seasonal in nature, with demand high during some periods and low during others. Sunscreen lotion and related products have a much higher demand in the spring and summer seasons than the fall and winter, though some demand will occur year round as people prepare for vacation. The DC handling this product may be short on space capacity as inventory builds up in advance of the primary selling season but be nearly empty during the off-season. Labor issues also arise—for example, not enough help is available to fulfill orders during the peak season but little work is available at other times. Without some ability to smooth out demand, it is difficult to effectively utilize the space and equipment resources and retain labor throughout the year. Thus, it is critical to balance the DC requirements of seasonal products with products that have alternate primary selling seasons and/or stable year-round demand products.

The successful expansion of specialized distribution facility roles that was discussed earlier is noteworthy but also creates a problem for organizations. As customers have learned that DCs are more than just storage facilities, the desire for additional capabilities and service has grown. Also, the trend toward lean operations and supply chains has prompted many customers to reduce inventory. They expect suppliers to provide smaller, more frequent, and faster fulfillment of orders. Together, these trends place a great deal of pressure on DCs to maximize speed and service while keeping costs under control. The solution is to build flexible fulfillment processes that can handle the varying requirements of different customer segments.

Distribution Planning and Strategy

Understanding the role of distribution in the supply chain is the foundation of effective fulfillment processes. The next step is to develop distribution strategies that are tailored to the products being handled, customer requirements, and available internal

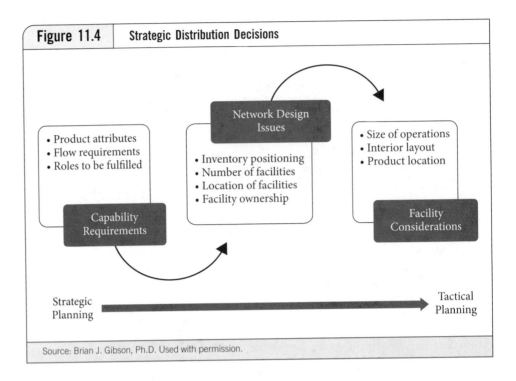

Figure 11.4 | **Strategic Distribution Decisions**

Network Design Issues

- Product attributes
- Flow requirements
- Roles to be fulfilled

Capability Requirements

- Inventory positioning
- Number of facilities
- Location of facilities
- Facility ownership

- Size of operations
- Interior layout
- Product location

Facility Considerations

Strategic Planning   Tactical Planning

Source: Brian J. Gibson, Ph.D. Used with permission.

expertise and resources. A series of interrelated distribution planning decisions must be made to ensure that the strategy can be executed at a reasonable cost while supporting supply chain demands. These planning issues, highlighted in Figure 11.4, are discussed next.

Capability Requirements

When establishing a distribution strategy, the first and most obvious consideration is the product. Product characteristics must drive the design of the distribution process. Issues such as product value, durability, temperature sensitivity, obsolescence, volume, and other factors must be considered just as they are in transportation decision making. For example, raw materials (coal and timber) can often be held in outdoor stockpiles and transferred as needed to the production facility. The same distribution process would be totally inappropriate for consumer products (ice cream and iPods), which need to be distributed quickly, shielded from the environment, and protected against theft and damage. Hence, it is critical to match distribution processes to the products involved to protect product integrity, promote customer service and satisfaction, and provide greater control of the inventory.

Another issue that has a major impact on the distribution strategy and network structure is the product flow requirements of the supply chain. Two options are available: (1) direct shipment of goods from the manufacturer to retailer or retailer to consumer or (2) movement of goods through distribution facilities to customers.

Direct shipping operations bypass distribution facilities, fulfilling retail store requests from the primary production point (manufacturer's factory or warehouse) rather than interim distribution facilities that hold inventory. Similarly, Internet retailers directly distribute goods to the end consumer without the need for retail outlets. Direct shipping avoids the need to build and operate distribution facilities, reduces inventory in the system, and often compresses order cycle time. Direct shipping works particularly well when customers place orders for truckload quantities or when product perishability is an issue.

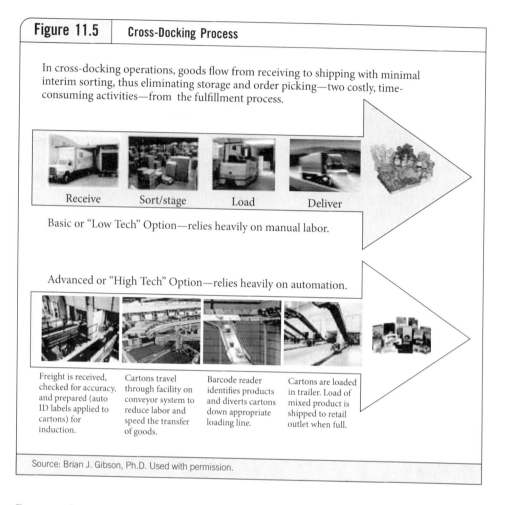

Figure 11.5 | Cross-Docking Process

In cross-docking operations, goods flow from receiving to shipping with minimal interim sorting, thus eliminating storage and order picking—two costly, time-consuming activities—from the fulfillment process.

Receive   Sort/stage   Load   Deliver

Basic or "Low Tech" Option—relies heavily on manual labor.

Advanced or "High Tech" Option—relies heavily on automation.

Freight is received, checked for accuracy, and prepared (auto ID labels applied to cartons) for induction.

Cartons travel through facility on conveyor system to reduce labor and speed the transfer of goods.

Barcode reader identifies products and diverts cartons down appropriate loading line.

Cartons are loaded in trailer. Load of mixed product is shipped to retail outlet when full.

Source: Brian J. Gibson, Ph.D. Used with permission.

For example, it is better to have bread and milk delivered directly to a grocery store than to a DC as they are high-volume products and direct shipping maximizes product shelf life.

On the downside, it is expensive to deliver small quantities to buyers (reduced transportation efficiencies), and there is limited safety stock readily available to protect against demand surges. Furthermore, many companies are not capable of fulfilling orders for case and individual unit quantities. Thus, it is important to consider product characteristics, demand volume and variability, and related issues before making the decision to establish a direct shipping strategy.

Properly planned distribution facilities can address the shortcomings of direct shipping. These facilities, including traditional warehouses, DCs, and cross-docking facilities, provide the supply chain with additional capabilities. Warehouses and DCs can hold goods in anticipation of customer orders, provide a buffer of safety stock to protect against contingencies, and handle small quantity orders efficiently from transportation and fulfillment standpoints. Cross-docks can provide a high-velocity alternative to direct shipping at lower transportation cost with product mixing capabilities. Figure 11.5 provides additional insight on cross-docking.

Of course, it is necessary to analyze the inventory, transportation, and service tradeoffs before choosing between direct shipping and the use of distribution facilities. The ultimate answer may be to employ a combination of the two strategies to ensure distribution efficiency and customer satisfaction. Many companies, like Walmart and Target, use a wide variety of distribution methods to accommodate variation in product volume, size, and supplier proximity.

The other key capability requirement—supply chain roles to be fulfilled—has been highlighted in an earlier section of the chapter. The specific capabilities needed by the supply chain should drive the network design strategies and facility planning. For example, the need for accumulation, sortation, allocation, and assortment functionalities will lead to a distribution strategy centered on traditional DCs and warehouse facilities that store and mix goods. On the other hand, a need for value-added, nontraditional roles such as product customization or repackaging will drive the development of flow-though facilities that operate as much like an assembly line as a DC.

Network Design Issues

Understanding the distribution capabilities required by a supply chain takes much of the guesswork out of the network design phase. If you know the types of activities that must be completed, the volume of product flows, and the expectations of customers, it is far easier to create a network that will perform well. This phase of strategic planning involves the determination of inventory positioning, the number and location of distribution facilities, and the ownership of facilities in the network.

Inventory positioning focuses on the issue of where inventory is located within the supply chain. One strategy is to hold a centralized stock of inventory at a single location such as the origin point or some other advantageous location in the supply chain. Product is distributed to customers across the network from this central stocking point. The benefit of this consolidation strategy is greater control over the inventory and reduced demand variability due to risk pooling. The central or national inventory pool supports higher in-stock availability, though there is a need for less safety stock.[3]

The drawback of centralized inventory is the long distance to customers, which typically extends lead times and results in higher transportation costs. Despite these drawbacks, manufacturers of high-value, low-weight products such as prescription pharmaceuticals often rely on one strategically placed inventory pool. The transportation costs associated with next-day and second-day order delivery are offset by the reductions in inventory carrying costs, the enhanced visibility of product flows, and the improved control over order-filling processes, product pedigree issues, and recall events.

The alternate inventory positioning strategy is to hold product in multiple customer-facing positions. Stocking inventory regionally or locally helps to reduce customer delivery costs and order cycle time. Product is positioned closer to demand points and can be readily dispatched to meet customer requirements. This decentralized inventory strategy works well for high-volume, low-cost products with low demand uncertainty such as laundry detergent, pet food, and cereal.

The decentralized inventory strategy is not without challenges. First, more facilities are required to stock the product, leading to higher handling costs, the risk of product damage, and the potential for product pilferage, not to mention the additional expenses of running the facilities. Also, average inventory levels will rise as each facility will have to hold safety stock to cover demand variation within the region. To combat these issues, some organizations have shifted toward more centralized distribution systems with fewer stocking points.[4]

Which inventory positioning strategy is best? There is no single answer, and many organizations use both strategies. For example, Amazon.com decentralizes inventories of books on the best seller list but centralizes slow-moving, out-of-print books. Ultimately, this strategy is based on product attributes, customer expectations and power, and competitors' actions. Other factors such as transportation prices, inventory carrying costs, and other supply chain expenses also affect inventory positioning strategy.

The second and third network design issues focus on the number and locations of distribution facilities within the supply chain. The required number of facilities will be driven by inventory positioning strategy. The greater the centralization of the inventory, the fewer the number of facilities needed to distribute the product. Market scope also impacts the decision. Small- and medium-sized companies with a regional market area often will need only one distribution facility, whereas large companies with national or global market areas need to consider using multiple facilities, some of which may have different distribution roles.

Determining the number of facilities needed for a supply chain involves the evaluation of cost tradeoffs with other functional areas. Figure 11.6 depicts the impact of increasing the number of warehouses on other logistics functional costs. As the number of warehouses increases, transportation cost and the cost of lost sales decline, though inventory and warehousing costs increase. Overall, total cost will generally decline. However, total costs begin to rise as increasing inventory and warehousing costs offset decreasing transportation costs and the cost of lost sales. Of course, the total cost curve and the range of warehouses it reflects will be different for each company.

- **Transportation costs**—Consolidation of inbound freight into truckload quantities achieves lower transportation rates per hundredweight and reduced transportation costs. On the outbound side, increasing the number of warehouses

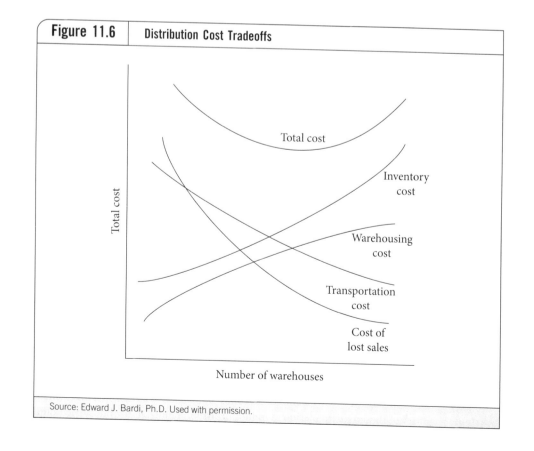

Figure 11.6 | **Distribution Cost Tradeoffs**

Total cost

Inventory cost

Warehousing cost

Transportation cost

Cost of lost sales

Total cost

Number of warehouses

brings the warehouses closer to the customer and market area, reducing both transportation distance and costs.

- **Cost of lost sales**—An increase in the number of facilities improves customer proximity and inventory availability. This facilitates faster order cycle time and more complete orders. Fewer customers will be compelled to find substitute products or take their business to other suppliers, thus reducing defections and lost sales.

- **Warehousing costs**—These costs increase because the total amount of space increases with a larger number of warehouses. For example, splitting a 200,000-square-foot facility in half will likely require two facilities of more than 100,000 square feet each. Office space, equipment storage, and other facilities have similar footprints in two facilities as in one, while aisles require a higher proportion of space in the two smaller warehouses.

- **Inventory costs**—As discussed earlier, an increased number of stocking points increases the overall safety stock levels and inventory carrying costs in the supply chain. Likewise, as companies increase product variety, additional inventory and storage space will be needed.

After settling on the number of distribution facilities, the issue of facility location arises. Though general heuristics (rules of thumb) such as locating high-service facilities near markets and raw materials mixing close to suppliers are valuable, it is important to pursue a desired level of customer service at the least possible logistics cost. Analyzing the DC's intended function, sources and volume of supply, customer locations and demand patterns, and related fulfillment costs will lead to more effective location selection than rules of thumb alone. Similar to other strategic distribution issues, this analysis should consider functional tradeoffs and leverage network design models and software tools. Chapter 12 provides a detailed discussion of facility location analysis.

The final piece of a network design strategy is the facility ownership question—should an organization own and operate private distribution facilities or contract with third-party logistics providers for distribution services? This issue is difficult to address without first determining facility roles, numbers, and locations. After these issues have been resolved, it is easier to understand the scope of tasks to be undertaken and to evaluate the organization's options for handling distribution requirements. They essentially have three choices: (1) private facilities, (2) public facilities, and (3) contract facilities.

Private DCs are internal facilities owned by the organization producing or owning the goods. The focus of the facility is to store goods and distribute them to customers. Owning and operating facilities provide the organization with greater control over fulfillment processes and inventory. Also, economies of scale can be achieved if the volume of activity is high enough. If this is the case, the cost per unit delivered to the customer is less, and the retailer can charge a lower price or maintain a higher profit margin. Private facilities are company assets that can be depreciated and can also provide a source of income by renting or leasing excess space to those who need storage facilities.

In order to make a private distribution cost-effective, the facility needs high product throughput, requires stable demand, and should be located in or near a dense market area. Additionally, the organization must have distribution expertise, the resources to build facilities, and the desire to operate them. If these attributes are not present, the firm should look to third party logistics (3PL) service providers to handle distribution and warehousing.

Public warehousing is the traditional external distribution option. A public warehouse rents out space to individuals or firms needing storage capacity. Additional service offerings vary by 3PL provider. Some provide a wide array of services including packaging, labeling, testing, inventory maintenance, delivery, data processing, and pricing to different types of customers. Others focus more on providing short-term storage solutions for specific types of goods—general merchandise, refrigerated goods, household goods, and bulk storage. Public warehousing capacity is often rented on a short-term, transactional basis without significant commitments or unique service requirements.

Contract warehousing is a customized version of public warehousing in which an external company provides a combination of distribution services that the organization itself has traditionally provided. These 3PL providers dedicate space, labor, and equipment to a client's specific product needs with the goal of providing integrated, accurate distribution services. These facilities can meet the specialized handling requirements for critical products such as pharmaceuticals, electronics, and high-value manufactured goods. The customized nature of contract facilities leads to strong relationships between the 3PLs and a small group of highly important clients.

These external distribution services should be considered for several reasons. First, buying the services on an as-needed basis alleviates capital investment in private distribution facilities. Second, short-term commitments for 3PL capacity maintain maximum distribution network flexibility. If demand shifts to another region, you are not locked into a long-term lease or facility ownership. Instead, you simply lease the needed capacity in the new market. Another benefit of outsourcing distribution responsibilities is that you do not have to manage the personnel issues (hiring, training, benefits, etc.) associated with owning and operating the facility. Essentially, distribution becomes a variable cost activity that is run by 3PL experts who can often leverage their investments and capacity across multiple customers.

Choosing between private and 3PL distribution options requires significant planning and analysis. On a financial basis, the selection decision boils down to the volume of product being moved through the supply chain. Figure 11.7 highlights the variable-cost-only nature of purchased 3PL distribution services versus the fixed-cost-plus-lower-variable-cost structure of private operations. At low throughput volumes, the 3PL cost structure has a distinct advantage but eventually loses out to the private distribution cost structure as throughput volume increases.

Figure 11.7	Distribution Cost Comparison

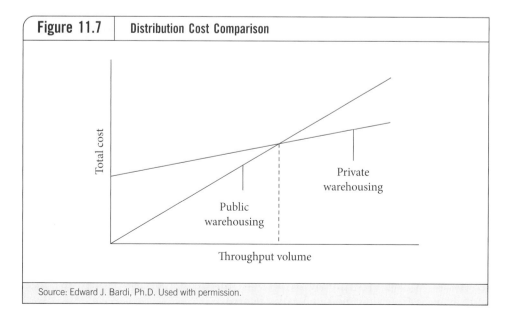

Source: Edward J. Bardi, Ph.D. Used with permission.

Table 11.2	Factors Affecting Distribution Facility Ownership	
FIRM CHARACTERISTICS	FAVORS PRIVATE DISTRIBUTION	FAVORS 3PL DISTRIBUTION
Throughput volume	Higher	Lower
Demand variability	Stable	Fluctuating
Market density	Higher	Lower
Special physical control needs	Yes	No
Security requirements	Higher	Lower
Customer service requirements	Higher	Lower
Multiple use needs	Yes	No
Source: Brian J. Gibson, Ph.D. Used with permission.		

Of course, cost is not the only consideration in this strategic "make versus buy" decision. Service factors and demand characteristics must be also be analyzed. The primary issues are summarized in Table 11.2.

Facility Considerations

When an organization chooses to outsource the distribution function to 3PL providers, facility design strategies shift to these service suppliers. However, when the facilities are privately owned and operated, a great deal of planning is required. The organization must determine the size of each facility in the distribution network, the interior layout of the facilities, and product locations within the facility.

It is important to carefully assess the situation and make competent decisions before facilities are built. Once completed, it is expensive and operationally disruptive to modify structures, layouts, and flows.

Leading organizations are also bringing sustainability considerations into the facility design process. The Supply Chain Sustainability feature describes how Walmart is designing DCs with lower environmental impacts.

The first facility consideration is to determine the size of each operation within the network. This decision is driven by the role, number, and location of facilities established in the network design phase. Typically, the more facilities in the distribution network, the smaller they need to be. Note that facilities do not have to be the exact same size, function, or layout.

Each facility must be large enough to accommodate the distribution activities that will be performed within the four walls. Traditional warehouses require storage space. It is important to use the full volume of the cubic storage space as efficiently as possible. This means making use of the vertical and horizontal capacity within the facility.

Space is also needed to interface with the transportation network. Most inbound goods are unloaded directly from trailers into the facility and received prior to storage. An area is needed to receive and inspect the goods, as well as stage pallets of product before storage. Outbound goods may need to be sorted, staged, and consolidated prior to loading. The volume and frequency of orders moving through the facility are critical in determining receiving and shipping space needs.

Supply Chain Technology

Walmart's Environmentally Friendly DCs

Sustainability has become a major concern for many organizations. For them, supply chain management presents a prime opportunity for conserving resources, reducing waste, and cutting greenhouse gas emissions.

Walmart has been a leading proponent of sustainability and has set aggressive goals. In 2005, the company set a goal to reduce greenhouse gases at its stores and DCs by 20 percent by 2012. During the first three years of the initiative, the emissions created by these facilities have been reduced by 5.1 percent.

Numerous projects have been undertaken around the world to reduce Walmart's impact on the environment. Three DC initiatives highlight the company's drive for sustainable operations.

The Apple Valley DC in California relies upon solar power for much of its energy resources. The project consists of more than 5,300 ground-mounted solar panels that cover nearly seven acres. The panels will generate more than 2 million kilowatt-hours of power, equal to the amount of electricity used by 156 average U.S. homes annually.

In Brazil, Walmart built a high-efficiency DC with an on-site solar power system to serve the building. The facility also uses skylights to provide natural lighting during working hours and features a "green wall" that uses plant growth to reflect heat.

The 450,000-square foot refrigerated DC in Balzac, Alberta, Canada will be 60 percent more efficient than a traditional Walmart facility. This building will be one of the most energy-efficient DCs in North America. A 225-kilowatt wind turbine generates needed power, solar panels produce hot water, hydrogen fuel cells power the materials handling equipment, and high-efficiency LED lighting is used throughout the facility.

Source: Mary Aichlmayr, "Leading Change," *Material Handling and Logistics* (April 2010), p. 13; "Wal-Mart Canada Adding Energy Efficient DC, Solar, Wind," *Environmental Leader* (February 11, 2010), retrieved October 14, 2010 from http://www.environmentalleader.com/2010/02/11/wal-mart-canada-adding-energy-efficient-dc-solar-wind/; *Walmart Global Sustainability Report: 2010 Update,* retrieved October 14, 2010 from http://walmartstores.com/sites/sustainabilityreport/2010/

Additional space is required for order picking and assembly. The amount needed depends on order volume and the product's nature, along with the materials-handling equipment used in the facility. Proper layout of the space used for these activities is critical to efficient operations and customer service.

Space may need to be allocated to three additional functions. First, an area may be needed for processing rework and returns. Second, office space is needed for administrative and clerical activities. Finally, space must be planned for miscellaneous requirements—break rooms, locker rooms, meeting rooms, equipment storage and maintenance, utilities, and other activities.

Demand forecasts for the region to be served by the facility will drive the sizing process as follows:

1. Develop a demand forecast; prepare an estimate in units for a relevant sales period (usually 30 days) by product category. Then the company will need to determine each item's order quantity, usually including some allowance for safety stock.

2. Convert the units into cubic footage requirements, which may need to include pallets and usually include an allowance of 10 to 15 percent for growth over the relevant period. At this point, the company has an estimate of basic storage space requirements.

3. Add space needs for aisles and other fulfillment activities (receiving, shipping, order picking, assembly, etc.). Traditional distribution facilities devote up to one-third of total space to these nonstorage functions.

The broader the set of activities to be handled within the facility, the more challenging it is to accurately determine space requirements. Many companies use computer simulations to analyze these needs. Effective software packages will factor in a vast number of variables and future growth forecasts when projecting space requirements.

After the facility size is determined, attention shifts to the layout of the operations within the distribution operation. The company must make decisions regarding aisle space, shelving, materials-handling equipment, and the interior dimensions of the facility. Table 11.3 highlights general principles for designing the interior of a facility.

Using these general principles as a guide, organizations design the interior of the distribution facility to support timely, accurate, and efficient customer order fulfillment. A number of objectives must be kept in mind during the planning process, with utilization of the facility's cubic capacity being first and foremost on the list. One storage area design feature that lends itself to this objective is the use of larger storage bays with more limited access. The turnover or throughput level will affect the storage bays' actual size. For example, when turnover is very low, as in supply warehouses, the bays can be wide and deep, with limited access, and the aisles can be narrow. Increased turnover necessitates quick access for better customer service and, consequently, smaller bays and wider aisles.

Product protection is another key objective. The layout must accommodate the physical characteristics of the products being handled. For example, hazardous materials such as explosives, flammable items, and oxidizing items must be separated from other items so as to eliminate the possibility of damage. Also, high-value goods must be safeguarded against pilferage, and temperature-sensitive products must receive proper refrigeration or heat. Finally, distribution personnel should avoid stacking or storing light or fragile items near other items that could cause damage.

Table 11.3	Facility Layout Principles
PRINCIPLE	**BENEFITS**
Use a one-story facility	• Provides more usable space per investment dollar • Results in lower construction costs than multistory facilities
Use vertical capacity	• Reduces building footprint and land requirements
Minimize aisle space	• Provides more storage and processing capacity
Use direct product flows	• Avoids backtracking and costly travel time
Use efficient materials-handling equipment	• Improves labor productivity and safety • Reduces travel time
Use an appropriate product storage plan	• Maximizes space utilization and product protection

Source: Brian J. Gibson, Ph.D. Used with permission.

Proper use of automation and materials-handling equipment is an important goal. Both offer great potential to improve distribution efficiency. Careful planning should include consideration of the risks of investing in automation—obsolescence due to rapid technological change, market fluctuations, and return on the large investment. Mechanized materials-handling equipment generally works best when items are regular in shape and easily handled, when order selection is the middle range of activity, and when product moves in high volumes with few fluctuations. A detailed discussion of materials-handling principles and tools is provided in Appendix 11A.

Another objective is process flexibility. The facility design should not be so permanent as to limit the facility from handling new product lines and providing value added services when new requests emerge. For example, reconfigurable racking and multifunctional materials-handling equipment can prevent the building from becoming obsolete if demand patterns change significantly. Such capabilities make the layout more dynamic and open to improvement.

Continuous improvement is the ultimate facility objective. An organization should not design an initial layout and then assume that it will work perfectly. Goals and standards for costs, order-handling efficiency, and customer service must be set and monitored on a regular basis. If measurements reveal that optimal facility performance is not being achieved, steps must be taken to improve productivity. Distribution performance measurement is discussed later in the chapter.

The final facility consideration is product placement within the facility. Before order fulfillment operations begin, goods must be located or slotted in the facility. **Slotting** is defined as the placement of product in a facility for the purpose of optimizing materials-handling and space efficiency. The main objective of slotting is to minimize, or in some instances even eliminate, travel and the amount of time that a stock-keeping unit is handled. This is important because travel and other nonproductive tasks can account for up to 60 percent of distribution labor hours.

Three criteria are commonly used to slot product within a distribution facility: (1) popularity, (2) unit size, and (3) cube. The popularity criterion locates popular items (most units ordered in a given time period) near the shipping area and the unpopular items (fewer units ordered) away from the shipping area. The benefit is reduced order-picking time, as less effort is required to travel to the most frequently ordered items.

The unit size criterion suggests that small-size items (item cubic dimensions) be located near the shipping area and larger-size items be placed farther away from the shipping area. By locating smaller-size items near the shipping area, more items can be stored near the shipping area, which reduces the order picker travel distance and order-picking time. The cube criterion is a variation of unit size in that the items with smaller total cubic space requirements (item cube multiplied by the number of items held) are located near the shipping area. The logic is the same as that used for unit size.

Why focus on slotting criteria and strategy? Proper product slotting can improve labor productivity and generate other advantages for the organization and its customers. Several benefits will be generated by effective product slotting:

- **Picking productivity**—Travel time can often account for up to 60 percent of a picker's daily activity. A good product slotting strategy can reduce travel time, thereby reducing picking labor.

- **Efficient replenishment**—By sizing the pick face location based upon a standard unit of measure (case, pallet) for the product in question, you can significantly reduce the labor required to replenish the location.
- **Work balancing**—By balancing activity across multiple pick zones you reduce congestion in the zones, improve material flow, and reduce the total response time for a given order or batch of orders.
- **Load building**—To minimize product damage, heavy product is located at the beginning of the pick path ahead of crushable product. Product may also be located based on case size to facilitate pallet building.
- **Accuracy**—Similar products are separated to minimize the opportunity for picking errors.
- **Ergonomics**—High velocity products are placed in a "golden zone" to reduce bending and reaching activity. Heavy or oversized items are placed on lower levels in the pick zone or placed in a separate zone where material handling equipment can be utilized.
- **Preconsolidation**—By storing and picking product by family group, you may be able reduce downstream sorting and consolidation activity. This is particularly important in a retail environment to facilitate efficient restocking at the stores.[5]

As this list suggests, proper product slotting is a foundation of facility productivity and sets the stage for a variety of other benefits. However, slotting is not a one-time, start-up event. Changing business environments and product demand fluctuation may eventually lead to disorganization and improperly slotted product. Hence, it is important for organizations to regularly monitor and adjust product locations as needed to maintain optimal facility performance.

Distribution Execution

Distribution strategy and planning activities set the stage for day-to-day operation of the facility. They facilitate effective execution of product movement and storage, order fulfillment, and value-added services on behalf of customers. This section will focus on the processes that take place within DCs, warehouses, and cross-dock facilities. For the purpose of this discussion, we will segment the processes into two categories—product-handling functions and support functions.

Product-Handling Functions

The primary facility operations focus on the movement and storage of product. Storage is the more traditional and obvious function, while movement may seem unimportant. However, maintaining proper product flows through efficient short-distance moves within the facility is a critical aspect of distribution. Goods arriving at DCs and cross-docks must often move through the building rapidly to fulfill customer orders and maintain high inventory turnover. Hence, effective in-facility movement supports strong customer service and high inventory velocity, which reduces holding costs; lowers loss, damage, or obsolescence risks; and holds storage capacity requirements in check.

As shown in Figure 11.8, product handling involves five primary processes: (1) receiving—transferring goods into the facility from the transport network, (2) put-away—moving goods into storage locations, (3) order picking—selecting goods for customer

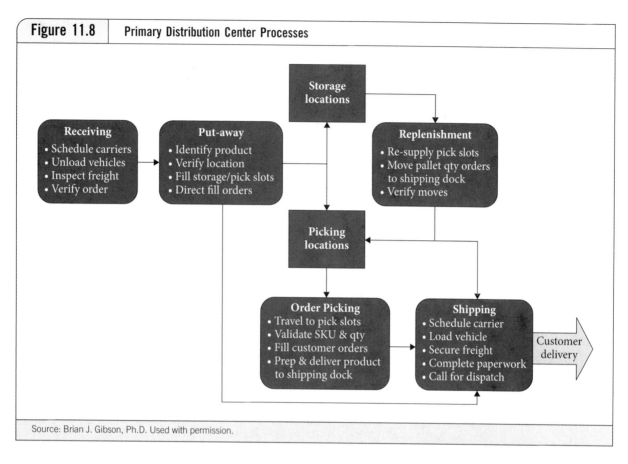

Figure 11.8 | **Primary Distribution Center Processes**

Source: Brian J. Gibson, Ph.D. Used with permission.

orders, (4) replenishment—moving product from storage locations to picking slots, and (5) shipping—loading goods for delivery to the customer. All five involve short-distance movement of product, while put-away also focuses on the storage activity.

At the receiving operation, the inbound carrier is scheduled to deliver the goods at a specific time so as to improve labor productivity and unloading efficiency. The goods are unloaded from the delivery vehicle onto the receiving dock. During the process, receiving clerks check the goods in to ensure that they match the purchase order and packing slips. Once on the dock, the goods are sorted by SKU, stacked on pallets to the correct ti-hi (where *ti* is the number of cartons stored on a layer and *hi* is the number of layers on the pallet), and secured using tape or shrink-wrap. The delivery is also inspected for damage and shortages. Problems are noted on the carrier's delivery receipt, and the receipt is signed. Prior to transfer, the items are tagged with pallet labels that assign storage locations in the facility or designate the goods for direct transfer to the shipping dock if needed to immediately fill a customer order.

The put-away operation focuses on the physical movement of product from the receiving dock to assigned storage locations in the facility. Forklift operators check the pallet configuration to validate quantities and product safety, verify the storage location on the pallet label, pick up the pallet, and scan the bar code on the pallet label. The product is moved to the proper storage location (or sometimes the picking location, if the product is new or the slot is empty) and placed in the rack. It is critical that the forklift operator verify that product is being put in the correct location or it may become lost among the vast number of pallet locations and similar looking boxes. After the process is completed, inventory records are updated to reflect receipt of the item, its storage location, and availability for customer order.

There are two keys to achieving an accurate, productive flow of goods into the facility. First, receiving clerks must be well trained to evaluate incoming goods and match product with carrier counts, vendor documentation, and the purchase order. Failure to do so will lead to a mismatch between the physical inventory and what is recorded in the system. This will subsequently lead to order-filling problems. Second, coordination of the receiving and put-away operations is needed. Most receiving docks have limited floor capacity, so pallets must be cleared away quickly to ensure that there is space to unload additional deliveries. One way to achieve coordination is to cross-train workers so that they can be shifted back and forth between receiving clerk and put-away forklift operator functions. Another option is to stagger the shift start time so that the receiving process is started early and work is generated for the later start time of the put-away function.

The order-picking process focuses on the selection of goods to fulfill customer orders. Order fulfillment personnel travel through the facility from pick slot to pick slot and pull the requested quantity of each product identified on the pick list. The pick list may be generated as a paper checklist, labels that are placed on the carton, a computer display, or a voice-activated picking system. Once picked, the items may be labeled and put on a conveyor system for transfer to the shipping area or assembled on a pallet or cart designated for the customer. If the latter method is used, the order fulfillment personnel transfer the order to the shipment staging area and prepare it for delivery. The items are secured to the pallet or cart by means of tape, stretch wrap, or strapping, and a shipping label is created and attached. Finally, the complete customer order is staged in a predesignated area for loading onto the appropriate outbound delivery vehicle.

For many organizations, order picking is the most labor-intensive and expensive distribution activity, accounting for 55 to 65 percent of DC operating costs. This function requires a great deal of travel throughout the facility and the handling of individual cases or units within cases. Thus, it is important for managers to focus on creating a productive, safe, and accurate order-picking operation, if the function is to be done correctly and at the lowest possible cost. Table 11.4 highlights a variety of industry practices that are used to improve picking productivity.[6]

To alleviate labor-intensive picking operations, some organizations are embracing warehouse automation. Although it requires a large capital investment, high-tech materials-handling equipment improves picking speed and accuracy, reduces labor costs, and alleviates work injuries. These benefits are critical, given the demand for distribution speed and the aging workforce in many countries. Automation is discussed in more detail in Appendix 11A, as well as in the On the Line feature that follows here.

On the Line

Goods-to-Person Puts a Different Spin on Order Picking

Back in the day, there was one thing about order fulfillment operations you could pretty much take for granted. When it came to gathering items for orders, the people did the walking and the equipment stayed put.

That's no longer a safe assumption. Today, a growing number of companies are taking the opposite tack. Instead of sending workers out to retrieve goods, they're using automated materials-handling equipment to deliver items to order pickers who remain in a fixed spot. This approach, known as a goods-to-person system, isn't new. In fact, it's been around for several decades. But it's attracting increased attention these days, particularly from high-volume operations that do a lot of piece picking.

What's driving much of the interest in this approach is its potential to enhance productivity. Suppliers of goods-to-person systems say the equipment can boost pick rates as high as 1,000 lines per hour. Part of the reason is that workers spend less time traveling and more time order picking, making them more productive. Another part is that automated systems offer capabilities like product sequencing that help streamline the work flow.

There are other benefits as well. For one thing, these systems save space. Goods-to-person set-ups allow for denser storage and eliminate the need for traditional pick faces, reducing overall storage space requirements. For another, they boost accuracy. With goods-to-person systems, only the goods needed for orders are delivered to operators, cutting down on the chances workers will pick the wrong items.

Other advantages include improved ergonomics and safety. Under this approach, workers no longer have to carry cases from place to place; the storage machines and conveyors do the heavy lifting. In addition, lift truck traffic is reduced, resulting in a safer work environment.

As for equipment, goods-to-person systems come in a variety of forms and configurations. They can incorporate pallet-based (unit load) automated storage and retrieval systems (AS/RS), tote-based miniload systems, carousels (both horizontal and vertical), robots, and vertical lift modules.

To date, goods-to-person picking has been successfully employed in a range of industries, including retail, pharmaceutical, grocery, apparel, industrial parts, meat, dairy, and medical. Next PLC, one of the United Kingdom's largest clothing retailers, has successfully adopted this approach.

NEXT PLC

When it needed to boost logistics productivity, Next decided to give goods-to-person picking a go. It installed an AS/RS that is connected to high-rate put stations at its DC in South Elmsall, England. The gambit paid off. Once the new system was in place, picking productivity increased by 300 percent.

The system, which was supplied by Dematic, stores fast-moving apparel items, footwear, accessories, and home goods. When needed for orders, products are automatically retrieved and conveyed to one of the system's 20 put stations. Within each station, 24 order totes are staged, each representing a different store.

Workers follow a light-directed process to select items and place them into the proper totes. The remaining product is then sent back to the storage system until needed. Completed orders are pushed off onto takeaway conveyors that whisk them to shipping.

The result is a fast, productive system for filling store orders. Workers are able to pick up to 1,000 items per hour, which is three times the rate achieved back when they had to search the shelves for products.

Source: Adapted from David Maloney, "Goods to Person Puts a Different Spin on Order Picking," *DC Velocity* (October 2010). Reprinted with permission.

Table 11.4	Best Practices in Order Picking

PRINCIPLE	BEST PRACTICES
Minimize travel time	• Sequence pick patterns and pick lists so that order fillers make one trip through the facility without backtracking. • Use batch picking. Order fillers select multiple orders during a single pass through the facility. • Use zone picking. Order fillers work in a limited area, selecting the parts of orders within their zone.
Maximize time spent picking product	• Reduce or eliminate paperwork to keep order fillers on task. Use voice or light-directed picking systems instead of paper orders. • Keep like items together to facilitate fast pallet building, reduce order rehandling, and avoid product damage. • Have necessary tools and equipment readily available.
Facilitate accurate order picking	• Provide clean and well-lighted picking areas with ample space for order pickers to perform tasks. • Clearly identify all pick locations with labels or placards that can be read from a distance. • Use systems that require validation of order-picking location and quantity before order filler is directed to next location.
Leverage materials-handling equipment	• Use carousels and automated storage/retrieval solutions lines to move product to the picker, reducing search and travel time. • Use conveyor lines to move product from picking areas to shipping area, eliminating back and forth travel. • Use forklifts and pallet jacks to handle bulk items and large quantities. This will promote safety and reduce picking time.
Minimize idle time	• Deploy inventory based on activity profiles, spreading out fast-moving products to facilitate access and reduce congestion. • Develop and enforce time standards for order-picking operation. • Maintain adequate inventory levels in pick slots so that product is available for order fillers to grab on their initial pass.

Source: Adapted from *The Journey to Warehousing Excellence*, (Raleigh NC: Tompkins Associates), Section 2.

The replenishment operation plays an important supporting role for order picking, moving product from storage locations in the facility to the designated pick slots. These storage locations are often inaccessible to the order fulfillment personnel, and specialized equipment is needed to retrieve the product. Replenishment forklift operators focus on keeping an adequate supply of product in each pick slot. When a pick slot is empty, the order fulfillment personnel will have to make a second trip to retrieve the required quantity of product. These additional trips are labor intensive and may cause split deliveries or delay the dispatch of customer orders. Hence, it is critical to synchronize order-picking and replenishment activities, shifting personnel back and forth between the functions as needed.

The final movement process occurs at the shipping operation. In some facilities, empty trailers are dropped at shipping dock doors and loaded as orders arrive from the picking operation. In other operations, a "live" loading process takes place when the outbound carrier arrives at the shipping dock. The goods are moved from the staging area to the loading dock, counted and inspected as required, and loaded into the carrier's vehicle. The carrier signs the bill of lading that has been prepared by the shipper, indicating receipt of the goods, and departs from the facility.

Though it appears to be more of a transportation-related activity, the shipping operation has a major impact on the success of distribution facilities. The shipping personnel must take steps to protect the freight from in-transit damage, accurately load orders into trailers, and complete work in a timely fashion to meet dispatch deadlines. They also need to utilize trailer space completely to reduce the cost of each trip. Collectively, these efforts augment the customer service and cost efficiency efforts of the other distribution operations.

Support Functions

While the product-handling functions account for the vast majority of the activity, labor, and cost in distribution facilities, a number of other administrative and management activities facilitate the successful execution of day-to-day operations. These support functions provide coordination between key processes and across the supply chain, protect the organization's inventory investment, and improve working conditions within the facility. Chief among these support functions are (1) inventory control; (2) safety, maintenance, and sanitation; (3) security; (4) performance analysis; and (5) information technology.

One of the most challenging activities in a distribution operation is to maintain control over the inventory. With product flowing in and out of the facility on a daily basis, it is critical to ensure that the inventory database accurately reflects what is actually inside the facility. Inventory control specialists and analysts resolve stock discrepancies, search for misplaced product, conduct cycle counts and quality audits, and make inventory adjustments. Their efforts improve the reliability of inventory reports so that when customers place product orders, the right quantities of the right products are available and accessible to the order fulfillment personnel. Additional discussion of inventory control is provided in Chapter 9.

Establishing a safe, clean, working environment is not only a management obligation but also a distribution productivity booster. The safety function focuses on preserving the health and welfare of distribution employees via an ergonomically sound working environment. Training employees on proper techniques for lifting, requiring industrial equipment training and licensing, and creating awareness of potential hazards will reduce costly workplace accidents and injuries. Preventive maintenance of equipment and timely repairs of problems also promote safe working conditions in the distribution facility. Finally, the sanitation function focuses on complying with regulatory standards and maintaining worker morale. Also, all three functions help keep product damage in check.

The security function seeks to protect the organization from merchandise theft and fraud. Numerous techniques can be used in the distribution facility to prevent losses. Physical tools such as trailer seals, security tags, and monitored processing areas are used to reduce inventory losses. Personnel procedures can also be effective deterrents against theft. Prescreening potential employees, conducting inspections and audits, and limiting access to the facility can be helpful. Finally, a security staff can monitor facility activity and investigate problems.

The management team is also responsible for evaluating and improving facility performance. Some organizations will have distribution analysts or software to measure productivity, quality, utilization, and costs for each aspect of the distribution process. A failure to monitor the performance of individual employees using labor standards and the accuracy of their work can lead to poor facility performance and low customer evaluations. Distribution measures are discussed in the next section.

Organizations rely heavily on information technology to receive, fill, and distribute customer orders. Access to a strong team of internal or external technology experts is needed to build stronger information-sharing processes and enhance visibility of inventory and orders. As discussed earlier, timely and accurate information is critical in the distribution environment. Specific software tools for distribution execution are discussed in an upcoming section of the chapter.

Together, these support functions facilitate product movement and storage within the distribution operation and the fulfillment of perfect orders. Without them, it would be difficult to protect workers and product from a host of challenges, maintain precise inventory records, or know how well the operation is performing. In short, the operation would quickly fall into disarray without the team of specialists behind the frontline managers and labor.

Distribution Metrics

The activities performed in the distribution function have a tangible output that can be readily evaluated. These evaluations are made through the measurement and analysis of distribution key performance indicators (KPIs). Customers use distribution KPIs to objectively assess the quality of service provided by the distribution operation, while management can appraise operational costs and productivity.

Many aspects of distribution performance can be evaluated. Important issues include cost efficiency, inventory accuracy, order fill rates, and capacity utilization, among others. KPIs can be used to evaluate current performance of internal and 3PL operations versus historical results, internal goals, and customer requirements. They can also be used to benchmark results against those achieved by competitors, world-class organizations, and other links in the supply chain.

The challenge lies in narrowing down the vast array of metrics available to a manageable number of KPIs that reflect the distribution requirements of a supply chain. Properly chosen KPIs provide numerous benefits—they help focus personnel on important fulfillment objectives, evaluate the impact of distribution process improvements, and keep distribution in line with corporate and supply chain goals.

The two primary categories of distribution KPIs include customer-facing measures and internal measures. Both internally and externally focused KPIs are needed to evaluate the success and impact of a distribution operation. Each type is discussed in the two sections that follow.

Customer-Facing Measures

When customers place an order, their goals are very simple—get the right product from the vendor in the quantity ordered at the expected time. Think about the last time you ordered something from a retail Web site—those were your primary goals, right? Thus, customer-facing KPIs must target reliability of the distribution processes to provide accurate, complete, and timely fulfillment of orders. Of course, the goal is to meet customer expectations for all three, delivering what would be considered a perfect order. If accomplished, companies will avoid rework and encourage customers to place future orders.

Order accuracy and **order completeness** KPIs are important to both the customer and the organization. Simply stated, customers want to receive the exact products and quantities that they ordered, not substitute items, incorrectly shipped items, or wrong quantities. These KPIs are measured as ratios of correct received to total ordered. Order accuracy evaluates the number of items ordered delivered correctly versus the number ordered. Order completeness is typically evaluated by an order fill rate KPI that compares the quantity received to the quantity ordered.

These metrics not only impact customer satisfaction, but they also highlight the accuracy (or lack thereof) of the order fulfillment process. If customers frequently receive the wrong products and/or the wrong quantities, the accuracy of facility inventory levels will also be negatively affected. If product is frequently out of stock and orders cannot be fulfilled, then poor forecasting may be the culprit. In either case, the resulting order accuracy and fill rate problems will result in lost sales, costly returns, and dissatisfied customers. Continuous monitoring of these metrics is important, as is fast reaction when problems are discovered.

Timeliness is a critical component of customer service. You may think of timeliness as being a transportation issue, but the distribution operation also plays a key role in delivering goods to customers on schedule. Order picking, preparation, and shipping each impact order cycle time. If these processes are not completed in a timely fashion, it may not be possible for the transportation system to make up the lost time. Therefore, it is very important to monitor the time required to process orders, from initial receipt until release to the transportation provider. Setting goals and measuring KPIs related to order processing time average, range, and standard deviation will direct attention toward improvement of order fulfillment velocity.

Industry-leading companies are now evaluating the combined impact of these KPIs via a metric called the **perfect order index (POI)**. This measure indicates that four basic elements are in place to promote successful fulfillment of customer orders. To be considered a perfect order, the right items must be (1) delivered to the right place; (2) at the right time; (3) in defect-free condition; and (4) with the correct documentation, pricing, and invoicing.[7] A service failure on any component means that the order is not counted as perfect and indicates a need for improvement.

Internal Measures

While service quality is the foundation of customer satisfaction with the fulfillment process, internal performance is also critical. Organizations need to balance customer expectations with the cost to process orders. If distribution costs are not kept low in proportion to the value of the goods, the organization will not be successful. These costs are kept low through effective utilization of assets and productive execution of distribution processes. A variety of internal KPIs help organizations pursue these outcomes.

Distribution cost efficiency is critical, given the magnitude of U.S. warehousing and distribution-related costs—$119 billion in 2009.[8] This is true whether functions are handled in house or outsourced to 3PL providers. **Aggregate cost efficiency** measures focus on the total distribution spending versus goal or budget. Item-level KPIs focus on the distribution expense per unit of measure (e.g., cost per pallet, case, or order). It is a simple calculation of total distribution cost divided by the number of units processed.

Understanding what is spent to process each unit in a customer's order highlights the impact of distribution on the overall cost of goods. This KPI also provides a baseline from which cost improvement efforts can be made.

Asset utilization is a very important aspect of private distribution facilities. Organizations spend significant sums of money to build distribution facilities and outfit them with materials-handling equipment and technology. If the facility sits half empty, the company has wasted time and money on a poorly utilized asset. Space utilization is measured as a percentage of capacity used to capacity available in cubic feet or storage slots. An oft-cited goal is to consistently use 80 to 85 percent of a DC's capacity, which provides some available space for peak season volume.

Equipment utilization KPIs can be used by managers to assess the need for additional forklifts, conveyors, and related equipment. Spending on new equipment should not occur unless comparisons of equipment up time (number of hours equipment was available to use versus total hours required) and utilization (number of hours used versus total hours equipment was available) reveal a real need. These KPIs provide an objective indication that equipment is effectively used, sitting idle, or offline for repair.

Resource productivity impacts distribution cost and the ability of the operation to maximize throughput on a consistent basis. With distribution costs averaging nearly 10 percent of a sales dollar, productivity improvements will have a notable impact on the bottom line of the profit and loss statement. Productivity is measured as the ratio of real output to real input. An example of this is the number of units processed per labor hour, a widely used productivity KPI. Productivity KPIs and goals help distribution managers evaluate facility performance, estimate how much volume can be handled by the facility, and schedule labor. These easy-to-measure KPIs also provide early warning signals of distribution problems that must be addressed.

Resource efficiency measures compare distribution activity completion time versus expected time. Engineered standards are created by breaking down a task into small elements that can be timed by a stopwatch. Allowances are added for fatigue and personal needs to determine an accurate, standardized measure of time for an operation. Efficiency is then measured as a ratio of actual time required for task completion to the engineered standard time allowed for the task. This KPI can be used to evaluate an individual employee's ability to accomplish key tasks and the overall efficiency of operations. The engineered standards can be used by management to set and communicate objective efficiency standards for each distribution function.[9]

During this discussion of distribution metrics, we have focused on important KPI categories. We have also provided examples of specific KPIs that can be used to improve fulfillment performance. Table 11.5 provides an effective summary of this topic. It highlights widely used distribution KPIs and performance benchmarks identified by 559 distribution managers and executives in a 2010 industry survey. Note that the list includes both customer-facing and internal KPIs.

Distribution Technology

While the distribution environment is dependent upon effective product flows, it also requires timely, accurate flows of information within distribution facilities and across the supply chain. Information must be shared regarding customer orders, inventory levels, condition, location within the facility, inbound deliveries, labor performance, and more.

Table 11.5	Distribution Center Metrics and Benchmarks	
MEASURE USED	**MEDIAN PERFORMANCE LEVEL**	**BEST IN CLASS PERFORMANCE LEVEL**
Inventory shrink	0.2%	< .001%
Damage rate	0.2%	< .007%
Out of stock (lost sales)	1.4%	< .001%
Distribution cost as proportion of cost of goods sold	5.1%	< 2.3%
Annual workforce turnover	6.8%	< 0.8%
Dock-to-stock cycle time	9.1 hours	< 2.3 hours
Cases picking productivity	142.5 cases per hour	> 281.4 cases per hour

Source: Karl Manrodt, Joseph Tillman, and Kate Vitasek, "A Bright Side to Dark Times," *DC Velocity* (April 2010), pp. 42–44. Reproduced by permission.

Virtually every distribution strategy and process discussed in this chapter would be easier to plan, execute, and evaluate with ready access to relevant information. Fortunately, distribution managers no longer need to manage vast amounts of information on paper and in their heads. Software and information technology tools are available to support distribution control and decision making. In this final section of the chapter, the primary technologies are presented.

Warehouse Management Systems

The core software used to manage fulfillment processes is called warehouse management systems (WMS), a mature technology dating back to the 1970s.[10] Widely used to support all types of distribution operations, WMS is a software control system that improves product movement and storage operations through efficient management of information and completion of distribution tasks. The goal is to achieve a high level of control, inventory accuracy, and productivity through directed picking, directed replenishment, and directed put-away.

A WMS is more than a simple database that provides stock location information. Instead, it is an integrated package whose components often include radio-frequency (RF) communications, dedicated localized computer hardware, and the necessary applications software. The detailed setup and processing within a WMS can vary significantly from one software vendor to another; however, the basic logic will use a combination of item, location, quantity, unit of measure, and order information to determine where to stock, where to pick, and in what sequence to perform these operations.[11]

Beyond the main functionalities, WMS can also provide value-added capabilities and support a variety of supply chain activities. Advanced systems generate performance reports; support paperless processes; enable integration of materials-handling equipment, picking systems, and sorting systems; leverage wireless communication tools; and support automatic identification equipment data collection (see the Supply Chain Technology feature that follows below). Other value-added capabilities include the following:

- **Labor management**—The ability to link WMS with a related labor tracking module allows the organization to create assignments based on engineered time standards, monitor the productivity of each employee, and audit the quality of their work. These labor-reporting capabilities support performance analysis and the use of incentive programs, and they help identify employees in need of additional training.

- **Task interleaving**—This process involves mixing dissimilar tasks such as put-away and replenishment. In large warehouses, WMS-based task interleaving can greatly reduce travel time, not only increasing productivity but also reducing wear on the lift trucks and saving on energy costs by reducing lift truck fuel consumption.

- **Systems integration**—The ability to interface the WMS with the enterprise resource planning (ERP) system, order management systems, and transportation management will provide a strong flow of information across the organization and the supply chain. Inventory availability, order status, advanced shipping notification, and delivery tracking are a few of the critical visibility benefits created by integration. This shared information can be used for distribution planning purposes.

- **Activity-based costing/billing**—Financial functionality is an important WMS capability for understanding costs and assigning expenses to distribution customers. Primarily designed for 3PL operations, activity-based billing allows them to calculate billable fees based on specific activities. For example, 3PL providers can assign transaction fees for each receipt and shipment transaction, as well as fees for storage and other value-added activities.

- **Multifunction distribution**—A strong WMS will support a variety of distribution methods, shipment sizes, and the execution of value-added services. The ability to support traditional case pick distribution and cross-docking, retailer orders and individual consumer orders, and light assembly and kitting operations creates flexibility for the distribution operation and the supply chain.

Improved productivity, efficiency, and accuracy are key WMS benefits. By keeping track of item locations in the facility, the WMS reduces wasted efforts associated with warehouse personnel hunting for an item. This improves labor productivity, reduces the number of personnel required, and improves the order-picking accuracy. The WMS also provides essential information that enables businesses to quickly make accurate decisions that are based on up-to-date information. In addition, these systems improve space utilization by determining the optimal storage patterns to maximize space utilization. Finally, the WMS provides improved managerial control and effectiveness through point-of-work confirmation, accountability, performance measurement, and what-if scenario planning.

Supply Chain Technology   *Moving Coca-Cola by Voice*

Order picking with voice is undergoing yet another transformation.

Since its pioneering days in the 1990s, voice picking consisted of predominantly proprietary hardware and software solutions, such as those by offered Vocollect, using mobile computers embedded with speaker-dependent speech engines.

Then in the early 2000s, vendors such as Voxware started moving away from proprietary hardware and shifted to more open architecture solutions that they embedded in commercial, off-the-shelf mobile computing devices such as those marketed by Motorola and LXE. This open hardware era saw an increase in speaker-independent technologies and the rise in multimodal functionality allowing devices to capture data in multiple ways—from voice and scanning to radio frequency identification (RFID).

Both proprietary solutions and open hardware approaches physically require a mobile computer when picking. But over the past three years, the proliferation of high-performance wireless networks and Voice over Internet Protocol (VoIP) phone systems has ushered in what could be a new era in voice. Coca-Cola Enterprises (CCE), partnering with Cisco and Datria, helped to innovate this network-based system.

With this approach, there's significant savings in hardware costs, because a company like CCE doesn't have to buy expensive wearable computers for each of its users. Instead, pickers can use a less expensive wireless phone to connect to the WMS and other enterprise systems.

CCE is the world's largest marketer, producer, and distributor of Coca-Cola products, shipping more than two billion cases in 2009 from more than 300 distribution centers. Over the past few years, however, changing consumer tastes for flavored water, new juices, and energy drinks resulted in a fourfold increase in SKUs, many with similar packaging. This made the assembly of mixed pallets challenging, with accuracy levels dropping below the desired 99.8 percent set by Walmart and other customers, even with the use of additional checkers.

"We are a lean, six-sigma company," says Michael Jacks, CCE's senior manager for logistics and transportation systems. "Additional checking is waste and we had to eliminate waste. We needed a solution that improved accuracy."

But accuracy wasn't the only issue. There was also the pressure to handle larger volumes without increasing headcount or square footage. It didn't help that warehouse picking positions were not exactly the easiest jobs. "It's hard, it's hot, and most of our picking is done at night. We are constantly hiring and retraining," notes Jacks.

In 2007, the business presented Jacks and his team with a solution: voice picking. While they agreed that voice is the way to go, navigating the different technologies to find the voice solution that best fits CCE's vision was a completely different story. "We took a step back, did our due diligence. We looked at all the vendors in the system in addition to talking to our strategic partners."

Cisco introduced CCE to Datria in March 2007, and together they innovated a new approach using regular VoIP-based wireless phones and wireless networks. Pickers used a Cisco 7921 wireless IP phone to call into a server and in real-time receive spoken instructions on where, what, and how many cartons to pick, while speaking confirmations when tasks were correctly completed.

In June and July 2007, CCE deployed two side-by-side pilots at two separate facilities, pitting this new approach against the traditional approach of using wearable computers. They eventually selected the VoIP-based approach after the second pilot.

By October 2008, CCE had successfully deployed a groundbreaking VoIP-based voice-picking solution to 2,600 pickers in 100 of its largest facilities—each with more than 5 million cases shipped.

But, of course, there were lessons learned along the way. In order to design the network for voice effectively, about 40 percent more access points had to be installed. Matching the power settings of the phones to those of the access points enabled CCE to get 10-hour shifts out of standard batteries. The team is now looking to replace corded headsets with Bluetooth devices.

According to Jacks, it's been a gift that keeps on giving. By going with the less expensive wireless phones and off-the-shelf headsets, CCE reported savings of $2 million to $4 million in capital expenses. Accuracy has been at a consistent 99.9 percent with some locations reporting a 100 percent accuracy rate.

As a result, 80 percent of checkers were deemed redundant and consequently re-assigned; and being a speaker-independent system, there was no need to record voice templates—further reducing training time from days to hours.

The best part of the initiative? In 2009, CCE was named Walmart's Supplier of the Year.

Source: Adapted from Maida Napolitano, "Three Voices, Three Solutions," *Logistics Management* (July 2010), pp. 40–43. Reproduced by permission.

Numerous companies supply WMS solutions, ranging from major ERP vendors that integrate WMS capabilities with their other supply chain software to specialists that focus primarily on high-end WMS systems. Another option is to develop a customized WMS in house. The choice between an off-the-shelf and a customized solution is difficult because of the fast pace of change in the industry—a custom system designed today may become outdated quickly, and the extra cost of the customization may not be warranted. However, off-the-shelf versions tend to drive distribution processes rather than be tailored to the facility's existing processes. Thus, flexibility can be lost with these systems. The challenge is to decide which option best integrates an organization's existing supply chain technology and supports its information requirements.

Automatic Identification Tools

Automatic identification (Auto-ID) describes technologies that help machines identify objects such as bar codes, smart cards, voice recognition, biometric technologies, radio-frequency identification (RFID), and others. The WMS utilizes Auto-ID data capture technologies, such as barcode scanners, mobile computers, wireless local area networks (LANs), and RFID to accurately gather information and monitor the flow of products. Once data have been collected, a batch synchronization process or real-time wireless transmission is completed with the central WMS database. The WMS database can then provide useful reports about the status of goods in the facility.

Barcodes and RFID are the tools of choice in distribution to help track, locate, and move product quickly—with near perfect accuracy rates to consumers. Barcodes have been used in retail industry distribution applications for more than three decades. A barcode is a series of parallel black and white bars, both of varying widths, whose sequence represents letters or numbers. This sequence is a code that scanners can translate into important information such as a shipment's origin, the product type, the place of manufacture, and the product's price. Barcode systems are simple to use and accurate, and they can store large amounts of information.

In distribution applications, barcoding improves data collection speed and accuracy, reduces receiving operations time and data collection labor, and helps to integrate data collection with other areas. This creates stronger information flows and inventory control. Items can be moved more quickly into the DC, and personnel can select and prepare orders much more rapidly.

RFID tags, which consist of silicon chips and an antenna that can transmit data to a wireless receiver, are being used to track everything from jeans to cars. Unlike barcodes, which need to be scanned manually and read individually, RFID tags do not require line-of-sight for reading.

In the distribution environment, it is possible to automatically read hundreds of tags a second as the product travels within the field of a wireless reading device. Not only can these tags be read faster than barcodes, but they also contain more information so they can recall items more efficiently.[12] Despite the promise, RFID still faces key barriers (tag cost, read range, privacy, etc.) to widespread adoption. Chapter 6 provides additional details regarding RFID.

While new functionalities are being added frequently, it is important for an organization to assess its needs before adding new capabilities. Many organizations can be very successful with basic WMS and Auto-ID capabilities. Combined, these tools facilitate fast, accurate, low-cost fulfillment of customer orders. They are proven, cost effective tools that help distribution managers make better decisions, achieve maximum throughput, and support customer requirements.

SUMMARY

Distribution managers play a critical role in the supply chain, focusing on the flow of product rather than storage. Fulfilling customer orders accurately and quickly while achieving the lowest possible cost is a balancing game that distribution managers must play daily. They must coordinate people, processes, capacity, and technology to achieve customer satisfaction, meet internal goals, and provide value-added services to the supply chain.

Managing the distribution system for maximum supply chain impact requires considerable planning, coordination of fulfillment strategy with the execution of distribution operations, analysis of key metrics, and information sharing. Additional concepts from this chapter include the following:

- Distribution operations perform inventory handling, storage, and processing activities to create time and place utility for the supply chain.

- A variety of supply chain challenges—balancing supply and demand, protecting against uncertainty, and promoting transportation economies, among others—can be addressed by distribution facilities.

- Four primary functions are carried out by traditional distribution facilities: (1) accumulation, (2) sortation, (3) allocation, and (4) assortment.

- Distribution operations are taking on value-adding roles—assembly, kitting, product postponement, sequencing, etc.—to complement their basic functionality and to support evolving supply chain needs.

- Tradeoffs must be made between space, equipment, and people—the primary resources available to distribution managers.

- It is critical to match distribution processes to the items being handled to protect product integrity, promote customer service and satisfaction, and provide greater control of the inventory.

- Distribution network design issues involve centralization/decentralization of inventory, the number and location of facilities, and facility ownership.

- Effective facility planning—operational size, layout, and product placement—positively impacts labor productivity and response time.

- Distribution execution involves five primary processes related to the handling and storage of product: (1) receiving, (2) put-away, (3) order picking, (4) replenishment, and (5) shipping.

- Fulfillment support functions provide coordination between key processes and across the supply chain, protect the organization's inventory investment, and improve working conditions within the facility.

- Distribution KPIs address asset utilization, labor productivity, and cost efficiency of the operation, as well as customer service quality issues and the ultimate goal of perfect order fulfillment.

- Warehouse management systems software solutions improve product movement and storage operations through efficient management of information and completion of distribution tasks.

- Barcodes and RFID are the automatic identification tools of choice in distribution to help track, locate, and move product quickly—with near-perfect accuracy rates to their consumers.

STUDY QUESTIONS

1. Discuss the role of distribution in the supply chain. Provide examples of how distribution operations can positively and negatively impact supply chain performance.

2. Compare and contrast the four primary functions of a DC: accumulation, sortation, allocation, and assortment.

3. Discuss the primary tradeoffs that must be made between distribution and other logistics activities.

4. Describe the major challenges faced by distribution managers in the current environment.

5. What are the primary capabilities, advantages, and disadvantages of direct distribution, DCs, and cross-docks?

6. Contract warehousing use is popular among many large manufacturers. Why would a company such as Unilever, which produces a wide variety of consumer goods, move toward this form of distribution?

7. Using company Web sites, compare the distribution service offerings for the following 3PL organizations:

   a. Exel (http://www.exel.com) and AmeriCold Logistics (http://www.americoldrealty.com)

   b. GENCO ATC (http://www.genco.com) and Caterpillar Logistics Services (http://logistics.cat.com)

8. When designing a DC, what interior layout objectives and slotting principles must be considered? Why?

9. Identify and describe the five primary product-handling functions in a DC.

10. What are the key support functions in a DC? Why are they important?

11. How would a distribution operation monitor the quality of service provided by a 3PL service provider? What types of metrics would be used to measure private distribution operations?

12. Using Internet search engines, identify three WMS solutions providers. Describe the capabilities and supply chain impact that their tools promise.

NOTES

1. Patrick Burnson, "2010 State of Logistics: Make Your Move," *Logistics Management* (July 2010), pp. 22–26.

2. Arnold Maltz and Nicole DeHoratius, *Warehousing: The Evolution Continues* (Oakbrook, IL: Warehousing Education and Research Council, 2004).

3. David Simchi-Levi, Philip Kaminsky, and Edith Simchi-Levi, *Designing and Managing the Supply Chain*, 3rd ed. (New York: McGraw-Hill, Irwin, 2008), 232.

4. Stuart Smith, "Why Convert Distribution to a Hub and Spoke Model," *CPE Management 101* (February 22, 2010). Retrieved October 22, 2010 from http://blog.mintek.com/Cable_CPE_Management/bid/34385/Why-Convert-Distribution-to-a-Hub-and-Spoke-Model

5. "Product Slotting—Inventory Profiling," *CEI Logistics*, (2007). Retrieved October 20, 2010 from http://www.ceilogistics.com/Solutions/product-slotting.htm

6. John M. Hill, "Accurate Order Picking Counts More Than Ever," *Modern Materials Handling* (April 4, 2007).

7. David Blanchard, "The Perfect Order," *Industry Week* (January 2007). Retrieved February 18, 2011 from http://www.industryweek.com/articles/the_perfect_order_13211.aspx

8. Patrick Burnson, "2010 State of Logistics: Make Your Move," *Logistics Management* (July 2010), pp. 22–26.

9. Martin Murray, "Measures of Warehouse Productivity," *About.com: Logistics/Supply Chain*. Retrieved October 21, 2010 from http://logistics.about.com/od/supplychainmodels/a/measures.htm

10. Joan Nystrom and Dan Gilmore, "WMS: Core of the Integrated Logistics Suite," *Supply Chain Digest Letter* (July 2010), pp. 1–9.

11. Dave Piasecki, "Warehouse Management Systems," *Inventoryops.com*. Retrieved October 21, 2010, from http://www.inventoryops.com/warehouse_management_systems.htm

12. Rob McGregor, "The Benefits of RFID Technology," *LogisticsIT.com* (March 22, 2007). Retrieved October 21, 2010 from http://www.logisticsit.com/absolutenm/templates/article-print.aspx?articleid=2883&zoneid=7

CASE 11.1
BathKing Industries

Chip Norek, president of BathKing Industries (BKI), is reading the latest financial report. As he reviews this information, Norek recalls the company's early days and the struggle to get retailers to stock the company's line of bathroom vanities, mirrors, and light fixtures. Today, the problem is quite different. The company is straining to produce enough product to meet retailer demand.

BKI manufactures a variety of bathroom accessories, including vanities (medicine chests), mirrors, lighting fixtures, and shelving. The products are made of rust- and chip-resistant molded plastic and come in a variety of modern designs and colors. The plastic construction permits BKI to produce a high-quality bathroom accessory at an affordable price.

In the late 1990s, Norek focused the company's marketing attention on the large home center chain stores: Home Depot, Lowe's, and their smaller competitors. Today, more than 80 percent of BKI's sales are to these retail chains, and they account for 95 percent of its growth. Without these key customers, BKI would still be a small, struggling manufacturer.

Norek's pleasant memories quickly fade to the realities of dealing with these large chain retailers. In the past two years, BKI has been required to comply with the customers' RFID initiatives, provide advanced shipping notifications, and improve inventory visibility. The latest request from one of the smaller chain stores is for BKI to reduce cycle time by shipping orders directly to the stores.

Currently, BKI's national DC processes and ships a weekly order for each of the chain store's three regional DCs (RDCs) via national truckload carriers. Product is then allocated by the RDCs to individual stores and delivered by their private fleet. Under the proposed arrangement, each store will be ordering separately, and BKI is to process the order and deliver it within five working days.

Joe Rutner, director of logistics, reviewed the request and delivered some sobering news to Norek. He indicated that order processing costs and freight costs would certainly increase. His team would now have to process smaller, case-quantity orders for each store versus pallet-quantity orders from the RDCs. Also, BKI would have to use more costly less-than-truckload service and deliver all the way to the stores.

Norek didn't relish the thought of spending more money on order fulfillment as the customer wasn't huge and had no interest in paying more for the product. He was also worried that other retailers might make similar requests. So Norek asked Rutner to develop a plan that would satisfy customers without cutting into BKI's margins too heavily.

Rutner came back with the concept of establishing a six-facility RDC network for BKI. The DCs would be located in high-demand areas within each region. He touted the network's ability to process orders faster and deliver product cheaper than the current BKI facility. The facilities would be able to handle case picking, pallet cross-docking, and some value-added services. Rutner went on to say that each RDC would maintain only a minimal level of safety stock and that the company's overall inventory would decrease.

Norek is skeptical of this plan. He feels that it would increase capital expenses, inventory levels, and transportation costs. He is not even certain it would meet the five-day delivery time requirements.

CASE QUESTIONS

1. Analyze the logistics service and cost constraints imposed on BKI by the chain store's request.

2. What is your opinion of Joe Rutner's proposal for establishing a series of company-owned RDCs?

3. If BKI moves forward with the RDC plan, what facility ownership structure do you recommend? Why?

4. Develop a process map depicting the product and information flows in Rutner's proposal.

Source: Brian J. Gibson, Ph.D. Used with permission.

CASE 11.2

Tele-Distributors Incorporated

Tele-Distributors Incorporated (TDI)—a distributor of exercise equipment, kitchen gadgets, and small appliances that are promoted on late-night infomercials—has been a successful organization but is facing some challenges in its DC operations. Some performance levels among its key performance indicators—order fill rate, fulfillment accuracy, order-picking productivity, distribution costs as a percentage of cost of goods sold, and damage rates—are trending in the wrong direction according to the third quarter report.

KEY PERFORMANCE INDICATOR	Q3 CURRENT YEAR	Q2 CURRENT YEAR	Q3 PREVIOUS YEAR
Order fill rate	95.4%	96.8%	93.9%
Out of stock rate	2.2%	1.8%	1.1%
Order-picking productivity	165.1 cases per hour	171.2 cases per hour	164.3 cases per hour
Distribution cost	3.7%	4.0%	4.5%
Damage rate	0.9%	0.7%	0.6%

In light of the current challenges, Nick Newton, TDI's director of distribution, has called a meeting with his staff. He opened the meeting with a brief statement: "I appreciate your attendance today. Our company has been growing rapidly and we seem to be taking care of customers but there are a few problems to address. Just look at the report data in the summary table. We have to deliver on the promises that Billy Blaze makes in our infomercials."

"I agree," replied Cam Chizik, TDI's senior distribution analyst. "Our order fill rate is dropping and that won't make customers happy. However, I like our performance in terms of out-of-stock and damage rates. We can't expect to be perfect every time and they are darn close to best-in-class performance levels."

"Gene, what do you think?" asked Newton.

Gene Fairley, the company's distribution manager, replied, "I don't think that we should find any decrease in the numbers to be acceptable. Why should we allow order-picking productivity to decline? And, we have to do something about the lower distribution cost percentage."

"So what can we do about these problems?" asked Newton. "Any ideas for improvement?"

"We really need to get away from our paper-based processes," suggested Fairley. "It is time for us to get into the twenty-first century and adopt a warehouse management system. It will help us better manage the inventory and our people."

"No offense Gene, but the DC is laid out in a confusing fashion with quite a bit of wasted space," said Chizik. "The order pickers seem to walk around in circles when fulfilling orders and they do everything by hand. We need to adopt the best distribution practices for facility layout and order picking."

"Excellent ideas," replied Newton. "I want you to investigate these opportunities and report back to me next Monday. Meeting adjourned."

CASE QUESTIONS

1. Evaluate Chizik's statements regarding performance. Do you agree or disagree with them? Does TDI achieve best-in-class performance levels according to Table 11.5?

2. Evaluate Fairley's statements regarding performance. Do you agree or disagree with them?

3. What benefits could TDI gain by adopting a warehouse management system?

4. What facility layout principles and order-picking practices should TDI adopt to improve distribution performance?

Source: Brian J. Gibson, Ph.D. Used with permission.

APPENDIX 11A
Materials Handling

Distribution centers (DCs) are under intense pressure to manage materials handling in a way that allows them to fulfill orders rapidly, accurately, safely, and economically. This need for speed and efficiency makes it very difficult for organizations to rely exclusively on manual labor to complete the key distribution functions of accumulation, sortation, allocation, and assortment. Instead, equipment can be used to reduce or eliminate manual labor for materials handling.

Generally speaking, materials handling focuses on the activities, equipment, and procedures related to the movement, storage, protection, and control of materials in a system. In logistics, the focus of materials handling is efficient short-distance movement of products and materials within the confines of a DC, factory, cross-dock, transportation terminal, or store. Adapting the customer-oriented "seven Rs" definition of logistics (Chapter 2) would yield the following:

> *Materials handling uses the right method to provide the right amount of the right material at the right place, at the right time, in the right sequence, in the right position, in the right condition, and at the right cost.*

To achieve the seven Rs of materials handling within a DC, specially designed equipment is used most often to accomplish short-distance product movement. Properly selected, this equipment improves labor productivity for receiving, put-away, replenishment, order picking, and shipping activities; increases space utilization; and improves DC order cycle time.

Objectives and Principles of Materials Handling

The general objective of materials handling is to create a more productive, efficient, and safe operation. To achieve a proper balance between service and cost, safety and productivity, and volume and capacity, logistics professionals must effectively manage for the four critical dimensions of materials handling: (1) movement, (2) time, (3) quantity, and (4) space.

The *movement* dimension of materials handling involves the conveyance of goods into, through, and out of DCs. Logistics professionals must select the proper combination of labor and equipment to achieve efficient flows.

The *time* dimension of materials handling is concerned with preparing goods for production or for customer order fulfillment. The longer it takes to get raw materials to production, the greater the chance of work stoppage, higher inventories, and increased storage space. Likewise, the longer it takes to move finished goods to the shipping area, the longer the order cycle time and the lower the customer service.

The *quantity* dimension addresses the varying usage and delivery rate of raw materials and finished goods, respectively. Materials-handling systems are designed to ensure that the correct quantity of product is moved to meet the needs of production and customers.

The *space* dimension of the DC focuses on the capacity constraints of the facility. Properly chosen materials handling equipment and systems allow an organization to use both the horizontal and vertical space effectively. For example, high reach forklifts

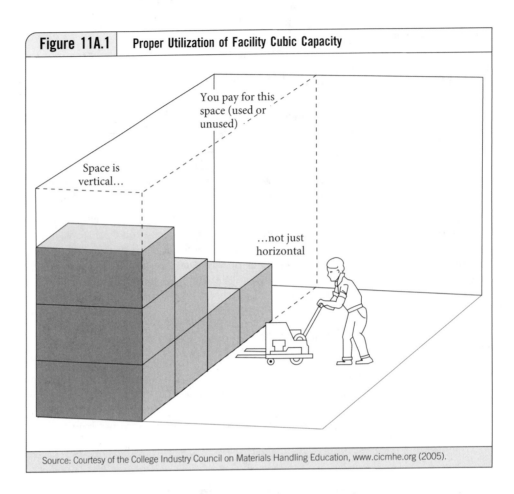

Figure 11A.1 | **Proper Utilization of Facility Cubic Capacity**

You pay for this space (used or unused)

Space is vertical...

...not just horizontal

Source: Courtesy of the College Industry Council on Materials Handling Education, www.cicmhe.org (2005).

can extend to heights of 25 to 30 feet, thereby increasing the vertical capacity utilization of the DC. Figure 11A.1 illustrates the importance of vertical space.

Finding the proper balance between these interrelated dimensions requires significant planning of materials handling and analysis of the many options for mixing space, equipment, and people. Fortunately, these challenges have been addressed by the Material Handling Industry of America in a set of guidelines called the *Ten Principles of Materials Handling*. Table 11A.1 identifies and summarizes the key points of these standards. Logistics professionals apply them on a daily basis when designing and managing DC operations.

These principles are important and interrelated. In the twenty-first century, materials handling helps companies minimize distribution facility investment, reduce expenses, and support supply chain requirements. It also helps organizations overcome some of the labor challenges associated with an aging workforce.

Materials-Handling Equipment[1]

Effective materials handling requires the effective use of different types of mechanical and automated equipment to move goods whenever movement and handling requirements, volume, and cost tradeoffs justify the investment. The Material Handling Industry of America's recent automation survey revealed that the majority of companies are making capital investments in material handling equipment and automation to improve distribution facility performance.[2]

Table 11A.1	The Ten Principles of Material Handling

1. **Planning Principle**. All material handling should be the result of a deliberate plan where the needs, performance objectives, and functional specifications of the proposed methods are completely defined at the outset.

2. **Standardization Principle.** Material handling methods, equipment, controls, and software should be standardized within the limits of achieving overall performance objectives and without sacrificing needed flexibility, modularity, and throughput.

3. **Work Principle.** Material handling work should be minimized without sacrificing productivity or the level of service required of the operation.

4. **Ergonomic Principle.** Human capabilities and limitations must be recognized and respected in the design of material handling tasks and equipment to ensure safe and effective operations.

5. **Unit Load Principle.** Unit loads shall be appropriately sized and configured in a way which achieves the material flow and inventory objectives at each stage in the supply chain.

6. **Space Utilization Principle.** Effective and efficient use must be made of all available space.

7. **System Principle.** Material movement and storage activities should be fully integrated to form a coordinated, operational system which spans receiving, inspection, storage, production, assembly, packaging, unitizing, order selection, shipping, transportation and the handling of returns.

8. **Automation Principle.** Material handling operations should be mechanized and/or automated where feasible to improve operational efficiency, increase responsiveness, improve consistency and predictability, decrease operating costs, and eliminate repetitive or potentially unsafe manual labor.

9. **Environmental Principle.** Environmental impact and energy consumption should be considered as criteria when designing or selecting alternative equipment and materials-handling systems.

10. **Life Cycle Cost Principle.** A thorough economic analysis should account for the entire life cycle of all material handling equipment and resulting systems.

Source: Material Handling Institute, *The Ten Principles of Material Handling*. Retrieved February 25, 2011, from http://www.mhia.org/industrygroups/cicmhe/resources/guidelines/principles. Reproduced by permission.

Choosing the right equipment is a multifaceted task. To reduce purchase, maintenance, and operating costs, materials-handling equipment should be standardized. It is also important to employ adaptable, flexible equipment that can be used for a variety of tasks and applications. Finally, the equipment should have a minimal environmental impact and a low ratio of deadweight to payload, and it must be properly suited to the goods flowing through the DC.

The College-Industry Council of Material Handling Education classifies materials-handling equipment into five major categories: (1) transport equipment, (2) positioning equipment, (3) unit load formation equipment, (4) storage equipment, and (5) identification and control equipment. This taxonomy is not intended to be all-inclusive, but it does provide an overview of the equipment commonly seen in distribution centers. Each category of equipment is briefly described below, with examples provided.

Transport equipment moves material from one location to another within a DC. This type of equipment improves product flows through the facility, minimizes labor effort and time, and reduces dwell time. Figure 11A.2 presents different types of transport equipment.

Forklifts and other industrial trucks are used to move materials over variable paths, with no restrictions on the area covered by the movement. For example, personnel use industrial trucks to unload arriving freight from trailers, move product from dock to various storage areas, and load outbound vehicles. Pallet jacks allow order pickers to

Figure 11A.2	Materials Transport Equipment

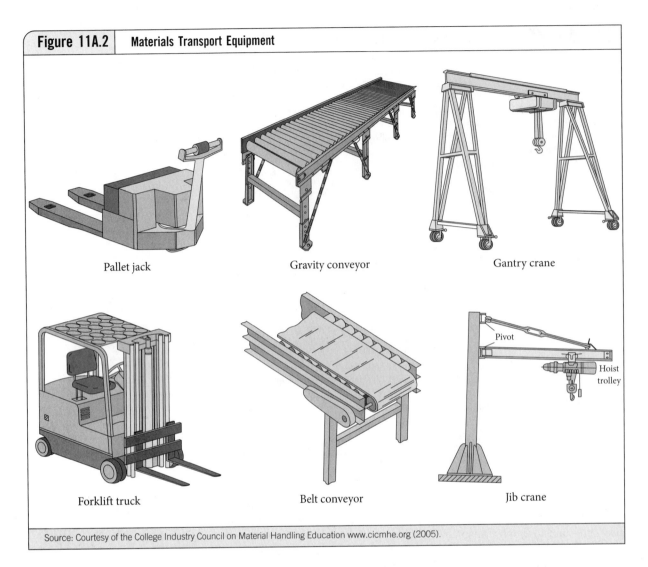

Pallet jack   Gravity conveyor   Gantry crane

Forklift truck   Belt conveyor   Jib crane

Source: Courtesy of the College Industry Council on Material Handling Education www.cicmhe.org (2005).

assemble orders directly on pallets and efficiently move to subsequent pick locations. Automatic guided vehicles (AGVs) are machines that connect receiving, storing, manufacturing, and shipping. AGVs can either roam freely or move on a fixed path, with computers that make traffic control decisions. Essentially, AGVs travel around the warehouse or manufacturing plant carrying various items to a particular programmed destination. Since these AGVs do not require a driver, labor costs are reduced.

Conveyors are used to move materials over a fixed path between specific points in a DC. They are beneficial when there is adequate volume and frequency of movement between points to warrant the investment. Numerous types of conveyors are used to accomplish labor-free flows. Primary classifications include unit load or bulk load conveyors; overhead, on-floor, or in-floor location; and gravity or motorized power. A variety of automated sortation conveyors also ease labor requirements in the DC.

Cranes are used to move loads over variable paths within a restricted area of the DC or factory. They are more flexible than conveyors, have the ability to move goods both vertically and horizontally, and can handle oddly shaped loads. Cranes make sense when there is limited volume and the cost of installing conveyors is not feasible.

| Figure 11A.3 | Product Positioning Equipment |

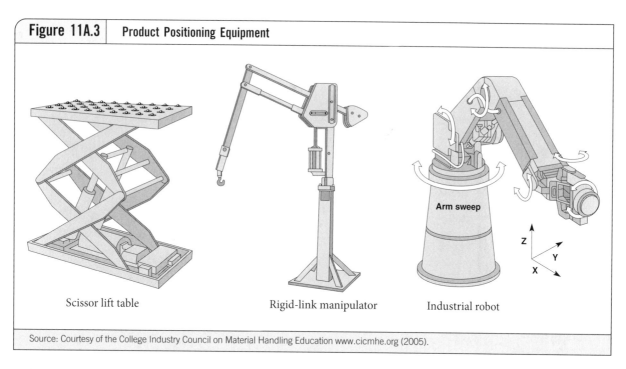

Scissor lift table   Rigid-link manipulator   Industrial robot

Source: Courtesy of the College Industry Council on Material Handling Education www.cicmhe.org (2005).

Positioning equipment is used to handle material at a single location so that it is in the correct position for subsequent handling, machining, transport, or storage. Unlike transport equipment, positioning equipment is usually used for materials handling at a single work-place. Examples of positioning equipment include lift/turn/tilt tables, manipulators, hoists, and industrial robots. Figure 11A.3 presents different types of positioning equipment.

This equipment is beneficial in that it raises productivity by moving, lifting, and positioning goods with limited manual labor. It also protects quality and limits damage to heavy products by reducing the need for troublesome manual handling. Finally, positioning equipment reduces the potential for worker fatigue and injuries.

Unit load formation equipment restricts materials so that they maintain their integrity when moved or stored as a single load. Pallets are one type of unit load formation equipment that enables a DC to leverage standardized transport equipment such as fork-lifts. Container-load be handled at the same time, thereby reducing the number of trips required and, potentially, reducing handling costs, loading and unloading times, and product damage. Crates, bags, bins, slipsheets, and stretch-wrap are also used to create unit loads. Figure 11A.4 presents common examples of unit load formation equipment.

Storage equipment allows companies to hold materials economically over a period of time. The goal of racks, automatic storage/retrieval systems (AS/RS), carousels, and mezzanines is to resourcefully use the vertical and horizontal space in the DC. Storage capacity also gives the company an opportunity to purchase goods in bulk for quantity discounts, hedge against anticipated price increases, and provide a buffer against demand spikes. Transportation efficiencies can be gained when a company can purchase and store container load quantities of goods. Properly laid out storage systems can enhance the speed, accuracy, and cost-effectiveness of the order-picking process.

Storage equipment can be segmented into two types: picker-to-part and part-to-picker. Picker-to-part storage systems require the order picker to travel to the product storage location. Examples of picker-to-part storage equipment include bin shelving,

Figure 11A.4 | Unit Load Formation Equipment

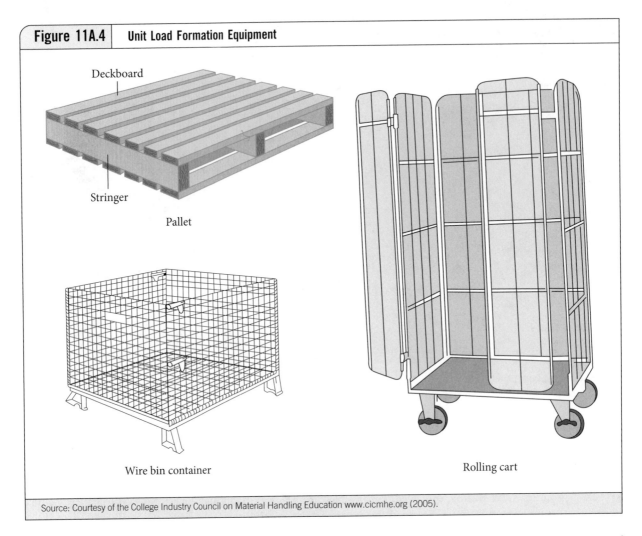

Deckboard

Stringer

Pallet

Wire bin container

Rolling cart

modular storage drawers, racks, and mezzanines. Figure 11A.5 displays various types of picker-to-part storage equipment.

Racks are made up of rails and load-supporting upright beams. Pallets of product are placed on the beams and held until needed. Multiple rack options exist: selective (single-deep, narrow aisle, or double-deep), flow-through, drive-in, drive-through, push-back, and cantilever are most commonly used in DCs.

Mezzanines are double-layered storage systems that utilize a second level of bin shelving, modular storage cabinets, flow racks, or carousels above the first storage level. Instead of using up square footage space, the mezzanine adds a second level to utilize DC cubic capacity more efficiently and allow order picking to take place on both levels. Steel grating usually divides the two levels, which workers access by stairs. Because the mezzanine is not part of the building's actual construction, its location is flexible.

In part-to-picker storage systems, the pick location travels through an automated machine to the picker. Examples include carousels and AS/RS. These systems have a higher initial cost than picker-to-part systems, but utilizing automated storage and retrieval equipment speeds up order-picking operations, improves inventory control, and increases profits. Part-to-picker systems minimize travel time. Figure 11A.6 displays various types of part-to-picker storage equipment.

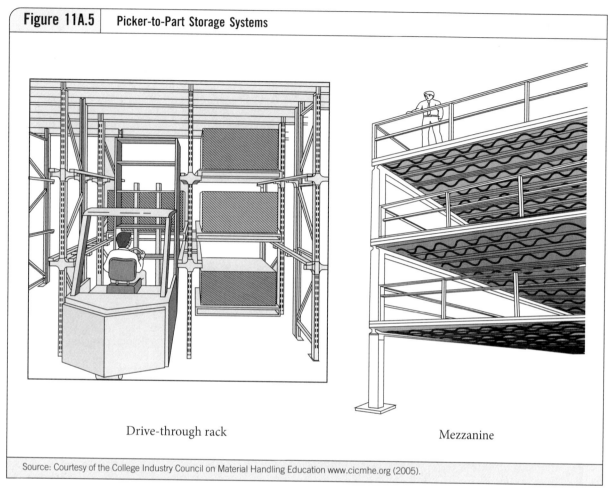

| Figure 11A.5 | Picker-to-Part Storage Systems |

Drive-through rack   Mezzanine

Source: Courtesy of the College Industry Council on Material Handling Education www.cicmhe.org (2005).

Carousels are shelves or bins linked together through a mechanical device that stores and rotates items for order picking. Horizontal carousels are a linked series of bins that rotate around a vertical axis. A computer locates a needed part and rotates the carousel until the part location stops in front of the order picker's fixed position. Automated systems attempt to minimize wait times and maximize order-picking times. Industries that use horizontal carousels include aviation, electronic, paper, and pharmaceutical.

Vertical carousels are enclosed for cleanliness and security and the carousel rotates around a horizontal axis. The vertical carousel operates on a continuous lift principle, rotating the necessary items to the order picker's work station. This vertical storage approach cuts floor space use by 60 percent and increases picking productivity by up to 300 percent over racks and shelving of equal capacity. Some industries that use vertical carousels include electronics, automotive, aerospace, and computer.

AS/RS are among the most technically advanced storage and order-picking equipment used in distribution. They efficiently use storage space and achieve the highest accuracy rate in order picking. The AS/RS machine travels both horizontally and vertically to storage locations in an aisle, carrying item storage containers to and from an order-picking station at the end of the aisle. At the order-picking station, the order picker programs the correct item-picking sequence. The AS/RS machine retrieves the next container in the sequence, while the order picker obtains items from the present container. AS/RS are space and labor efficient but are very expensive to purchase and install.

| Figure 11A.6 | Part-to-Picker Storage Systems |

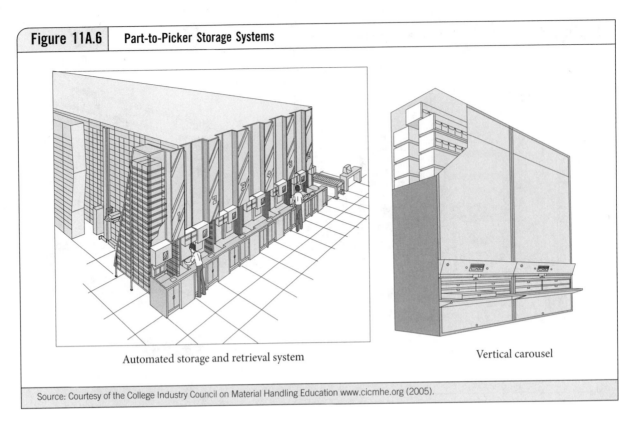

Automated storage and retrieval system   Vertical carousel

Source: Courtesy of the College Industry Council on Material Handling Education www.cicmhe.org (2005).

Identification and control equipment collects and communicates information that is used to coordinate the flow of materials within a facility and between a facility and its suppliers and customers. Automatic identification tools—bar codes, magnetic stripes, and radio frequency identification tags—capture data with little or no human intervention. These tools are discussed in Chapter 11. Other critical control tools include portable data terminals to capture and store information, as well as electronic data interchange tools and supply chain software that facilitate the transfer of information.

SUMMARY

Materials handling is very important to the efficient operation of DCs and other logistics facilities. The equipment and tools discussed in this appendix facilitate internal flows of goods from receiving to shipping. The key to success is selecting the appropriate equipment for the type and volume of product being distributed by the facility. Ultimately, effective selection and application of materials-handling principles to daily operations will improve capacity utilization, employee productivity, and fulfillment speed.

NOTES

1. This section is derived from the College-Industry Council of Material Handling Education's *Material Handling Equipment Taxonomy*. Retrieved February 25, 2011 from http://www.mhia.org/industrygroups/cicmhe/resources/mhe_tax.htm

2. Trebilcock, Bob, "Looking for Automation," *Logistics Management*, February 2011, p. 53.

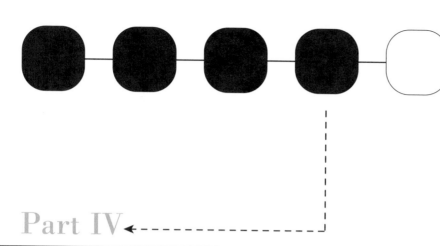

Part IV

Achieving desired objectives is a challenging and formidable task for any logistics or supply chain manager. Successful firms will be those that identify and utilize new, innovative, and value-added approaches to logistics and supply chain management.

Chapter 12 examines issues relating to supply chain network design and facility location. Considering the need to keep today's logistics and supply chain systems up to date, an understanding of analytical approaches proves to be of value. Additionally, it is important to realize how transportation economics can affect optimum or preferred locations for logistics and supply chain facilities.

Chapter 13 provides valuable perspectives on the topics of purchasing, procurement, and strategic sourcing in a supply chain context. Included are the principles and processes of effective sourcing management and the value to companies of having effective and productive relationships with product suppliers and suppliers of logistics services.

Chapter 14 highlights key aspects of manufacturing as they relate to logistics and supply chain management. Given the changes that have occurred in the overall business environment, such as the move to contract manufacturing and offshoring of manufacturing, the link between logistics and manufacturing has become a critical element of overall supply chain success.

Chapter 15 looks at opportunities relating to the effective management of reverse logistics flows. Overall, there are great opportunities in most organizations to improve the effectiveness of managing reverse flows of product for returns, repairs, etc.

Chapter 12

SUPPLY CHAIN NETWORK ANALYSIS AND DESIGN

Learning Objectives

After reading this chapter, you should be able to do the following:

- Understand the critical need to evaluate the structure and functioning of logistics/supply chain networks, and for making changes and improvements as appropriate.

- Identify factors that suggest a need to redesign a logistics/supply chain network.

- Structure an effective process for logistics/supply chain network design.

- Be aware of key locational determinants, both regional/national/global and site-specific, and the impacts they may have on prospective locational alternatives.

- Describe the different types of modeling approaches that may be used to gain insight into logistics/supply chain network design and facility location decision making.

- Apply the simple grid or center-of-gravity approach to facility location.

- Discuss certain ways in which transportation alternatives and transportation costs may affect the location decision.

Supply Chain Profile

Volkswagen Opens U.S. Production Facility in Chattanooga, Tennessee

On July 15, 2008, Volkswagen Group of America Inc. announced that it would build a U.S. automotive production facility in Chattanooga, Tennessee, to produce a car designed specifically for the North American consumer and to invest $1 billion in the U.S. and regional economies. The announcement was an important element of the company's overall U.S. strategy of connecting with its customers, increasing its competitiveness, and tripling its U.S. customer base in the next decade.

According to Prof. Martin Winterkorn, CEO of Volkswagen AG, "Volkswagen will be extremely active there. This plant represents a milestone in Volkswagen's growth strategy. We will be selling 800,000 Volkswagens in the U.S. by 2018, and this new site will play a key role. This, along with our growth strategy, is a prerequisite for the economic success of the company in the dollar region. We look forward to establishing an important mainstay for ourselves when we become the biggest European carmaker there."

Plans were made to build the facility in the Enterprise South Industrial Park, located 12 miles northeast of downtown Chattanooga, and adjacent to Interstate 75. The 1,350-acre site is 100 percent owned by the city of Chattanooga and Hamilton County and is certified as an industrial megasite by the Tennessee Valley Authority. Production has been scheduled to begin in early 2011.

According to Phil Bredesen, former Governor of the State of Tennessee, "I believe Volkswagen chose Tennessee because of our shared values, our commitment to innovation, and our strong respect for the environment. This project will have a significant impact on the economy of Tennessee and the region for decades to come."

"We started with a vision of transforming an idle Army facility into the source of thousands of family-wage jobs," said Claude Ramsey, former Mayor of Hamilton County. Chattanooga City Mayor Ron Littlefield indicated that both Volkswagen and Chattanooga are serious about environmental sustainability and twenty-first century manufacturing. U.S. Senator Lamar Alexander suggested it was an ideal marriage of one of the world's most admired companies and one of America's most livable cities, and would help to keep Tennessee on the road to becoming the No. 1 state in auto jobs.

With the new plant, Volkswagen will bring about 2,000 direct jobs to the area, plus a significant number of jobs in related sectors. Volkswagen of America received an attractive, comprehensive package of incentives for the new facility from Governor Bredesen's office and from the Tennessee Department of Economic and Community Development. The statutory incentives are tied to job creation and capital investment. Additional support includes assistance for public infrastructure and job training, each designed to ensure the local economy best leverages Volkswagen's investment to benefit the local work force and ensure the facility's success.

"This area has a deep base of well-trained labor, with excellent engineering and manufacturing programs at the universities and technical colleges," added Stefan Jacoby, former President and CEO of Volkswagen Group of America. "Thanks to the visionary leaders and people of Chattanooga, we're confident that the values of this area are compatible with our own, and we envision a long and productive partnership."

Introduction

As firms continue to search for new ways to lower costs and improve service to their customers, the issue of where to locate logistics and manufacturing facilities has never been more complex or critical. In addition to enhancing the efficiency and effectiveness of a logistics/supply chain operation, the redesign of a firm's overall network can help to differentiate a firm in the marketplace. Considering the increasingly dynamic aspects of today's business world, companies are continually seeking new and improved approaches to network design and operation. Several examples illustrate this type of success:

- A leading pharmaceutical distributor with nationwide service reduced its logistics network from more than 60 to 20 distribution centers, while offering its customers a selection of service responses from which to choose (for example, same-day delivery, regular service, and so on).

- A prominent office products company shrunk its network of distribution facilities from 11 to 3, while substantially increasing the level of cross-docking activity with its customers and significantly improving logistical customer service.

- A direct-selling company with a national distribution capability reengineered its customer service operation and eliminated a major distribution point, which resulted in significant reductions to its fixed assets and operating expenses, at the same time differentiating its services to meet a recognized range of customer requirements.

- As a result of the merger of two large grocery industry manufacturers, the combined logistics network consisted of 54 distribution centers across the United States. Following careful study and analysis, with a look to the future, the company consolidated its network into 15 strategically located facilities. This move significantly reduced the company's overall logistics costs and improved service levels to its customers.

- A major consumer products retailer developed a very large import distribution center to accommodate inbound shipments of products from its global manufacturing sites.

- A global semiconductor products manufacturer consolidated its logistics network into a single, global distribution center in Singapore and engaged a third-party supplier of express logistics services to manage its overall distribution activity. The end results included lower cost, improved service, and a new way for the firm to differentiate itself in the marketplace.

- As levels of international trade fluctuate, this results in changing volumes of freight shipped to and from various global port facilities. These variations frequently have significant impacts on the structure and functioning of global supply chains, and the relative roles of various alternative port facilities.

While there are also examples of the opposite situation, in which firms have justifiably expanded their logistics networks and increased the number of distribution facilities, the move to consolidate existing systems is far more prevalent. Assuming that a firm considers the impact of such a decision on total logistics cost, it is not unusual for the inventory cost savings associated with consolidating facilities to outweigh any additional transportation expense involved with moving product to the customer. Also, the use of currently available information technology, coupled with the time-sensitive capabilities of many suppliers of transportation service, can mean that such a move enhances responsiveness and the levels of service experienced by customers.

This chapter first looks at several strategic aspects of logistics/supply chain network design. While it may sometimes be that "change for the sake of change" is helpful, a number of prominent factors may suggest that a redesign of the network may be necessary. Next, the process of logistics/supply chain network redesign is examined in detail. This content provides a useful framework for understanding the key steps that must be included in a comprehensive approach to network design and facility location.

Following these discussions, attention shifts to several major locational determinants. These factors may be either regionally focused or site-specific. Also included is a summary of current trends governing site selection. The chapter concludes with coverage of several modeling approaches that can be used to provide insight into the issues of logistics/supply chain network design and facility location. Several examples of transportation-specific factors are also considered.

The Need for Long-Range Planning

In the short term, a firm's logistics/supply chain network and the locations of its key facilities are relatively fixed, and the logistics managers must operate within the constraints imposed by the facility locations. Site availability, leases, contracts, and investments make changing facility locations impractical in the short term. In the long term, however, the design of the overall network must be thought of as variable. Management decisions can and should be made to change the network to meet the logistics requirements imposed by customers, suppliers, competitive changes, and the realities of the supply chain itself.

In addition, the decisions as to network design and facility location that are made today will have implications far into the future. A facility properly located under today's economic, competitive, and technological conditions may not be at an optimum location under future conditions. Also, today's facility location decision will have a significant effect on future costs in such areas as logistics, marketing, manufacturing, and finance. Thus, the facility location decision must seriously consider anticipated business conditions and acknowledge a critical need to be flexible and responsive to customer needs as they may change in the future. This latter concern heightens the attractiveness of the third-party logistics option for many logistics operations today.

The Strategic Importance of Logistics/Supply Chain Network Design

Why analyze the logistics/supply chain network? In essence, the answer lies in the fact that all businesses operate in a very dynamic environment in which change is the only constant. Characteristics of consumer and industrial-buyer demand, technology, competition, markets, and suppliers are constantly changing. As a result, businesses must redeploy their resources in response to and in anticipation of this ever-changing environment.

Considering the rate at which change is occurring, it is questionable whether any existing logistics/supply chain network can be truly up to date. Any network that has been in existence for a number of years is certainly a candidate for reevaluation and potential redesign. Even if the existing system is not functionally obsolete, an analysis of the existing network will probably uncover new opportunities to reduce cost and/or improve service.

This section focuses attention on several types of change that may suggest a need to reevaluate and/or redesign a firm's logistics network. While not all of these factors will affect any single firm at the same time, they represent some of the more frequently changing elements of the business environment that affect logistics and supply chain management.

Changing Customer Service Requirements

As was discussed in Chapters 1–3 and 7–8, the logistical requirements of customers are changing in numerous ways. As a result, the need to reevaluate and redesign logistics/supply chain networks is of great contemporary interest. While some customers have intensified their demands for more efficient and low-cost logistics services, others are seeking relationships with suppliers who can take logistical capabilities and performance to new, unprecedented levels.

While customer service requirements may be subject to change, the types of customers served may also evolve over time. Consider, for example, the case of food manufacturers that have distributed their product to independent stores and regional retail chains for many years and recently added mass merchants to their list of customers. Another example is that of manufacturers of stationery who traditionally served a multitude of customers, from small retail to club stores, but that now focus primarily on distributors of office supply products. In these examples, change has occurred at both the customer and supply chain levels, with significant impacts on lead times, order size and frequency, and associated activities such as shipment notification, marking and tagging, and packaging.

Shifting Locations of Customer and/or Supply Markets

Considering that manufacturing and logistics facilities are positioned in the supply chain between customer and supply markets, any changes in these markets should cause a firm to reevaluate its logistics network. When the U.S. population shifted to the southeast and southwest, for example, new warehouses and distribution facilities followed the changing geo-location trends. As a result, cities such as Atlanta, Dallas, Las Vegas, Reno/Sparks, and Memphis have become popular distribution center locations for companies serving these increasing population centers.

On the supply side, the service and cost requirements of the automobile industry's movement to JIT-based manufacturing have forced companies to examine the locations of logistics facilities. Many product suppliers to the automotive industry, for example, have selected nearby points for manufacturing and/or parts distribution facilities. Considering the growing, global nature of parts sourcing, automotive industry firms are also focusing on streamlining their global supply chains to achieve objectives relating to efficiency and effectiveness.

Also on the global scene, changes such as the unification initiatives of the European Union, the continued searches for lower-cost manufacturing, and the growing economic importance of China and the Asia-Pacific area in general have forced many companies to examine facility locations in terms of their suitability for competition in these rapidly developing markets. In addition to reconfiguring their overall logistics/supply chain networks, firms facing these challenges have taken steps such as establishing branch operations in these newly popular geographies and entering into joint agreements with companies that are located in and already have a significant business presence in these areas.

Change in Corporate Ownership

A relatively common occurrence today is for a firm to experience an ownership-related change associated with a merger, an acquisition, or a divestiture. In such instances, many companies choose to be proactive and to conduct a formal evaluation of new versus previous logistics/supply chain networks in advance of such a change. This is very helpful in terms of making sure that the newly merged or newly independent firm will have fully anticipated the logistics and supply chain impacts of the change in corporate ownership. In other instances, those having management responsibility for logistics and supply chain activities may be the last ones to find out about the impending change, and the role of network design immediately takes on a defensive posture.

Even if these logistics impacts are not part of the planning process, it is critical for firms to reassess their logistics/supply chain networks following ownership-related changes such as those identified in the preceding paragraph. Without sufficient advance planning, such changes increase the likelihood that the new operation is duplicating effort and incurring unnecessary logistics expense.

Examples of mergers/acquisitions that over time have had significant implications for logistics/supply chain network design include Pfizer's acquisition of Warner Lambert and then Wyeth, Procter & Gamble's acquisition of Gillette, the Heinz/HP Foods merger, Energizer's purchase of Schick, the acquisition of DuPont Pharmaceuticals Corporation by Bristol-Myers Squibb, the acquisition of Compaq by Hewlett-Packard Company, the acquisition of Quaker Oats Company by Pepsi, and the merger of two large petroleum-industry companies to form Exxon Mobil Corporation. In fact, one of the driving factors of some of these examples are the synergies that exist or can be created as a result of the merger or acquisition.

Cost Pressures

A major priority for many firms today is to figure out new and innovative ways to take cost out of their key business processes, including those relating to logistics. In such instances, a reevaluation of the logistics network and the functioning of the overall supply chain can frequently help to uncover new sources of such savings. Whether the answer lies in reducing cost in transportation, inventory, warehousing, or another area, a detailed examination of the current system versus alternative approaches can be exceptionally useful.

On a global basis, labor wage rates have a significant impact on the location of manufacturing and logistics operations. In recent history, economic activity has evolved to lower-wage rate locations such as the BRIC countries (Brazil, Russia, India, and China), while contemporary areas of global interest include countries such as the VISTA countries (Vietnam, Indonesia, South Africa, Turkey, and Argentina). One interesting example of the movement to new global locations was the decision made by Intel Corporation in 2006 to build a $300 million semiconductor assembly and test facility in Ho Chi Minh City, Vietnam.[1] Also, and while wage rates in some countries such as those mentioned above have risen to some extent, recent trends have not significantly reduced the gap with comparable figures from the United States.[2]

Companies considering plant modernization needs also sometimes benefit from a comprehensive cost analysis, which might accompany a reevaluation of the logistics network. A firm considering an investment of millions of dollars in an existing plant must ask, "Is this the proper location for a plant, given the current and future customer and vendor locations?"

Competitive Capabilities

Another factor relates to competitive pressures that may force a company to examine its logistics service levels and the costs generated by its network of logistics facilities. To remain competitive in the marketplace or to develop a competitive advantage, a company should frequently examine the relative locations of its facilities toward the goal of improving service and/or lowering costs. Companies often conduct this network review in light of newly developed transport alternatives.

For example, many firms locate distribution facilities near the hub operations of companies such as FedEx and UPS so that access to time-critical, express transportation services will be facilitated. This strategy is particularly appropriate for inventories of high-value, time-sensitive products that may need to be shipped on a moment's notice. The resulting service levels are higher, and the total cost of the comprehensive, express logistics services is lower than the total cost would be of warehousing the needed inventories at various locations throughout the company's logistics network. Essentially, the centralization of such inventories at strategically selected locations reduces the overall cost of logistics and significantly improves responsiveness in terms of delivery times. Additionally, the same result may be achieved through the use of a high-quality logistics provider, such as Forward Air Corporation, that specializes in airport-to-airport transportation of service-sensitive shipments and other value-added logistics solutions and logistics services.[3]

Corporate Organizational Change

It is not unusual for logistics/supply chain network design to become a topic of discussion at the same time that a firm considers any major corporate organizational change, such as downsizing. In such instances, the strategic functioning of the firm's logistics network is viewed as something that must be protected and even enhanced through the process of organizational change.

Logistics/Supply Chain Network Design

An organization must consider many factors as it approaches the task of determining the optimum design of its logistics/supply chain network. These factors are identified and discussed at a later point in this chapter. At the outset, however, it is important to realize that the task of designing an appropriate logistics/supply chain network should be coordinated closely with the corporate and overall business strategies that may be in place. Since the process of designing or redesigning a firm's logistics/supply chain network can be complex, it is discussed in the context of a major corporate reengineering process.

Figure 12.1 identifies the six major steps that are recommended for a comprehensive logistics/supply chain network design process. Each of these steps is discussed in detail in the following paragraphs.

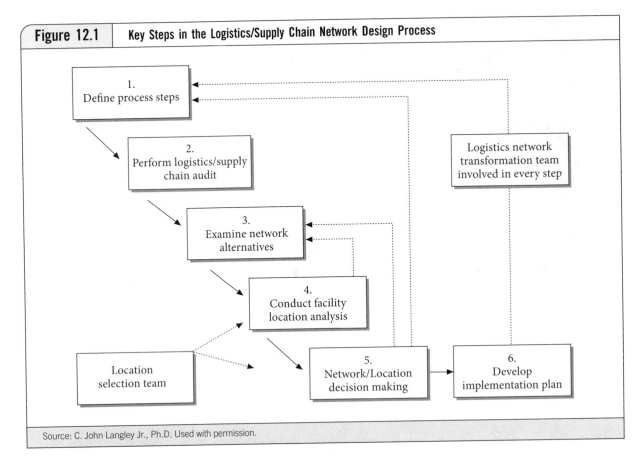

Figure 12.1 | **Key Steps in the Logistics/Supply Chain Network Design Process**

Source: C. John Langley Jr., Ph.D. Used with permission.

Step 1: Define the Logistics/Supply Chain Network Design Process

Of initial importance is the formation of a logistics/supply chain network transformation team to be responsible for all elements of the network design process. This team will first need to become aware of overall corporate and business strategies and the underlying business needs of the firm and the supply chains in which it is a participant.

Also in this step, it is important to establish the parameters and objectives of the network design or redesign process itself. An awareness of the expectations of senior management, for example, is essential to the effective progress of the overall improvement process. Issues pertaining to the availability of needed resources in the areas of funding, people, and systems must be understood at an early stage in the process.

An additional topic to be addressed early on is the potential involvement of third-party suppliers of logistics services as a means of achieving the firm's logistics objectives. This consideration is critical, since it will expand the mindset of the network design team to include a consideration of logistics/supply chain network solutions that may involve externally provided as well as proprietary logistics resources.

Step 2: Perform a Logistics/Supply Chain Audit

The logistics/supply chain audit provides members of the transformation team with a comprehensive perspective on the firm's logistics process. In addition, it helps to gather

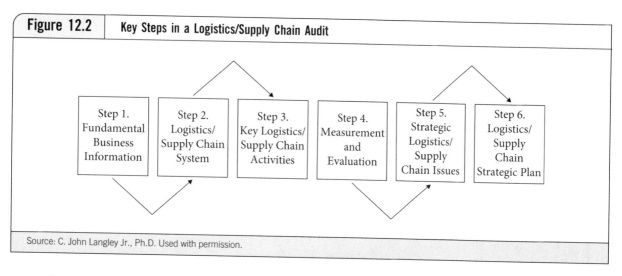

Figure 12.2 | Key Steps in a Logistics/Supply Chain Audit

Source: C. John Langley Jr., Ph.D. Used with permission.

essential types of information that will be useful throughout future steps in the redesign process. Figure 12.2 indicates a number of key steps that should be included in a logistics/supply chain audit. Listed here are examples of the types of information that should become available as a result of this audit:

- Customer requirements and key environmental factors
- Key logistics goals and objectives
- Profile of the current logistics/supply chain network and the firm's positioning in respective supply chain(s)
- Understanding of key logistic/supply chain activities and processes
- Benchmark, or target, values for logistics/supply chain costs and key performance measurements
- Identification of gaps between current and desired logistics/supply chain performance (qualitative and quantitative)
- Key objectives for logistics/supply chain network design, expressed in terms that will facilitate measurement

Step 3: Examine the Logistics/Supply Chain Network Alternatives

The next step is to examine the available alternatives for the logistics/supply chain network. This involves applying suitable quantitative models to the current logistics system as well as to the alternative systems and approaches under consideration. The use of these models provides considerable insight into the functioning and cost/service effectiveness of the various possible networks. Essentially, the principal modeling approach will be optimization, simulation, heuristic, or some combination of these three approaches that are explored in detail later in this chapter. Briefly, optimization approaches search for "best" solutions, simulation models replicate the functioning of the logistics/supply chain network, and heuristic techniques are able to accommodate broad problem definitions but do not provide optimum solutions.

Once an appropriate modeling procedure has been selected, it should be used to help identify a logistics/supply chain network that is consistent with the key objectives identified during the audit phase. Although, at first, transformation teams often look to the model to suggest answers to the key questions that have been raised, they quickly realize that the modeling effort is likely to produce more insight than answers.

Once preliminary design solutions have been identified, subsequent "what-if types of analysis should be conducted to test the sensitivity of recommended network designs to changes in key logistics variables. The results of this step should provide a useful set of recommendations for the number and general location of logistics facilities that will help to meet the desired objectives.

Also, at this point in the network design process, it is critical to understand the geographical parameters of the logistics/supply chain under study. Although a domestic or regional perspective has been the focus of many network design projects to date, there are an increasing number of projects in which a multinational or global perspective is necessary. State-of-the-art network design processes are currently capable of dealing with the logistics/supply chain needs of this broader geographical setting.

Step 4: Conduct a Facility Location Analysis

Once a general configuration of the desired logistics/supply chain network has been recommended, the next task is to carefully analyze the attributes of specific regions and locales that are candidates for sites of logistics facilities, distribution centers, cross-docking operations, etc. These analyses will have both quantitative and qualitative aspects. Many of the quantitative elements have already been incorporated into Step 3 of the modeling effort. The qualitative aspects, to be discussed in a later section of this chapter, include such considerations as labor climate, transportation issues, proximity to markets and customers, quality of life, taxes and industrial development incentives, supplier networks, land costs and utilities, overall supply chain and logistics infrastructure, and company preference.

The effort in this step will be facilitated by the formation of a location selection team, which will collect information on specific attributes such as those identified earlier. In addition, this team should be able to examine potential sites in terms of local factors such as topography, geology, and facility design. To supplement internally available resources, the firm may wish to engage the services of a consulting firm that specializes in assisting clients with the process of selecting a location.

The first screening by the location selection team usually eliminates areas that are uneconomical from a logistics perspective, thereby reducing the number of alternatives. For example, consider the number of potential distribution center sites in the southeastern United States. Applying the logistics/supply chain location determinant, the team may find that the optimum location is in the Tennessee/Georgia area. This definitely reduces the number of potential sites and enables the team to direct the location analysis toward a specific area. Or, if the decision situation is in more a global setting, the initial screening may focus attention on potential locations in the Southern China area—with further resolution to be provided through more in-depth analysis.

Step 5: Make Decisions Regarding Network and Facility Location

Next, the network and specific sites for logistics facilities recommended in Steps 3 and 4 should be evaluated for consistency with the design criteria that were identified in Step 1. This step should confirm the types of change that are needed to the firm's logistics network and should do so in the context of overall supply chain positioning.

Although the feasibility of involving third-party suppliers should have been incorporated into the alternatives that were evaluated in the two preceding steps, the decision to involve external suppliers will have cost and service implications as well as strategic ones.

Step 6: Develop an Implementation Plan

Once the overall direction has been established, the development of an effective implementation plan, or "blueprint for change," is critical. This plan should serve as a useful road map for moving from the current logistics/supply chain network to the desired new one. Since it was known from the beginning that this transformation process was likely to produce recommendations for significant change, it is important that the firm commit the resources necessary to assure a smooth, timely implementation, and the continuous improvement of the network decisions that will have been made.

Major Locational Determinants

The focus of Step 4 in the logistics/supply chain network redesign process is on analyzing the attributes of specific regions and areas that are candidates for sites of logistics facilities. Table 12.1 lists a number of major locational determinants for both national/regional and site-specific locations. While these factors are listed in general order of importance, the relative weighting applied to each depends on the details of the specific location decision under consideration.

The importance of major locational determinants varies among industries and among individual companies within specific industries. For example, labor-intensive industries such as textiles, furniture, and household appliances place significant emphasis on the availability and cost of labor in both regional and local market areas. Alternatively, manufacturers of high-tech products such as computers and peripherals, semiconductors, and engineering and scientific instruments place great emphasis on ensuring the availability of a highly qualified workforce with very specific technical skills and, as discussed earlier, proximity to customer markets. For industries such as drugs, beverages, and printing and publishing, in which competition or logistics costs are significant, other logistics variables are critical.

Table 12.1	Major Locational Determinants
NATIONAL/REGIONAL DETERMINANTS	**SITE-SPECIFIC DETERMINANTS**
• Labor climate	• Transportation access
• Availability of transportation	— Truck
— Services	— Air
— Infrastructure	— Rail
• Proximity to markets and customers	— Water
• Quality of life	• Inside/outside metropolitan area
• Taxes and industrial development incentives	• Availability of workforce
• Supplier networks	• Land costs and taxes
• Land costs and utilities	• Utilities
• Company preference	

Source: C. John Langley Jr., Ph.D. Used with permission.

Key Factors for Consideration

This discussion focuses attention on the regional determinants shown in Table 12.1. Because the site-specific determinants cannot be generalized as readily, this level of detail should be acquired and evaluated through the efforts of the location selection team.

Labor Climate

Location decision makers consider a number of factors in determining the labor climate of an area, region, or country. Given the typically labor-intensive nature of many logistics/supply chain operations, the cost and availability of labor are major issues of concern. Other factors to be considered include the workforce's degree of unionization, skill level, work ethic, productivity, and the enthusiasm of local public officials. The existence of right-to-work laws in certain states (which prohibit union membership as a condition of employment) and the unionization of major area employers reveal the area workforce's degree of unionization. Government information regarding work stoppages, productivity (value added per employee), and skill levels is available for most areas. Data regarding hourly earnings by industry and occupation are available from governmental agencies.

Another labor-related factor to be considered is the rate of unemployment in the local areas under consideration. While many other factors may seem to be quite acceptable, low levels of unemployment may require a firm to significantly increase its projected hourly wage scales to attract qualified workers. This sometimes unexpected increase may affect the overall attractiveness of a particular local area under consideration. The location study team will need to visit areas of potential interest to gather impressions and study attitudes regarding work ethic, absenteeism, potential labor-management issues, and the cooperativeness of state and local public officials.

Transportation Services and Infrastructure

Given the need by many firms for high-quality, capable transportation services, this factor is of great significance in many location decisions. Depending on the product type and industry to be served, a suitable location may require one or more of the following features: interstate highway access, availability of intermodal or local rail facilities, convenience of a major airport facility, proximity to inland or ocean port facilities, and so on. The number of serving carriers and the breadth of overall transport capabilities are factors that may need to be evaluated. Availability of capable transportation services and issues relating to transportation infrastructure may vary widely among regions of the world. In China, for example, investments in transportation infrastructure have been a key priority since they are viewed as being needed to sustain economic development.[4] For this reason, this topic deserves very deliberate and careful consideration in any network design decision.

Considering the significant service improvements that have been made in recent years by many transportation firms, most regional and local areas are strong in at least one or more areas related to transportation. For certain high-value, low-weight products, such as computers, semiconductors, and electronic equipment, the location decision may focus on identifying a single national or international geographical area from which to distribute the company's entire manufactured output. Given the time-sensitive logistics services available today from firms such as FedEx, UPS, DHL, and the postal services of many countries, this strategy is becoming more prevalent.

Also, on a global basis, it is important to assess the infrastructure capabilities of various geographies and countries. For example, the logistics and transportation road structure in China is continually improving, whereas there are longer-lasting highway deficiencies in parts of India that would be a relevant factor in a logistics/supply chain location decision.

Proximity to Markets and Customers

The nearness-to-market factor usually considers both logistics and competitive variables. Logistics variables include the availability of transportation, freight cost, and the geographical market size that can be served, for example, on a same-day or next-morning basis. The greater the number of customer firms within the market area, the greater the competitive advantage offered by the proposed location.

Although many companies place a high priority on locating logistics facilities near markets and customers, an overly complex logistics/supply chain network can be disadvantageous from a cost perspective. Also, the availability of high-quality transportation services and capable information technologies has resulted in an expansion of the geographical areas that can be served in a timely manner from key logistics facilities. In an extended sense, this has resulted in the enhanced role of global sourcing and global marketing, depending on the service needs of customers. Today's global logistics/supply chain capabilities may be enhanced to meet even more rigorous service levels that are established and expected by customers.

Quality of Life

A particular region's or area's quality of life is difficult to quantify, but it does affect the well-being of employees and the quality of work they are expected to perform. The quality-of-life factor is more important to companies that must attract and retain a mobile professional and technical workforce capable of moving to any location. Such a situation is common in the high-tech industry, especially in a company's research and development operations. The *Places Rated Almanac*[5] rates the quality of life in metropolitan areas in terms of climate, housing costs, health care and environment, crime, passenger transportation, education, recreation, the arts, and economic opportunities. Another useful source of information is *Cities Ranked and Rated.*[6]

Taxes and Industrial Development Incentives

It is important to have advance knowledge of state and local taxes that apply to businesses and individuals. Prevailing business taxes, including revenue or income taxes, inventory taxes, property taxes, and so on, will have a significant impact on the cost of operating a business in the area under consideration. Personal taxes that may affect the attractiveness of a particular region or local area include taxes on income and property, as well as applicable sales taxes, excise taxes, and so forth.

Another significant factor is the availability of industrial development incentives, which are used to entice companies to locate in a particular area. Examples include tax incentives (reduced rates or tax abatements on property, inventory, sales, etc.), financing arrangements (state loans or state-guaranteed loans), reduced water and sewage rates, and rent-free buildings that are built by the community to the company's specifications. Most countries, states, provinces, cities, etc., have an industrial development commission that provides information about state and local inducements. In addition, early contact and discussions with representatives of the state and local-area banking institutions and

On the Line

Global Sourcing and Manufacturing Compel Companies to Rethink U.S. Distribution Networks

When faced with finding new suppliers and providing new products for their customers, companies are turning more and more to solutions involving the use of outsourced logistics services. A typical scenario might look like the case of a company that sells shower curtain/curtain ring sets to retailers across the country. For many years, it has been sourcing these goods from a supplier in Mexico and processing shipments in its Dallas/Ft. Worth distribution center. Now, its largest customer, based in California, wants a unique, special curtain set it can private label.

The company finds the ideal item from a supplier in South Korea. Not only is it exactly what the customer wants, this premium item is less expensive than the company's usual sets. The South Korean supplier does not manufacture curtain rings, but a supplier is found in China that sells them for a fraction of the cost. The shipment from South Korea will enter the country through the Port of Tacoma; the Chinese goods through the Port of Long Beach.

In the old, centralized DC network, the company's response would include the following steps:

- Hire carriers to transport the goods from Tacoma and Long Beach to its DC in Dallas/Ft. Worth.
- Bundle and label the goods.
- Ship the finished goods back to the customer's warehouse in Los Angeles.

By the time it reaches the customer, the cost of transportation has made the premium product less profitable than its standard sets.

Under the scenario that would involve the use of outsourced logistics services, the overall process would include the following steps:

- Short-haul carriers transport the goods from Tacoma and Long Beach to a DC in Sacramento.
- There, the sets are assembled and compliance labeled.
- The finished goods are shipped to the customer's LA warehouse.

The new product now retains its healthy profit margin and the goods reach the customer in a fraction of the time, improving customer service. A simple example such as this illustrates a setting where an innovative solution to a sourcing issue may produce highly beneficial results.

Source: Adapted from "Outsourcing Distribution Centers Offers More Flexibility, Less Risk," White Paper published by Ryder Supply Chain Solutions, Ryder System, Inc., 2008, pp. 7–8. Copyright © 2008 by Syder Systems, Inc. All rights reserved. Reproduced by permission.

financial communities will provide a wide range of useful information, as well as commitments regarding financing and other services.

In 2006, Honda Motor Company announced its plans to build a $550 million automotive assembly plant in southeastern Indiana to help meet a growing demand in North America for its vehicles. Although four other sites were in contention for this location decision, Indiana offered $141.5 million in incentives to the company, which included tax credits and abatements, training assistance, and a promise to expedite the needed highway interchange upgrades that would facilitate transportation in the vicinity of the plant site.[7] A very interesting global example of the use of tax reductions and industrial development incentives is evidenced by the Shanghai Waigaoqiao Free Trade Zone, located in the Pudong New Area, Shanghai, China.[8] This facility was established in 1990 and includes total space of 10,000 square kilometers; its customers include companies such as Intel, Hewlett-Packard, Philips, IBM, and Emerson Electric. Interestingly, companies locating in the Waigaoqiao Free Trade Zone are given five years of preferential tax treatment. Instead of paying the corporate tax ratio of 15 percent, the tax rate to be paid starts at 8 percent and increases over the five-year period to the full 15 percent.

Supplier Networks

In the case of a manufacturing facility, the availability and cost of raw materials and component parts are of significance, as well as the cost of transporting these materials to the proposed plant site. For a distribution center, it is important to know how the proposed facility sites will fit with the geographic locations of key supplier facilities. In either instance, the cost and service sensitivity of the inbound movements from suppliers must be considered.

As an example, consider the case of Lear Corporation, a company that supplied seats for certain Ford Motor Company truck plants. Essentially, the seats were manufactured in sequence so that they could go right off the delivery vehicle onto the Ford assembly line in the order in which they would be installed. Faced with the need to expand, and knowing that its existing plant was landlocked, Lear chose a new plant site that was 10 minutes away from one plant and 20 minutes from the other. As a result, for 20 hours per day, trucks loaded with seats left the Lear factory every 15 minutes. According to Lear company officials, the location was about as far away from the customer as it can afford and still deliver true, just-in-time (JIT) deliveries.

Land Costs and Utilities

Depending on the type of facility under consideration, issues relating to the cost of land and the availability of needed utilities are more or less critical. In the case of a manufacturing plant or distribution center, for example, a certain minimum acreage or parcel size may be needed for current use as well as future expansion. This represents a potentially significant expense. Factors such as local building codes and cost of construction are important to consider. Also, the availability and expense of utilities such as electrical power, sewage, and industrial waste disposal need to be factored into the decision-making process.

Company Preference

Aside from all of the preceding types of factors, a company, or its CEO for that matter, may prefer a certain region and/or local area for the location of a logistics facility. For example, a company may prefer to locate all new facilities in rural areas within 50 miles of a major metropolitan area. Or a company may wish to locate its facilities in areas where competitors already have a presence. In other instances, a firm may wish to locate facilities in an area where it may enjoy common access with other firms to benefits such as a skilled labor supply, excellent marketing resources, or proximity to key supplier industries. This determinant is referred to as **agglomeration**, a phenomenon that sometimes explains why certain firms tend to co-locate facilities. As the trend toward globalization continues to develop in the business world today, it will be interesting to see the growth and expansion of agglomeration to achieve various types of synergies.

Current Trends Governing Site Selection

A number of trends in today's logistics environment may have a significant effect on decisions involving logistics facility location. Included among these are the following:

- Strategic positioning of inventories, such that fast-moving, profitable items may be located at "market-facing" logistics facilities. Slower-moving, less-profitable items may be located at more regional, or national, facilities. These examples are consistent with implementation of effective inventory segmentation strategies.

- Aside from a general trend toward the elimination of many wholesaler/distributor operations, companies are moving to greater use of "customer-direct" delivery from manufacturing and other upstream supply chain locations. Many times, this bypasses and diminishes the need for complete networks of distribution facilities. Increased use of drop shipments provides deliveries of product direct from manufacturing to the customer, thus eliminating the need for intermediate distribution capabilities.

- There is a growing use of and need for strategically located cross-docking facilities that serve as transfer points for consolidated shipments that need to be disaggregated or mixed into typically smaller shipments for delivery to individual customers. An example of this would be the consolidation of multiple-vendor shipments into full trailer loads being shipped to retail stores or points of use. Applied to inbound movements, this concept can significantly reduce the need for inbound consolidation facilities.

- Due diligence for location and site selection decisions is placing great emphasis on access to major airports and/or ocean ports for import and export shipments.

- Greater use of providers of third-party-logistics services, who may assume part or all of the responsibility for moving a firm's products to its customers, and/or moving its inbound parts and materials to its manufacturing process. In the global setting, many of these companies are developing specialized abilities to facilitate the movements of import and export shipments.

Modeling Approaches

This section focuses broadly on the topic of modeling approaches that can provide insight into the choice of a logistics/supply chain network design. As such, the techniques discussed here are applicable to a wide range of issues pertaining to the locations of plants, distribution centers, and customers and to the flows of product and information to support the functioning of the logistics/supply chain network. These apply to network design decisions that may be made on a domestic and/or global basis. The principal modeling approaches to be covered are optimization, simulation, and heuristic models. Detailed coverage of the grid method for facility location is included as part of the discussion of heuristic modeling approaches.

As was indicated previously, the use of appropriate modeling techniques will facilitate a comparison of the functioning and cost/service effectiveness of current versus proposed logistics/supply chain networks. Once an appropriate modeling procedure has been selected, it should be used to help identify a logistics network that is consistent with the key objectives identified earlier in the logistics/supply chain network redesign process.

After preliminary solutions have been identified, subsequent what-if types of analyses should be conducted to test the sensitivity of the recommended network designs to changes in key logistics/supply chain variables.

Optimization Models

The **optimization model** is based on precise mathematical procedures that are guaranteed to find the "best," or optimum, solution, given the mathematical definition of the problem under evaluation. This means that it can be proved mathematically that the resulting solution is the best. The simple EOQ model, discussed earlier, is an example of a technique that produces an optimum solution.

While recognizing relevant constraints, optimization approaches essentially select an optimal course of action from a number of feasible alternatives. The optimization models in use today incorporate such techniques as mathematical programming (linear, integer, dynamic, mixed-integer linear, etc.), enumeration, sequencing, and the use of calculus.[9] Many of these have been incorporated into software packages that are commercially available.

Figure 12.3 lists the types of issues that maybe addressed through the use of optimization techniques There are several advantages to using this overall type of approach:

- The user is guaranteed to have the best solution possible for a given set of assumptions and data.
- Many complex model structures can be handled correctly.
- The analysis and evaluation of all alternatives that are generated result in a more efficient analysis.
- Reliable run-to-run comparisons can be made since the best solution is guaranteed for each run.
- Cost or profit savings between the optimum and heuristic solution can be significant.[10]

Figure 12.3	Representative Strategic/Managerial Issues Relevant to Logistics/Supply Chain Network Modeling

I. **System Structure Issues**

    A. Number and Location of Raw Material Suppliers

    B. Number and Location of Plants

    C. Number and Location of Production Lines

    D. Number and Location of DCs

    E. Assignment of Plants to Suppliers

        1. DCs to Plants or Other DCs

        2. Customers to Plants or DCs

II. **Facility Ownership Issues**

    A. Owned

    B. Leased

    C. Public

III. **Facility Mission Issues**

    A. Raw Materials Suppliers

        1. Procurement Levels

        2. Costs and Capacities

    B. Plant Locations

        1. Manufacturing Levels

            a. Intermediate Products

            b. Finished Products

        2. Costs and Capacities

    C. DC Locations

        1. Throughput Levels

        2. Costs and Capacities

IV. **What-If Issues**

    A. Business Decision/Policy Issues

        1. Supply Chain Vulnerability

        2. Multi-Division Mergers

        3. Facility Capacity Changes

        4. Transportation Policy

        5. Seasonal Demand/Supply

        6. International Trade

        7. Customer Profitability

        8. Product Introductions/Deletions

        9. Alternative Networks

      10. Implementation Analysis

    B. Environmental Issues

        1. Economic Climate

        2. Competitive Pressures

        3. Disaster Planning

    C. Sensitivity Issues

        1. Cost versus Customer Service

        2. Cost versus Number of DCs

        3. Parametric Analysis of Inputs

Source: SAILS: Strategic Analysis of Integrated Logistics Systems (Manassas, VA: Insight, Inc. 2006). Reproduced by permission.

The classic objective of a network design model has been to establish the number, location, and size of finished goods distribution centers and associated product flows so as to minimize costs and maintain or improve customer service. Now the mandate is to design the *entire supply chain*, from source of raw materials to the final customer. This emerging view encompasses procurement, multiple stages or processes of manufacturing, distribution center functions, and all related transportation flows. The supply chain function is increasingly viewed as a competitive weapon, not just a service provider;

cost minimization is being supplanted by profit maximization (or enhancing shareholder equity); and national borders are dissolving. In short, answering network design questions today is virtually impossible without the help of very powerful decision support tools. There are just too many data to assimilate, and the combinations of facilities and support patterns number in the trillions. Fortunately, help is readily available for coping with this class of decision problems.[11]

One of the optimization techniques that has traditionally received significant attention is linear programming (LP). This approach is most useful for linking facilities in a network where supply and demand limitations at plants, distribution centers, or market areas must be treated as constraints. Given an objective function that focuses attention on, for example, minimizing total cost, LP defines the optimum facility distribution pattern consistent with the problem's demand-supply constraints. Although this technique is actually quite useful, its applicability is limited due to the need for the problem formulation to be deterministic and capable of linear approximation. Also, the use of LP itself does not allow for consideration of fixed as well as variable costs of operating logistics facilities.

On a more advanced scale, the use of mixed-integer linear programming allows consideration of issues such as fixed and variable costs, capacity constraints, economies of scale, cross-product limitations, and unique sourcing requirements. One of the leading models of this type is **Strategic Analysis of Integrated Logistics Systems (SAILS)**, developed by Insight, Inc. Figure 12.4 illustrates the supply chain complexity that may

Figure 12.4	**Supply Chain Complexity**

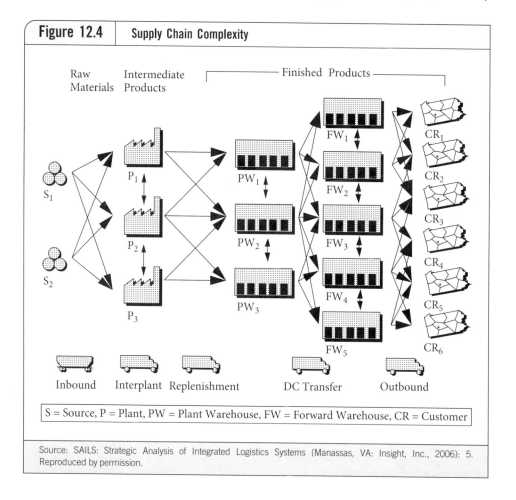

S = Source, P = Plant, PW = Plant Warehouse, FW = Forward Warehouse, CR = Customer

Source: SAILS: Strategic Analysis of Integrated Logistics Systems (Manassas, VA: Insight, Inc., 2006): 5. Reproduced by permission.

be addressed by a capable network optimization model such as SAILS. In brief, SAILS is a fully integrated decision support system that can be used to build, modify, solve, and interpret sophisticated strategic supply chain design models. Although SAILS is an off-the-shelf software package, it may be easily customized through an extensive array of model building, input data, and processing options to meet the requirements of a particular problem formulation. Although SAILS was designed originally to analyze *strategic* issues that involve longer-term resource commitments, many users have successfully addressed *tactical* issues as well, such as first-level production planning, production line balancing, seasonal pre-build, etc.[12] At press time for the publication of this textbook, Insight had planned the release of a significantly-enhanced version of SAILS to be known as ISCO (Insight Supply Chain Optimizer). Although ISCO is not a totally new product, the evolutionary enhancements to SAILS will position it to be a very significant, new addition to Insight's suite of supply chain planning solutions.

Once a modeling database has been created, either simple or complex, the use of SAILS facilitates the rapid generation and evaluation of many alternate scenarios for analysis.[13] Numerous shipment planning controls also permit the user to evaluate the network impact of various shipment planning options such as pooling, stop-offs, pickups, and direct plant shipments. SAILS is a highly flexible logistics modeling tool that can be used for a range of problems from the very simple to those in which data may exist in the form of millions of shipment transactions. When a given modeling scenario has been generated, SAILS utilizes mixed-integer linear programming, along with an advanced technique called **network factorization**, to produce an optimum solution. Typical data inputs to SAILS include customer demand (either forecast or historical); aggregated product and customer identification; facility data for plants and DCs; transportation options and rates; and policy considerations such as shipment planning rules, DC inventory constraints, and customer service requirements.

Although optimization approaches typically require significant computer resources, the availability of capable systems today has greatly facilitated their ease of use. Along with improvements in model design and solver technologies, future approaches should be even more convenient for general use by those involved with the design and analysis of logistics/supply chain networks.

In addition to improved analytical techniques, the availability of insightful visual representations of logistics networks has enhanced our ability to gain insight into network alternatives. Figure 12.5 is an example of the types of "geo-mapping" alternatives that are currently available.

Simulation Models

The second approach to logistics/supply chain network design includes the development and use of **simulation models.** Simulation is defined as "the process of designing a model of a real system and conducting experiments with this model for the purpose either of understanding the behavior of the system or of evaluating various strategies within the limits imposed by a criterion or set of criteria for the operation of the system."[14] Network simulation involves developing a computer representation of the logistics/supply chain network and then observing the cost and service characteristics of the network as cost structures, constraints, and other factors are varied. It has been stated that the process of simulation is "nothing more or less than the technique of performing *sampling experiments* on the model of the system."[15]

For location analysis, the use of simulation allows the decision maker to test the effect of alternative locations upon costs and service levels. The modeling requires extensive data

---

Figure 12.5 | **Example Geographical-Mapping Representations**

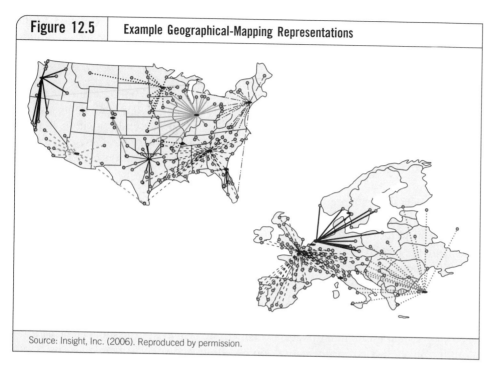

---

collection and analysis to determine how system factors such as transportation, warehousing, inventory, materials handling, and labor costs interact. The simulation process evaluates the decision maker's selected sites to determine respective costs. Simulation does not guarantee an optimum solution but simply evaluates the alternatives that are fed into it.[16] A critical characteristic of a simulation tool is whether it is static or dynamic in nature. A dynamic tool will not only incorporate a multiperiod time perspective but also update system status for each time period based on the results of the previous time periods.

According to Ballou, simulation has value in business network planning.[17] Although it does not search directly for the best warehouse configuration, its problem description can be very rich, including cost functions that are nonlinear (inventory), stepwise (labor costs), and discontinuous (quantity discounts). Simulation continues to be used as a stand-alone approach but also is used as a supplemental methodology within other search-oriented approaches. If for no other reason, simulation is needed to replicate, or cost out, the current logistics/supply chain network of a firm so that potential improvements from location analysis can be compared to it.

Although simulation models are not designed to produce optimum solutions, they are very capable in terms of their ability to incorporate relatively comprehensive and detailed problem descriptions. Sometimes an optimization approach is used first to identify and evaluate feasible network design alternatives, and then highly customized simulation models are used to focus on the exact logistics network that will best meet the desired objectives.

Heuristic Models

Heuristic models are able to accommodate broad problem definitions, but they do not provide an optimum solution. The use of a heuristic approach can help to reduce a problem to a manageable size and search automatically through various alternatives in an attempt to find a better solution. As is indicated in the discussion of the grid technique that follows, heuristic approaches can provide a good approximation to the least-cost location in a complex decision problem. To reduce the number of location alternatives, the decision maker should incorporate into the heuristic program site characteristics considered to be optimal.

For example, the location team may consider a desirable warehouse site to be (1) within 20 miles of a major market area, (2) at least 250 miles from other company distribution centers, (3) within three miles of an interstate highway, and (4) within 40 miles of a major airport facility. The heuristic model searches for sites with these characteristics, thus reducing the number of alternative sites to those the decision maker considers practical.

Additionally, heuristic decision rules are sometimes incorporated into the decision-making process in what may appear to be "rules of thumb." Examples might include requirements to locate distribution centers at or near points of demand, to supply customers from the nearest distribution facility, to choose as the next distribution site the one that will produce the greatest cost savings, or to serve all customers within a 24-hour delivery time.[18]

As we are reminded by Ratliff and Nulty,[19] sometimes the word *heuristics* implies a "seat-of-the-pants" solution approach, involving little or no intelligence or sophistication. They suggest that this is unfortunate, as many times analytical heuristics can be as technically sophisticated as mathematical optimization approaches. Many heuristics are based on mathematical optimization models and algorithms, such as using practical rules to formulate a mathematical optimization model. A powerful heuristic approach is to modify a mixed-integer program by temporarily assuming the integer variables to be linear in nature, thus creating an approximate but much more solvable model. Then the solution to this model is used as a basis for constructing a solution to the integer problem.

Potential Supply Chain Modeling Pitfalls to Avoid

According to Bender, a number of common pitfalls should be avoided in designing and implementing an optimum worldwide supply chain.[20] Recognizing these in advance should help to maximize the value to be achieved through use of appropriate mathematical techniques for supply chain network design.

- **Short-term horizon.** Unless modeling features are designed, implemented, and used with a long-term perspective, significant suboptimization is likely to occur.

- **Too little or too much detail.** Too little detail can make it difficult to implement results due to insufficient information; too much detail can create unnecessary complexity, making it difficult to understand the results and more difficult to implement effectively.

- **Thinking in two dimensions.** While the use of two-dimensional maps certainly helps to provide insight into supply chain problems, the geometry of the networks may ignore cost and geographical dispersions of demand. Over significant distances, and particularly for global supply chain analyses, the curvature of the earth may distort distance calculations, in which case needed adjustments must be made.

- **Using published costs.** Many published costs tend to represent "list" prices that need to be modified to reflect what may result after significant negotiations occur between buyers and sellers of transport services.

Supply Chain Technology

Supply Chain Network Design in an Era of Dynamic Costs

The topic of supply chain network design is of great significance to Dr. Jeffrey Karrenbauer, president and founding director of Insight, Inc., and J. Michael Kilgore, president and CEO of Chainalytics. The following comments reflect some of the thoughts of Dan Gilmore, editor of *Supply Chain Digest*, following the chance to speak in detail with both Jeff and Mike.

According to both Karrenbauer and Kilgore, a significant change such as increases in oil prices really does affect how you have to think about supply chain network design. In some cases the responses accentuate principles they have long been espousing, in some cases adding new wrinkles.

According to Kilgore, one impact is that many companies will need to redo or at least tweak their networks designs more often. "An increasing number of companies are recognizing the need to replan their networks more frequently, and adjust the strategy on at least an annual basis," Kilgore said. "When you combine the constant changes in business strategy with all the uncertainties in the supply chain right now, including the cost and dynamics of transportation, very few networks are good for more than about 12 months."

"You always forecast demand, but now you'll have to forecast costs in much the same way," Karrenbauer said. "What could look good in the short term could turn out to be really bad under a different set of cost assumptions. In the past, you could use a fairly static level of costs in the model, but now that's very dangerous. You need to evaluate a number of cost scenarios over multiple periods. That's not often done."

Some observations and recommendations were offered by these two industry experts:

- More and more companies may move to hedging transportation costs through the proxy of hedging oil prices. Being able to lock in a known cost of transportation for a period of time (say a year) provides additional stability in terms of designing logistics and supply chain networks.

- To maintain margins, it may be necessary at times to "fire" some customers, or at least to raise their prices to maintain margins. Alternatively, it may be necessary to offer a different level of service to be better-aligned with the price actually being paid.

- If you can reduce the number of manufacturing SKUs that need to be forecast, produced, and replenished to stocking points, it can significantly reduce the cost of transportation, in addition to creating other benefits.

- Private fleets may be under pressure. "Companies are frankly often less than honest about the real cost of private fleets," Karrenbauer noted. As the cost of fuel fluctuates, the appropriateness of a private fleet may change accordingly.

- The trade-offs between inventory and transportation will continue to migrate. Until recently, with lower transportation costs, the focus was more on inventory reduction. Now, companies will have to rethink that equation, and plan for how to adjust that balance if transport costs continue to soar.

According to Dan Gilmore, at the end of the day what all this says is that flexibility—the agile supply chain—is simply more necessary than ever.

- **Inaccurate or incomplete costs.** Analyses based on insufficiently accurate information lead to invalid results; inaccurate cost forecasts result in suboptimal allocations of resources, typically leading to seriously flawed strategies.

- **Fluctuating model inputs.** Given the prevailing uncertainties in many of the relevant inputs to today's network design models, it is important to conduct sensitivity analyses to be aware of the potential wide swings in key model inputs.

- **Use of erroneous analytical techniques.** The selected techniques and approaches should be matched with the level of precision desired; the identification of modeling objectives is an important forerunner to the selection of the techniques to be utilized.

- **Lack of appropriate robustness analysis.** Since most or all model inputs have at least an element of uncertainty, it is important to understand the consequences that could result from variation in actual behavior of key model inputs; robustness analysis can help to ensure the practicality and validity of the results from the selected analyses.

Example of a Heuristic Modeling Approach: The Grid Technique

Although other factors are also important, the availability and expense of transportation services are commonly included in location analyses. While transportation itself can represent a significant cost, decision makers should strive to make the final decision on the basis of the full range of relevant cost factors, as well as on the customer service implications of the network alternative being evaluated.

The grid technique is a simplistic, but well-known, heuristic approach to help companies with multiple markets and multiple supply points determine a least-cost facility location. Essentially, the grid technique attempts to determine a fixed facility (such as a plant or distribution center) location that represents the least-cost center for moving inbound materials and outbound product within a geographic grid. The technique determines the low-cost "center of gravity" for moving raw materials and finished goods.

This technique assumes that the raw materials sources and finished goods markets are fixed and that a company knows the amount of each product it consumes or sells. The technique then superimposes a grid upon the geographic area containing the raw materials sources and finished goods markets. The grid's zero point corresponds to an exact geographic location, as do the grid's other points. Thus, the company can identify each source and market by its grid coordinates.

Figure 12.6 is an example of a supply source and market environment for a company that is deciding where to locate a plant. The company, which has located supply sources and markets on the map and has superimposed a grid system over the source-market area, purchases raw materials from sources in Buffalo, Memphis, and St. Louis—S_1, S_2 and S_3, respectively. The new plant will serve five markets: Atlanta, Boston, Jacksonville, Philadelphia, and New York—M_1, M_2, M_3, M_4, and M_5, respectively.

The technique defines each source and market location in terms of its horizontal and vertical grid coordinates. For example, the Jacksonville market (M_3) has a horizontal grid coordinate of 800 and a vertical grid coordinate of 300. The Buffalo source is located at grid coordinates 700 horizontal and 1,125 vertical.

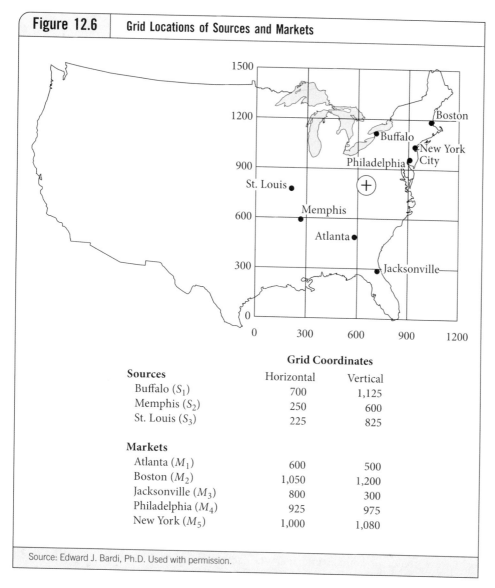

Figure 12.6 | **Grid Locations of Sources and Markets**

Grid Coordinates

Sources	Horizontal	Vertical
Buffalo (S_1)	700	1,125
Memphis (S_2)	250	600
St. Louis (S_3)	225	825

Markets		
Atlanta (M_1)	600	500
Boston (M_2)	1,050	1,200
Jacksonville (M_3)	800	300
Philadelphia (M_4)	925	975
New York (M_5)	1,000	1,080

Source: Edward J. Bardi, Ph.D. Used with permission.

We can visualize this technique's underlying concept as a series of strings to which are attached weights corresponding to the weight of raw materials the company consumes at each source and of finished goods the company sells at each market. The strings are threaded through holes in a flat plane; the holes correspond to the source and market locations. The strings' other ends are tied together, and the weights exert their respective pulls on the knot. The strings' knotted ends will finally reach equilibrium; this equilibrium will be the center of mass, or the ton-mile center.

We can compute this concept mathematically, finding the ton-mile center, or center of mass, as follows:

$$C = \frac{\sum\limits_{1}^{m} d_i S_i + \sum\limits_{1}^{n} D_i M_i}{\sum\limits_{1}^{m} S_i + \sum\limits_{1}^{n} M_i}$$

where

d_i = Center of mass, or ton–mile center
d_i = Distance from 0 point on grid to the grid location of raw material i
D_i = Distance from 0 point on grid to the grid location of finished good i
S_i = Weight (volume) of raw materials purchased at source i
M_i = Weight (volume) of finished goods sold in market i

This equation will generate the least-cost location if transportation rates for raw materials and finished goods are the same. But transportation rates vary among commodities, and the ton-mile center equation does not reflect differences in the costs of moving commodities. The transportation rate pulls the location toward the location of the commodity with the higher rate. Thus, the higher rates of finished goods will draw the least-cost location toward the finished goods market and thereby reduce the distance the company moves these higher-rated goods. This will increase the distance the company transports lower-rated raw materials.

Thus, we must incorporate into our analysis the transportation rates of different products. This modification is as follows:

$$C = \frac{\sum\limits_{1}^{m} r_i d_i S_i + \sum\limits_{1}^{n} R_i M_i}{\sum\limits_{1}^{m} r_i S_i + \sum\limits_{1}^{n} R_i M_i}$$

where

r_i = Raw materials rate/distance unit for raw material i
R_i = Finished goods transportation rate/distance unit for finished good i

r_i and R_i are the transportation rates per distance unit, and we assume them to be linear with respect to distance. This assumption does not correspond to the tapering principle of rates (to be discussed later in this chapter), but it does simplify the analysis.

Plant Location Example

Table 12.2 presents relevant data for a plant location example, as well as the grid technique solution using a computer spreadsheet program. The grid coordinates of the raw materials sources and markets correspond to their locations on the grid in Figure 12.6. For simplicity, we will assume that this company produces only one type of finished good, so that each finished good's transportation rate is the same.

To determine the least-cost center on the grid, we must compute two grid coordinates, one for moving the commodities along the horizontal axis and one for moving them along the vertical axis. We compute the two coordinates by using the grid technique formula for each direction.

Table 12.2 provides this example's computations. The two columns at the far right contain the calculations that the grid technique equation indicates. The first calculations column contains the calculations for the horizontal numerator, or the sum of the rate times the horizontal grid coordinate times the tonnage for each raw materials source and market. The calculations at the bottom of Table 12.2 indicate the numerator and denominator of the grid technique equation.

As Table 12.2 indicates, the plant location's least-cost center in this example is 655 in the horizontal direction and 826 in the vertical direction. We measure both distances from the grid's zero point. Figure 12.6 indicates the least-cost center as point +. The

Table 12.2	Grid Technique Analysis of Plant Location Example					
SOURCES/ MARKETS	RATE $/TON-MILE (A)	TONS (B)	GRID COORDINATES		CALCULATIONS	
			HORIZONTAL	VERTICAL	(A) × (B) × HORIZONTAL	(A) × (B) × VERTICAL
Buffalo (S_1)	$0.90	500	700	1,125	315,000	506,250
Memphis (S_2)	$0.95	300	250	600	71,250	171,000
St. Louis (S_3)	$0.85	700	225	825	133,875	490,875
		1,500			520,125	1,168,125
Atlanta (M_1)	$1.50	225	600	500	202,500	168,750
Boston (M_2)	$1.50	150	1,050	1,200	236,250	270,000
Jacksonville (M_3)	$1.50	250	800	300	300,000	112,500
Philadelphia (M_4)	$1.50	175	925	975	242,813	255,938
New York (M_5)	$1.50	300	1,000	1,080	450,000	486,000
TOTALS		1,100			1,431,563	1,293,188
					HORIZONTAL	VERTICAL
			Numerator: $\Sigma(r \times d \times S) =$		520,125	1,168,125
			$+\Sigma(R \times D \times M) =$		1,431,563	1,293,188
			Sum		1,951,688	2,461,313
			Denominator: $\Sigma(r \times S) =$		1,330	1,330
			$+\Sigma(R \times M) =$		1,650	1,650
			Sum		2,980	2,980
			Grid Center		655	826

Source: Edward J. Bardi, Ph.D. Used with permission.

least-cost location for the plant is in southeastern Ohio or northwestern West Virginia in the Wheeling-Parkersburg area.

The preceding example applied the grid technique to a plant location. Companies can use the technique to solve warehousing location problems as well. The company follows the same procedure, but the company's plants are the raw materials sources.

Advantages

The grid technique's strengths are in its simplicity and its ability to provide a starting point for location analysis. Computationally, the technique is relatively easy to use. A company can generate the necessary data from sales figures, purchase records, and transportation documents (either the bill of lading or the freight bill). More exact market and source location coding is possible, as is modifying the rate–distance relationship quantification. A computer can easily handle such refinements.

The grid technique also provides a starting point for making a location decision. Although transportation cost is not the only locational determinant, use of the grid technique can help at an early stage in the network design process by helping the decision maker to focus on an area or areas that are logistically advantageous. For example, use of the grid technique may suggest that a distribution center located in The Netherlands may be logistically advantageous to serve as a point of distribution for shipments destined to points of final delivery in Western Europe. This is a great step forward in the location decision process, as further steps in the process may help to identify preferred locations within the broader area that is targeted.

Limitations

The grid technique has limitations that the decision maker must recognize. First, it is a static approach, and the solution is optimum for only one point in time. Changes in the volumes a company purchases or sells, changes in transportation rates, or changes in raw materials sources or market locations will shift the least-cost location. Second, the technique assumes linear transportation rates, whereas actual transportation rates increase with distance but less than proportionally. Third, the technique does not consider the topographic conditions existing at the optimum location; for example, the recommended site may be in the middle of a lake. Fourth, it does not consider the proper direction of movement; most moves occur along a straight line between two points, not "vertically" and then "horizontally."

Sensitivity Analysis

As mentioned in the preceding paragraph, the grid technique is a static approach; the computed location is valid only for the situation analyzed. If the transportation rates, market and source locations, and volumes change, then the least-cost location changes.

Sensitivity analysis enables the decision maker to ask what-if questions and measure the resulting impact on the least-cost location. For example, the decision maker may examine the least-cost location in light of a five-year sales projection by inserting the estimated market sales volumes into the grid technique equation and determining the least-cost location. Other what-if scenarios could include adding new markets and/or sources, eliminating markets and/or sources, and switching transportation modes, thereby changing rates.

Tables 12.3 and 12.4 perform two sensitivity analyses for the original problem in Table 12.2. The first what-if scenario considers switching from rail to truck to serve the Jacksonville market; the switch entails a 50 percent rate increase. The data in Table 12.3 show that the rate increase shifts the least-cost location toward Jacksonville; that is, the new location grid coordinates are 664 and 795, or east and south of the original location (655, 826). Therefore, a rate increase will pull the least-cost location toward the market or supply source experiencing the increase.

The second what-if sensitivity analysis considers the elimination of a Buffalo supply source and increasing by 500 tons the amount the example company purchases from Memphis. Table 12.4 shows the effect of this sourcing change. With Memphis supplying all the material the company formerly purchased from Buffalo, the new least-cost location moves toward Memphis, or south and west of the original location. Similarly, a new market or a market experiencing a sales volume increase will draw the least-cost location.

We can conclude from these sensitivity analyses that the rates, product volumes, and source/market locations do affect a plant's least-cost location. The least-cost location

Table 12.3	Impact of Transportation Rate Change on Least-Cost Location					
SOURCES/ MARKETS	**RATE $/TON-MILE (A)**	**TONS (B)**	**GRID COORDINATES**		**CALCULATIONS**	
			HORIZONTAL	**VERTICAL**	**(A) × (B) × HORIZONTAL**	**(A) × (B) × VERTICAL**
Buffalo (S_1)	$0.90	500	700	1,125	315,000	506,250
Memphis (S_2)	$0.95	300	250	600	71,250	171,000
St. Louis (S_3)	$0.85	700	225	825	133,875	490,875
		1,500			520,125	1,168,125
Atlanta (M_1)	$1.50	225	600	500	202,500	168,750
Boston (M_2)	$1.50	150	1,050	1,200	236,250	270,000
Jacksonville (M_3)	$2.25	250	800	300	450,000	168,750
Philadelphia (M_4)	$1.50	175	925	975	242,813	255,938
New York (M_5)	$1.50	300	1,000	1,080	450,000	486,000
	TOTALS	1,100			1,581,563	1,349,438
					HORIZONTAL	**VERTICAL**
			Numerator: $\Sigma (r \times d \times S) =$		520,125	1,168,125
			$+ \Sigma (R \times D \times M) =$		1,581,563	1,349,438
			Sum		2,101,688	2,517,563
			Denominator: $\Sigma (r \times S) =$		1,330	1,330
			$+ \Sigma (R \times M) =$		1,838	1,838
			Sum		3,168	3,168
			Grid Center		664	795

Source: Edward J. Bardi, Ph.D. Used with permission.

moves toward a market or source experiencing a rate or volume increase, and away from the market or source experiencing a decrease. Introducing a new market or source pulls the location toward the additional market or source.

Application to Warehouse Location in a City

A special case exists for applying the grid technique to the location of a warehouse in a city. The situation's uniqueness comes from the blanket rate structure, which applies the same rate from an origin to any point within the city or commercial zone. Thus, any location within a city's commercial zone incurs the same inbound transportation cost from a company's mix of suppliers used; that is, the cost of moving supplies to a warehouse within the same city does not affect the location decision.

Since the supply volumes moving into the warehouse do not affect the location decision, the least-cost warehouse location within a city considers the cost of moving finished

Table 12.4   Impact of Supply Source Change on Least-Cost Location

SOURCES/ MARKETS	RATE $/TON-MILE (A)	TONS (B)	GRID COORDINATES		CALCULATIONS	
			HORIZONTAL	VERTICAL	(A) × (B) × HORIZONTAL	(A) × (B) × VERTICAL
Buffalo (S_1)	$0.90	0	700	1,125	0	0
Memphis (S_2)	$0.95	800	250	600	190,000	456,000
St. Louis (S_3)	$0.85	700	225	825	133,875	490,875
		1,500			323,875	946,875
Atlanta (M_1)	$1.50	225	600	500	202,500	168,750
Boston (M_2)	$1.50	150	1,050	1,200	236,250	270,000
Jacksonville (M_3)	$2.25	250	800	300	450,000	168,750
Philadelphia (M_4)	$1.50	175	925	975	242,813	255,938
New York (M_5)	$1.50	300	1,000	1,080	450,000	486,000
TOTALS		1,100			1,581,563	1,349,438
					HORIZONTAL	VERTICAL
			Numerator: $\Sigma (r \times d \times S) =$		323,875	946,875
			$+\Sigma (R \times D \times M) =$		1,581,563	1,349,438
			Sum		1,905,438	2,296,313
			Denominator: $\Sigma (r \times S) =$		1,355	1,355
			$+\Sigma (R \times M) =$		1,838	1,838
			Sum		3,193	3,193
			Grid Center		597	719

goods from the warehouse to the customers. We modify the grid technique equation as follows:

$$C = \frac{\sum_{1}^{n} R_i D_i M_i}{\sum_{1}^{n} R_i M_i}$$

If we assume that the cost of distributing (.R) the commodity throughout the city is the same, .R cancels out, reducing the equation to a ton-mile center as follows:

$$C = \frac{\sum_{i}^{n} D_i M_i}{\sum_{1}^{n} M_i}$$

As before, this modified grid technique enables the decision maker to eliminate certain areas of the city and to concentrate the analysis upon sites in the general vicinity of the least-cost location's grid coordinates. To determine a specific site for the warehouse, the decision maker must consider land and facility availability, expressway systems, and highway access in this general vicinity.

Transportation Pragmatics[21]

The previous discussion showed the importance of the transportation factor in the facility location decision. We simplified the rate structure focus on the transportation factor's locational pull. In this section, we examine how dropping these transportation simplifications affects facility location, directing attention specifically toward tapering rates, blanket rates, commercial zones, foreign trade zones, and in-transit privileges.

Tapering Rates

As we pointed out earlier, transportation rates increase with distance but not in direct proportion to distance. This **tapering-rate principle** results from the carrier's ability to spread certain fixed shipment costs, such as loading, billing, and handling, over a greater number of miles. As noted by Edgar M. Hoover, a tapering rate in a one-source, one-market situation pulls the location to either the source or the market but not to a point in between.

To illustrate this effect, consider the data in Table 12.5 and Figure 12.7. In this example, we assume the rates to be constant (the same) for raw materials supplied at S and finished products sold at M. The rates in Table 12.5 increase with distance but not proportionally. For example, the shipping rate from S is $2.00 for 50 miles and $3.00 for 100 miles, a distance increase of 100 percent but a rate increase of only 50 percent.

Table 12.5 and Figure 12.7 indicate that a location at either S or M will result in a total rate of $3.70. At any other location, the total rate is higher. Thus, the tapering rate pulls the location toward the source or the market.

Dropping rate constancy between raw materials and finished goods draws the location toward M, the market. In Table 12.6 and Figure 12.8, the rates for moving the finished product into the market are higher than those for moving raw materials. The location having the least total transportation cost is at M, where the total transportation rate is $3.70.

Blanket Rates

A noted exception to the preceding rate structure is the **blanket rate.** The blanket rate does not increase with distance; it remains the same from one origin to all points in the blanket area. The carriers establish such rates to ensure a competitive price for a product

Table 12.5	Locational Effects of Tapering Rates with Constant Rate Assumption			
DISTANCE FROM *S* (MILES)	TRANSPORT RATE FROM *S*	DISTANCE TO *M* (MILES)	TRANSPORT RATE TO *M*	TOTAL TRANSPORT RATE
0	$0.00	200	$3.70	$3.70
50	2.00	150	3.50	5.50
100	3.00	100	3.00	6.00
150	3.50	50	2.00	5.50
200	3.70	0	0.00	3.70

Source: Edward J. Bardi, Ph.D. Used with permission.

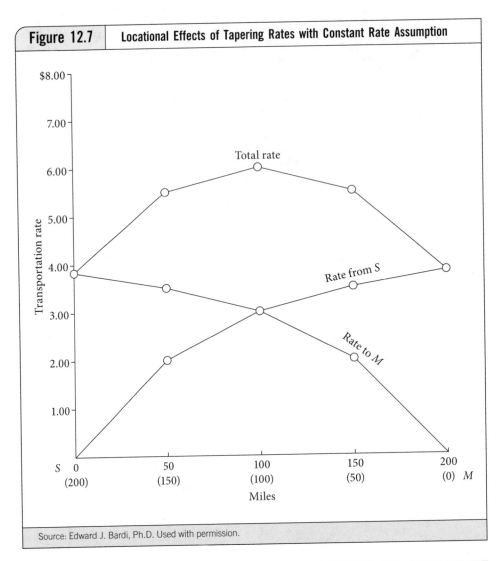

Figure 12.7 | **Locational Effects of Tapering Rates with Constant Rate Assumption**

Source: Edward J. Bardi, Ph.D. Used with permission.

Table 12.6 | **Locational Effects of Tapering Rates without Constant Rate Assumption**

DISTANCE FROM S (MILES)	TRANSPORT RATE FROM S	DISTANCE TO M (MILES)	TRANSPORT RATE TO M	TOTAL TRANSPORT RATE
0	$0.00	200	$5.20	$5.20
50	2.00	150	5.00	7.00
100	3.00	100	4.50	7.50
150	3.50	50	3.50	7.00
200	3.70	0	0.00	3.70

Source: Edward J. Bardi, Ph.D. Used with permission.

in a given area, thereby ensuring demand for the product and its transportation. An example of a blanket rate would be the same rate on wine traveling from the West Coast to all points east of the Rocky Mountains, enabling the West Coast wine to compete with imported wines entering the East Coast.

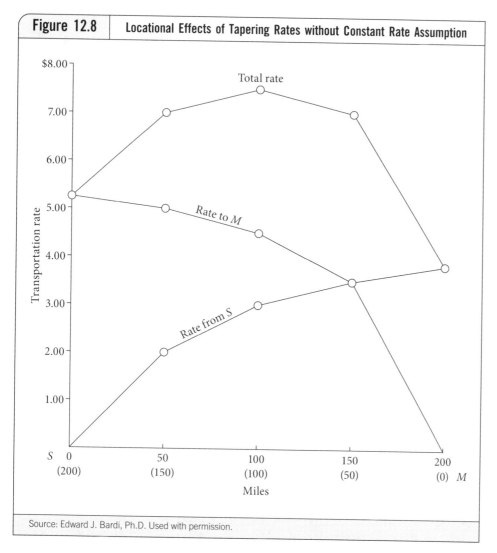

Figure 12.8 | **Locational Effects of Tapering Rates without Constant Rate Assumption**

Source: Edward J. Bardi, Ph.D. Used with permission.

The blanket rate eliminates any transportation cost advantage or disadvantage that companies associate with a given location. In the case of the wine blanket rates, the West Coast wine producers can effectively compete in the East Coast market area with East Coast and foreign producers. The blanket rate, then, is a mutation of the basic rate-distance relationship that eliminates the transportation rate as a locational determinant; it is the exception rather than the rule in transportation rates.

Commercial Zones

A specific blanket area is the **commercial zone**, the transportation definition of a particular city or town. It includes the municipality itself plus various surrounding areas. The commercial zone rates that carriers quote to a particular town or city also apply to points in the surrounding area within the commercial zone.

The commercial zone's locational impact appears near the end of the location decision process when a company selects a specific site. If the specific site is beyond the limits of a municipality's commercial zone, rates that apply to the city do not apply to the site. Also, a site outside the commercial zone reduces carrier availability, especially the availability of motor carriers that define their operating scopes in terms of point-to-point operations.

Foreign Trade Zones[22]

As previously discussed, a **foreign trade zone (FTZ)** is a geographic area into which importers can enter a product and hold it without paying duties—and only paying duties or customs when is it shipped into U.S. customs territory. A variety of activities can be conducted in an FTZ, including assembling, packaging, destroying, storing, cleaning, exhibiting, distributing, sorting, grading, testing, labeling, repairing, combining with foreign or domestic content, or processing.[23] Advantages of FTZs include the following:

- Deferred customs duties and federal excise taxes on imports
- No duties or quota payments on re-exported materials
- Choice of duty rates paid—based either on the rate for component parts or for the finished product
- Exemption from state and local inventory taxes or foreign and domestic goods that are to be exported

The availability of FTZ benefits can impact the design of a firm's logistics network. For example, Ryder Group operates a foreign trade zone, Kelly USA, on the former Kelly Air Force Base in San Antonio, Texas. The Trade Processing Center operated by Ryder is a 40,000-square-foot facility with an on-site Mexican freight broker who serves as a liaison between Ryder's U.S. and Mexican operations. Also, the complex operates seven days a week with door-to-door services for over-the-road trucking, rail, air, and ocean transport of goods.

Another example of how a foreign trade zone can help a company is Foreign Trade Zone 50 in Long Beach, California.[24] This involves an electronics company that imports 40,000 electrical capacitors per year from Asia at a value of $200 per unit or 9.6 percent duty rate. The company requested permission to manipulate the merchandise (e.g., open cartons, perform quality control inspections, and repackage cartons) prior to re-exportation to Mexico. The final product then is exported to a free zone within a Mexican maquiladora for manufacturing of the finished goods. The company benefits from duty elimination within Foreign Trade Zone 50 and realizes a yearly zone savings of U.S. $768,000.

Other well-known companies that utilize foreign trade zones include Northrop Grumman, Kawasaki Motors Manufacturing Corp., BMW Manufacturing Corp., General Electric Co., JVC America, and Caterpillar, Inc.[25]

Transit Privileges

Basically, the **transit privilege** permits the shipper to stop a shipment in transit and to perform some function that physically changes the product's characteristic. The lower through rate from origin to final destination (the tapering-rate principle) applies, rather than the higher combination of rates from origin to transit point and from transit point to final destination.

The transit privilege essentially makes intermediate locations, rather than just origins or destinations, optimum. The transit privilege eliminates any geographic disadvantage that companies associate with a producer's location. The intermediate point the carrier designates as a transit point enjoys the lower, long-distance through rate that applies at either the origin or the destination.

Like the blanket rate, the transit privilege is not available at all locations or for all commodities—only those sites and commodities the carrier specifies. If a commodity benefits from the availability of a transit privilege, the limited points specified by the carrier will be prime facility location alternatives.

SUMMARY

- The logistics/supply chain network design decision is of great strategic importance to logistics, the firm as a whole, and the supply chain. This decision is becoming increasingly important due to trends related to the globalization of manufacturing, marketing, sourcing, and procurement.
- A number of factors may suggest the need to redesign the logistics/supply chain network.
- A formal, structured process for network design is preferable; the potential impacts on cost and service justify a significant effort toward following a sound process.
- Numerous factors may affect the design of a logistics network and the location of specific facilities within the context of the network.
- Principal modeling approaches to gain insight into the topic of logistics/supply chain network design include optimization, simulation, and heuristic models.
- The grid method represents a useful way to obtain a good, but not necessarily optimal, solution to a logistics facility location problem.
- The availability and cost of transportation affect the location decision in a number of significant and unique ways.

STUDY QUESTIONS

1. In what ways can the design of a firm's logistics/supply chain network affect its ability to create value for customers through efficiency, effectiveness, and differentiation?

2. What are the steps in the process of logistics/supply chain network design? Of these steps, which are most relevant to the task of selecting a specific site for a logistics facility?

3. Discuss the factors that cause a company to analyze the design of a logistics/supply chain network or to reconsider the location of a particular facility.

4. Why are most location decisions analyzed by a team of managers instead of a single person? What types of teams are suggested as being helpful to the task of logistics network redesign?

5. What are the major locational determinants, and how does each affect the location decision?

6. What is the difference between a regional/national location decision, and in what ways do the determinants of each differ?

7. Discuss the role of logistics variables in the decision as to where to locate a plant or distribution center.

8. What are the principal types of modeling techniques that apply to the task of logistics/supply chain network design and facility location? What are the strengths and limitations of each?

9. Describe the grid technique. What is its purpose, and how does it lead to the making of a decision? What are its strengths and limitations?

10. Using the grid technique, determine the least-cost location for the following problems:

(a)

	TONS	RATE	GRID COORDINATES (H, V)
S_1	200	0.50	2, 14
S_2	300	0.60	6, 10
M_1	100	1.00	2, 2
M_2	100	2.00	10, 14
M_3	100	1.00	14, 18
M_4	100	2.00	14, 6

	Tons	Rate	Grid Coordinates (H,V)
S_1	200	0.50	2, 14
S_2	300	0.60	6, 10
M_1	100	1.00	2, 2
M_2	100	2.00	10, 14
M_3	100	1.00	14, 18
M_4	100	2.00	14, 6

(b)

CUSTOMER	TONS	GRID COORDINATES (H, V)
A	100	1, 11
B	300	7, 11
C	200	5, 9
D	500	7, 7
E	1,000	1, 1

Customer	Tons	Grid Coordinates (H,V)
A	100	1, 11
B	300	7, 11
C	200	5, 9
D	500	7, 7
E	1,000	1, 1

11. Explain how tapering rates, blanket rates, commercial zones, foreign trade zones, and in-transit privileges affect the facility location decision.

NOTES

1. http://www.industryweek.com, Article ID 12125.

2. Morgan Stanley, 2006.

3. For example, see http://www.forwardair.com

4. Figures relating to the development of transportation infrastructure in China suggest that in the 50 years from 1949 to 1999, road length in China increased 16 times, highway and expressways increased by 15 times, and seaport terminals increased by 7.6 times By the end of 1999, passenger transportation had increased by 100 times that of 1949 and cargo transportation increased 155 times. Adapted from Charles Guowen Wang, *CSCMP Global Perspectives China* (Oak Brook, IL: Council of Supply Chain Management Professionals, 2006) and the official Web site of the China Ministry of Communications.

5. David Savageau, *Places Rated Almanac* (Washington, DC: Places Rated Books, LLC, 2011).

6. Bert Sperling and Peter Sander, *Cities Ranked and Rated: More Than 400 Metropolitan Areas Evaluated in the US and Canada*, 2nd ed. (Hoboken, NJ: Wiley Publishing Company, 2009).

7. *Knoxville News Sentinel* (June 29, 2006): 1.

8. *Investing in Waigaoqiao Free Trade Zone*, Shanghai Waigaoqiao Free Trade Zone United Development Co., Ltd., 2005.

9. Ronald H. Ballou, *Business Logistics Management*, 3rd ed. (Englewood Cliffs, NJ: Prentice-Hall, 1992): 297.

10. Richard F. Powers, "Optimization Models for Logistics Decisions," *Journal of Business Logistics* 10, No 1 (1989): 106.

11. SAILS Strategic Analysis of Integrated Logistics Systems (Manassas, VA Insight, Inc., 2006).

12. Ibid.

13. Ibid.

14. Robert E. Shannon, *Systems Simulation: The Art and Science* (Englewood Cliffs, NJ: Prentice-Hall, 1975): 1.

15. Frederick S. Hillier and Gerald J. Lieberman, *Introduction to Operations Research*, 3rd ed. (San Francisco, CA: Holden-Day, Inc., 1980): 643.

16. For an excellent overview of simulation modeling, see Donald J. Bowersox and David J. Closs, "Simulation in Logistics: A Review of Present Practice and a Look to the Future," *Journal of Business Logistics* 10, No. 1 (1989): 133–148.

17. Ronald H. Ballou, "Logistics Network Design: Modeling and Informational Considerations," *The International Journal of Logistics Managements* 6, No. 2 (1995): 47.

18. For additional examples and a comprehensive perspective on heuristic modeling, see Ronald H. Ballou, "Heuristics Rules of Thumb for Logistics Decision Making," *Journal of Business Logistics* 10, No. 1 (1989): 122–132.

19. Donald H. Ratliff and William G. Nulty, *Logistics Composite Modeling* (Atlanta, GA: Ratliff and Nulty, 1996): 38.

20. The content of this section has been adapted from Paul S. Bender, "How to Design an Optimum Supply Chain," *Supply Chain Management Review* (Spring 1997): 79–80.

21. Portions of this section are adapted from Edward J. Taaffe and Howard L. Gauthier Jr., *Geography of Transportation* (Englewood Cliffs, NJ: Prentice-Hall, 1973): 41–43.

22. Margaret Gordetsky, "Ryder Puts Customers in the Foreign Trade Zone," *Transport Topics* (August 28, 2000): 26.

23. Trade Information Center, http://www.la.ita.doc.gov/ftzpage/tic.html

24. Retrieved from http://www.expansionmanagement.com/cmd/articledetail/articleid/15924/default.asp

25. Ibid.

CASE 12.1

Johnson & Johnson

Healthcare consumer packaged goods giant Johnson & Johnson's (J&J) European operations were comprised of 12 distribution centers in seven countries. The company's initial analysis showed there was little or no consolidation among facilities. The facilities had high operational costs (U.S. $10 million+), but transportation costs were relatively low (U.S. $6 million+). The distribution centers were geographically located to help meet the specific needs and service expectations of their European customers. Since J&J is always on the lookout for ways to streamline and improve its supply chain practices, it was very interested in ways to improve its manufacturing and distribution activities in Europe.

An initial result of applying the network optimization software was a reduction in the number of distribution centers from 12 to 2. Although this scenario was accompanied by increases in the transportation costs to customer locations, overall systems costs decreased by U.S. $7 million. Given the strategic importance of maintaining acceptably high levels of customer service, however, it was important to incorporate the requirement of retaining reasonable customer service levels (i.e., one-day service for some customers, with two-day service for others) into the formulation of the network optimization model. In addition, it also was necessary for the model to consider factors such as the expense of long-term leases, etc.

Subsequently, a network optimization model that responded to the issues discussed above was developed and utilized. The end result included a reduction in the number of distribution centers from 12 to 5, which translated into a decrease in facility costs from U.S. $10.1 million to U.S. $3.9 million. Although transportation costs increased slightly—from U.S. $6.6 million to U.S. $7.6 million, the overall network experienced a system savings of approximately U.S. $5 million. At the same time, the optimized network was able to meet customer service objectives such as those outlined above.

CASE QUESTIONS

1. What factors help to explain why J&J historically had as many as 12 distribution centers in Europe?

2. What steps in the logistics/supply chain network design process discussed in this chapter would have been most relevant to the task faced by J&J in Europe?

3. Are there other factors that the network optimization study should have considered?

4. This case study focuses on the shipments from distribution centers to customer locations. What factors on the supply side, or inbound-to-DC-side, would be relevant to the analysis that was conducted?

Source: Adapted from Insight, Inc. (2006). Reproduced by permission.

CASE 12.2
Fireside Tire Company

Fireside Tire Company, a manufacturer of radial tires for sport utility vehicles, sells its products in the automotive aftermarket and distributes them throughout the United States. Fireside has three tire production plants located in Allentown, Pennsylvania; Toledo, Ohio; and Macomb, Illinois (see map). Normally, Fireside ships tires from its plants to distribution centers, but truckload-size purchases typically are transported directly from plants to customer locations. All shipments to a region move under truck-load rates applying to a minimum weight of 40,000 pounds, or 400 cwt.

Fireside management is concerned about the most economical location for a distribution center to serve its southeastern region, consisting of North Carolina, South Carolina, Georgia, Florida, Mississippi, Alabama, and southeastern Tennessee. Although an Atlanta distribution center currently serves this region, Fireside management is concerned that the Atlanta location is not the most logistically sound alternative.

To help the logistics department conduct an analysis of this region's distribution center location using the grid method, Fireside's transportation department developed the following data based on projections for 2012:

	2012 SHIPMENTS TO ATLANTA			GRID COORDINATES	
FROM	CWT	RATE/CWT	MILEAGE	HORIZONTAL	VERTICAL
Toledo	15,000	$2.20	640	1,360	1,160
Macomb	5,000	2.43	735	980	1,070
Allentown	11,000	2.52	780	1,840	1,150

2012 SHIPMENTS FROM ATLANTA		GRID COORDINATES	
TO	CWT	HORIZONTAL	VERTICAL
Chattanooga	2,700	1,350	650
Atlanta	3,500	1,400	600
Tampa	4,300	1,570	220
Birmingham	2,800	1,260	580
Miami	5,300	1,740	90
Jacksonville	5,100	1,600	450
Columbia	2,200	1,600	650
Charlotte	2,900	1,590	740
Raleigh/Durham	2,200	1,700	800

The transportation department also determined that total freight expenditures from the Atlanta distribution center during 2012 were $217,000 and that the average shipment distance was 330 miles.

CASE QUESTIONS

1. Based on the available information, is Atlanta the best location for a distribution center to serve the southeastern region? If not, what would you recommend?

2. The Fireside transportation department projects a 25 percent rate increase in 2013 from all of its transportation providers. How will this affect the southeastern location?

3. Marketing anticipates that the Raleigh/Durham market will grow by 3,000 cwt in 2014, and that Fireside will serve the growth from Allentown. How will this affect Atlanta as a location?

Chapter 13

SOURCING MATERIALS AND SERVICES

Learning Objectives

After reading this chapter, you should be able to do the following:

- Understand the role and nature of purchasing, procurement, and strategic sourcing in a supply chain context.

- Consider the importance of types and of items and services purchased to the sourcing and procurement processes.

- Understand the strategic sourcing process.

- Recognize principles and approaches for the effective management of sourcing and procurement activities.

- Appreciate the importance of companies having effective relationships with suppliers and understand the value of supplier organizations having certain certifications and registrations.

- Examine the issue of procurement price and the relevance of total landed cost (TLC).

- Be aware of contemporary advances in the areas of e-sourcing and e-procurement.

Supply Chain Profile   *Achieving Greater Cost Savings for Global Manufacturers Through Merger of Supply Chain Service Providers*

In July 2009, Elemica, a leading global supply chain services provider, and RubberNetwork, a global sourcing and supply chain company announced that they had merged. The combined company, which continued to operate under the name Elemica, provides even greater supply chain efficiencies and cost savings for global manufacturers who are looking to gain a competitive advantage in today's challenging marketplace. Positive results from the merger were expected quickly as the combined product portfolio provides a complete suite of capabilities to unlock cash in the supply chain for the company's clients.

Elemica is a leader in supply chain integration and execution, with a significant presence in the chemical industry. RubberNetwork is the leader in sourcing and supply chain integration for the global tire and rubber industry. The two highly complementary companies joined forces to deliver closer collaboration for global manufacturing supply chain partners. RubberNetwork's comprehensive sourcing services united with Elemica's robust supply chain network will be valuable to the combined client base as well as new customers that the company is expecting to sign.

Elemica and RubberNetwork enable collaboration for buyers, suppliers, and logistics service providers and facilitate stronger relationships through exceptional business-to-business integration. Cost reduction and performance improvement goals for their customers are enhanced through the integration of the companies' individual capabilities. Ultimately, Elemica will have approximately 2,500 partners connected to its supply chain network. The company integrates dissimilar business systems into one unified network across all customers, suppliers, and third party providers, irrespective of company size or industry, helping companies cut structural costs from the supply chain. Savings are realized through seamless execution of business processes such as order-to-invoice, procure-to-pay, and logistics, resulting in error reduction and lowered inventories. Sourcing services allow customers to reduce procurement costs primarily for indirect materials and services using online bidding technology, negotiation strategies, and targeted benchmarking.

The global footprint of the merged company includes offices in Atlanta, Amsterdam, Frankfurt, London, Seoul, Shanghai, Singapore, and Tokyo. Headquarters remain in Exton, Pennsylvania.

Source: Adapted from press release titled "Elemica and RubberNetwork Merge," July 31, 2009, available at www.elemica.com. Reproduced by permission.

Introduction

Logistics and supply chain managers are looking for ways to drive more value from their purchasing and procurement operations. Whether it may be pressure from demanding customers, the emergence of lower-cost competition from global sources, or the complexity of supply chains, executives are finding that the time-honored emphasis on low-cost purchasing just isn't cutting it anymore.

As a result, the topics of purchasing, procurement, and strategic sourcing are all receiving considerable attention as organizations try to improve the overall efficiency and effectiveness of their supply chains. While the definitions provided below are intended to aid understanding of some of the similarities, differences, and linkages between purchasing, procurement, and strategic sourcing, it is not uncommon in practice for these terms to be used somewhat interchangeably at times.

- **Purchasing:** The transactional function of buying products and services. In a business setting, this commonly involves the placement and processing of a purchase order. Typically, this activity follows the conduct of a formal sourcing process.

- **Procurement:** Refers to the process of managing a broad range of processes that are associated with a company's need to procure goods and services that are required to manufacture a product (direct) or to operate the organization (indirect). Example activities within the procurement process include product/service sourcing, supplier selection, price negotiation, contract management, transaction management, and supplier performance management.

- **Strategic sourcing:** Essentially, the strategic sourcing process is broader and more comprehensive than the procurement process. Strategic sourcing takes the process further, focuses more on supply chain impacts of procurement and purchasing decisions, and works cross-functionally within the business to help achieve the organization's overall business goals.

Based on a review of these definitions, it is important to consider purchasing simply as an activity (albeit an important one), while procurement and strategic sourcing are best described as processes. Figure 13.1 identifies five examples of ways in which strategic sourcing is a more comprehensive concept: (1) consolidation and leveraging of purchasing power—to concentrate larger volumes of purchases into fewer suppliers or fewer purchasing transactions; (2) emphasis on value—rather than acquisition cost alone; (3) more meaningful supplier relationships; (4) attention directed to process improvement; and (5) enhanced teamwork and professionalism—to include suppliers and customers, as appropriate.

Figure 13.1	Unique Aspects of Strategic Sourcing

1. **Consolidation and Leveraging of Purchasing Power:** If every department or division in an organization were to make independent purchasing decisions, the end result would be more costly than if the purchases were coordinated. Looking broadly at everything purchased by an organization, significant savings may be achieved through the consolidation of purchasing power and leveraging larger volumes of purchases with fewer total suppliers.

2. **Emphasis on Value:** Far too frequently, organizations place the highest priority on trying to procure needed items at the lowest possible cost. In so doing, opportunities may be missed to achieve greater value, for example, through reduced costs over the life cycle of the product. Buying a copier/fax/scan machine on the basis of acquisition cost alone would effectively neglect the long-term costs that may be associated with toner, repairs, etc.

3. **More Meaningful Supplier Relationships:** Strategic sourcing benefits from developing sound business relationships with many types of suppliers. Depending on the type of purchase being considered, the development of truly collaborative relationships can be very effective.

4. **Attention Directed to Process Improvement:** Strategic sourcing looks beyond the need for effective purchasing practices and focuses attention on the business processes that are related to the particular purchase being considered. Additionally, reformulation and streamlining of purchasing processes are key elements of strategic sourcing.

5. **Enhanced Teamwork and Professionalism:** The concept of teamwork is essential to the success of strategic sourcing. Through the use of cross-functional teams that may include representatives of supplier and customer organizations, the benefits of strategic sourcing may be realized.

Source: C. John Langley Jr., Ph.D. Used with permission.

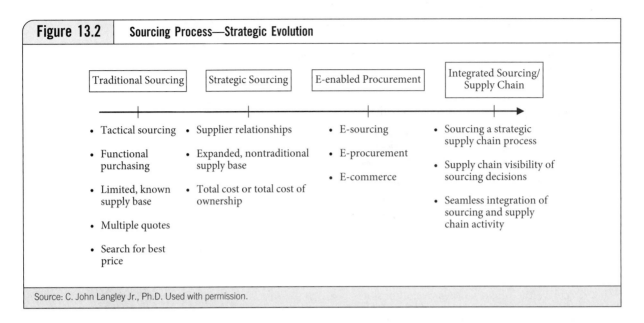

Figure 13.2 | Sourcing Process—Strategic Evolution

Traditional Sourcing Strategic Sourcing E-enabled Procurement Integrated Sourcing/ Supply Chain

- Tactical sourcing
- Functional purchasing
- Limited, known supply base
- Multiple quotes
- Search for best price

- Supplier relationships
- Expanded, nontraditional supply base
- Total cost or total cost of ownership

- E-sourcing
- E-procurement
- E-commerce

- Sourcing a strategic supply chain process
- Supply chain visibility of sourcing decisions
- Seamless integration of sourcing and supply chain activity

Source: C. John Langley Jr., Ph.D. Used with permission.

Figure 13.2 suggests a strategic evolution to the sourcing process. This diagram highlights not only the trend from traditional/tactical sourcing to strategic sourcing, but ultimately to e-enabled procurement and integration of sourcing and supply chain. Regardless of the terminology used to describe the future state, it is clear there is a high priority on developing and enhancing approaches to procurement and sourcing that create additional value for organizations, their customers, and their suppliers. Michael Porter, in his value chain, identified the strategic importance of procurement, since it includes such activities as qualifying new suppliers, procuring different types of inputs, and monitoring supplier performance.[1] As such, procurement serves as a critical link between members of the supply chain.

Types and Importance of Items and Service Purchased[2]

The products and services purchased by a company are not all the same. Some products are more important and require greater procurement attention. Applying the same procurement strategies, tactics, and resources to supplying a computer manufacturer with paper clips and computer chips overlooks the differences in the critical nature of each item to the firm's survival and profitability. That is, the computer company can survive without paper clips but not without computer chips.

The quadrant technique enables the supply chain manager to assess the importance of each product or service being purchased. This technique utilizes a two-by-two matrix to determine a procured item's relative importance on the basis of value and risk. The criteria used to delineate importance are value or profit potential and risk or uniqueness.

The value criterion examines product or service features that enhance profits for the final product and the firm's ability to maintain a competitive advantage in the marketplace. For example, a computer chip that is faster or an operating system that is more user friendly will make the computer more desirable, thereby increasing demand for the product and, consequently, increasing profits. Alternatively, the addition of a gold-plated paper clip to the computer instruction manual probably will not increase computer sales or solidify a competitive advantage in the marketplace.

Risk reflects the chance of failure, nonacceptance in the marketplace, delivery failures, and source nonavailability. The risk of a paper clip failure is really not a significant risk for a computer manufacturer. That is, if a paper clip fails to hold a number of pieces of paper together, the operation of the company's computer should not be affected. However, if a computer chip fails, the computer will not operate, and the marketplace will respond in a negative way. Thus, the computer chip poses a greater risk than the paper clip to a computer manufacturer.

Figure 13.3 depicts the value risk quadrant and categorizes item importance. Items of low risk, low value are identified as generics; those of low risk, high value are commodities. Products or services that are high risk, low value are distinctives; while those of high risk, high value are criticals.

Generics are low-risk, low-value items and services that typically do not enter the final product. Items such as office supplies and maintenance, repair, and operating items (MRO) are examples of generics. The administrative and acquisition processing costs are more significant than the purchase price of generics, and, for some generics, the administration and processing costs may exceed the price paid for the item or service. The strategic procurement thrust for generics is to streamline the procurement process to reduce the cost associated with purchasing generics. For example, the use of purchasing cards (corporate credit cards) reduces the number of checks written and the administrative costs associated with check payment, bank verification, and so on.

Commodities are items or services that are low in risk but high in value. Basic production materials (bolts), basic packaging (exterior box), and transportation services are examples of commodities that enhance the profitability of the company but pose a low risk. These items and services are fundamental to the company's finished product, thus making their value high. Risk is low because commodities are not unique items, and there are many sources of supply. Because commodities are not unique, there is little brand distinction, and price is a significant distinguishing factor. Freight and inventory are major procurement cost considerations for commodities. The procurement strategies used for commodities include volume purchasing to reduce price and just-in-time systems to lower inventory costs.

Figure 13.3	**Item Procurement Importance Matrix**

Distinctives	Criticals
• High risk, low value • Engineered items	• High risk, high value • Unique items • Items critical to final product
Generics	Commodities
• Low risk, low value • Office supplies • MRO items	• Low risk, high value • Basic production items • Basic packaging • Logistics services

Risk (vertical axis) — Value or Profit Potential (horizontal axis)

Source: C. John Langley Jr., Ph.D. Used with permission.

Distinctives are high-risk, low-value items and services such as engineered items, parts that are available from only a limited number of suppliers, or items that have a long lead time. The company's customers are unaware of or do not care about the uniqueness of distinctives, but these products pose a threat to continued operation and/or high procurement cost. A stockout of distinctives results in stopping the production line or changing the production schedule to work around a stocked-out item; both tactics increase production costs. Alternatively, using premium supply sources or premium transportation will eliminate the stockout, but procurement costs will increase. The strategic focus for distinctives is developing a standardization program to eliminate or reduce the uniqueness of the distinctives, thereby changing these items to generics.

Finally, **criticals** are high-risk, high-value items that give the final product a competitive advantage in the marketplace. As noted earlier, the computer chip used may give the computer a unique speed that differentiates it from all competitors. This unique computer chip increases the computer's value to the customer, and the risk of nonavailability is customer dissatisfaction and reduced sales. Criticals, in part, determine the customer's ultimate cost of using the finished product—in our example, the computer. The procurement strategy for criticals is to strengthen their value through use of new technologies, simplification, close supplier relations, and/or value-added alterations. The focus of critical procurement is on innovation to make the critical item provide greater market value to the finished product.

The preceding discussion of the quadrant technique emphasizes that not all items and services purchased are of equal importance. It also suggests that the supply chain manager must utilize varying procurement strategies based on the value and risk of the item. Greater resources and attention should be directed toward procuring criticals than toward generics. For example, one full-time procurement specialist may be assigned to purchasing one critical item—say, a computer chip—whereas one full-time person may be assigned to the purchase of hundreds of generics—office supplies.

Figure 13.4 helps to understand the three types of buy situations that may occur. The first is that of capital goods that may represent a longer-term investment for an organization that may require significant financial planning. The second is that of re-buys, which are repeat purchases that may either be identical to historical purchases (standard) or some variation thereof (modified). The third is that of maintenance, repair, and operations items that are needed for the continuing operation of the company and its supply chain activities.

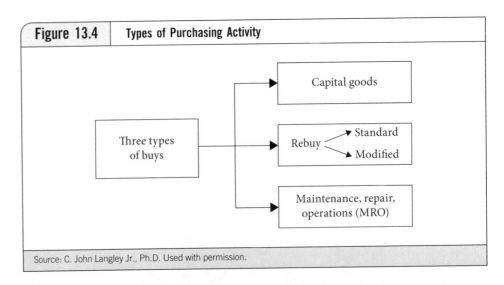

| **Figure 13.4** | **Types of Purchasing Activity** |

Source: C. John Langley Jr., Ph.D. Used with permission.

Strategic Sourcing Methodology[3]

As indicated previously, strategic sourcing as a process is far more broad and comprehensive than procurement. Figure 13.5 provides details concerning a seven-step methodology that better describes the strategic sourcing process. Overall, the process commences with the formation of a steering committee and a sourcing team, includes the development and execution of an appropriate sourcing strategy, and provides a direction for ongoing efforts in the contexts of transition, integration, and measurement and improvement of performance. The following sections provide additional details on key steps in this process.

To help guide the strategic sourcing process, five core principles are recognized as key drivers to achieve the desired levels of value. These principles are as follows:

- **Assess the total value**—Emphasis must go beyond acquisition cost and evaluate total cost of ownership and the value of the supplier relationship.

- **Develop individual sourcing strategies**—Individual spend categories need customized sourcing strategies.

- **Evaluate internal requirements**—Requirements and specifications must be thoroughly assessed and rationalized as part of the sourcing process.

- **Focus on supplier economics**—Suppliers' economics must be understood before identifying buying tactics such as volume leveraging, price unbundling, or price adjustment mechanisms.

- **Drive continuous improvement**—Strategic sourcing initiatives should be a subset of the continuous improvement process for the procurement and sourcing organizations.

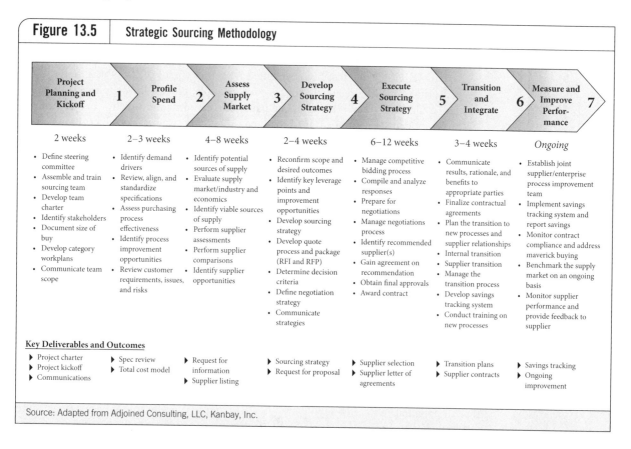

Figure 13.5 — Strategic Sourcing Methodology

Source: Adapted from Adjoined Consulting, LLC, Kanbay, Inc.

Seven key steps are included in the overall strategic sourcing methodology, as shown in Figure 13.5.

Step 1: Project Planning and Kickoff

This step suggests that a formal start to the strategic sourcing process is warranted. Included here are the formation of a steering committee to guide and oversee the overall strategic sourcing process, and a sourcing team to have direct involvement with all elements relating to the development and execution of the chosen sourcing strategy or strategies. In addition to establishing the parameters and organization of the overall strategic sourcing process, this step should identify key stakeholders in the process and also provide an initial documentation of the scope and scale of the products and services that are purchased and of relevance to the process.

Step 2: Profile Spend

The purposes of this step are to develop an accurate understanding of requirements and specifications for needed products and services and to assess opportunities for improvement of purchasing and procurement processes. Among the activities to be included in this step are the following:

- **Identify or reevaluate needs.** A procurement transaction is usually initiated in response to either a new or an existing need of a user (by an individual or department within the buyer's firm). In some instances, existing needs must be reevaluated because they change. In either case, once the need is identified, the procurement process can begin. The need can be identified by any of a variety of functional areas in the firm or even by someone outside the firm, for example, by customers.

- **Define and evaluate user requirements.** Once the need has been determined, its requirement must be represented by some type of measurable criteria. The criteria may be relatively simple—for example, criteria for copy machine paper could be 8 1/2 by 11-inch white paper of a certain bond weight—or they may be very complex if the company is buying a highly technical product. Using these criteria, the sourcing professional can communicate the user's needs to potential suppliers.

- **Decide whether to make or buy.** Before outside suppliers are solicited, the buying firm must decide whether it will make or buy the product or service to satisfy the user's needs. Even with a "make" decision, however, the buying firm will usually have to purchase some types of inputs from outside suppliers. This step has become much more important today, when more companies are outsourcing in order to focus upon their core activities.

This step also should develop a structured "spend analysis." This analysis should help to understand spend by supplier, category, and internal user and to profile current sourcing approaches and areas for improvement. The end result should include recommendations for improvement of the overall sourcing process and likely financial benefits.

Step 3: Assess Supply Market

This is a very critical step in the strategic sourcing process, as it involves making sure that all potential sources of supply are identified and that useful mechanisms are in place for meaningful comparisons of alternative supply sources. A few perspectives on this step are as follows:

- A thorough assessment of a supply market will include a comprehensive market analysis. A source of supply can operate in a purely competitive market (many suppliers), an oligopolistic market (a few large suppliers), or a monopolistic market (one supplier). Knowing the type of market will help the procurement professional determine the number of suppliers in the market, where the power/dependence balance lies, and which method of buying might be most effective—negotiations, competitive bidding, and so on. The information about market type is not always apparent, and some research may be necessary using standard reference sources such as *Moody's* or information from a trade association.

- It is important to identify all possible suppliers that might be able to satisfy the user's needs—including suppliers that the buying firm has not used previously. Again, identifying all possible suppliers, especially with today's global environment, can be a challenge and may require some research. If the company is small, it may rely on more common secondary sources of such information, such as local buying guides, Internet searches, etc.

- Prescreen all possible sources. When defining and evaluating user requirements (as described in the second activity), it is important to differentiate between demands and desires. Demands for a product or service are those characteristics that are critical to the user; desires are those that are not as critical and are therefore negotiable. Prescreening reduces the pool of possible suppliers to those that can satisfy the user's demands. In some instances, prescreening can be a relatively simple task. For example, in the case of the copy paper, the supplier will have it on hand regularly or will not have it available dependably. With parts for a computer, the situation may require a series of tests by internal engineering staff.

This step also should recognize the need to simplify purchasing complexity and whenever possible rationalize products. In addition, attention should be directed to developing a detailed understanding and analysis of pricing, identifying opportunities to consolidate buying and create leverage, and redefining and modernizing supplier relationships. Making sure that objectives such as these are met should help to provide a comprehensive and meaningful supply market assessment.

Step 4: Develop Sourcing Strategy

Prior to embarking on the task of supplier selection, it is important to fully develop a sourcing strategy that defines the parameters of the process and the steps to be followed. Figure 13.6 provides an overview of the supplier portfolio screening process; it spans Steps 3-5 in the strategic sourcing process. Of particular interest in this process are the steps related to initial supplier research and screening, development of a responsive request for information (RFI) and request for proposal (RFP), site visits with follow-up discussions, and supplier selection.

- The purpose of the RFI is to establish whether a supplier has the capabilities and interest to be considered further in the sourcing process and is potentially able to meet the customer's business requirements. Examples of information that may be requested in an RFI include company background, financial stability, markets covered, manufacturing and distribution facilities, research and development, and quality systems. RFIs generally focus attention on

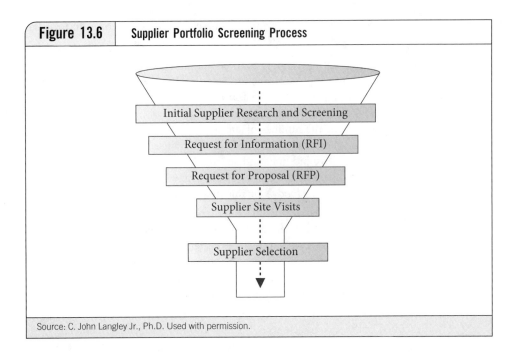

Figure 13.6 | **Supplier Portfolio Screening Process**

Initial Supplier Research and Screening

Request for Information (RFI)

Request for Proposal (RFP)

Supplier Site Visits

Supplier Selection

Source: C. John Langley Jr., Ph.D. Used with permission.

non-price information that may be of interest and relevance to the buying organization.

- The RFP provides specific information as to what the buying company would like to source and asks potential suppliers for details as to how they would respond to the request. Included in this response would be substantive information as to the specific products and services to be provided, as well as pricing information.

The sourcing strategy also should include supplier selection criteria and a process for evaluating submissions from multiple suppliers. The selection criteria should relate directly to the previously established objectives to be met by the formal strategic sourcing process. Examples of supplier selection criteria are shown in Figure 13.7.

Step 5: Execute Sourcing Strategy

Essentially, this step begins with an evaluation of the suppliers that remain following the RFI and RFP processes and culminates in the award of a contract. With the pool of suppliers reduced to those that can meet the user's demands, it is now possible to determine which supplier or suppliers can best meet the user's negotiable requirements, or desires. This activity may be accomplished through the use of competitive bidding if the procurement item or items are fairly simple or standard and there is a sufficient number of potential vendors. If these conditions do not exist, more elaborate evaluation may be necessary, using engineering tests or simulated end-use situations, for example, to test seat belts for cars.

Clearly, the most important part of this step is to choose a supplier (or suppliers, depending on the objectives of the sourcing decision). The choice of supplier also determines the relationship that will exist between the buying and supplying firms and how the mechanics of this relationship will be structured and implemented.

This activity determines how relationships may be maintained with suppliers who are not selected.

Figure 13.7	Overview of Vendor Selection Criteria

Quality
- Technical specifications
- Chemical and physical properties
- Design
- Product life
- Ease of repair
- Maintenance
- Dependability

Reliability
- On-time delivery
- Performance history
- Warranty and replacement policies

Risk
- Cost risk
- Potential for supply uncertainty
- Lead time risk and uncertainty

Capability
- Production capability
- Technical capability
- Management
- Operating controls
- Labor relations

Financial
- Price of products
- Financial stability

Desirable Qualities
- Vendor attitude and cultural compatibility
- Training aids
- Packaging
- Vendor location

Source: C. John Langley Jr., Ph.D. Used with permission.

Step 6: Transition and Integrate

Important elements of this step are the finalization of the contractual agreement, planning the transition process, and receipt or delivery of the product or service. This activity occurs with the first attempt by the supplier or suppliers to satisfy the user's needs. The completion of this activity also begins the generation of performance data to be used for the next step in the strategic sourcing process.

Other helpful elements of this step include the development of a savings tracking system and training on new processes that may be related to the products or services that have been procured.

Step 7: Measure and Improve Performance

A very important step in the strategic sourcing process is the measurement and improvement of supplier performance. Basically, this involves making a postpurchase performance evaluation. Once the product has been delivered or the service performed, the supplier's performance must be evaluated to determine whether it has truly satisfied the user's needs. This also is the control activity. If supplier performance did not satisfy the user's needs, the causes for this variance must be determined and the proper corrective actions implemented.

One final comment relating to the strategic sourcing process is that all of the activities identified in this section may be subject to influences beyond the control of the procurement professional. These influences can determine how effectively each activity is performed. They include intraorganizational and interorganizational factors and external factors such as governmental influences. For example, a change in marketing needs or manufacturing process may require repeating all or some of the activities identified before the first iteration is completed. Financial failure of a potential vendor will also cause problems and necessitate repeated activities.

Managing Sourcing and Procurement Processes

Managing the sourcing and procurement process can be difficult for a multitude of reasons, ranging from inflexible organizational structures to inflexible organizational cultures. However, most firms should find the process relatively straightforward. What must be remembered when dealing with these activities is that all firms are different and will have different requirements for the procurement process. A four-step approach can be used and adapted to a firm's particular needs. To maximize effectiveness, the following steps may be considered:

1. **Determine the type of purchase.** In the strategic sourcing process, identifying the type of purchase will many times dictate the complexity of the entire process. Of the three types of purchasing activity discussed earlier in Figure 13.4, for example, the straight rebuy situation would involve only minimal additional effort in terms of procurement activities. Alternatively, the modified rebuy, and certainly the new buy situations, would involve significantly more effort.

2. **Determine the necessary levels of investment.** The strategic sourcing process requires two major types of investments by the firm: time and information. Time is expended by the individuals involved in making the purchase; the more complex and important the purchase, the more time must be spent on it, especially if it is a new buy. Information can be both internal and external to the firm. Internal information is gathered concerning user requirements and the implications that the purchase will have for the firm. External information concerning the input to be purchased may be gathered from supply chain members, potential suppliers, and others. The more complex and important the purchase, the more information is needed for the procurement process to be effective.

   By determining the type of purchase (which is also a function of the user's needs), the procurement professional can determine the levels of investment necessary in the procurement process. Problems can occur when not enough or too much investment is made to satisfy a particular user's needs. Determining the level of investment needed in time and information to adequately meet a user's requirements is a firm-specific process. Once the level of investment is decided, the strategic sourcing process can take place.

3. **Perform the procurement process.** This is a relatively easy step to describe but can be a complex step to perform, depending on the situation. It includes performing those activities necessary to effectively make a purchase and satisfy the user's requirements. This step also allows the procurement professional to collect data on the time and information actually used in making a specific purchase. The ability to measure the actual investment and how well a user's needs were satisfied is important to the final step in managing the strategic sourcing process.

4. **Evaluate the effectiveness of the strategic sourcing process.** This is a control step that asks two questions: (1) Were the user's needs satisfied? and (2) Was the investment necessary? Remember, the goal is to invest only enough time and information to exactly satisfy the user's needs. If the process was not effective, the cause could be traced to not enough investment, not performing the proper activities, or mistakes made in performing one or more of the activities. In any case, when the strategic sourcing process is less effective than would be desired, the cause(s) must be identified and corrective actions taken to make sure that future sourcing strategies will prove to be effective. If the purchase satisfied the user's needs at the proper level of investment, the strategic sourcing process may be deemed to be effective and can serve as a reference for future purchases.

Thus, although the procurement process is complex, it can be managed effectively as long as the manager develops some systematic approach for implementing it. A key factor in achieving efficiency and effectiveness in this area is the development of successful supplier (vendor) relationships. In fact, many professional procurement/materials managers agree that today's global marketplace requires developing strong supplier relationships in order to create and sustain a competitive advantage. Companies such as NCR and Motorola go so far as to refer to suppliers (vendors) as partners and/or stakeholders in their company. When vendors are "partners," companies tend to rely more upon them to provide input into product design, engineering assistance, quality control, and so on.

Supplier Selection

As discussed previously, Figure 13.7 provides an overview of the supplier selection criteria. The most important factor in vendor selection is usually **quality**. As was indicated earlier, quality often refers to the specifications that a user desires in an item (technical specifications, chemical or physical properties, or design, for example). The procurement professional compares the actual quality of a supplier's product with the specifications the user desires. In actuality, quality includes additional factors such as life of the product, ease of repair, maintenance requirements, ease of use, and dependability. In today's Six Sigma and lean environments, not only are quality standards higher, but suppliers are typically counted upon to take major responsibility for quality.

Reliability comprises on-time delivery and performance history, the second- and third-ranked factors for most procurement professionals. To prevent production line shutdowns resulting from longer-than-expected lead times, the buyer requires consistent, on-time deliveries. Also, the performance life of the procured product directly affects the quality of the final product, the manufacturer's warranty claims, and repeat sales. Finally, in cases of material malfunction, the buying firm considers the supplier's warranty and claim procedure a reliability measure. Reliability is often considered a part of a total quality management program. It should also be noted that the growing reliance upon foreign suppliers presents some special challenges to the achievement of reliability because of the distances involved.

A factor of great contemporary relevance is **risk**.[4] One way this may occur is if there is likely variability in the cost of purchased products or services that may result in higher prices. Other ways in which risk may occur include supply uncertainties and unusual variation in delivery lead times. In either case, the result may be that the purchased products or services are not available when and where they are needed, thus introducing additional cost to develop appropriate countermeasures.

The fourth major supplier selection criterion, **capability**, considers the potential supplier's production facilities and capacity, technical capability, management and organizational capabilities, and operating controls. These factors indicate the supplier's ability to provide a needed quality and quantity of material in a timely manner. The evaluation includes not only the supplier's physical capability to provide the material the user needs, but also the supplier's capability to do so consistently over an extended time period. The buying firm may answer this long-run supply concern by considering the supplier's labor relations record. A record of supplier-labor unrest resulting in strikes may indicate that the supplier is unable to provide the material quantity the user desires over a long time period. A firm that buys from this supplier will incur increased inventory costs for storing material in preparation for likely disruptions in the supplier's business due to labor strife. Again, sourcing from global suppliers makes this assessment more challenging.

Financial considerations constitute the fifth major supplier selection criterion. In addition to price, the buying firm considers the supplier's financial position. Financially unstable suppliers pose possible disruptions in a long-run continued supply of material. By declaring bankruptcy, a supplier that supplies materials critical to a final product could stop a buyer's production. This criterion has become especially important in purchasing transportation service from truckload motor carriers. With the trend toward companies utilizing a smaller number of carriers, the financial failure of such a supplier is a major problem and source of disruption in a supply chain.

Desirable capabilities include several that may be helpful depending on the type of purchase being made and the type of relationship desired between the customer and the supplier. Although the buyer might find the supplier's attitude difficult to quantify, attitude does affect the supplier selection decision. A negative attitude, for example, may eliminate a supplier for a buyer's consideration. The impression or image that the supplier projects has a similar effect on supplier selection, as well as cultural compatibility. The importance of training aids and packaging will depend on the material the buyer is purchasing. For example, packaging is important to buyers of easily damaged material, such as glass, but not important to buyers purchasing a commodity that is not easily damaged, such as coal. Training aids would be significant to a firm selecting suppliers to supply technical machinery such as computers and robots but not to a firm seeking office supplies. Likewise, a buyer would consider the availability of repair service more important when buying technical machinery.

Another supplier selection factor is geographical location. This factor addresses the issue of whether to buy from local or distant suppliers. Transportation cost is one obvious aspect of this issue. Other factors, such as the ability to fill rush orders, meet delivery dates, provide shorter delivery times, and utilize greater supplier–buyer cooperation, favor the use of local suppliers. However, distant suppliers may provide lower prices, greater technical ability, greater supply reliability, and higher quality. This is again a choice faced more frequently in today's global environment.

The relative importance of the supplier selection factors will depend upon the material the buyer is purchasing. When a buyer purchases a computer, for example, technical capability and training aids may be more important than price, delivery, and warranties.

On the Line

IBM Achieves Success via Improved Purchasing and Strategic Sourcing

When Gene Richter was offered the position of IBM's chief procurement officer during the company's turnaround, he felt it was an opportunity he couldn't turn down—"the chance to save a national treasure." But IBM purchasing had a terrible reputation among its suppliers as being arrogant, short-sighted, and pushy. Richter knew that in order to meet Chairman Louis Gerstner's revival plans, Big Blue needed cash, and lots of it—money to fuel R&D's idea factory and build new products.

Richter moved quickly to change suppliers' perceptions of IBM as a partner. About 54 percent of annual revenues was spent in 1999 with outside suppliers; that number was expected to rise so supplier support was critical. Internally, he established centers of commodity expertise, ordered buyers to create written commodity plans, and offered incentives to purchasing professionals to find the lowest possible prices and acquire the most efficient technologies on the market.

In six years, the IBM team racked up a long list of paybacks on their supply chain investments, ranging from savings of US $9 billion, to improved satisfaction ratings by internal clients of 89, up from 43; Internet purchases increased from $0 to $13 billion; and contracts cropped from 40-plus pages to six.

The overall popularity of IBM compared to other customers improved among suppliers, from five or six out of seven or eight competitors, to first place four years later. The culmination of IBM's supply management turnaround resulted in Lou Gerstner awarding (for the first time ever) the Chairman's Award to the procurement team.

Other examples illustrate the power of supply chain management to mine the incredible payback. Motorola's supply management team saved the company US $600 million in 18 months. Honda purchasing eliminated 25 percent of the cost of the 1998 Accord, an achievement that significantly increased market share, by diligently cutting costs before they were incurred during the design phase. John Deere and Delphi's strategic sourcing operations likewise have realized millions in hard dollar savings.

While many purchasing professionals concentrate on a few sure-fire cost reduction approaches, including supplier rationalization and Internet buying, the area of logistics and distribution grows in value and opportunity. Generally, logistics costs may represent an average of approximately 10 percent of total sales.

Source: Adapted from "Discovering the Incredible Payback," *CSCMP Supply Chain Comment* (Oak Brook, IL Council of Supply Chain Management Professionals, May/June 2005). Reproduced by permission.

Conversely, a buyer of office supplies would probably emphasize price and delivery more than other factors.

All of the criteria just discussed are important or can be important in certain procurement situations. However, the one criterion that generates the most discussion and/or frustration for procurement specialists is price or cost. Therefore, some extended discussion of this criterion is necessary.

Supplier/Vendor Evaluation and Relationships

Many successful companies have recognized the key role that sourcing and procurement play in supply chain management and that supplier/vendor relationships are a vital part of successful procurement strategies. "Good suppliers do not grow on trees" is an adage that is often quoted by procurement professionals. This is especially true when companies reduce the total number of their suppliers, frequently in conjunction with Six Sigma and lean programs, or just-in-time (JIT) production and inventory systems.

The strategy to utilize a smaller number of suppliers/vendors frequently means an alliance or partnership with suppliers/vendors because of the need to ensure an adequate supply of quality materials over time at an optimum total acquired cost. The partnership/alliance concept encompasses more than just the procurement process, since partnerships are being developed today throughout the supply chain by companies. For example, partnerships are also evolving with transportation companies, contract logistics companies (third-party providers), and channel members.

At this stage, suffice it to say that procurement professionals today recognize that quality management necessitates quality materials and parts. That is, the final product is only as good as the parts that are used in the process. Also, we need to recognize that the customer satisfaction process begins with procurement.

Another dimension of the supplier relationship is that procurement contributes to the competitive advantage of the company, whether the advantage is one of low cost, differentiation, or a niche orientation (using Porter's generic strategies).[5] Therefore, the procurement management program has to be consistent with the overall competitive advantage that a company is seeking to attain in the marketplace. For example, Honda or Toyota would be expected to approach procurement differently than would Mercedes-Benz or Audi.

Certifications and Registrations[6]

A topic of interest to many buyers of products and services is the extent to which potential suppliers have achieved excellence in terms of process management and continuous improvement. As a result, over time several techniques and approaches have been developed that address issues relating to soundness of processes, results achieved, and continuous improvement. A few of the more prevalent approaches are briefly discussed next.

- **Total Quality Management**—Arising in the 1980s in response to Japanese competition and the teachings of Dr. W. Edwards Deming, TQM represented a strategy in which entire organizations were focused on an examination of process variability and continuous improvement. This approach, which was very popular into the mid-1990s, included a goal of improving a company's quality to only three defects per million through systematic incremental change in processes and careful statistical measurement of outcomes.

- **Six Sigma**—Is similar to TQM in its focus on techniques for solving problems and using statistical methods to improve processes. But whereas TQM emphasizes employee involvement for the total organization, the Six Sigma approach involves training experts (known as green belts and black belts) who work on solving important problems while they teach others in the company.

- **ISO 9000**—A program started in 1987 by the International Organization for Standardization. It has an objective of making sure that companies have standard processes in place that they follow: "Document what you do and do what you document." ISO 9000 involves a third-party registration program (not dissimilar to Underwriters Laboratories—a very well-known registrar) certifying that companies are following documented processes.

Aside from the fact that these approaches typically require very significant commitments in terms of time, effort, and expense, buying organizations need to look closely to make sure that participation in these programs actually produces results that are of tangible value. While it is encouraging to know that certain potential suppliers have committed their organizations to approaches such as these, one needs to be sure to document the benefits and improvements that are likely to be created as a result.

The Special Case of Procurement Price[7]

We begin by identifying the four generic sources of prices in procurement situations. This is somewhat basic but important to understand. The discussion of price becomes more complex when one adds an analysis of total acquired cost or value in the procurement process from a supply chain perspective. Total acquired cost and value are discussed after our description of price sources.

Sources of Price

Purchasing managers utilize four basic procedures to determine potential vendors' prices: (1) commodity markets, (2) price lists, (3) price quotations, and (4) negotiations. Commodity markets exist for basic raw materials such as grain, oil, sugar, and natural resources including coal and lumber. In these markets, the forces of supply and demand determine the price that all potential vendors will charge. Reductions in the supply of these materials or increases in demand usually result in increased prices; the converse is true for increases in supply or decreases in demand.

Price lists are published prices that are generally used with standardized products such as gasoline or office supplies. The vendor's catalog, electronic or hard copy, describes the items available and lists their prices. Depending on the status, buyers may receive a purchaser discount from the list price. For example, a vendor may give a 10 percent discount to small-volume buyers (less than $1,000 per month) and a 35 percent discount to large-volume buyers (more than $10,000 per month).

Purchasers use the price quotation method for both standard and specially items. It is particularly useful in promoting competition among suppliers. The process begins with the buyer sending potential vendors requests for quotes (RFQ). An RFQ contains all the necessary information regarding the specifications the purchaser requires and the manner in which potential suppliers are to present their offers. In turn, the vendors examine the cost they will incur in producing the material, considering the quantity the purchaser will order, the purchase's duration, and other factors that will affect the vendor's profitability. Finally, the purchaser compares the vendor's quoted price and offer specifications with those of other vendors.

The fourth procedure, negotiation, is useful when the other methods do not apply or have failed. Negotiation is particularly effective when the buyer is interested in a strategic alliance or long-term relationship. The negotiation process can be time consuming, but the potential benefits can be significant in terms of price and quality. Negotiation is becoming more widely used by logistics managers who buy goods and logistics services.

The objective of the procurement process is to purchase goods and services at the "best" price, which may not be the lowest price per unit at the vendor source. This is particularly true from a global supply chain perspective. In all four settings, the base price needs to be evaluated in a total acquired cost context.

A generalized spectrum of expanding procurement approaches to the supply chain concept is presented in Figure 13.8. At the first level, the firm evaluates procurement and logistics functions simply on the basis of lowest price or lowest cost, without strong regard to the total costs to the firm. In this context, it is difficult to achieve a total cost savings unless a manager or group becomes directly responsible for the two or more interfacing functions that might offer a total cost savings. As a company attempts to move from the lowest base or unit price to taking a supply chain perspective to create highest value, the procurement function becomes more strategic in nature.

For customer satisfaction, all costs and factors that affect costs and create value should be captured in the total acquired cost. As Figure 13.8 indicates, a hierarchy of costs and other factors builds upward from raw materials through manufacturing, to distribution, to final marketing and selection and use by the ultimate customer in order to determine total procurement cost and the highest total value.

For the buyer, the total procurement price is more than just the basic purchase price, as indicated in Figure 13.9. The following discussion starts with the base cost and delineates the additional direct and indirect costs that need to be considered:

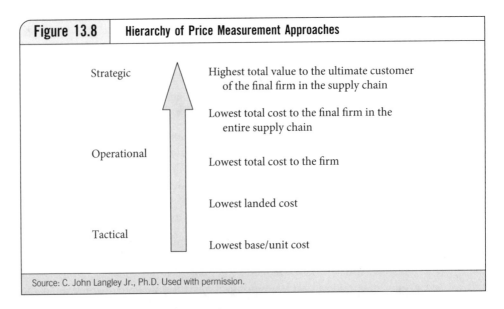

Figure 13.8	**Hierarchy of Price Measurement Approaches**

Strategic — Highest total value to the ultimate customer of the final firm in the supply chain

Lowest total cost to the final firm in the entire supply chain

Operational — Lowest total cost to the firm

Lowest landed cost

Tactical — Lowest base/unit cost

Source: C. John Langley Jr., Ph.D. Used with permission.

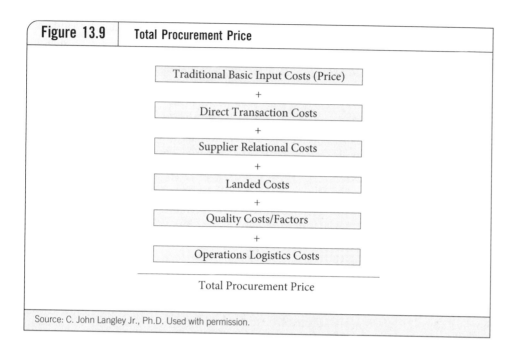

Figure 13.9 | Total Procurement Price

Traditional Basic Input Costs (Price)

+

Direct Transaction Costs

+

Supplier Relational Costs

+

Landed Costs

+

Quality Costs/Factors

+

Operations Logistics Costs

Total Procurement Price

Source: C. John Langley Jr., Ph.D. Used with permission.

Traditional Basic Input Costs

This is the primary price of the product or materials as paid by the firm. It is the traditional price buyers seek through bidding, through negotiating, or in requests for quotes. It is easily measured, and it has long been the hallmark against which buyer performance is measured; but, in a supply chain setting, it is only one factor for the firm to evaluate and consider in the acquisition process.

Direct Transaction Costs

These are the costs of detecting, transmitting the need for, and processing the material flow in order to acquire the goods. They include the process of detecting inventory need, requisitioning, preparing and transmitting the order documentation to the supplier, receiving the acknowledgment, handling shipping documents, and receiving information about input to inventory. This area was made more efficient with the advent of internal electronic mail systems that automated the purchasing-requisition and order-transmission process. Users inside the firm use electronic means to transmit their needs to purchasing. EDI and the Internet are extensions of this process outbound to the supplier.

The use of blanket or systems contracting can also reduce transaction costs. These include direct ordering by users to suppliers, single consolidated billing, and user inspection and checking. Direct transaction costs are overhead types of costs that are not easily visible, but they represent time and effort that are not available for more productive value-added activities. Suppliers and interfacing carriers that reduce the need for these activities represent value to the buying firm.

Supplier Relational Costs

These are the costs of creating and maintaining a relationship with a supplier. They include travel, supplier education, and the establishment of planning and operational links between purchasing and the supplier's order-entry operation, as well as other links, including those related to traffic, engineering, research, and product development in both firms. In traditional purchasing settings, this includes the process of evaluating and certifying a supplier for quality and preferred supplier programs.

Landed Costs

The inbound transportation flow includes two key cost elements: the actual transportation cost and the sales/FOB terms. There are four different transportation options with inbound movements—supplier-selected for-hire carrier or private carrier and buyer-selected for-hire carrier or private carrier.

The sales terms define which firm owns the goods during transportation as well as invoice payment requirements. Transportation terms pertain to the carrier in the move between the supplier and buyer firm. There are nearly a dozen possible transportation terms that include different carrier payment and loss and damage claim options. Each one presents different relative costs to each party in the linkage; for supply chain purposes, the one that can perform the task or own the goods at the lowest overall cost has an advantage that can contribute to the overall chain. Both sales and transportation terms must be considered, and different direct costs, responsibilities, and indirect implicit costs of cash flow are affected by each one of them.

Quality Costs/Factors

Quality pertains to the conformance of goods to a desired specification. It includes the cost of conformance, nonconformance, appraisal, and ultimate use costs. The required quality specification is often balanced against what the supplier can easily provide nearly 100 percent of the time. Often, a product specification that is extremely tight requires extra costs but results in higher quality, which may reduce total cost.

Operations Logistics Costs

This group includes the following four key areas:

- Receiving and make-ready costs are the costs of those flow activities occurring between the inbound transportation delivery of a good and its availability for use by production or other processes. These include the cost of unpacking, inspecting, counting, sorting, grading, removing and disposing of packaging materials (strapping, banding, stretch-shrink wrapping, pallets, etc.), and moving the good to the use point. A streamlined system such as direct forklift delivery to a production line is an example of an efficient receiving/make-ready process. Some leading edge carriers provide information links to the firm that include inspection checks, sequencing of the loads, and final count checks so that receiving processes can be reduced or eliminated.

- Lot-size costs directly affect space requirements, handling flow, unit price, and related cash flows. These are a major cost of inventories.

- Production costs can be affected by suppliers of even seemingly similar goods. Extruded plastic for high-quality towel rods is an example. The plastic is an extruded tube that must be inflated with air and slipped over a metal or wooden rod. Original raw materials quality, differing production processes, and in-transit humidity can cause two suppliers' goods to affect the production line significantly. One might allow assembly of 200 units per hour, while another might split or not form properly, wasting 10 percent of the sleeves and requiring the production line to operate at a slower speed. Thus, each one has a different cost of production operation.

- Logistics costs are also important in both upstream and downstream settings. These are cost factors that are affected by product size, weight, cube, and shape and their resulting impact upon transportation, handling, storage, and damage costs. Purchased goods and packaging materials have a direct bearing on these subsequent process costs.

All firms in the supply chain add cost and, hopefully, value to a product as it moves through the supply chain. Value is added by reducing total acquired cost or by enhancing the function of the product. Each firm in the supply chain can contribute to or detract from these factors. The key is to focus downstream in the supply chain, but it is also important to note the key role that the procurement process can play at each point along the supply chain by being aware of a product's total acquired cost. Ideally, the focus should be upon the total value at the end of the supply chain. Therefore, the analysis should also include indirect financial costs (payment terms), tactical input costs (vendor capabilities), and strategic business factors (factors that cause customers to buy the product).

Total Landed Cost (TLC)

As indicated in Figure 13.10, purchase or acquisition cost is only the tip of the iceberg when the analysis is broadened to encompass factors that would better relate to the total landed cost (TLC). This concept represents the sum of all costs associated with making and delivering products to the point where they are needed. In effect, this perspective brings into play a few considerations that are helpful to the supplier selection process. Among those that are highlighted are life cycle costs, inventory costs, strategic sourcing costs, transaction costs, quality costs, technology costs, and management costs.

Figure 13.10	Understanding Total Landed Cost (TLC)

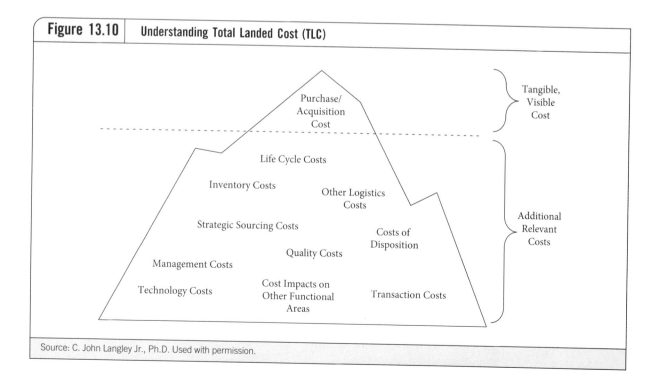

Source: C. John Langley Jr., Ph.D. Used with permission.

Figure 13.11	**Conducting a Cost Comparison of Alternative Sourcing Options**		
DESTINATION COUNTRY – SWITZERLAND	**COUNTRY OF ORIGIN**		
PRICE COMPONENTS - all prices in Euros	**CHINA**	**VIETNAM**	**EU**
Net purchasing price for a specific volume of the product from 3 different suppliers	10,000	8,000	12,000
Total transportation cost to Switzerland – Ocean freight from China/Vietnam – Road freight within Europe	4,000	6,000	1,200
Customs according trade agreement	1,000	1,500	n.a.
VAT (Switzerland 7.6%) based on value of goods	1,140	1,178	1,003
Total Landed Cost	16,140	16,678	14,203

Source: C. John Langley Jr. and Capgemini (2010). *Third Party Logistics: Results and Findings of the 15th Annual 3PL Study.*

Figure 13.11 illustrates how important it is to consider types of cost that are in addition to the purchase price for needed product. Interestingly, the product prices are lowest in Vietnam and highest in the EU, but after transportation, customs, and VAT costs are included, sourcing from the EU is the least expensive and from Vietnam the most expensive. Although this is a relatively straightforward example, it reinforces the importance of looking beyond the price of the products themselves when trying to make a cost-effective sourcing decision.

e-Sourcing and e-Procurement

Obviously, the computer and Internet have created some dramatic changes in the business world and in the everyday activities of consumers. For example, it has become quite common for individual consumers to research products and services, locate retail and e-retail suppliers, purchase goods and services, and track the delivery of shipments—all electronically and in the convenience of their own home. Interestingly, estimates are that U.S. online retail sales are expected to reach $250 billion by 2014, according to Forrester Research.[8]

Of great relevance to the topic of this chapter, procurement was found to be the business process that made the greatest early application of e-commerce. Initially, companies utilized electronic data interchange (EDI) technology to connect with their major customers to process purchase orders, send notifications of shipment, and transfer funds. However, EDI technology has proven to be more costly than desired and requires special technology to implement. The advent of the publicly available Internet has eliminated the investment and technology problems associated with EDI and opened the door to increased application of e-commerce techniques to the areas of procurement and sourcing.

For purposes of this discussion, **e-procurement** and **e-sourcing** will refer to the use of electronic capabilities to conduct activities and processes relating to procurement and sourcing. Figure 13.12 provides a number of common functionalities that relate to e-procurement and e-sourcing.

Figure 13.12 | e-Sourcing and e-Procurement

- **Industry Analysis and Supplier Identification:** Provides valuable information on supplier industries and facilitates development of candidate supplier lists for specific commodities, geographies, and product types.
- **Analytical Tools:** Supplier selection, bid, spend, and performance management analytics.
- **Management of RFI/RFQ/RFP Processes:** Electronic support for the preparation, submission, and evaluation of these repetitive processes.
- **Requisition and Purchase Order Process:** Provides needed automation of purchase order and of item selection from central resources such as online catalogs.
- **Online Negotiations:** Supports real-time sourcing, for example, through online bidding or reverse auction.
- **Collaboration Tools:** Supports collaborative sourcing with other functions and divisions in same organization, with other organizations, and interaction and electronic connections with suppliers.
- **Logistics Procurement:** Assumes responsibility for e-procurement of logistics services such as transportation, forwarding, etc. Utilizes a growing number of tools and technologies, for example, online bidding, to facilitate and improve efficiency of logistics procurement processes.
- **Project Management Capabilities:** Standardizes and improves issues related to cost, quality, and time.
- **Knowledge Management:** Provides centralized, computerized availability of past, current, and future information relating to purchasing and sourcing activities. Serves as knowledge resource for those who are involved in e-sourcing and e-procurement.
- **Contract Management:** Fulfills needs relating to legal contracts or agreements with suppliers.

Source: C. John Langley Jr., Ph.D. Used with permission.

Which of These Solutions Should Be Considered[9]

According to Norek and Favre, strategic sourcing solutions should be considered for any entity that has a significant amount of spending with outside suppliers (over $50 million total). The spend should also be segmented into categories (e.g., sheet steel, contractor services) and sorted in descending dollars so only the top dollar spend categories are candidates for a strategic sourcing solution (the number of significant categories will go up for firms with a larger amount of spending). For smaller companies, a hosted solution (software run by the software company, behind their firewall) is less expensive and more manageable. For larger companies with higher usage, the software is typically purchased outright.

Transactional procurement systems are typically used to reduce the time and effort associated with the tactical aspects of procurement, such as requisition and purchase order creation, as well as the approval and payment processes. Companies with 10,000 purchase transactions or more per year should consider transactional procurement solutions. Companies with fewer transactions who don't purchase a solution outright can take advantage of supplier Internet sites for business-to-business transactions—for example, ordering office supplies or work gloves directly from a supplier's Web site using a purchasing card.

Data management and analytics are valuable for medium to large companies with a large number of part numbers and supplier information. They are especially valuable for companies with multiple locations and/or divisions where data are not currently managed centrally. With data standardization, companies can find common suppliers and items across divisions and locations, allowing them to aggregate spend volumes and achieve discounts.

Advantages

The advantages of e-commerce procurement are shown in Figure 13.13. An obvious advantage is the lowering of procurement operating costs. The reduction of paperwork and the associated cost of paper processing, filing, and storing is a major cost-saving area of e-commerce. Many companies have a goal of being paperless, but few have obtained that goal at this time.

Another paper reduction possible with e-commerce is electronic funds transfer. Paying vendor invoices electronically eliminates the cost of preparing, mailing, filing, and storage of the checks. Estimates of the cost of writing a check vary from a low of $10 to a high of $85, the majority of this cost being the cost of accounts payable personnel.

Reduced sourcing time means increased productivity because a procurement specialist spends less time per order and can place more orders in a given time period. Likewise, the seller utilizing e-commerce can increase the productivity of customer service representatives. Many of the questions asked by the buyer can be answered online, thereby saving time for both the buyer and seller personnel.

Given the real-time nature of e-commerce information, sellers have up-to-date information on demand and can adjust production/purchases to meet the current demand level. This same real-time information enables the buyer to establish controls that will coordinate purchase quantities with requirement quantities and monitor spending levels. That is, the buyer is now in the position of monitoring the quantity of an item ordered,

---

Figure 13.13	**Advantages of Electronic Procurement**

Lower Operating Costs
- Reduce paperwork
- Reduce sourcing time
- Improve control over inventory and spending

Improve Procurement and Sourcing Efficiency
- Find new supply sources
- Improve communications
- Improve personnel use
- Lower cycle times

Reduce Procurement Prices
- Improve comparison shopping
- Reduce overall prices paid

Source: C. John Langley Jr., Ph.D. Used with permission.

received, and on hand; comparing it to the amount needed; and doing this in a real-time mode. The same is true for monitoring spending activities against budgeted amounts.

Electronic procurement affords efficiency in the process by utilizing fewer resources to produce a given level of purchases. With a click of the mouse, a purchasing manager can search the world for alternative supply sources of a product or service. With another click, the manager can then ascertain information about the sources identified through the electronic search. All of this research is done in the office without phone calls, additional personnel, or outside sources.

A significant efficiency factor of e-commerce is improved communications. The buyer can secure information from the vendor's company—product line, prices, and product availability. The seller can obtain information regarding requests for proposals, blueprints, technical specifications, and purchase requirements from the buyer. Also, the seller can improve customer service by communicating the status of the order, giving the buyer advance notice of any delays in the order fulfillment due to stockout conditions or transportation. As noted earlier, e-commerce permits the seller to gain real-time information to more accurately predict demand.

This improved communication via e-commerce aids in reducing order cycle time. All the time elements incorporated in order cycle time are reduced. The time to place the order is reduced to seconds. The buyer knows prior to placing an order whether the vendor has product available. The seller monitors demand instantaneously and is in a better position to adjust supply with current demand and to reduce or eliminate a stockout condition.

Better use of procurement personnel is made possible by relieving them of the clerical tasks associated with processing the order, such as manually preparing purchase orders, mailing them to the vendor, and checking the status of the order via phone. The procurement manager is now free to focus attention on the long-term strategic procurement issues such as long-term item availability, opportunities for supply chain efficiencies, innovative products, and so on.

Reduced procurement prices have resulted from the ability of a buyer to gain access to pricing information from more potential vendors. With more vendors bidding for the business, the buyers are finding lower prices forthcoming. In addition, the procurement manager has the ability to view online the qualities of different vendor products and services, making comparison much easier. The overall effect of increased comparison shopping and increased number of potential vendors is lower prices.

Disadvantages

Like most things in life, e-commerce does have some drawbacks. The most frequently voiced concern about using the Internet for procurement is security. Examples of attacks on e-commerce companies, such as Amazon.com and eBay where computers were overloaded with orders and operations were stopped, give many executives much concern about e-commerce security. Also, there is concern regarding the vulnerability of credit card numbers transmitted over the Internet or stored on a vendor's system to theft by a computer hacker.

Another problem is the lack of face-to-face contact between the buyer and seller. Buying and selling via e-commerce reduces the ability to build close supplier relationships. This can be overcome by making a concerted effort to develop and enhance personal communications with the vendor.

Supply Chain Technology

Transportation Sourcing – Innovative Approaches to Bid Optimization

Prevailing business conditions make it essential for shippers to be economical in their selection of specific carriers to serve individual freight lanes in their networks. Thus, new and improved methods for transportation sourcing and lane assignments have been developed and successfully implemented. These approaches assume that if transportation providers have an opportunity to bid simultaneously on multiple lanes, and/or pre-specified packages or combinations of lanes, results will be a significant improved. Earlier bidding strategies asked providers to state their prices for individual lanes only, and then the shipper's task was to select the "lowest price" carrier for each individual lane. This traditional approach generally resulted overall in higher-costs for transportation than decisions based on use of the newer technologies.

The results of using these enhanced bidding techniques are a win-win for both shippers and carriers. Shippers see improvements in the efficiency and effectiveness of their transportation operations, and cost-savings from awarding greater volumes of business to a smaller number of providers. Carriers benefit through improved capacity utilization, more strategic routing of vehicles and drivers, greater opportunities for continuous improvement, and overall improved alignment between carrier business objectives and shippers' transportation needs.

Industry-leading technologies for transportation bid optimization are available from many commercial suppliers such as CombineNet (www.combinet.com), Infor (www.infor.com), JDA Software (www.jda.com), Manhattan Associates (www.manh.com), Oracle (www.oracle.com) and Sterling Commerce – an IBM Company (www.sterlingcommerce.com).

Source: C. John Langley Jr., Ph.D. Used with permission.

Other concerns deal with technology. More specifically, there are concerns with the lack of standard protocols, system reliability, and technology problems. Lastly, there is reluctance on the part of some to invest the time and money to learn the new technology. For the most part, these concerns are diminishing daily as new and improved technology is developed and the business community demands the use of e-commerce.

e-Commerce Models[10]

The four basic types of e-commerce business models used in procurement and sourcing are **sell-side system**, **electronic marketplace**, **buy-side system**, and **online trading community**. The following comments and examples clarify each of their roles:

- **Sell-side system:** Online businesses selling to individual companies or consumers. Examples include OfficeMax (www.officemax.com), Staples (www.staples.com), Xpedx (www.xpedx.com), Best Buy (www.bestbuy.com), Wal-Mart (www.walmart.com), and CNET (www.cnet.com). An increasing number of sell-side Web sites provide buyer login capabilities that allow storing of information concerning buying preferences, buying history, etc., for future reference.

- **Electronic marketplace:** A seller-operated service that consists of a number of electronic catalogs from vendors within a market. The electronic marketplace provides a one-stop sourcing site for buyers who can examine the offerings of multiple vendors at one Internet location. Examples include Expedia.com (www.expedia.com), PlasticsNet (www.plasticsnet.com), ThomasNet (www.thomasnet.com), Froogle (www.froogle.google.com), Amazon (www.amazon.com), eBay (www.ebay.com), and Hotwire (www.hotwire.com).

- **Buy-side system:** A buyer-controlled e-procurement or e-commerce service that is housed on the buyer's system and is administered by the buyer, who typically pre-approves the suppliers who have access to the system, and the process of the suppliers' products and services that have been prenegotiated. These systems permit tracking and controlling procurement spending and help to reduce unauthorized purchases. However, the cost of buy-side systems is frequently high due to the cost of developing and administering the system with a large number of suppliers. For this reason, most buy-side systems are usually in the domain of large companies. An interesting example of a buy-side system is Elemica, discussed in the Supply Chain Profile at the beginning of this chapter.

- **Online trading community:** A system maintained by a third-party technology vendor where multiple buyers and multiple sellers in a given market can conduct business. The difference between the online trading community and the electronic marketplace is that the electronic marketplace is focused on providing information about sellers, whereas the online community permits the buyers and sellers to conduct business transactions.

The online trading company also may be viewed as an electronic auction. In such instances, the buyer indicates the type of product, quantity, and so on, desired; and the sellers respond. In a downward auction, the buyer states a maximum time period to receive the best bid from potential vendors. At the end of the time period, the buyer selects the vendor(s) with the lowest price and will conduct negotiations, if necessary, to finalize the transaction. Examples of online trading companies include Travelocity (www.travelocity.com), Priceline (www.priceline.com), eBay (www.ebay.com), and NTE (www.nte.net).

Other examples of online trading communities are E2open (www.e2open.com), which focuses on high-tech and electronics, and Agentics (www.agentics.com), a global retail industry.

Electronic procurement is here and will continue to grow. It will not replace all procurement activities, but it could reach 80 percent or more of a company's total purchase order activity. Electronic procurement focuses on the processing of orders and maintaining a source of real-time information for better decision making. Procurement specialists focus on selecting vendors, negotiating prices, monitoring quality, and developing supplier relations.

SUMMARY

- Expertise in the areas of purchasing, procurement, and strategic sourcing is essential to the success of supply chain management.

- Different procurement and sourcing strategies are related to the risk and value or profit potential from needed products and services. Not all purchased items are of equal importance. Using the criteria of risk and value, the quadrant technique classifies items into four categories: generics, commodities, distinctives, and criticals. Generics have low risk, low value; commodities have low risk, high value; distinctives have high risk, low value; and criticals have high risk, high value.

- The strategic sourcing process consists of seven steps that include project planning and kickoff, profile spend, assess supply market, develop sourcing strategy, execute sourcing strategy, transition and integrate, and measure and improve performance.

- Keys to effective management of the procurement and sourcing processes include determining the type of purchase, determining the necessary levels of investment, performing the procurement process, and evaluating the effectiveness of the process.

- A number of key factors should be considered in the supplier selection and evaluation process, including certifications and registrations such as TQM, Six Sigma, and ISO 9000.

- Extensive effort should be expended to research and understand procurement price and total landed cost (TLC).

- e-sourcing and e-procurement practices and technologies are helping to enhance the effectiveness and efficiency of traditional buying processes. In addition, a number of e-commerce model types have been developed and are becoming very popular: sell-side, electronic marketplace, buy-side, and online trading community systems. Overall, the advantages of e-sourcing and e-procurement include lower operating costs, improved efficiency, and reduced prices.

STUDY QUESTIONS

1. Describe and discuss the differences and relationships between purchasing, procurement, and strategic sourcing. How have these concepts evolved?

2. Using the quadrant or risk/value technique, categorize the importance of the following items for an automobile manufacturer: engine, tires, gasoline, paper for the employee newsletter, a uniquely designed and engineered muffler, and rail car service to dealers. Describe the rationale you used to ascertain each categorization.

3. The strategic sourcing process can be described in terms of a series of steps that should be used in the purchase of goods and services. Briefly discuss these steps.

4. Maximizing the effectiveness of the procurement process is a major goal of an organization. What steps can be taken to help ensure that the process is maximized?

5. A key part of the procurement process is the selection of suppliers. What criteria are commonly used in this selection process? Which criteria should be given the highest priority? Why?

6. What is meant by supplier "certifications and registrations"? Of what relevance are these to the supplier selection process?

7. How should companies evaluate suppliers?

8. What are the major sources of prices in the purchase of goods? Under what circumstances would these sources be utilized?

9. What are the components of total acquired cost? Is it realistic to expect companies to consider all of these components?

10. Discuss the advantages and disadvantages of using e-commerce in the procurement process.

11. Describe the different types of e-commerce business models available for procurement and point out their respective benefits and disadvantages.

NOTES

1. Michael E. Porter, *Competitive Advantage* (New York Free Press, 1985), 16.

2. This section is adapted from Joseph L. Cavinato, "Quadrant Technique Key to Effective Acquisition and Access," *ARDC Spectrum, Report #11* (State College, PA: Acquisition Research and Development Center).

3. The strategic sourcing process discussed in this section was developed at Adjoined Consulting, LLC (now Kanbay, Inc.). Used with permission.

4. The relevance of risk is becoming more apparent in today's supply chain decision making. One source where this factor is discussed meaningfully is Mark Crone, "Are Global Supply Chains Too Risky?" *Supply Chain Management Review* (May/June 2006): 28–35.

5. Porter, 33–34.

6. The content of this section is adapted from Knowledge@Wharton (December 9, 2005).

7. This section is adapted from J. L. Cavinato, "A Total Cost/Value Model for Supply Chain Competitiveness," *Journal of Business Logistics,* Vol. 13, No. 2 (1992): 285–299.

8. Retrieved from www.forrester.com.

9. The content of this section is from Christopher D. Norek and Donavon Favre, "Procurement Solutions: What Might Work for You," *Logistics Quarterly* (March 2006): 25–26.

10. The content of this section is adapted from Mark Vigoroso, "Buyers Prepare for Brave New World of E-Commerce," *Purchasing* (April 22, 1999).

CASE 13.1

South Face

South Face is a global manufacturer of winter and summer outdoor sports apparel. Its winter line predominantly includes outerwear such as ski jackets, fleece, windbreakers, and footwear. Its summer line is somewhat different and includes running attire (shorts and shirts), windbreakers, backpacks, hydration systems, and footwear. The company is headquartered in Vail, Colorado, but does business principally through retailers in North America, Europe, and Australia. In addition, South Face has established itself as a well-known Internet retailer of its full product line. Overall, South Face is viewed as a trend-setter and is one of the most profitable firms in the industry.

At the present time, South Face uses contract manufacturers in China, Taiwan, Korea, and Vietnam to make most of the items in its product line. Typical manufacturing lead times are anywhere from 4 to 12 months, depending on the type of product being manufactured and the complexity and range of materials needed to manufacture individual items. Both air and ocean are used for shipments to the destination countries, with the mode selection being largely a function of the urgency of the shipment. South Face maintains company-owned distribution centers in Denver, Colorado; Atlanta, Georgia; Amsterdam, Netherlands; Hamburg, Germany; and Melbourne, Australia.

As a practical matter, the alternating seasonal product lines manufactured by South Face help to ensure year-round utilization of its contract manufacturing capacity and its company-owned distribution centers. Over the past few years, South Face has experienced a number of areas of concern, including the following:

- Intensifying competition from other manufacturers of similar winter and summer outdoor sportswear. Given the attractive profit margins on many of its products, a number of new competitors have emerged in recent years.

- Inaccuracy of demand forecasts across both the winter and summer lines of products and the geographies served. Coupled with unexpected variations in the length, consistency, and cost of transportation services, this has resulted from time to time in stock-outs of needed items at retail stores.

- The need for a meaningful, strategic sourcing process that can help to better guide the approaches taken by South Face with regard to the supply side of its business.

- Evidence that the contract manufacturers employed by South Face are also manufacturing illegal, knock-off merchandise that is being sold through "gray market" channels.

To help address some of the supply chain issues facing South Face, Mercer Wilde has recently been hired as the new senior vice president of supply chain. He has taken time so far to visit the company's global facilities and to become aware of the situation, problems, and concerns that are faced by the company. Mercer will be asked to address the following types of questions.

CASE QUESTIONS

1. Based on your knowledge of the global business environment and the positioning of South Face with regard to its markets and supply sources, what do you think are some of the major global issues that will be relevant to the area of strategic sourcing?

2. What are the impacts of less-than-perfect demand forecasts for South Face products, and of volatility in the length and cost of transport services used to move its products from contract manufacturers to DCs? What should be done to mitigate these problem areas?

3. What elements of the strategic sourcing process do you feel are the top candidates for improvement at South Face, and why?

4. How would you respond to the assertion that some of your contract manufacturers are involved in producing illegal merchandise that ends up competing with the branded merchandise of South Face?

Source: C. John Langley Jr., Ph.D. Used with permission.

CASE 13.2

Durable Vinyl Siding Corporation

Durable Vinyl Siding Corporation (DVS) is a leading U.S. manufacturer of vinyl siding products for home and commercial buildings. In 2006, the company had record sales of $250 million—a 15 percent increase over 2005 and the tenth year of double-digit growth. Mark Talbott, president, was very pleased with the positive sales figures for 2006 but was becoming concerned about the trend of the bottom-line numbers. During the past five years, the net profit margin had slipped from 7.2 percent in 2001 to 4.5 percent in 2006.

At the monthly executive team meeting, Mark pointed out the downward trend of net profits and challenged the team to increase the bottom line by 1 to 2 percentage points for the next year. Mark pointed out to the team members that price pressure from competing siding companies and increasing costs were the primary reasons for the declining profit margins. He asked each team member to develop a strategic plan to accomplish the profit goals.

Margaret Klisure, director of sourcing and procurement, was reviewing the purchasing data that had been gathered in preparation for developing a purchasing strategic plan. Procurement costs had increased from 57 percent of sales in 1996 to 65 percent of sales in 2006, a period of time during which the size of the procurement staff increased by five people.

DVS now manufactures 1,500 stock-keeping units (SKUs) and purchases over 5,000 SKUs of materials to support the manufacture, sale, and delivery of its finished goods line. The items purchased include vinyl base products, paints, office supplies, packaging, lumber for pallets, warehouse equipment, maintenance and operating items, and transportation services. In total, DVS spent $162.5 million in 2006 for these items and the operation of the procurement department. For each 1.0 percent reduction in procurement expenditures, Margaret calculated an increase of 0.65 percent in net profits (assuming $250 million in sales).

The purchasing department operation was basically the same as it was in 1996. Margaret was recently appointed director of sourcing and procurement following the retirement of the previous director who had been the head of purchasing since the founding of the company over 20 years before. Although most of the purchasing/procurement tasks are completed manually, computers are used for internal control of inventory levels and for printing invoices. There is no procurement computer system in place, and there is no use of e-commerce for purchasing. The purchasing staff consists primarily of buyers who are assigned to particular product groups; for example, a person is responsible for purchasing all the vinyl raw materials, one person purchases transportation, and so on.

Over the years, the buyers have become very skilled at gaining price concessions from vendors. However, this has created some very serious warehousing problems for DVS. For example, last week, Mark Talbott called an emergency meeting with the directors of manufacturing, warehousing, sales, and purchasing to seek a solution to the overcrowding in the warehouse. The warehouse was completely full, forcing DVS to go off site to store finished goods. A review of the items stored in the warehouse indicated that there was a 6-month supply of corrugated packaging material, a 10-month supply of paints, and a 4-month supply of lumber. Also, the inventory levels of over 50 percent of the finished good SKUs exceeded a two-year supply at current sales levels.

With only one warehouse in the system, DVS had to optimize the utilization of this facility. If DVS had to use an outside warehouse for short-term storage, it incurred a 15 percent penalty in the form of higher storage, order picking, and transportation costs. In addition, the cost of capital rose last year because of the actions of the Federal Reserve, and the total purchasing expenditure included the cost of money tied up in inventory.

Margaret also knew that the buyers' productivity was declining because the annual number of orders per buyer was declining in light of the addition of staff last year. The buyers noted the need for more time to research potential vendors and to maintain good vendor relations as the prime reasons for the lower productivity.

Margaret's primary objective was to reduce procurement costs while maintaining the product quality and efficiency of procurement. Price concessions from vendors did not appear to be a major source of cost savings, particularly for the basic vinyl raw materials. She concluded that the primary areas for efficiency enhancements were in computerization and e-commerce.

CASE QUESTIONS

1. What organizational changes would you suggest for DVS procurement?

2. What types of computerization changes would you recommend?

3. How would e-commerce benefit DVS procurement?

4. Would you recommend the same computer and e-commerce strategies for all 5,000 SKUs purchased? If not, how would these strategies differ?

5. What strategies do you suggest for maintaining procurement service levels?

Source: Edward J. Bardi, Ph.D. Used with permission.

Chapter 14

OPERATIONS—PRODUCING GOODS AND SERVICES

Learning Objectives

After reading this chapter, you should be able to do the following:

- Discuss the strategic value-adding role operations plays in the supply chain.
- Explain the concept of a transformation process and its application to goods and services.
- Appreciate the tradeoffs and challenges involved in production operations.
- Understand the primary production strategies and types of planning.
- Discuss the primary assembly processes and production methods for goods creation.
- Describe the various production process layouts.
- Explain the role of productivity and quality metrics for improving operations performance.
- Know how information technology supports efficient production of goods and services.

Supply Chain Profile   *Ford: Putting on the Top Hat*

For the past several years, automakers have been reducing product development and engineering costs through the reuse of parts and platforms. In several cases, this has resulted in products that look alike, with little differentiation between vehicle brands, save for interior trim packaging and optional equipment. But this has changed, in large part due to advances in computer-aided design and flexible manufacturing systems. Now automakers can reuse the basic architecture and structure of a vehicle but then put vastly different body styles, or top hats, over them. Ford is the latest automaker to join the top hat revolution and it is moving aggressively forward with plans to use fewer global architectures over multiple vehicle segments to improve profitability and operational efficiency.

"At Ford, we view the top hat as being the upper body structure of the vehicle which is set on a common set of underpinnings. The upper body could be a number of variants from a crossover to a sedan or coupe," says Bruce Hettle, executive director of manufacturing at Ford, who points out that because they're reusing the base, they get economies of scale, but because of the different top hats, the customer gets extensive product differentiation. Sounds simple, right? Think again. Implementing a comprehensive and successful top hat strategy requires a complete change in process from the start of design through to manufacturing job one. It isn't as simple as buying the latest PLM software or flexible manufacturing cell.

Ford is making huge changes to the way it conducts its product development activities to accommodate increased reliance on more top hats based on fewer architectures. The automaker has revamped its entire product development, engineering, and manufacturing disciplines to encourage early communication throughout the product development phase, ensuring that vehicle architectures can accommodate numerous top hats before freezing platform dimensions and having to make costly modifications down the road.

"We do not have separate product development and manufacturing functions at Ford anymore. Both functions are fully collocated," says Hettle. The automaker is also shifting to a "gold standard" streamlined global bill of design, process, and materials focused on just two vehicle architectures: unitized bodies and frame-based vehicles, with complete commonality between every vehicle within these architecture segments by 2012, including manufacturing sequences.

"Prior to this approach, we would have one or two vehicles in an assembly site, but now the plan calls for 3, 4, or 5 differentiated products," Hettle says. As an example, Ford is investing $100 million in flexible tooling to move production of its Lincoln Navigator and Ford Expedition full-size SUVs to its Louisville, Kentucky, truck plant in spring 2009 alongside the Super Duty pickup to maximize efficiency at the plant, which was dedicated solely to the Super Duty. "Once we make these investments we will be able to build the new Super Duty model along with the next Navigator and Expedition and fluctuate that mix up and down so when the new Super Duty is launched we can run that product all out and reduce the number of Navigators and Expeditions and vice versa," Hettle adds.

Relocation of the Navigator and Expedition has freed up capacity at Michigan Truck for Ford to respond quickly to changing market conditions in the United States and move its European C-segment–based vehicles—Focus, C-Max and Kuga—into the plant beginning in early 2010. Unlike prior product relocations, Ford will only have to invest $75 million to retool the plant for the shift because the automaker put $300 million into the plant in 2005 for flexible tooling in the body shop, which can be easily reconfigured to accommodate the smaller unibody-based vehicles and their top hats. "The way we configured the original body shop is that 80 percent of the infrastructure was non-vehicle specific, allowing those pieces to remain in place. The other 20 percent that requires changes are the fixtures that touch the sheet metal along with minor modifications to the paint shop," Hettle says.

This approach to forethought is a critical part to executing a successful top hat strategy, and Ford will push the boundaries even further with its Fiesta B-segment vehicle platform, which will include crossover and MPV body style variants after 2010 sharing a singular global design built in plants with identical tooling and layouts. "There will no longer be a reliance on regional designs and processes," Hettle says.

Top hats may help to improve the bottom line through increased reuse, but there are limits to the benefits. Building too many variants—more than six or seven at one facility—could inject excessive complexity into the manufacturing process, thus eliminating the cost savings generated when only three or four variants are built. Likewise, only building two variants could lead to problems if both vehicles are failures in the marketplace. Still, failure to implement a cohesive top hat strategy is like leaving money on the table, and in this day and age that's a massive waste of potential resources.

Source: Adapted from Kevin M. Kelly, "Ford: Putting on the Top Hat," *Automotive Design & Production,* (January 2009), pp. 25, 27. Reproduced by permission.

Introduction

Operations focus on the "make/build" portion of the supply chain. They focus on production of goods and services needed to fulfill customer requirements. Production involves the transformation of inputs into outputs that customers demand. For example, a computer manufacturer like Lenovo or Apple assembles a set of components (processor, memory, hard drive, etc.) into the ThinkPad or iMac that you configure. Likewise, a hospital emergency room has knowledgeable doctors and nurses to transform an injured person (the input) back to a healthy state (the output).

In the execution of these processes, production facilities must interact with supply chain functions that have been discussed in previous chapters. Both manufacturers and service providers need ready access to inventories of key inputs from their suppliers. Lenovo and Apple need hardware and software to build computers that are functional when they are removed from the box. The doctors and nurses require diagnostic equipment, medical supplies, and pharmaceutical products to evaluate and treat the patient. Hence, there's a critical link between supply management, inventory, inbound transportation, and production operations.

Also, operations create the outputs that are distributed through supply chain networks. Consumer demand for computers cannot be satisfied without production of the physical goods. Production schedules must be coordinated with delivery schedules and transportation methods to ensure that inventory is received when promised. Ambulances and delivery vehicles may be needed to transport treated patients and home care equipment to their residences. Thus, it is easy to understand why production operations are part of the supply chain and cannot be conducted independently. All activities in the purchase, production, and delivery of goods and services need to be synchronized to ensure consistent, efficient product and service flows.

This is no easy task, as highlighted by the Ford example in the Supply Chain Profile. To remain competitive, automobile manufacturers and other organizations must continually strive to provide variety and quality at a reasonable production cost. This chapter focuses on the need to balance flexibility and responsiveness with efficiency during the transformation process, as well as the critical links between production processes and other supply chain activities. We will discuss the planning and development of production capabilities, as well as the processes, metrics, and technologies that support efficient product and service operations. Throughout the chapter, you will gain an understanding of the roles that production strategies and methods play in the creation of the inventories needed to fulfill customer demand.

The Role of Production Operations in Supply Chain Management (SCM)

When you think about it, many of the supply chain and logistics activities discussed in previous chapters focus on operations—procurement operations that provide access to materials, transportation operations that support the flow of goods, distribution operations that streamline order fulfillment, and so on. Collectively, they create time and place utilities. However, the potential contributions of goods manufacturing and service production to supply chain effectiveness are often overlooked because they focus on a different, but also important, dimension of economic utility called **form utility**. All the activities and processes involved in changing the appearance or composition of a good or service—component fabrication, product assembly, and service request execution—focus on creating form utility. The goal is to make the product or service more attractive to potential and actual users so that demand is created.

Of course, a great product design or form utility is important, but not enough to guarantee success. Form utility drives the need for supply chain capabilities (i.e., time and place utilities). When Microsoft introduces a product like the Kinect for Xbox 360, they need integrated supply chain processes to fulfill customer demand for the gaming system. It is imperative to procure key materials quickly, marshal production resources and capacity to assemble the components, and move the finished goods to retailers in sufficient quantities to meet demand. Otherwise, the door opens for competitors to hijack potential Kinect customers to their offerings.

It takes a great deal of effort and coordination to run an effective production operation that is supported by and also supports the supply chain. Processes must be effectively designed and flawlessly executed, supply chain tradeoffs must be understood and made, and economies of scale need to be achieved, all while the organization addresses competitive challenges and other problems. Consider the success of the Apple iPhone. A great product design, procurement–assembly–distribution synchronization, and savvy marketing all contributed to the success of this commercial juggernaut. Rapid execution of the "plan/buy/make/move" supply chain processes is essential to meeting global demand for this innovative smartphone.

With the vital connection between production and SCM established, we'll take a deeper look at the details of production operations.

Production Process Functionality

Manufacturers, contract assemblers, and service providers all engage in production processes. Whether they make sandwiches, laser printers, or bank loans, these organizations perform a group of related activities during which inputs are transformed into outputs.

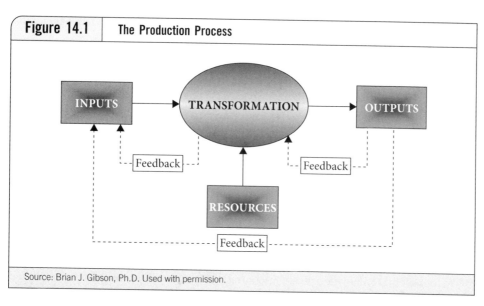

Figure 14.1 | The Production Process

Source: Brian J. Gibson, Ph.D. Used with permission.

This production process, as shown in Figure 14.1, also uses resources such as facilities, equipment, knowledge, labor, and capital to support the transformation. Feedback of key information is used to make adjustments within the process (e.g., speed up or slow down the purchase of inputs and the production of outputs according to changes in demand requirements) in an attempt to synchronize production more closely to demand. Ignoring these feedback signals will lead to excess inventory of unpopular products or inventory shortages of hot items.

While the basic input–transformation–output principle applies to all production processes, no two are organized exactly alike or perform to the same level. For example Pizza Hut, McDonald's, and Subway each make fast food but have slightly different product strategies that drive their process design and assembly methods. Pizza Hut and Subway offer assemble-to-order products that are created from a variety of available components (e.g., pre-sliced meats, cheeses, and vegetables) when you place an order. McDonald's produces products in anticipation of demand using standardized product components. As you might expect, assemble-to-order methods tend to be more complex, be more labor intensive, and require longer processing time than the mass-production-oriented, make-to-stock operations. Process capacity (how much can be produced) is also impacted by product type and production methods.

Process functionality also plays a role in the success of an organization. The ability to perform different processes from those of competitors to create unique products and services can create a competitive advantage. For example, eBay became an online powerhouse by developing auction processes that are vastly different from traditional methods. On the other hand, the ability to perform common processes better than the competition can generate efficiencies and lower costs for the organization. Southwest Airlines is a good example of a company that provides the same basic passenger flight services as its competition, but at a lower operating cost. As long as the level of service and quality of output meets customer expectations, either focus can help the organization reach its goals.

Production Tradeoffs

One of the most important issues for supply chain professionals to understand is the tradeoffs involved within production operations and between production operations, other supply chain functions, and corporate strategy. All decisions are interrelated and can impact costs, productivity, and quality in other areas. In the next few paragraphs, common tradeoffs are discussed.

The volume–variety tradeoff is a primary issue in production. Higher volume leads to lower cost per unit of output, according to the long-established economies of scale principle. In situations where production processes have high fixed costs and equipment like chemical production or paper manufacturing, it makes sense to pursue volume. In contrast, processes that can produce a range of products are said to have **economies of scope**. These flexible capabilities are important in situations where efficient, low-volume production runs of a wide variety of products are required to meet changing customer demand.[1] Organizations should evaluate their product, process, and demand characteristics to determine their relative need for variety versus volume.

Fundamental tradeoffs between responsiveness and efficiency arise when production facility decisions are made. Centralized production facilities provide operating cost and inventory efficiencies, while regional production facilities allow companies to be closer to customers and more responsive. Larger facilities with excess capacity provide the flexibility to respond to demand spikes. In contrast, smaller facilities that are better utilized will be more cost efficient. Finally, the operating methodology used by the facility impacts this tradeoff. Product-focused facilities that perform many processes on a single product type will tend to be more responsive than process-focused facilities that concentrate on a few functions across multiple product types. The latter type of facility will be more efficient at its limited scope of activities.[2]

Tradeoffs between production processes for goods and the costs involved in manufacturing them must also be understood. Production and supply chain costs vary for make-to-stock, assemble-to-order, and build-to-order products. As Figure 14.2 highlights,

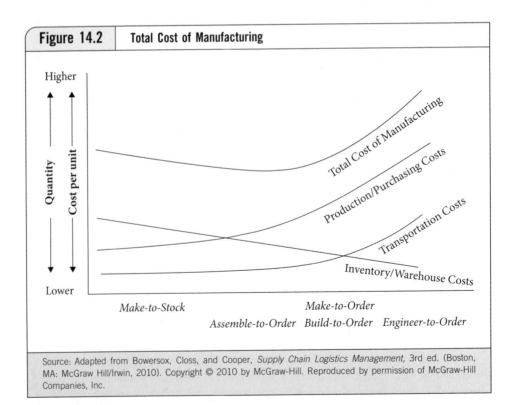

Figure 14.2 | **Total Cost of Manufacturing**

build-to-order products incur the highest total cost of manufacturing due to the lower production economies of scale and higher transportation costs. On the other hand, make-to-stock production processes have lower total costs due to higher volumes and lower transportation costs. One should not forget that while make-to-stock may be cheaper from a total cost of manufacturing standpoint, the method may sacrifice customer service, responsiveness, and variety.[3]

Another consideration is whether to conduct your own production operations or to outsource production to external suppliers. The make-versus-buy decision can be very complex and involves sacrifice whichever way the company chooses to go. Internal production processes are more directly visible and should be easier to control from a quality standpoint. Outsourced production may lead to lower product costs and allow the company to focus its resources on other, more strategic needs.

An organization needs to understand and evaluate the tradeoffs and comparative costs of producing or purchasing goods before making a final decision. Once outsourced, supplier quality and service must be monitored. Toyota's high-profile safety-related recalls in 2010 for "unintended acceleration" were caused, in part, by the throttle pedal assemblies made by an external supplier.[4]

Finally, traditional wisdom suggests that production operations cannot strive to be all things to all people and tradeoffs must be made. That is, when designing and executing production processes, they should focus on one or two competitive dimensions: low cost, high quality (features and reliability), fast delivery speed, high delivery reliability, ability to cope with demand change, or the flexibility to offer variety. Proponents logically argue that an operation cannot excel simultaneously on all six competitive dimensions due to inherent conflicts between the strategies and too many compromises would be required.[5] However, research by Accenture and others has shown that world-class organizations can improve performance along multiple dimensions without making extensive performance tradeoffs or sacrifices.[6] Procter & Gamble (P&G) is one of these world-class companies. Perennially ranked in the top five of the AMR Supply Chain Top 25, P&G is at the forefront of demand-driven SCM, specialized production operations in emerging markets, commodity hedging upstream for key inputs, and environmental responsibility.[7]

Production Challenges

To say that production is a dynamic field would be a severe understatement. Operations managers face numerous challenges and tradeoffs that must be managed successfully if the organization and supply chain are to achieve their performance goals. These challenges were highlighted by Ferrari and Parker in a *Supply Chain Management Review* article: "Intensified competition, more demanding customers, and relentless pressure for efficiency as well as adaptability are driving significant changes across many manufacturing industry settings."[8] According to the authors, long-term profitable growth is dependent on manufacturing and supply chain organizations' abilities to address these challenges through process innovation.

Competitive pressures are a major challenge for many established manufacturers and service providers. As the global reach of supply chains makes it possible to source product from nearly anywhere in the world, companies need to continually update their production capabilities and develop innovative responses to upstart competitors. The U.S. automobile industry is a prime example. Not only do General Motors and Ford need to compete with Toyota's lean production capabilities and Honda's product quality, but U.S. manufacturers must also develop an effective response to low-cost producers like Hyundai and Kia. A "business as usual" approach will lead to further deterioration of market share and supply chain woes for these organizations.

Customers' demand for choice and rapidly changing tastes make life difficult for product makers. For many products, it is no longer possible to focus on mass production and the Henry Ford approach to customization: "People can have the Model T in any color—so long as it's black." The expectation today of customized products that meet the specifications of individual buyers requires far different production processes than the assembly methods needed for standardized goods. The shrinking life cycle of products today also renders long production runs of these common goods obsolete. In response, companies like Dell and Nike have developed responsive capabilities by building supply chains around assemble-to-order production capabilities. Today, you can design your own Nike shoes at NikeiD.com.

While the use of responsive, small quantity production processes is growing, company executives still demand productivity and efficiency. They expect operations managers to employ processes that are *both* financially efficient and responsive to demand. Leanness and adaptability are requirements for success, though many organizations struggle to make the transition from traditional production methods and strategies to more contemporary ones that can better balance product quality, process flexibility, fulfillment speed, and execution costs.

Certainly, operations managers face many other operations challenges. Labor availability and productivity issues, synchronization of activities with the supply chain, and capital costs are just a few of the additional obstacles that must be overcome. The next section discusses planning methods and strategies used for product and service operations. Thoughtful, advanced preparation of production processes that consider these difficult challenges and tradeoffs will elevate an organization's prospects for growth and profitability.

Operations Strategy and Planning

A great deal of planning, preparation, and engagement of multiple parties is required for production operations to make a positive contribution to supply chain effectiveness. Strategies that encompass product/service characteristics, internal capabilities, customer expectations, and competitive issues must be developed. From these strategies, long- to short-range production plans are created, followed by the implementation of product assembly/service delivery processes.

Production Strategies

Over the last 30 years, significant development and shifts have occurred in production strategy. Many organizations have advanced from forecast-driven production strategies to demand-driven approaches. These companies strive to be lean, flexible, or adaptive; wait for customers to pull products to the market; and rely on much smaller stockpiles of inventory. The demand-driven strategies are vastly different from the efficiency-focused, mass-production concepts that dominated production strategies from the early part of the twentieth century until the 1970s. Figure 14.3 provides a general timeline and description of the evolution of production strategies. We will discuss each major strategy in detail.

Figure 14.3	Evolution of Production Strategies			
	1970s	*1980s*	*1990s*	*2000+*
Strategy	Mass Production	Lean Manufacturing	Flexible Manufacturing	Adaptive Manufacturing
Market Differentiator	Cost Inventory Protection	Quality Waste Reduction	Availability Leverage Resources	Velocity Real-time Execution
Process Option	Make-to-stock	Assemble-to-order	+ Build-to-order + Engineer-to-order	Hybrids
Materials Release	Push	Pull	Pull	Pull
Performance Focus	Production Throughput	Cost Management	Segment Market Share	Customer Satisfaction

Source: Adapted from *Manufacturing Strategy: An Adaptive Perspective* (Newton Square, PA: SAP AG, 2003).

In the era of mass production, operations strategy focused on efficiency and scale. The strategy of choice for mass production is a push-based system that relies on long-term forecasts for production planning and decision making. This methodology works well if demand is constant with limited variability throughout the year. Processes can be established to fulfill this stable demand without the need for excess or just-in-case capacity, and production throughput can be maximized.

In reality, few companies enjoy perfectly stable demand for their products and the related opportunity to maintain level production that is quickly consumed. More often, organizations must deal with demand variation. In these situations, goods are produced to stock according to the forecast and finished goods inventory or production backlogs are used to accommodate variation. Inventories accrue during lower-demand seasons, and the stockpile is reduced during peak seasons. If production can't keep up with demand during these high-demand periods, then a backlog of orders will start to accumulate and be worked down as orders decline.

The push-based strategy works well for supply chains that focus on the immediate delivery of off-the-shelf, low-cost, standardized goods. Coca-Cola soft drinks and Levi's jeans are examples of make-to-stock products that fit these criteria. As long as trading partners seek these low-priced stock items in reasonable volume, the producer can profitably use this production strategy.

Push-based supply chains are not without challenges. Operating from forecasts that are derived from supply chain partners' predictions may limit the producer's responsiveness. Without visibility to actual end-consumer demand, the producer will be slow to react to changes in the marketplace. The result may be continued production of items whose demand is dropping and may soon be obsolete. Alternatively, the producer may fail to recognize changing customer requirements and ramp up production of desired goods. The ultimate impact will be missed opportunities, unrecoverable costs, and/or missed revenues.

The other problem with basing production on supply chain partners' forecasts is the potential for the bullwhip effect to occur. Under this phenomenon, forecast errors are magnified and demand variability increases as orders move upstream from retailers to distributors to producers. The producers have to complete larger and more variable production batches to supply the often-changing downstream orders. This can lead to inefficient resource utilization as production capacity is not consistently engaged—sometimes being overworked, other times being idled.[9]

The 1980s ushered in the era of lean production to address the changing demand environment and the shortcomings of push-based, mass-production strategies. Lean production is an integrated set of activities designed to minimize the movement and use of raw materials, work-in-process, and finished goods inventories during production. The goal is to have materials arrive at the needed location just in time for rapid processing and flow through the system. A principal focus of lean manufacturing is to minimize all forms of waste and to produce quality products without the need for rework. The lean philosophy is largely based on the **Toyota production system (TPS)**, which seeks to develop and redesign production processes to remove overburden (*muri*), smooth production (*mura*), and eliminate waste (*muda*). Table 14.1 describes the seven types of *muda* targeted for elimination in the TPS.

Lean production relies on pull-based systems to coordinate production and distribution with actual customer demand rather than a potentially error-laden forecast of demand. In a pull system, the producer only responds to customer demand. No action is taken until an order is placed or a purchase is made. The order signal sets the production process into motion to quickly assemble the requested item (which may be an assemble-to-order product that is tailored to the customer) and move it toward the point of demand. The technology tools discussed in Chapter 6—point-of-sale scanning, electronic data interchange, the Internet, and auto-ID tags—support pull-based systems by providing visibility of demand. This allows quick action to be taken for the purpose of minimizing customer order cycle time.

One of the main benefits of a lean, pull-based system is the reduction of waste. Manufacturers don't have to build inventory in anticipation of demand or without knowledge of customer orders. This will limit the problems of overproduction, excess

Table 14.1	TPS Seven Deadly Wastes
WASTE	**DESCRIPTION**
Overproduction	Making more parts than you can sell.
Delays	Waiting for processing, parts sitting in storage, etc.
Transporting	Excessive movement of parts to various storage locations, from process to process, etc.
Overprocessing	Doing more "work" to a part than is required.
Inventory	Committing money and storage space to parts not sold.
Motion	Moving parts more than the minimum needed to complete and ship them.
Making defective parts	Creating parts that cannot be sold "as is" or that must be reworked, etc.

Source: Ta'Ichi Ohno, *Toyota Production System: Beyond Large-Scale Production* (New York, NY: Productivity Press, 1988).

inventory, and unnecessary processing. The bullwhip effect is also reduced when all supply chain partners function based on customer demand. This helps to reduce variation in the system and shrink lead times. Other benefits include an enhanced ability to manage resources and a reduction in system costs compared to push-based systems.[10]

Many computer companies, like Dell, rely on pull-based systems to manufacture desktop computers. Rather than trying to predict what customers will order, Dell waits until specific orders are received via its Web site or call center. Needed components are rapidly obtained from suppliers and third-party warehouses, assembled to customer specifications, and shipped via a customer's chosen delivery method. Dell does not waste effort building computers and putting them into inventory with the hope of a customer wanting that particular model. Organizations whose products have similar characteristics—higher value, customizable, short life cycle—can also benefit from the pull-based strategy.

A few challenges are inherent in the pull-based strategy. In some cases, customers want immediate access to products and don't want to wait for production and delivery (basic necessities like milk and bread are good examples). Also, it can be difficult to achieve economies of scale in assemble-to-order and build-to-order product operations, making them more expensive to produce. Finally, companies short on technological capabilities would find it difficult to achieve the supply chain visibility and synchronization needed in pull-based systems.

Although many companies have made significant gains during the evolution from mass production to lean production processes, perfection has not been achieved. Industry experts suggest that the shortcomings of lean processes need to be addressed if significant further progress is to be made. Lack of flexibility and inadequate information systems are frequently cited as significant barriers to achieving manufacturing responsiveness and true flexibility.[11]

Flexible manufacturing emerged in the early 1990s in response to the production challenges described earlier in this chapter—product proliferation, shorter life cycles, faster competitors, and more sophisticated customers. The purpose of this strategy is to build some flexibility into the production system in order to react effectively to markets characterized by frequent volume changes and rapid product evolution.[12]

One type of reactive capability is **machine flexibility**. Under this strategy, general purpose machines and equipment staffed by cross-trained workers provide the ability to produce different types of products as well as change the order of operations executed on a product. In the automobile industry, Honda leads the way. To respond to changes in economic conditions, Honda shuffles production among different plants and also makes different models in one plant. Within minutes, technicians change production line settings and adjust equipment, so that production can shift from cars to sport utility vehicles. Other manufacturers take weeks to make similar changes.[13]

Another type of reactive capability (there are eight in all) is called **routing flexibility**, which provides managers with production options and the ability to adapt to changing needs. In its simplest terms, routing flexibility provides managers with a choice between machines for a part's next operation.[14] This capability is valuable for overcoming machine breakdowns so that production can continue for the given products. It also creates opportunities to flow products through alternate routes within the production facility. Under these scenarios, the system has the ability to absorb large-scale changes, such as in volume, capacity, or capability.

A primary advantage of the flexible manufacturing strategy is the ability to leverage production resources (e.g., time and effort) in support of different transformation processes. It also takes advantage of the capabilities of strong vendors, information technology, and highly trained indirect staff. The desired outcome is the achievement of economies of scope where small batches of a large variety of products can be produced cost effectively. Other benefits include improved productivity, quality, and labor cost due to higher automation, as well as shorter preparation and setup time for new products.

For all its benefits, the flexible strategy is not perfect. Its main flaw is cost, as companies find it expensive to purchase multipurpose or adjustable equipment. Building excess flexible capacity into the system is also a costly proposition. In addition, the promise of productivity increases doesn't always pan out in flexible operations.[15] Finally, inadequate information systems are frequently cited as significant barriers to achieving manufacturing responsiveness and true flexibility.[16]

Given these issues, many organizations have adopted an outsourcing strategy for some or all of their production operations. Business process outsourcing involves the farming out of any internal process—payroll, transportation, or production—to a third party. Contract manufacturers provide outsourced production and assembly services just as a third-party logistics firm provides distribution, warehousing, and transportation services (see Chapter 4). Should the activity be relocated to a contract manufacturer in another country, it is commonly called **offshoring**. Today, a popular location for offshore production is China, though the country's rising labor costs and quality challenges may drive production elsewhere.[17]

The business case for outsourcing varies by situation, but the reasons often focus on cost and capacity issues. The outsourcing strategy commonly provides a more viable means to variable capacity at a lower cost than the flexibility strategy.[18] Other reasons for production outsourcing include the following:

- The ability to focus on core competencies by getting rid of peripheral ones
- Lack of in-house resources
- Getting work done more efficiently or effectively
- Increased flexibility to meet changing business and commercial conditions
- Tighter control of budget through predictable costs
- Lower ongoing investment in internal infrastructure
- Access to innovation and thought leadership[19]

While outsourcing has proven to be a valuable strategy whose popularity has grown dramatically, it is important to conduct a full analysis of the benefits and drawbacks of offshoring. Moving production offshore raises transportation costs, inventory carrying costs of goods in transit, customs costs, and some hidden expenses. As production spreads out among multiple facilities in different countries, it becomes more difficult to maintain visibility and synchronize activities. Finally, companies may lose control over quality, intellectual property rights, and customer relationships. The On the Line feature below focuses on Whirlpool's analysis and decision to "on-shore" appliance production.

A newly launched twenty-first century addition to production strategy is **adaptive manufacturing,** which leverages lean manufacturing strategies, Six Sigma best practices, and real-time actionable intelligence from the factory floor. The adaptive approach rejects traditional reliance on standard lead times and long-range forecasts in favor of a more demand-driven approach in which the supply side quickly senses and responds to what customers want.[20] The result is increased production flexibility and demand fulfillment velocity.

On the Line

Whirlpool's On-Shore Production Decision

According to a September 1, 2010, *Wall Street Journal* article by Bob Tita, Whirlpool plans to build a new factory in Cleveland, Tennessee, on the site of a 100-year-old oven factory. The new facility will be "the centerpiece of a $300 million upgrade of domestic manufacturing facilities" for the company. The article goes on to say: "The move highlights a shift by even export-driven U.S. manufacturers away from low-cost overseas locales in favor of rationalizing domestic operations to boost productivity." In Whirlpool's case, the company had considered building the factory in Mexico.

The move toward manufacturing or sourcing products closer to home has been happening for a few years, accelerated in part by the record-high oil prices in 2008 (which caused transportation costs to skyrocket), demand for faster lead times, and quality issues in foreign factories that have triggered a continuous wave of recalls.

In their January 2009 *Supply Chain Management Review* article, John Ferreira and Len Prokopets from Archstone Consulting argue that a thorough sourcing analysis would reveal that offshoring no longer makes sense for many companies. Ferreira and Prokopets offered this analysis:

> Just when thousands of manufacturers thought that offshoring a significant portion of their manufacturing and supply operations has given them competitive parity, the game may be changing again. The same factors that made offshoring a sure-fire tactic for reducing costs have shifted dramatically and now are eroding many of those savings. As a result, on-shore and near-shore production is now viable and competitive in many cases.

Manufacturers may thus want to hit the hold button before moving more of their supply operations offshore; many manufacturers are finding that the numbers just don't add up anymore. In fact, a significant percentage of U.S. manufacturers are seriously reconsidering their production and sourcing strategies and even beginning to return manufacturing that they had once moved to low-cost countries.

The article about Whirlpool reveals two important points. First, Whirlpool has linked product design and development with its manufacturing strategy and factory design. By building washers with more easily changeable components, Whirlpool will be able to assemble multiple models and brands from the same plant.

"Just about everything can be changed out," said Frank Nekic, manager of washing machine development. "You can take one motor and replace it with another. It was much more difficult to create variations within the washers we had."

The second key point in the article is the value Whirlpool placed on employee knowledge and experience in making its sourcing decision. Preserving the Cleveland employees' training and experience in lean manufacturing was a major consideration in choosing the site, according to Al Holaday, vice president for North American manufacturing.

"Everyone can pretty much duplicate the manufacturing process," Holaday said. "What I can't do is duplicate the experienced work force."

Kudos to Whirlpool for making employee knowledge and experience a "major consideration" in its decision to build its new factory in Tennessee. It's not always easy to place a financial value on employee talent, but everyone knows that inexperience and lack of training ultimately translates into productivity, quality, and recall issues, which can be very costly, difficult and time consuming to fix, especially from half-a-world away.

Source: Adapted from Adrian Gonzalez, "Whirlpool, On-shore Production, and Employee Talent," *ARC's Logistics Viewpoint* (September 1, 2010). Retrieved from http://logisticsviewpoints.com/2010/09/01/whirlpool-on-shore-production-and-employee-talent/. Reproduced by permission.

Technology is a key facilitator of flexibility and velocity. Properly deployed systems link factory processes, production equipment, and production systems to supply chain operations.[21] These linkages and real-time information are critical for sensing supply chain and manufacturing exceptions and quickly responding with appropriate actions.[22]

Though it has not gained widespread adoption, the adaptive manufacturing strategy provides numerous benefits. Adaptive manufacturing users are realizing significant benefits, including reductions in inventory, production cycle time, quality issues, and cost.[23] The "morph on the fly" capabilities of adaptive manufacturing are also well-suited to handle the chaotic swings in demand and economic uncertainty that have become commonplace.[24]

Each of these five strategies has a role in today's supply chain, including the traditional mass-production, push-based strategy. Newer manufacturing strategies will not completely replace the older ones. Rather, the goal is to link the strengths of the traditional strategies with the enhanced capabilities of the innovative strategies to meet customer requirements. Manufacturers must develop strategic solutions that are appropriate for the product being made, the volume and variability of demand, and the capabilities of the manufacturer. The wider the range of products and customers is, the more likely the organization will be to run a hybrid system that leverages multiple strategies.

Production Planning[25]

With a strategy or combination of strategies defined, an organization turns its attention toward the planning aspects of production. During the planning process, operations managers continually try to balance inputs, capacity (resources), and outputs so as to not create waste. Excess inputs and outputs create unnecessary inventory, while excess capacity leads to higher than necessary production costs. On the flip side, shortages of inputs will starve the production process and reduce output. Capacity shortages lead to overwork of machines and labor that may result in quality problems.

This section briefly discusses two types of planning: **capacity planning** and **materials planning**. Three planning timeframes are also covered: (1) **long-range plans**, which span a year or more, focus on major decisions regarding capacity and aggregate production plans; (2) **medium-range plans,** which span 6 to 18 months and involve tactical decisions regarding employment levels and similar issues; and (3) **short-range plans,** which range from a few days to a few weeks, and deal with specific issues and the details of production—quantities of items to be produced, schedules, and sequences. The major planning activities are identified in Figure 14.4.

Capacity planning focuses on determining the appropriate production levels that the company is capable of completing. **Capacity** is the maximum amount of work that an organization is capable of completing in a given period of time. It will help the company determine if changing customer demand can be met or if a discrepancy exists. A discrepancy between capacity and demands results in an inefficiency, either in underutilized resources or unfulfilled customer requirements. The goal of capacity planning is to minimize this discrepancy.

Resource requirements planning (RRP) is a long-run, macro-level planning tool. It helps the operations leaders determine whether aggregate resources are capable of satisfying the aggregate production plan. Gross labor hours and machine hours are the primary focus at this level of planning. If the RRP reveals inadequate resource levels, capacity expansion may be initiated via new facilities, capital equipment, or contract

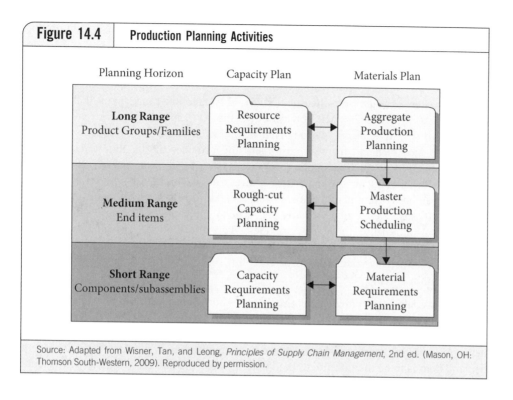

Figure 14.4	Production Planning Activities

Source: Adapted from Wisner, Tan, and Leong, *Principles of Supply Chain Management*, 2nd ed. (Mason, OH: Thomson South-Western, 2009). Reproduced by permission.

manufacturer resources. Otherwise, the aggregate production plan must be revised downward to make it feasible within the constraints of the available resources.

The next step is to create a **rough-cut capacity plan (RCCP),** a process that checks the feasibility of the master production schedule. The medium-range RCCP takes the master production schedule and converts it from production to capacity required and then compares it to available capacity for each production period. If the RCCP and master production schedule are in sync, the schedule is set. If not, capacity can be adjusted through the planned use of overtime, subcontracting, resource expansion, or routing flexibility to meet production needs. Alternatively, the schedule can be revised downward.

Finally, **capacity requirements planning (CRP)** is used to check the feasibility of the materials requirement plan. This short-range capacity planning technique determines, in detail, the amount of labor and equipment resources that were needed to accomplish production requirements. Even though RCCP may indicate that sufficient capacity exists to execute the master production schedule, CRP may show that capacity is insufficient during specific time periods.

Materials planning, in general, focuses on balancing of future supply and demand. It involves managing sales forecasts, creating master schedules, and running materials requirement planning tools.

The **aggregate production plan (APP)** is a long-range materials plan that translates annual business plans, marketing plans, and forecasts into a production plan for all products produced by a facility. The anticipated demand is used to set the facility's output rate, workforce size, utilization and inventory, and backlog levels. The planning horizon for the APP is a year or more and is continuously rolled forward to allow the company to analyze future capacity requirements on an ongoing basis. The objective of the APP is to develop a game plan that is capable of producing enough finished goods within product families or groups each period to meet the sales goal. Of course, the APP must work within the production capacity constraints while controlling the use of financial resources for labor costs, machine setup and operating costs, inventory costs, and related expenses.

The **master production schedule (MPS)** is a medium-range plan that is more detailed than the APP. The MPS breaks down the APP, listing the exact end items to be produced within a specific period. That is, the MPS defines the production quantity required to meet demand from all customers and provides the baseline for computing the requirements (production, staffing, inventory, etc.) for all time-phased end items. It also serves as an input to the materials requirement plan, which computes component and subassembly requirements. Thus, effective execution of the MPS helps avoid parts shortages, costly expediting, last-minute scheduling, and inefficient allocation of resources. Additionally, the MPS provides vital information regarding production availability. This information can help the organization use capacity more effectively in handling customer demand changes or accepting additional orders for completion and delivery within specific periods.

The **materials requirement plan (MRP)** is a short-range materials plan that converts information regarding end-items in the MPS into a set of time-phased component and part requirements. MRP focuses on scheduling and placing orders for dependent demand items so that they are available in the exact quantities on the date the independent demand item is to be manufactured. Lead time for ordering and receiving these dependent demand items must also be factored into the MRP process. Dependent demand items are components of finished goods—raw materials, component parts, and subassemblies—for which the amount of inventory needed depends on the level of production of the final product. For example, in a plant that manufactures motorcycles, dependent demand inventory items include aluminum, tires, seats, and exhaust system components.

For MRP to provide effective planning knowledge, the following three sets of information are needed:

1. Independent demand information—The MPS-defined demand for the final product or component.

2. Parent-component relationship—The bill of materials (BOM) inclusive listing of all component parts and assemblies that make up the final product, including the planning factor and lead-time information. The BOM effectively provides the "recipe" of component quantities and assembly sequence for making the final product.

3. Inventory status of the final product and all components—Information regarding net inventory requirements (gross requirements minus on-hand inventory). Orders for needed components are placed to ensure that orders are released on time for creating higher-level components as scheduled.

The goal of all these materials planning tools, especially MRP, is to provide useful information for operations decision makers. Solid production information regarding scheduled receipts, on-hand inventories, net requirements, and planned order releases is necessary for effective execution of assembly operations and timely fulfillment of customer orders. Recall that an understanding of capacity is the other piece of the production puzzle. You need both effective production and capacity planning to put an organization's production strategies to successful use. Otherwise, it will be difficult to meet customer deadlines with quality products that are made in the most cost-efficient manner possible.

Production Execution Decisions

The production strategy and planning outcomes, along with product characteristics, influence the execution methods used for day-to-day operations. Effective selection of assembly processes can help an organization manage its variability of demand. Products with consistent demand patterns require far different manufacturing methods than do products whose demand is affected by seasonality, short life cycles, and competitors' goods. Organizations must also establish facility layouts and production flows that are well matched to demand volume and manufacturing requirements. And organizations must use proper packaging to safely handle and transport the production outputs. This section will address these three topics that impact day-to-day production performance.

Assembly Processes

Earlier in the chapter, we alluded to products that are built either according to plan or to demand. Their production occurs via either a **make-to-stock (MTS)** or a **make-to-order (MTO)** manufacturing process. MTO can be segmented into three variations: **assemble-to-order (ATO)**, **build-to-order (BTO)**, and **engineer-to-order (ETO)**. Each process is appropriate for some types of products. Selection is driven by the current state of the business environment, the need for the supply chain to manage demand variation, and the product's level of standardization and production complexity.

Make-to-stock is the traditional production method where end-item products are finished before receipt of a customer order. In these mass-production processes, customer orders are filled from finished goods inventories, and production orders are used to replenish finished goods inventories. This generally makes production scheduling easier, supports cost-effective manufacturing with economies of scale, and enables the manufacturer to quickly fill orders from finished goods inventory. Accurate forecasting and inventory control are critical issues in MTS, and warehousing of end products is the norm.

In this build-ahead production approach, production plans are driven by historical demand information in combination with sales forecast information. This approach is good for high-volume products where the demand is predictable or requires production in advance of seasonal demand. MTS is an ideal method for continuous process manufacturing and works well for commodity-based end products such as chemicals, pharmaceuticals, and paper products.

Assemble-to-order product assembly commences after receipt of a customer's order. The finished ATO product is generally a combination of common components and a limited number of options or accessories made available to the customer. The individual components are often stocked in anticipation of demand, but the finished goods are not assembled until customers place orders for their desired products.

ATO is useful in repetitive manufacturing situations where a large number of end products (based on the selection of options and accessories) can be assembled from common components. Automobiles and personal computers are good examples of ATO products that allow for limited consumer choice. As the On the Line feature below explains, ATO can even be applied to chocolate bar production. Key benefits of this production process versus MTS include lower finished goods inventory, greater ability to adapt to changing demand, streamlined forecasting for components rather than finished goods, and higher levels of customer engagement.

On the Line   *Creating Your Own Chocolate Bar*

Have you ever had a craving for a tasty chocolate treat that just doesn't exist in any store? Short of going to the kitchen and testing your skills as a candy maker, that custom creation is just a passing thought. Correct?

Thanks to three entrepreneurs, the situation has changed and you can now design chocolate bars without making a mess of your kitchen. The team at Chocomize (i.e., *chocolate* plus *customize*) adapted the assemble-to-order concept made famous by Dell computers to candy bars. The company offers three basic chocolate options and over 90 ingredients ranging from traditional nuts to exotic herbs and spices. A base bar with five ingredients can be configured into 15 billion unique combinations!

The process is as easy as 1 – 2 – 3:

- Choose a flavor of chocolate for the base—dark, milk, or white.
- Choose up to five ingredients from the list of 90 options—main categories include fruits, nuts and seeds, herbs and spices, candy, decorations and others (including bacon, beef jerky, and potato chips).
- Place your order—put your custom chocolate bar in the shopping basket, pay with a credit card, and wait for your chocolate creation to arrive.

The design-to-delivery process takes four business days or less and your candy bar is delivered to your doorstep via the U.S. Postal Service. The chocolate bars start at $3.85 and ingredient prices range from 40 cents for sea salt to $3.90 for 24-karat gold flakes. Flat-rate shipping fees are charged to each order.

"Our whole concept is that customers can customize their own chocolate rather than getting a mass-produced combination that everyone else gets and someone else thinks up," says Eric Heinbockel, one of the company founders, in a May 2010 *Candy Industry* article. "We chose this concept because we think that mass customization is the future for many industries, thanks to the buying power of the Internet."

Sources: "Three Guys and a Chocolate Bar," *Candy Industry* (May 2010): RC18; and "The Story Behind our Candy Chocolate Bars" *Chocomize.com*. Retrieved September 2, 2010 from: http://www.chocomize .com/personalized-chocolate-bar-story.

The build-to-order production approach also delays assembly until a confirmed order is received for the product. The end-item finished product is a combination of standard and custom-designed components that meet the unique needs of a specific customer. It differs from ATO in the higher level of customization and lower volume level of production. BTO is considered a good choice for products that require some custom configuration, such as a private jet where the aircraft is a standard model but the customer specifies the avionics and interior design. It is also effective for situations where holding finished goods inventories in anticipation of demand is very expensive.

A primary benefit of the BTO approach is its ability to handle variety and meet customers' product specifications. Like ATO, BTO requires little or no finished goods inventory, which means carrying costs and product obsolescence rates are low. On the other hand, demand fluctuations can cause extreme swings in BTO manufacturing capacity utilization, setup costs can be high, and lead times are relatively long, because orders are not filled from readily available inventory.[26] The manufacturer also faces the challenge of deciding how much capacity to reserve in each production period for BTO products and what lead time should be quoted for each item.

Engineer-to-order production focuses on the creation of highly tailored products for customers whose specifications require unique engineering design or significant customization. In this manufacturing environment, no two products are identical, and each order requires detailed cost estimates and tailored pricing. Each customer order results in a unique set of part numbers, bill of materials, and routings that tend to be complex with long lead times. Components and raw materials may be stocked but are not assembled into the finished good until a customer order is received and the product is designed.

Also known as *project manufacturing*, successful ETO initiatives depend on effective collaboration between all supply chain participants. Customers must be involved throughout the entire design and production process. Supplier engagement is also a critical aspect of ETO production. The materials required by the manufacturer can be very unique or ordered infrequently. Working together, engineering, purchasing, and suppliers can compress the lead time for these inputs and help keep production on schedule. ETO products include capital equipment, industrial machinery, and complex items in the aerospace and defense industries. Table 14.2 summarizes the role and benefits of ETO relative to the other MTO options.

Some firms rely exclusively on MTO processes, while others employ only the MTS method. Given the widespread proliferation of products, a number of manufacturers take a hybrid approach, where some items are built to stock and others are built to order. **Delayed differentiation** is a hybrid strategy in which a common product platform is built to stock. It is later differentiated by assigning to it certain customer-specific features, only after demand is realized. Hence, manufacturing occurs in two stages: (1) an MTS stage, where one or more undifferentiated platforms are produced and stocked, and (2) an ATO stage, where product differentiation takes place in response to specific customer orders. For example, Benetton has sweaters made in a neutral color (MTS stage) and waits until customer preferences emerge. Then, the sweaters are dyed with specific colors (ATO stage).

Delayed differentiation carries several benefits. Maintaining stocks of semifinished goods reduces order cycle time relative to BTO or ETO production. Since many different end products have common parts, lower levels of semifinished goods inventory are

Table 14.2	Comparison of Make-to-Order (MTO) Options		
	ATO	**BTO**	**ETO**
Level of customization	Limited	Moderate	Total
Cost of finished goods	Moderate	High	Very high
Order fulfillment speed	Days to weeks	Weeks to months	Month to years
Production process complexity	Moderate	High	Extreme
Example products	Personal computers Automobiles	Computer servers Private jets	Stadium JumboTron Nuclear power plant
Source: Brian J. Gibson, Ph.D. Used with permission.			

needed. Furthermore, investment in semifinished inventories is smaller when compared with the option to maintain a similar amount of finished goods inventory. There is also the benefit of having better demand information before committing generic semifinished products to unique end products. Additional benefits from delayed differentiation include streamlining the MTS segment of the production process and simplification of production scheduling, sequencing, and raw materials purchasing. However, implementing delayed differentiation also carries extra materials costs due to the need for redundant or more expensive parts.[27]

Production Process Layout

One of the key drivers of how production activities will be carried out is **facility layout**—the arrangement of machines, storage areas, and other resources within the four walls of a manufacturing or an assembly facility. The layout is influenced by the production strategy and assembly process employed by the organization. Product characteristics (weight, fragility, size) and demand characteristics (volume and variability) also play a role in the layout decision, as do service commitments, production mix issues, and facility costs.

A thorough analysis of these issues will often lead to an obvious and ideal layout choice. The goal of process layout selection is to ensure that production activities are carried out as efficiently and effectively as possible. An appropriate, successful layout is one that does the following:

- Reduces bottlenecks in moving people or materials.
- Minimizes materials-handling costs.
- Reduces hazards to personnel.
- Utilizes labor efficiently.
- Increases morale and ease of supervision.
- Utilizes available space effectively and efficiently.
- Provides flexibility.
- Facilitates coordination and face-to-face communication.[28]

Production process layouts generally fit into a spectrum of work flow that moves from projects to continuous processes. This spectrum is highlighted in Figure 14.5 according to the product standardization and product volume requirements of each layout. Additionally, as you move from project to continuous process layout, note the following characteristics:

- Labor skill requirements decrease.
- Material requirements become better known.
- High-capacity utilization becomes more important to controlling costs.
- Product flexibility declines.
- Ability to adapt rapidly to changing market conditions diminishes.

A **project layout** is a fixed location layout where the product remains in place for the duration of production. Materials and labor are moved to this production site. For example, assembly of a cruise ship would take place in a dry dock in which the entire process from construction of the hull to the installation of the propulsion system and on-board facilities would take place. Areas on site will be designated for supporting activities such as materials staging, subassembly construction, site access for specialized equipment, and

---

Figure 14.5 | **Facility Layout Matrix**

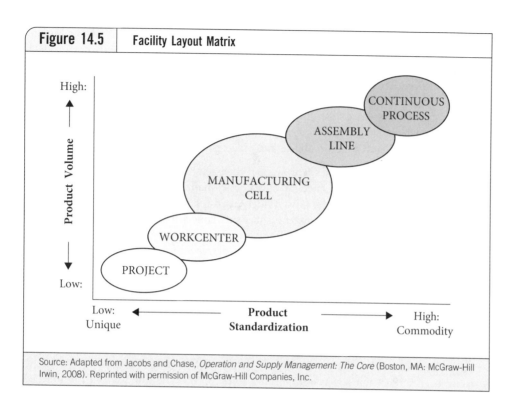

Source: Adapted from Jacobs and Chase, *Operation and Supply Management: The Core* (Boston, MA: McGraw-Hill Irwin, 2008). Reprinted with permission of McGraw-Hill Companies, Inc.

---

a project management area. Similar layouts are used for road construction, home building, and other major projects.

A **workcenter** is a process-focused layout that groups together similar equipment or functions. The materials move from department to department for completion of similar activities and tasks. For example, a manufacturer of towels may have different departments focused on individual operations related to textile production—yarn spinning, weaving, dyeing, cutting, and sewing. This layout provides flexibility in that equipment and personnel can be used where they are needed, lower equipment investment is needed, and supervisors gain expertise in their functions. The downsides of the workcenter layout are related to the materials-handling and movement costs, worker idle time between tasks, and the cost of training and developing a highly skilled workforce that can move between areas.

The **manufacturing cell** is another process-focused layout that dedicates production areas to a narrow range of products that are similar in processing requirements. Setting up a manufacturing cell involves four activities: (1) identifying families of parts with similar flow paths, (2) grouping machines into cells based on part families, (3) arranging cells so materials movement is minimized, and (4) locating large shared machines at the point of use. When properly implemented, cellular manufacturing provides higher production efficiency, reduces waste, lowers inventory levels, shortens production cycle times, and improves customer response time. This type of layout is widely used for fabrication operations and production of mobile phones, computer chips, and automotive subassemblies.

An **assembly line** is a product-focused layout in which machines and workers are arranged according to the progressive sequence of operations need to make a product. Often used for mass production of goods, the assembly steps are completed at workstations that are typically linked by materials-handling equipment. An assembly line can begin as many different lines, each devoted to a different component of a product, with the lines converging upon one another, becoming fewer until only one line is left for the final product. The key to success is control, matching the assembly line speed to the skills of the workforce and the complexity of the assembly processes being performed. Assembly lines are cost efficient, eliminate cross flows and backtracking, limit the amount of work in process, and streamline production time. This type of layout is appropriate for appliances, automobiles, and video game consoles.

Continuous process facilities are similar to assembly lines, with product flowing through a predetermined sequence of stops. The main difference is the continuous, rather than discrete, nature of the flow. Widely used for high-volume, standardized products like chemicals, paper products, and soft drink concentrate, these highly automated, capital-intensive facilities need to run almost nonstop to gain maximum efficiency. This layout is not without challenges. The equipment is large and fixed in nature, limiting the flexibility of continuous processes to meet changing requirements. Also, finished goods inventories can be high as companies are likely to continue to run the production line during low-demand periods.

Packaging

As product comes off the assembly line, the handoff from production operations to logistics begins. Packaging plays important roles in the smooth transfer of finished goods from the plant to the distribution center and customer locations. Package design issues can affect labor and facility efficiency. Well-designed packaging facilitates efficient handling and shipping of the products, keeping landed costs in check. Proper packaging protects the integrity and quality of the goods just produced. And customized packaging can provide another level of product differentiation sought by the customer. These packaging-focused links between production operations and logistics, along with the materials used, are worthy of a brief discussion.

Package design impacts an organization's ability to use space and equipment. The design must promote effective space utilization in the production facility and distribution centers. Package shape, strength, and materials impact the ability to use the full cubic capacity (both horizontal and vertical space) of facilities. Hence, it is common to use square or rectangular boxes or containers with adequate strength to support stacking. The physical dimensions of products and packaging must fall within the capabilities of existing materials-handling equipment at the factory, distribution centers, and customer locations. Poor package design leads to costly and potentially dangerous manual handling of products.

A major packaging concern is the ease of handling in relation to materials handling and transportation. Handling ease is quite important to the production manager, whose labor must be used to place the goods in the packages. It is also important to logistics managers who need product to be handled quickly and without wasted effort. Large packages, for example, may be desirable from a production perspective, but the size and weight of the contents might cause problems when transferring product into and out of transportation equipment. Also, packaging design should take pallet and transportation vehicle capacity into account, so as to fully utilize these assets. Failure to do so will lead to the costly consequence of "shipping air" rather than product, driving up the cost of goods.

Another primary concern is protecting the goods in the package. In the production facility, adequate packaging is needed to protect goods as they move through the facility. Products falling off conveyor lines or packages being hit with a forklift are just two examples of dangers that must be factored into the design process. Protection is important when logistics service providers transport products. Protection can also mean protecting products from contamination resulting from contact with other goods, water damage, temperature changes, pilferage, and shocks in handling and transport. Packaging must support the weight of products stacked above it or provide even weight distribution within the package to facilitate manual and automatic materials handling.

With customer service playing an ever-increasing role in the supply chain, companies need to integrate their packages with customers' materials-handling equipment. A special package that can interface with a customer's innovative equipment will help move product quickly through the supply chain, keeping costs down, product availability strong, and customer satisfaction high. In contrast, incompatible packaging and equipment will lead to inefficient receiving and storage. It may also increase the potential for product damage. In these situations, customer service value may be lost.

Also, packaging plays a key role in providing information about the package contents. Information provision is also important to production and logistics personnel in their day-to-day execution responsibilities. Properly identified packages and reusable containers make it easier for production personnel to locate goods needed by the workcenter or assembly line. Goods stored in a distribution center must bear the proper identification so that order pickers can locate them easily and correctly for customer orders. Barcodes, RFID tags, and other auto-ID tools can be attached to or built into the packaging to make product information more readily accessible.

Accomplishing these key goals is dependent upon finding the right materials for exterior packaging and interior cushioning materials. It is important to use materials that are economical, strong, and sustainable. Durable packaging materials like wood and metal—which are expensive and add excess weight to the product—are instead being replaced by softer packaging materials—recycled cardboard, polyethylene bags, and biodegradable cushioning materials made from cornstarch and soy—in an effort to reduce cost and waste. Dell has even begun to use bamboo in its packaging, as highlighted in the Supply Chain Sustainability box that follows below.

The sustainability mantra of reduce, reuse, recycle is not lost on other manufacturers who are embracing these new packaging technologies. In fact, the global market for sustainable packaging is projected to reach $142.42 billion by 2015. Growth drivers include increased awareness about environmental hazards related to disposal and recycling of packaging wastes, government initiatives to minimize greenhouse gas emissions, and stringent regulations.[29] According to the Sustainable Packaging Coalition, sustainable packaging meets several criteria:

- It is beneficial, safe, and healthy for individuals and communities throughout its life cycle.
- It meets market criteria for performance and cost.
- It is sourced, manufactured, transported, and recycled using renewable energy.
- It optimizes the use of renewable or recycled source materials.
- It is manufactured using clean production technologies and best practices.
- It is made from materials healthy in all probable end-of-life scenarios.
- It is physically designed to optimize materials and energy.
- It is effectively recovered and utilized in biological and/or industrial closed loop cycles.[30]

Supply Chain Sustainability	Dell's Three Cs Packaging Strategy

In its effort to make product packaging more convenient for customers and to have less of an impact on the planet, Dell has eliminated the use of more than 18.2 million pounds of packaging material since 2008. For perspective, that's approximately the same weight as 226 fully-loaded 18-wheelers or almost 4,184 small pick-ups.

The reductions, reported in Dell's 2009 Corporate Responsibility report, result from the company's "three Cs" packaging strategy, which focuses on the cube (packaging volume), content (what it's made of), and curbside recyclability of its packaging materials.

Dell revealed it has made significant progress toward its packaging content and curbside recyclability targets. Since 2008, the company has increased the amount of recycled content in its packaging to approximately 32 percent. Dell is now 94 percent of the way to achieving its stated goal of increasing recycled content in packaging to 35 percent by 2010, a 40 percent increase over 2008 levels. And more than half (57 percent) of Dell's packaging materials can now be conveniently recycled by customers using their local curbside pick-up programs. The company is aiming for that number to be 75 percent by the end of 2012.

In December 2008, Dell announced a plan to revolutionize computer packaging. To achieve this goal, the company is implementing a strategy based on the three Cs:

- **Cube**—Reducing the size of product packaging has required changes ranging from the simple (putting fewer items—disks, catalogs, etc.—in the box, allowing for smaller packaging and a more straightforward "out-of-box" experience for customers) to using engineering tools to run various "what if" scenarios. With these tools, Dell has optimized its Inspiron 15 laptop packaging so that 63 laptops fit on each shipping pallet, up from 54. More laptops on each pallet means more laptops fit into each vehicle, which can result in fewer shipping vehicles and less shipping-related environmental impact.

- **Content**—Dell has significantly increased the amount of recycled content that goes into its packaging. For heavier products that require sturdy support, the company has increased its use of recycled foam versus using virgin product. Dell has also increased its use of postconsumer recycled (PCR) plastics from items such as milk jugs and detergent bottles. The company has integrated the equivalent of more than 9.5 million half-gallon milk jugs into its packaging. That's enough to stretch from Florida to Maine—more than 1,500 miles.

  In November 2009, Dell was the first technology company to integrate bamboo into its packaging portfolio. Bamboo is a strong, renewable and compostable material that serves as a great alternative to the molded paper pulp, foams and corrugated cardboard often used in packaging. Starting with its Inspiron Mini 10 and 10v netbooks, the company has since extended the use of bamboo packaging to include its new five-inch hybrid device, Streak, and a number of its Inspiron laptops.

- **Curbside**—Dell aims to make being "green" easy and cost-effective for its customers. Using product packaging that is curbside recyclable is part of that commitment. To reach its goal, Dell increasingly selects recyclable materials for its packaging, including PCR plastics and molded paper pulp.

While highly renewable and compostable, bamboo packaging isn't yet accepted by many municipal packaging programs today. Dell is teaming with Georgia Pacific, Unisource Global Services, and Environmental Packaging International in an effort to certify its bamboo packaging for recycling.

Source: "Dell Eliminates Use of 18.2 Million Pounds of Packaging Since 2008," *Packaging Digest* (August 24, 2010). Copyright 2010 by CANON COMMUNICATIONS LLC. Reproduced with permission of CANON COMMUNICATIONS LLC via Copyright Clearance Center.

Production Metrics[31]

Throughout this chapter, we have discussed the evolution of production operations from assembly-line-focused, mass-production processes to more lean and flexible manufacturing approaches. The problem is that many organizations continue to monitor production performance as if the goal were strictly to make product to stock at the lowest possible labor cost. This has led to the use of measurements and key performance indicators (KPIs) that do not support operational strategies, organizational objectives, or customer requirements. Thus, it is important to avoid three mistakes when establishing production metrics:

- Using KPIs that are too narrow—Avoid metrics that focus on discrete events as indicators of overall success of the process. For example, labor cost is sometimes studied in detail and used as a surrogate for overall cost. It is only one component of total cost and must be combined with other data to be meaningful.

- Encouraging wrong outcomes—Eliminate measurements that promote activity rather than needed output. Be wary of standard cost accounting measures that lead to good direct labor efficiency, high machine utilization, and continuous production. They may also produce unneeded inventory and high overhead expenses.

- Focusing on issues that are not key priorities—Shun narrowly focused, short-sighted production goals that are disconnected from the overall strategy of the organization. For example, the goal of reducing year-over-year manufacturing costs may not be realistic for a lean production environment.

So, what should operations managers do to ensure that they are measuring the right things in the right way? They should align operations metrics with corporate objectives, leading people toward behaviors and goals that are important to the overall success of the organization. They should keep the metrics program straightforward, limiting the number of metrics used to a maximum of five or six per team or function and focus on KPIs that can be easily compiled and updated. They should also measure the performance of individual activities as key inputs to manufacturing and supply chain performance goals. The key is to follow the "five golden metrics" of manufacturing that impact an organization's bottom line: (1) total cost, (2) total cycle time, (3) delivery performance, (4) quality, and (5) safety.

Total Cost

The most meaningful measurement of **total cost** is on a cash basis. All money spent on manufacturing must be summarized and the total compared to the previous period, rather than to a flexible budget or a plan. What matters is whether the total cash spent on manufacturing (including sales, general, and administrative expense) was more or less than it was in the previous period. The cost figure should exclude arbitrary allocations and major capital investment spending and adjust expenses for accounts receivables and payables. This allows manufacturing performance to be evaluated as if payment were made at the time materials and services were delivered and payment were collected at the time finished goods were shipped to an outside customer.

Total Cycle Time

Total cycle time is a measure of manufacturing performance that is calculated by studying major purchased components and determining the total days on hand of each one. The total days on hand is the sum of all of such components in the plant regardless of form, with the only exception being low-cost, bulk items. Components in their original purchased state, embedded in assemblies or subassemblies, in a modified state in work-in-process inventory, or embedded in a finished product should be included in the sum.

The total days on hand figure is divided by the planned shipments per day for all products that require that component. For example, if there are 5,000 of a component in the plant in all its various forms, and it goes into two final products that are each projected to ship 100 per day, the cycle time for that component is 5,000/200 = 25 days. The total cycle time for the plant or for an individual value stream within the plant is the cycle time of the component with the greatest cycle time.

Delivery Performance

Delivery performance is the percentage of customer orders shipped when the customer requested them to be shipped. It should not be modified to accommodate company policies or shipping promises. It is purely a metric of manufacturing's ability to meet customer requirements.

Quality

The definition of **quality** will vary by company, but it must focus on quality from the perspective of the customer. As a result, customer returns or warranty claims are a good basis for this metric rather than a summary of internal quality metrics (e.g., defect rates or first pass yield). It is important to realize that internal metrics are only important to the extent that they provide information that management can use to minimize cost, improve flow, and pursue customer quality requirements.

Safety

The standard metrics of accident/incident frequency, severity, and cost are important to monitor, with continuous improvement (i.e., reduction) as the goal. Frequency can be measured in the number of accidents and the number of OSHA-recordable accidents. Severity involves the number of lost workdays or the number of days of workers' compensation paid. Financial impact can be evaluated via the cost of injuries and injuries as a percentage of manufacturing cost.

Effective performance measurement is the compass that guides management toward meaningful results at the process level, results that will tie in directly with the company's goals.[32] World-class manufacturers continually track process performance factors that impact success. They work to gain balanced improvement of the five golden metrics of production while supporting overall supply chain KPIs (e.g., order-to-delivery cycle time, throughput, inventory levels, operating expenses, and customer satisfaction).

Production Technology

As production operations become more and more complex—receiving inputs from a wider variety of suppliers, producing goods in smaller batches, and delivering a larger range of outputs—technology is needed to keep the facility running at peak performance. The enterprise resource planning systems and supply chain technologies discussed in earlier chapters help improve operational efficiency and support basic plant scheduling

Table 14.3	MES Key Functionality

FUNCTION	DESCRIPTION
Resource allocation and status	Manages resources including machines, tools, labor skills, materials, other equipment, and other entities such as documents that must be available in order for work to start at the operation.
Operations/detail scheduling	Sequences work based on priorities, characteristics, and/or recipes associated with specific production units at an operation which, when scheduled in sequence properly, minimize setup.
Dispatching production units	Manages flow of production units in the form of jobs, orders, batches, lots, and work orders. The information is presented in the sequence in which the work needs to be done and changes in real time as needed.
Document control	Controls records/forms that must be maintained with the production unit, including work instructions, recipes, drawings, standard operation procedures, engineering change notices.
Data collection/ acquisition	This function provides an interface link to obtain the intraoperational production and parametric data that populate the forms and records attached to the production unit.
Labor management	Provides up-to-the-minute tracking of people in terms of time and attendance reporting, current assignments, type of activity (direct versus indirect).
Quality management	Provides real-time analysis of measurements collected from manufacturing to ensure proper product quality control, to identify problems requiring attention, and to recommend corrective actions.
Process management	Monitors production and either automatically corrects or provides decision support to operators for correcting and improving in-process activities.
Maintenance management	Tracks and directs the activities of maintenance personnel to maintain the equipment, schedules periodic or preventive maintenance, and responds to immediate problems.
Product tracking and genealogy	Provides the visibility to where work is at all times and its disposition. Status information may include who is working on it, inputs used, production conditions, and any exceptions related to the product.
Performance analysis	Provides real-time reporting of manufacturing operations results. Tracks resource utilization and availability, product unit cycle time, conformance to schedule, etc., versus goals and past performance.

Source: Manufacturing Execution Solutions Association International, *MES Functionalities & MRP to MES Data Flow Possibilities*. Retrieved February 25, 2011 from http://www.glbinc.com/MESMRP_Data_Flow.pdf

for production, material use, inventory levels, and delivery. However, they don't effectively link the factory to the supply chain or ensure that operations are being managed proactively. Other tools must be linked to these systems to create flexible and adaptive production processes that are capable of responding in real time to changing market dynamics.

Manufacturers across all industries understand the importance of sharing real-time information across their extended manufacturing and supply chain network. Enhanced manufacturing visibility and responsiveness can provide significant competitive advantage in terms of fulfilling customer demand faster while increasing profitability and shareholder value.[33] These organizations are using **manufacturing execution systems (MES)** to link ERP systems and supply chain applications to ensure that operations are being managed in real time. In the most basic terms, an MES system controls, manages and reports on manufacturing processes with very detailed and serialized information at a granular level.[34]

MES derives its name from its inherent purpose of providing intelligent process control through an electronic system designed to execute instructions to control manufacturing operations. The goal is to supply a continuous flow of meaningful instructions, and most importantly, for those instructions to be carried out correctly and reliably. An effective MES provides manufacturing planning information, supports the day-to-day execution of operations, and provides production process control. Table 14.3 highlights the primary functions of MES.

Here's how the functionality works in a collaborative manufacturing environment: the MES receives an order from the ERP system and then makes an intelligent decision on where to produce the orders. This decision is based on facility capabilities, capacity, and price. Next, the MES publishes the instructions for the best way to manufacture the product for the parties involved in the manufacturing process. Finally, the details of production performance are tracked via KPIs and dashboards in real time, allowing managers or the system to react to changes and problems in a timely fashion.[35]

Although MES has been in existence for years, the market for these software systems is growing. AMR Research estimates that MES sales are a $1 billion market annually and will increase 5 to 6 percent per year.[36] Driving the growth of MES are the following benefits: improved visibility and traceability, reduced lead time and manufacturing costs, increased equipment uptime, reduced scrap and waste, reduced inventory levels, fewer problem orders, and more accurate cost analysis.[37]

What is the future of MES? AMR Research identifies five capabilities that will define the next generation MES:

- **Quality management**—Future MES will create their own solutions with the ability to not just catch defects but perform root cause analysis of why those defects happened.

- **Scheduling**—Solutions that couple MES with fast scheduling capabilities will be able to respond more quickly to changes in customer demand, supplier constraints, and constraints in manufacturing capacity or quality.

- **Product and process lifecycle management**—Top MES will link research and development, engineering and manufacturing together.

- **Activity-based costing and profit velocity**—These solutions will allow a manufacturer to analyze product manufacturability, costs, and contribution to profit.

- **Operations intelligence**—Future MES will be able to take current system data and use it for data mining, modeling, and simulation functionality.[38]

SUMMARY

The key concept from this chapter is the critical and codependent link between production operations and logistics. Just as your heart and arteries need to work together to move blood through your circulatory system, production and logistics must work in concert to move product through the supply chain. For their part, production managers must coordinate demand information, inputs, and resources to transform them into outputs (products and materials) that are desired by customers. The faster and more flexible the transformation processes are, the more responsive the production operation can be to changing conditions and disruptions. This in turn makes the supply chain more dynamic and competitive.

Additional topics from the chapter include the following:

- Production operations include all activities and processes involved in changing the composition of a good or service—component fabrication, product assembly, and service request execution—for the purpose of creating form utility.

- Numerous tradeoffs must be made regarding production: volume versus variety, responsiveness, or efficiency; make or outsource; and focusing on a few versus many competitive dimensions.

- Intensified competition, more demanding customers, and relentless pressure for efficiency as well as adaptability are driving significant changes across many manufacturing industry settings.

- There have been significant developments and shifts in production strategy. Organizations have advanced from forecast-driven mass production to demand-driven, lean, flexible, and adaptive approaches.

- Capacity planning and materials planning are used to balance inputs, capacity (resources), and outputs so that customer demand can be fulfilled without creating waste.

- Most manufacturers use a combination of make-to-stock and make-to-order production methods to satisfy demand for their products.

- Within the make-to-order method, companies can leverage assemble-to-order, build-to-order, or engineer-to-order options, based on product complexity and uniqueness.

- Facility layout involves the arrangement of machines, storage areas, and other resources within the four walls of a manufacturing or an assembly facility.

- Facility layout is influenced by the product characteristics, production strategy, and assembly process employed by the organization.

- Packaging plays important roles in the smooth, safe, and economical transfer of finished goods from the plant to the distribution center and customer locations.

- Sustainability is a key consideration in packaging selection, and companies are turning to recyclable and reusable materials for exterior and interior packaging.

- Production KPIs must be linked to corporate goals and objectives, customer requirements, and overall performance of the production operation.

- Critical production KPIs address total cost, total cycle time, delivery performance, quality, and safety.

- Manufacturing execution systems software solutions improve an organization's ability to manage production operations and make them more responsive to disruptions, challenges, and changing marketplace conditions.

STUDY QUESTIONS

1. Discuss the role of production operations in the supply chain. Provide examples of how effective/ineffective production operations impact supply chain performance.

2. Describe the major challenges faced by production managers in the current environment.

3. Compare and contrast push-based production strategies with pull-based production strategies. What are the primary capabilities, advantages, and disadvantages of each?

4. Outsourcing is a popular supply chain strategy. Discuss the reasons for and against an organization outsourcing its production processes.

5. Describe the differences between capacity planning and materials planning.

6. Discuss the concept of delayed differentiation and why it is considered to be a hybrid approach to product assembly. What types of products can benefit from delayed differentiation?

7. Using the Business and Company Resource Center (http://academic.cengage.com/bcrc) and company Web sites, compare the supply chain and contract manufacturing services provided by the following organizations:

   a. Flextronics (http://www.flextronics.com) and Ditan Corporation (http://www.ditan.com)

   b. Accupac (http://www.accupac.com) and Jabil Circuit (http://www.jabil.com)

   c. ModusLink (http://www.moduslink.com) and Cott Corporation (http://www.cott.com)

8. Identify and discuss the most appropriate assembly process and facility layout for each of the following products:

   a. Coke Zero concentrate

   b. Harley-Davidson motorcycle

   c. Microsoft Xbox 360

9. Describe the characteristics of good production metrics and the types of KPIs that companies should monitor.

10. Using the Business and Company Resource Center (http://academic.cengage.com/bcrc) and search engines, identify two MES solutions providers. Describe the capabilities and supply chain impact that their tools promise.

NOTES

1. Donald J. Bowersox, David J. Closs, and M. Bixby Cooper, *Supply Chain Logistics Management*, 3rd ed. (Boston, MA: McGraw-Hill, 2010), 91.

2. Sunil Chopra and Peter Meindl, *Supply Chain Management, Strategy, Planning, and Operations*, 4th ed. (Upper Saddle River, NJ: Pearson Prentice Hall, 2010), 45.

3. Donald J. Bowersox, David J. Closs, and M. Bixby Cooper, *Supply Chain Logistics Management*, 3rd ed. (Boston, MA: McGraw-Hill, 2010), 93–94.

4. "Business: The Machine that Ran Too Hot; Toyota's Overstretched Supply Chain," *The Economist* (February 27, 2010): 74.

5. F. Robert Jacobs and Richard B. Chase, *Operations and Supply Management: The Core* (Boston, MA: McGraw-Hill Irwin, 2008), 11–14.

6. Mandyam Srinivasan, *Streamlined: 14 Principles for Building and Managing the Lean Supply Chain* (Mason, OH: Thomson South-Western, 2004), 101.

7. Kevin O'Mara and Debra Hofman, "The AMR Supply Chain Top 25 for 2010," *Gartner.com* (June2, 2010). Retrieved September 2, 2010 from http://www.gartner.com/DisplayDocument?ref=clientFriendlyUrl&id=1379613.

8. Bob Ferrari and Bob Parker, "Digging for Innovation," *Supply Chain Management Review* (November 2006), pp. 48–54.

9. David Simchi-Levi, Philip Kaminsky, and Edith Simchi-Levi, *Designing and Managing the Supply Chain: Concepts, Strategies, and Case Studies*, 3rd ed. (Boston, MA: McGraw-Hill Irwin, 2008), 153–154.

10. Ibid., 188–89.

11. Kevin O'Brien, "Value-Chain Report—Next Generation Manufacturing," *IndustryWeek.com* (September 10, 2001). Retrieved September 2, 2010, from http://www.industryweek.com/articles/value-chain_report_-_next_generation_manufacturing_2167.aspx.

12. Tullio Tolio, ed., *Design of Flexible Production Systems: Methodologies and Tools* (Berlin, Germany: Springer-Verlag, 2009), 1.

13. Kate Linebaugh, "Honda's Flexible Plants Provide Edge," *Wall Street Journal* (September 23, 2008), B1.

14. Felix S. Chan, "The Effects of Routing Flexibility on a Flexible Manufacturing System," *International Journal of Computer Integrated Manufacturing*, Vol. 14, No. 5 (2001).

15. *Manufacturing Strategy: An Adaptive Perspective* (Newtown Square, PA: SAP AG, 2003). Retrieved September 2, 2010, from http://www.sap.com/solutions/business-suite/scm/pdf/BWP_Mnf_Strategy.pdf.

16. O'Brien, "Value-Chain Report—Next Generation Manufacturing."

17. Paul Davidson, "Some Manufacturing Headed Back to USA," *USA Today* (August 6, 2010).

18. *Manufacturing Strategy: An Adaptive Perspective*.

19. Stephanie Overby, "ABC: An Introduction to Outsourcing," *CIO.com* (2007). Retrieved September 2, 2010, from http://www.cio.com/article/40380/Outsourcing_Definition_and_Solutions.

20. Roberto Michel, "Adaptive Manufacturing Moves In," *Modern Materials Handling* (September 2006): 29–31.

21. *Manufacturing Strategy: An Adaptive Perspective*.

22. Andy Dé, "Adaptive Manufacturing," *SAP Info* (October 2005): 30–32.

23. O'Brien, "Value-Chain Report—Next Generation Manufacturing."

24. Fred Hapgood, "Factories of the Future: Machines that 'See' Parts on Assembly Lines, 3-D Printers that Prototype Products in Hours—Let's Take a Look at Adaptive Manufacturing," *CIO* (January 2007): 1.

25. This section is adapted from Joel D. Wisner, Keah-Choon Tan, and G. Keong Leong, *Principles of Supply Chain Management: A Balanced Approach,* 2nd ed. (Mason, OH: Thomson South-Western, 2009), chap. 6.

26. MIT Center for Transportation and Logistics, "Solving Production Puzzles," *Supply Chain Frontiers* (July 2007). Retrieved September 3, 2010, from http://ctl.mit.edu/library/solving_production_puzzles.

27. Saif Benjaafar, "Make-to-Order, Make-to-Stock, or Delay Product Differentiation? A Common Framework for Modeling and Analysis," *IIE Transactions* (June 2004), pp. 529–546.

28. Henry C. Co, "Facility Design and Layout." Retrieved September 3, 2010, from www.csupomona.edu/~hco/POM/05FaciltyDesignLayout.ppt.

29. "Global Sustainable Packaging Market to Reach Nearly $143B by 2015," *Environmental Leader* (August 12, 2010). Retrieved September 5, 2010, from http://www.environmentalleader.com/2010/08/12/global-sustainable-packaging-market-to-reach-nearly-142b-by-2015/.

30. Sustainable Packaging Coalition, *Definition of Sustainable Packaging Version 2.0* (October 2009). Retrieved September 5, 2010, from http://sustainablepackaging.org/uploads/Documents/Definition%20of%20Sustainable%20Packaigng.pdf.

31. Unless noted otherwise, information in this section is adapted from Bill Waddell, "Manufacturing's Five Golden Metrics," *Lean Directions: The e-Newsletter of Lean Manufacturing* (October 10, 2006). Retrieved September 6, 2010, from http://www.sme.org/cgi-bin/get-newsletter.pl?LEAN&20061010&2.

32. "Performance Measurement Metrics for Success." Retrieved September 5, 2010, from http://www.rmdonovan.com/performance_measurement.htm.

33. Joe Bellini, "Extending Supply Chain Execution in Production to Improve Fulfillment," *Supply and Demand Chain Executive*. Retrieved September 6, 2010, from http://www.sdcexec.com/online/article.jsp?id=8014.

34. Bob Trebilcock, "Managing Manufacturing with MES," *Modern Materials Handling* (September 2009), pp. 32–34.

35. Bob Trebilcock, "The Year of MES," *Modern Materials Handling: Warehouse Management Edition* (January 2005), pp. 72–74.

36. Trebilcock, "Managing Manufacturing with MES."

37. David Blanchard, "Five Benefits of MES," *Industry Week* (April 1, 2009). Retrieved September 6, 2010 from http://www.industryweek.com/articles/five_benefits_of_an_mes_18701.aspx

38. Bob Trebilcock, "Next Generation MES," *Modern Materials Handling* (September 2009), p. 34.

CASE 14.1

Elvis Golf Ltd

Elvis Golf Ltd. (EGL) manufactures the King 460cc driver, a $79 clone of a far more expensive golf club from a well-known brand. The King is manufactured at the company's small Memphis, Tennessee, factory and is shipped to major sporting goods retailers. EGL has always relied upon a mass production strategy to gain economies of scale and high labor productivity. This strategy is coupled with a make-to-stock assembly process, and goods are produced in anticipation of demand.

The company has experienced a sales slump over the last three quarters. In response, EGL sent their sales team to the World Golf Expo, a major trade show in the golf industry. The goal of this first-time trip to the Expo was to boost awareness of the King, gain retailer feedback, and generate orders. The sales team set up a display booth and had plenty of literature to distribute.

The trip wasn't successful from an order standpoint, but the sales team gained valuable insights from the Expo attendees. At a post-trip meeting, the following information was shared with EGL executive management:

- Retailers liked the novelty and price of our product but having only one model available—a right-handed, 43-inch, 10-degree loft, steel shaft driver with a tacky grip—limits the market appeal.

- Competitors at the event were offering semicustomizable clubs similar to the King at a $119 price point. Options included left-handed clubs, a choice of three different grips, steel or graphite shaft, and six shaft length/flex combinations.

- A few retailers commented that sales would explode if EGL offered an optional package deal—the King, a blue suede head cover, and a golf hat with "Elvis" written on it.

Tom Parker, the company CEO, was intrigued by the customization angle. He liked the higher price and believed that the input component costs wouldn't be much higher than the current model of the King. "Let's get started right away," he said.

"But that will add great complexity to our supply chain and production operations," replied Pat Boone, vice president of manufacturing. He noted that the company would now have to manufacture 72 different models based on all the possible configurations of club heads, shaft types, shaft length/flex options, and grips. "Creating a forecast will be a nightmare and we'll have to hold finished goods inventory of every model," he added. "And don't get me started on that package deal mess either. Blue suede head covers, how tacky is that?"

"Well, Mr. Boone, you'd better figure it out," replied Parker. He went on to talk about the need for EGL to adopt a more modern and agile manufacturing strategy. "We need to respond to our customers, and offering semicustomized clubs sounds like a good idea to me," he added. "If that is too much to ask, then I may need to think about outsourcing our manufacturing and become a sporting goods marketing company like Nike."

"I want your production plan on my desk in one week," said Parker as he walked out of the meeting.

CASE QUESTIONS

1. In terms of production strategy, should Boone stick with mass production or try something else? Explain.

2. Is the make-to-stock assembly process well-suited to Parker's desire to make semi-customized clubs? What other assembly options could be considered?

3. What do you think of Parker's idea to outsource the manufacturing of the King?

4. Develop a brief proposal for the production plan requested by Parker. Discuss your recommended production strategy, assembly process, other considerations, and the benefits/drawbacks of your proposal.

Source: Brian J. Gibson, Ph.D. Used with permission.

CASE 14.2

Team HDX

Harry Limmer, vice president of manufacturing for Point Electronics Corporation (PEC), is both excited and apprehensive. PEC is four months away from the most important industry event of the year, the Consumer Electronics Show. At this trade show, PEC will roll out the most advanced line of HDTV equipment available (3-D capabilities, microthin glass, noninterlaced 1080z format, digital surround sound, and more) at prices that will average $250 less than competing models. The company has staked its future on this rollout, and demand is expected to skyrocket—if Limmer and his team can get enough units into the supply chain by the release date.

The HDTV monitors are to be assembled at PEC's facility in Juarez, Mexico. Key components and subsystems come from the following locations:

- Signal reception system—Circuits Unlimited is assembling the high-tech tuners and amplifiers needed to translate digital broadcasts in its Rome, New York, facility.

- Sound system—PEC's nearby El Paso, Texas, plant builds the sound system.

- TV control system and remote—MicroSolutions of Seoul, Korea, provides the internal microprocessor that governs tuning, program selection, and other key functions.

- Power supply system—Grupo PEC, the Mexico City–based subsidiary of PEC will be used.

- Glass panel—The low-cost, microthin LCD display glass is being manufactured by Suny, a new Jakarta, Indonesia, joint-venture of two major electronics companies.

During the weekly conference call with members of Team HDX (suppliers, PEC facility managers, and Limmer's corporate staff), most of the updates from suppliers were positive. However, certain items piqued Limmer's attention throughout the call.

Cliff Randall, director of operations at Juarez, noted that all the materials-handling and production equipment had arrived and the facility was ready to be retrofitted from its original tube television production setup to HDTV assembly. He suggested that the new configuration remain consistent with the existing workstation setup to avoid employee retraining. "We're still making televisions, not computers," noted Randall.

Brent Defee, Limmer's production analyst, gave an update on the expected margins for the new HDTV line. "I've been studying our expected labor cost per unit for the assembly of the new products, and it compares very favorably to our CRT television manufacturing facility in Bonham, Germany," stated Defee with confidence. "That old facility was vertically integrated, making almost all the components in-house."

Limmer was most distressed by the lack of input from the Suny team member. When pressed on the issue of microthin glass panel production and delivery dates, the Suny representative said that all was going according to plan. He was downplaying the fact that they were experiencing a 15 percent defect rate for the new panels, mostly due to damage during handling and transport to the warehouse. "Not to worry," the representative quickly added. "We produce a variety of glass panels based on forecasts and will substitute as necessary from our existing inventory to fill your orders. Shipping will commence next week."

After ending the conference call, Limmer grows more and more anxious. He is skeptical of Randall's plan and can't help but think that Defee's focus is off base. Most importantly, Limmer is really concerned about those glass panels and the lack of concern on the Suny representative's part. He is thinking about getting on the next flight to Jakarta and taking a tour of the factory and warehouse to see what is going on.

CASE QUESTIONS

1. Analyze the recommendation made by Randall regarding the facility setup. Would you tell Limmer to follow this recommendation or go with another setup? Why?

2. What is your opinion of Defee's selection of the labor cost KPI? Is it on target or somehow flawed?

3. Should Limmer get on that flight to Jakarta? If he makes the trip, what should he investigate on his tour?

4. Develop a process map depicting the product flows for the HDTV supply chain, and note the potential problem areas that may impact the success of Team HDX.

Chapter 15

SUPPLY CHAIN SUSTAINABILITY

Learning Objectives

After reading this chapter, you should be able to do the following:

- Appreciate the importance of sustainable supply chains for the protection of the ecology of the planet.

- Understand how effective supply chain management can contribute to sustainability.

- Discuss why it is economically and politically important to manage supply chains as sustainably as possible.

- Appreciate why sustainability and social responsibility are the "new normal" for managing supply chains.

- Understand the established frameworks for sustainable supply chains.

- Discuss the importance and challenges of reverse flows in supply chains.

- Understand why there has been a significant increase in the number and volume of items moving in reverse flows and supply chains.

- Explain the eight major categories of reverse flows and understand the three major forces that drive reverse supply chains.

- Discuss the differences between reverse logistics systems and closed-loop supply chains as well as value streams and waste streams for reverse logistics.

Supply Chain Profile   *Trash to Treasure Foundation: A Sequel*

Chris Norton and Lloyd Huck were meeting to discuss what had been accomplished during the previous five years and make plans for the next five years. They were both pleased with the success of the Trash to Treasure Foundation, but they recognized that there were some challenges and issues to be resolved as they looked to the future. They realized that there were some opportunities to grow and increase the scope of their activities, but some changes were necessary. Many organizations and the general public were more aware of the ecological challenges the world faced and the need to adapt supply chains for returns, reuse, and recycling. Chris and Lloyd had to capitalize on this increased awareness without losing momentum.

BACKGROUND

Chris Norton and Lloyd Huck were friends in graduate school and were reunited when they met in an airport terminal. Chris was in the consulting business and had developed an expertise in helping organizations establish reverse logistics systems for product returns. He explained to Lloyd why he had developed a passion for this area. As Lloyd listened to Chris he recalled an article that he had read in the Knoxville newspaper about a growing problem at the University of Tennessee when students left their dorm rooms and apartments. The problem was that students left all types of clothing, small appliances, athletic equipment, TVs, computers, and related items behind when moving out. The items ranged from needing repair to being still in their unopened, original boxes. The University of Tennessee hired temporary personnel to remove these items, and then they were hauled to a landfill for a "tipping fee." In spite of increased efforts to mitigate this problem, the University reported that the volume of discarded items was growing and the associated costs were escalating. The newspaper article reported that this was also a problem at other colleges and universities.

Chris was immediately interested in this report because he saw an opportunity to use his experience and expertise to help solve the problem. Lloyd got interested because of his business experience with discount store operations. He felt that there was an opportunity not only to cover the cost of removing the items but also to develop a revenue stream for student scholarships. The "icing on the cake" was the reduction in items going to the landfill, which would be a so-called green impact. They both envisioned what could be called a win-win-win opportunity.

They decided to visit the University of Tennessee campus at the end of the next school year along with several other universities where they had contacts to see the extent of the problem and opportunity firsthand. During their visit, they became even more enthusiastic. Their second and third visits to Penn State and Auburn solidified their conclusion about the opportunity. However, they also recognized some of the challenges. At the University of Tennessee, where the landfill tipping fees were about $42.00 per ton and 80 to 100 tons were being hauled to the landfill, the total cost after adding direct labor and hauling costs was in excess of $15,000. They estimated that the resale value of the items, even with substantial discounts, could reach $65,000 to $70,000.

They convinced the vice president of business affairs at Penn State to allow them to organize and implement their "Trash to Treasure" program with the cooperation of the university and student leaders. They netted $60,000 with the first venture after paying about $16,000 in direct costs.

CURRENT SITUATION

After five years, the Trash to Treasure program had been initiated at 12 large universities, and scholarship contributions were averaging about $65,000 per year at each of the schools—and the ecological impact could be higher if the benefits could be accurately measured. Needless to say, the administrators and students at the various academic institutions were enthusiastic if not ecstatic at the success of the effort.

Chris and Lloyd established a Trash to Treasure Foundation shortly after their first program for tax and risk reasons. Thus far they had been able to minimize overhead costs by volunteering their services as officers of the foundation. They were also able to minimize their direct costs by using student, faculty, and staff volunteers during the three- to five-day period that the sales were conducted. Both Chris and Lloyd saw that there were opportunities at many other colleges and universities around the country. Also, they expanded their efforts at Auburn, Penn State, and University of Tennessee to include off-campus student housing as well as fraternities and sororities.

FUTURE DIRECTIONS

Both Chris and Lloyd felt that they were at an important point with the foundation. As suggested above, there were opportunities for expansion to other academic institutions, but expansion was also possible at the current locations by adding other types of student housing at nine of the current universities. Also, student lenders at Penn State recommended that they investigate the possibility of implementing a comparable program at the current universities in the dining halls to reclaim leftover food for local charities and also a composting program for scraps and other food waste. However, there would not be a revenue stream for food reverse flows as there was for the Trash to Treasure programs. This food recovery would be entirely philanthropic and need student-volunteer effort on a continual basis. There were probably other opportunities also, for example, cleaning up trash and recovering usable items at athletic event venues.

In addition to the above opportunities, Chris and Lloyd were challenged to find enough time away from their "daytime" jobs to handle the current operations. They had developed an operating model blueprint that they distributed free of charge to interested universities. This blueprint would allow each institution to operate independently. However, they realized that they were able to improve the efficiency and increase the effectiveness at the current institutions by their coordination efforts and the collaboration and sharing among the universities. They felt obligated to consider some full-time employees.

As you read this chapter and reflect upon the previous chapters, think about the possibilities for the expansion of the Trash to Treasure Foundation and its organizational challenges. It is an interesting and practical opportunity with many options.

Source: John J. Coyle, DBA. Used with permission.

Introduction

The interest in sustainability and so-called green supply chains has increased since the publication of the previous edition of this text. Consequently, the focus of this chapter has been expanded from focusing upon reverse flows in a supply chain to also include a more general overview of sustainability. Reverse and closed-loop logistics systems and supply chains are an important part of sustainability, but there are other aspects of how supply chains are operated and function that impact the ecology and environment and should be considered.

One might question why there has been an increased interest in sustainability among profit-oriented companies. There was a time when any discussion about sustainability or green supply chains was likely to be linked with increased cost and loss of efficiency.

While there may well be additional expenses or additional investment, there are many opportunities to be "green" and be able to lower cost. This is especially true if a broader perspective rather than just recycling and disposal is taken. For example, several years ago, P&G and Walmart decided to reduce the size of the plastic bottles used for liquid detergent by reducing the water content of the liquid to make it more concentrated. There was some customer resistance at first because it appeared that the same price was being charged for less product. However, P&G was able to convince customers that they would achieve the same results with about 50 percent less of the liquid detergent. Once the customers accepted this concept, the impact was dramatic. Transportation costs were reduced by lower weight and volume, that is, weight-density was improved, resulting in lower rates (see Chapter 10). Packaging costs and warehousing costs were lowered with the smaller container size. Store productivity improved with less required shelf space and easier handling. Another example is Supervalu, a large grocery retail and wholesale company, and Wegmans, a large regional grocery chain. They saved thousands of dollars annually by putting more items in each bag or even avoiding using a bag in some cases. This was a simple cost-saving strategy with a positive sustainability impact.

In addition to the economic rationale for sustainability illustrated by these examples, there is a growing sense of urgency among private and public organizations, as well as consumers, about the necessity to take action to operate in a sustainable manner and thereby protect our ecology and environment. At this point, it is appropriate to provide a framework for discussing and evaluating sustainable supply chains.[1]

Supply Chain Sustainability Framework

As suggested above, organizational supply chains are faced with a myriad of challenges to operate efficiently that are also consistent with the objective of improving sustainability. The challenges range from global climate change to diminishing raw material resources and loss of habitat and species. There is a growing recognition of a universal need or mandate to address environmental actions among scientists, consumers, businesses, not-for-profit organizations and government agencies.[2]

From a business and supply chain perspective, sustainability practices are usually based upon a recognition that industrial systems need to be in harmony with nature by not depleting resources beyond their replacement or regeneration rate, with special emphasis upon reducing wasteful practices—in other words, developing supply chain procedures that meet demand in the growing global markets and at the same time promote positive ecological impacts throughout the supply chain. Hence the need for sustainable supply chain management and green supply chains. Table 15.1 presents definitions and frameworks for sustainable supply chain management from various authors.

The definitions and frameworks presented in Table 15.1 illustrate the multiple product and process elements in a supply chain where sustainability is the focus. It also conveys some of the functional aspects of supply chains such as procurement, operations, transportation, and distribution. The diversity of views presented by the various authors illustrates the complexity of sustainable supply chain management, which leads individual companies or organizations to develop customized versions combining elements from several frameworks. Nevertheless, the outcomes are beneficial to society overall as the attempt is made to develop a sustainability framework and related practices.[3]

Table 15.1	Definitions and Frameworks for Sustainable Supply Chain Management
AUTHOR(S)	**DEFINITIONS AND FRAMEWORKS**
Hervani, Helms, and Sarkis (2005)	Green supply chain management (GSCM) = green purchasing + green manufacturing/materials management + green distribution/marketing + reverse logistics. Of these, reverse logistics "closes the loop" of a typical forward supply chain and includes reuse, remanufacturing, and/or recycling of materials into new materials or other products which have value in the marketplace.
Kleindorfer, Singhal, and Van Wassenhove (2005)	Sustainability includes environmental management, closed-loop supply chains, and a broad perspective on the triple-bottom-line (3BL) of the three Ps that integrates profit, people, and the planet into the culture, strategy, and operations of companies.
Linton, Klassan, and Jayaraman (2007)	Sustainability integrates issues and flows that extend beyond the core of supply chain management to incorporate product design, manufacturing by-products, by-products produced during product use, product life extension, product end-of-life, and recovery processes at end-of-life.
Srivastava (2007)	Green supply chain is the integration of environmental thinking into supply chain management, including product design, material sourcing and selection, manufacturing processes, delivery of the final product to the consumers as well as end-of-life management of the product after its useful life.
Pagell and Wu (2009)	To be truly sustainable a supply chain would at worst do no net harm to natural or social systems while still producing a profit over an extended period of time; a truly sustainable supply chain could, customers willing, continue to do business forever.
Sharma et al. (2010)	Sustainable market framework is based on two major objectives in sustaining environments, namely: (1) reducing surplus supply in which firms do not manufacture more units than are required (over-produce), thus leading to lower levels of product needing to be disposed (that may need recycling or remanufacturing) and a more sustainable environment, and (2) reducing reverse supply in which firms need to develop repairable products as well as more complete recycling and remanufacturing strategies.

Source: E. A. Thomchick and K. Ruamsook, Working Paper, March 2010, Center for Supply Chain Research, Penn State University, pp. 4–5.

It would be useful, however, to also consider the various supply chain initiatives on a broad functional basis, for example, inbound functions, production or operations functions, and outbound functions. The inbound functions would be comprised of green procurement strategies addressing such issues as waste reduction, environmental sourcing, and minimizing waste of hazardous materials. Green procurement usually requires collaboration with suppliers or vendors.

The production or operations functions would include clean and lean production methodologies, designing for the environment, total quality environment management, and various product end-of-life practices, which are becoming increasingly popular in organizations as they move aggressively to achieve sustainability goals. On the outbound side of the supply chain, the initiatives include green marketing and environment-friendly packaging, warehousing, and transportation. The transportation function is usually a critical part of this effort since it can cause a large carbon footprint. Related transportation strategies can include mode selection (e.g., rail as opposed to truck), fuel sources, routing, scheduling to reduce partial loads and empty backhauls, and so forth.[4]

Table 15.2	Sustainability Approaches
Reuse	Reuse often requires disassembly, which is a systematic method of separating a product into constituent parts, components, subassemblies, or other component parts. The parts or components may be reassembled for reuse after cleaning, checking, and repair, or the individual components may be reused.
Remanufacturing	Remanufacturing essentially means that a product or part is returned to the market as "good as new." Auto parts, tires, and electronics are frequently remanufactured.
Reconditioning	Reconditioning usually means returning used products to working order but not "good as new."
Recycling	Recycling generally refers to the secondary use of materials. It usually includes glass bottles, cans, newspapers, corrugated material, tires, etc. The recycling is usually performed for individual households by municipal government agencies.

Source: Center for Supply Chain Research, Penn State University.

These transportation-related strategies have received growing attention from restaurant chains such as Subway and McDonalds. These transportation strategies are both cost efficient and ecologically sound.

In this general discussion, mention should also be made of reverse logistics systems and closed-loop logistics or supply chain systems. Both reverse and closed-loop systems are important strategies that impact sustainability in a positive manner. Both will be discussed in detail later in this chapter. At this point, consideration needs to be given to the so-called R's of sustainability: reuse, remanufacturing, refurbishing, and recycling. Table 15.2 provides a brief description of each of the R's.

It is important to note that sustainability strategies are being designed today also from a business-related or economic perspective as opposed to a public relations approach, as was frequently done in the past. The global, competitive environment requires a broad-based collaborative effort among organizations in a supply chain along with governmental support. Sustainability is a complex issue that will continue to be challenging.

The recycling of consumer and industrial waste has become very widespread, and materials are being reused in a variety of creative forms. Often recycling results in the creation of an entirely new product, for instance, automobile tires into door mats and flooring material. At this point, reverse logistics and closed-loop systems will be discussed in detail since they have become such an important part of the sustainability efforts of business and government organizations.

Reverse Logistics Systems

A basic or simple supply chain was illustrated in Chapter 1. The description of this supply chain indicated that there were four important flows to manage: materials, information, financials, and demand. Furthermore, the figure demonstrated that three of the flows could be two-directional. Materials typically flow "downstream" in a supply chain from raw materials sources to the ultimate consumer with value being added to the product along the way. **Reverse flows** can move back through the supply chain for a variety of reasons. Consequently, a number of terms including *reverse logistics systems,* *product recovery systems, product return networks, enterprise returns management,* and others have been used to indicate the growth in the volume and importance of returns and the need for their efficient and effective management.

Several observations are important at the outset of this section about reverse flows. The forward flow in the supply chain typically has received the most attention since it is so important in terms of customer service, revenue, and cash flow. The reverse direction has often been regarded as a necessary evil or at best a cost center that needs continual scrutiny to control and reduce.

Traditionally, reverse flows were not viewed as adding value for customers or revenue for the manufacturer or producer. In other words, product returns were viewed as a "waste stream," not as a potential value stream. One of the objectives of this chapter is to examine reverse product flows as a potential value stream for a company or an organization. It should be noted that Internet sales have contributed significantly to the increase in reverse flows. Why?

The second observation is that information and financials (cash) are also an important dimension of reverse logistics and closed-loop supply chains. It was stated in Chapter 1 and other chapters that information is power. Good information contributes to efficiency and effectiveness because it facilitates the flow through the supply chain and reduces uncertainty. Unfortunately, the power of information systems and technology has not received enough emphasis in return flows. Cash or value from returns also needs to be a focus for organizations if they are to receive all the benefits that can come from managing reverse flows. This requires more proactive management to obtain such benefits for companies. Some examples of more proactive approaches have already been discussed in this chapter.

A third observation is that global supply chains present challenges and opportunities for reverse flows. Some European countries have been very proactive in passing so-called **green laws**, primarily for environmental reasons, which means that companies doing business in these countries must be cognizant of these regulations and policies. The green laws usually require reverse flows, for example returning packaging materials. Some underdeveloped countries are very lenient in these areas, which may raise ethical issues for companies doing business in these countries. The differences among countries and the complexity of global supply chains mandate a critical evaluation and analysis of the issues associated with global reverse flows.

The next section will explore the importance and magnitude of the reverse flows of products. This will be followed by definitions and classification of reverse flows. Finally, an overview of the rationale and appropriate management of reverse flows will be provided.

Importance and Magnitude of Reverse Flows

Some individuals consider reverse flows for logistics and supply chains as a relatively new phenomenon. In actuality, reverse flows have been a part of logistics and supply chains for many years. Consumer goods companies and transportation companies have always dealt with damaged products that often required returns at some level. For example, many warehouses had a section set aside to repackage cases where only part of the case was damaged. Transportation companies dealt with customers who would not accept damaged products, and they accepted liability for the value of the damaged products. To offset their lost revenue, the transportation companies would usually attempt to sell such products to salvage operators for eventual resale. Historically, beverage bottlers refilled empty bottles for which a deposit may have been paid at the customer level. The empty bottles were returned from the retail level to the beverage bottler. Engines have been repaired and recycled for airlines and other large equipment operations. These repairs required a reverse flow to a centralized location where maintenance would be performed.

Many additional traditional examples of reuse, recycling, and so forth could be offered to make the case that reverse flows have been a part of the business operations of some companies for many years. The recent increased focus on reverse flows is attributable to the significant increase in volume of reverse flows.

According to some experts, a large percentage of what is sold may be returned. No one has an exact measure, and the percentage will vary among industries, but it is estimated that returns can range from a low of about 3 percent to a staggering 50 percent in some sectors.[5] AMR Research estimates that U.S. retailers lose 3 to 5 percent of their gross sales to returns and that this accounts for about 4.5 percent of the cost of logistics.[6] In the consumer electronics industry, the average return rate is estimated at 8.5 percent and in the apparel industry at 19.4 percent. Some additional sector data on returns indicate the following: catalog retailing, 30 percent; durable goods (TVs, refrigerators, etc.), about 4 percent; book industry, 10–20 percent; and music and entertainment, 10–20 percent.[7]

As the preceding data indicate, returns are a significant issue in some industries, and this trend appears to be increasing. The relevant question at this point is: Why are the volumes of returns increasing? Several reasons seem to explain the increase.

At the retail level (where most returns originate), Internet returns are about double the counter sale returns. It seems safe to conclude that as Internet sales increase relative to traditional sales, the volume of returns will increase. Another reason for the increase is the customer service policies of some of the large retailers, which make the acceptance of returns ridiculously easy (e.g., "no questions asked," "no receipts necessary," "no time limits," etc.). The problem is then shifted back to the product manufacturer, which has to accept the return and usually deduct the original price from the invoice. As indicated previously, consumer recycling programs have increased in many cities and towns to protect landfills. Also, the high obsolescence rate in technological products has contributed to the growth in reverse flows.

For purposes of further discussion and analysis, the following eight categories of reverse flows are offered:

1. Products that have failed or are unwanted, damaged, or defective but that can be repaired or remanufactured and resold

2. Products that are old, obsolete, or near the end of their shelf life but that still have some value for salvage or resale

3. Products that are unsold from retailers, usually referred to as overstocks, that have resale value

4. Products being recalled due to a safety or quality defect that may be repaired or salvaged

5. Products needing "plug and replace" repair before being put back in service

6. Products that can be recycled, such as pallets, containers, and computer inkjet cartridges

7. Products or parts that can be remanufactured and resold

8. Scrap metal that can be recovered and used as a raw material for further manufacturing

Given the reasons listed earlier for reverse flows, it is not difficult to understand why reverse flows in supply chains have increased, along with present challenges and opportunities for sustainable actions. Other examples or types of reverse flows could be listed, but the above-listed examples should suffice to validate their importance and magnitude. The next sections provide several definitions, illustrations, and explanations of reverse flows systems.

On the Line

Staples Shows Business Value of Environmental Initiatives

In addition to helping the energy industry to deliver its renewable products more efficiently, supply chain managers can make a vital contribution to reducing energy consumption in their own operations. While a focus on energy reduction is typically part of an environmental commitment, it can bring in some cash at the same time. For example, Staples set a 2010 goal to bring its U.S. carbon footprint 7 percent below 2001 levels on an absolute basis. On the journey toward that goal, the $23 billion retailer has realized that some initiatives not only have environmental benefits but also improve margins and mitigate energy risks into the future.

Conservation efforts at DCs were employed around the clock, with skylights to harvest daylight during the day and infrared motion sensors to turn on the lights only when needed at night. Installation of variable-speed motors and intelligent control systems not only conserve energy but also reduce maintenance costs. To manage HVAC consumption, Staples added reflective roofing material to reduce heat gain inside the building and also lower the air inlet temperatures on the rooftop air conditioners. Conservation efforts have lowered operating consumption of electricity by 15 percent per square foot since 2001.

Staples also is using its DC roofs to aggressively pursue solar power. Through long-term purchase agreements with Sun Edison, the company has already installed 27 projects representing 4.5 MW of power and plans to more than double that. Staples is now producing the most expensive power onsite with costs well below the market price of the grid during peak hours. Further, any excess power can be sold back to the grid at this peak price. Onsite generation also offers a long-term hedge against electric grid costs that in many markets are driven by natural gas prices and could potentially include significant costs to build out future transmission capacity.

At its retail stores, Staples is working with a third party to manage consumption by slightly adjusting lighting and HVAC loads. This enables participation in demand-response markets where the grid operator pays Staples for its capability in times of peak demand. Grid operators are also beginning to create energy efficiency markets that pay large industrial or commercial customers for permanent reduction in electricity usage—a potential revenue stream to further capitalize on Staples' DC conservation efforts.

Though a smaller part of Staples' carbon footprint, transportation has not been ignored. Installing speed regulators on their Isuzu trucks saved the company 540,000 gallons of diesel, reduced operating expense by $2 million, and cut CO_2 emissions by 12 million lbs. In the summer of 2009 Staples received its first plug-in electric trucks from Smith Electric.

Source: Jarred Goentzel, "Delivering on the Promise of Green Energy," *Supply Chain Management Review*, January/February 2010, p. 16.

Reverse Logistics Systems versus Closed Loops

As indicated previously, many terms are used in describing the activities associated with managing reverse flows in a supply chain. Two of these terms are used more frequently and for the purposes of this text are defined as follows:[8]

- **Reverse logistics**—The process of moving or transporting goods *from* their final forward destination for the purpose of capturing value or for proper disposal.

- **Closed-loop supply chains**—Designed and managed to explicitly consider both forward and reverse flows activities in a supply chain.

While these two terms are sometimes used interchangeably, they do have differences. Reverse logistics involves the processes for sending new or used products "back up stream" for repair, reuse, refurbishing, resale, recycling, scrap or salvage. The items in a reverse logistics system are usually returned to a central location for processing. The processing typically involves transporting, receiving, testing, inspecting, and sorting for appropriate action (e.g., repair, refurbishing, or resale). The facility and related processes may be provided by a third-party logistics (3PL) company. The reverse flows may be done independently of the original manufacturer, that is, the system was not designed and managed for forward and reverse flows.

The closed-loop supply chain, on the other hand, is explicitly designed and managed for both flows. In the closed-loop supply chain, the manufacturer is proactive in the processes, and the emphasis is on reducing cost and capturing value. The ultimate goal is for everything to be reused or recycled (i.e., nothing wasted). Several examples are offered here to illustrate closed-loop supply chains.

Figure 15.1 shows a closed-loop supply chain for cartridge returns. This illustration depicts the program that Xerox introduced in 1991 and expanded in 1998. Customers can return the cartridges in prepaid mailers. The cartridges have to be cleaned and inspected before refilling.[9] The original system for the rental movies by Netflix was a closed-loop system, as was the system designed by RedBox.

Figure 15.2 depicts a closed-loop supply chain for single-use cameras. Kodak instituted such a program in the early 1990s to allow the recycling and reuse of parts for its

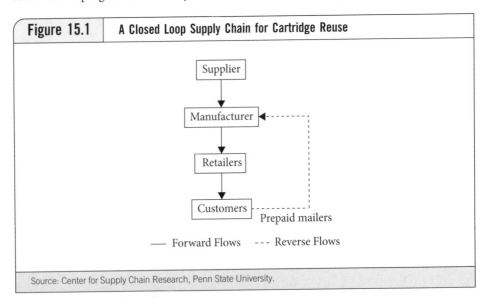

| Figure 15.1 | A Closed Loop Supply Chain for Cartridge Reuse |

Source: Center for Supply Chain Research, Penn State University.

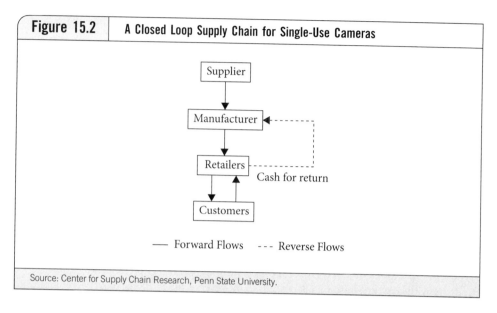

Figure 15.2 | **A Closed Loop Supply Chain for Single-Use Cameras**

Source: Center for Supply Chain Research, Penn State University.

disposable cameras. The process starts with the customer returning the camera to the photo-finisher to develop the film. The photo-finisher batches the cameras to send to a collection center, where they are sorted for shipment to a subcontractor who cleans, disassembles, and inspects them for shipment to a Kodak facility for reloading and resale. The final product containing remanufactured parts and recycled material is indistinguishable to consumers.[10]

The closed-loop supply chain for commercial tire retreading is depicted in Figure 15.3. Frequently, the fleet manager for a trucking fleet, particularly if it is a large fleet, will make arrangements directly with a tire retreader. After receipt of the casings, the retreader will usually retread the same casings and return the retreaded tire to the trucking fleet. This makes the job of balancing supply and demand much easier. For smaller fleet operations, the manager will usually make arrangements with a reseller or tire dealer who will pick up

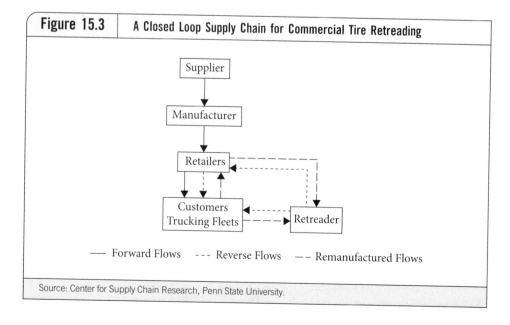

Figure 15.3 | **A Closed Loop Supply Chain for Commercial Tire Retreading**

Source: Center for Supply Chain Research, Penn State University.

the casings for delivery to the tire retreader and subsequently deliver them back to the fleet. Closed-loop supply chains are also in place for passenger tires. They are more complex because of the need to consolidate casings from retailers, garages, and brokers, which are sold in batches to the retreader. The retreader then has to sell the remanufactured tires, which can present some challenges. Consequently, the balancing of supply and demand is not as easy as it is with commercial tires, and sometimes the retreader has a problem maintaining profitability on passenger tires.[11]

The examples of closed-loop supply chains illustrate the characteristics previously described, namely, that they are explicitly designed and managed for both forward and reverse flows to reduce cost and capture value. While they do not achieve 100 percent return of forward flows, they do recapture a significant percentage. Companies gain an economic and a societal benefit by not having to dispose of the items in landfills. More complex examples of closed-loop supply chains can be found. Xerox, for example, initiated what it called a waste-free system in 1991 for photocopiers that has been very successful. This system involves forward flows, reverse flows, and remanufactured flows. In Europe, Xerox has a closed-loop supply chain that handles copiers, printers, and office products with a return rate of 65 percent. The reverse flows items may be repaired, be remanufactured, or have parts remanufactured—all with eventual resale. The fourth option in reverse flows is to recycle and dispose where the product has no value.[12]

In contrast to closed-loop supply chains, the reverse logistics process is frequently much more challenging to operate, or it is more difficult to develop a viable value stream. Items may have to be collected from geographically diverse locations, and some items may be considered hazardous materials. The latter could necessitate special handling for collection and disposal. Frequently, the testing, sorting, grading, and inspection are complex and time consuming. Similarly, remanufacturing or reconditioning can be complex and challenging.[13] Resale after remanufacturing may be difficult. In spite of the challenges, companies have come to recognize value stream opportunities if reverse flows are managed carefully and proactively. Major retailers and their suppliers have become proactive in developing more effective reverse flow systems to capture value.

For reverse logistics programs, the three major forces are customer service, environmental issues, and economic benefits. As indicated, the reverse or return processes are substantial in some industries. Understanding the major forces for the reverse flows is important for gaining insight into the challenges and opportunities for efficiency and effectiveness.

Customer Returns

A variety of reasons for customer returns can be given (as indicated previously), including defective or unwanted items, warranty problems, recalls, and misshipments. Given the potential magnitude of such returns, managing the product return process can have a substantial impact on a company's profit and loss statement. The internal channel for return flows will differ depending on the reason for the return. The alternatives include reinventory for resale, repair or refurbish for return to the customer, or reinventory for resale or disposal.[14] Industries with high return percentages, such as magazines, books, greeting cards, newspapers, catalog and internal sales, and so forth require internal processes as indicated earlier. Managing these processes efficiently and effectively can have a positive impact on the profit and loss statement. The handling of customer return issues can also have a positive customer service benefit when returns are handled expeditiously with timely cash or credit issuance or product replacement (i.e., it can offer a competitive advantage).[15] The super-retailers (Walmart, Target, Best Buy, etc.) have used this approach as a key element in their customer service policies. It has, however, also contributed to the increase in reverse flows. Companies need to have a balanced approach that accommodates legitimate returns but discourages needless returns. Many retailers have returned to a more conservative approach with product returns to reduce costs.

Environmental Challenges

Recycling and environmental concerns are frequently viewed simultaneously because of their association with regulatory policy at the local, state, and federal level. Social concerns stimulate the development of more environmentally friendly products, new standards, and publicly provided recycling programs. It may be surprising to some individuals, but corporations play an active role in this area as part of their focus on ethics and social responsibility. In fact, the term *triple bottom line* of the three P's—profit, people and the planet (also known as "the three pillars")—has gained in popularity with corporations, governments, and activist groups in the twenty-first century. The triple bottom line integrates the three P's into the culture, strategy, and operations of

---

On the Line   *Triple Bottom Line*

The term *triple bottom line* (3BL) dates back to the mid 1990s when management think tank AccountAbility coined and began using the term in its work. The idea behind the 3BL paradigm is that a corporation's ultimate success or health can and should be measured not just by the traditional financial bottom line but also by its social, ethical, and environmental performance. The term found public currency with the 1997 publication of the British edition of John Elkington's *Cannibals with Forks: The Triple Bottom Line of 21st Century Business*. There are in fact very few references to the term before this date, and many (including the man himself) claim that Elkington coined it. By the turn of the millennium, the term had spread like wildfire. The Internet search engine Google returns roughly 25,200 Web pages that mention the term. The phrase *triple bottom line* also occurs in 67 articles in the *Financial Times* in the year preceding June 2002.

The apparent novelty of 3BL lies in its supporters' contention that the overall fulfillment of obligations to communities, employees, customers, and suppliers (to name but four stakeholders) should be measured, calculated, audited, and reported—just as the financial performance of public companies has been for more than a century. Organizations such as the Global Reporting Initiative and AccountAbility have embraced and promoted the 3BL concept for use in the corporate world. And corporations are listening. Companies as significant as AT&T, Dow Chemicals, Shell, and British Telecom have used 3BL terminology in their press releases, annual reports, and other documents. Not surprisingly, most of the big accounting firms are now using the concept approvingly and offering services to help firms that want to measure, report, or audit their two additional "bottom lines." Similarly, there is now a sizable portion of the investment industry devoted to screening companies on the basis of their social and environmental performance, and many of these explicitly use the language of 3BL. Governments, government departments, and political parties are also well represented in the growing documentation of those advocating or accepting 3BL principles.

Source: Norman, Wayne, and MacDonald, Chris (2004), "Getting to the Bottom of 'Triple Bottom Line,'" *Business Ethics Quarterly*, Vol. 14, No. 2, pp. 243–262.

companies and thus captures an expanded spectrum of values and criteria for measuring organizational success to include economic, ecological, and social factors.

In addition to the public relations value of such corporate policies, some evidence suggests that when corporations work with their suppliers to reduce waste, reduce pollution, and improve overall "eco-efficiency," they have also been able to improve product quality, cut production times, and increase productivity.[16] The discussion of closed-loop supply chains is an indication of a more proactive approach by companies to be environmentally responsible and use these strategies to enhance their overall financial viability.

Fueled by the growing sense of urgency for environmental action among scientists, consumers, and most governments around the world, the concept of closed-loop supply chain has gained momentum on a global scale. International organizations such as the United Nations and the International Standardization Organization (ISO) initiate frameworks and tools to promote integration of environmental thinking into business practices. For example, the United Nations University/Institute of Advanced Studies launched Zero Emissions Research Initiative (ZERI) in 1994, which was renamed Zero Emissions Forum in 1999. ZERI promoted the concept that all industrial inputs can be completely converted into a final product and that waste products can be converted into value-added inputs for another chain of production. Similarly, ISO first published ISO 14001 in 1996, specifying the operational requirements for an environmental management system that can guide the environmental activities of organizations in most industries.[17]

Economic Value

In reverse logistics systems as well as closed-loop supply chains, economic benefits have become an important emphasis for businesses and even some nonprofit organizations. The potential for viewing reverse flows as a value stream as opposed to a waste stream was identified in a study published over 30 years ago[18] and further amplified in a White Paper published by the Council of Logistics Management.[19] Both studies pointed out that economic benefits can be the primary driver for the establishment of explicit reverse flow processes not otherwise required by customer service (product returns) and governmental requirements. In other words, recycling for reuse and remanufacture has the potential to be a profitable scenario and a value stream. This has become particularly true in industries that have experienced increasing cost of raw materials, such as the steel industry.

Making reverse flows profitable, however, is a challenge as well as an opportunity. Managing such flows for economic benefit requires careful articulation of the processes and detailed analysis of the costs to determine whether the cost–benefit tradeoffs are positive. The mistake that is commonly made is the assumption that the processes are the same as forward flows and therefore the costs are the same. These assumption will lead to false conclusions.

Achieving a Value Stream for Reverse Flows

The challenge indicated in the previous section of making certain that the proactive management of reverse flows represents an opportunity for enhancing profits through cost reduction or increased revenue is a consideration for both closed-loop supply chains and reverse logistics systems.

From a manufacturing perspective, it may appear to be more costly to remanufacture or refurbish the materials obtained through reverse flows systems than to produce a new product from basic materials or components. Frequently, much of the additional cost is associated with the returns process. Time and distance are often the major cost contributors associated with capturing returns and their residual value.[20] Interestingly, transportation expense is the largest cost component of reverse flows and frequently represents 25 percent or more of the total cost.[21] Using transportation management tools and technology to improve and monitor the transportation network can lower this cost through better scheduling of pickups and deliveries and consolidation of loads to achieve scale economies.

As suggested earlier, one of the major challenges is the estimation of the total cost of the return flow processes. Companies typically have detailed costs associated with forward transportation flow and use historical averages of ton-mile costs to estimate budget costs for the future. In addition, the handling costs associated with returns can be higher because of the sorting, packaging, and random sizes that are typically associated with this activity. As companies gain experience, they can usually reduce handling costs.

Some companies are using activity-based costing (ABC) as a tool to delineate the true costs associated with reverse flows. Quantification of the costs must include all costs associated with the returns processes—labor, transportation, storage and inventory carrying costs, materials handling, packaging, transactional and documentary costs, and appropriate overhead costs. Conversely, accounting for the actual cost savings associated with the materials from reverse flows is important for the tradeoff analysis to determine the economic value added (or the lack thereof).[22]

Once the evaluation for economic value has been completed, it is important to consider the barriers that may impede the implementation of the reverse flows program. These barriers may be internal or external and may include the following:[23]

- Priority relative to other issues and potential projects or programs in the organization
- Inattention or lack of "buy-in" from top-level management in the organization
- Financial resources necessary for operations and asset infrastructure
- Personnel resources required to develop and implement the reverse flows program
- Adequacy of material and information systems to support the returns program
- Local, state, and federal restrictions or regulations

The development and implementation of the articulated and managed reverse flows process requires careful consideration of the preceding list of internal and external barriers. Some organizations may encounter additional barriers. Also, global supply chains may have some additional barriers, but even if they do not, the listed barriers may be more complex on a global basis. Companies that have successfully implemented reverse flows programs give careful consideration to this list of potential barriers prior to attempting to start a program.

The strategic and tactical issues identified earlier for making a reverse flows program a value stream, as opposed to a waste stream, have led some companies to consider a third-party logistics company once the potential program has been rationalized and economically justified. The growth in number and sophistication of 3PLs in the last two decades has made this a very viable option. In fact, some 3PLs specialize in returns and reverse systems. This type of outsourcing may be beneficial for many reasons, as outlined in more detail in Chapter 11, but some discussion of the 3PL alternative is appropriate at this point.

As indicated earlier, reverse or closed-loop systems are often very different from forward flow systems. Since managing reverse flows may not be a core competency of an organization, it could be a natural candidate for outsourcing. Obviously, the economic value added of utilizing a 3PL has to be considered. (Chapter 4 provides a framework for such an evaluation.) 3PLs can offer some special advantages for global supply chains with information technology that provides visibility of inventory. This is particularly critical when dealing with time-sensitive products such as computers and related peripherals, copy equipment, cell phones, and other personal communication equipment. These products have short life cycles and high obsolescence risk. The value of time for such products is a key consideration in the returns process. Time delays can be very costly in terms of recapturing the value of such product assets.

Total life cycle considerations (TLC) are figuring more prominently into reverse flows management programs and into the 3PL evaluation. It is estimated, for example, that a new printer can lose 20 percent of its value while waiting for disposition.[24] A product's time value function is an important consideration for asset recovery decisions. In fact, just reducing time delays in the reverse flows process can result in significant value being added.[25] The time-sensitive products clearly indicate the importance of logistics processes for reverse flows programs, but even for products with longer life cycles and less risk of obsolescence, logistics processes play a key role in the efficiency of the reverse flows program and the potential for recovering assets that will allow economic value to be added. This is particularly true for retailers and one of the reasons why some of the large mass merchandisers utilize 3PLs so extensively. It was previously pointed out that customer returns at the retail level can reach 50 percent in some instances. Speed and efficient reverse logistics processes are essential in such cases to maximize the value of the returns stream.[26]

Managing Reverse Flows in a Supply Chain

The effective and efficient management of reverse flows in a supply chain requires the careful consideration of a number of key activities or issues. As indicated previously, proactive management of reverse flows can impact the financial position of a company quite positively. On the other hand, the opposite can be true if reverse flows are mismanaged or not carefully managed. The Reverse Logistics Educational Council has recommended careful consideration of the following:

- **Avoidance**—Producing high-quality products and developing processes to minimize or eliminate returns

- **Gatekeeping**—Checking and screening merchandise at the entry point into the reverse flows process to eliminate unnecessary returns or minimize handling

- **Reducing reverse cycle times**—Analyzing processes to enable and facilitate compression of time for returns to enhance value recapture

- **Information systems**—Developing effective information systems to improve product visibility, reduce uncertainty, and maximize economies of scale

- **Returns centers**—Developing optimum locations and facility layouts for returns centers to facilitate network flow

Supply Chain Technology

Improving Reverse Flows with Technology

A key to successful returns management is an asset recovery program that reduces losses or even generates revenue. Genco, a third-party logistics provider and returns specialist, operates 94 facilities in the United States and Canada with a combined 26.3 million square feet of space. At these high-tech returns processing centers, technicians and testers, in what the company calls a value inspection process, determine the most cost-effective means for disposition of goods. After deciding which foods fall under warranty or are covered by other business rules or contract provisions between the retailer and manufacturer, a disposition channel is chosen, and the goods are sent along conveyors to the right staging area. Many manufacturers offer off-invoice discounts based on assumed rates of defective products rather than take products back. It makes sense for both parties, given that most goods are manufactured overseas.

For products not tossed or returned to the manufacturer, Genco maintains a global network of liquidation channels that includes salvage buyers, online auction partners, B2B (business-to-business) exchanges, fixed-price offerings, and category and bulk salvage. There are three types of buyers in the "gray market." The first type, online auction sites like eBay, accounts for only about 10 percent of liquidated goods because of the high costs of selling goods online. The second gray market channel, which accounts for around 20 percent of returned goods, is comprised of buyers that Chris Greve (an executive vice president with Genco) categorized as "mom-and-pop resellers" who purchase goods by the pallet or partial truckload and resell them through flea markets and other channels. Dominating the liquidation market are cash-rich buyers who can write checks worth millions of dollars on the spot for multiple containers of consumer goods.

Genco clients include a virtual who's-who of global pharmaceutical, retail, and consumer goods and electronics manufacturers, and the value inspection process reduces their reconciliation and administrative costs; reduces unauthorized returns, freight costs, and operational costs; and fits into overall supply chain strategies by providing enhanced visibility.

"Being able to disposition products correctly is the biggest contribution a reverse logistics network can make to a company."

At UPS Supply Chain Solutions, the postsales supply chain is broken out into two buckets: consumer returns to stores and online retailers, and service parts logistics. Both demand far faster cycle times than companies are accustomed to. Today, consumers expect that laptops, cell phones, and other electronics devices will be repaired and returned in ever-shrinking time frames; whether it's a network server or photocopy machine, delivery windows for service parts and technicians can be as short as one hour.

Source: David Biederman, *Traffic World, Inc.* (September 4, 2006): 1, Commonwealth Business Media.

- **Remanufacture or refurbishment**—Preparing and repairing a product for resale as is usually done in closed loop supply chains to maximize value recapture
- **Asset recovery**—Classifying and disposing of returned items, surplus, scrap, and obsolete items to maximize returns and minimize cost
- **Pricing**—Negotiating the best price for products being returned and resold

- **Outsourcing**—Considering a relationship with a third-party organization to handle and manage reverse flows in cases where existing personnel, infrastructure, experience, or capital may not be adequate to implement a successful program
- **Zero returns**—Developing a policy to exclude returns by giving a returns allowance or "destroying" the product in the field
- **Financial management**—Developing guidelines and financial procedures to properly account for charges against sales and related financial issues when items are returned by customers

SUMMARY

- Sustainability has become an increasingly important objective for private-sector, for-profit organizations in the twenty-first century.

- Initially organizations focused upon sustainability because of political and public pressure and their recognition of the importance of their social responsibility.

- In recent years there has been a growing recognition of the economic opportunity to reduce cost and improve profit positions.

- Sustainability is a challenging and complex issue because of the diversity of views on the topic, but some supply chain professionals have found it useful to consider sustainability on a broad functional basis—inbound functions, production and operation functions, and outbound or distribution functions.

- Transportation is frequently a critical part of a sustainability effort since it has the potential of leaving such a large carbon footprint. Various transportation strategies that are both cost efficient and ecologically sound can be used to mitigate this challenge.

- The so-called R's of sustainability include: reuse, remanufacturing, refurbishing, and recycling. The R's are unique but can be used in a comprehensive program where they are complimentary to each other.

- The R's can be an important component of a recycling program to create a value stream for the organization to enhance profitability.

- Recycling is often part of a reverse flow logistics system or closed-loop logistics system, and both have grown in importance as reverse flow volumes have increased during the last two decades.

- The major forces impacting the growth in reverse flow volumes have been customer returns, environmental policies, and economic benefits for organizations.

- When designing an efficient and effective returns flow program, consideration must be given to the variety of the returns and the development of procedures and processes for each one.

- An analysis of the benefits of a reverse or return flows program is dependent upon the development of the true costs associated with such a program and comparing them to a realistic measure of the benefits.

STUDY QUESTIONS

1. Why is sustainability such a complex and challenging issue for organizations? How can they simplify these challenges from a supply chain perspective?

2. Compare and contrast the so-called R's of sustainability.

3. Distinguish between a value stream and a waste stream for reverse flows. Give examples of each.

4. Reverse flows were usually viewed as a necessary cost by business organizations. Why? Has this attitude changed? Why?

5. What special challenges and opportunities are presented for reverse flows by globalization? What do you think is the biggest challenge and the greatest opportunity? Why?

6. Some individuals argue that reverse flows programs are a relatively new phenomenon, but others state that reverse flows programs have been in existence for many years. What is your position on this issue? Why?

7. Explain the eight major categories of reverse flows and their importance.

8. Compare and contrast reverse logistics systems and closed-loop supply chains and give examples of each. Are there more opportunities for closed-loop systems?

9. Customer returns, particularly at the retail level, have increased dramatically. What factors have contributed to this increase? What recommendations would you implement to decrease this volume?

10. Evaluate the Trash to Treasure program discussed at the beginning of this chapter in terms of advantages, disadvantages, and long-run potential for expansion and financial viability. What are your recommendations for improvement?

NOTES

1. Evelyn A. Thomchick and Kusumal Ruamsook, "Frameworks and State of Environmentally Sustainable Supply Chain Management," Working Paper, March 2010, Center for Supply Chain Research, Penn State University.

2. Ibid., p. 2.

3. Ibid., pp 3–5.

4. Ibid., pp. 9–11.

5. Christopher D. Norek, "Returns Management: Throwing It into Reverse," *DC Velocity* (January 2003): 54–58.

6. Ibid.

7. Christopher D. Norek, "Returns Management: Making Order out of Chaos," *Supply Chain Management Review* (May/June 2002): 34–37.

8. Dale S. Rogers and Ronald S. Tibben-Lembke, *Going Backwards: Reverse Logistics Trends and Practices* (Reverse Logistics Executive Council, 1998): 2.

9. V. Daniel, R. Guide, and Luk N. Van Wassenhove, *Business Aspects of Closed-Loop Supply Chains* (Pittsburgh, PA: Carnegie Mellon University Press, 2003): 17–27.

10. Ibid.

11. Ibid.

12. Ibid.

13. Ibid.

14. Rogers and Tibben-Lembke, op. cit., p. 37.

15. Ibid., p. 17.

16. Linda C. Angell and Robert D. Klassen, "Integrating Environmental Issues into the Mainstream," *Journal of Operations Management* (March 2000): 64.

17. Peter M. Senge, Benyamin B. Lichtenstein, Katrin Kaufer, Hilar Bradbury, and John S. Carroll, "Collaborating for Systematic Change," *MIT Sloan Management Review*, Vol. 48, No. 2 (2007): 44–53.

18. Joseph P. Guiltiman and Nonyelu G. Nwekoye, "Developing Distribution Channels and Systems in the Emerging Recycling Industries," *International Journal of Physical Distribution*, Vol. 6, No. 1 (1975): 28.

19. James R. Stock, *Reverse Logistics* (Oak Brook, IL: Council of Logistics Management, 1992): 1–27.

20. John A. Effelson, *The Development of Reverse Logistics Processes in a Global Business Environment*, M.S. Thesis, (Pennsylvania State University, May 1999): 14–16.

21. Stock, op. cit, p. 76.

22. Effelson, op. cit., pp. 16–17.

23. Rogers and Tibben-Lembke, op. cit., pp. 32–35.

24. Guide and Van Wassonhove, op. cit.

25. Ibid.

26. Rogers and Tibben-Lembke, op. cit., p. 7.

CASE 15.1

Fitness Retreads, LLP: A Sequel

Terry Edwards, Sandy Knight, and Andy Reisinger, partners in Core Fitness, were meeting in the conference room of their athletic club in State College, Pennsylvania, to discuss their new venture, which was based on the R's of recycle, repair, refurbish, reuse, and resale or scrap. Andy Reisinger admitted that when they initiated this venture as a complimentary business to their network of fitness and health clubs in Central Pennsylvania, he was very skeptical and thought that it would detract from their primary business activity of providing upscale facilities and exercise equipment and related programs for adults. What had started as what he considered to be a bad idea of one of the other partners, Terry Edwards, was showing promising growth and a steady stream of new revenue.

Background

Core Fitness was an established organization with health and fitness facilities in five communities in central Pennsylvania. The business had grown on a steady basis since it was established in 1985, and it now was operating seven clubs in these five communities. It had three clubs in State College because of the size of the student body (45,000) enrolled at Penn State and the population of professionals in the surrounding areas. In 2007, the business seemed to be stagnating in terms of memberships and revenues. It had initiated a number of group exercise programs, such as boot camps, karate, and Pilates, but the business was not experiencing the growth that the partners had anticipated.

Terry Edwards, the partner responsible for procurement and maintenance of equipment, had purchased some used equipment from a bankrupt club in the Pittsburgh area, which had saved Core Fitness at least $15,000 after paying the purchase price and the costs associated with repairing and refurbishing the equipment to an "as new" status. Terry decided to repair the equipment that they were replacing instead of having it hauled away to a landfill. Terry had to buy new parts as well as having the equipment repaired, but he was able to sell the equipment to individuals for their home gyms and make a good profit. The success of these two related activities led Terry to recommend that Core Fitness start a new complementary business of buying used equipment for refurbishing, repair, and resale either to individuals or other businesses.

Current Situation

Terry Edwards responded to Andy Reisinger's comments by thanking him and expressing appreciation for his support at the outset of their new venture. Terry reported that "Fitness Retreads" had experienced remarkable and steady growth in revenues over the five previous years. He was able to utilize their two mechanics on a full-time basis and had to add a third full-time individual to accommodate their growth during the past two years.

Terry felt that there were some additional opportunities that the company could exploit. For example, it had been contacted by competitors and clubs in other areas about providing repair service for their equipment and possibly selling them equipment that had been prepared for resale. Thus far, the company had only been selling to individuals and local businesses with facilities for employees.

Sandy Knight, who was responsible for club programs for members and some of the marketing, reported that the core business was again experiencing a growth in membership and increase revenues. She felt that the group fitness programs and an HMO-sponsored program (Silver Sneakers) for retirees at the university had a very positive impact, but she also felt that the new enterprise allowed them to add equipment and keep all of their equipment in an excellent state of repair, which was very beneficial and gave Core Fitness a competitive edge in its market area.

Terry thanked her for her compliments and added an important caveat, namely, that they were going to need more space if they expanded the business of Fitness Retreads. Andy, who had been quiet since his initial comment, joined in again by stating his support of expanding Fitness Retreads and that he felt that there were additional opportunities besides those offered by Terry. He also stated that he felt that there were some excellent real estate options in the local area for purchase or lease. He felt that they should move Fitness Retreads from the space in one of their State College facilities to the new space and use the existing space for equipment or activities for the expanded demand of their core business.

CASE QUESTIONS

1. What is your evaluation of the various proposals made by the partners of Core Fitness and Fitness Retreads? What challenges and issues do they face? What factors in the current environment favor their proposed activities?

2. What other suggestions would you make for expanding Fitness Retreads? Why?

REFERENCES

Biehl, M., Edmund Praton, and Matthew J. Realff, "Assuming Performance and Uncertainty in Developing Carpet Reverse Logistics Systems," *Computers and Operation Research*, Vol. 34 (2007): 443–463.

Breen, Liz, "A Preliminary Analysis of Customer Compliances in Reverse Logistics Practices," *Management Research News*, Vol. 29, No. 9 (UK, 2006): 532–551.

Chan, H. K., "A Proactive and Collaborative Approach to Reverse Logistics—A Case Study," *Production Planning and Control*, Vol. 18, No. 4 (June 2007): 350–360.

Geeker, Rachel, and M. W. Vigoroso, "Industry Best Practices in Reverse Logistics," *Aberdeen Group* (January 2007): 1–26.

Norek, Christopher, "Returns Management," *Supply Chain Management Review* (May/June 2002): 35–42.

Rogers, Dale S., and Ronald S. Tibben-Lembke, "An Overview of Reverse Logistics Practices," *Journal of Business Logistics*, Vol. 22, No. 2 (2001): 129–48.

Rogers, Dale S., and Ronald S. Tibben-Lembke, "Returns Management and Reverse Logistics for Competitive Advantage," *CSCMP Explores*, Vol. 3 (Winter 2006): 1–15.

Rogers, Dale S., Douglas M. Lambert, Keely Croxton, and Sebastian Garcia-Dastugue, "The Returns Management Process," *International Journal of Logistics Management*, Vol. 13, No. 2 (2002): 1–18.

Savaskan, R. Canan, and Luk N. Van Wassenhove, "Reverse Channel Design: The Case of Competing Retailers," *Management Science*, Vol. 52, No. 1 (January 2006): 1–14.

Srivastava, Samir K., and Rajiv K. Srivastava, "Managing Product Returns for Reverse Logistics," *International Journal of Physical Distribution and Logistics Management*, Vol. 36, No. 7 (2006): 524–546.

Tibben-Lembke, Ronald S., "Strategic Use of the Secondary Market for Retail Consumer Goods," *California Management Review*, Vol. 45, No. 2 (Winter 2004): 90–104.

Source: John J. Coyle, DBA. Used with permission.

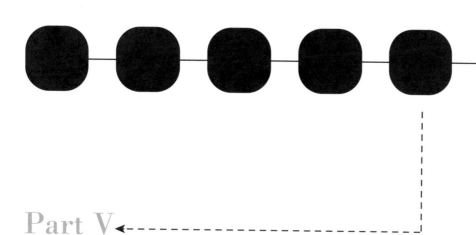

Part V

For many reasons, it is essential for logistics, supply chain, and corporate executives to be thinking continuously about how to grow revenue and enhance profitability. Based on information discussed throughout this text, there are ample ways for effective management of logistics and supply chain activities to help with the imperatives of cost reduction. The real value of effective supply chain management (SCM), however, moves into the strategic realm of revenue growth. Companies are finding out that excellence in logistics and SCM, if properly managed and directed, can help to grow the top line as well as the bottom line.

This concluding chapter deals generally with the topic of supply chain transformation and how companies can mobilize their efforts to create maximum value for their organizations and for the supply chains in which they operate. **Chapter 16** focuses on several major types of supply chain strategies: differentiation, financial, technology-based, relationship-based, and global. Sound, calculated approaches in each of these areas should help to magnify the corporate benefits of investments in logistics and SCM. Finally, the chapter discusses the need for supply chain transformation and some of the steps that accomplish this objective.

Chapter 16

STRATEGIC CHALLENGES AND CHANGE FOR SUPPLY CHAINS

Learning Objectives

After reading this chapter, you should be able to do the following:

- Understand current and future strategic challenges for supply chains.
- Identify principles for supply chain success.
- Appreciate the CEO's viewpoint on and expectations of supply chain management.
- Understand how supply chain management can help to grow revenues, as well as contain costs.
- Appreciate several major types of supply chain strategies: differentiation, financial, technology-based, relationship-based, and global.
- Name several examples of companies that have successfully developed global supply chain strategies that help to differentiate themselves from the competition.
- Describe the need for supply chain transformation and some of the steps that are important to accomplish this objective.

Supply Chain Profile

From Bean to Cup: How Starbucks Transformed Its Supply Chain

It takes a well-run supply chain to ensure that a barista pours a good cup of Starbucks coffee. That's because the journey from bean to cup is a complicated one. Coffee and other merchandise must be sourced from around the globe and then successfully delivered to the Starbucks Corporation's 16,700 retail stores, which serve some 50 million customers in 51 countries each week.

In 2008, Starbucks wasn't sure that its supply chain was meeting that goal. One clue that things were not quite right: The company's operational costs were rising even though sales were cooling. Between October 2007 and October 2008, for example, supply chain expenses in the United States rose from US $750 million to more than US $825 million, yet sales for U.S. stores that had been open for at least one year dropped by 10 percent during that same period.

In part, Starbucks was a victim of its own success. Because the company was opening stores around the world at a rapid pace, the supply chain organization had to focus on keeping up with that expansion. As a result, the costs of running the supply chain—the operating expenses - were rising very steeply.

STARBUCKS' SUPPLY CHAIN OBJECTIVES

To transform its supply chain, the coffee retailer established three key objectives: (1) reorganize its supply chain organization; (2) reduce its cost to serve stores and improve execution; and (3) lay the foundation for future supply chain capability

The first step of the transformation plan, reorganizing Starbucks' supply chain organization, got under way in late 2008. According to Peter D. Gibbons, executive vice president of global supply chain operations, that involved taking a complex structure and simplifying it so that every job fell into one of four basic supply chain functions: (1) plan, (2) source, (3) make, and (4) deliver. For instance, anybody involved in planning—be it production planning, replenishment, or new product launches—was placed in the planning group. Sourcing activities were grouped into two areas: coffee and "non-coffee" procurement. (Starbucks spends US $600 million on coffee each year. Purchases of other items, such as dairy products, baked goods, store furniture, and paper goods, total US $2.5 billion annually.) All manufacturing, whether done in-house or by contract manufacturers, was assigned to the "make" functional unit. And finally, all personnel working in transportation, distribution, and customer service were assigned to the "deliver" group.

After the supply chain functions were reorganized, the various departments turned their attention to the second objective of the supply chain transformation: reducing costs and improving efficiencies. As part of that effort, the sourcing group worked on identifying the cost drivers that were pushing up prices. "We went out to understand the contracts we had, the prices we were paying, and the shipping costs, and we began breaking items down by ingredient rather than just purchase price," Gibbons says. "We built more effective 'should cost' models, including benchmarking ingredients and processes, which showed that we could negotiate better prices."

Although Starbucks has a raft of metrics for evaluating supply chain performance, it focuses on four high-level categories to create consistency and balance across the global supply chain team: (1) safety in operations, (2) service measured by on-time delivery and order fill rates, (3) total end-to-end supply chain costs, and (4) enterprise savings. The last category refers to cost savings that come from areas outside logistics, such as procurement, marketing, or research and development.

To sustain that momentum for improvement and to ensure a future flow of talent into the organization, Starbucks recently began the third step of the transformation plan, to recruit top graduates of supply chain education programs and to provide ongoing training for its existing employees to help them further develop their supply chain knowledge and skills. "We want to make sure we have thought leaders [in our supply chain organization]," Gibbons says. Starbucks considers this initiative to be so important, in fact, that Gibbons now spends 40 to 50 percent of his time on developing, hiring, and retaining supply chain talent. The infusion of new recruits will allow Starbucks to stay focused on its supply chain mission of delivering products with a high level of service at the lowest possible cost to its stores in the United States and around the globe.

ONE WORLD—ONE LOGISTICS SYSTEM

Overall, a priority on the creation of a single, global logistics system was important for Starbucks because of its far-flung supply chain. The company generally brings coffee beans from Latin America, Africa, and Asia to the United States and Europe in ocean containers. From the port of entry, the green (unroasted) beans are trucked to six storage sites, either at a roasting plant or nearby. After the beans are roasted and packaged, the finished product is trucked to regional distribution centers, which range from 200,000 to 300,000 square feet in size. Starbucks runs five regional distribution centers (DCs) in the United States; two are company-owned and the other three are operated by third-party logistics companies (3PLs). It also has two distribution centers in Europe and two in Asia, all of which are managed by 3PLs. Coffee, however, is only one of many products held at these warehouses. They also handle other items required by Starbucks' retail outlets—everything from furniture to cappuccino mix.

Also, the manufacturing group developed a more efficient model for delivering coffee beans to its processing plants, with the goal of manufacturing in the region where the product is sold. Starbucks already owned three coffee plants in the United States, in Kent, Washington; Minden, Nevada; and York, Pennsylvania. In 2009, the company added a fourth U.S. plant, in Columbia, South Carolina. The benefits of that approach were quickly apparent; regionalizing its coffee production allowed Starbucks to reduce its transportation costs and lead times, says Gibbons. Moreover, once the new facility was up and running, all of the U.S. coffee plants were able to switch from seven-day operations to five days.

Because delivery costs and execution are intertwined, Gibbons and his team set about improving both. One of their first steps was to build a global map of Starbucks' transportation expenditures—no easy task, because it involved gathering all supply chain costs by region and by customer, Gibbons says. An analysis of those expenditures allowed Starbucks to winnow its transportation carriers, retaining only those that provided the best service.

EARNING THE COMPANY'S CONFIDENCE

In Gibbons' eyes, the transformation effort has been a success. "Today there's a lot of confidence in our supply chain to execute every day, to make 70,000 deliveries a week, to get new products to market, and to manage product transitions, new product introductions, and promotions," he observes. "No one is going to listen to us talking about supply chain strategy if we can't deliver service, quality, and cost on a daily basis."

Introduction

As the concluding chapter in this edition, it is important to provide a capstone or an integration of the content of this book and to establish a perspective on future issues and challenges that will face supply chains and supply chain managers. Thus, this chapter is organized around four main topics: (1) principles of supply chain management (SCM), (2) CEOs' perspectives and expectations for supply chain management, (3) key areas of supply chain strategy, and (4) supply chain transformation—how to get from where we are now to where we need to be in the future.

Principles of Supply Chain Management[1]

Figure 16.1 lists the seven principles of supply chain management that were discussed in an article that appeared in the very first issue of *Supply Chain Management Review* (SCMR). According to Frank Quinn, editor of the SCMR, this was the most requested article in the 10-year history of the publication; it provided a clear and compelling case for excellence in supply chain management.[2] Further, Mr. Quinn added that the insights provided in the article remained remarkably fresh 10 years later.

In addition, Figure 16.1 provides a perspective on each of the seven principles and the extent to which each may be expected to contribute to the objectives of revenue growth, asset utilization, and cost reduction.

Principle 1: Segment Customers Based on Service Needs

Essentially, this principle suggests a departure from traditional approaches to customer segmentation based on industry, product, or trade channel to an approach that segments customers based on logistics and supply chain needs. Examples would include service requirements, fulfillment priorities, frequency of service, etc. Also, it is important to make sure that supply chain services are delivered at a profit and that accounts align appropriately with service packages. According to the authors, one successful food manufacturer aggressively marketed vendor-managed inventory to all customer segments and boosted sales as a result. Regrettably, subsequent activity-based cost analysis found that one segment actually lost nine cents a case on an operating margin basis.

Principle 2: Customize the Logistics Network

Historically, many companies have designed logistics and supply chain capabilities to meet the average service requirements of all customers, or maybe to satisfy the toughest requirements of an individual customer segment. This principle stresses the need to develop supply chain approaches that are responsive to the needs of individual customer segments. These approaches are more likely to involve greater complexity and flexibility and will require the involvement of real-time decision support tools.

Principle 3: Listen to Signals of Market Demand and Plan Accordingly

In contrast to traditional forecasting approaches that sometimes result in multiple departments creating separate forecasts for the same products, the objective here is to see that demand planning is responsive to and aligned with market signals such as point-of-sale information. Also, by seeing that demand planning involves both customers

Figure 16.1 | Principles of Supply Chain Management and Financial Outcomes

Relationship between supply chain principles and financial outcomes

Seven Principles	Revenue Growth	Asset Utilization	Cost Reduction
1. Segment Customer Based on Needs	High	Medium	Medium
2. Customize Logistics Network	Medium	High	Medium
3. Listen to Market Signals And Plan Accordingly	Low	High	Medium
4. Differentiate Products Closer to Customers	Low	Medium	High
5. Source Strategically	Low	Medium	High
6. Develop Supply Chain Technology Strategy*	Medium	High	Medium
7. Adopt Channel-Spanning Measures	High	High	High

● High   ◐ Medium   ○ Low

*Information technology provides the infrastructure required to capture benefits across the supply chain

Source: David L. Anderson, Frank F. Britt, and Donavon J. Favre, "The Seven Principles of Supply Chain Management," *Supply Chain Management Review* (April 2007): 46. Copyright © 2007 Reed Business, a division of Reed Elsevier. Reproduced by permission.

and suppliers, this collaborative approach improves the effectiveness of sales and operations planning.

Principle 4: Differentiate Products Closer to the Customer

When successfully implemented, this principle helps to improve customer service via fewer stockouts and also takes significant inventory carrying cost out of the supply chain. By postponing product differentiation to the latest possible moment and by gaining greater understanding and control of cycle times, supply chain efficiency and effectiveness will be positively impacted.

Principle 5: Source Strategically

Although customers of all types should have fact-based knowledge of the cost of purchased products and services, over the long term, suppliers' cost experiences will be passed along to customers in terms of higher prices. Excellent supply chain management requires customers and suppliers to work together in a creative, positive way to meet overall supply chain objectives. This may involve short-term competitive bids, entering into long-term contracts and strategic supplier relationships, outsourcing, and even vertical integration.

Principle 6: Develop a Supply Chainwide Technology Strategy

The priority here is to replace inflexible, poorly integrated transactional systems with enterprise-wide systems. Instead of using transactional systems that capture large quantities of data that are difficult to assimilate and utilize, this approach will help to translate available data into actionable intelligence that can enhance real-world operations.

Principle 7: Adopt Channel-Spanning Performance Measures

When individual companies in a supply chain ask the question: How are we doing? the response should be in the context of the overall supply chain. While it is important for individual organizations to meet their corporate objectives, the realization of supply chain objectives will be essential to the long-term success of the individual participants. Thus, it is essential for these companies to work toward the same goals by understanding what each brings to the supply chain and showing how to leverage complementary assets and skills to the greatest advantage of the supply chain.

In response to the comment that "the insights (from this article) remained remarkably fresh 10 years later," lead author Dr. David L. Anderson wrote that he went back and reread the article to see if he agreed. His assessment is captured in the following points:[3]

1. **The seven principles basically survive the test of time.** Although I might include some thoughts around global supply chain risks, add a section on insourcing/outsourcing strategies, update the case studies, and tighten up the procurement strategy discussion, I still believe companies cannot go wrong by adopting these principles as the basis of their supply chain strategies.

2. **We still have a long way to go on supply chain strategy implementation.** The fact that the principles are still relatively fresh implies that many companies have not done the best job implementing strategies that underlie the principles.

3. **Technology and data will be the major game changer going forward.** UPC, RFID, and GPS-related data were not around when we wrote the article. The growing availability of "real-time" supply chain data as well as the tools to enable us to use the data in planning and executing supply chains will be the key factor that separates the winners and losers in supply chain management over the coming decade.

Focus of Supply Chain Management

One of the greatest challenges for supply chain managers is to get other corporate leaders to appreciate the potential impact that effective supply chain management can have on their businesses. This challenge stems from the preoccupation of many corporate executives with growth for their companies, sometimes at the expense of maintaining short-term service levels and achieving longer-term objectives.

In a timely and relevant article, Richard Thompson, Donald Eisenstein, and Timothy Stratman address this very problem and discuss some of the ways that supply chain leaders can position their organizations to meet their objectives and also contribute to corporate growth imperatives.[4] To become contributing players to the growth agenda, the authors suggest three areas in which supply chain leaders need to focus: (1) think beyond cost, (2) develop world-class collaboration skills, and (3) aggressively grow your personal leadership capabilities.

Getting to Growth: Think Beyond Cost

To better understand how high-level executives perceive the challenge of growing their business profitably, a study was conducted of Chicago-based CEOs representing companies having annual sales ranging from $50 million to more than $20 billion, across a variety of industries. Additionally, interviews were held with many of the CEOs to better understand and interpret the study findings.

Figures 16.2, 16.3, and 16.4 show some of the results of this study that suggest the basic challenge is to help CEOs understand the significant contribution that excellence

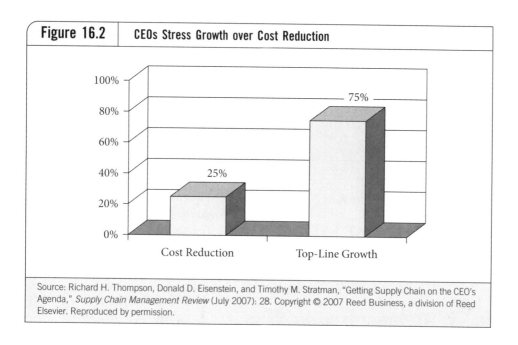

Figure 16.2 | **CEOs Stress Growth over Cost Reduction**

Source: Richard H. Thompson, Donald D. Eisenstein, and Timothy M. Stratman, "Getting Supply Chain on the CEO's Agenda," *Supply Chain Management Review* (July 2007): 28. Copyright © 2007 Reed Business, a division of Reed Elsevier. Reproduced by permission.

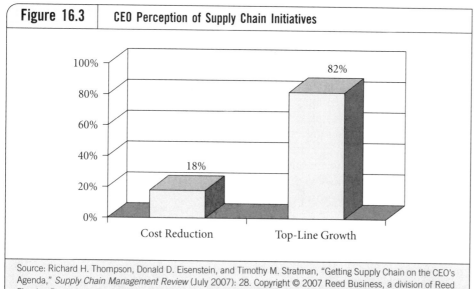

Figure 16.3 | **CEO Perception of Supply Chain Initiatives**

Source: Richard H. Thompson, Donald D. Eisenstein, and Timothy M. Stratman, "Getting Supply Chain on the CEO's Agenda," *Supply Chain Management Review* (July 2007): 28. Copyright © 2007 Reed Business, a division of Reed Elsevier. Reproduced by permission.

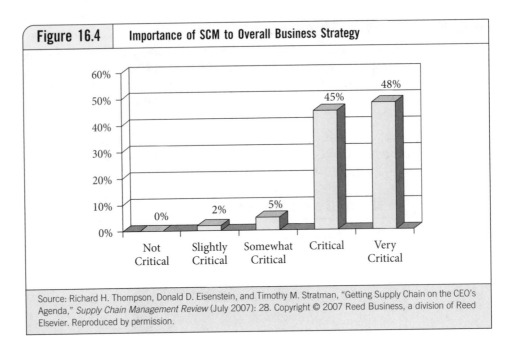

Figure 16.4 | **Importance of SCM to Overall Business Strategy**

Source: Richard H. Thompson, Donald D. Eisenstein, and Timothy M. Stratman, "Getting Supply Chain on the CEO's Agenda," *Supply Chain Management Review* (July 2007): 28. Copyright © 2007 Reed Business, a division of Reed Elsevier. Reproduced by permission.

in SCM can have on corporate growth initiatives. According to Figure 16.2, three of four CEOs surveyed indicated their top priority is on top-line growth, rather than on cost reduction. Figure 16.3, however, indicates that 82 percent of the same CEOs view SCM initiatives as being primarily focused on cost reduction, in contrast to top-line growth. Based on this information, there appears to be a gap between corporate priorities and the ways in which effective SCM can contribute to the achievement of these priorities.

Figure 16.4 shows that 93 percent of these same executives identified supply chain management as being either critical or very critical to their overall business strategy. Clearly, the challenge for supply chain managers is to work with their CEOs and to instill a sense of urgency as to how excellence in SCM can be recognized.

The authors offer a few thoughts as to what supply chain managers can do to get their CEOs thinking about SCM more in terms of growth than cost reduction. The first step is to *communicate the relationship between supply chain competency and growth.* A recent study conducted by the MIT Center for Transportation and Logistics did this effectively, finding that "… focusing supply chains on achieving customer objectives rather than reducing near-term costs and inventories can have a greater impact on a company's financial performance. Leading enterprises integrate elements of supply chain management with customer-facing and revenue-generating capabilities."[5] Essentially, this requires that supply chain management be viewed as central to the enterprise, rather than as an overlooked back-office function. Also, SCM must be viewed as a competitive differentiator that helps to ensure profitable growth.

Next is a recommendation that supply chain executives *move beyond a mindset focused primarily on delivering the "right product, at the right place, at the right time, at the lowest cost" to one more oriented toward growth.* This broader mindset is required to profitably grow market share, acquire new customers, and expand into new markets. Also, to heighten the challenge, it is not sufficient to simply grow the business; corporate earnings must grow as well.

Supply chain executives should modify their traditional mindset from thinking with an "inside-out" perspective to one that is "outside-in." Historically, management of supply chains involved strong analytical orientations and process management, which required linear thinking to help identify and drive out inefficiencies in a process. Even those who suggest that their leadership "starts with the customer or the demand signal" sometimes remain trapped in a linear thinking model as they work to optimize the existing supply chain network. While the outside-in approach may very well start with the customer, key questions to be asked revolve around the issue of why a customer prefers a particular company and how that company's supply chain should align itself to meet these preferences. Responding to these questions requires taking a more holistic view of the overall business and developing a complete understanding of what kinds of value are created by each participant in the supply chain. Then, the imperative shifts to designing or redesigning the supply chain to better deliver the value, rather than optimizing the current-state network built around existing assets.

Develop World-Class Collaboration Skills

Although this topic was discussed initially in Chapter 4 of this book, the second key to being a growth contributor is to develop world-class collaboration skills. While many corporate CEOs view collaboration as a key to fostering growth, they also recognize the challenges to successful collaboration. Based on interviews conducted with corporate CEOs, the following success factors were recognized as being central to accomplishing this objective:

- **Define the benefits of collaboration**—Participants need to understand and quantify the benefits of collaboration to the overall supply chain and then recognize how individual participants will benefit from the collaboration.

- **Make the investment**—Individual participants in a collaborative effort must be willing to invest to make collaboration a reality and to consider investments that may need to go beyond the borders of their own organizations.

- **Earn trust and create mutual ownership**—All partners in the collaboration need to become vested in the collaboration efforts and develop a sense of ownership in the initiative. This ownership needs to go well beyond any formal contract that may pertain to the relationship, as collaborations that are constrained by the terms of a contract are likely to fail.

- **Dedicate "A" players**—Involvement of the "best and brightest" people in the involved organization will greatly assist in achieving the goals of a collaborative relationship.

In the words of the authors, "business people have been trained traditionally to maximize their self-interest. Successful collaboration requires analytical and business savvy—but just as important is psychological savvy. It is the people or emotional side of the equation that is most difficult and fragile. The good news for supply chain leaders is that from a people and process standpoint, they are in a great position to get the collaboration ball moving. And, the CEO will be watching."[6]

Grow Your Leadership Capabilities

The recommendation here is that supply chain executives develop and exercise their leadership capabilities on a day-to-day basis. As a result, supply chain executives should set their personal objectives to include being viewed as exceptionally engaging, persuasive, visible, and customer-focused members of the executive team. This is a great contrast to the traditional roles of many supply chain managers who were less visible and less involved with sales and marketing processes and direct customer interaction.

To help grow leadership capabilities and achieve recognition of this by others in the organization, the authors offer four suggestions: (1) get out of your office and

On the Line   *Best Buy's Supply Chain Transformation*

Rarely has a major shift in a company's strategy relied so heavily on the supply chain. Best Buy is reimagining its big-box retail concept to focus intensively on customer needs, and the company's supply chain is an integral part of the new vision. No longer will the supply chain simply push high volumes of product out of factories and into stores—a task at which it excels, by the way. Now, it will emphasize agility, responsiveness, and accuracy, pinpointing smaller, sales floor-ready deliveries to meet the changing desires of specific customer segments. In effect, the supply chain is becoming a customer-facing unit.

The Richfield, Minnesota-based retailer, a $27 billion market leader in consumer electronics with more than 700 stores in 49 states, faced several related challenges. For one thing, Walmart and Target were chipping away at its core businesses—consumer electronics, home office equipment, entertainment software, and appliances. For another, as the population ages, consumers are putting more emphasis on service and support and less on the gee-whiz technical aspects of products. Third, the company found that 33 percent of the people visiting its stores were leaving dissatisfied. Best Buy's broad focus just wasn't meeting its needs.

Best Buy executives realized they needed to reposition the company for future growth. The one-size-fits-all approach clearly was not the answer. So Best Buy developed a strategy that focused on satisfying the needs of eight distinct demographic segments and the desires of customers in those segments. That meant giving up the idea that Best Buy stores had to have similar product mixes and layouts; instead, each store would carry products for all the segments but focus on one or two groups. It also meant taking a greater role in helping consumers understand and make choices about the increasingly numerous and complicated products that are constantly being rushed to market nowadays.

The strategy, dubbed "customer-centricity," entails seeing the customer experience from the consumer's perspective and investing in new store formats that are tailored to the buying intentions of the demographic segments—affluent professionals, active younger males, family men, and busy suburban moms, to name a few. Store format is no trivial matter. Even the details can have a big impact on sales. Small appliances that appeal to suburban moms, for instance, began selling much better at a California store after they were moved from high shelves, where they were among major appliances, to a low rack in a prominent location.

Best Buy's supply chain is an inseparable part of the new strategy. To support the company's transformation, the supply chain is changing in several important ways. Included are better information flow—particularly to managers who may take corrective action when necessary, seeing that floor layout is responsive to consumers' needs in individual stores, and trying to reduce the number of nonsales activities in which store personnel are involved. Also, supply chain efficiencies are sought through higher delivery frequency and smaller shipments, streamlined network or distribution centers and stores, and improved forecasting.

opportunistically interact with customers—raise your profile and visibility; (2) demonstrate strong listening skills, particularly with customers—and then use what you have heard to identify customer values and problems and to design appropriate responses; (3) rely on influence—make sure that your voice is heard and that people feel compelled to implement your suggestions; and (4) develop your personal leadership brand, one that reflects a strong growth bias.

Supply Chain Strategies

The next several sections provide details concerning five high-priority areas in which it is important to develop effective logistics and supply chain strategies. Included are differentiation, financial, technology, relationship, and global strategies. Although this list is not intended to be exhaustive, success in each of these areas will contribute to the objective of seeing supply chain capabilities contribute to corporate growth.

Differentiation Strategies

Simply stated, this strategy refers to the extent to which the supply chain approach of a particular company may be different and unique and thus differentiate it from those of competing organizations. The basic concept underlying **differentiation** is to see that supply chain capabilities are viewed by customers as being sufficiently effective and unique to distinguish an organization in the marketplace. At the same time, those customers may hopefully be willing to pay a premium price for the product or service offerings that are involved. While supply chain capabilities may have been regarded traditionally as part of the "augmented" or "value-added" product or service, successful organizations today may count supply chain excellence as part of their core capabilities.

To a large extent, differentiation materializes in some combination of price and service. You can probably think of examples from personal experience in which you have paid for a higher-priced product because of its perceived extra value to you. From a strategic perspective, differentiation requires good supply chain planning and execution to deliver on high-quality customer service. This may mean making deliveries on an appointment basis with very tight time windows for deliveries; being available and responsive 24 hours a day, seven days a week to receive orders; planning for inventory replenishment in a manner that will virtually ensure in-stock availability of items in a retail store; or perhaps making sure easy-to-use alternatives are available when post-purchase returns or repairs are needed.

Although supply chains may strive for differentiation in many ways, this section will elaborate briefly on elements of time-based strategies, ones that typically have short- and long-term positive effects on levels of customer service that are delivered by supply chains.

Time-Based Strategies

Most people have heard the old adage "Time is money." The value of time can be measured in a number of different ways. For example, adapting an inventory model to include alternative means of transportation can demonstrate that transportation choices that result in faster, more consistent transit times can help to reduce inventory and warehousing costs. Even though a faster mode of transportation may be more expensive, the net impact of savings in inventory and warehousing costs would be a reduction in total costs. This is an example of an effective strategy that is based on the tradeoffs between transportation, inventory, and warehousing costs. Coupled with improved speed and lessened variability of transit times, these impacts will help to reduce the length of the "cash-to-cash" cycle that is experienced.[7] This metric is becoming one of the more sought-after measures of overall supply chain performance.

Supply chain strategies that shorten the length of the order and/or replenishment cycle have been the focus of much attention in recent years. Time-compression strategies have also received attention in the previous chapters in this text when inventory, transportation, warehousing, and so on, were discussed. Some more general aspects of time reduction are discussed in the following section.

Supply Chain Technology

Technology a Key Requirement for Supply Chain Success

The availability and use of capable information technologies are now recognized as essential competencies for supply chain success. Additionally, various types of supply chain functionality (e.g., TMS, WMS, global trade management, sourcing, supply chain visibility, network modeling and optimization), have now made their way into the software suites offered by major vendors of broad-based, ERP (Enterprise Resource Planning) technology systems. Although the life cycle of the supply chain software sector began with the emergence of individual companies that focused on specific types of software, many of these companies are now part of broader-based firms with larger software footprints. At the same time that we have seen a growing number of large providers that represent a wide range of supply chain functionality, there remain a large number of technology providers that focus on specialized subsets of supply chain functionality.

The effective implementation of supply chain software can be very challenging, and so there are many issues that must be anticipated and planned-for. Some of these are highlighted below

Define the benefits of collaboration—Given that any strategic initiative must relate to the goals and objectives of the overall business and of the supply chain, it is essential that any IT initiative be well-aligned with business and supply chain needs.

Make the investment—Successful IT implementations require critical levels of IT knowledge and capability within the user business organization. This will be important not only from the perspective of being a capable buyer and user of technology-based services, but also from the point of view of successful implementation within the supply chain organization.

Earn trust and create mutual ownership—Considering the boundary-spanning dimension of supply chain management, effective internal and external collaboration is essential for the successful implementation of supply chain technologies.

Dedicate "A" players—Useful supply chain data not only needs to be available and accessible, but shared and used between supply chain partners and between process areas within the user organization.

Dedicate "A" players—The supply chain IT space continues to exhibit impressive growth in terms of breadth and depth of concepts and technologies. So, the growth of newer approaches such as software-as-a-service (SaaS) and cloud computing will have significant impacts on state-of-the-art in the design and use of supply chain information systems.

Corporate and supply chain leadership must ensure the success of IT-based supply chain initiatives. Coupled with making sure there is alignment among all of the people involved with supply chain IT initiatives, achieving "buy-in" and commitment from all concerned will be a key to success.

Source: C. John Langley Jr., Ph.D. Used with permission.

Reducing Cycle Time

Reductions in cycle time are based on three factors: processes, information, and decision making. If SCM is viewed as a series of processes, then those processes being performed faster will reduce cycle time, with the associated benefits already mentioned.

Another important source of reductions in cycle time is faster provision of information. The utilization of faster, more efficient forms of order transmission—use of the Internet, for example—can significantly reduce the time needed to complete the transaction. Also, the use of contemporary information technologies is becoming increasingly attractive as technology costs have been declining significantly. Timely, accurate information about sales, orders, inventory levels, transportation service, and so on, leads to shorter cycle times and also reduces uncertainty about what is happening, which leads to lower inventory levels by reducing the need for safety stock. Thus, information has become a source of significant savings to many companies.

The final factor in reducing cycle time is decision making. In some organizations, this is the most important of the three factors. The critical issue is to empower individuals to make decisions relevant to their areas of expertise and responsibility. All too frequently, multiple levels of approval must be received before a decision can be made. The important point is that preexisting levels of needed approval slow down the decision-making process, which can, in turn, lengthen the order cycle. Flat, lean organizations that are becoming more common in today's business environment are frequently characterized by delegated decision making, which emphasizes decision making at the so-called "action" level, such as that of the customer service representative. While decision making at the lowest possible level in the company can lead to the making of some mistakes, the experience of companies like Procter & Gamble and others suggests that the risk is justified in terms of the time that is saved and the improvement that often takes place with respect to customer responsiveness.

Time-Reduction Logistics Initiatives

Contemporary concern for visibility of product throughout the supply chain has also renewed our emphasis on the utilization of information technologies for product tracking and tracing, optical scanning, barcoding, stock location, and so forth. In short, the imperative is for firms to develop the ability to know where all products may happen to be at any point in time. This information is needed not for its own sake but, more importantly, so that companies know when shipments may be late, need expediting, and so on.

Finally, interest has grown recently in the area of leveraging the power of effective demand planning and forecasting to more meaningfully move from "push" to "pull." Improved ability to diagnose and even anticipate customers' needs enables the logistics and supply chain processes to make a much more valuable contribution to the achievement of corporate goals and objectives. Recent interest in collaborative planning, forecasting, and replenishment (CPFR)[8] also serves as an example of a highly useful, contemporary technology.

Increasingly, companies continue to change from the traditional push approach to a pull approach, which is a demand-responsive system. The switch requires a major change in corporate culture that is frequently difficult to achieve. Not only does the change require a switch to a flexible, quick-change manufacturing environment, necessitating retraining of the manufacturing employees, but it also requires that manufacturing operate at a less-than-optimal cost from time to time. An additional aspect of pull systems is that some companies use the concept of postponement to achieve a system that is close to a pure pull system. As was indicated earlier, postponement involves not completely finishing products until an order is received. The auto industry, for example, uses a form of postponement by building basic component packages, such as wiring harnesses, in advance of orders and then assembling the auto to final specifications. Considering the fast pace of technological change, the practice of postponement is essential to the success of many businesses in the computer and high-tech industries.

Overall, leading-edge companies have used a number of initiatives to improve their competitive position by reducing cycle time, thus producing significant benefits in terms of efficiency and effectiveness. Time-reduction strategies, because of their potential to reduce costs, improve cash flow, and enhance customer service, have been the focus of much attention and have enabled companies to gain a competitive advantage.

Financial Strategies

Clearly, the most compelling **financial strategy** is the pursuit of operational efficiency. By placing a priority on cost control, performance effectiveness and efficiency, and viable measurement strategies, companies are able to improve financial performance. Coupled with the identification and leveraging of corporate core competencies, focusing attention on metrics such as return on assets (ROA) and return on investment (ROI) facilitates the achievement of financial objectives.

Inventory Productivity

One class of assets that already receives significant attention is inventory, and major strategies are in place at many firms to reduce inventory levels without diminishing levels of customer service (or preferably, increasing levels of customer service). Initiatives such as just-in-time (JIT), vendor-managed inventory (VMI), and continuous replenishment (CRP) are examples of popular approaches. When appropriately designed and implemented, initiatives such as these lead not only to inventory reductions for the company at hand but also to overall supply chain performance.

Facility Utilization

One of the major trends in supply chain facility management is to more effectively utilize the capacity of various types of supply chain facilities. Whether they be supplier locations, plants, warehouses, distribution centers, or customer locations, the objective is the same—to see that these facilities are utilized to an extent that will produce close to optimal efficiencies. In addition, high priority is placed on making sure that all supply chain facilities create value not only for the individual organizations, but also for the supply chain in a broad sense. For example, if manufacturer to customer deliveries would be more efficient and effective than moving all products through an intermediary distribution center, then that should be the selected alternative. This strategy not only contributes to improved facility utilization, it does so by reducing or eliminating the need for certain types of facilities.

Equipment Utilization Strategies

Another area of asset investment for companies is logistics-related equipment such as materials-handling equipment used in warehouses and transportation equipment that is leased or owned by a company. Some reduction in the amount of this equipment has occurred because of the decrease in the number of distribution centers, discussed briefly in the previous section. Companies have rationalized their facilities and improved their throughput, utilizing the initiatives discussed previously. In other words, as companies have reduced the number of warehouse facilities that they operate, there has been a natural reduction in the materials-handling equipment that is necessary. Also, the use of technology-based devices such as handheld computers, barcode scanning devices, radio-frequency communications in logistics facilities, and RFID has caused a general reduction in the need for additional assets to move and store product.

In addition, transportation equipment is an important area in terms of asset invest-ment. This has been another area of improvement for many companies. Since deregula-tion, many companies have reevaluated their position with respect to equipment ownership. Contract rates with railroads and motor carriers, more specialized service and equipment, lower rates, and so on, have led companies to turn increasingly to the commercial sector for needed transportation services.

Outsourcing

As discussed in significant detail in Chapter 4, the use of outsourced logistics services has grown in popularity. Once a strategy that focused primarily on the commercial procurement of tangible, asset-based services such as transportation and warehousing, outsourcing now has grown into areas that are both strategic and customer focused. Thus, recent studies have cited growth in services available from the outsourced logistics sector such as freight bill auditing and payment, customer service, information technol-ogy, and light manufacturing and assembly. As a result, this increasingly popular alterna-tive has led many firms such as Walmart, General Motors, DuPont, Nabisco, Procter & Gamble, General Electric, and others to use the services of capable third-party logistics providers (3PLs).

The decision to utilize third-party or contract logistics companies has been fostered in part by the interest in reducing asset investment to improve asset productivity. An interesting aspect of 3PL use is that, while a customer may use a 3PL to help reduce commitment to its assets, the 3PL may focus its activity on managing the availability of logistics services and hopefully procure the best available asset-based services from selected contractors. Another rationale is the trend mentioned earlier of focusing on core competencies as a strategy to operate more effectively and efficiently. Essentially, a company might feel that its expertise or core competency may, for example, be produc-ing and marketing cookies and crackers. While it may be very capable of providing necessary inbound and outbound logistics services to support its products, the company may be even more effective if it focuses on its two core competencies. While this rationale is commonly used to support the decision to use a 3PL, the move can be even more attractive if it can be demonstrated that, additionally, there will be cost savings and or improved asset productivity.

The relevance of using a 3PL becomes even clearer as increasing numbers of businesses get involved significantly in global commerce. The ability of outsourced logistics services providers to facilitate the complexity of international trade is of great advantage to customers. Thus, most businesses involved in global commerce turn at least in some measure to the capabilities of 3PLs.

As a concluding comment regarding the use of 3PL providers, there has been a continuing trend toward the involvement of 4PL™ providers.[9] Aside from managing a number of 3PL operations, a 4PL is looked to for the provision of competencies relating to knowledge availability, information technology, and skills in forming and sustaining successful supply chain relationships. Although the use of 4PLs has met with uneven success so far, it appears that the concept has significant validity and that further refinements will make it more viable in the future. Most likely, a future direction in the area of a "control tower" approach will be a productive direction for the continued growth of 4PL services.

Technology-Based Strategies

It has been evident for some time that the realization of future logistics and supply chain goals will depend significantly on the further development and utilization of information technologies. Whether they are in the form of hardware, software, or connectivity, these technologies will be the springboard for progress and innovation. Looking back at the content of this text, there are numerous areas in which evolving information technologies have been highlighted and discussed. Chapter 6 was devoted fully to a treatment of contemporary information technologies that impact logistics and supply chain management. Rather than try to repeat or summarize those key points, this section is directed toward some of the more significant future trends in technology and their likely impacts.

Innovative Growth Areas in Supply Chain Technology[10]

Observers of the supply chain technology space will confirm that there has been no shortage of innovations that have occurred in this area in recent years. Aside from the fact that an economic recession occurred in the 2008–2010 time frame, growth in this market has been in the vicinity of 5 percent annually. So to provide some perspective on future areas of growth for the supply chain software market, this section focuses on several areas wherein innovative developments were cited by Steve Banker, director of supply chain management for ARC Advisory Group.

Demand Signal Depositories

Basically, this is a shelf-level collaboration solution between consumer goods manufacturers and retailers, wherein the manufacturers pull in the point-of-sale (POS) data and other data that minimizes the bullwhip effect. Essentially, this provides the manufacturers with supplies of downstream data, direct from the retailers that are much more useful than the predominantly used data relating to withdrawals from retailer warehouses and distribution centers. The availability of demand signal data helps to improve forecasting, allows for better transportation planning and better warehouse capacity decisions. While there are challenges to be worked out with this approach, such as the cleaning and preparation of large amounts of retail sales data, there is great potential to generate significant cost savings and service improvements in the supply chain.

Warehouse Technology

Of great note here are the robotic forms of material handling that are far more flexible than have been available in the past. In essence, their capabilities to move around, operate a mechanical limb, sense and manipulate their environment, and exhibit intelligent behavior are transforming the ways that warehouses and distribution centers operate. In addition to operational improvements, the flexibility of robotic alternatives provides a materials-handling solution that involves much less risk than traditional methods.

Software as a Service (SaaS), GPS, and Cloud Computing

These technologies, collectively, should assist significantly in achieving enhanced supply chain flexibility and facilitating network-type solutions. In addition to the extension of SaaS from its current primary application in transportation to other supply chain activities, the utilization of GPS can help by providing better tracking of shipments and transportation equipment over broad geographic regions. As only time will tell, cloud computing should provide supply chain managers access to more powerful and functional types of software with less inconvenience of dealing with unnecessary firewalls, etc.

RFID (Radio Frequency Identification)

As a technology that was introduced in recent years, the use of RFID has fallen far short of initial expectations. With early encouragement by organizations such as Walmart and the U.S. Department of Defense, top suppliers had been required to develop RFID capabilities. While the initial ambitions were that the use of RFID would have significant impacts on the functioning of overall supply chains, the principal uses were seen to be far more narrow—for example, achieving visibility for in-store merchandise, etc. Perhaps the greatest accomplishment for now from the introduction of RFID is that the value of supply chain visibility was reinforced. So future advances, whether RFID-based or not, will focus on the continued improvement of supply chain visibility.

ERP (Enterprise Resource Planning) Systems

Currently, we are seeing a significant development of supply chain functionality by ERP vendors, and the integration of these capabilities with the power of the ERP systems. Among the key benefits from the involvement of ERP will be the enhancements of business intelligence—in particular, scorecarding and dashboards. In addition, the integration of ERP systems with S&OP and budgeting processes will provide great benefit to the management of supply chains.

Relationship-Based Strategies

An area of significant strategic interest is that of relationships and relationship formation in logistics and supply chain processes. Although the preceding chapters have provided a number of perspectives on this topic, experience to date suggests that major challenges lie ahead with respect to our ability to develop and sustain effective relationships. As indicated earlier, one of the major attributes of using the services of a 3PL or 4PL is that these types of firms specialize in a number of areas, including relationship management. Thus, this area represents a critical challenge for future logistics and supply chain managers. Therefore, the remainder of this section focuses on collaboration—a concept that has great potential value, but which has proven to be very elusive in terms of successful implementation.

Collaboration

As discussed earlier in Chapter 4, collaboration occurs when companies work together for mutual benefit. Since it is difficult to imagine very many logistics or supply chain improvements that involve only one firm, the need for effective relationships is obvious. Collaboration goes well beyond vague expressions of partnership and aligned interests. It means that companies leverage each other on an operational basis so that together they perform better than they did separately. It creates a synergistic business environment in which the sum of the parts is greater than the whole.

Figure 16.5	Elements of Successful Collaboration
1.	Well-understood goals and objectives
2.	Trust and commitment
3.	Corporate compatibility
4.	Communication
5.	Shared decision making and ability to reach consensus on matters of importance
6.	Equitable sharing of gains, losses, and investments
7.	Overall benefits to involved parties greater than could be obtained alone
8.	Effective measurements and measurement strategies
9.	Strategic plan for collaborative relationship

Source: C. John Langley Jr., Ph.D. Used with permission.

Figure 16.5 summarizes a number of elements of successful supply chain collaborations. While no such list could possibly be exhaustive, the listed elements are central to successful collaboration.[11]

Well-Understood Goals and Objectives

Members of the collaboration need to understand their individual organizational objectives and then be willing to share these openly with each other. From this point forward, the involved parties will find it easier to meaningfully discuss the objectives of the relationship and how they can create value for each other and for the extended customers and suppliers who are involved in the supply chain.

Trust and Commitment

Widely recognized as a fundamental relationship building block, trust may be thought of as "reliance on and trust in one's partner."[12] Both trust and commitment have great relevance because they encourage companies to (1) work at preserving relationship investments by cooperating with exchange partners; (2) resist the temptation of alternatives that may have a short-term attractiveness, in favor of agreed-upon priorities that may have longer-term benefit; and (3) view potentially high-risk action as being prudent because of the belief that partners may not always act opportunistically.[13]

Corporate Compatibility

Of greatest importance here is that the relationship include a sharing of vision, goals, objectives, and cultures. Facilitating mechanisms include meaningful alignment of individuals and processes, identification of executive and operational champions, and executive visits to supply chain locations on a regular basis.

Communication

Regular communication and sharing/use of information are central to an effective collaborative relationship. For example, the sharing and use of forecasting information can be of great value to other supply chain participants. Additionally, regular meetings with representatives of involved organizations are of great help.

Shared Decision Making and Ability to Reach Consensus on Matters of Importance

Matters that are related to the success of the relationship should be treated jointly by all involved organizations. Also, participants should try to avoid micro-management of one another's activities and give one another the latitude to successfully perform the responsibilities upon which they have agreed.

Equitable Sharing of Gains, Losses, and Investments

Although many organizations demonstrate a dedication to their individual objectives, successful collaborations require the development of mechanisms to share gains, losses, and investments. Continuity of the willingness to share will be dependent on all parties developing knowledge of the benefits that result from the sharing (both financial and nonfinancial) and a belief that the sharing has been equitable to all parties involved.

Overall Benefits to Involved Parties Greater Than Could Be Obtained Alone

To be sustainable over the longer term, successful collaborations need to create benefits for the involved parties that exceed what those organizations could accomplish individually.

Effective Measurements and Measurement Strategies

Understandably, a dedication by all involved participants in a collaboration to measurements and the development of measurement strategies will be a key to the success of the relationship. Essentially, key performance indicators (KPIs) that require ownership and commitment to the objectives by all involved parties are needed.

Strategic Plan for Collaborative Relationship

Successful collaborations are not without their challenges and difficulties. Thus, the development of a strategic plan for the relationship itself should be of great value. As part of the process of developing the strategic plan, a checklist for successful collaboration should be developed, and everyone involved must realize that a successful collaboration should last longer than the people who are involved in its formation.

Impact of Collaboration on Business Processes

In the context of users of 3PL services and how they are viewed by customers, Table 16.1 identifies business processes and the extent to which customers feel they would benefit from improved collaboration with 3PLs.[14] Table 16.1 demonstrates that the greatest potential benefits of collaboration seem to be associated with business processes such as inventory management, customer order management, customer service, and supplier order management. Generally, the greatest benefits are related areas that affect suppliers and customers, lead to inventory efficiencies, and relate to S&OP.

Financial vs. Nonfinancial Benefits of Collaboration

Regarding this topic, an interesting question is whether the costs of collaboration are exceeded by the benefits—in essence, whether collaboration pays for itself. Although there certainly are pitfalls to avoid, there are significant opportunities to form collaborative efforts that are financially successful. Among the observations included in the above-referenced study are that organizations involved in a collaboration should each achieve a

Table 16.1	Business Processes That Would Benefit from Improved Collaboration with 3PLs	
BUSINESS PROCESS		**ALL REGIONS**
Inventory management		51%
Customer order management		49
Customer service		43
Supplier order management		41
International trade logistics		38
Sales and operations planning		36
Supply planning		33
Repair/returns management		29
Compliance (e.g., Sarbanes-Oxley, customs)		29
Demand planning		26
Accounts payable/receivable processes		18
Manufacturing scheduling		17
Product launch		16
Warranty management		12

Note: Figures refer to percentages of study respondents indicating business processes would benefit from improved collaboration with 3PLs.

Source: C. John Langley Jr. and Capgemini, LLC, *12th Annual Third-Party Logistics Study* (2007). Reproduced by permission.

balanced cost-reduction strategy and that KPIs for involved parties should be aligned with drivers of total economic value for the collaboration and the supply chain.[15]

As a concluding thought on the importance of collaboration, we must think about the overall challenge of managing supply chains. To be successful, all supply chain organizations must work with each other in a manner that provides the greatest value for themselves, as well as the end-use customer or consumer. Similarly, it is important for organizations throughout the supply chain to form relationships that will produce success for not only each organization and its trading partners but also for the supply chain as a whole.

Global Strategies

In June 2010, McKinsey & Company published a document that focused on the global forces that they feel are shaping the business landscape.[16] Their advice is that any business managers who ignore these forces do so at their peril. The concluding section of this text thus highlights these global forces that will define the coming era and provides a commentary indicating the direct impact and significance of each to the domain of supply chain management. The global forces and their definitions are credited to McKinsey & Company, while the commentaries for supply chain management (SCM) have been added by the authors.

- **The Great Rebalancing**—The coming decade will be the first in 200 years when emerging-market countries contribute more growth than the developed ones. This growth will not only create a wave of new middle-class consumers but also drive profound innovations in product design, market infrastructure, and value chains.
  - ◦ *SCM Commentary:* This force places great pressure on supply chains to adapt their capabilities to respond to consumer and business needs in emerging countries and regions. This will require a rethinking and recalibration of generally accepted supply chain practices to the unique needs and requirements of these new markets and sources of supply.

- **The Productivity Imperative**—Developed-world economies will need to generate pronounced gains in productivity to power continued economic growth. The most dramatic innovations in the Western world are likely to be those that accelerate economic productivity.
  - ◦ *SCM Commentary:* Supply chain capabilities in developed countries and regions have been improving significantly in recent years. The pursuit of continued productivity improvements will require that market-leading supply chains step up the pace of innovation and the extent to which they differentiate themselves from competing supply chains.

- **The Global Grid**—The global economy is growing ever more connected. Complex flows of capital, goods, information, and people are creating an interlinked network that spans geographies, social groups, and economies in ways that permit large-scale interactions at any moment. This expanding grid is seeding new business models and accelerating the pace of innovation. It also makes destabilizing cycles of volatility more likely.
  - ◦ *SCM Commentary:* In essence, this force sets the agenda for the future of global supply chains, and makes it essential that global supply chains must be functionally well-connected. Desirable results will include global shipment management and visibility, and the ability to create a single point of control for the functioning of global supply chains.

- **Pricing the Planet**—A collision is shaping up among the rising demand for resources, constrained supplies, and changing social attitudes toward environmental protection. The next decade will see an increased focus on resource productivity, the emergence of substantial clean-tech industries, and regulatory initiatives.
  - ◦ *SCM Commentary:* Supply chains of the future must be able to compete in a more complex business environment. Given that many of the basic assumptions about the way business is conducted are in the process of change, the ability of individual supply chains to be agile and responsive to these changes will be a key component of success.

- **The Market State**—The often contradictory demands of driving economic growth and providing the necessary safety nets to maintain social stability have put governments under extraordinary pressure. Globalization applies additional heat: How will distinctly national entities govern in an increasingly globalized world?
  - ◦ *SCM Commentary:* Considering the extent to which many levels of government are becoming more involved in regulating and controlling business practices, a clear key to success will be the ability of individual supply chains

to function effectively in this new business environment. Given that many governmental decisions are made with the idea of moving toward social equity, the challenges to businesses and supply chains will become correspondingly more difficult. The long-term stability of our businesses and supply chains will continue to be directly related to their ability to create value for their consumers, customers, and stakeholders.

Supply Chain Transformation

Much of this textbook has focused on the priorities and processes that can lead to improved supply chain management. A very critical step, however, is to determine how an organization can transform itself to one that meets and exceeds these future objectives. Perhaps the experience of Motorola will lend some insight into how this may be accomplished.

Motorola[17]

Motorola, a *Fortune* 100 telecommunications company best known for its cellular phones, is transforming a collection of separate, independent operations into an integrated and cost-effective global supply chain. One of its objectives was to link supply chains strung across the globe to achieve efficiencies in logistics, manufacturing, procurement, and quality. Motorola's vision of a supply chain that would support growth and create value focused on three Cs: cost, cash, and customer service. Cost improvements help Motorola price its products to win business. Freeing up cash through efficiency improvements provides capital for business growth and acquisitions. And finally, customer service enables the company to retain existing customers and gain new ones.

Over time, Motorola had developed numerous product categories and a far-flung, multifaceted supply chain structure. For example, operations in the following major divisions essentially were dispersed across the world: Mobile Devices unit, Connected Home Solutions business, and Networks & Enterprise division. As recently as 2004, the company was sourcing from 47 countries, and the six business units it had at the time rarely shared facilities or resources.

The impetus for supply chain transformation came in 2004 when the heads of Motorola's various business unit supply chains approached the company's CEO and recommended that the multinational company streamline its supply chain. Consequently, the six business units were consolidated into four, and priority was placed on the objective that product design, procurement, manufacturing, logistics, and customer service all work in sync.

The integration was kicked off by identifying six priorities that the company would pursue simultaneously. These are listed in Figure 16.6. A few comments regarding each element are provided.

- **Element 1: Identify "best in class" processes that can be rapidly replicated throughout the organization.** Central to this priority is to establish idea-sharing across divisions and to create a culture where teams across Motorola steal shamelessly from one another.
- **Element 2: Rationalize the supplier base and strengthen relationships with the remaining key suppliers.** Motorola developed a Rapid Sourcing Initiative, under which all business units would treat vendors in a consistent way. A high priority

Figure 16.6	Key Elements in Motorola's Integrated Supply Chain Strategy

1. Identify "best in class" processes that can be rapidly replicated throughout the organization.

2. Rationalize the supplier base and strengthen relationships with the remaining key suppliers.

3. Set quality expectations for suppliers and institute a performance scorecard system to measure compliance with standards.

4. Optimize manufacturing and logistics operations.

5. Focus information technology spending on projects benefiting all business units.

6. Create a culture of action in order to drive organizational efficiency.

Source: James A. Cooke, "Metamorphosis of a Supply Chain," *CSCMP's Supply Chain Quarterly* (Quarter 2, 2007): 36. Reproduced by permission of *CSCMP's Supply Chain Quarterly*, Supply Chain Media, LLC, Copyright 2007; http://www.supplychainquarterly.com.

was placed on finding ways for vendors to reduce cost and then pass the savings along to Motorola in the form of lower prices.

- **Element 3: Set quality expectations for suppliers and institute a performance scorecard system to measure compliance with standards.** To put an end to quality problems that were sometimes referred to at Motorola as "spills," suppliers that wished to continue doing business with Motorola were required to develop quality renewal plans to ensure craftsmanship. Also, the company instituted a performance scorecard system to measure compliance with its procurement standards.

- **Element 4: Optimize manufacturing and logistics operations.** This element involved strategic consolidation of plants and warehouses across the operating divisions. The kind of problem this would help solve was in evidence in Tianjin, China, where five different Motorola business units were using the same facility, yet all five were running different information technology systems and three had separate loading docks.

- **Element 5: Focus information technology spending on projects benefiting all business units.** As a purposeful move away from IT projects that were designed to benefit individual business units, there was a shift toward projects that help various parts of the company run in sync.

- **Element 6: Create a culture of action in order to drive organizational efficiency.** Key to success here was a shift in orientation from talking to doing. Results suggest this change has been met with success.

Overall, Motorola's supply chain transformation has met with success. Customer service levels have improved markedly, and delivery times for shipments to customers have become shorter and more consistent. In terms of cost, Motorola's Integrated Supply Chain initiative produced a 40 percent improvement in material expenses, product quality, and manufacturing efficiency from 2004 to 2006. Also, inventory turns have increased markedly over this same time frame.

The future for Motorola entails a continued focus on key metrics, such as inventory turns, productivity per employee, and further reductions in manufacturing and logistics costs as a percentage of sales. Coupled with great transparency to those metrics and full accountability, Motorola is well positioned for future success. Perhaps the greatest facilitator of the company's success, however, is that the value of having a great supply chain is recognized at the highest levels.

SUMMARY

- Several principles of supply chain management are able to retain their relevance over time.

- It is essential to expect that effective supply chain management will be able to help grow revenues as well as contain costs. Among the skills needed for success in this endeavor are supply chain leadership skills.

- Several types of strategy are imperative to the success of supply chain management including differentiation, financial, technology-based, relationship-based, and global strategies.

- The strategy of differentiation is needed to establish a particular company and its supply chain as being different and unique.

- Financial strategies not only help improve the efficiency of supply chain operations, they also help managers understand and document the financial value created by supply chain management. Included as an example of financial strategy, but which is also an operational strategy, is outsourcing of logistics and supply chain activities.

- The emergence of new and innovative technology-based strategies will result in dramatic changes to the ways we manage logistics and supply chain activities.

- Supply chain success will be facilitated by the development of effective, collaborative relationships between supply chain participants.

- The ability of organizations to develop and implement effective global supply chain strategies will be of great importance. Also, a growing number of organizations have achieved excellence in this area.

- Perhaps the most important area is that of supply chain transformation—how an organization can transform itself into one that meets and exceeds future goals and objectives.

STUDY QUESTIONS

1. To what extent have the seven principles of supply chain management remained current? What are some of the major changes that have occurred since they were first developed?

2. Why do corporate CEOs tend to stress growth over cost reduction, yet think of supply chain management more as an area for cost reduction?

3. Explain the objective and benefits of differentiation-based logistics and supply chain strategies. What are some examples of strategies that are included in this category?

4. What are the objectives of financial-based strategies? In what ways does outsourcing some or all logistics and supply chain activities help to accomplish these objectives?

5. What are some areas in which future development of supply chain information technologies is most likely?

6. To what extent is collaboration a necessary condition for supply chain success? What do you consider to be some of the more important elements of supply chain collaboration?

7. Describe some examples of success in the area of global supply chain management.

8. What are some of the priorities that organizations should consider as they strive for success with the challenge of supply chain transformation?

NOTES

1. Comments in this section about each of the seven principles of supply chain management are based on the content of David L. Anderson, Frank F. Britt, and Donavon J. Favre, "The Seven Principles of Supply Chain Management," *Supply Chain Management Review* (April 2007): 41–46.

2. Ibid., 41.

3. Dr. David L. Anderson, managing director, Supply Chain Ventures, LLC, http://www.supplychainventures.com.

4. Much of the content of this section has been adapted with permission from Richard H. Thompson, Donald E. Eisenstein, and Timothy M. Stratman, "Getting SCM on the CEO's Agenda," *Supply Chain Management Review* (July 1, 2007): 26–33.

5. Ibid., 27.

6. Ibid., 30.

7. Cash-to-cash cycle may be defined as the time it takes to convert a dollar's worth of raw materials into a dollar's worth of sales in the marketplace.

8. For further information on CPFR, see http://www.cpfr.org or http://www.vies.org.

9. The term 4PL™ is a registered trademark of Accenture, Inc.

10. The content of this section has been adapted from SCMR Staff, "Technology Outlook: 2010 and Beyond, An Interview with Steve Banker," *Supply Chain Management Review*, January 1, 2010.

11. The organization of this section benefited from a discussion of key relationship marketing elements as presented by A. Michael Knemeyer, Thomas M. Corsi, and Paul R. Murphy, "Logistics Outsourcing Relationships: Customer Perspectives," *Journal of Business Logistics*, Vol. 24, No. 1 (2003): 77–109.

12. Ibid, 80.

13. Ibid.

14. These results are taken from C. John Langley Jr. and Capgemini, LLC, *12th Annual Third-Party Logistics Study* (2007). The study involved an analysis of customers of 3PLs across several key regions of the world.

15. Ibid.

16. Portions of this section were adapted from Peter Bisson, Elizabeth Stephenson, and S. Patrick Viguerine, "Global Forces: An Introduction," *McKinsey Quarterly*, June 2010.

17. Much of the content of this section is adapted from James A. Cooke, "Metamorphosis of a Supply Chain," *CSCMP's Supply Chain Quarterly* (Quarter 2, 2007): 34–38. Reproduced by permission of *CSCMP's Supply Chain Quarterly*, Supply Chain Media, LLC, Copyright 2007, http://www.supplychainquarterly.com.

CASE 16.1

Tommy Hilfiger and Li & Fung

Tommy Hilfiger, the well-known designer and marketer of casual fashions, recently sold its global sourcing group to Li & Fung, a buying agency for consumer goods with its headquarters in Hong Kong. At the time of the sale, Tommy Hilfiger sourced principally from Hong Kong, Taiwan, India, Bangladesh, Sri Lanka, Tunisia, the United States, and Honduras.

The transfer of Tommy Hilfiger's sourcing operations to Li & Fung was intended to capture significant synergies with the existing network of Li & Fung, which was well entrenched in China, specifically with 19 offices on the mainland alone. Additionally, the purchase by Li & Fung will strengthen its portfolio of sourcing business and ultimately provide leverage to work with other brands.[1]

This transaction should be viewed as a very significant decision by Tommy Hilfiger to opt for an outsourced solution to its strategic sourcing needs. In the words of the CEO of the Tommy Hilfiger Group, "Our own operated buying offices have contributed tremendously to the development of our business to date, but we believe that to take things forward we can benefit tremendously from the integration of these offices within the greater network of Li & Fung, with over 70 offices in over 40 countries and territories, including as many as 19 offices in China alone."[2]

CASE QUESTIONS

1. What reasons do you think led Tommy Hilfiger to consider this unique approach to transfer its sourcing operations to Li & Fung?

2. If you were a supply chain executive at Tommy Hilfiger, what steps or approaches would you consider taking to make sure you did not lose control over the inbound logistics portion of your overall supply chain?

3. If you were an executive at Li & Fung, what future strategic business decisions and directions do you think would be appropriate to consider—both for Tommy Hilfiger and for other clients?

NOTES

1. China Supply Chai Council (2007).

2. *Supply Chain Digest* (February 21, 2007).

Source: C. John Langley Jr., Ph.D. Used with permission.

CASE 16.2

Peerless Products, Inc.

Imagine that Peerless Products, Inc., a well-known manufacturer of consumer electronics, decides to expand its manufacturing in China. The CEO assigns the task to the vice president of manufacturing, and within two years, the company has a plant up and running in Guangdong. Unfortunately, however, Peerless has no overall end-to-end supply chain capability to account for the fact that its lead times have increased by four weeks. This, in turn, has an impact on how the company sells its products, takes orders, plans distribution, sizes warehousing, and manages inbound and outbound logistics throughout the global markets being served by the Chinese plant.

In short, although the company has lowered its product costs, it has increased its supply chain risk and possibly raised its total cost of ownership—taking into account the impact on lost sales. According to Accenture, Inc., risk in the context of global operations may be placed into three buckets: uncontrollable (such as geopolitical instability or natural disasters), somewhat controllable (volatility of fuel prices, for example), and controllable (for instance, forecasting accuracy or the performance of supply chain partners). Based on a study of 300 companies, however, Accenture found that the more controllable factors constitute the greatest sources of disruption. Up to 35 percent of respondents reported being impacted by natural disasters and 20 percent by geopolitical turmoil. But 38 percent indicated they felt the effects of their supply chain partners' poor performance, and 33 percent had been hurt by logistics complexity, for instance. The consequences of failing to manage those risks are costly indeed, as negative impacts may be experienced in metrics such as sales, return on sales, operating income, return on assets, and inventories.

Although few companies have mastered the management of risk in global operations, many are trying. For example, more than 60 percent of the executives who participated in the global operations study conducted by Accenture indicated that their organizations were manufacturing locally and globally and that they are using contingent suppliers and/or logistics providers. Half said they are intentionally establishing a geographically distributed supply base, and more than half cited increases in inventories and safety stock. Furthermore, 49 percent claimed to have a formal supply chain risk management program in place already.

CASE QUESTIONS

1. Assume you are the CEO of Peerless Products and that you are aware of your company's lack of overall end-to-end supply chain capability. What are some of the high-level, adverse impacts on your business that may occur?

2. What steps would you recommend be taken to help avoid the types of adverse impacts identified above?

3. As CEO, what would be your expectations of the company's vice president of supply chain with respect to the potential problems at hand? How would you compare and contrast expectations of the vice president of supply chain with those of the vice president of manufacturing?

Source: Adapted from Jaume Ferrer, Johan Karlbert, and Jamie Hintlian, "Integration: The Key to Global Success," *Supply Chain Management Review* (March 2007): 26–27. Copyright © 2007 Reed Business Information, a division of Reed Elsevier. Reproduced by permission.

Subject Index

Note: Italicized page numbers indicate illustrations or boxes text.

Name Index

Note: Italicized page numbers indicate illustrations or boxes text.

A

ABC Power Tools, 324–327, 332–335, 338
Aberdeen Group, 189, 199, *209*, 212, *256–257*
Abott, Jeff, 196
Accelerated Solutions Environment, 124
Accenture, Inc., *133, 229*, 593, 675
AccountAbility, 635
Achieving Supply Chain Excellence *through* Technology, *216*
Agility, Inc., 119
Ahold, 10
Aichlmayr, Mary, 479
AIMS Logistics, 120
Aimi, Greg, *129*
Airborne Express, *96*
Amazon.com, 207, 254, 308, 578
American Railcar Inc., *439*
AMR Research, 193, 630
AMR Supply Chain Top 25, 593
Anderson, David L., *653*
APL, *95*
A. P. Moller, *95*
Apple, 84, 88, 189, 590
ARC Advisory Group, *70, 175*, 189, *209, 216*
Arizona State University, *147*
Armbruster, Richard, *439*
Armstrong & Associates, Inc, 121, *122, 123*
AT&T, 635
AT&T/Bell, 12
Auburn University, *162*

B

Ballou, Ronald H., 533
Bardi, Edward J., *142–144, 452*
BathKing Industries, 499
BAX Global, *96*
Beierlein, Jean, 29, *226*, 314
Beierlein, Jim, 81
Benchmarking Partners, *209*
Berman, Jeff, *39, 70*
Best Buy, 257, 401, 578, 634–635, 658
Biederman, David, *437, 639*
Blackwell, Kristina, 227
Blackwell, Roger D., 227
BMW Manufacturing Corp., *122*, 546
BNSF Railway, 408
Bob's Custom BBQs, 448
Boeing, 371
Boone, Pat, 619
Bower, Beth, *226*
Bowersox, Donald J., 592
Boyst, William M., III, *366*
BP, 413
Bredesen, Phil, 514
Breiner, Adrienne, 140
Bristol-Myers Squibb, 518
British Airways, *96*
British Telecom, 635
Britt, Frank F., *653*
Bureau of Customs and Border Protection, 404

Bureau of Transportation Statistics, *405*
Burnson, Patrick, 400
Byline Industries, 314

C

Canadian Pacific Railway, 421
Capgemini LLC, 123, *124, 125, 126, 127, 130, 131, 132, 133, 134, 192, 195, 196, 574, 668*
Carrefour, 10
Carter, Philip, *147–148*
Cass Information Systems, 120
Caterpillar, Inc., *295*, 308, 546
Caterpillar Logistics, 119, 120, *295*
Catnap Pet Products (CPP), 221
Central PA Distribution and Warehouse, 182
Central Transport, Inc., 29
Center for Strategic Supply Research, *147*
Center for Supply Chain Research, 243
Central Region of Nittany Bank, *318*
Centre for Monitoring Indian Economy Pvt. Ltd. (CMIE), 44
Chase, Richard B., *607*
China Shipping (CSCL), *95*
Chizik, Cam, 501
Chocomize, 604
C. H. Robinson, 120
CIO, 199
Circuit City, 257
Circuits Unlimited, 621
Cisco, *492–493*
Clarion University, *318*
Clark, Dick, 325
CLGN Book Distributors.com, *142–144*, 157, *159, 164, 165, 166, 167, 168, 169, 170, 171, 172, 175*
Closs, David J., 592
CMA CGM Group, *95*
CNET, 578
Coca-Cola Enterprises, *492–493*, 595
Coglianese, Vinny, *226*
CoLinx LLC, 138–139
College-Industry Council of Material Handling, 505
Communicating the Value of Supply Chain Management to Your CEO (CSCMP), *162*
Compaq, 518
Computer Sciences Corporation (CSC), 194
Container Corporation of India Ltd. (Concor), 44
Cooke, James A., *209, 651, 671*
Cooper, M. Bixby, 592
Core Fitness, 644
COSCO Container Line, *95*
Council of Logistics Management, *305*
Council of Supply Chain Management Professionals (CSCMP), 35, *162, 305, 320, 322*
Covenant Transport, Inc., 121
Cox, Sharon, *142–144*
Coyle, John J., *452*
Craftsman Tools, 308
Craig, Kenny, 387
C. R. Bard, 204
CSX Transportation, 408, 417
Cube Route, *209*